the Grey Cup

A HISTORY

GRAHAM KELLY

JOHNSON GORMAN PUBLISHERS

The Publishers
Johnson Gorman Publishers
3669 – 41 Avenue
Red Deer Alberta Canada T4N 2X7

Acknowledgments
Cover and text design by Boldface Technologies.
Cover image by courtesy of the Canadian Football Hall of Fame. All text photos courtesy of the Canadian Football Hall of Fame except page 373 courtesy of Craig Robertson/ Canada Wide and pages 468 and 470 courtesy of Reuters.
Printed and bound in Canada by Friesens for Johnson Gorman Publishers.

Financial support provided by the Alberta Foundation for the Arts, a beneficiary of the Lottery Fund of the Government of Alberta.

COMMITTED TO THE DEVELOPMENT OF CULTURE AND THE ARTS

Canadian Cataloguing in Publication Data
Kelly, Graham, 1942–
The Grey Cup
Includes index.
ISBN 0-921835-53-1
1. Grey Cup (Football)—History. 2. Canadian Football League—History.
I. Title. GV948.K44 1999 796.335'648 C99-910987-1

5 4 3 2 1

ACKNOWLEDGMENTS

I wish to thank all the players, coaches, managers and officials who made this book possible, especially Stan Schwartz, Wally Buono, Cal Murphy, Don Matthews, Ray Jauch, Jack Gotta, Bob Ackles, Frank Morris, Annis Stukus, the late Johnny Bright, Jack Parker, Hugh Campbell, Dan Kepley, Ron Lancaster, Alan Ford, Ralph Sazio, Allan McEachern, Al Wilson, Lui Passaglia, Less Browne, Dave Richie, Norm Fieldgate, Dave Berry, Pete Thodas, Norm Kwong, Herm Harrison, Wayne Harris, Matt Finlay, Mark McLoughlin, Dave Sapunjis, John Hufnagel, Will Johnson, Willie Burden, Jeff Garcia, Doug Flutie, Dave Fennell, Dan Bass, Rod Connop, Dave Cutler, Dave Ridgway, Glen Suitor, Kent Austin, Gary Brandt, Wayne Shaw, Dale West, Ron Atchison, Bill Clarke, Glen Dobbs, Jeff Fairholm, Danny McManus, Don Narcisse, John Gregory, Bill Baker, Paul Dojack, John Ireland, Bob Cameron, Chris Walby, Stan Mikawos, Ken Ploen, Leo Lewis, Steve Patrick, Norm Rauhaus, Frank Rigney, the late Bernie Faloney, John Barrow, Garney Henley, Angelo Mosca, Don Sutherin, Joe Zuger, the late Harold Ballard, Hal Patterson, Sam Etcheverry, Red O'Quinn, Bob Geary, Mark Kosmos, Russ Jackson, Ron Stewart, Bob Simpson, George Brancato, Bob O'Billovich, Greg Marshall, Dick Adams, Mike Eben, Leo Cahill, Don Moen, Adam Rita, Matt Dunigan, Hank Ilesic, Joe Krol and the late Fritzie Hansen, as well as past and present Canadian Football League officials Jake Gaudaur, Larry Smith, Jim Neish and Jeff Giles. All went above and beyond the call of duty in helping me assemble the material for this project.

I particularly wish to thank super secretaries Shirley Richardson and Joanne Galdwell for the help they gave me in so many ways. Deep appreciation also to friend Dave Carnegy, who came to my rescue more than once when I hit the wrong key and my software crashed.

I am deeply indebted to my publisher, Dennis Johnson, who provided encouragement, hope and essential advice.

Finally I wish to thank my family. Without the constant support and encouragement of my dear wife, Lorena, sons David and Robert and my late daughter-in-law, Pamela, this book would not have been possible.

—GRAHAM KELLY
JULY 1999

To Lorena, Mom and Dad, and Leo
for loving me and the game.

CONTENTS

PREFACE

I was raised in Saskatchewan, where the word *fan* really is a shortened form of "fanatic." In the Wheat Province to be anything less than fanatic about football is unthinkable, so I may therefore be excused, I hope, for unapologetically declaring myself a true fan of Canadian football. The first Grey Cup I can really remember much about was the 1953 match-up between Winnipeg and Hamilton. I was 11 years old when I sat with my dad in the kitchen of our Regina home, listening to the voice of Hamilton broadcaster Norm Marshall. With Hamilton leading 12–6, Indian Jack Jacobs brought the Bombers down the field on one final drive. The game on the line, Jacobs threw to Tom Casey on the 1-yard line. Lou Kusserow made a bone-crushing tackle to save the day for the Tiger-Cats. That first memory, like so many that have followed, was made all the more poignant by the last-minute heroics that have characterized the national classic. So many Grey Cups have been won on the last play of the game.

The following year was the first time I witnessed the Grey Cup on television. Edmonton and Montreal met for the first of their eight battles for the national championship. It, too, was a thriller with Jackie Parker scooping up Chuck Hunsinger's fumble at the last minute and running the length of the field to score. Bob Dean's convert won the game 26–25 for the underdog Eskimos.

In 1956–57 I was the waterboy and assistant equipment guy with the Saskatchewan Roughriders. The '56 team was one of the best ever, and I dreamed being on the sidelines as the Green and White went on to trimuph in the national classic. Unfortunately for my Grey Cup aspirations, the Eskimos of that season and era were even better. Then tragedy struck in December of that year, when four of our players died in a plane crash returning from the All-Star game in Vancouver. The entire province mourned, underlining again how important football is to Saskatchewan. Since then it has been my privilege to be part of 24 Grey Cups, beginning in 1974, when Les Alouettes defeated Edmonton 20–7 on a rain-soaked field in Vancouver. Every one has been just as special in its own way. Some have been memorable for their weather, a few more for antics off the field than on, but most have been notable for the sheer unpredicatability that, if anything, is the hallmark of our distinctly Canadian brand of football. Across the years I've witnessed players, coaches and fans in states of elation and despair and everything in between. And I've never yet come away from a Grey Cup game being less a believer in Canadian football.

As a product of Saskatchewan, I was, of course, particularly moved by the 1989 thriller, when Dave Ridgway kicked the Riders to victory on the last play of the game. Just before the end, a Hamilton writer turned to me and said, "You know, it's been such a great game, it doesn't matter who wins or loses."

"If you're from Saskatchewan," I replied, "it's a matter of life and death!"

That year I, like so many thousands of other Saskatchewan fans, was driven by more than the normal fanaticism. Next to the Dirty Thirties, the decade of the '80s was the worst in Saskatchewan history. It was a time of darkness and despair as low grain prices and searing drought caused record numbers of farmers to go bankrupt. The population of the province fell as young people headed west in search of a better life. Even suicides rose dramatically.

No solace was found on the football field. After making the play-offs 15 straight years with Ron Lancaster and George Reed, the Roughriders experienced their own drought, missing postseason play a record 11 seasons in a row. Finally the dry spell ended in 1988 when General Manager Bill Baker and Coach John Gregory put together a play-off team that one year later would win the Grey Cup.

The Riders finished third in 1989 but upset Calgary and Edmonton and headed for Toronto to play in the inaugural Grey Cup at the eighth wonder of the world, the SkyDome. Hamilton and Saskatchewan put on the greatest display in Grey Cup history, scoring a record 83 points, including Dave Ridgway's winning field goal on the last play of the game.

Because of the recession that had gripped Saskatchewan for so many years, winning the Grey Cup was truly a magic moment to be cherished and shared by everybody in the province. As one, the people of Saskatchewan reveled in their moment of glory. Finally some good news. They were the champions—and champions of something they cared deeply about.

Coach John Gregory, reflecting on that wonderful time, said, "The fan support was great. I was really proud for the Saskatchewan people who supported the team so strongly. It was interesting how it affected everybody from the farmers to the meat cutters to the presidents of banks."

After the game I went down to the Rider dressing room and offered my congratulations to John Gregory and Kent Austin. I gave a big hug and a handshake to Bill Baker, the CFL Commissioner at the time but in reality the architect of that championship Rider team. It had been 33 years since I'd first dreamed of being in the dressing room after the Roughriders had won the Cup, and I was finally there. I then walked on air back to my hotel room. There my sons, David and Robert—David's wife, Pamela—her dad, Bill Alinks—and her brother, Paul, gave me a standing ovation when I entered the room. Never had a win been so enjoyable, the memories so warm. It was the last time we would all be together—and what better time could there have been to be together?

The 1998 game was very special as well. I knew how much pressure the Calgary Stampeders were under to win the Grey Cup. Though the dominant team in the league of the '90s, the Stampeders had but one championship to their credit. Wally Buono, Stan Schwartz and the rest of the organization were so deserving of success. So was Mark McLoughlin, the place-kicker, a native of Winnipeg, whose dad had died the year before. How fitting it was for him to kick the field goal that won the Grey Cup against a courageous team of Tiger-Cats.

This trip down Grey Cup memory lane is the story of the players, coaches, executives and officials who have made the Grey Cup a true national classic. Across the 27 years that I've covered the game, it has been my privilege, with tape recorder in hand, to interview many of them at length. They include men who were involved in the Grey Cup from 1929 to the present—men like Harry Veiner from the '20s, Fritzie Hansen and Annis Stukus from the '30s, Joe Krol, Ken Charlton, Dave Berry and Rod Pantages from the '40s, and the majority of the greats of the second half of the century, whose names are too numerous to mention. For me, they brought to life what were otherwise simply the game stories and statistics of the Grey Cup. They also provided valuable insights into the making of great athletes and championship teams.

Throughout the hundreds of hours of interviews, I have been deeply impressed with the honesty and forthrightness of the men of the game. Quick to accept the blame for failure, slow to take credit for success, they told it like it was. Jackie Parker, after reading the chapter concerning the Edmonton Eskimos, commented, "Everything you've written seems to be pretty well the way it happened." My hope is that my judgment has been accurate throughout and that the stories of the many people who have contributed to making the Grey Cup a true national classic will bring the games of the past to life for readers of this book.

INTRODUCTION

HAD GOVERNOR GENERAL ALBERT HENRY GEORGE Grey forseen the place the trophy bearing his name would come to occupy in the hearts Canadians, he might have have shown more enthusiasm for the game of football. Apparently the Earl wanted the trophy to go to the Canadian senior hockey champions, but Montreal entrepreneur Sir H. Montagu Allan beat him to the punch and put up a mug himself. Quite likely an aide suggested that the trophy intended for hockey be awarded to the amateur football champion instead, and Grey agreed. Earl Grey, born in England in 1851, known more as a patron of the arts than a sportsman, probably never saw a Canadian football game.

The first Grey Cup game was played December 4, 1909, between the Toronto Parkdales and the University of Toronto, Varsity winning 26–6 before 3,807 people. They did not, however, receive the Cup until March of the following year because Grey's staff forgot to have the $48 trophy made. The oversight was corrected, Birk's Jewellers performed their task and the Cup was presented to the University of Toronto in due course.

From that inauspicious beginning, the Grey Cup became a truly national event in 1921, when the Edmonton Eskimos became the first team from the West to challenge for the trophy. Drubbed 23–0 by the Argonauts, the Eskimos had several American college players on the team who had difficulty

Hugh Gall and Jack Maynard starred for the University of Toronto in the 1910 Grey Cup.

with the rules of the Canadian game and who were repeatedly penalized for interference. If that wasn't enough, Canada's Athlete of the Half Century, Lionel Conacher, scored 15 points before retiring from the game at the end of the third quarter in order play hockey that night for the Maple Leafs.

The following year the Eskimos, renamed the Elks and with a new sponsor, returned to the Grey Cup, losing to Queen's University 13–1. It would be 30 years before an Edmonton team competed again for the national symbol of football supremacy.

In 1923 the Elks reverted to their original name, and the club folded after losing the Alberta Rugby Football Championship to Calgary in 1924. The team emerged again in 1928 and became the Boosters, playing in brand new Clarke Stadium, which would serve them until 1978. Lasting only a year, the Boosters were reborn eight years later as the Eskimos, clad in blue and white. That reincarnation lasted two years, after which the Eskimos folded again until 1949.

Football grew in popularity throughout the 1920s and 1930s. To attract more fans teams began signing American players, the forward pass was introduced, various rule changes were made, and in 1948, thanks to Calgarians, the Grey

Cup became a true national festival, bringing together Canadians from all walks of life to have fun. Staid old Hogtown had never witnessed anything like the scene as Calgarians flipped flapjacks on the steps of city hall and rode horses through the lobby of the prestigious Royal York Hotel.

Throughout the '30s, '40s and into the CFL's first golden age in the '50s, the Grey Cup featured some of the most entertaining football ever played at any level in any league. There was Red Storey's incredible three-touchdown performance in 1938; Parker, Bright and Kwong versus Etcheverry, O'Quinn and Patterson in the mid-1950s and the tremendous rivalry between Winnipeg and Hamilton featuring Hall of Famers like Frank Rigney, Ken Ploen, Leo Lewis, Bernie Faloney, John Barrow, Garney Henley and Angelo "The Meanie" Mosca. The '60s saw Lancaster and Reed against Jackson and Stewart; the '70s, Wilkinson, McGowan and Cutler taking on Rodgers, Wade, Buono and Sweet. The 1980s featured the likes of Moon, Holloway, Minter, the Gizmo, Bass, Fernandez, Browne, Fenerty, Ilesic, Dunigan and Austen. The '90s have had their share of Grey Cup heroes with players like Battle, Pless, Flutie, Sapunjis, McManus and the Pinball.

Throughout the 1980s and '90s, no matter how desperate the situation for the Canadian Football League, the Grey Cup has been its salvation. The first major crisis in confidence came when the Montreal Alouettes folded on June 24, 1987. That year's Grey Cup, as well as those of 1988–89, were marvelous contests decided in the last minute, the total margin of victory in the three games a mere six points. Those Grey Cups brought the CFL through its darkest hour.

The same was true in the 1990s, when the American challengers from Baltimore were rebuffed in 1994 as Lui Passaglia kicked the B.C. Lions to a thrilling last-second victory. Baltimore took the Cup south the following year before the the short-lived experiment of American expansion ended in 1996, giving the CFL another black eye. When the faithful gathered in Hamilton that year to watch the Argos and Eskimos contest the eighty-fourth Grey Cup many thought it would be the last. Days later the Ottawa Rough Riders ceased operation and most of the teams were losing money.

But the venerable old league refused to die. Although the 1997 match-up between Saskatchewan and Toronto wasn't a thriller like the three before it, the fact that the Roughriders came from third place to be there fired the football imagination. In 1998 another Cinderella team, the Hamilton Tiger-Cats, made it to the Grey Cup, losing in yet another cliff-hanger to Calgary on a last-second Mark McLoughlin field goal.

Over its 89-year history the Grey Cup has come to occupy a special place in the hearts of Canadians. Come the end of November, more of them settle down in front of their television sets to watch the Grey Cup than any other sporting event.

In a day and age when the rookie minimum in the National Hockey League is seven times more than the top salary in the Canadian Football League and a major league pitcher signs for over $10 million a season, the Grey Cup represents to many Canadians the values of common sense and proportion as well as old-fashioned down-home hospitality and fun.

The Grey Cup isn't about money. And it's not a matter of life and death (unless you're from Saskatchewan). It's a celebration, a time to party, the only time Canadians from coast to coast assemble to celebrate a truly and distinctly Canadian sporting event.

Bud Grant coached in six Grey Cups and four Super Bowls. Quoting a former prime minister, Grant said, "It was an event that everyone went to or was interested in. John Diefenbaker said the Grey Cup was the greatest unifying force in Canada in bringing East and West together."

Because in recent years it has been a widespread perception that the Canadian Football League has been on its deathbed, many commentators have ignored the fact that the Grey Cup game usually records the largest television audience of all sporting events televised in Canada, including the Super Bowl. Part of the reason, of course, is that the NFL championship should be called the Super Bore because most of those games have been blowouts, whereas the Grey Cup is generally decided by last-minute heroics, whether it be the dramatic run by Jackie Parker in 1954, Winnipeg and Hamilton's overtime battle in 1961 and the Fog Bowl of 1962, the McQuay fumble of 1971, the dramatic miss on a frozen field in Calgary in 1975, the heartbreak for Saskatchewan fans when Tony Gabriel caught the Cup-clinching touchdown in 1976 or Michael Gray's interception of a Matt Dunigan pass to preserve the win for Winnipeg over B.C. in 1988.

What about all those Grey Cups won by a last-minute kick? There was Joe Krol's punt in 1947, Bob Dean's convert in '54, rookie Ian Sunter's win for Hamilton over Saskatchewan in 1972, Dave Ridgway's turning of the tables on Hamilton in 1989, Dave Cutler preventing the biggest upset in sports history by kicking the winning field goal for Edmonton against Ottawa in 1981. Lui Passaglia preserved our national honor by repelling the American invasion from Baltimore in 1994, and, of course, Mark McLoughlin, his guardian angel father looking over his shoulder, won for the Stampeders on the last play of the 1998 Grey Cup.

Certainly there have been difficulties for the Canadian Football League. The CFL shies away from staging the Grey Cup in Canada's largest city, fearing a low turn-out even though in southern Ontario Canadian football comes out on top in television ratings when going head to head with the NFL. This is quite an achievement considering the enormous marketing machine of the National Football League.

The CFL has proved it is the little engine that could. It is, after all, the only professional sports league in North America that has direct competition. The NHL, NBA and the major leagues of baseball do not. Given that reality, the league has done very well indeed. It has not only endured but has been restored to health and approaches the new millennium with confidence. The Grey Cup, its symbol of sporting supremacy, remains the most cherished Canadian sporting tradition and an integral part of our culture. Much of the credit goes to Canadians' ongoing love affair with the Grey Cup.

CHAPTER 1

Edmonton and Montreal

The Rivalry and the Revelry

ARGUABLY THE GREATEST TEAM IN THE HISTORY OF Canadian football was the Edmonton aggregation that won five straight Grey Cups between 1978 and 1982. Since reentering the Western Conference in 1949, the Eskimos have been the dominant force in Canadian football, making the play-offs 42 times in 48 years and appearing in the Western Final on 33 occasions. They haven't missed postseason play since 1971 and have won 11 of their 21 Grey Cup appearances.

The list goes on. There are 21 Eskimos in the Canadian Football Hall of Fame. Eskimos have won 32 Schenley and league awards. Ray Jauch, Hugh Campbell and Ron Lancaster have won the Stukus Trophy.

Eight of Edmonton's 21 Grey Cup appearances have been against the Montreal Alouettes. In the first of these in the 1950s, football fans thrilled to the tremendous battles fought between some of the greatest players the game has ever known, such as Jackie Parker, Normie Kwong and Johnny Bright of Edmonton and Les Alouettes' Sam "The Rifle" Etcheverry, Pat Abruzzi and Red O'Quinn. The teams renewed their rivalry in the 1970s when Ray Jauch and Hugh Campbell fashioned the dynasty that beat the Als three times.

In 1921 the Eskimos were the first team from the West to challenge for the Grey Cup, losing 23–0 to the Argonauts. Under the name Elks, the same team returned to the Grey Cup the following year, losing this time to Queen's 13–1.

It would be 30 years before an Edmonton team competed for the national championship again. During those 30 years the Eskimos had an on-again, off-again history, folding after losing the Alberta Rugby Football Championship to Calgary in 1924, emerging again in 1928. In 1920 the Eskimos became the Boosters, playing the Western Rugby League in a brand new Clarke Stadium, the football facility in Edmonton until 1978. The Boosters lasted only a year but were reborn eight years later as the Eskimos, clad in blue and white. That reincarnation lasted two years.

In 1949 the Edmonton Eskimos were reorganized, adopted green and gold as their colors and joined the Western Interprovincial Football Union. This time they were not only here to stay, but they were to become the flagship team of Canadian football and one of the most successful organizations in all of professional sport.

In the East, Montreal was one of the original members of the Interprovincial Union, or Big Four, organized in 1907, but it wasn't until 1931 that they became the first non-Ontario team to represent the East in the Grey Cup, when their Winged Wheelers defeated the Regina Roughriders 22–0. That doesn't mean good football wasn't played in that city before 1931. Under the direction of Frank Shaughnessy, McGill was probably the best team in the country from 1912–19, but he showed no interest in competing for the Grey Cup because that would interfere with his players' studies.

Frank Shaughnessy dramatically changed the face of Canadian football by bringing in blocking for running backs, the huddle and using a secondary instead of having all the defenders on the line. When the forward pass was approved in 1931, Shaughnessy brought Warren Stevens from Syracuse to run the Montreal passing attack. After the Winged Wheelers initial win over Regina, a team representing Montreal didn't get to the Grey Cup until 1949.

That same year, back in Edmonton, the Eskimos asked Annis Stukus to become their coach and general manager. At first he didn't take the offer seriously. "I coached interfaculty football in Toronto. My gofer was a guy from the School of Dentistry who later moved to Edmonton, Dr. Bill Quigley. I got a letter from him during the winter of 1949. It said, 'Stuke, they are talking about starting up football, and I've offered your name as a possible candidate.'

"I wrote back a facetious letter that said, 'I understand you guys have found

The Montreal Winged Wheelers beat the Regina Roughriders 22–0 to win the 1931 Grey Cup.

oil out there and with an oil well or two, a guy's willing to start anything.' Then I forgot about it.

"About a month later I got a letter saying, 'We're looking at your application to coach the Edmonton Eskimos, and we'd like to talk to you.' I thought, 'When the hell did I apply for your coaching job?'

"In those days we only had five imports, and if you didn't have the Canadians, good-bye! I knew where the Canadians were and Edmonton knew it. They talked me into taking the job, and I convinced my wife."

Upon arriving in Edmonton Stukus wondered what he had gotten into. "I had my hands full with a lot of help from a board of directors that included four or five former football players. When I finally got out to Clarke Stadium, I found out they only had 2,700 bleacher seats—and we're going to play pro football?

"They condemned the stands at the race track, and one of our directors had the job of tearing them down. I asked him to take them down piecemeal and move them over to the east side of Clarke Stadium so we got at least 7,700 seats."

On a budget of $45,000 Stukus began putting a club together, winning four games in 1949 and finishing third. One of the great characters of the game,

Stukus, a marketing genius ahead of his time, staged promotions that made the team a profit when it wasn't yet delivering on the field.

With more money in the coffers, Stukus went hunting for football players and found them in Toronto. Frank Morris was one of them. "In 1949, my last year with Argos," Morris recalled, "I was selling beer for Labatt Breweries. I was in the Town Tavern on one of my calls and Stuke was in there recruiting Dougie Pyzer and Don Durno. There were four or five guys at the table. I sat down and joined them, set up a round of Labatt's and got talking. Somebody casually said, 'Why don't you come out west and play football?'

"I had some reasons for doing that. I kidded Stuke about it. Finally he said, 'If you want to come out, you just let me know.' So I let him know.

"We had Doug Pyzer, Don Durno, Bill Briggs, Mike King and Frank Hickey. Bill Zock came out in 1951."

It wasn't the only time Edmonton built a winner from ex-Argos. In 1993 they swung the biggest trade in CFL history with Toronto and promptly won the Grey Cup. The Argos finished last.

Head Coach Annis Stukus also was the place-kicker. He was so sure he wouldn't be hit in that position that he didn't wear pads or a helmet. He didn't even remove his gold wristwatch before kicking. Legend has it that in a game against Winnipeg in 1951, Buddy Tinsely broke through on a point after, blocking the kick and sending Stukus flying in one direction and his watch in another.

No way, Stuke said. "It didn't happen. They never scratched that watch. In our training camp I had about eight or nine guys kicking converts and field goals. I thought I'd better take a look to see what they could do with someone coming down their throats. I discovered I didn't have anyone who could get the ball over the line of scrimmage.

"My brother Bill said, 'What about you?' I said, 'I haven't kicked a ball in anger in four years, and I've got enough headaches.' He said again, 'What are you going to do? You know how important kicking is.'

"So all of a sudden I'm doing laps and windsprints after practice. One night I went all the way around the track without dying, so I was ready.

"I didn't wear pads for one reason: so I wouldn't stay out there. You're 37 or 38 years old and you figure you can still play? Yeah, sure.

"We're out there for the warm-up before an exhibition game, and I wore my wristwatch to make sure we didn't stay out there longer than 18 minutes. We scored early against Montreal, and I went out for my first convert in four years. I had my wristwatch on and I got a brilliant idea.

"I said to the guys in the huddle, 'Fellas, you know I don't believe in fines for mistakes. But this wristwatch is worth 85 bucks, and if anything happens to it while I'm out here, each one of you will buy me a new one.' The Montreal players didn't get their breath past the line of scrimmage. I kicked that field goal and won the game, which really helped us with season ticket sales. That watch went through 39 football games without a scratch. My daughter took it to school one day and came back with the strap. The kids were looking at it, and somewhere along the line, they dropped it."

As coach and place-kicker, Stukus compiled a record of 19 wins and 23 losses, making the play-offs in 1950 and '51, after which he returned to his sports writing job at the *Toronto Star*. His successor in Edmonton in 1952 was another controversial, colorful character, Frank Filchock. Filchock had come to Canada from the NFL, where he had been banned for failing to report an attempted bribe. After playing for the Hamilton Tigers in 1947–48, he moved on to Montreal, leading the Alouettes to a Grey Cup win over Calgary the following year. He went west in 1951, sharing the Eskimos' quarterbacking duties with Lindy Berry before becoming head coach in 1952.

Although one of the greatest passers who ever lived, Filchock didn't look like much of an athlete with his big ears, twinkling eyes and funny-shaped head set on a short, rotund body. Adding to the absurdity was his penchant for wearing a red toque during practices in July while clenching a cigar between his teeth.

The biggest rap on Filchock as coach was that he didn't take the game seriously enough. He loved to have the guys playing touch football rather than scrimmaging with full gear. Some thought his training camps were country clubs. However, 25 years later, Hugh Campbell and Don Matthews introduced the same idea into the Edmonton operation, eschewing heavy hitting in practice.

Eskimo guard Frank Morris was an unabashed Filchock fan. "We ran what everyone thought were really short practices. But we were always out ahead of time and did a lot of things, including a touch football game, which meant we got a whole lot of running in. Actual practice was minimal. Frank handled people really well."

Normie Kwong also remembered his 1952 head coach fondly. "Frank Filchock was one of the boys. He was a lot of fun to play for.

"I had a streak of fumbling the first time I carried the ball in three games in a row. The practice after the third game, Frank came out after the warm-up, presented me with the ball and taped it to my arm. He made me carry it the rest of the week that way. I don't think I fumbled the rest of the year."

In 1952, Flichock's first year as head coach, the order of finish in the West was Winnipeg first, Edmonton second, Calgary third. After beating Calgary in the semifinal, the Eskimos upset Winnipeg to make their first Grey Cup appearance in 30 years, but victory would elude them. Normie Kwong succinctly summarized the 1952 season: "We stumbled through the league somehow, won the West and got down East. It was kind of a shock to be there, and then Toronto out-coached us and beat us."

Poor play selection late in the game cost Edmonton dearly. Early on, the Eskimos unleashed a powerful running attack with Normie Kwong, Rollie Miles and Rod Pantages. In the first quarter Pantages fumbled out of bounds on the Argo 1-yard line, resulting in a 10-yard penalty, but Kwong ran into the end zone two plays later.

With six minutes to go in the fourth quarter and trailing 15–11, the Esks, scrimmaging from the Argo 54, marched relentlessly down the Varsity Stadium field. Miles carried for 14 yards, Pantages for 11 and Miles again for 13, bringing the ball to the enemy 16. Then, inexplicably, Coach Filchock and quarterback

Claude Arnold went to the air. On the first down Arnold couldn't find an open receiver and threw the ball into the ground, an incomplete pass under U.S. rules, a fumble according to ours. A few minutes later Sculler quarterback Nobby Wirkowski put the icing on the cake with a touchdown pass to Zeke O'Connor. The final score was 21–11.

At the end of the 1952 campaign, Filchock was fired, replaced by Darrell Royal. The Eskimos of 1953 were led by Tulsa All-American Billy Vessels, who won the first ever Schenley Award over teammate Rollie Miles. Most people believed that the award rightly should have gone to Miles but that he wasn't selected by football reporters because of racism.

There were very few black players in the league in 1953, and they certainly weren't welcome at country and other private clubs in Edmonton or elsewhere. Football reporters in Edmonton quite likely didn't appreciate Miles' outspokenness on racial matters. However, it wasn't all that clear-cut because Billy Vessels did have an outstanding year. But, as Normie Kwong commented, "Conditions in the country then weren't conducive to a person of color winning awards."

Rollie Miles road to football stardom in Edmonton was a long and unusual one. He had originally come to Regina in 1951 to play baseball. Although the Roughriders were aware of his football abilities, they weren't interested in signing him because he was black. A more tolerant management attitude and bad weather landed this gifted athlete in Edmonton. "We had some games in Edmonton," Miles explained. "There were a couple of rain-outs, and I got involved with the Eskimos."

Annis Stukus signed him. "We'd had a scrimmage and I lost a couple of backs," he recalled. "Don Fleming, who was covering baseball at Renfrew, phoned me up and said, 'Stuke, there's a kid here with the Regina Caps who is an All-American football player. He's got a bad ankle, but he's stolen seven bases so far.'

"I told Fleming to ask him to stay over and I'd fly him back to Regina. Miles came out to practice and I took a look at him and thought, 'Ho–ho–ho, this guy's been around a football field once or twice.' Next night he was back again. I was running a shortside play. I couldn't get a guy who could run to his left and throw a pass. I hear a voice behind me say, 'Hey, coach, I can run that.' I turned around and there was Miles in uniform. The way he ran it, you'd think I had been dreaming of Rollie Miles when I designed that play."

"I signed him. After about four or five games, I tore up the paper and signed him to a three-year contract for a lot more money. I knew I had something."

The "China Clipper" Normie Kwong battles in a losing cause as the Toronto Argonauts defeated the Edmonton Eskimos in 1952.

During a distinguished 11-year career in which he proved himself probably the most versatile player in the history of Canadian football, Miles was a Western All-Star eight times, three each at running and defensive back, twice as a linebacker. In 1954 he made the All-Star team on both sides of the ball. Miles played in five Grey Cups, winning three, and was elected to the Hall of Fame in 1980. Yet Rollie Miles never won a Schenley Award. His year should have been 1953, when the award went to the All-American from Tulsa, Billy Vessels. Parker and Bright came along the next year, and no one begrudged them the Schenley.

Recalling that time, Miles said, "I would say that when I played with Billy I did the things that he did, and I did some of them better. I played some of the things better, and I think he realized that."

Did racism prevent Rollie Miles from winning a well-deserved Schenley Award?

"I'm not saying it, but I think that could be a ring," he said. "Billy told me that in '53. Racism I would say was part of it."

Frank "Pop" Ivy took over the Eskimo coaching reins in 1954. Billy Vessels left for the Baltimore Colts, but Johnny Bright arrived from Calgary. Other newcomers were Roger Nelson, Earl Lindley and All-Americans Maryland quarterback Bernie Faloney and Mississippi running back James Dickinson Parker. Nine members of that 1954 team are in the Hall of Fame.

With such a lineup the 1950s saw some of the best football ever played in

Canada. Partly that was the result of CFL teams paying better than the NFL. That is why so many All-Americans and NFL veterans still in their prime came north. A third of Edmonton's starting imports had been All-Americans.

In the 1954 campaign, Edmonton tied Saskatchewan for first place, getting top spot by winning one more game. After beating the Bombers in the Western Final, they defeated the Ontario Rugby Football Union (ORFU) champion Kitchener Waterloo Dutchmen to advance to the Grey Cup. It was the last time the ORFU competed for the trophy.

Facing the Eskimos for the Cup were the heavily favored Montreal Alouettes. Torontonians Lew Hayman and financial backer Eric Cradock had started the Als in 1946 with help from Leo Dandurand and Joe Ryan. In the Alouettes' first year of operation, they finished first but lost the Eastern Final to Toronto 12–6.

Three years later, led by Frank Filchock, seven-time All-Star Herb Trawick and Virgil Wagner, the Als beat Calgary 28–15 to win their first Grey Cup. Montreal then missed the play-offs the next three years, falling to 2–10 in 1952 when Douglas "Peahead" Walker came from Wake Forest as coach. Early arrivals were Sam Etcheverry, Red O'Quinn, Tex Coulter, Tom Hugo, Doug McNichol and Alex Webster. The much-improved Als tied Hamilton for first in 1953 but lost the final.

Sam the Rifle Versus Old Spaghetti Legs

In 1954, with newly acquired receiver Hal Patterson aboard, Montreal finished first and went on to meet the Eskimos in the Grey Cup in the second of ten times they would face Alberta clubs for the Grey Cup, eight versus Edmonton, the other two against Calgary.

The 1954 Grey Cup was a tremendous offensive display featuring some of the greatest players the game has ever known. Montreal set the still-standing record of 656 yards total offense. Receiver Red O'Quinn was magnificent for Montreal, catching 13 passes for 316 yards, the longest being a 90-yarder for a touchdown—all records yet to be broken. Together the two teams ran up 1,090 yards, the second highest total in Grey Cup history. The same two teams set the record the following year with 1,115 yards in total offense, and in 1956 they racked up the third highest total in Grey Cup history with 1,018 total yards.

O'Quinn had joined the Alouettes in 1952 when Walker traded Bill George to the Chicago Bears for him. The 1954 Grey Cup was the greatest game of his career. O'Quinn described the 90-yard pass and run. "Sam called an audible.

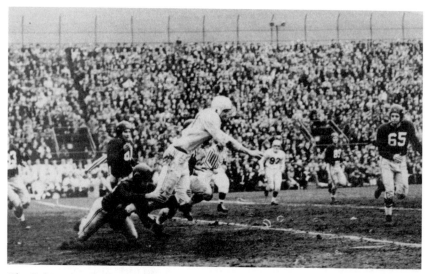

The Eskimos and Alouettes put on one of the greatest displays of offense in Grey Cup history in 1954.

We had what we called a Flare Pass, where he would take the ball from the center and jump up in the air and throw it to me on a quick slant across the middle—a quick pass between the linebackers.

"Pop Ivy had been working with Rollie Miles and Jackie Parker to intercept it. They had seen the films. The Eskimos thought they were going to come up and intercept it, but they overshot me, and I went through there and put a hand out and the ball stuck. I was off and running. I managed to make it to the goal line before Miles and Parker could get turned around and catch me.

"My other catches were all about 15 or 20 yards. Sam was hitting me as quick as I turned. It was just a great day. We were having a grand old time, but unfortunately we lost the game."

Over the years a few great or controversial plays stand out as being crucial in determining the outcome of the game. The Alouettes' 1954 Grey Cup loss was decided by the Hunsinger play. Chuck Hunsinger was an Alouette halfback. On the fateful play he tried to pass (his version) or fumbled (the Eskimo and official version). Jackie Parker scooped up the ball and ran 90 yards for a touchdown. The play tied the game at 25.

"I've got the film here," said Frankie Morris. "They still show stop-action of Hunsinger with the ball up. The Alouettes made the point that it was a pass—that it should have been ruled an incomplete pass, not a fumble. But he

Chuck Hunsinger picks up 30 yards on that fateful day in November 1954.

was carrying the ball. He kind of jumped up in the air. I think it was Ted Tully who hit him. In the stop-action shot, it looks like he's going to push the ball with his right hand on a lateral, a pass. But he got hit. The ball came free and, of course, Jackie picked the ball up and ran the rest of the way for the touchdown.

"If I were a Montreal player, I'd say yeah, he was passing the ball, but as an Eskimo I'd say no. If you saw it, you'd say it could have been called either way. Thank God the officials called it our way."

In an 1978 interview the late Johnny Bright was unequivocal about what happened. "I was playing right cornerback, Jackie Parker was playing right defensive halfback behind me, and that time Roland Prather was playing the defensive end.

"On the previous play Montreal ran an Inside Counter on which Prather got blocked out. I was on the looping position as a linebacker, and I filled the hole. Because they had been alternating these kind of plays, Prather said to me, 'Watch it, John. They're going to come outside.'

"At the time when Prather closed down, I came across very flat or tight to the end when the pitch was made to Hunsinger. I think when I showed up, Hunsinger looked up to see what had happened and the ball was in his hands and then across his hands.

"The odd thing about that is if the ball had bounced toward the line of scrimmage, it would have bounced right to me and I would have picked it up and been on the run. Rather, it bounced parallel to the line of scrimmage and Jackie was filling on the outside and it bounced to him."

Many considered the Eskimo victory a fluke. Bright had an answer for that. "Had the score at that time been 24–0 or 24–14, that touchdown would have done nothing but put us a little closer. But the touchdown tied it up. If the Alouettes were such a great team and we were able to tie it up, we must have been competitive with them."

Jackie Parker, one of the greatest offensive performers in U.S. college and Canadian football history, is best remembered for that defensive play in the 1954 Grey Cup. Parker recalled what happened. "They were trying an end run, and Rollie, Prather and Ted Tully got through and hit Hunsinger simultaneously. The ball popped out and I happened to be there. I picked it up and started running.

"I don't think it was an attempted forward pass, but I don't know that. It looked like our players got through quickly, stopped the end run and kind of stripped the ball.

"Hunsinger got hit behind the line of scrimmage, but one of his offensive linemen was in the vicinity. Being a very astute football player, Hunsinger might have tried to pitch it back to him, but he didn't really have a chance."

Montreal receiver Red O'Quinn looked back on that fateful day, recalling a prophetic Hunsinger comment. "I was on the bus going from the Royal York out to the stadium, and I was sitting beside Chuck Hunsinger. Everyone was so keyed up about the game. Chuck was sitting beside me and said, 'The only thing I don't want is to be a goat. I don't want to mess up.' It turned out that it was the biggest mess-up of his career.

"Today he laughs about it and says, 'If it hadn't been for that play, I'd have been long forgotten.'

"It was really a forward pass, O'Quinn argued. "Chuck tried to push the ball

"Spaghetti Legs" Jackie Parker recovers Chuck Hunsinger's fumble and runs to pay-dirt in the Eskimos' first-ever Grey Cup victory.

forward to Ray Cicia, who was a guard pulling around. Jim Staton had missed his block on the tackle, and the tackle came through and was right in Chuck's face from the time he got the ball.

"Chuck did the wrong thing. He panicked and tried to throw it forward to Cicia. It didn't work out. The ball was on the ground, Parker came through like a shot, picked it up and was gone. Etcheverry couldn't catch him."

As far as Red O'Quinn was concerned, the Hunsinger fumble wasn't the only key play of the ball game. "Herb Trawick was covering a punt. It hit the receiver right in the chest and bounced out. Trawick came along, picked it up on the dead run and ran for a touchdown. But the officials ruled it a dead ball at the point it hit the receiver."

Parker's 90-yard run tied it up, but it was up to kicker Bob Dean to win the game by kicking the extra point. Dean hadn't missed all year, but even the convert attempt was dramatic because center Eagle Keys was out of the game. Keys was a study in courage in that game. Despite an injury he limped onto the field to snap the ball for a Bob Dean field goal and two converts. By the time Parker made his dramatic run, Keys could not continue.

Bright recalled that crucial moment. "Eagle Keys was the starting center, but he had a broken leg. For all the converts up to that point in the game, Keys had been the center. So here we are changing the center. All of a sudden I think we were in awe. When the snap count was being called, someone said, 'Let's not mess it up fellows. No mistakes. Let's block.'"

Bill Briggs snapped the ball, the convert was made and the Grey Cup was won by a point.

Edmonton's quarterback that day was Bernie Faloney, who would play in seven more Grey Cups with Hamilton. He recalled one unsung hero of the Eskimos' victory. "There was a little guy by the name of Glen Lippman, who scored a touchdown," Faloney remembered. "Glen really hadn't played much offense, but Rollie Miles was playing with a hurt.

"Parker and I were playing defense in the fourth quarter, and Jackie intercepted a pass, giving us the ball. We started moving down the field. Jackie had a good run, and I had a good option run. There was a short pass to Keeper McWhinney.

"And then Glen Lippman was there. We called a sweep and that little guy ran about 25 yards right into the end zone. That put us in the position where Jackie's score could tie the game."

In 1955 the Eskimos and Alouettes met again, this time at Empire Stadium in Vancouver, the first time the Grey Cup was played in Western Canada. Montreal was 9–3 that year and barely edged out Toronto in the Big Four final 38–36.

Although the Alouettes were a marvelous passing team, fullback Pat Abbruzzi had won the Schenley Outstanding Player Award as a rookie. In Abbruzzi's 49 games as an Alouette, he picked up 3,749 yards and scored 39 touchdowns in just two years, including 20 in 1956, a record that stood for 38 years until Calgary's Allen Pitts tallied 21.

The Eskimos breezed through the regular season, running up a record setting 14 wins against 2 losses. They beat the Bombers two straight in the final. As Bright explained, they were a team on a mission. "Come hell or high water there was no way we were going to lose the play-offs to Winnipeg because we had to go back and thrash Montreal.

"Montreal had made comments that the Grey Cup game was a million dollar classic, but this was the first time a nickel-and-dime team had shown up. They said we had no business even being in the same ball park with them—that we had won on a fluke the year before. They never had given us credit."

Miles agreed. "We didn't get much respect. Even after we won in 1954, we still didn't get much respect."

Said Parker, "We'd been the team that went down and won a Grey Cup in '54 and everybody thought we weren't very good. But we *were* a good football team. We had a lot of really excellent players who gave it all they had. Even though we won the '54 Grey Cup, it was considered a fluke. When we beat Montreal again in 1955 that was the best one for me because we kind of said, 'Hey, we're not that bad.'"

The 1955 Grey Cup match-up was the army versus the air force. Bright and Kwong rolled over the Alouettes like Sherman tanks, Kwong running for 145 yards and Bright for 82. Both scored two touchdowns. Edmonton set a single-game rushing record of 438 yards, which they broke the following year. Montreal's Sam Etcheverry threw for an incredible 508 yards, a record that still stands.

Abbruzzi scored a touchdown for the Alouettes. Hal Patterson got the other two although he didn't play the last quarter and a half because, he said, he "got hit in the head and was a little woozy."

The Eskimos went to the dressing room at half time down 19–18. The Alouettes didn't score another point. Johnny Bright broke the game open in the third quarter. "There hadn't been very many long gains made running," he recalled. "We were 42 yards out, and we ran what we called a 41 Counter. I broke it the 42 yards for a touchdown, which put us up to stay.

"Later in the game we were on the 8-yard line and Jackie called a 38 Pitchout. Montreal had a mouthy back by name of J.C. Caroline, who later became an all-pro defensive back with the Chicago Bears. He had been stating what he would do to me.

"I turned the corner on the pitch. I ran over J.C. and knocked him out and scored a touchdown. From there on nobody challenged me very much in that game."

Kwong's record of 30 carries in the 1955 game still stands. His 145 yards is

Joey Pal and Johnny Bright fight for the ball in the Grey Cup, the first ever to be played in the West.

the second best in Grey Cup history, and he is third on the all-time list for Grey Cup rushing yardage behind Leo Lewis and George Reed.

Despite his impressive performance Kwong's fondest memory is of the win over Montreal the year before. "The 1954 game was most satisfying because we were such underdogs and we won the thing. It was more fun to win because we were so downgraded and we showed them."

The Eskimos also showed the Alouettes in the 1956 Grey Cup. Tied 20–20 in the third quarter, the Edmonton team went on to win 50–27. Jackie Parker scored three touchdowns and a single. Johnny Bright was magnificent, rushing for 171 yards, a still-standing record. It was probably the greatest game he ever played.

The legendary Johnny Bright.

"In that particular game, with Rollie Miles hurt, Norm and I carried almost all the offensive load. I caught nine of nine passes. I had two touchdowns," said Bright. "I went in and played one quarter of defensive ball, recovered a fumble, knocked a pass down and intercepted one. In 1956 I made more of a contribution to the overall success of the team than at any other time. That was the greatest satisfaction I had."

The Eskimo quarterback in that game was Don Getty, one of only two Canadians to have won the Grey Cup since the end of World War II. (Joe Krol wasn't a quarterback.)

"One thing I was very pleased about as a Canadian quarterback," said Alberta's future premier, "was that in the Western Final and the Grey Cup we scored over 100 points. I was very proud of that. I think that's the real measure of a quarterback: Can you get the ball in the end zone?"

Why did they thrash Montreal so thoroughly? "They were a tremendous club," Getty argued. "But we won because, the week we were practicing in London, Ivy put in a system we hadn't used all year. We were going to go at the touch of the guard's hands to the ground, and the ends and tackles had to race up there. I was going to call for the ball the instant I got behind the center. So we had kind of a rolling start. We were by the big, heavy guys like Doug McNichol, Tex Coulter and Jim Staton before they had a chance to exercise their weight advantage against us. That was very effective. We just wore them down.

"They were ahead in the third quarter, but by then they were running out of steam and we were going faster and faster. Ivy didn't put in the system to blow them away but because we were stale. He thought we needed to work on something new."

Said the Alouette's Red O'Quinn, "They outsmarted us. They came out almost on the dead run and never did stop. They snapped the ball while everybody was moving. They had it timed perfectly. Everything was a quick count."

Eskimo guard Frank Morris believed that Montreal's lack of strategy was crucial to Edmonton's success in the 1955 and '56 Grey Cups. "We played them three years in a row, and every year we set our offense to go against the defense that they had run the year before. We thought they would make some changes, but three years in a row they never changed a damn thing."

"Our biggest mistake was not changing our defense," admitted Sam "The Rifle" Etcheverry. "We held to the same defense in all three Grey Cup games against them. We just came out on the field and tried to outscore them and not worry about defense."

"They weren't a better team," lamented Alouette Hal Patterson. "They just out-coached us. We had only two defenses, a 5–4 and a 5–2. We didn't have anything else, and we pretty well got picked apart."

The losses were a bitter disappointment for Etcheverry. The University of Denver product passed for 25,582 yards in seven years of recorded statistics, completing 1,630 passes for 174 touchdowns and a 57 percent average. No statistics were kept in 1952 and '53, his first two seasons in the league. He is the tenth-ranked passer of all time and a brilliant Grey Cup performer.

He described his feelings about the big game. "When you haven't won the Grey Cup, it is something that sticks with you the rest of your life. It's something that always comes up. People remember it. It comes up in my business. Some people are very critical that I never won the Grey Cup as a player. You know," he said, "every person in your home stands is not automatically on your side."

Were the 1956 Eskimos the greatest CFL team of all time? "I would have said the '57 one," replied Getty. "We could have been undefeated, but Pop Ivy rested the imports the last two games of the year. In a way that may have hurt us. We weren't sharp the last two games. Then there was a 17-day break between our last game and the Conference Final. We couldn't bear down and Winnipeg won.

"We broke all the offensive records that year, and yet right at the end we weren't able to score. I think the score was 2–2 at the end of regulation time, and Winnipeg won it on a fumble on the opening kickoff in overtime. That was my biggest disappointment—not going to the Grey Cup in 1957."

Johnny Bright shook his head in wonder when he recalled the 1957 Western Final against Winnipeg. "We had 495 yards total offense to Winnipeg's 140, and we couldn't score. We fumbled. We tried nine field goals in that game and never got a single point. We had incompleted passes; we dropped balls. They beat us without scoring an offensive touchdown. It's always been a mystery to me."

The outcome of the Western Final was no mystery to guard Frank Morris. "We always thought referee Cliff Roseborough and another Winnipeg official were the key men in that game. Every time we got into scoring position we got a penalty. I call it puck luck. We didn't have it."

The tables were turned in 1960, a year that was a mirror image of 1957. That year the Bombers breezed through the regular season 14–2, the same tally as Edmonton in '57. After exchanging play-off wins, the right to represent the West in the Grey Cup all came down to the third game.

The Bombers led 2–1 late in the fourth quarter. With the ball on their own 25-yard line, Winnipeg quarterback Ken Ploen, playing with a broken hand, fumbled the ball. The Esks recovered and kicked a field goal to win. The greatest Eskimo team didn't get to the Cup in 1957, and the greatest Bomber team didn't make it three years later.

But the Eskimos were in no shape to contest a Grey Cup against Ottawa. "We were so battered that we could have had a 10-week break and not been at full strength physically," Bright recalled. "I had two very severe charley horses. I had to stay at the University of Alberta Hospital, and they had to drain the blood off in order to get my legs down so I could walk. So I arrived in British Columbia late Thursday night and had a 40-minute workout with the team on Friday and tried to play on Saturday.

"Kwong was hurt. Parker had a bad shoulder. I don't think Rollie Miles played in that game or didn't play very much of it. Nat Dye, our defensive end, couldn't play, so we played Jim Toon, who had only been in four games all year."

Normie Kwong had another problem. "I realized that I wasn't in that great shape," he admitted. "I didn't really play to my expectations and came in really kind of tired that day. I was out of condition, and I had worked a little harder the day before than I should have. I told them all I was retiring, and the other players said this is going to be your last practice and we really want to see you run. Also, that Grey Cup was in Vancouver and I was recently married. I was going around visiting in-laws more than I should have been."

Said Don Getty, "We had such an emotional high beating Winnipeg because we had lost to them for three years. It was such an emotional high that the Grey Cup seemed incidental."

Instead of Bright, Kwong and Parker dominating the ground game, Ottawa's diminutive running back Ron Stewart led the Rough Riders to a 16–6 victory. The three Eskimo stars combined for a grand total of only 22 yards. Russ Jackson threw a touchdown pass to Bill Sowalski and Kaye Vaughn, winner of the 1960 Schenley Award for Outstanding Lineman, scored the other Rider major on a fumble recovery. The Eskimos were never really in it.

Said Eagle Keys, "Ottawa played a man-to-man defense against us, which we really hadn't seen in the West. We weren't really prepared."

"That did turn out to be a problem," allowed Parker. "Mind you, we got away from it late in the game and came very close to coming back and winning. They stopped us up pretty good on our running game, so we went to the passing game later. We had a chance to win it, but we just weren't good enough. Ottawa deserved to win. They played very well on defense—very well."

Jackie Parker assessed the first great era of Edmonton Eskimo football, which came to an end with the loss of the 1960 Grey Cup game. "We had some of the best players on our team that I ever played with or have been around," said Parker. "There was nobody we had who didn't excel. It was a team with excellent players.

"We had a family feeling. Wherever one went, everybody went. If we had a house party or barbecue, everybody showed up. We had a lot of fun together. If a team is all together, and they like each other, you can't beat that."

During the 1960s both the Alouettes and Eskimos experienced prolonged failure. Montreal had only one winning season, Edmonton four. Normie Kwong retired in 1960, Miles in '61 and Bright two years later. In 1963 Edmonton traded Jackie Parker to Toronto for Joe Hernandez, Zeke Smith, Jon Rechner, Mike Wicklum and Bill Mitchell plus $15,000.

Parker handled his departure with his usual magnanimity. "I didn't particularly want to leave Edmonton, but my brother was living in Eastern Canada. It looked to me like it was the best thing at the time for the Eskimos. The trade was just part of the game."

After the 1963 season another of the old guard departed when Head Coach Eagle Keys was fired, a victim of the club's record as well as a number of players' wives leaking information to the media about discontent in the dressing room. An honest man without guile, Keys was deeply hurt, leaving Edmonton a sadder but wiser man. He was replaced by Neil Armstrong.

Norm Kimball and Ray Jauch

The 1960s, however, weren't entirely a lost decade for the Eskimos to the extent that two personnel moves were made that laid the foundation of the greatest dynasty in Canadian football history. The first, in 1966, saw Norm Kimball named general manager. The second, in 1970, came when Ray Jauch was named head coach.

Born February 11, 1938, in Mendota, Illinois, Jauch graduated from Iowa in 1960 and joined the Winnipeg Blue Bombers. His playing career ended abruptly during the 1961 Grey Cup when he blew his Achilles tendon, the only player in Grey Cup history to do so. He remained in Winnipeg to coach junior football before returning to Iowa. In 1966 Neil Armstrong hired him as an assistant.

Armstrong's Eskimos made the play-offs in 1966 and the two following years, but finished each time a distant third to Saskatchewan or Calgary. They didn't win a play-off game. When the Eskimos slipped to fourth, Armstrong was given his walking papers.

At only 32 years old, Ray Jauch took over and began to build a better football team. General Manager Norm Kimball explained why he hired him. "I thought that he was very competitive, a bright young guy. He wanted to win so badly that I knew he would work hard to get it done."

In Jauch's rookie season in 1970, the Eskimos finished second, and he won the CFL's Coach of the Year Award. He wasn't satisfied, though, and was particularly upset with the attitude of some of his players before the team's semifinal loss against Calgary. "Although we were in the play-offs, the guys all had their cars packed and in the parking lot, ready to go home. I thought that was a bunch of garbage. I wanted them to have to walk down the street the next day. It's a matter of attitude, of playing harder, of having to face the fans rather than getting out of town."

Jauch was determined to build a team with a tougher attitude. "The players had to learn that if they did something negative, like take a penalty, it would affect the whole team. They'd been disciplined before, but it was individual rather than team discipline. They felt if they did something wrong, they were only hurting themselves. To change that attitude in my first year or two, I punished the whole team for what an individual would do. That was wrong, but it drove home the idea of team responsibility. If a guy wasn't going to comply, he had to understand he wasn't going to be there. Consequently I think we built a team attitude and came together as a team."

Jauch went from hero to bum in a matter of months with the Eskimos finishing last in 1971 with a record of 6–10. They haven't missed the play-offs since. Nevertheless, Jauch built his team of men with character. "What I look for in an athlete is honesty," he insisted. "If you can get honest people who will give you everything they've got every time out, and you know exactly what they can do, then you can form a plan, you can do something. My philosophy has always been to find the best players with the right attitude—self-motivators. Those people take care of themselves."

Jauch's journey to the top of the Western Conference began in a strange way. "When I took over," he confided, "I knew we just had to beat Saskatchewan at something. We went through '70 and '71 and they were tough. During the off-season we had a basketball team and played a charity game at the University of Alberta against the Roughriders.

"I told the guys before the game, 'Listen, I don't give a damn, we're going to beat these guys at something. I don't care what it is—checkers or whatever—but we're going to beat these guys and, by golly, let's go out and beat them at basketball. Let's get this thing started.' We won the basketball game. From then on the team had a winning attitude."

One of the new players Jauch brought in was Bobby Taylor, a pugnacious, abrasive receiver from the Hamilton Tiger-Cats. "When we got Taylor in '72," Jauch said, "he gave us the toughness we didn't have. He got into a fight with Dave Skrein on the sidelines in Regina. The Saskatchewan players jumped in, and immediately Ty Walls and Larry Watkins grabbed Bobby and were protecting him against the whole Roughrider team. Bobby Taylor had a great attitude. His attitude had a lot to do with our success."

The Quarterback

Attitude and character also came with Tom Wilkinson, who was signed by the Eskimos in 1972. To say he was unprepossessing would be an understatement. He would have easily stumped the panel on *What's My Line?*

The great middle linebacker Dan Kepley recalled his first encounter with the man who would lead the Esks to the promised land. "I got into Edmonton October 1975. Wilkinson came walking up to me. He was a little chunky. He had that double lip of Skoal and a Styrofoam cup, and he was spittin' and chokin'. He said, 'Nice to meet you. I'm the quarterback.'

"I said, 'Yeah, sure, you're my quarterback. I just left Roger Staubach and Clint Longly, and you're my quarterback?' I thought he was the equipment manager."

Kepley soon learned that looks can be deceiving. "He wasn't pretty, but he was effective. I still hold Wilkie as probably the best all-around athlete I have ever seen in my life. The best. He was drafted by major league baseball. He can shoot the eyes out of a basketball. He shoots pool, he bowls, he knows every card game, he's a Ping-Pong player, he plays golf. He was an A squash and racquetball player. He is the most intelligent athlete I have ever met."

During his 15-year CFL career, Wilkinson completed 1,613 of 2,662 passes for 22,579 yards and 154 touchdowns. His percentage completion rate of 60.6 is the fourth best in league history. Wilkinson was the CFL All-Star quarterback in 1974, '78 and '79. He won the Schenley Most Outstanding Player Award in 1974. When Edmonton instituted the Wall of Honour at Commonwealth Stadium in 1982, Wilkinson was the first name on it. He entered the CFL Hall of Fame in 1987.

Wilkie began his pro career in 1966 with the Toronto Rifles of the Continental League. When the Rifles' coach, Leo Cahill, went to the Argos the following year, he took Wilkinson with him.

In 1971 Cahill signed Joe Theismann and shipped Wilkinson to the Lions. Argo owner John Bassett simply didn't believe Wilkie looked like a quarterback. He was cut by the Lions in favor of Don Moorhead after spending the season riding the pine.

"Wilkinson called me," explained Ray Jauch. "We had Lemmerman at the time, but I really didn't have a backup. I had Dave Syme. Tom said he was driving to Grey Bull, Wyoming, and wanted to know if I was looking for a backup quarterback. I said sure, come on by. So he did. He still lives in Edmonton. He never did get to Grey Bull."

Jauch really didn't know what he was getting in Wilkinson, Jauch confessed. "I really didn't—not until I walked into the locker room with him and I could see the reaction of the players. He brought a desire, a willingness to put himself secondary to everything else. Tom was a great team player right from the start. I could sense that when we first got him. The players loved to play with him and for him."

Matt Dunigan was one of Wilkinson's admiring successors. "It's not so much stature as makeup. He could motivate guys in ways they never thought imaginable. He had an intuitive ability to analyze people precisely and get the most out of them in any situation he faced. Regardless of whether he was the number one or number two quarterback, he was there, holding it together. He was the glue."

Hugh Campbell, who coached Wilkinson from 1977–81, recognized the same quality in Wilkinson. "Wilkinson was our number one leader. He had great athletic ability that was somewhat camouflaged with his build, being short and a little bit squatty. But he was a competitor at the highest level. He had all the things you were looking for. He was the single best leader I've ever been around as far as team play goes."

After bouncing around the league for five years and getting nowhere, a lesser man would have called it quits. Not Wilkinson. "You want to prove to yourself that you were right," he said. "The thing is, though, you've got to get on a good ball club. I wanted to take one more shot at it, and I took the shot here in Edmonton.

"Edmonton had a fine football team. If my last shot had been with a team that had a poor offensive line, I maybe wouldn't have been able to prove myself. You've got to get the time to deliver the ball, and you've got to have excellent receivers, which we had. I'm not trying to belittle my own position, I'm just saying good quarterbacks have been with teams that weren't that good and, as a result, they haven't done that well."

Kicker Dave Cutler recalled the team's change in attitude that came with Wilkinson. "Ray Jauch started the idea of putting the team first. The biggest move Ray made was bringing in Tom Wilkinson. Wilkie and Bobby Taylor were really team guys, and they taught us all to put the team first and be unselfish. Jauch let them do that. That's part of good coaching, to encourage leadership to develop within the team."

One of Wilkinson's favorite targets was receiver George McGowan. In 1971

Jauch brought McGowan to training camp as a defensive back but soon realized he had the potential to be a receiver. He liked McGowan's aggressiveness toward the ball. He had a good year in 1971 and improved in '72. The next year he won the Schenley Award.

McGowan credited Wilkinson with his transformation from average receiver to superstar. "Wilkinson—that's what turned it around right there for the Eskimos and me also. I was a late bloomer. We had that happen in Edmonton in all kinds of positions. Look at the people we got from British Columbia: Tom Wilkinson, Larry Highbaugh, Ron Estay, Bob Howse, Wayne Matherne. Sometimes the conditions, the surroundings, the city you're in change a ballplayer."

The Kicker

Dave Cutler was the first kicker to make the CFL Hall of Fame (1988). The Simon Fraser grad spent 16 years in the CFL from 1969–84. His 464 field goals and 2,237 total points place him fifth in all-time scoring. Cutler is the most prolific scorer in Grey Cup history with 72 points.

In 1974 Ray Jauch discussed the importance of Dave Cutler to the dynasty the Eskimos became. "It is our basic philosophy that if we can get the ball to the other team's 43-yard line, then Dave has a very good chance to make a field goal. From 50 yards out, his chances of making it are about half and half. With that type of percentage you're willing to take a chance."

Working the other side of kicks was Edmonton's premier kickoff return man, Larry Highbaugh, who had a career average of 35 yards per carry, still the best mark in CFL history. In 1974 Highbaugh averaged an incredible 43.3 yards per return.

What a scenario! Highbaugh would run back the kickoff to his own 50-yard line, Wilkinson would complete a couple of 7-yarders and Cutler would kick a field goal. Opponents quickly found themselves on the wrong end of the scoreboard.

And yet Cutler's magnificent career was almost nipped very prematurely in the bud.

"In 1969, my rookie year, I was lucky they paid me two cents to play. Then in 1970 I was very lucky in training camp because my holder had once held for George Blanda, and Blanda credited him with getting him into place-kicking. So I started to get better. But I missed a convert in Vancouver, and soon after, I had a field goal blocked. Jauch then told Peter Kempf to get ready to kick, but

Kempf didn't have his shoe on, so I was sent out again to kick from the 43. I sunk it and I was back on track. That kick turned my career around."

When Jauch was reminded that he almost cut one of the greatest place-kickers in CFL history, he laughed. "We always weren't so smart, were we? Thank God Kempf couldn't find his shoe."

Cutler was totally devoted to his craft, studying wind currents, temperatures, field conditions, anything that might have an effect upon his kicking. He kept a record of every kick.

"The winds change. In the summer the winds are usually north–south and all the stadiums are north–south. But during the late fall the winds blow east–west, and so you get more swirl late in."

Cutler's powers of concentration were total. "When I'm at my best," he explained while still playing, "I don't hear anything. All the other teams yell at you that they're going to break your neck or something, but I don't hear anything. It's as if someone has left the volume on loud on a stereo set and someone switches the power on—it just blows you out. That is exactly the feeling I get after I kick the ball. The crowd all of a sudden comes on again. It's really weird. It really blows your mind sometimes."

Cutler relished the opportunity to kick a game-winning field goal. "You look forward to getting in there and kicking. You don't worry about failing. You only think of winning. I loved to win. When I could feel the team momentum build toward victory and my part in that momentum, then I could really go after a field goal. All I wanted was a chance to do my job."

Grey Cup 1973

Two years after missing the 1971 play-offs, Jauch had his Eskimos on their way to the Grey Cup. Unfortunately Tom Wilkinson and Bruce Lemmerman were hurt. Ottawa's starter, Jerry Keeling, also was on the sidelines. The man of the hour would be Rough Rider second-stringer Rick Cassata, who led his team to a 22–18 victory.

Near the end of the opening quarter, Wilkinson rolled to his right around the Ottawa 12-yard line and was trying to get out of bounds. Linebacker Jerry Campbell hit him in the face mask with a forearm, driving him to the turf, and Wayne Smith came in late with a shot to the ribs. Dick Adams also hit him. Wilkinson left the game with broken ribs, replaced by Bruce Lemmerman, who had torn up his elbow during the Western Final. Lemmerman ripped it open again during the course of the game, forcing Wilkinson to return in the fourth quarter.

Certainly Ottawa played well defensively, but injuries seemed to be the key to the game's outcome. Tight-end Tyrone Walls dropped several passes because of a broken hand. Ray Jauch has no doubt about the difference in that game. "Wilkie could play, but we knew if he took one hit it was all over. I knew that if they got Wilkie out of there we were in trouble. Then Wayne Smith got him on the sidelines. Bruce went in to play on sheer guts. He shouldn't have been playing. Then he got hit and Wilkie had to go back in. If we had had a couple of healthy quarterbacks, I think we would have had a good shot at them."

Play it Again, Sam

The 1960s also were years of futility for the Alouettes, brought about by the disastrous Etcheverry–Patterson–Faloney–Paquette trade at the beginning of the decade. Despite stars like Don Clark and George Dixon, who won the Schenley Award for Most Outstanding Player in 1962, fans refused to forgive the Alouettes' owner, Ted Workman, for dispatching their heroes to hated Hamilton. Averaging only four wins per year, the Als didn't win a single play-off game after 1962. Coaches Perry Moss, Jim Trimble, Darrell Mudra and O. Kay Dalton couldn't turn the team around.

In 1970 the Alouettes' new owner, Sam Berger, hired Red O'Quinn as general manager and Sam Etcheverry as head coach. The club finished third but got by Toronto and Hamilton to advance to the Grey Cup against third-place Calgary, who had pulled off a stunning upset over 14–2 Saskatchewan. It was the first time two third-place teams played for the Grey Cup.

Every coach will tell his players to have a good time before a championship game but not to do anything to embarrass themselves or the club. Etcheverry had to deal with every coach's worst nightmare when starting receiver Bob McCarthy and star running back Dennis Duncan, who had led the Alouettes in scoring for three seasons and in rushing twice, went one step too far. Just before the semifinal, Etcheverry was forced to cut them both.

Red O'Quinn recalled what happened. "Duncan and McCarthy were in a nightclub the night before the game and got into a brawl. It was reported to *The Gazette*, everybody got hold of it and so Sam had no choice."

An outside linebacker on that team was Mark Kosmos, who would go on to play in three more Grey Cups with two different teams. He supported Etcheverry's decision. "Dennis Duncan and Bob McCarthy were tremendous contributors to our team. I remember being shocked by it all, but we had so much respect for Sam that whatever he did was okay with us."

Minus two important contributors to the team, the Alouettes prepared to play the Grey Cup game in a sea of mud. The field had been resodded the week before, Kosmos recalled. "The turf was ripping up in almost two-foot squares. After a play you'd reach down, grab the thing and spread it out, almost like you were making your bed. They had laid it in big squares like that, thinking the weight would keep it down, but it didn't work."

The Stampeders took advantage of the first break of the game when they converted a fumbled punt into a Hugh McKinnis touchdown. Soon after, a long Montreal march stalled deep in Calgary territory. The Als gambled on third and one. Moses Denson was tackled below the waist by Terry Wilson. The quick thinking halfback then tossed the ball to Ted Alfin in the end zone.

Said Kosmos, "The pitch went to Moses, and we thought he was going to take it in. All of a sudden he was trapped in the backfield. Somebody had him by the leg, but it was such a sloppy field the guy couldn't get up. Moses cocked his arm and threw it. Ted's back there and it's the biggest play of the game. Today he'd be ruled in the grasp, and the play would be whistled dead."

The teams traded field goals before Alouette Tom Pullen scored on a 7-yard running play after being set up by an interception by Al Phaneuf, who picked off two that day, a record he shares with eight others.

In the fourth quarter Sonny Wade passed to Gerry Lefevbre for a touchdown. The final score was 23–10 in favor of the Alouettes. If there was any doubt about Etcheverry's decision to cut the quarrelsome Duncan and McCarthy it was erased.

Defensive back Gene Gaines, who had come over to Montreal from Ottawa, looked back at his third Grey Cup win in a row. "That was kind of a Cinderella one. We were a team that probably everybody thought wouldn't gel, but we came together at the right time. The exciting thing about it was that we were the first team to finish third and win the Grey Cup."

Mark Kosmos cited an unusual reason for their success. "I think one thing that made us a better club than our ability would indicate was the fact that we knew so little. We had 16 or 18 rookies. We didn't know who the Calgary guys were, so when we went out there we didn't have the same respect for them that we might have had if we had idolized them as kids."

The marriage made in heaven between owner Sam Berger and Montreal greats Etcheverry and O'Quinn didn't last long. Both left in 1972. Asked why he had left the general manager's job in Ottawa to take over the Alouettes, he replied, "Stupidity, I guess. Ego more than anything. The Alouettes had been going through all that mess and turmoil over there, and I wanted to straighten it out because I'd had some great years in Montreal.

"We got along fine the first year and it was Utopia. We won the Grey Cup. Unfortunately we had no place to go but down. Sam Berger stayed out of the operation the first year because he had lost an eye and was quite ill. But when he got well he started getting into everything. He interfered so much that we just couldn't live together. I left in July of 1972."

Having never won it as a player, it would be reasonable to assume Sam Etcheverry regarded winning the Grey Cup as a coach the crowning achievement of a distinguished career. Not so, said Sam. "I enjoyed playing in the Grey Cup more than winning it as a coach. My coaching experience with the Alouettes wasn't a good one even though we won the Grey Cup. We didn't have a good season. We were just fortunate to put four good games together and win it all. But it was an unhappy experience for me. I regret ever having coached the Alouettes."

Why was Etcheverry so bitter? Gene Gaines explained, "As things went along, a lot of things occurred, and he wasn't well supported by the management."

The Rivalry (and Revelry) Begins

Succeeding Etcheverry in Montreal was Marv Levy, who had been special teams coach with the Washington Redskins. In five seasons with the Alouettes, he would compile a record of 50–34–4, including two Grey Cup victories over Edmonton.

The first match-up took place in Vancouver, November 24, 1974. Rainfall was so heavy that tractors with huge roller brushes had to be used to push water off the artificial turf at Empire Stadium. Although most of the fans were under the roof, the players were soaked to the skin minutes after taking the field. Still, the game was played with tremendous intensity and surprising speed.

Although the Eskimos appeared healthy, Tom Wilkinson had an injured shoulder. That year Wilkie had won the Schenley Outstanding Player Award and was the All-Canadian quarterback.

Though strong offensively, the Eskimos were not formidable on the other side of the ball. The front four was solid with the likes of Ron Estay, John

Lagrone, Bruce Smith and Ron Forwick, but the linebacking and secondary were pretty green with the exceptions of Larry Highbaugh and Dick Dupuis. The defense bent but didn't break. Bending was all Alouette place-kicker Don Sweet needed in a game in which field goals were the order of the day.

Sweet tried eight, making four (a record he broke three years later) and a single. He also converted Montreal's only touchdown scored on Larry Sherrer's second quarter 5-yard run. Earlier in the game Edmonton had moved into a 7–0 lead on Wilkinson's 8-yard pass to Calvin Harrell. Montreal shut out the Eskimos the rest of the way to record a 20–7 victory.

Once again the Eskimos lost their starting quarterback because of a late hit. With the ball on the Alouette 23, Glen Weir nailed Wilkinson, and Junior Ah You piled on. Montreal was assessed 15 yards, bringing the ball to the 8. The Eskimos scored their only touchdown on the next play, but Wilkinson left the game and didn't return. He was replaced by Bruce Lemmerman.

"We were in pretty good shape going into the Grey Cup," recalled Ray Jauch, "and then Wilkinson got hurt on the first series we went in and scored on. Well, you could say, 'You're all right. You've still got Lemmerman.' but Wilkinson had just won the Outstanding Player Award, he had established himself as our leader, our number one quarterback, and then we lost him. From a morale standpoint that had as much effect on us as anything.

"But you never want to complain about injuries in a Grey Cup when you lose because some day you're going to play in a Grey Cup when you're not going to have anyone hurt and you lose and then what excuse are you going to fall back on?

"Our offensive line had a hard time with the Alouette's defensive line. That was one of the factors that caused us to lose. But in both '73 and '74, we came out and played well until our quarterbacks got hurt."

A star for the Easterners that day was Johnny Rodgers. Twice Larry Highbaugh was called for holding because he couldn't handle Rodger's dashes through the secondary.

Rodgers joined the Alouettes in 1973, one of the most exciting, heralded players to come into the league in years. A Heisman Trophy winner from Nebraska, he was everybody's All-American. He rushed, caught passes and was spectacular on punt and kickoff returns. Rodgers surprised almost everybody by spurning an offer from the San Diego Chargers in favor of the wider field in Montreal. He won the Schenley Rookie of the Year Award.

Rodgers also made a statement during the season that was taken out of context and made him sound like a blowhard. When asked if he would be a superstar in the CFL, he replied that if that came to pass, he wanted to be an ordinary superstar, one who never lost the common touch and remembered his roots. All the reporter passed on was the term "ordinary superstar" with no explanation of what Rodgers really meant.

In his four-year CFL career Rodgers made All-Canadian three times, twice as a receiver and once as a running back. In 1974 he led the league with 1,024 yards on 60 receptions. He picked up 492 yards rushing and 291 yards on kickoff returns. In 1975 he picked up 2,054 all-purpose yards. He was runner-up to Wilkinson in 1974 and Willie Burden in 1975 for the Outstanding Player Award.

Playing in his first Grey Cup in 1974 was Montreal native and future CFL Commissioner Larry Smith. For Smith just playing for the hometown team was a dream come true. "From the time I was a little kid I wanted to be an Alouette. I collected all the Bank of Montreal cards of the players. It was a dream."

Because he was so excited Smith didn't remember much about his first Grey Cup. "I started the game. I was so excited the next thing I remember was the end of the game. As a young player I was in awe the whole game."

The same year also was the first Grey Cup for fellow Montrealer Wally Buono. "I look back at 1974 in Vancouver with a lot of fond memories. It rained every day that week, but it didn't really affect us at all because we were really pumped up for the game. One of our emotional leaders was Marv Luster, a very intense player, who really got the guys riled. We came out and played a tough game."

Back in Edmonton Ray Jauch retooled his team for the 1975 season, adding Canadian players who would be part of Edmonton's success for years to come. Home-brew rookies from the previous year included Dave Fennell, John Konohowski, Stu Lang and Dale Potter. In 1975 Bill Stevenson, Tom Towns and Pete Lavorato joined the team.

For the third straight year the Eskimos finished first and defeated Saskatchewan in the Western Final, a cold, foggy day at Clarke Stadium. Two of Edmonton's four regular season losses that year had come at the hands of the Roughriders, so Jauch called for drastic measures, significantly changing his defenses. "We did some different rotations in the secondary," he said. "We used different coverages than we used before. We only rushed three guys sometimes in order to cover everybody. Ronnie would take his normal reads, go to dump the ball off and we would have a guy right there in his face. It might have been the first time a three-man rush was used."

In 1975 Montreal finished second to Ottawa but still advanced to the Cup, which was held in Calgary for the first time.

Baby, It's Cold Outside

When the Grey Cup game was awarded to Calgary, the major concern was what the weather would be like. The organizing committee produced charts proving the weather could be quite nice on November 23. It wasn't.

The week didn't start out that way. The first four days the weather was beautiful. On the Thursday evening, when the Schenley awards were staged, people walked the streets without a coat. The fancy coats were all inside.

The nominees for the Most Outstanding Player Award were hometown hero Willie Burden, who had set a new rushing record of 1,896 yards despite his team's fourth-place finish, and the Ordinary Superstar. The normally reserved Willie was decked out in a baby blue tux. Not to be outdone, Rodgers donned a plush red velvet tuxedo with matching cape and a Three Musketeers hat. Willie won the award. Edmonton's Charlie Turner won the offensive lineman award.

The weather turned cold on Friday and colder Saturday. On game day all male metal chimpanzees were judiciously moved indoors, and the temperature at game time was –10°C. Add the wind chill and it was likely at least –30°C, the coldest Grey Cup in CFL history. Despite the weather McMahon Stadium was full half an hour before the kickoff. Fun-loving fans eager to watch the pregame show got more than they bargained for. As the bands were playing, a streaker took to the field and did a dance that lasted several minutes. For a few seconds people thought she was part of the show. Soon she was corralled by stadium security staff and the proceedings could begin.

The playing conditions turned the game into a defensive struggle. It was only the third Grey Cup in which no touchdowns were scored (the others were in 1933 and 1937). It was the first one since 1945 in which all points were scored by Canadians, and it was the only Grey Cup in which the points were scored by just one player on each side. The final score was Dave Cutler 9, Don Sweet 8.

Sweet kicked the Alouettes into the lead with a 30-yarder in the first quarter. Cutler replied from 40 yards. Near the end of the half Sweet set a Grey Cup record with a 47-yarder and added a single. Montreal led 7–3 at the half.

In the second half Cutler booted one from 25 yards out. On the final play of the third quarter, he broke Sweet's record from 52 yards. Edmonton was ahead 9–7 going into the final 15 minutes, but Montreal had the wind.

In the dying minutes of the fourth quarter Sonny Wade replaced Jimmy Jones at quarterback and marched his team downfield. Larry Smith picked up 26 yards on a screen pass, and Joe Petty made a razzle-dazzle play for a 46-yard gain. Steve Ferrughelli and Johnny Rodgers made it third and seven on the 12-yard line. Trailing by 2 points with a minute left, the Alouettes naturally opted for a field goal.

Wayne Conrad snapped the ball back to Jimmy Jones, who dropped it. Already moving forward, Sweet kicked the ball on the ground. It squibbed into the end zone, where the Eskimos conceded a single point.

After the game Jimmy Jones and Montreal owner Sam Berger were a contrast in class. Jones blamed Conrad and anyone else involved—everyone but himself. Berger, tears in his eyes, thanked his players for giving him a wonderful season.

Alouette linebacker Wally Buono deeply admired the owner. "Sam Berger was a great owner because he really cared for the players and he really liked being around the players. He was always very fair.

"I remember when we went to Vancouver for the Grey Cup in 1974, and they put us in an out-of-the way place by the city dump. It wasn't a very nice hotel.

"Sam Berger came the next morning and was really upset about it. He told us to pack up, and we went to the Bayshore. He said we were a first-class team and deserved first-class accommodation."

The Eskimos Dan Kepley, arguably the greatest middle linebacker to play Canadian football, had special memories of that Grey Cup because it was his first. "I had no idea what a Grey Cup was. But I knew I had to win that game just to pay for the down-filled jackets and clothes I had to buy my dad and his best friend when they came up for the game.

"I knew Canadians were a little crazy when all of a sudden I saw that woman streaking. Tom Wilkinson went out to the center of the field with the other captains for the coin toss and said to Montreal's captain, Junior Ah You, 'Wasn't that your wife?' That really started things off well. Junior didn't have much of a sense of humor."

After the missed field goal, 45 seconds remained. It was imperative that Edmonton retain possession by picking up a first down. Ray Jauch figured that sequence was just as important to victory as the the Alouettes' missed field goal. "Near the end of the game we were going into the wind. We still needed a first down, and Wilkie's gutsy run got one for us. We were able to run the clock out."

According to Wilkinson the wind during the game was a bigger factor than the cold. "When you were playing you didn't notice the cold all that much, but the wind you did notice, especially from my perspective as a quarterback. I was quite concerned about it because the wind could hold the ball up very easily."

The Alouettes' Gene Gaines thought Edmonton took advantage of their opportunities and Montreal did not. Wally Buono concurred with that assessment. "We felt we had really outplayed them. We had ample opportunities to put the game away even at the end when a chip shot of a field goal would have won it for us. We had the game very much under control, but then Johnny Rodgers fumbled a punt. Another time, going into score, Rodgers fumbled the ball again.

"And then everyone can remember the last-second field goal we missed. It was really caused by Jimmy Jones not being able to put the ball down, not Don Sweet missing it. It wasn't a very good hold because his hands were cold." He sighed. "It wasn't our day."

But it was a very good day for Larry Smith in a losing cause. He caught 8 passes for 183 yards. "I was used to the cold weather. I was what they called a cold-weather back—slow and cold. All I had on was a little T-shirt, my shoulder pads and our summer mesh jersey. We didn't have our winter jerseys because they forgot to bring them.

"I didn't feel anything. I think I was frozen right through, but I was so pumped I really didn't notice the weather."

Smith thought about the field-goal attempt. "We were there. Then Jimmy Jones screwed up the hold and Don missed it. All of us thought we had it won because he was automatic. We never really felt we lost that Grey Cup. It was most disappointing.

"As a matter of fact I had just bought myself a 1975 Buick Century, and I was planning on paying it off with my Grey Cup winnings. When we missed the field goal, I went on GMAC for three years."

Dynasty, Edmonton Style

Both the Edmonton and Montreal teams slipped to third the following year. At the end of the 1976 season Ray Jauch startled the football world by deciding to leave coaching for the front office. "They told me that they were going to hire a director of football operations. They said I could do one or the other. I decided to take a look at the other side of it and get into the administrative end, which maybe was a mistake. I should have coached, but I didn't. Once I got into it that first year, I realized I wasn't ready to quit coaching."

The man chosen to succeed him was Hugh Campbell, former outstanding receiver with Saskatchewan. Campbell had been head coach at Whitworth College in Spokane, taking over a program in 1970 that was nearly extinct and building teams that won two-thirds of their games. He was selected Coach of the Year in the Pacific Northwest Conference three times. Still, coaching downy-cheeked collegians is one thing, looking after grizzled old pros another. When informed that no one had ever sussessfully made the head-coaching jump from small college to pro, he replied, "Gee, I didn't know that. Maybe I shouldn't have taken this job." His appointment was greeted with skepticism.

"It's true he didn't have a track record," admitted Jauch, "but I liked his approach to things. I thought he was the right kind of guy for our team. I wanted to hire someone I thought would come in, take what we had and build on it."

Jauch and General Manager Norm Kimball disagreed slightly about how Campbell was signed. "He wrote us a letter," said Jauch. "I looked at all the candidates. It was my job to hire a successor to myself and make a recommendation."

So it was Jauch's decision to hire Campbell? "No, that's not right," replied Kimball. "Ray was involved, certainly. I was the one who brought Hugh into the equation. Ray had to approve it, though. Actually the person who was probably more responsible than anybody was Earl Lunsford. Hugh had worked with him in Winnipeg as a guest coach. I talked to him about Hugh.

"Campbell was just a quality person. I liked the fact that he had head coaching experience and I knew him as a player. I knew he was a fierce competitor. I don't think you can be a coach without being a great competitor."

Campbell agreed. "I'm very competitive, and I want us to do our best with whatever hand is dealt. If you've got a year of injuries or something, you may not go all the way, but you still want to get the most you possibly can out of the players.

"My coaching pattern was really established at Whitworth. The amazing thing was how similar that was to the CFL in that the roster was small. You didn't have as many guys backing up positions. If there were injuries you had to make some things do. There were a lot of things that made me better prepared to come to the CFL.

"Whitworth was my education in coaching. There was nobody else to line the field, nobody else to raise the flag. My wife coached the cheerleaders. We did it all."

Campbell knew what was expected of him in Edmonton. "When I was hired Ray and Norm Kimball told me that one of the reasons they had selected me was that because I wasn't here as an assistant coach I would have a more open mind about new people and change.

"Ray told me the team needed a lot of changes and that was one reason he hired me instead of Vic Rapp. Vic, he said, wouldn't make the changes that had to be made. He had favorite players.

"The year before the team had not made it to the Grey Cup. They finished in third place. Ray felt there were some players who were aging, and it was hard to make those changes when you've had those players for years."

At age 36, Campbell was the youngest, greenest coach in the CFL. He immediately began the task of hiring assistants, favoring older men with a wealth of experience. "That was one of the things Jack Gotta told me at the time," Campbell confided. "By doing that you're not afraid of someone stabbing you in the back for your job. You get people around you who are experts at their positions. We went with Don Matthews as kind of an extra defensive coach under Leo McKillip, the coordinator. After one year I felt that Don knew enough about the CFL to take the job over. Don and I had a relationship that went back to Spokane when I was at Whitworth and he was coaching at Ferris High School.

"I knew that Don could be the coordinator, but I didn't think he should be it right off the bat because he needed to know the league. So he came in and then Leo went with Ray Jauch to Winnipeg and it worked out great for us."

Don Matthews had no coaching experience beyond the high-school level, except for a graduate assistantship at the University of Idaho. Some people thought Campbell had taken leave of his senses.

"When I hired Don Matthews, the headline in the Edmonton paper was 'Campbell Hires High School Coach.' They said it was a big negative that we had a high-school coach. What about all the guys that have coached pro ball that are looking for jobs right now, they asked? But I knew Don was special.

"Joe Faragalli—I had been a guest coach in Winnipeg so I had seen him coach. I knew that his style of offense with no tight-end was the coming thing in the CFL. I wanted Leo McKillip for carry over from the team before because he would be the coach that knew the players. Cal Murphy I'd known for a long time. We hired him the second year I was here."

"You've got to have two things in assistant coaches: one is that they've got to have ability, knowledge and creativity and be able to get something done. But, two, you've got to have a group that can work together harmoniously. They don't have to be friends. They don't have to drink together. But they do have to respect one another's abilities."

"At half time assistant coaches can't be telling the defense one thing, the offense another and the punt protection team that they almost had a punt blocked. I don't want to come in at half time and have to be a diplomat. I want to be able to tell a coach to get that punt protection straightened out or get more pressure on the quarterback or get our running game going. I don't want an assistant coach sulking because he thinks I don't appreciate him or I've hurt his feelings. We've got to trust each other enough that I can just say what's on my mind. I've never known a coaching staff that hasn't had fights. There is no business with so much pressure."

New defensive coordinator Don Matthews' greatest player was Dan Kepley, who remembered his coach fondly. "He is the most innovative, flexible defensive coach that I've ever seen. He would come up with some incredible schemes. I ran the show for him on the field. If I came back to him and told him I didn't think something was going to work unless we moved this guy and I did this and that guy did that, he'd say go do it.

"He wasn't a guy who would come in and say this is my system, you play it. He would observe each one of us and then design defenses around our abilities. He would not put us in a bad light."

Hugh Campbell

When Hugh Campbell took over the Eskimos, he had very definite ideas about what should be done and how to do it. "Involve yourself with the most talented and best people you can," he concluded. What I honestly think was a strong point in my coaching was that I had a passion for making sure that people got to contribute the most they could, not just for their happiness but also for my selfishness so that everything would be as good as possible. I believe in getting the right people and having them be thinkers and contributors.

"In Canadian football you only have 20 seconds between plays instead of 45

Mastermind and master builder Hugh Campbell.

in the NFL. There will be times when something happens and you don't have time to write a book about it—the guys on the field have to decide what to do. If you give a player the confidence and allow him to make decisions, it is not a big shock the last three minutes of a game to be doing that.

"The players I've coached knew they were allowed to make decisions, free in the knowledge that if they made a mistake they were not going to get traded that night. And so they did better under stress. I feel the team that is completely drilled and mechanical is ill-prepared.

"When I was thinking about being a coach, I learned most from Eagle Keys but certainly from others as well. I admired Bud Grant from a distance. I never played for him, but I watched the way he handled players and his remarks about players in interviews. I learned a lot from him about communication.

"I was genuinely interested in each player. Never a week went by when I didn't have a good discussion with a player about his life and goals and whether he was getting to where he wanted to go. Plus every day I thought about how every player was going to get better at that practice.

"My job, I felt, was coordinating the coaches and players and striving for perfection, really striving for improvement every day. What I brought to the team was not letting anything slip through the cracks."

Born May 21, 1941, in San Jose, California, Campbell was raised with his brother in a neighboring suburb called Saratoga. His father was a grocer who dealt with people from all walks of life and Campbell acquired qualities of infinite kindness, patience and common sense.

"The thing my parents gave me was that they were as close as any people I've known to being without prejudice of any kind, be it wealth or color or religion or whatever. My father was always very, very understanding. My mother was very competitive, and I think I have a blend of those characteristics."

With the full support of Kimball and Jauch, Campbell decided to change direction. Slowly, surely and deliberately, Campbell fashioned a dynasty. "Too many teams put their Canadians at the receiver positions, and because they were always worried about protecting the quarterback, they used two or three imports on the offensive line."

The Eskimos had three import offensive linemen when Campbell arrived. "The first thing we did was trade away some Canadian offensive linemen for defensive lineman David Boone, receiver Angelo Santucci and defensive back David Montagano. The trade worked out really well because it set the tone and theory for what we were going to do. It had to do with the philosophy that we were going to win on defense and sell tickets on offense.

"In anything I say I don't want to downgrade the person we traded away. We ended up a year later completing the process. We had Charlie Turner and Willie Martin still left as offensive linemen. We gave Hamilton their choice of either of those guys for Mike Wilson.

"We were having some trouble with a guy named Reggie Lewis at Calgary, and we really intended to replace both those guys, but to make it look good and be legitimate with Hamilton, we gave them their choice. The next year we took Wilson, who played as an import for us. We never heard from Reggie Lewis anymore. Wilson could handle him.

"By then Hector Pothier got old enough to play out there at tackle.

"I think it was about the middle of the third season that we finally went to an All-Canadian line. The thing I think I brought to the Eskimos was playing an All-Canadian offensive line.

"Then we got Neil Lumsden for Bruce Lemmerman when I guaranteed

Hamilton they would make the Grey Cup if they had Bruce as their quarterback. I loved and respected Lemmerman as a player, but we had Wilkinson and Moon, so I felt we could give up one of our really good quarterbacks for an outstanding Canadian player like Neil."

In 1977 the Eskimos finished in a three-way tie for first with the Lions and Blue Bombers. Edmonton got the bye.

Lui Passaglia kicked his Lions past the Bombers in the semifinal, but the Eskimos crushed them 38–1 to return to the Grey Cup at Olympic Stadium against Montreal. On paper the Alouettes and Eskimos were pretty evenly matched. It was reasonable to expect a close game.

Staples Anyone?

Events, however, conspired against the Eskimos. Like Calgary in 1975, the weather in Montreal was reasonably pleasant the first half of the week. The Thursday night marked the twenty-fifth anniversary of the Schenley Awards, and Johnny Bright gave a moving speech to an appreciative audience. Then a blizzard hit the city, dumping tremendous amounts of snow on Olympic Stadium. At that time the Big O wasn't closed in, so the field was exposed. The stadium workers put salt on the snow to melt it. When the temperature plunged the next day, the field turned into a sheet of ice. Despite the billion dollars spent on the Olympic Stadium they had no tarpaulin.

Despite a transit strike, a record crowd of 68,205 watched what should have been an excellent football game. Instead they were treated to a sorry spectacle resulting from the incompetence of Olmypic Stadium officials. The score ended 41–6. For the sake of the crowd, it was a good thing the home team had the 41.

The shellacking absorbed by Hugh Campbell's Eskimos was the third worst in league history. What surprised the crowd was how the Alouettes handled the slippery field with ease while the Eskimos were floundering. Sonny Wade unleashed an aerial attack, completing 22 of 40 passes for 340 yards and 3 touchdowns. Don Sweet set two records, one by kicking six field goals (equaled by Paul Osbaldiston in 1986 and Sean Fleming in 1993) and another for total points (23), which still stands. Edmonton had a miserable day.

During Grey Cup week, Alouette coach Marv Levy had cloistered his team away, thinking only about football. Rumor had it they were staying in a monastery. "It was pretty close to being a monastery," recalled the Alouettes' Larry Smith. "The only difference is that we didn't have the Bible right in front of us."

If the Eastern champions were essentially inaccessible, the Eskimos were highly visible everywhere, including the lobby bar at the Chateau Champlain, as loose and carefree as a bunch of kids when school's out.

Montreal's Wally Buono discounted that as a factor in the Edmonton loss. "Probably Edmonton had done that all year. Their lifestyle didn't prevent them from winning a lot of football games and getting to the Grey Cup. So come Sunday afternoon, how should it matter what you did the night before or two nights before if that's what you've been doing all year?"

"We know they were going out every night of that week," recalled Larry Smith. "Our guys stopped going out three nights before the game."

Buono agreed. "Marv Levy was very much in control. He didn't allow us to do a whole lot—maybe the first day or two—but come Thursday, he tabooed everything."

It was only natural to examine a number of factors to explain the Eskimos' lopsided loss. It couldn't have been the field conditions or the –9°C temperature because the conditions were the same for both teams.

What had made the difference, it turned out, was that the Alouettes had put heavy-duty staples on their shoes in order to get a grip on the ice. They worked perfectly, giving the Montrealers a significant edge. According to Buono the architect of the idea was Tony Proudfoot. "The big thing for us was seeing what shoes would be adequate. Tony—very ingenious, always thinking—felt we needed something steel-tipped to cut through the crust of the ice. He came up with the staples idea.

"All we did was get two staples and cross them. You put them on the outer part of the shoe where you get the grip. I think it was a psychological edge more than anything else."

"Tony Proudfoot had the idea," Gene Gaines confirmed. "He said this is really effective. So he popped some staples into his shoes, and then some other guys grabbed a staple gun and went *boom, boom, boom.* We found out during the first half that they were effective. At half time everyone else had them in their shoes."

Edmonton's Dan Kepley wasn't buying it. "We were set up. The ice and snow were going to come, and all of a sudden there just happened to be staple guns all around the place. I mean, if Custer had known the Indians were on the other side, he wouldn't have walked over there.

"We had one of the fastest teams position by position that I can remember,

The Staple Bowl, Grey Cup 1977.

but we just had too many Americans and too many brothers who didn't know what to do on ice. It was the most embarrassing thing I had experienced. I won the Schenley that year, but that achievement was completely obliterated by what happened to us that game."

Alouette Larry Smith begged to differ. "If Dan is using the staples as an excuse, that's a little odd—41–6 is a fairly dominant score. The way I looked at

Montreal's Vernon Perry still holds the record for the longest Grey Cup interception return set November 27, 1977.

it, Edmonton was highly charged, highly emotional, but as a group they were a little cocky. We knew they were more talented in many areas than we were, but we felt we may have had just a slight bit more character in terms of the mental toughness of our team."

Als' Assistant Coach Cal Murphy had another idea. "I don't know if it was the staples so much as the way the turf was laid. In Montreal, if you were going toward the scoreboard end, the turf lay that way. If you tried to stop and the field was slick, your feet would go right out from under you. When we were heading toward the scoreboard, we would run the football because we had the traction. When we had to go away from the scoreboard, we threw the ball more. But keep in mind that Sonny Wade had an outstanding game, and when he was hot there weren't many guys any better."

Wally Buono had no doubt why Montreal won. "We didn't win because of the staples — we won because we were a better football team. We had beaten the Eskimos in Edmonton that year. We had a closely knit group of guys who really played hard and intensely. That's why we won."

Of the five Alouette Grey Cup teams, Buono thought the 1977 edition was the best. "We had a great defense under Dick Roach. We never allowed a team to score more than 20 points on us. That's a pretty good record by itself. We had excellent special teams.

"Offensively Marv was always very conservative, but there were very few turnovers. "We had John O'Leary, Ed George, Dan Yochum, Dave Braggins, Brock Aynsley, Ray Watrin, Peter Della Riva, Larry Smith, Sonny Wade, Joe Barnes. On defense we had Glen Weir, Junior Ah You, Carl Crennell, Chuck Zapek, Vernon Perry, Dickie Harris, Tony Proudfoot, Jim Burrow, Randy Rhino. The guys had a great sense of pride, a great willingness to go out and pay the price to win. They had a great sense of confidence in one another that no matter what, they were going to win."

The 1977 season was Marv Levy's last in Montreal. He was succeeded by Joe Scanella.

When asked why the Als were unable to repeat in 1978, Larry Smith replied, "We didn't have Marv Levy, who would allow us to change things and do things on our own. When Scanella came, he started to take that initiative away. He was an autocratic coach. We lost the feeling we had under Marv.

"Marv encouraged people and gave them their space. He had great assistant coaches, delegated well and was a fantastic manager. That's why Marv was still so successful at Buffalo."

Wally Buono really admired Levy. "No matter what your role was, he made you feel that you were a very important part of the team because he allowed you to have input. He allowed the players to be a big part of the preparation. He let the defensive players call all the defenses. He let the offensive players control what plays they ran.

"Scanella was totally opposite. He took no input at all from the players. We had a lot of veterans at that time who were very sharp and who really wanted to be part of the game plan decision-making. They felt it was just as much their team as anyone else's. That was a source of conflict.

"Marv was much more relaxed and seldom raised his voice to anybody. The guys just went out and played. Scanella was always hollering."

Back in Edmonton Hugh Campbell took his 1977 Grey Cup defeat in stride. "After winning the West I felt that we had done as well as we could possibly do," he confessed. "However, that game served as our motivation for five straight Grey Cups."

Let the Good Times Roll

From the moment the 1978 training camp began, the Eskimos desperately wanted a return Grey Cup match with the Alouettes. They knew about the staples and felt they'd been had.

Campbell also felt the team needed to improve. "We didn't have the speed I wanted. Our receivers were Donny Warrington and Stu Lang, George McGowan (who had a very sore knee) and John Konihowski. In my second year we had Tom Scott, Waddell Smith and Brian Fryer to go with them."

Scott had been traded by the Bombers to Edmonton for Joe Poplawski. Scott ranks second behind Brian Kelly as Edmonton's best all-time receiver with 426 receptions for 7,160 yards and 58 touchdowns. He was All-Canadian four times. He ranks third in league history for touchdown passes, fifth in yardage and seventh in receptions. He averaged 985 yards a season.

Scott became one of the greatest receivers in Grey Cup history. The Washington State grad caught 26 passes, second only to Hal Patterson. He is third in yardage behind Patterson and Red O'Quinn. He caught 12 for 174 yards in the 1980 Grey Cup against Hamilton, the second-best performance ever. He caught four career Grey Cup touchdown passes, tying with Patterson for second behind Brian Kelly. Scott's record three touchdown catches in the 1980 Cup match still stands. Strangely, he is nowhere to be found in the record book for play-off games.

Fellow receiver Waddell Smith became the fifth best receiver in Eskimo history, catching 343 passes for 5,542 yards. Only Kelly and Scott had more touchdown passes.

The Eskimos fielded a powerful lineup in 1978. In addition to their corps of receivers, running back Jim Germany was coming off a 1,004-yard season. Tom Wilkinson and Bruce Lemmerman were joined by a Rose Bowl hero named Warren Moon. The offensive line was solid.

Although finishing last in the West in total offense, Edmonton scored the most points in the league. They became a big-play team.

The defense was the best in the West with Dave Fennell, David Boone, Ron Estay and York Hentschel on the line, Dan Kepley, Tom Towns and Dale Potter behind it and one of the best secondaries in the history of Canadian football with Larry Highbaugh, Joe Hollimon, Ed Jones, Greg Butler and Pete Lavorato.

In spite of their talent, the Eskimos didn't find 1978 a cakewalk, for the Stampeders, who had finished last the previous year, were revitalized under Jack

All-time Grey Cup interception leader, the Eskimos' Joe Hollimon.

Gotta and challenged for first place. The Esks ended up on top with a record of 10–4–2, the Stamps second at 9–4–3. Edmonton beat Calgary in the final 26–13 and moved on to the rematch with Montreal played at Toronto's CNE Stadium.

"Our team was very well motivated," said Campbell. "Montreal was an excellent football team with a bunch of old pros who had been there, and we had a mixture of very young and very old players. Not only were we hungry, we were pretty talented."

Dan Kepley described the atmosphere that afternoon. "There was really a tremendous amount of revenge involved. It was one of the most physical games I can remember. There was so much hitting going on, and it was constant. Normally, when the plays are away from you, you don't get that involved. That day there were guys flying around everywhere. It was a really tough defensive struggle that we won 20–13."

Jim Germany and Dave Cutler staked Edmonton to a 10–0 lead in the first quarter. Cutler added 7 more points compared to 3 by Don Sweet. Going into the fourth quarter trailing 17–3, Montreal closed the gap when Joe Barnes ran

10 yards for a touchdown and Sweet added another field goal. The rally fell short when Cutler wrapped things up with another 3-pointer during the last minute of play. For the first time in 14 years a Western team had won a Grey Cup on eastern soil.

The following year the two teams met again in Montreal, their fifth meeting in six years and their last. Both had won the Cup twice.

That year a red-headed rookie from Washington State named Brian Kelly arrived in Edmonton. Over a nine-year career, Kelly caught 575 passes for 11,169 yards and 97 touchdowns, the second-most majors ever by a receiver and third overall. Kelly averaged 1,241 yards a season. Only Calgary's Allen Pitts has done better.

Kelly was inducted into the CFL Hall of Fame a mere four years after he retired. Why was he so good? With a twinkle in his bright blue eyes, Kelly replied, "It helps to have a good quarterback. That is one very important characteristic, a quarterback who can put the ball on the money all the time without putting the receiver at risk. Warren Moon can do that.

"It is just hard work like any other job—long hours, using your brain, studying the game and your opponents. You have to know your opponent's strengths and weaknesses. You then formulate a game plan about how you exploit him. I also think good eyesight is a key. The last time I was tested I read the bottom line of the chart."

Like other great athletes Kelly finds it difficult to understand or describe why he is able to play so well. "Sometimes things happen on the field, and after, you wonder if you can really do things like that."

He did focus on one particular talent he possessed. "I'm not very fast, but I have some quickness. I can change directions. I can get a guy turning, and the instant he turns, I know it. I can then shift to go the other way before he even thinks about recovering. That is something I've never worked on—I just have it. I can't explain it."

To listen to him you would believe his Hall of Fame career was really a lucky accident. "I had made the decision in college that I wasn't going to pursue a professional football career. I had never even given Canada a thought, but then Hugh Campbell called me one day and asked me if I wanted to come up. I figured it would only be four weeks out of my life to find out if I could make it or not and so I said well, what the heck. I wasn't planning on doing that many other things, so I came to Edmonton."

Edmonton's Brian Kelly caught a record five Grey Cup touchdown passes.

Despite the great offenses of both the Alouettes and the Eskimos, the 1979 Grey Cup was again a tough, defensive struggle. The Alouettes won all the game awards, but the Eskimos got the Grey Cup by a score of 17–9. The Alouettes couldn't get the ball into the end zone, settling for three Don Sweet field goals.

The Eskimos relied on two big plays for victory. In the first quarter Tom Wilkinson hooked up with Waddell Smith on a 43-yard pass and run for a touchdown. Smith was so wide open he could have crawled into the end zone.

In the third quarter Sweet's field goals gave the home team a 9–7 lead, and Hugh Campbell responded by changing quarterbacks. Warren Moon came in and threw a touchdown strike to slotback Tom Scott. Cutler closed out third quarter and game scoring with a 38-yard field goal.

The quarterback switch was normal procedure for Campbell. "Moon and Wilkie shared most of the games that year. It had nothing to do with who was playing well. They had their personal contest. They each got to play half a game.

"In the six years I coached, we started three different quarterbacks in the

Grey Cup: Wilkie, Warren and Bruce. Bruce is one name that gets left out too much outside of Edmonton. People in Edmonton appreciate the fact that he won a lot of games."

Throughout their losing effort, the Alouettes were convinced the Eskimos had a thirteenth man on their side: the head referee. Montreal was penalized 15 times for 145 yards, Edmonton 5 times for only 25 yards. The play that particularly upset Montreal came in the last minute of the first half. Keith Baker returned a punt 85 yards for a touchdown that was disallowed when Gerry Datillio was called for a clip. Instead of going into the dressing room with momentum on their side, the Alouettes were angry and dispirited.

"I thought that was a cheap call," recalled Larry Smith. "That would have brought us back to 17–14 or whatever."

"It was a low-scoring game," Buono recalled. "What was most disappointing was that Keith Baker returned a punt for a touchdown and the officials called it back for a very marginal clip. That might have been the deciding play."

Dan Kepley believed that the Alouettes' checkered past had finally caught up with them. "Montreal was always notorious for taking absolutely stupid penalties at the wrong time. That one cost them dearly."

Alouette Gene Gaines agreed. "We were our own worst enemy. We created our own problems. All three stars of the game were Alouettes: David Green, 142 yards rushing, linebacker Tom Cousineau and Don Sweet. If we had played a little smarter, we would have been more successful."

Smith had another explanation. "We never got started. We were lacking gas in that game. It was our fifth Grey Cup in six years, and we didn't play with a lot of emotion. The signs of dissension with Joe Scanella were showing, and we did not have the same unity and spirit we'd had with Marv Levy."

After their Grey Cup loss in 1979, the Alouettes were competitive for one more year, going 8–8 before losing to Hamilton in the Eastern Final. But all was not well. Scanella, called the Italian Ayotollah by his players, responded to a player revolt by cutting All-Stars Danny Yochum, Gordie Judges and Don Sweet. At the end of the 1980 campaign, Peter Della Riva and Dickie Harris were given their walking papers.

Della Riva returned the following year when the Als were short of receivers as a result of sending Keith Baker to Hamilton for the rights to Vince Ferragamo, who was needed to replace Joe Barnes, who had been traded to Saskatchewan. Scanella also cut Randy Rhino.

Sam Berger sold the team to flamboyant entrepreneur Nelson Skalbania, who signed NFL stars Billy "White Shoes" Johnson, a return man from Houston, Chicago Bear receiver James Scott, Los Angeles Ram Super Bowl quarterback Vince Ferragamo, as well as Keith Gary and David Overstreet, the first-round draft choices of Pittsburgh and Miami.

La Grande Fizzle

But what should have been a powerhouse on the field and a bonanza at the box office turned into a nightmare. Linebacker Tom Cousineau was lost to injury, and Vince Ferragamo couldn't or wouldn't adjust to the Canadian game. By the end of July the Alouettes were 1–3. They were winless in August, outscored 146 to 50. After losing 58–2 to Winnipeg, the erratic Skalbania gave Scanella a two-year contract extension. Two games later he fired him. He was succeeded by former Saskatchewan coach Jim Eddy. After managing only two more wins, Eddy also was fired.

It is generally believed that Skalbania's high-priced American players were duds, but the record doesn't entirely support this opinion. After all, David Overstreet won the Eastern rushing title, James Scott led the East in receiving and Johnson was third in punt returns. Ferragamo was fourth in the CFL in completions and yardage but threw 25 interceptions and only 7 touchdown passes.

During the off-season the affairs of the Alouettes resembled a comic opera, the major aria entitled "Uncertainty." First George Allen came in but quickly departed. Then Harry Ornest seemed to be representing the team and immediately cast off the high-priced American help, receiving nothing in return. Finally the Bronfman family, owner of the Expos and Seagrams, rescued the Alouettes, who were reborn as Les Concordes. Joe Galat became the head coach.

When Les Concordes went to training camp in 1982, they faced enormous difficulties. Because they didn't know if they would be operating, they couldn't sign players or sell season tickets. A further complication was the fact that Sam Berger hadn't received full payment for the team from Skalbania.

"Only 6,000 people renewed their tickets," said Assistant General Manager Bob Geary. "Mr. Sam Berger put a monkey wrench into our operation. Mr. Bronfman took over the team on May 16, but even after that I couldn't find anyone who could sign a check until May 24, four days before the opening of training camp. We had the money in the bank, but we didn't have the authorization to go ahead until Mr. Berger released the veterans' contracts that he had seized."

Geary felt the biggest problem facing the franchise was the indifference of French Canadian fans. "For us to get their support, we must win. Marv Levy used to say when the gate was down that people would not come out unless we had a left-handed French-Canadian quarterback who could win. The French Canadian is a winner. If the Expos and Canadiens don't win, he doesn't come out. That's the kind of fan he is. So we must win."

Les Concordes didn't. To sell tickets the Bronfmans convinced Sam Etcheverry to join the club as president and general manager. Although still bitter about the way the team had treated him in the past, he loved Montreal football and very reluctantly agreed to come aboard.

Etcheverry worked himself to exhaustion by going everywhere in Quebec to sell a team that faced incredible challenges. Attendance was as bad as the team on the field. Though there were signs of progress, they were not enough for the Bronfmans. On July 7, 1983, Etcheverry was fired. Poor communication, they said.

By 1985 Montreal managed to finish 8–8 under Joe Galat, who was replaced by Gary Durchik. Under the Alouette banner again in 1986, the club regressed to a 4–14 mark, missing the play-offs. Durchik was fired, replaced in December 1986 by the happy warrior, Joe Faragalli.

Faragalli had been brought in by the Alouettes' new president and chief operating officer Norm Kimball, who had retired from the Eskimos after the 1985 season. Charles Bronfman and IMASCO wanted out of the football business so they brought Kimball on board in March 1986.

That summer CFL Commissioner Doug Mitchell had been ecstatic. "If someone had told me a year ago not to worry about Montreal because Norm Kimball will move from Edmonton to the Alouettes, I would send them for tests. This could never happen. It would be so good for the league it would be beyond comprehension. But it did happen. Things in Montreal have improved dramatically."

One year later Kimball and former Eskimo president Jim Hole assumed ownership of the Alouettes and prepared for the 1987 season. With Kimball the Alouettes had the best and most experienced football man in the country. Bob Geary and Faragalli had put together a contender on the field. The only missing ingredient was fans.

Kimball and Hole made the decision to fold. On June 24, 1987, the Alouettes were no more. Canada's second largest city would be without the CFL for nine years until the defending Grey Cup champion Baltimore Stallions crossed the border in 1996.

Business as Usual

The Eskimos began the decade of the 1980s on their usual winning note, finishing 13–3 and becoming the first team in CFL history to score over 500 points. Dave Cutler led the league in scoring, Jim Germany picked up 1,019 yards rushing, Tom Scott and Brian Kelly caught 121 passes for over 2,000 yards and Warren Moon was second only to Schenley winner Dieter Brock in passing. Hank Ilesic had the best punting average, and Larry Highbaugh led the league in punt returns. Ed Jones was number one in interceptions. Nine Eskimos made the All-Canadian team and a dozen were Western Conference All-Stars.

The 1980 edition of the Eskimos defeated the Blue Bombers 34–24 in the Western Final 34–24 in Edmonton. From there they went on meet the Tiger-Cats in one of the few clear Grey Cup mismatches. Edmonton's third straight Grey Cup was won 48–10, the most lopsided score since Queen's University drubbed Regina 54–0 in 1923.

By this time Warren Moon had displaced Wilkinson as the starting quarterback. During the season he completed 181 passes for 3,127 yards and 25 touchdowns, at the time an Eskimo record. Tom Wilkinson wasn't exactly confined to the pine, hitting the target 83 times for 1,060 yards.

During the Grey Cup game, Moon completed 21 of 33 passes for 398 yards and three touchdowns. The Eskimos netted 606 yards to Hamilton's 201. Tom Scott caught three touchdown passes.

The Best Ever?

Many believe that the following year's edition of the Eskimos, who went 14–1–1, were the greatest team in CFL history. Warren Moon had a passing percentage of 62.6, completing 237 for 3,959 yards and 27 touchdowns, second to Dieter Brock. Dave Cutler established five career records. Moon and Wilkinson combined to set a new passing yardage record of 5,289. The Esks also scored 576 points, the most ever in a season.

In the Western Final Dave Cutler kicked five field goals as the Eskimos downed the Leos 22–16 and advanced to the Grey Cup for the fifth straight year. Their opponent was the Ottawa Rough Riders, clearly the poorest Cup contender the franchise ever faced. The Eskimos had won 14 games, Ottawa 5. Edmonton averaged 17 points per game more than Ottawa and surrendered 10 less. Ottawa's leading rusher, Richard Crump, had but 440 yards. Their leading receiver, Tony Gabriel, second in the East with 73 receptions for 1,006 yards would have ranked eleventh in the West. The Riders used four quarterbacks, the most successful being Jordan Case, who completed 129 passes. Moon hit for almost double that number.

An Ottawa victory was unthinkable, and it would have been the greatest upset in the history of Canadian sports. But it almost happened as the ridiculed Rough Riders gave Edmonton all they could handle.

The Eskimos were a team on a mission. No other club had won four straight Grey Cups. That goal was uppermost in Warren Moon's mind although he also was thinking about the Schenley. "Winning the fourth straight Grey Cup is the big thing, of course," he said. "Winning the Schenley is out of my hands because the winner isn't selected by my peers. The media picks them, and they tend only to look at statistics.

"My stats won't be as great as Brock or Clements because I won't play a whole game whereas they will. When we get ahead I come out and Wilkie comes in.

"But statistics don't tell the whole story. Brock should have scored more points than he did when you consider the number of passes he completed and yards gained. The most important thing is points scored and games won."

Moon's assessment was correct. Brock won his second Schenley that year.

Warren Moon celebrated his twenty-fifth birthday four days before the 1981 Grey Cup. His winning percentage was .790. Though obviously a consistent performer, he came out flat against Ottawa.

The Rough Riders, however, led by the inspired quarterbacking of Julius Caesar Watts, drove for two first-quarter Gerry Organ field goals. Jim Reid finished off an Ottawa drive with a 1-yard touchdown, putting the underdogs into a 13–0 lead at the end of the opening quarter.

Early in the second quarter Sam Platt capped another Ottawa drive with a 14-yard run. All the Eskimo offense could muster in the opening half was a single when Dave Cutler missed a 24-yard field-goal attempt. Even Mr. Automatic couldn't hit the broad side of a barn door.

Just before the end of the half, Campbell pulled Moon and sent in the forgotten Tom Wilkinson. With a 7-yard pass here and a Jim Germany run there,

Wilkie strung together a few first downs and kicked the sputtering offense into life. This gave the Esks some semblance of optimism when they headed for the dressing room down 20–1.

Early in the second half, Dan Kepley and Dave Fennell made crushing tackles and stopped the Riders cold. Soon after, the great Eskimo offense made a dent in Ottawa's stalwart group of defenders. First Jim Germany ran for a touchdown, and after holding Ottawa on the subsequent possession, Warren Moon, returning to the quarterbacking duties, drove his team to the goal line again, where he went over on a quarterback sneak. At the end of the third quarter, Ottawa led by 5.

Gerry Organ upped the Rough Riders' lead to 8 with a 28-yard field goal halfway through the final quarter. Shortly after, Moon scored again and with the 2-point conversion to Marco Cyncar, the Eskimos tied the game.

Near the end, the Riders' J.C. Watts threw to Tony Gabriel on the 55, but Gabriel was called for offensive interference. With the penalty Ottawa was hemmed in deep and had to kick. Twice before, Ottawa had had great field position after punt returns nullified by clipping calls.

Starting around midfield Moon quickly marched the Eskimos to the Rider 20. Dave Cutler kicked the winning field goal with 3 seconds left on the clock. Edmonton had become the first team to win four straight Grey Cups. The ridiculed Riders went home defeated but with heads held high.

What did Campbell do at half time to shake his team out of the doldrums? "The big adjustment at half time was mental," he recalled. "Wilkie had already adjusted us going into the second half. Wilkie had gone into the game because Warren Moon wasn't doing anything, nor was the entire team. Wilkie went in and moved the football.

"At half time we discussed in a businesslike way what we had to do for a shorter time than normal and in an emotional way for a longer time than normal.

"We ended half time by saying we had to win the third quarter. (Edmonton outscored Ottawa 14–0.) Most teams believe they have to win the fourth quarter, but I've always thought that if you win the third, the fourth will take care of itself.

"I couldn't have drawn that game up better. I wouldn't have felt satisfied blowing Ottawa away like we did to Hamilton the year before. That's what everyone expected. For my personal selfishness it was wonderful to have a close game, to have all the decisions to make, be really involved and be able to win it on the last play. I preferred to win it with us making a field goal rather than them missing one."

To many observers, Wilkinson had been the key to turning the game around. Assistant Coach Don Matthews demurred. "We couldn't get anything going in the first half so Tom Wilkinson went in for Warren Moon. Wilkie picked up a couple of first downs, and so people think he turned the game around. He didn't. Warren Moon came back in for the second half and was magnificent. Moon won the game."

But at the heart of the matter was the fact that Moon was given the opportunity to win the game because of the tremendous second-half play of the defense, led by Dan Kepley, who that week had won his third Schenley Award for Outstanding Defensive Player. He harried Ottawa's Watts into throwing two key interceptions. Kepley played like a man possessed.

"It was the Grey Cup that we just *had* to win," said Kepley. "In December of 1980 my friend Donny Warrington was killed in a car accident. The following season our whole team dedicated itself to winning the Grey Cup for Donny. We wore a patch with Number 21 on our jerseys.

"Donny was just an incredible individual. He would do anything, just absolutely anything for this ball club. He didn't care if he ever read his name in the paper. He gave you 250 percent.

"I nicknamed him Jeep because he drove around in the wintertime in an old Jeep, wearing a big parka. He was an outdoorsman, a real man's man. He loved to fish and hunt. When he was killed, it was a horrible thing. To this day I wear the '81 Grey Cup ring every day, and when I put the ring on in the morning, I always say hi to him. Every morning."

Dan Kepley saluted the unselfish attitude of Tom Wilkinson. "Warren Moon had started and was having a very tough time. Wilkie went in and got some first downs and gave Junior, as Wilkie called Warren, enough time to stand on the sidelines, watching the defense to see what was happening out there. Warren came back in and played well.

"After being such a great quarterback and being a starter all those years, Wilkie was still prepared to school Warren and teach him absolutely everything he knew about the game. Wilkie was also prepared to step down and leave the limelight to Warren."

What did Moon think he learned from Wilkinson? "Not as much as people think," he confided. "I've learned a lot by watching him, by seeing how he does things, but our styles are different. People criticized him for his physique, but all he did was win. I've got great respect for his accomplishments."

The Speech

For three complete seasons, 1979–81, the Eskimos lost a grand total of six games. This was a team used to winning. But how would they handle losing? What would happen if their backs were to the wall? At the halfway mark of the 1982 season, the Eskimos faced the Stampeders in the Labour Day Classic at McMahon Stadium. Calgary won 32–20, leaving the Grey Cup champions in last place with a record of 3–5.

Gene Gaines was an Eskimo assistant coach that year. "We had a rough year at the beginning," he said. "We had a good team, but we weren't playing well together as a team. We were trying to go up a hill that had a lot of Vaseline on it."

The injury bug had struck. Brian Kelly and Marco Cyncar missed parts of the 1982 season, as did the unassuming, usually overlooked running back Jim Germany. It was no coincidence that the team returned to its winning ways when he returned.

"Once we were able get our running attack back, it solidified things all around for us," explained Gaines. "We were pretty solid defensively, but it is the offense that takes the pressure off your defense. When Germany came back the whole team performed much better."

Over seven seasons, the New Mexico grad ran for 5,730 yards and scored 58 rushing touchdowns. His value to the team wasn't really appreciated until he was injured. Did that bother him? "To get the notoriety due to an injury really did affect me somewhat. I thought it was a little bit unfair to get recognition that way. There have been running backs who come into the league and lead in rushing and then they have an off year or are gone. Over the years I was a consistent running back in Canada."

Germany's accomplishments are impressive, especially considering that he played on a team that lived and died with the pass. "The running attack for the Eskimos is nothing more than a down to give the receivers a chance to catch their breath," Germany said. "I have to try to break every play, think touchdown on every play. This situation has made me a better running back."

Just as important to the team was Germany's tremendous blocking ability. His absence was the main reason Warren Moon was sacked so often during the first half of the 1982 season. "That is what they missed when I was injured. Kevin Cole did a really good job, but if Kevin's man didn't come he would go out into the pattern, whereas I would pick up whoever was leaking through. My getting out into the pattern was just to be a safety valve."

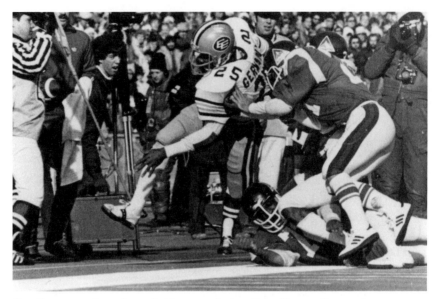

Jim Germany plows through Alouettes during Grey Cup 1978.

The Eskimo comeback began minutes after their Labour Day loss to Calgary. Hugh Campbell addressed the troops. "I said to the team that I hadn't given up, but that we had lost all our margin for error. We had to virtually win every game just to make the play-offs.

"I said we were capable of doing that, and any players who didn't think we could, I would guarantee them their contracts. All they had to do was step forward and say they wanted out. I promised them they would still get paid, but I needed them out of the way because we were going to the Grey Cup.

"The players did a lot of talking among themselves, and as a group we all agreed to play the best football possible and let the chips fall where they may. We then won 10 sudden-death games in a row, including the Grey Cup in Toronto against the hometown team. The odds against doing that are phenomenal."

One of the few rookies on the Eskimo club that year was Laurier graduate Rod Connop, who went on to win the award for Outstanding Offensive Lineman in 1989 and to be an All-Star seven times. "I remember that speech well," Connop said. "It *was* something. Instead of letting the media in after the game, he closed the door and spent the next 20 minutes explaining things the way he saw them. When people talk about great turning points in seasons, they always mention Hugh Campbell's speech."

Connop then added a qualification. "It just so happened that Jim Germany and Brian Kelly came back in the lineup. We played with Kevin Cole, who could run the ball but didn't have the understanding of the offense and couldn't block as well as Jim Germany.

"Cole had been diagnosed with dyslexia and it was literally a nightmare for him to learn his plays. If he went the right way, you had maybe a chance of the play working as long as it didn't involve him blocking.

"People never understood how good Germany was because he did everything so easily, so smoothly. He wasn't flashy so he didn't stand out. Anyway, after Labour Day the team basically got healthy for the first time that year."

Practically nothing went wrong the rest of the way. The Roughriders collapsed, Calgary's defense fell apart and British Columbia lost both their quarterbacks. Edmonton ended the season tied for first place with Winnipeg.

In the Western Final, which ended 24–21 for Edmonton, Bomber Trevor Kennerd was as cold as the weather. If he had been able to contribute even the minimum performance expected of a professional, the Eskimo Grey Cup streak would have ended at four.

The man of the hour in 1982 was Warren Moon, who threw for 5,000 yards, the first quarterback in CFL history to achieve the mark. He completed 333 passes, 36 for touchdowns. But his record-setting performance still didn't win him the Schenley Award. That went to Toronto's Condredge Holloway, who didn't even lead the East in passing. It's hard to win when you aren't nominated. The Eskimos chose Tommy Scott instead. James "Quick" Parker won for Outstanding Defensive Player.

It was cold, wet, windy and miserable for the last Grey Cup game played at the CNE, November 28, 1982, won by Edmonton 32–16.

For Hugh Campbell it would be his last Grey Cup as a CFL coach. Soon after he began his odyssey to the United States, first as coach of the Los Angeles Express of the USFL and then as the head man in Houston with the NFL Oilers. As beloved as any coach could ever have been, the players desperately wanted Campbell's CFL coaching career to end on a winning note.

Edmonton opened the scoring against the Good Ship Argonaut with a Dave Cutler 38-yard field goal. Minutes later Condredge Holloway hit Emanuel Tolbert on a hitch pattern. He turned up field and ran 84 yards for a touchdown. Cutler added another field goal, but Toronto took the lead again when Terry Greer scored on a 10-yard pass from Holloway.

Before the half ended, Cutler struck again, and Brian Kelly picked up a major to put the Eskimos into a 20–14 lead. Neil Lumsden added a major, and Cutler kicked a fourth field goal, giving him a record-setting Grey Cup career total of 18. All Toronto could muster in the second half was a safety touch.

Hugh Campbell said, "Toronto had a good team. They hadn't been there for a long time, and they were playing at home. A lot of people don't realize how hard it is to beat a team in a Grey Cup in their home stadium. Before we won in 1978, no Western team since 1964 had won a Grey Cup on Eastern soil, let alone in the other guy's home stadium. We won five in a row on Eastern soil and two of them in the other guy's home stadium. It is rare for a team to do that."

For rookie Rod Connop, the outcome was never in doubt. "At no time during that game did I think Toronto was going to win. It was a case of being blissfully ignorant because of being young. All I thought was that I just couldn't let the guys down and we would win the game. Warren Moon, Tommy Scott, Dan Kepley and Dave Fennell were just too great, too talented, too awesome not to win that game. The one thing that sticks out was that it was pouring rain, which wasn't affecting us in the slightest, but it was affecting the Argonauts."

Warren Moon won the Grey Cup Outstanding Player Award and Dave Fennell won the other two for top defender and top Canadian. Of all his Grey Cups, 1982 was the best. "I think winning the Grey Cup in 1982 was the most satisfying because at Labour Day everyone had written us off. People were calling for Coach Campbell to be fired. The finger was being pointed at a number of players for not performing properly.

"We went through a little bit of soul-searching. Then we won 10 straight games. That was a team accomplishment. I think I'm prouder of that than anything. It is the ability of a team to overcome adversity that is really the mark of a champion. It's easy to be a front-runner. What really counts is your ability to pick yourself up when you're down."

Fennell never tired of winning the Grey Cup. "The challenge after a team matures becomes quite different," he explained. "It's sort of like having sex five times a night. The first time is always the most exciting. You're not quite as enthusiastic the fifth time as the first, but it's still great."

The win was particularly special for Connop. "I was a rookie starting for the Edmonton Eskimos in my hometown of Toronto against the Argonauts. I had lots and lots of family and friends come out to that game. It was perfect. In my very first year I went home and played the hometown team and beat them.

"However, I was a little disappointed because the veterans were so used to winning that it was almost anticlimactic for them, whereas I was so wound up and excited. I felt like I was the only one. That game connected me to the Eskimo dynasty. That made it special."

The Anatomy of a Dynasty

Words that repeatedly crop up when speaking of the great Eskimo teams of the late '70s and early '80s are *esprit de corps, self-sacrifice* and *attitude.* "We spoke in plurals," said Dan Kepley. "It was *we.* There wasn't any *me.* We had a lot of guys who were great athletes—and even greater people—who checked their egos at the door. We had one thing as a common goal and that was to go out and win football games. We didn't care who got the credit.

"We had fun. We weren't so caught up in the money as a lot of people these days are. There wasn't a lot of money. There were a couple of guys who were going to make big money. Somebody like Warren Moon was going to make a lot of money. And we wanted Warren to make a lot of money. If he made a lot of money he was happy when he walked on the field, and it definitely reflected in the way he played."

Said Gene Gaines, "Any problems that occurred within the football team, the players themselves rectified. They kind of controlled everything. They stepped in because they had great respect and admiration for the team and for one another. If someone didn't show that respect, they let him know about it, telling him, 'What we have here is good, and you're not going to tear it down.' Great teams have camaraderie, that family feeling for one another, that permeates the whole organization."

"During those six years that I was the head coach," reflected Campbell, "we had real good players, which was the most important thing. But I think that history has proved that just having really good players doesn't guarantee you a championship. I think what we did as an organization is that we got everyone to pull in the same direction and do it repeatedly. We never took a deep breath and said we've arrived. We kept being driven for six consecutive years.

"I coached for six years here, and for the first five years, we did better than the Eskimos had done the year before. I felt great pressure every time we won because everybody was expecting us to win all the more.

"The sixth year was kind of the *coup de grace,* when we lost all those players offensively and ended up being in last place on Labour Day. The team not only showed it could play from being in front but also showed that when they were down and out, and people had written us off, that we could come from behind and consistently, week after week, never get blown out—always being there, never blowing a lead in the fourth quarter. In Canadian football, teams get beat a lot in the fourth quarter.

"A lot of people look back and say, gosh, you won all those games, you must have dominated all the time, but that wasn't the case at all. If you look at the record, we were behind at least four of those six years at half time in the Western Final. The Eskimos were a team that just kept coming at you.

"The main thing that made us good was that everybody worked together. If someone wasn't team-oriented, we asked him to move along. Sometimes we played against guys that were stars, but we'd rather have had them be a star somewhere else than a distraction here."

Campbell never took success for granted. "Norm Kimball and I were both committed to the fact that we were going to always have the best possible team we could have with whatever hand was dealt to us.

"I never said 'We've got to do what we did last year.' I always said, 'We've got to do better.' We always looked at the two or three weakest links of the team—even if they were pretty darned good—and replaced them.

"So every single year we've had four to six changes on our team. Every year! Even after a championship we'd come back the next year and there'd be some changes. Two or three would happen early and others at the last cut.

"We felt if we made changes we weren't going to grow old as a team. People would remember Tom Wilkinson, Bob Howse and Dave Cutler and say you had the same old guys all the time. Most people don't realize we didn't have Howse or Wilkinson at the end."

Hugh Campbell is a kind, decent man who found it very difficult to tell players their careers with the Eskimos were over. "The most miserable thing in my life has been releasing players. The way I lived with myself is that the decision was what I honestly thought would give us the best chance to win the most games possible. I never kept a guy because he was with us last year and made the play that won the Grey Cup for us. My decision was based on what would give us the best chance to win.

Of nine-year veteran defensive end and four-time All-Star Ron Estay, Campbell said, "I can remember watching a film of Ron Estay and tears coming to my eyes when I realized I was going to be cutting him that afternoon.

Frankly, Don Matthews didn't see it. Assistant coaches are wonderful, and he did more than I did, but I was neutral. I wasn't defense, I wasn't offense, I wasn't special teams. I was head coach. My decision wasn't prejudiced."

Campbell used a hands-on approach. "I wasn't like some coaches who tried to be distant and authoritarian. I was more of a guy who got involved with them and tried to squeeze every ounce of their brainpower first and their energy second toward having a better team and at no time asking them to sacrifice their family.

"We even incorporated their families. Their wives were part of the Eskimo family. When it came time for the wives to sacrifice for their husbands when it was play-off time and everything was doubled and practices were harder, the wives felt they were a part of it. There wasn't the griping at home there might have been when it came to play-off time."

Kepley agreed with Coach Campbell's assessment of the Eskimos success. "What we did together as a team affected our performance on Sunday afternoon. Generally everybody liked everybody. Everybody got along very, very well. The one thing that really made us strong was that there was unconditional respect on Sunday afternoon that each man was going to do his job.

"We socialized a lot together. We talked about personal issues and we had a lot of fun. We genuinely became incredibly close. The theme song we played for a number of years was 'We Are Family'—and we were.

"Our wives and girlfriends got to know each other. Our children socialized with each other. When we went to Grey Cups our parents got to know each other. Our grandparents got to know each other. They started looking forward to the next Grey Cup so they could see each other again.

"There were a lot of players who sacrificed a lot of their bodies. It seems to be too easy to say, 'I've got a hamstring pull or my shoulder hurts a little bit so I'm not playing!' We didn't have guys like that.

"We had guys who believed that if they were supposedly the best players in this league, and they were the champions, then they should show up for the party on Sunday afternoon. And they did."

The players also showed up for another kind of party that encouraged solidarity. "We had some rituals and traditions. The day after the game, after the practice, we'd go to an old bar here in Edmonton called the Grand Hotel. We had a requirement that you had to show up. Everybody used to.

"You didn't have to drink. Everybody would ante up and we'd buy beer, pop, hotdogs and sit around and bullshit. We'd talk a little bit about football and about life.

Campbell recalled that the coaches also were involved. "The offensive line had what they called a carbo pack, where they'd have a big meal, and Cal Murphy would go with them. I told them I thought it would be good if they invited someone from another group on the team—maybe a defensive coach or back, for example. They did, having a guest, so to speak, every week. Each group did that."

Said Dan Kepley, "Ray Jauch started the whole thing, and Hugh Campbell picked up the ball in '77. They treated us as men and put responsibility on us. They gave us the best facilities, travel, hotels, food. Campbell and Kimball did everything possible to give us the best opportunity to be a winning football team. We had to supply the effort and the ability.

"We policed ourselves. If someone was getting out of line, was getting ready to upset the apple cart, we pulled him aside and took care of it."

Dan Kepley

Hugh Campbell's Eskimos had an outstanding linebacking corps with Dan Kepley in the middle and Canadians Tom Towns and Dale Potter on the outside. Kepley, an All-American from East Carolina, was a victim of the NFL's passion for measurement and statistics. "I was a small middle linebacker," he said. "I was not 6'3", 235–240 pounds like the computer said you had to be to play in the NFL. Being 6' and 215 pounds is not that impressive.

"The day after the NFL draft, I signed as a free agent with the Dallas Cowboys. I was their last cut. The decision came down to me or a first-round draft pick by name of Hollywood Henderson. There was no way that I was going to beat out a first-round draft pick because that wouldn't have looked very good for Dallas.

"After the last cut every other NFL team had their rosters set, and I bounced to Cleveland and Denver. I thought maybe I might have a chance to hook on the reserve list with Denver because they were looking for an extra linebacker, but in their last exhibition game they lost a couple of defensive backs, so they decided to go with another defensive back instead.

"I was getting ready to sign with the Charlotte Hornets of the World Football League when Frankie Morris called me. He told me the Eskimos had just lost their starting middle linebacker, Sam Britts, and asked if was I interested in coming up and giving it a try. I said sure.

"I had no idea where Edmonton was. I just knew it was an opportunity to keep playing football. I came in on a Thursday and started against Calgary in Clarke Stadium on Saturday. Being 21 years old and coming into a new place, my adrenaline was really pumping."

Kepley was All-Canadian five of his 10 years in Edmonton. He won the Schenley three times and is on the Eskimo Wall of Honour. He gave new meaning to the idea of playing with pain. "Broken bones are just an occupational hazard," he explained. "I've checked myself out of hospitals, I've shot myself up with Novocain and Xylocain. All of my fingers have been broken once and some twice. Three have been operated on. My knee can tell you if it is going to rain tomorrow. In 1982 I tore a rotator cuff in my shoulder the third day of training camp. I wasn't going to tell anybody at the time because I was afraid I would lose my job.

"I played the whole season on a couple of shots of Novocain every game. The shoulder would separate probably 15–20 times a game. It would just come out of the socket."

His linebacking mates Tom Towns and Dale Potter were no slouches either. In 1980 all three made the Western All-Star team. Potter came out of the University of Ottawa and Towns was a hometown boy from the University of Alberta. Potter was voted the Outstanding Canadian and Defensive Player of the 1980 Grey Cup game.

"Wonderful players!" said Campbell. "Towns and Potter never missed. They were always out there banging away and consistent. The hearts of the team were Brian Fryer, Stu Lang and Angelo Santucci on offense and, on defense, Potter and Towns. These guys never got big recognition because they weren't big stars, but they were big stars to me."

The Kimball Way

The key to success of any professional team is the general manager. The man who put the dynasty together in Edmonton was Norm Kimball, inducted into the CFL Hall of Fame in 1991. Before joining the Eskimos in 1961 as coordinator of minor football, Kimball spent nine years working for the National Cash Register Company and coaching minor and junior football. It was Kimball who introduced the system of seeking out local talent.

"We started by having camps and recognizing who the younger, talented people were," Kimball explained. "Then we started distributing information to colleges, primarily in the northwest, and after that it was self-feeding. We'd had some success and they started coming to us rather than us having to go to them."

When reminded that other teams weren't operating that way at the time, Kimball replied, "You don't want to say that you are better than other people. I think we worked harder. We made sure that we scouted properly. We made sure that we put the system in place.

"It's like any business. In the final analysis you do the things that you have to do to be good. And so you pay attention to detail. We didn't do everything well right away, but eventually we were pretty good at it."

It wasn't easy. "I was relatively younger and tried to bring in new ideas. It took some time for our organization to understand what we had to do to get it done, too. You know, to have the willingness to expend funds and to do the things that were necessary to become a winner. The '80s were different than the '50s and therefore everyone had to adjust."

When the team was losing in the early years, too many executives were hanging around. One club president even wanted to get involved in preparing the game plan. "Those things happened in the early years, no question about it," he admitted. "I think that's just transitional. Everybody wants to get the job done, and until you learn how, those kinds of things happen."

Kimball's management philosophy was simple but effective. "The whole idea is to get the best people you possibly can, let them do their jobs and do everything you can to help them. That's what a manager's responsibility is. The easiest way to achieve that is to get the best people to start with. We were fortunate in being able to do that. I don't think there is any question that for a long period of time we had the best talent in the league. A lot of people worked very hard to achieve that. Frankie Morris, Ray Neuman, the coaches Ray Jauch and Hugh Campbell. The board of directors kept their hands off the football club. They were certainly welcome to be there, but they weren't involved in the operation."

Frankie Morris agreed that meddling directors could spoil a potentially good fooball club. "There has to be a complete division," he insisted. "That was one of the best things Norm Kimball did. Shortly after I joined the Eskimos, he said, 'Management is here, the football team is here and the executive is over there.' We had three complete divisions.

"We certainly talked about things, but the personnel department was the personnel department and the coaching staff was tied directly into the team.

The executive took care of all the other things. That was what turned the team around. When Norm ensured those divisions, things took off and we never looked back."

Kimball denies that money was a key factor in building the Edmonton dynasty. "We were about in the middle of the pack as far as spending was concerned," he insisted. "We certainly didn't have the top payroll. But we sometimes spent money in different places. We spent more money on scouting than other teams. We stayed in the best places, we traveled the best way, we did everything to make it better for the individual, and then we asked a lot of him.

Super Scout

Nowhere was Kimball's philosophy more apparent than in the scouting system. The best ever were Ray Neuman and Frankie Morris. Norm Kimball hired both of them. "Ray did a great job," Kimball recalled. "We always had people coming in, especially at quarterback. We were never in a position that if somebody went down, we couldn't replace him. That's one of the things that was critical.

"Frank Morris had a great ability to deal with young people. I saw that when he was working at the University of Alberta. He was absolutely outstanding in dealing with our Canadian prospects and in college scouting."

Morris described his art. "You have to know people. You have one guy you talk to and he won't tell you anything. You have another guy who tells you everything and another guy who does a lot of stick handling. I did some things that I think were a little different. I got to know a whole lot of trainers and equipment people. They enjoy talking to you. I got a lot of good information from them. If you want to really know a kid's character, ask the trainer or equipment man."

What gave Edmonton the edge? "You know, for a long time when I would go across the country, I didn't see a whole lot of people from other teams."

Morris loved the work. "I like people. I made every effort to help as many people as I could. I tried to establish really good relationships between the team and the kids and make it as easy and pleasant for them as possible.

"Prospects still had to be realistic and realize they had to come in and bust their butts. I think I gave them an honest view of what they had to do to make the club. I thoroughly enjoyed my scouting career."

"I've told this story many times over about our Argonaut club of 1947 and the great Eskimo teams of the '50s, '70s and '80s. I've always said the parts were interchangeable. Same types of individuals: a bunch of guys who liked to play hard. They liked one another, they got along real well, they had a whole lot of pride and were a heck of a pile of good athletes. I was lucky to be associated with three groups of guys like that. It was marvelous.

"There was an atmosphere. It's funny. When I'd go to visit NFL clubs I could walk on to their training site and, honest to God, when I walked in the door I almost knew immediately whether it was a winning or a losing situation — just the atmosphere around those places.

"That's what the Eskimos had. People would come in and feel like a winner. I don't know how you define that, but I really think it was true."

According to Rod Connop those people stayed, which was an important factor in contributing to the Eskimos' success. "We're probably the leaders in the league in terms of our out-of-town players who make Edmonton their home. When you become part of the community, you have that much more drive to do well because you've got to live in that community. That has had a real bearing on Edmonton's success."

Old Soldiers Never Die

After the 1982 season Hugh Campbell left for the USFL. His assistants also left Edmonton. Cal Murphy became head coach in Winnipeg while Don Matthews took over the Lions. Gene Gaines went with Campbell. Campbell would lead the Los Angeles Express and the Houston Oilers before returning to the Igloo in 1986.

Despite outstanding performances by Warren Moon, Brian Kelly and Tom Scott, the 1983 Eskimos finished at 8–8, tied for third with Calgary. They lost the semifinal to Winnipeg.

In an uncharacteristic move, Norm Kimball had hired the wrong coach in Pete Ketella, who had been the offensive coordinator for Bart Starr's Green Bay Packers. Ketella had no CFL experience. Still, the season began on a promising note.

"We're not coming in here to change everything," Ketella said. "This team has been very successful winning Grey Cups. It is easier for us to adjust to the players than it is for them to completely change to a new way of thinking."

The team also was loaded with veterans. The only concern was replacing Hank Ilesic, who had left Edmonton over a contract dispute. But the Eskimos were nevertheless an aging football team.

The Eskimos of 1983 picked up 450 more yards of total offense than the year before but scored 96 fewer points. They scored 13 fewer touchdowns despite the heroics of Warren Moon, who ran for 527 yards and completed 380 of 664 passes for 5,648 yards (both records) and 31 touchdowns. In his last year in the CFL, he won his only Schenley.

That same year Brian Kelly and Tom Scott led the West in receiving with 184 catches for 3,046 yards and 20 touchdowns. Scott set a career record for receiving touchdowns (85) and Larry Highbaugh for interceptions (66). Dave Cutler established career records for most points (2,114), field goals (444), converts, (580) and singles (202). The team set a new single-season high of 5,887 yards in total offense.

At the halfway mark of the season, Winnipeg, B.C. and Calgary were tied for first with 10 points. Edmonton had 8. The Esks were only one win away from first place—not bad for a team in transition.

Instead of rewarding Pete Ketella with a contract extension or at least a public pat on the back, Kimball fired him. "I don't want to be negative about it," said Norm Kimball. "I thought Pete had a good background and had a lot of ability, but when it came to taking all the responsibility of the head coach's job, he just didn't seem to be able to get the job done.

"I hired Pete Ketella and that was a mistake. I think Pete was a good man, but you don't know what's going to happen in the future unless they've had previous experience."

Connop agreed with Kimball. "Now that I look back, hiring Ketella was a mistake, but I don't know who Kimball could have put in there. Whoever it was would be in for a tough ride because difficult decisions had to be made about veterans who had probably reached the end of the road but had just won five Grey Cups.

"Pete Ketella wanted to be his own coach, but he didn't want to alienate that veteran core, so he was terrified of cutting a vet for a younger guy, even though the veteran was actually going to weaken the team.

"He did some strange things. He'd go out on the field at six-thirty in the morning with a bucket of sand and a little garden shovel, going around looking for little divots in the grass made at practice the day before. He'd fill them in.

"The guys see the head coach doing that kind of stuff and wonder about it. I think he started to lose it early on although I didn't realize it at the time because I was just a young guy who had played exactly 16 pro games in my career."

To bring the team back into line with Eskimo values and traditions, Kimball turned to his old friend and golfing partner, Eskimo icon Jackie Parker. Parker had joined the B.C. Lions as an assistant coach in 1968, and when Jim Champion was fired the following year, he took over as head coach and did a credible job. In 1971 Parker became the general manager and hired his buddy Eagle Keys as head coach. In 1975, with the team mired in last place, both Parker and Keys were fired.

Parker returned to Edmonton. He answered Kimball's call as a favor to his friend and the football team that had been such an important part of his life. If hiring Ketella had been a mistake, replacing him with Parker was a stroke of genius, typical of Kimball's wonderful insights about people. "Jack probably did one of the best coaching jobs that anybody ever did for us," Kimball said, "at a time when it would have been very easy for us to go the other way. Parker deserves a lot of credit for what he accomplished in that interim period when our team got older, when we were replacing people and when we were trying to turn it around."

It wasn't easy, as Parker explained. "The guys that were great players for Edmonton over the years are still very good friends of mine, but I had to tell them they couldn't play anymore, which is hard to do. Some realize on their own that their careers are finished, but most don't. So they have to be told. It was very difficult."

Parker's record was the same as Ketella's, 4–4. During the off-season, Parker began to rebuild. He had to replace Warren Moon, James Parker, Ed Jones, Larry Highbaugh, Jim Germany, Dave Fennell, Waddell Smith, Tom Scott, Gary Hayes and Dale Potter. The following year Tom Towns, Dan Kepley and Dave Cutler retired.

Matt Dunigan

Crucial to rebuilding the fortunes of the Eskimos was the quarterback, and the scouting system produced another great one. Matt Dunigan explained how he came to Edmonton in 1983. "Ray Neuman, the Eskimos' U.S. pro scout, contacted me while I was at Louisiana Tech. It was at the beginning of my senior year, and he said that the Eskimos would be looking at me through the year and that I was on their negotiating list. One thing led to another, and at the end of the season, the Eskimos and I came to terms."

Dunigan was a talented quarterback who was nevertheless used to being overlooked. "I really didn't think I would be drafted by the NFL. I hadn't set any hopes. I just concentrated on my senior year and doing everything I could. It was a surprise that the Eskimos were looking at me. I considered it a blessing. I feel very fortunate to have had a career in the pros."

Dunigan has always demonstrated real poise and leadership ability. "Those qualities are very important in a quarterback, and I don't think people put enough emphasis on them. It seems like the NFL just looks at your stature and physical attributes. A lot of times a big heart, poise and leadership will overcome a lot of things."

Dunigan quickly established himself in the CFL. As a backup to Moon in 1983, he completed 14 of 26 passes for 239 yards. In 1984 he was fourth in the league, hitting on 220 of 412 attempts for 3,273 yards and 21 touchdowns. He finished fourth in rushing with 732 yards, displaying a recklessness that has cost him dearly in injuries throughout his career. He didn't apologize for his approach.

"I realize that if I run with the football my career will be shortened. But running is a skill you must have in Canadian football because when it's second and 10 and nobody's open — and that happens a lot — you just can't throw the ball away. You've got to make something happen."

In 1996, after suffering his twelfth concussion, he said, "I just play the game consistently like I think it should be played, stripping the label of quarterback off my back and going out there and doing what I can as a football player. I think that's the most important thing that I've tried to bring to the field week in and week out, year after year."

In 1985 Dunigan was fifth in passing, fourth in rushing and made All-Canadian. For the third straight year, Edmonton finished third. Because of an injury, Dunigan didn't play in the semifinal, which Edmonton lost to Winnipeg 22–15.

The following season the Eskimos returned to the top with a record of 13–4–1, but on an ominous note, their leading receivers were running backs Milson Jones and Chris Skinner. Dunigan was third in the league in passing. The team lost only once at home.

The league changed its play-off format that year so that the top teams would qualify for the play-offs. Calgary finished fourth with 22 points, 14 more than the third-place team in the East, so they made postseason play, losing to the Eskimos 27–18. Edmonton then crushed the Lions 41–5, setting the stage for a thoroughly wretched Grey Cup experience.

Despite being overwhelming favorites, the Eskimos were humiliated by Hamilton 39–15 in the 1986 Grey Cup. Usually when a team wins by a big margin, they do so on the strength of overwhelming offense. But it was the Hamilton defense that savaged the Eskimos that day in one of the most ferocious displays ever witnessed in a Grey Cup. Grover Covington, Mike Walker and Mitchell Price ripped the Edmonton offensive line apart and then did all manner of unspeakable things to Matt Dunigan and whoever was unfortunate enough to be in their path.

Things started to go wrong the moment the Eskimos left the dressing room. When the players were introduced, they were greeted by thunderous boos from the largely B.C. crowd, still smarting over the defeat of their beloved Lions the week before. Clearly the fans favored Hamilton.

On Edmonton's very first play, Grover Covington laid an enormous hit on Dunigan, knocking the ball loose for Mitchell Price. On the next play Hamilton quarterback Mike Kerrigan hit Steve Stapler for a touchdown.

Connop explained what happened. "Hector Pothier got suspended [for a drug conviction] and a player [Leo Blanchard, eight-year veteran and All-Canadian that year at guard] switched from the right side over to Hector's left tackle spot and just never adjusted.

"On the first series of the game, Dunigan was rolling to our left, and in our scheme your job is to basically protect a gap. We were both supposed to turn to the outside, but the left tackle turned toward me. Grover Covington was coming off the edge because no one was blocking him. I dove out and got my head snapped across by his knee."

Minutes later, Mark Streeter blocked a punt and Jim Rockford recovered for another Hamilton touchdown. Two Edmonton misses, two Hamilton touchdowns.

Less than four minutes later, after a Kerrigan-to-Stapler pass that covered 43 yards, Paul Osbaldiston kicked the Ti-Cats into a 17-point lead. Osbaldiston tied Don Sweet's Grey Cup record of 6 field goals and added 3 converts.

The score was 29–0 at the half and 36–0 by the 13-minute mark of the third quarter, when Damon Allen finally got the Westerners on the scoreboard with a 6-yard run for a touchdown.

The Eskimos rounded out their scoring when Allen threw to Brian Kelly in the end zone and added a 2-point convert. In the dying moments of the travesty, Osbaldiston rubbed salt in the wound with a final field goal. The Eskimos allowed 10 sacks and gave up 10 turnovers, equaling the record for miscues set in 1957 by Winnipeg.

Jackie Parker explained the defeat. "We had to change our offensive line around. That really killed us because Hamilton was a really good defensive team. Plus the fact that Hamilton had been there two years in a row. We'd played them twice during the year and beaten them, but we tried to tell everybody that these guys had been there two years—they know what's happening in this Grey Cup thing.

"While we couldn't get any offense going, Mike Kerrigan had a really good day. He was getting rid of the ball fast."

General Manager Hugh Campbell said, "We knew we were really the underdog. We knew we had a problem on the offensive line. We had covered it up for two weeks on an icy field. The key for us was to make some plays early and put off for as long as possible Hamilton finding out how superior they were to us. But they found out real quickly."

Quarterback Dunigan seconded the motion. "It was like a track meet to see who could get to me first. I was sacked 10 times and had to have my knee and elbow operated on after the game. They got good pressure on the quarterback and we had some turnovers."

"That's part of being a quarterback," said Eskimo linebacker Dan Bass, offering a contrary opinion. "You have to call a different game then. You've got to do something else that works. A good team will find something that will work. The Ti-Cats were coming through and getting sacks. Whenever you're playing on your heels, it's tough. You're playing their game. We were never able to get back the momentum that we needed to get back in the game."

The seventy-fifth anniversary of the Grey Cup came in 1987 and was contested appropriately enough by Edmonton and Toronto. Both teams had appeared in the national classic more often than their division rivals. Both teams were steeped in Grey Cup tradition.

The football year began in a pall of gloom when Norm Kimball announced the demise of the Montreal Alouettes on June 24. When the Als shut their doors, confidence in the CFL reached an all-time low. Attendance had peaked in 1978 at 2,914,387 and would bottom out 10 years later at 2,048,441. In less than a decade the league went from its golden age to the verge of collapse. The old league desperately needed a great Grey Cup. They got it.

The year began on an ominous note for Edmonton when Jackie Parker had to relinquish his position because of ulcers. Typically he treated his misfortune with equanimity. "My problem with the ulcer was just too much," he explained. "I couldn't have stayed on that year. It was disappointing because I felt that the team, after three or four years, was as good as anybody. But it was the time for me to get out. Joe Faragalli came in and did a nice job, and we won, which was great. I was really very, very happy about that."

"Jackie Parker was a great coach," Connop recalled. "I was so disappointed when he had to retire. When we won the Grey Cup that year Jackie didn't get enough credit. We were the team that he had put together."

Dunigan remembered Parker's quiet leadership style. "Without saying much, Jackie certainly put you in a position to realize what was expected of you. That's what made him such a great player and a great coach. The man commanded instant respect. He still does. That's a special gift."

Papa Joe

When faced with a coaching crisis, Hugh Campbell reached into the Eskimo past, hiring his former assistant Joe Faragalli, who was at the helm of the Alouettes when they folded, as head coach. Campbell said he wanted someone familiar with the Eskimo tradition, the community, the team's will to win.

The Philadelphian from Villanova had begun his CFL coaching career as an assistant with Winnipeg from 1967–70. After a short stint in U.S. college ball, he returned to the Bombers from 1974–76 before serving as Campbell's offensive coordinator for four years.

At the age of 54, Faragalli finally had his first head coaching job when he took over a Saskatchewan Roughrider team that went 2–14 in 1980. He led them to a 9–7 mark, for which he was named the CFL's Coach of the Year. He was fired two years later.

Under Faragalli the 1987 Eskimos scored a league record of 617 points. Because of injuries they had to replace most of the secondary, and for much of the season they had the worst pass defense in the league. But come play-off time the new people had adjusted and the Eskimos were loaded for lion.

In his CFL swan song, Brian Kelly had led all receivers with 1,626 yards on 68 catches and 13 touchdowns. He became the all-time leader in touchdown pass receptions with 97, moving past former teammate Tom Scott. In total touchdowns he is third behind George Reed, who tallied 40 more, and Allen Pitts. Kelly was All-Canadian in 1987 and runner-up to Tom Clements for the Most Outstanding Player Award.

The Eskimos beat Calgary in the Western Semifinal and then knocked off B.C. in the Western Final. Again the Grey Cup was played in Vancouver.

The first quarter of the national classic was one of missed opportunities for the Argonauts. Lance Chomyc was wide on a field-goal attempt. Henry Williams returned it to his 22. Minutes later Toronto lined up for another 3-pointer. Again Chomyc missed the mark. Again Henry Williams caught the ball. Gizmo took caught the ball 5 yards behind his goal line and then exploded out of the end zone and down the sideline to midfield. He then changed direction, crossed the field and sped down the other sideline to the end zone, his 115-yard touchdown run the longest return in Grey Cup history. Edmonton led 7–0.

"Most of the time, if there's less than 5 yards or they miss it to the far right or left, I bring it out," Williams explained. "If they miss it deep, I usually down the ball. That time Chomyc missed it farther to the left, but I had enough time because the ball got down there pretty quickly. The first guy I had to get around was an offensive lineman, and once I got around him there was a clear side-line. I could run it up there. After, I jumped over Larry Wruck on the sideline to celebrate."

The Argos got on the scoreboard before the quarter ended when Chomyc finally split the uprights from 34 yards out. Rookie Eskimo kicker Jerry Kauric from the Windsor junior team replied two minutes into the second quarter to give his team a 10–3 lead.

Toronto struck back with a vengeance when Gilbert Renfroe hit rookie sensation Gil Fenerty on a 61-yard pass and run for a touchdown. Shortly after, Darnell Clash intercepted Matt Dunigan. The Argos went on a 78-yard drive, capped off by Fenerty's 4-yard plunge for the major.

The Argo defense wasn't finished. On the next series Dunigan fumbled after being hit by Glen Kulka. Linebacker Doug "Tank" Landry scooped it up and ran 54 yards for the score. With just over two minutes left in the half, the Argos had a commanding 24–10 lead.

"It was a concussion," Dunigan recalled. "Kulka put a forearm across my chest and slammed me to the ground. When Glen hit me there was no way that I could go out there and do the things I was required to do as a leader and a quarterback. Unlike getting your bell rung, you can't play through a concussion."

Dunigan was replaced by Damon Allen.

Just before the teams headed for their dressing rooms, another rookie figured prominently in the outcome of the game when Eskimo Stanley Blair blocked a Hank Ilesic punt. Starting on the Argo 40, Allen hit Milson Jones out of the backfield for 17 yards. Jones then ran the ball down to the 6. Allen then converted the blocked kick into a touchdown with a 7-yard pass to Marco Cyncar, halving the Argo lead.

Early in the third quarter, Allen marched the Eskimos into field-goal range using screen passes to Brian Kelly and Stephen Jones. Toronto led by 4 points.

Turnabout being fair play, Argo quarterback Gilbert Renfroe was driven from the game by an injury. Both starting quarterbacks were out, the only time that has happened in Grey Cup history. Renfroe, who had gone 9 for 19 and 153 yards, was replaced by Danny Barrett.

The only other scoring in the third quarter came on a 50-yard Lance Chomyc field goal and a Kauric single when he missed a 39-yard attempt. This set up a wild and woolly final stanza that saw the lead change five times. First of all, Brian Kelly caught a touchdown pass, setting a new mark for Grey Cup touchdown receptions at five. Then Chomyc booted the Argos back into the lead with a 32-yard field goal.

Allen responded by leading the Eskimos 80 yards on 6 plays for a touchdown, which he scored on a 17-yard run around his left end. Barrett brought the Boatmen back to the enemy 25. After a wide-open Darrell Smith dropped a pass on the 11, Barrett scampered the 25 yards for the touchdown. The Argos opted for the 2-point convert but failed. Toronto led by a point with 2:47 remaining in regulation time.

Eskimo Rod Connop explained what happened on the major. "On our defense we were missing a key guy, Tom Tunei. We had a guy named Gary Palumbus playing defensive end. He was a really good physical football player, but he had only been there five or six games and didn't know our system. Barrett saw that our defensive end was lined up in the wrong spot and he just took off. There was nobody there."

Tom Richards returned the Argo kickoff 16 yards to his 21. Allen threw to Stephen Jones for 21 yards, and Milson Jones picked up 23 more on 2 plays, bringing the Esks to the Toronto 45. An incomplete pass and a 3-yard run set the stage for Jerry Kauric to be the hero of the day. He banged it through from 49 yards out with 25 seconds left on the clock. The Eskimos had won their tenth Grey Cup 38–36.

How does a great defensive ballplayer feel in a shoot-out like the 1987 Grey Cup? "Just hanging on," said Dan Bass. "It's not good. Everybody has pride. The offense wants to score 40 points, the defense wants to shut the opposition down. But sometimes you have to realize that the other team is playing well and that

The Eskimos James Zachery (left) and Dan Kearns pose with the Cup after defeating Toronto 38–36 in the 1987 thriller.

big plays are going to happen that particular day. You're just hoping that when the chance comes to make a big play, you can do it and come out on top."

The seventy-fifth Grey Cup was just what the doctor ordered for the troubled CFL. "That was a huge game," said Hugh Campbell. "At the very end it didn't matter whether Toronto won or we won. The fact that the game was so close extended the life of the CFL, which right then was in real jeopardy. The people in Toronto got really excited over this great game. It was a bit of a wake-up call in Eastern Canada about the CFL."

Although 1988 was a rebuilding year, the Eskimos finished first with a 11–7 record, identical to that of the Roughriders. Campbell had made a blockbuster trade with B.C., sending Matt Dunigan to the Lions for receiver Jim Sandusky. Edmonton had to deal a quarterback, replace the retired Kelly and secure the future of the football team.

"Both Damon Allen and Dunigan are outstanding," said Faragalli at the time, "but neither wanted to share playing time, so I had a problem. This year is no problem, but I could conceivably wind up in 1989 without an experienced quarterback. Neither one was signed. Now I have my quarterback for the future."

Dunigan wasn't surprised he was traded because, he said, "I knew I might be traded once I took the position that I did in Edmonton. That is, if things didn't work out financially the way we anticipated, I said I'd retire and try baseball, which I had been dreaming about for many years.

"When that didn't work out, I reinstated myself in the CFL and shortly afterward I was traded to B.C. That was pretty much a given because of our difference of opinion and philosophy."

The trade was typical of the Eskimos front-office acumen. The immediate exchange was Sandusky for Dunigan. At the end of the season, the Lions would protect *two* players and Dunigan. Edmonton could then choose anyone they wanted from the B.C. roster. The Lions would then protect two more players and Edmonton would select again. The Esks chose Gregg Stumon, Andre Francis, Jeff Braswell and Reggie Taylor. Part of the deal was B.C.'s 1989 first-round draft choice, who turned out to be Leroy Blugh.

The All-Canadian Stumon stayed in Edmonton one year, Francis and Braswell two. Taylor made All-Canadian in 1989. The undisciplined Braswell ultimately cost Faragalli his job. Blugh is still in Edmonton.

Despite the trades the 1988 Eskimos were poor offensively. Rookie pivot Tracy Ham and Damon Allen took turns on the injury list with the veteran missing nearly half the season. Only Jim Sandusky cracked the top 10 receiver list. Ham was the team's leading rusher. Home-field advantage in the final didn't help as B.C. thumped Edmonton 37–19.

In 1989 the Eskimos won more games than any team in CFL history, finishing first with a record of 16–2, 12 points ahead of second-place Calgary. They set records for scoring (644) and yards gained (7,951). They had the second-best takeaway–giveaway differential in CFL history at +40.

And yet it was the 9–9 Roughriders who went to the Grey Cup that year after knocking off the highly favored Eskimos 32–21 at Commonwealth Stadium. The Eskimos wouldn't win a play-off game at home for another six years.

Gone from the Eskimos were the winning qualities of camaraderie, pride and team discipline. Players such as Jeff Braswell and Enis Jackson led the league in penalties, which cost them the Western Final. "It's not so much the penalties but the results of the penalties," Faragalli explained. "When we got beat in the final, it was two penalties that kept their drives alive.

"When you take a lot of penalties and win, you tend to overlook it. When you win 16 games, the trap is that you say we're aggressive and we're naturally going to get those penalties. But that's baloney. The day comes when the penalties cost you a ball game. Come the play-offs, the penalties get you beat."

"Exactly," agreed Dan Bass. "Sometimes you can win and the small things don't bother you. Maybe you've been taking a stupid penalty here or there, but you can get away with it because the other team is on its heels so much. But then all of a sudden you get a bad break and the other team capitalizes on it—boom. It changes the tide very quickly. And that's basically what happened in the final.

"We'd had some problems before, but we were able to beat the odds. Then, in that particular game, they cost us. A lot of people talked about this team as the best ever, but it doesn't mean diddly unless you win the Grey Cup."

In 1990 the Eskimos had turned a corner and were the second least penalized team in the league. They returned to the Grey Cup. But their success masked fundamental problems that Faragalli didn't deal with. On September 21 the Eskimos were 9–3. They then lost four in a row and five of six, falling into second place by losing to the Stampeders 34–32 on the final game of the regular season.

In the semifinal Edmonton avenged their 1989 loss to the Roughriders by winning 43–27. Bass had 15 postseason tackles including a record-setting 11 against Saskatchewan. The Eskimos then went down to Calgary and dispatched the Stampeders 43–23 before moving on to Vancouver and the worst Grey Cup shellacking they have ever suffered.

Edmonton began the game on a promising note by marching from their 32-yard line to the Bomber 20 in seven plays. Tracy Ham went back to pass on first down. The Bombers' Greg Battle exchanged positions with safety Dave Bovell and intercepted at the 1-yard line. He returned the ball to the Edmonton 53. The referee tacked on 10 yards for unsportsmanlike conduct. Trevor Kennard kicked Winnipeg into a 3-point lead.

On second down on Edmonton's ensuing possession, Blake Marshall fumbled at the 43. Five plays later, Tom Burgess hit Lee Hull deep in the end zone for a touchdown. From two Edmonton turnovers, Winnipeg put 10 points on the board.

On Winnipeg's opening drive of the second quarter, Mark Mathis recovered a Robert Mimbs' fumble, but all Edmonton could do was kick a single.

With one second left on the clock, the Eskimos closed out the first half with a 37-yard Ray Macoritti field goal. Despite turnovers and other miscues, they were only trailing by six.

But on Edmonton's first possession in the second half, Greg Battle did it again, picking off Ham and running 32 yards to the end zone. Thus began the most productive quarter of scoring in Grey Cup history as the Bombers tallied 28 points, leading 38–10 after three quarters.

In the final stanza the Bombers added a safety touch, a field goal and a Rick House touchdown. Edmonton responded with a touchdown pass from Tracy Ham to Larry Ray Willis. The debacle was over. Winnipeg 50, Edmonton 11.

Tracy Ham said it all. "Rather than thinking like professionals about what we had to do to get back in the game, we let the turnovers demoralize us. We got beat by a better club—there's no doubt about that. They outplayed us in every phase of the game."

General Manager Hugh Campbell observed, "I think we were completely outmanned. Morale-wise, we were outplayed. We just had some things that were screwed up about us. The team, to its credit, despite all the things that were wrong, upset Calgary in the Western Final in Calgary to go to the Grey Cup, but it was not one of our better teams in any way."

In 1990 the team whose second name was solidarity was uncharacteristically torn by dissension over issues of team discipline and Coach Faragalli's unwillingness to take corrective action.

There has been no finer person in professional sport than Joe Faragalli. His willingness to give one last chance to those who had worn out their welcome elsewhere was well known throughout the league. Unfortunately some players took advantage of his good nature, ultimately costing him his job first in Regina and then Edmonton. Hugh Campbell's loyalty is equally legendary. To fire Faragalli meant the situation in the Igloo was desperate.

The main offender was Jeff Braswell. Braswell had begun his career with B.C. in 1988. Traded to the Eskimos in 1989 as part of the Dunigan deal, Braswell spent two years in green and gold. A trash-talking, in-your-face player, he was ejected from a game in Regina for kicking a player who was down. If ever a player represented everything that the Edmonton Eskimo football club was not, it was Braswell, and Faragalli's reluctance to take action affected the entire team.

"We had a team that was in absolute turmoil within the locker room that year," Connop explained. "I don't understand why Faragalli protected Braswell. He would overlook a hundred bad things and point out the one good thing. It just made no sense. What Faragalli didn't see was the effect all the bad things were having on everybody else and how they were bringing the players down."

New head coach Ron Lancaster made getting rid of Braswell one of his first orders of business and shipped him to Ottawa in 1991 for receiver David Williams. Although hardly deep in talent, Ottawa released him in July. He signed as a free agent with Toronto that October and stayed one more season. At the age of 28 and in his prime, he was out of football.

During the 1990 season one of the league's most notorious malcontents, receiver Larry Ray Willis, also was added to the Edmonton mix. In six games with the Eskimos, he caught 14 passes for 193 yards.

"Yeah, he was a mistake," said Rod Connop. "Boy, that guy! We might have been the only team left in the CFL that would have given him a chance, and I think it was only because Coach Faragalli was so desperate to find some sort of weapon that we ended up with him."

"Sometimes you have to play with some guys who don't have the same feel for the game," said Dan Bass. "We had some guys with different philosophies— getting up, barking like a dog. It kind of takes away a lot of focus. Certain players play different ways because they realize that it's one way of getting their name in the paper and getting more hype," he added, almost diplomatically.

"In 1990 we had some of the players that weren't what we call Eskimos. They really caused us some problems—like a cancer."

General Manager Campbell was dismayed with the acrimony and turmoil surrounding his ball club and moved quickly to make changes. He announced that Faragalli, in his sixties, had decided to retire. Papa Joe appeared at the same press conference and made it clear that he was fired. Always an honest man, Faragalli refused to be part of the charade. He left the team he loved with head held high and with class.

The Lancaster Era Begins

Campbell first talked to Don Matthews about taking over the troubled team, but Matthews' wife didn't want to live in Edmonton. He then turned to his old Saskatchewan batterymate Ron Lancaster to clean up the team's act and restore Edmonton's reputation as a first-class organization.

After quarterbacking Saskatchewan for 16 years, Lancaster had retired to the sidelines in 1979. In two seasons he managed 4 victories in 32 tries. He then left to become a television analyst with the CBC. He agreed to return to coaching after an 11-year hiatus.

"It was something I always wanted to do," he explained. "Although I enjoyed my two years of coaching in Saskatchewan, I was out of it by the time I was starting to get a little bit of a feel for it. It nagged at me since then. I didn't want to be sitting around five years from now regretting that I didn't take another shot at it."

Did he accept Campbell's offer because he didn't want to be considered a failure at coaching? "Maybe subconsciously, but I don't look at it that way. I never really planned on playing football. Coaching is what I *always* wanted to do."

Campbell knew exactly what he wanted his old friend to do. "When I hired Ronnie I didn't even think it was a close call as to whether he could do the job. I thought that he really got shafted in Saskatchewan. I felt he had inherited a team that had just lost the best quarterback in league history and then had the guts to make the changes that had to be made. A whole bunch of those players were there for many years. He had that club going the right way so that the following year Joe Faragalli went in there and was Coach of the Year. I thought Ronnie had done a good job in Saskatchewan and I knew he would do a good job in Edmonton."

"But the biggest reason why I hired him was to reunite the team. I felt that the team had really gone sideways the year before. Ronnie came in and made some tough decisions, got rid of some guys, brought a certain work ethic and got the team going in the right direction. He got us working together."

"Throughout the years Edmonton has been the number one organization in the CFL," Lancaster said before the 1991 season. "It seems like everybody compared themselves with Edmonton. We would like that to return. I think if attitude becomes a problem, you're going to have problems both on and off the field. We don't want those problems in either place. We're hoping that we can put the ship on the right course.

"On the field we'll play within the rules. We'll play hard and tough. Off the field we'll conduct ourselves the way Eskimos should conduct themselves."

Rod Connop loved to play for Lancaster. "He's a great coach," he said. "He does exactly what I think needs to be done. He makes the personnel decisions, he sets the atmosphere, he sets the level of discipline and he lets his assistants take care of football-field related details. He takes care of the psychology of the game."

The second coming of Ron Lancaster was a tremendous success with the Eskimos finishing first with a record of 12–6. "Ronnie should be the Coach of the Year," enthused Hugh Campbell. "He got rid of all the big mouths and restored discipline. I was hoping he would do that and finish second or third. He did even better."

The Eskimos faced the Stampeders in the final, having lost at home to Calgary just once in the previous 10 years. Edmonton was ahead 36–31 in a thriller with just over a minute to go when Stampeder pivit Danny Barrett hit Pee Wee Smith for a long touchdown that catapulted Calgary into a 38–36 lead and the victory.

In Lancaster's second season at the helm, the Eskimos finished second to Calgary with a 10–8 record. They edged Saskatchewan in the semifinal and lost again in the last minute to Calgary when Shoeless Doug Flutie led the Stampeders back to the Grey Cup with a gut wrenching 23–22 win.

A first- and second-place finish and two last-minute defeats in the Western Final still add up to a pretty impressive record. But not in Edmonton. Campbell and Lancaster went for a massive overhaul and made the biggest trade in CFL history by swapping a total of 16 players with—who else?—Toronto.

Edmonton acquired Rickey Foggie, Darrell K. Smith, Don Wilson, Ed Berry, Bruce Dickson, Eddie Brown, J.P. Izquierdo and Len Johnson in exchange for Tracy Ham, Craig Ellis, Enis Jackson, Travis Oliver, John Davis, Ken Winey, Chris Johnstone and Cam Brousseau. The trade allowed Edmonton to shore up their weak secondary and give them the receivers they needed. Toronto needed a marquee player at quarterback to attract fans back to the SkyDome.

Only Enis Jackson and Travis Oliver lasted more than one season in double blue. The only player acquired by Edmonton who didn't pan out was Smith.

The key to the deal was Ham, who had won the Most Outstanding Player Award in 1989 and was still one of the premier performers in the Canadian Football League. Those who had listened carefully to Ham's coaches weren't surprised that Lancaster traded him. Said Joe Faragalli in 1990, "Tracy needs to learn to react to situations faster. He ran for over 1,000 yards. He should be throwing for more yards and not running as much. But his mechanics are getting better. When he came here in 1987, he had some terrible habits but

Michael Faragalli, the offensive coordinator, works with him every day through-out the season."

Before training camp in 1991, taking a page from Faragalli's book, Lancaster explained, "We're going to start from the beginning with Tracy. Even though he's got three years of experience, tremendous statistics and all that stuff, we're still going to approach it from the beginning, making sure he understands what he needs to know to play quarterback: reading defenses, moving the ball around to receivers so they can't gang up on a guy like Craig Ellis, when to throw, when to be careful, when to gamble — just what a quarterback's role is in the game of football. We're going to start right at the beginning even though we feel he's a little farther ahead than that."

One year later Lancaster's comments echoed the previous year: "We will again go back to the beginning with Ham when training camp starts to try and get him to be a complete quarterback."

Lancaster explained the trade. "Toronto initiated the deal. We traded Ham, one, to get some help we needed; two, it was time for the team to go in a new direction; and three, it was time for Tracy to make a move into a bigger market. His contract was coming up for renewal that year. With the salary cap that might have been a problem."

The deal was done January 28, 1993. In February Edmonton traded DeWayne Odum, Dechance Cameron and draft choice Michael O'Shea to the cash-strapped Hamilton Ti-Cats for Damon Allen. Lancaster introduced 11 new faces into his starting lineup. The Eskimos sputtered along offensively partly because when they weren't moving the ball, Lancaster yanked the quarterback.

On September 26 they were clobbered at home 52–14 by the Blue Bombers to put them in fourth place with a record of 7–6. A frustrated Damon Allen went to Lancaster and asked for the ball to be put in his hands. The coach agreed.

"After we lost to Winnipeg we said to heck with it, Damon you're going to start and finish and play this season down the line, and you're going to take us as far as we can go. And that's what we did.

"Also we simplified our offense," Lancaster continued, "going to a ball-control game with Lucius Floyd, who we picked off Saskatchewan's practice roster. He and Damon clicked, and our running game got going where Damon would either give it or keep it. Then the offense really got into sync, and we went 8–0 down the stretch."

The defense made the difference. "Guys like Malvin Hunter, Earl Martin,

Robert Holland, Ed Berry, Don Wilson, Glen Rogers, Tony Woods—all new faces. I thought our defensive coaches did a great job of scheming our defense to allow for individual play. Our defense was as sound as any in the league. It was tough."

The heart of that defense was Willie Pless. The University of Kansas graduate chose the CFL because, he said, "Being a smaller-type player, if I had chosen to go to the NFL, they were going to move me to a strong safety-type position. I felt I would have been out of place. Right there and then I chose to go to Toronto."

He made an immediate impact. In 1986, his first season in double blue, he was an Eastern and Canadian All-Star and the Eastern nominee and runner-up for the Schenley Outstanding Rookie Award.

In 1990 he was part of the trade to B.C. for Matt Dunigan. In 1991 he was acquired by the Eskimos as a free agent. He has been All-Western and All-Canadian every year of the decade. He is the all-time leader in Outstanding Defensive Player Awards with five.

Ron Lancaster ranked Willie Pless among the great linebackers. "Willie Pless is right up there with them," he said, "but in a different fashion. Willie Pless isn't a middle linebacker who is going to stand in there like Tom Brown and cover tackle to tackle. He's a unique linebacker in that he is only about 210 pounds, but he can run and he has a great ability for finding the football and making the play. If you want to rate him for tackling and making plays, he's as good as any of them. But he's not what people refer to as a true linebacker. He is a playmaker, and in our scheme of things, we allowed him to run and make plays."

Willie and the rest of the Eskimo gang were ready for the play-offs. They trounced Saskatchewan 51–13 in the semifinal and prepared to go to Calgary and face the 15–3 defending champion Stampeders.

The weather for the big game was the worst in living memory. A blizzard hit Calgary early in the week, and the terrible conditions continued unabated until Saturday morning. That afternoon and evening, Stan Schwartz's McMahon Stadium crew removed most of the snow, but early Sunday morning it snowed again. It was windy and bitterly cold. The field was covered with snow.

The weather conditions didn't hamper the Stampeders in the early going. With just over three minutes gone, Eskimo nemesis Pee Wee Smith ran a Glenn Harper punt back 64 yards for a touchdown. Halfway through the quarter Mark McLoughlin kicked Calgary into a 10–0 lead, the score at the end of the first.

In the second quarter Damon Allen teamed up with Jim Sandusky on a beautiful 73-yard pass and run for a touchdown. The Esks added a single, and the Stamps' McLoughlin kicked another field goal to close out the half at 13–8 for Calgary.

In the second half Allen hit Sandusky for his second touchdown, sending the Esks into a 15–13 lead at the end of the third quarter. In the final frame Allen threw a 32-yard touchdown strike to Eddie Brown and a 16-yarder to Jay Christianson. The Eskimo defense held the vaunted Stampeder offense to two points and drove a frozen Doug Flutie from the game.

Rod Connop dismissed the playing conditions as a factor that determined the outcome. "Everybody plays on the same field," he exclaimed. "I know people said Calgary was rolling. I think there were two teams basically stalemated, figuring each other out, and then in the second half the Stampeders cracked first and away we went. I don't think they were rolling. What did they have—a 5-point lead at the half?

"They were up 10–0 on us early, but not one guy on our team panicked because we had beaten them the last two times we had played them. In November of that year, the last game of the regular season, we had sat Damon Allen down in the first quarter and won 39–21. We beat them the game after Labour Day, too. We were very, very, very confident that this was going to be our year, at least in terms of beating Calgary."

The Eskimos remained in Calgary for the Grey Cup the following week against the Winnipeg Blue Bombers, a team that had manhandled them that season, crushing them 53–11 and 52–14. But the man responsible for the devastation of the Eskimos, Matt Dunigan, was out for the season with a torn Achilles tendon. His absence boosted Eskimo confidence.

"Matt had been a real Edmonton killer that year," allowed Connop. "But we were on an incredible roll. Still, as good as we felt about how we were playing, we felt maybe a little bit better because Matt wasn't there and we didn't have to worry about that threat. But by the same token, I think deep down we wanted Matt to be there because we thought there would be excuses when we won the game."

The absence of Dunigan didn't affect Lancaster's approach to the game. "But the players, let's face it, knew he wasn't playing. They knew he had tremendous success against us. From their standpoint, just knowing he wasn't going to be there gave them a psychological lift. A coach can't say, 'Because Matt's not

Sean Fleming kicked for 21 of Edmonton's 33 points as the Eskimos defeated the Blue Bombers 33–23 in 1993.

playing, that's going to help us.' If you start thinking that way, you're likely to get your rear end kicked."

In fact Dunigan's successor, Sammy Garza, completed 20 passes for 322 yards in the Grey Cup. The Esks' Damon Allen was good on 17 for 226 yards. Garza turned the ball over three times, Allen twice. Winnipeg's defense performed in sterling fashion. But often in Grey Cup competition the team that makes the fewest mistakes wins. Edmonton converted seven Winnipeg turnovers into 23 points and won their eleventh Grey Cup 33–23.

It seemed that Murphy's Law was bedeviling Winnipeg's head coach because whatever could go wrong did. Near the halfway mark of the opening quarter, Winnipeg center Nick Benjamin snapped the ball over punter Bob Cameron's head.

Deep in his own end, the veteran should have run to the end zone and conceded a safety touch. Instead he tried to kick the ball, it was blocked and Edmonton recovered on the 4-yard line. Lucius Floyd scored on the next play.

Blaise Bryant fumbled on the ensuing kickoff. Several plays later Damon Allen hit Jim Sandusky in the end zone. On Winnipeg's next possession, Garza was intercepted by Dan Murphy. Sean Fleming then kicked a 41-yard field goal. In five minutes Edmonton scored 17 points and the season of the 14–4 Bombers was over.

In the second quarter Edmonton upped their lead to 21–0 on the basis of a single by Fleming on a missed 59-yard field-goal attempt and a good 3-pointer from 26 yards out. But Winnipeg didn't give up. They got on the scoreboard when Michael Richardson plunged over from the 2-yard line. The teams exchanged field goals, making the score 24–10 at half time. Courageously fighting back, the Bombers outscored the Eskimos 23–12 throughout the rest of the game.

Winnipeg closed the gap in the third when Garza finished off a drive with a quarterback sneak for a touchdown. They were down 24–17 heading home.

Troy Westwood reduced the difference to 4 by kicking a 32-yarder at 4:19. Most of the crowd of 50,035 were Calgary fans lustily cheering the dramatic Blue Bomber comeback. And the Bombers might still have pulled it out had not David Williams dropped a pass in the end zone with three minutes left in the game. The Bombers had to settle for a field goal.

In the same frame Sammy Garza mysteriously dropped the ball on his 35. Fleming kicked his second field goal of the quarter. Fleming's record sixth field goal wrapped things up with six seconds left on the clock. The final score favored Edmonton 33–23.

Rod Connop analyzed the game. "What was important was the first quarter, when they had three turnovers and we scored two touchdowns and a field goal. Also, if I could pick one thing, it would be the last drive Damon put together for a field goal. We were up seven points. We got the ball with about three minutes left. We put together about a 9- or 10-play drive, keeping the ball in bounds almost the entire time. When we stalled on their 12-yard line and kicked a field goal, we were up 10 points with just a few seconds left in the game."

Winnipeg Coach Cal Murphy agreed. "We made one mistake on one play on that drive. Damon Allen broke outside, scrambled and hit Soles. We came off the thing for some unknown reason. It was such a big play for them. Up until then they were in the doo-doo, as they say."

Particularly in the third quarter, according to Connop. "We sort of swooned a bit in the third quarter. We had three series where we were two and out. Then we got ourselves relaxed, got back in there and were able to finish off.

"Sammy Garza played well. He had that one untimely fumble, but he moved the ball. We just played error free. We always turned our opportunities into points and gave as few opportunities as possible to the opposition."

Cal Murphy believed that, taking away those early errors, the Bombers played Edmonton straight up. "I know we did," he averred, chuckling ruefully. "I mean, I like Blaise Bryant, but he was a one-man wrecking crew. You know, the fumble, the penalties, everything else. But anyway, those things happen," he groaned.

"We picked that fumble up—and it was a fumble. Randolph picked it up and ran it in for what should have been a touchdown. I really felt at that point we had control of the football game.

"How often do you see David Williams drop a pass in the end zone? That's a touchdown. If we had got that, it would have been a different ball game. And Sammy Garza just dropped the ball. He started to run and the ball slipped out of his hands. It was just one of those things where you try to do too much at once."

Still, Murphy was proud of his team. "I wanted to win that thing so bad, but coming from devastation corner the way we did, I thought we played awfully well to come back."

The drive for the cup in 1993 was a bitter disappointment for Bomber Nose Tackle Stan Mikawos, hero of his first Grey Cup nine years earlier. "I really thought we had an opportunity to beat them again. Turnovers killed us. Before we knew it we were down 21 points. It is hard to come back against a good team. It was like the air just ran out of our tires."

Connop summed up how the Eskimos felt about Grey Cup 1993. "Is there anything more perfect than going down and beating the Calgary Stampeders in a year when they are supposed to win everything? They've got Doug Flutie and all those talented people, and we go into their own field and beat them and then move into their locker room for the week and win the Grey Cup in Calgary? I mean for an Edmontonian and an Edmonton football player that is the most perfect scenario you could imagine."

The Eskimos would win their next trip to the Grey Cup in similar fashion. For the Edmonton Eskimos, how sweet it's been.

Back to the Future

It had always been a dream of former league commissioner Larry Smith to bring the CFL back to Montreal. When the NFL returned to Baltimore, that dream became reality with the Grey Cup champion stallions arriving in Montreal, where they were 12–6 in their first year. After that favorable start the team was bought by New Yorker Robert Wetenhall, who then made Smith the president and CEO.

In a brilliant and daring move, Smith moved the team to outdoor Molson Stadium at McGill University. Although capacity was only 18,027, it was a fun place to watch football. Season ticket sales increased dramatically because football fans realized that was the only way to guarantee themselves a seat in a sold-out stadium.

In 1997 Dave Ritchie succeeded Bob Price as head coach, leading the Als to a record of 13–5 and a second-place finish. They lost the Eastern Final to Toronto 37–30. They were back the following year in the Final, only to lose a heartbreaker to Hamilton when Paul Osbaldiston kicked a field goal on the last play of the game. The score was 22–20.

For the 1999 campaign Charlie Taaffe took over as head coach when Ritchie went to Winnipeg. Under Taaffe's direction, the team continued to win, the ball park was full and Les Alouettes looked forward to the new millennium with confidence.

In May 1999 the nomadic Don Matthews returned to coach the Edmonton Eskimos. "I'm very happy here," he enthused. "Coming back to Edmonton was like coming home for me. I'm happy to be an Eskimo, where I started. I've been all over the place, and I can say the grass is not always greener in other places. I turn 60 next month. I want to win three more Grey Cups, starting in 1999."

Given Matthews penchant for success and prospect of Montreal producing a serious contender for many years to come, the chances are good that one of the great rivalries in Grey Cup history will soon be renewed.

CHAPTER 2

Winnipeg and Hamilton

Tales from Tough City

THE FIRST 30 YEARS OF THE SECOND HALF OF THE century featured tremendous rivalries in the CFL— Montreal and Edmonton and the '50s and '70s, Saskatchewan and Ottawa in the '60s. But perhaps the greatest battle of wills of them all was between the Winnipeg Blue Bombers of Bud Grant and Ralph Sazio–Jim Trimble Hamilton Tiger-Cats. Six times in nine years they met for the Grey Cup with Winnipeg coming out on top four times. The 1958 match-up between the two clubs, won by the Bombers 35–28, is still regarded by many as the greatest Grey Cup ever played. The teams clashed in the only overtime Grey Cup in 1961 and the famous Fog Bowl of the following the year, the only football game in Canadian history to be played over two days. Across the years of this rivalry, some of the greatest players in CFL history provided some of the most memorable moments the game has ever known.

Teams representing Hamilton have appeared in 28 Grey Cups, winning 14. Hamilton holds Grey Cup records for most points scored (569) and most touchdowns (68). Tiger-Cats Tommy Grant, John Barrow and Angelo Mosca have played in the most Grey Cups (9) a record shared with three others.

From the time the Hamilton Football Club was born November 3, 1869, in a room over a grocery store, the team took on the personality of the city where the fans are as tough as the players.

Hamilton's first Grey Cup was played before a hometown crowd of well over 12,000 in 1910 against the University of Toronto. Interest was so high that an unruly mob stormed past a line of Mounted Police and forced their way into the stadium. In 1912, the the team, then known as the Alerts won Hamilton's first Grey Cup. Fearing the worst after the game, the deputy police chief warned the fans to behave. They did. The police had good reason to fear, for earlier in the season Hamilton fans had been so upset over a loss to Ottawa they believed was caused by referee error that they threw sticks and stones at the official and chased him off the field. He then foolishly disguised himself in an Ottawa uniform. Soon after, the fans attacked the rival players. After the Alerts won the Grey Cup, they were expelled from the Canadian Rugby Football Union for unsportsmanlike behavior.

In 1913 the Alerts' cross-town rivals, the Tigers, won their first of 14 Grey Cups by destroying Toronto Parkdale 44–2, the second largest margin of victory in Grey Cup history. Ross Craig scored three touchdowns, setting a record now shared by Red Storey, Jackie Parker and Tom Scott. Two years later, the Tigers won their second Grey Cup by defeating the Toronto Rowing Club 13–7. So little offense was generated by both sides that a still-standing Grey Cup record was set. Each side punted 36 times! The only real excitement came as the game ended and Hogtown fans, not be outdone by Hamiltonians, tried to get at referee Red Dixon, who hid in the Toronto dressing room until the fans lost interest and went home.

The Tigers returned to the national championship for three straight years beginning in 1927, losing first 9–6 to Toronto Balmy Beach and then beating Regina 30–0 in 1928.

In 1929 the Tigers faced Regina again. That was year the forward pass was authorized if the quarterback tossed the pigskin from at least 5 yards behind the line of scrimmage and if the receiver did not catch the ball inside the opposition 25. If the pass was incomplete, it was a live ball, and the opposition could pick it up and run with it. Until the Grey Cup game, neither Hamilton nor Regina had made use of the forward pass.

Hoping to catch the Tigers by surprise, Regina's Jersey Jack Campbell threw 11 times, completing 8. Hamilton's Huck Welch passed to Jimmy Simpson, who lateraled to Cap Fear, who headed for the Roughrider end zone. The flea flicker was born. However, the referee nullified the touchdown on the grounds the pass had been completed within the Regina 25-yard line. Still, the Tigers beat the Westerners 14–6.

The Tigers won their last Grey Cup in 1932, scoring 25 points to the 6 of the Regina Roughriders, who were making their fifth straight appearance in the national final.

Nobody wanted to be the first Eastern team to lose the Grey Cup to the West, generally considered to be an untalented bunch of hicks. Imagine Hamilton's chagrin when Fritzie Hanson took the measure of them as Winnipeg won the West's first Grey Cup. Oh, the shame of it all.

The Whirlwind from the West

On June 10, 1930, the Winnipeg Rugby Club and Winnipeg St. John's amalgamated to create the Winnipegs. Their general manager, Joe Ryan, believed the only way his team would have a realistic chance to win the Grey Cup was to sign Americans. So, when the Winnipegs played a series of exhibition games against Minnesota and North Dakota university teams in In 1933–34, Ryan recruited heavily from their ranks, signing the nine Americans for a total of $7,500 the following year. Among those who came to Winnipeg was a North Dakota back named Fritzie Hansen.

Hansen explained how he came to Canada. "In 1932 and '33, Russ Rebholz, Greg Kabat and a couple of guys down East came up. Then the big push for imports came in 1935 in Winnipeg. They brought in seven Americans.

"Financially it wasn't that enticing, but the best job I could get coaching and teaching in the Dirty Thirties was 90 bucks a month. Then I got a contract in the mail from the Detroit Lions offering $125 a game if I made the team. I thought that was a hell of a lot of money for playing football. At the same time Bob Fritz, who was at Concordia College in Minnesota, just across the river from me, had been asked by Winnipeg to find some football players. People from Winnipeg came down to my hometown, Fargo, North Dakota, and they talked to me and some other fellows as well, and we all went up to Winnipeg."

Everything favored Hamilton in the Grey Cup played December 7, 1935. While the Winnipegs had struggled to get to the Grey Cup, the Tigers had breezed by Queen's and Sarnia. Hamilton also had home-field advantage, and to make matters worse for the Winnipeg's running attack, it was a miserable day. With a temperature of 3°C and rain, the gridiron was a sea of mud. But the day was to be Fritzie Hansen's finest hour as he led the West to victory 18–12.

A runner extraordinaire, Hansen overcame the treacherous field conditions, returning punts for more than 300 yards on seven returns, including a memorable 78-yard touchdown run through the entire Hamilton team. Because official statistics weren't kept then, Hansen is regrettably not credited with any Grey Cup records.

Neither did Hansen receive a bonus for winning the Grey Cup. "My first year I got a straight $125 a game," he recalled. "The next year I signed up for $1,500 a season. It doesn't sound like much, but everything is relative. I was able to get a pretty decent job at the same time, and, you know, $2,000 a year was pretty good pay in the Dirty Thirties."

The Winnipegs were given the sobriquet *Blue Bombers* that year by reporter Vince Leah, imitating Joe Louis, who was called the Brown Bomber.

In a comedy of errors the Blue Bombers lost the 1937 Cup to the Toronto Argonauts 4–3. Certainly, with players such as Red Storey, Annis and Bill Stukis, Bob Isbister and Teddy Morris, Toronto was a fine football team. But the football fates weren't smiling kindly on the Westerners that day when Argonaut Bill Stukus fumbled on his 7-yard line. Unable to determine who had the ball, referee Hec Crighton gave it to Toronto, reasoning they would be in dire straits if he didn't. Soon after, Stukus fumbled a punt in the end zone, which Winnipeg recovered, but the Bombers were penalized for no yards.

Later, when Argo Bud Marquardt blocked a kick, the ball bounced right into the arms of teammate Teddy Morris. When Winnipeg's Fritzie Hansen fumbled a punt, the ball bounced to Boatman Bill Bryers, and the term *Argo Bounce* was born.

The following year Winnipeg was done in by Toronto's redheaded whirlwind Alvin "Red" Storey, who came off the bench with his team trailing 7–6 in the fourth quarter. Storey scored three touchdowns in less than 12 minutes. His first touchdown came on a 38-yard run from scrimmage, the second on a short run set up by his own 37-yard interception return and the third came on a 12-yard run from scrimmage. He set up another major score by running 102 yards to the Winnipeg 4.

Fritzie Hansen remembered that day all too well. "We were badly hurt," he explained. "Greg Kabat was supposed to cover Red, but he was injured. Our coach, Reg Threlfall, wanted to take him out, but he wouldn't go. So they gave him a shot of Novocain in his leg. But he still couldn't move, and I couldn't get over there in time to stop Storey. Old Red had a great day, didn't he? But that was it for him. I see Red occasionally and he says, 'That was my day. I never had one before nor have I had one since.'"

Argo Annis Stukus remembered the 1938 Grey Cup game differently. "We were down 7–6 with 12 minutes to go, but we knew the game was over. It was just going to be a question of how many points. They outweighed us by about 20 to 40 pounds up front, so we ran a three-man end run to one side of the field, then back to the other side, kicked, got the ball back and ran it and ran it. We ran Winnipeg right into the ground. We were greyhounds. We just wore those big guys out.

"I was playing end at the time. We'd been running these end runs, and I was trying to block out Bud Marquardt. I couldn't catch the guy with a net, so I finally told my brother to switch to that C Formation of ours, where we pretended we were going wide but came back inside.

"I pretended I was going after Marquardt. Then I threw a cross-body block on him. Red Storey came off my fanny and went 38 yards for a touchdown while they were still chasing the wide man. And Marquardt, draped over me, said, 'Holy mackerel, this is a *long* day.' I said, 'I've got news for you. It's going to get longer.'"

So it wasn't a case of Red Storey coming off the bench when all was lost and heroically saving the day? "Oh, no," Stuke insisted. "Red was just the guy who was fresh. I started at quarterback and called a play, and for some reason Red froze. I waved to the bench and had him sent off, and the coach, Lew Hayman, as usual, forgot he wasn't in there. Hayman was a great guy to get you ready for a game, but come the day of the game, if we could have locked him up in a hotel room, we'd have won four or five straight Grey Cups.

"Anyway, I got winded and when I was about to go back in for the last 12 minutes, I asked Lew if I could take Red with me. Lew said that Red was already out there. I told him he had been sitting beside him on the bench all day. So Red went out there pissed off and fresh and tore them apart. He should have had four or five touchdowns!"

Winnipeg returned to the Grey Cup in 1939 for the third year in a row. They won a squeaker 8–7 in the first of only two match-ups ever against Ottawa, the other coming in 1941. A fumble by Rough Rider Orville Burke led to a first-half Winnipeg touchdown by Andy Bieber. Andy Tommy evened the score at 6. Greg Kabat missed a field goal but scored a single to Winnipeg a 7–6 lead in the fourth quarter. Tiny Herman punted for single to tie the score. From there the game was decided on one of those plays that is characteristic of only Canadian football.

Late in the game, Jeff Nicklin of Winnipeg recovered another fumble by

Orville Burke and ran it to the Ottawa 30-yard line. Tiny Herman punted into the end zone and Burke kicked it back. The ball dribbled off the side of his foot and went out of bounds at the Ottawa 9. Art Stevenson punted the ball through the enemy end zone for the winning single.

Although Fritzie Hansen didn't score a point in that Grey Cup, he was proud of what his team accomplished.

During the course of a game, regular season or play-off, Hansen would carry the ball 30 to 40 times as well as doing a full shift on defense. In his day the players went both ways the full 60 minutes, and a player who came out in one quarter couldn't return until the next quarter. Also, when a substitute came in, the referee would make sure he wasn't bringing in any messages. Said Annis Stukus, "That is how we learned our football. We were allowed to play and think instead of being treated like robots."

Hansen didn't like the move to specialists and the passing game that has characterized CFL football from the 1970s on. "I think football is going downhill," he said in 1980. "Now every play is geared to the pass. It's not my kind of football. A guy runs 20 yards and they have to give him oxygen. They've got more injuries now than equipment. I think the hitting was a lot better in my day. They were more tenacious. There were much tougher linemen.

"We didn't have any blocking, so the onus was on the backs themselves. The line had to be really good to hold off that initial charge. But we ran with a lot of power. They don't do that now. I still think a guy will come along some day with a single wing and kick the hell out of everybody."

Back in Hamilton, the Flying Wildcats came into existence in 1942 as a member of the Ontario Rugby Football Union (ORFU), the Big Four and Western Interprovincial Football Union having suspended operations until the end of the war.

The Wildcats weren't a service team and therefore had something of an advantage in recruiting and keeping players. "We didn't have any problems in keeping a team together," their rookie star Joe Krol explained. "We were all working in the wartime plants, and we were playing mostly service teams. The caliber of play wasn't as good because most of the good ballplayers were in the service all over the country and overseas."

On November 27, 1943, Krol outscored the Winnipeg RCAF Bombers 18–7 in the first quarter. Krol threw a touchdown pass to Doug Smith and kicked for 7 points of his own. The final score was 23–14. One of the Winnipeg touchdowns was scored by Dave Berry. "It was the first one I ever scored," he said. "We had a play called Banana Long. You ran out like a banana and then you cut to your left. You looked and the ball was there. The guy covering me was Joe Krol. I was lucky to fake him out of the ball park, and I caught the ball and ran with it.

"You've got to remember I was 21. I ran down the field and I ran through the end zone and I ran across the track and I hit the fence and I was still running. I was hardly excited at all. It was a 55-yard play, which was a record at the time."

In 1944 the Flying Wildcats lost 7–6 to St. Hyacinthe–Donnacona Navy.

In 1946–47 the Tigers were 2–22 and brought in quarterback Frank Filchock for an unheard of sum of $7,000. They tried to convince their Big Four brethren to go along with gate equalization to help pay his contract but were turned down. In 1948 the Tigers withdrew from the Big Four and joined the ORFU. They were replaced by the ORFU Wildcats.

The two Hamilton teams between them set records for futility that still stand, including the longest losing streak in league history (20 games) and the longest winless streak on the road (26). In 1949 they went 0–12.

The situation couldn't continue. In 1950—led by Ralph Cooper, F.M. Gibson, C.C. Lawson and Sam Manson—the Wildcats and Tigers amalgamated to become the Hamilton Tiger-Cats. For the better part of the next two decades, they were one of the greatest organizations in the history of Canadian sports. Only two other teams have appeared in five consecutive Grey Cups. Edmonton made it to six, 1977–82, and the Regina Roughriders to five, 1928–32.

Hamilton was successful because of solid front office management provided by Jake Gaudaur and Ralph Sazio. Sazio was involved in 12 of the Tiger-Cat's Grey Cup appearances, one as a player, five as an assistant, four as a head coach and two as a general manager.

After leaving Hamilton he joined the Argos as general manager in 1981, leading them to three Grey Cup appearances and one victory. As a coach Sazio's .707 winning percentage has been surpassed only by Hugh Campbell, Pop Ivy and Wally Buono. He was inducted into the CFL Hall of Fame March 5, 1988.

Golden Glory

Ralph Sazio has been one of the great men of Canadian football. Just as Norm Kimball was the thread of genius running through the Eskimos, so Sazio was with the Tiger-Cats. His first Grey Cup experience in 1953 marked the beginning of the rivalry between the Tiger-Cats and Winnipeg Blue Bombers. That year the Grey Cup matched the brilliant passing of Indian Jack Jacobs against Hamilton's tenacious defense.

Jacobs set a record by completing 31 of 48 passes, a mark that stood until Calgary's Danny Barrett hit for 34 out of 56 attempts while losing to Toronto in the 1991 Grey Cup. The only scoring in the first half came on an Ed Songin quarterback sneak that capped a long Hamilton drive featuring passes to Vito Regazzo and Lou Kusserow.

The Bombers' Gerry James opened the third quarter with a long kickoff return, giving his team excellent field position. Catching and running, Tom "Citation" Casey took the ball to the 1-yard line. James carried it over.

Ed Songin struck back, hitting Ragasso on a 50-yard pass and run for the touchdown. Hamilton led 12–6. The game appeared to be wrapped up when Cam Fraser kicked the Bombers deep, pinning them on their 5-yard line. But the remarkable Jacobs wasn't done. With passes to Andy Sokol, Neil Armstrong, Keith Pearce and Tom Casey, he marched the Bombers to the Ti-Cat 15.

Dick Huffman then executed the tackle eligible play, running the ball to the 5. Casey carried to the 3. On the last play of the game, Jacobs dropped back for his forty-eighth pass and threw to Casey on the goal line. Lou Kusserow timed his tackle perfectly, dislodging the ball from the startled receiver and giving the Hamilton the win.

When the big moment came, the Ti-Cats were ready. Jake Gaudaur explained. "I give Carl Voyles, our coach, an awful lot of credit. Films weren't very prominent in those days, even for coaching. Whatever ones we had were so gray and foggy you could hardly get any benefit from them. But the one thing that seemed to be apparent on the film we had was that any time the Winnipeg club got inside the 25-yard line, they would go to Tom Casey. So we had a "Casey" to practice against all week.

"Coach Voyles said, 'Risk a penalty if you have to, but get to this guy.' Lou Kusserow may have got there a little ahead of time, I don't know. It was a very close play. But he was coached to err on the side of committing a penalty."

Gaudaur was probably the only executive in league history to come down from the board room to take his place on the field. "I played in '50 and '51 for Hamilton, and we finished in first place each year, but we didn't go on to the Grey Cup. I didn't play in '52 because of my job responsibilities, so I resigned from the team and they made me a director of the Tiger-Cats.

Lou Kusserow hits Tom Casey at the 1-yard line to preserve Hamilton's 12–6 Grey Cup win over Winnipeg in 1953.

"The following year our center got hurt so I was induced at a board meeting one day to come out of retirement. I was glad I did because we won the Grey Cup that year. I played center and middle linebacker that day, and I was given the game ball.

"Winnipeg had a young player by the name of Steve Patrick. I was 245 pounds then, and he would have been an awful lot less. But he was so quick. I went back in the huddle early in the game and said, 'Look, to tell the truth, I can't block this cat. Call some draw plays. Let him come through. Knowing I can't stop him, I'll just take him whichever way he's going.'

"So we'd have a delay draw play and go the opposite way. Merle Hapes, the fullback, and I worked together on those plays. I didn't get the game ball because I was a great blocker. It's just that I took advantage of my inability to block that kid."

Indian Jack Jacob's passing totals were impressive, yet the Bombers only scored one touchdown in the 1953 match-up. With running backs like Tom Casey and Gerry James, some wondered why Winnipeg passed so much.

Bomber Buddy Tinsley had a theory. "Psychologically I thought the whole thing was that in the 1950 Grey Cup Jacobs couldn't throw, and he wanted to show everybody he could throw. Tom Casey was a great runner, a clutch player. I would have had Casey running the ball two out of four downs, the big fullback once and I'd have thrown once.

"But we were throwing the ball down on the goal line. We shouldn't have been doing that. That's hindsight, of course. I've never been known to be a good quarterback."

Calling his own game was something Jack Jacobs demanded, and the feuds between him and Coach George Trafton were legendary. The story goes that the 1952 Bombers were losing badly in Regina because Trafton refused to put Jacobs into the game. In the fourth quarter Trafton succumbed to the howls of protests from the players and sent the smoldering quarterback into the fray. He quickly engineered three touchdowns and won. An interesting story but according to Tinsley not true.

"We had a real beat-up team that week," Tinsley explained. "Trafton was going to keep everybody off and let us recuperate until the next week. But Regina didn't run away with us that day, and we figured we had a really good shot at it, so Trafton sent Jake in along with a few of the other boys who were hurt pretty bad."

The popular Oklahoman joined the Bombers in 1950 after seeing service with the Cleveland Rams, Washington Redskins and Green Bay Packers. Jacobs made All-Canadian his rookie year. He threw 1,330 passes, completing 770 for 11,094 yards and 104 touchdowns. After retiring in 1954 he coached the ORFU London Lords and was an assistant in Hamilton, Montreal and Edmonton.

For the Tiger-Cats' Jake Gaudaur, the 1953 Grey Cup finally marked the end of a playing career that had begun 13 years earlier. "After I retired for the second time, I became president of the club, and in 1956 I took on the general manager's job as well. In 1959 we got into an ownership situation, and I became the principal owner."

His first year in the general manager's job was a baptism of fire. "The first job I had to take on was to get us out of a $150,000 law suit that Chicago Bears' owner George Halas had filed against us in Florida. Carl Voyles had signed quarterback George Blanda and a linebacker named Frank Dempsey, as well as a running back—all first-line people under contract.

"The directors said, 'Get us out of this thing or we're gone as a franchise.'

When you have about $5,000 in the bank and a $150,000 judgment against you, you're finished. I went down to see the NFL commissioner, Bert Bell, at his home in Margate, New Jersey. We became great friends. We sat up all night and worked out an agreement by which all the raiding would be stopped."

The Coaches and Quarterbacks

In addition to establishing long-lasting peace with the National Football League, Gaudaur also found a coach to replace the departed Carl Voyles. "I had read in a newspaper that Jim Trimble had been let go by Philadelphia the year after he had been named Coach of the Year.

"Bert Bell had hired Trimble to coach the Eagles. He told me that Jim Trimble would coach interesting offense, that he'd be one of the greatest people I'd have to promote the team locally and nationally."

Trimble, a robust barrel-chested man with wavy greying hair and twinkling blue eyes, was bombastic, charming and fun. His players loved him. "Jim was a colorful guy," recalled Ti-Cat legend Angelo Mosca. "He wasn't a great X's and O's man, but he could coordinate and motivate. He had the people in place to do the coaching. I respected him then and still do today."

Hall of Famer John Barrow said, "I loved Jim Trimble. He was a great motivator, a great leader of men. Jim Trimble was probably the main reason I stayed in Canada."

Back in Winnipeg, Bud Grant took over the reins of the Blue Bombers in 1957. His teams would meet Hamilton in the Grey Cup six times in nine years while the Tiger-Cats would represent the East in the Grey Cup nine of the following 11 years, including five straight from 1961–65.

In 1957 Gaudaur signed future Hall of Famers John Barrow and Bernie Faloney as well as fullback Gerry McDougall and one of the toughest men to ever grace a Canadian gridiron, Ralph Goldston. The year before Gaudaur had brought in Hall of Famer Tommy Grant and one of the most talented players of all time, Chester "Cookie" Gilchrist.

With no scouting department, Gaudaur followed football news in American magazines, looking for new talent. "One of the best running backs we ever had up here was Gerry McDougall. I read in *Collier's Magazine*, one of the biggest magazines in the United States, how he had been kicked out of UCLA because of a panty raid. Here's a guy probably going to the NFL, but he's not going to be able to finish his schooling. So I had a friend of mine in Los Angeles look him up. I went down and signed him. When I got him up here I found that his mother had dual citizenship so he played as a Canadian."

The man who would lead the Tiger-Cat offense from 1957–64 was the second most prolific quarterback in Grey Cup history, University of Maryland All-American Bernie Faloney. Faloney came to Canada to play for the Edmonton Eskimos because of economics. "I was drafted by the San Francisco 49ers to play defensive halfback and backup quarterback," he explained. They offered me $9,000.

"The University of Maryland was number one in the country. Edmonton had hired a coach by name of Frank Ivy—Pop Ivy—who was with Oklahoma. Oklahoma was number two that year. We had played them in the Orange Bowl Game.

"Pop wanted to take his Split-T offense to Edmonton. He called me and said they would like to have me up there, and the contract, quite frankly, was much better. It was for $12,500. The Canadian dollar had a 10 percent premium at that time. For a kid getting out of university that was a lot of money to start out with."

Faloney would end up in Hamilton three years later because Edmonton made an uncharacteristic mistake. After playing one year in the green and gold, Faloney had to return to the U.S. for two years of mandatory military service. In 1957, when negotiation lists were first instituted in the CFL, Faloney was ready to return, but Edmonton neglected to put him on their list.

"I went into the Air Force for two years," Faloney said. "Teams had no negotiation list at that time, and you had to sign what was called a Canadian Rugby Union Card, which I never did sign. In essence I was a free agent. They started negotiation lists the year I got out of the Air Force and went to Hamilton.

"Edmonton neglected to put me on their list. Maybe they didn't want to because Jackie Parker and Don Getty were still there, and they didn't need a quarterback. Jim Trimble put me on the Ti-Cat's negotiation list, and that's how I ended up in Hamilton."

Over the course of his 12 years in the Canadian Football League, Faloney made the Eastern All-Star team five times. He won the Schenley Award for Most Outstanding Player in 1961.

Faloney's career statistics indicate that he was not a great passer. His percentage completion rate was 51.9 percent, and he ranks third all-time in interceptions with 201. Yet, until eclipsed by Flutie in 1997, Faloney was the most productive Grey Cup quarterback of all time. Ralph Sazio said, "Faloney was a hell of a competitor. If you put the money on the line, he was there.

"Toronto used to have a Triple A baseball team. They had a doubleheader. As part of the activities between the games, they had a few quarterbacks taking part in an throwing efficiency contest: how many balls they could get through a rubber tire. Bernie was up against some NFL quarterbacks who were pretty good. Everyone else had the form, bringing the ball from behind the ear, the release just right. Bernie would throw sidearm, and the ball would wobble, but he put in 9 out of 10 to win the prize. He's a competitor."

"He wasn't the greatest quarterback in the world," said Angelo Mosca, "but I'll tell you one thing, when you got to the 5-yard line you thought you were on the 1 because he was a believer in what he did and he had the confidence of his players and their respect."

Much the same could be said for Kenny Ploen, Faloney's Winnipeg rival throughout the late '50s and early '60s. Ploen had been named the 1957 Rose Bowl Player of the Game after leading Iowa to a 35–19 win over Oregon State. In his inaugural season in the CFL, he led the Bombers to a 12–4 second-place finish and made the Western Conference All-Star team. He went on to win four Grey Cups with the Bombers. "I attribute a lot of that success not only to the Canadian game but to bringing up the Iowa offense," he said. "Because of the wingbacks that were available here in Canada, we played the Wing-T with the roll-out options, the bootlegs and different things. It seemed to fit the Canadian game, particularly the wide field. No one had seen it up here too much, and it worked very effectively."

When asked about great Grey Cup performers, Winnipeg Coach Bud Grant said, "Kenny Ploen would be number one. He always had great games. Many times we used him both ways as a defensive back and a quarterback."

"He was a great athlete," recalled Tinsley. "He had good ability, tremendous desire. He had no regard for his personal physical well-being. When there was a first down to be made and 2 yards to go, he was going to run over the biggest damn tackle out there. There was no pussyfooting around. His passes may not have looked beautiful, but he completed a lot of them. If I had to pick a quarterback I had complete confidence in to win, I'd take Kenny Ploen."

Ploen gave most of the credit for his success to others. "We had some awfully good teams to play with. A good team can make a quarterback look pretty good, and a good quarterback who doesn't have much to work with can look pretty bad, too. Football is a team game.

"You get into the superstar system they publicize these days. A Flutie or a Dunigan are regarded as one-man teams and get paid a bunch of money. I'm sorry, but they are about as good as who they put around them."

Kenny Ploen set no records and won no awards. All he did was win.

Round One

In 1957 Hamilton finished first in the East. The Alouettes got by the Ottawa Rough Riders 24–15 in the semifinal, but Hamilton ended their domination of the Big Four by winning the two-game total-point final 56–11. It was a powerful, talent-laden, injury-free team that took on the black and blue Bombers in the Grey Cup.

Beat up when the game began, the Blue Bomber's situation went from bad to worse. Ploen hurt his knee, and running back Gerry James sustained a broken hand when he was stepped on. Another back, Dennis Mendyk, wore a cast to protect a broken wrist.

In the first quarter Mendyk was hit hard by Cookie Gilchrist and coughed up the ball. Ray "Bibbles" Bawel picked it up and ran 53 yards for a touchdown. A little later, Hamilton capitalized on one of four Gerry James fumbles and went 46 yards in four plays, the last one a 6-yard run for the score by Bernie Faloney. Gilchrist scored two more touchdowns. Gerry McDougall scored one.

An otherwise uncharacteristically dull game was made memorable by one of the strangest plays in Grey Cup history, the Bibbles Bawel incident. About 10 minutes into the fourth quarter, Bawel, a defensive back from Indiana who had arrived in Hamilton halfway through the season, picked off an errant Bomber pass and headed down the sideline to the end zone. He hadn't gotten very far before a fan near the Winnipeg bench stuck his foot out and tripped him. Bawel fell at the Winnipeg 42-yard line. Referee Paul Dojack marched the ball half the distance to the goal line. A couple of plays later Gilchirst carried it in.

"We didn't have a rule covering such an event at that time so I made a judgment call," recalled Dojack. "Bawel was pretty well on his way, there was no doubt about it. We had a little consultation and decided he could have very well gone in. But you couldn't give any particular penalty because you couldn't penalize a spectator even though he was on the sideline at the Winnipeg bench.

"We said half the distance to the goal line and time enough for three plays, which gave Hamilton ample opportunity to go in. The game was pretty much in hand at that time. The Tiger-Cats had a good lead."

"The guy who tripped him was a lawyer from Toronto," reminisced Ralph Sazio. "For years after, he corresponded with Bibbles, and I believe he sent him a watch one year."

Bomber defensive back Norm Rauhaus couldn't believe his eyes. "That guy ran right by me to get him. He was a lawyer from Toronto who'd just had one too many. Our trainer, Jim Ausley, almost nabbed him, but the guy got by him. There was no question Bibbles would have gone all the way."

The final score of 32–7 would indicate that Hamilton dominated the play that day. Yet the Bombers had more yards and first downs, and the Ti-Cats were only ahead 13–7 at the end of the third quarter. However, their 19 unanswered fourth-quarter points are the second-highest tally in Grey Cup history.

Hamilton pivot Faloney explained. "What happened in the fourth quarter was the result of the wear-them-down situation. We would pound and pound and pound, and in the fourth quarter everything came to fruition."

The Bombers' Steve Patrick pleaded that injuries had caused the Winnipeg loss. "We had about six guys out. Dennis Mendyk played with a cast that almost reached his elbow. Charlie Shepherd couldn't kick. We had somebody else punting. Our stats were better than Hamilton's, but we self-destructed in that game."

Norm Rauhaus said, "We were a very beat-up team. We probably surprised everybody, including ourselves, by beating Edmonton to make it to the Grey Cup. I think it was a question of us saying, 'Hey, our Grey Cup was beating Edmonton in Edmonton.'"

Bud Grant agreed. "In '57, after we'd beaten the Eskimos, we went to Toronto, but we only had half a team. We had fellows that couldn't play or only played a few plays. We were just lucky and happy to be there."

One of the Bomber casualties during the game was Kenny Ploen. "My knee gave out in the third quarter," he said. "We were pretty beat up going into that game. I wasn't particularly, but we'd lost a lot of our players in that rock 'em sock 'em series we had in the cold weather with Edmonton. We played five games in fourteen days to get to the Grey Cup.

"The score wasn't indicative of the game because I think we were down there about four times, and Gerry James fumbled every time we were ready to score. He was such a competitor that he never said anything, but we found out afterward he was playing with a broken hand."

A star of that Hamilton team was John Barrow, who made the All-Star team

Paul Dekker starred for the 1957 Grey Cup champion Hamilton Tiger-Cats.

on both offense and defense, something never accomplished before or since. Although regarded as one of the greatest defensive tackles of all time, he played in fact five different positions, making All-Star at every one of them.

Barrow was an All-American in high school and the University of Florida. The greatest defensive lineman ever to play in the CFL, he was an All-Star 12 straight years, four times on both sides of the ball. He was runner-up for the outstanding lineman award five times, and he won it in 1962. He was All-Canadian six straight years. Like Faloney, money lured him north of the border.

"In 1956 Jake Gaudaur and Jim Trimble approached me and said I was on their negotiation list. I decided to come to Hamilton because at that time the Canadian Football League was paying better than the National Football League and because I was very impressed with Jake and Jim.

"They sometimes neglected to tell you why the money was better. The fact of the matter was you had to go both ways. You had to play 60 minutes. But playing both ways back in those days was the accepted thing. You were glad to do it because you knew nobody could take your job.

"My first Grey Cup was in 1957, and it was the biggest thrill of my life, and, of course, we won. We had a very strong team."

Barrow's opponent for most of his Grey Cup years was another Hall of Famer, Frank Rigney, who remembered Barrow's talents. "I played against John Barrow in all five Grey Cups I was in. John was a great football player, and not just physically. He was a smart player, too. When you were playing against a fellow the caliber of Barrow, you had to figure out different ways to block him because you certainly couldn't block him one way regardless of what the play was."

A number three draft choice of the Philadelphia Eagles, Rigney was no slouch himself. After playing on the same Rose Bowl team as Ploen, Rigney joined the Bombers a year later. He explained why. "First of all, the money was better in Canada. Secondly you could also work, have a job and do better financially, which I did for 10 years.

"Then there was a very clear connection between Forest Evashesky at Iowa and Bud Grant, who was using Jerry Burns, who wound up being the head coach of the Vikings. Jerry had come to Winnipeg from Iowa to install the Iowa offense, the Wing-T. So it was a combination of things that brought me to Winnipeg. I certainly never regretted it."

That may not have been the case when he first arrived. "I didn't go to training camp with Winnipeg because I was in the army. I got up to Canada two and a half weeks late. I had to fly to Montreal the next morning with the team for a preseason game.

"Coach Grant gave me a playbook on the plane and said, 'Look, I'm not expecting you to learn the plays or anything, but we may use you on the kickoff team just to see if you want to play.'

"It wound up that Herb Gray got hurt very early in the game, and a couple of us were alternating at defensive end, a position I hadn't played a whole lot, certainly not on the wide field of the Canadian Football League. We got beat 53–0 by Montreal and, of course, nobody was talking to each other after the game.

"We got on the plane the next night and got off in Toronto. I said, 'What are we doing, changing planes?' They said, 'No, we're playing tomorrow.' I said, 'What the hell are you talking about, we played yesterday!' We got beat 28–6. I had been in Canada four days and lost two games 81–6. And we wound up *winning* the Grey Cup."

If the money was better than in the States, Rigney recalled it still wasn't that good. "I got a contract my rookie year in 1958 for $8,500. (I can't remember whether it was $8,000 plus a $500 signing bonus or $8,500 and a $500 bonus.) Supposedly it was the same contract that Big Daddy Lipscomb had with the Baltimore Colts—that's the way they sold me on the money being so outstanding.

"The next year, even after we had won the Grey Cup, they wouldn't even give me the 500 bucks they gave me for a signing bonus. I actually played my second year for less money than my first."

Although the American players were paid better, Buddy Tinsley felt Canadians were the strength of the ball club. "Fellows I played with like Cornell Piper and Ed Kotowich could have made any NFL team. They were as good a pair of running guards as there were. That's what made Winnipeg pretty strong in those years. We had so many good Canadians that played first-string. We not only had those two boys, there were others like Gordie Rowland and George Druxman."

Round Two

Hamilton's Ralph Sazio thought he had assembled such a strong team that they would win many Grey Cups in the years ahead. Instead they lost four straight to Winnipeg, beginning in 1958, one of the greatest Grey Cup games ever played.

"I thought we should have had a dynasty going after we beat Winnipeg in 1957," said Sazio. "I remember that in the '58 game in Vancouver we had the Winnipeg club hanging on the ropes, but they blocked that kick just before half time. Then came the Fog Bowl in 1962. We were the much superior team. We had the Bombers in our back pockets, and yet they won the next day. We had the momentum, but we just couldn't win. We should have had both those games."

"We had terrific rivalries," offered Winnipeg's Norm Rauhaus, "and there were top-notch football players on both sides that made big plays, but it seemed to me that either through conditioning or mental outlook we were a little tougher than the Tiger-Cats."

In 1958 the Bombers were healthy and raring to go. As if avenging their previous year's loss wasn't incentive enough, Hamilton Head Coach Jim Trimble added fuel to the fire by declaring, "We'll waffle them!"

Although Ploen had been the All-Star quarterback in 1957, rookie Jim Van Pelt from Michigan was at the helm in the 1958 Grey Cup.

"I started the season at quarterback but about the sixth game, I separated my shoulder at Calgary," said Ploen. "I sat out for six games and Jim, who was playing safety at the time, took over. When I got healthy I came back and played both ways. Jim stayed at quarterback, I played at offensive halfback and safety over on defense. We finished the year on that basis.

"In 1959 they stayed with Jim at quarterback, and they put me at safety right off the bat and played that way all through the year until the second-last game when Jim separated his shoulder in Edmonton. Rollie Miles hit him."

"Van Pelt looked like a little bitty kid down the street," recalled Tinsley. "But he was a really smart quarterback.

"He filled the breach when Kenny hurt his shoulder. Van Pelt took over at quarterback, and with a cast on a broken hand, Kenny played defense."

Hamilton did look like they might waffle the Bombers, jumping into an early 14-point lead when Gerry McDougall capped off a long drive with a touchdown. Minutes later, Winnipeg quarterback Jim Van Pelt fumbled, Ralph Goldston recovered and ran 75 yards to the end zone.

The Bombers replied when Van Pelt capped a 90-yard drive by sneaking over from the 1. In the second quarter he closed the gap by kicking two field goals.

Then Hamilton coach Trimble made a decision that defies explanation. On the last play of the first half, with the ball on his 13-yard line, he decided to

Jim Van Pelt stars in the 1958 Grey Cup.

punt! Norm Rauhaus broke through, blocked it and recovered the ball in the end zone. The Bombers went into the dressing room with a 20–14 lead.

"You could call it a coaching error," said Faloney. "Cam Fraser was our punter at that time, and I was doing some of the kicking as well. We were in a spread punt, supposedly, and Cam was in a tight punt. In the spread the punter is 15 yards back, in the tight, 12. Cam didn't get back where he was supposed to be, so he didn't have enough time to get the ball off. That really hurt us a lot."

Mosca was characteristically blunt. "We should have won the 1958 Grey Cup, but there was a bad coaching error before half time, punting the ball instead of grounding it."

Winnipeg's Norm Rauhaus described what happened. "I turned around and kind of hid myself on our defensive left, and I was fortunate enough to get through unscathed, block the punt and fall on it in the end zone. Fortunately for us it happened because we were getting beat pretty badly. We turned it around and won that game. For a young Canadian kid like me, doing something like that was very exciting."

Can one play a Grey Cup make or break? "We were winning the ball game prior to half time," explained Faloney. "When the punt was blocked and Winnipeg scored a touchdown, we went into the dressing room down points. That hurt us. We just didn't come back."

The ejection of Ralph Goldston didn't help matters either, when he was thrown out in the second quarter for punching Leo Lewis. "To me the toughest player who ever played in this league was Ralph Goldston," said Gaudaur. "But Ralph was capable of taking his aggressiveness beyond the point he should have. For example, the best trade I ever made was really years after the Etcheverry–Patterson thing. I traded Bernie Faloney, Ralph Goldston and Jackie Simpson to Montreal for Billy Ray Locklin, Chuck Walton, Billy Wayte and Teddy Page.

"The very first game we played against Montreal in Hamilton we had a running back named Willie Bethea. Goldston and Bethea had been very good friends when they played together in Montreal. The first time Willie carried the ball, Ralph just went up to him and drove him right in the mouth. Knocked him out. Ralph would do almost anything to win. He was the kind of football player I liked, to tell the truth."

Sazio thought the ejection was too severe. "That was ridiculous. It might have been a late hit . . . maybe. You'd have to question that. If you want to penalize him, fine, but you don't get rid of an American when you only have 11 or 12. And when you lose a guy of his ability, you're not just losing a defensive back. He was a backup fullback and a receiver. That was an absolute crime."

"He punched Leo Lewis," referee Dojack recalled. "It was just a regular punch, but we were pretty rigid on punches, forearms, kicking and that type of thing. That was the call by the sideline official, which meant a disqualification, and that was it. If an official said he used his fists, that was enough for me."

In the third quarter Charlie Shephard and Jim Van Pelt scored majors for Winnipeg while Faloney stormed back with two touchdown passes to Ron Howell. Because of a missed Winnipeg convert, when the third quarter drew to a close, Hamilton led 28–27. Early in the fourth the Bombers' Shephard tied the game with a single.

The game's outcome was decided by a little razzle-dazzle. Scrimmaging from the Ti-Cat 25-yard line, quarterback Jim Van Pelt threw to quarterback Kenny Ploen at the 1. Van Pelt then took it into the end zone. The final score was 35–28 with Van Pelt contributing 22 points, second best in Grey Cup history.

Hamilton's last possession saw Faloney lead his team into Winnipeg territory. With seconds left on the clock, Faloney was intercepted by Kenny Ploen after Steve Patrick broke through the line and tipped the pigskin. "They had thrown a long pass down the sideline, and I was able to intercept it near the goal line,"

Ron Latourelle, a Blue Bomber stand-out in five Grey Cups, 1957–59 and 1961–62.

Ploen smiled. "I lateraled to Norm Rauhaus, who was eventually tackled."

After winning the Grey Cup and playing two seasons with the Bombers, Van Pelt went back to the United States and never played football again. "Too bad we lost him," said Tinsley. "If we had those two quarterbacks, we'd have really steamrolled."

Of the four Grey Cups the Bombers won, 1958 was the most memorable. Bud Grant said, "Winnipeg hadn't won a Grey Cup in 18 years. After what we had gone through the year before and then playing Hamilton again and Jim Trimble (who'd been my coach in Philadelphia) saying they were going to waffle us, 1958 was the most satisfying."

Tinsley seconded the motion. "It was a long time coming. But I enjoyed all of them because of the hospitality and everything you go to. It was like a college atmosphere where the people get behind the team. The fans were always there, win or lose. They'd come out to the airport and greet the team. It was really nice that the fans did that."

Round Three

In the 1959 season Hamilton won 10 games for the third year in a row. In the Eastern Semifinal a rookie quarterback named Russ Jackson led Ottawa to a 43–0 rout of the Alouettes. His magic continued with a 17–5 win over Hamilton in the first of the two-game final, but the Ti-Cats rebounded to win the round 26–24. Meanwhile Winnipeg finished first in the West and dispatched the Eskimos two games straight in the Western Final. That same year was the inaugural Grey Cup for Toronto's CNE Stadium, hard by the shore of Lake Ontario.

After a rainfall the field was covered with a tarpaulin, which prevented the turf from drying. Come game day it was a spongy, soggy mess.

The only scoring in the first quarter of the national classic was a Bomber field goal by Gerry James. In the second quarter Vince Scott broke through to block a Winnipeg punt. The ball squirted away from Scott in the end zone, but Winnipeg recovered, surrendering only a point.

In the third quarter Steve Oneschuk kicked Hamilton into the lead with two field goals. The Bombers replied in the final quarter with a touchdown and four singles by Charlie Shephard and a major by Ernie Pitts. The final score was 21–7. It was not a great day for Hamilton.

"To be honest," recalled Bernie Faloney, "Winnipeg had the better team that year. They just bottled us up. When you can't get it moving offensively or defensively, it is just one of those days. We couldn't do anything right."

"It was pretty sloppy out there," said Ploen. "The turf wasn't too good. We were in control of that game from start to finish although we weren't that far ahead. The score wasn't indicative of our domination, but that's the way it goes sometimes. They always had a tough defense. They were big and strong and always made it tough."

The Hamilton–Winnipeg rivalry was put on hold for a year. The Bombers again finished first in 1960 but lost to Edmonton in the Western Final. Tinsley chuckled ruefully, "The two best teams that I played on were the '52 and '60 teams, but we didn't even go to the Grey Cup. We had a 14–2 record in 1960 and we got beaten by a snowstorm. We just fumbled. The score was 4–2—a hockey score. Nobody could do anything. You just can't play in a driving snowstorm."

Bomber Steve Patrick agreed. "The 1960 team was our best. We were 14–2 and would have beat the East easily, but we didn't go to the Grey Cup. Both play-off games in Winnipeg were in a snowstorm. It was about 18 below."

"The most disappointing year we had was 1960 when we had the best team in Canada," echoed Leo Lewis. "There is no doubt, no reservation about that. We should have gone to six Grey Cups in a row and won five in a row.

"That year we were more complacent than in other years. In the play-off final Edmonton beat us 4–2. We couldn't understand what was happening that day. We couldn't move the ball, we couldn't pass, we couldn't do anything. They couldn't either. Tommy Joe Coffey kicked a field goal with a few seconds left to beat us. It was so disappointing. Grown men cried in the dressing room."

No one felt worse than Kenny Ploen. "I had broken the back of my hand. We were leading 2–1 near the end of the game. They missed a field goal, we ran it out and then I fumbled it back to them. They faked a quick kick and got down into position. They got one more chance, and the second time Coffey put it through."

Bud Grant said, "I think our '60 team was the best team we had, the most dominant team. But the third game of the final we couldn't do anything. I remember Kenny Ploen fumbled on a quarterback sneak when we were ahead 2–1. All we had to do was run the clock out, but he fumbled. He had broken a bone in his left hand in the second game up in Edmonton.

"I remember standing on the sidelines thinking that my friends in the States are never going to understand a 2–1 football game. The score ended up 4–2, not much better, and Edmonton won. But that was probably our best team."

Say It Ain't So, Ted

In 1960 the Tiger-Cats ended an 11-year play-off run by tumbling into the Eastern cellar with a 4–10 record. The Alouettes had fared little better, finishing third at 5–9, and the stage was set for one of the most sensational trades in Canadian sports history: the Sam "The Rifle" Etcheverry and Hal Patterson trade. Jake Gaudaur masterminded the deal. "That year, 1960, Montreal had lost the play-off to Ottawa. I had read in the morning paper that Ted Workman [Montreal owner] was blaming Etcheverry.

"We had finished last that year. I picked up the phone on Tuesday and said to Workman, 'How about doing a straight trade: Etcheverry for Faloney.' And he said, 'That's great. Are you interested in Patterson as well?' I just about dropped off my chair.

"I said, 'Tell you what, Ted. I'll catch the first plane to Montreal. I'll call you from the airport to let you know of my arrival. You can pick me up and we can talk about it.'

"He picked me up at the airport and we went to his home. At that time I owned a General Motors car dealership, so I operated at times as a used car salesman. I decided to offer him Don Paquette, a very promising tough young-ster I really liked because at age 17, when he came to us, I could see him as a replacement for Pete Neumann. He wasn't very big, only 210 pounds, but he was very strong, very quick and fast and tough as hell.

"So I said, 'How about Don Paquette?' Workman said, 'That's fine.' That was it. That was the extent of the negotiations."

Why did Gaudaur want Sam Etcheverry? "I was thinking of attendance. I was thinking more of a promotional thing at that time. To me Sam Etcheverry was still a fantastic quarterback. He was deemed at that time to be better than Bernie Faloney. Whether he was or not might be difficult to prove."

Etcheverry refused to report to Hamilton, so the quarterback swap was off. The trade came down to the journeyman Don Paquette for one of the greatest receivers of all-time, Hal Patterson. While the deal certainly helped the Hamil-ton Tiger-Cats, it was the beginning of the end of football in Montreal, given that Sam Etcheverry and Hal Patterson were nearly as popular in Montreal as Jean Beliveau and Rocket Richard. Speculation about Workman's motives ran wild. Gaudaur, who had the greatest respect for the Alouette owner, had an explanation.

"Not too long after he got into the ownership of the Alouettes, he got into something called Moral Rearmament. He became obsessed with it—I mean absolutely obsessed with it. Players told me he would be in the dressing room preaching it.

"I think it is fine to be in Moral Rearmament or any religion you want, but I don't think you preach it in the dressing room of a football team.

"I remember on another occasion Workman got upset with a big Canadian defensive end, Doug McNichol, and he called and said, 'Do you want him?' But Workman had many good qualities. He deserves more credit than he has received as an administrator. But Ted was a paradox."

Part of Moral Rearmament was a kind of public confessional. The rumor at the time held that Mrs. Workman, also a believer, made some remarks that indicated her relationship with Etcheverry and Patterson was more than platonic. Gaudaur could not confirm or deny the rumor. "Whether there was any substance to the rumor," he concluded, "I guess we'll never know. But very definitely that might have been a factor in wanting to get rid of Etcheverry and Patterson."

Hal Patterson had a much different explanation. "When the season was over I told Coach Moss that if he was going to be there the next year, I didn't want to be there. I don't know whether that prompted the trade or not."

For Hamilton, as Gaudaur predicted, the trade was a success on the field and at the gate. "To demonstrate the irony of the thing," said Gaudaur, "Patterson joined us and sold out our stadium the next year, and Bernie won the Most Outstanding Player Award."

For Hamilton pivot Bernie Faloney, news of the trade was distressing. "I was very upset," he said. "Actually I found out about it from a sportscast. Then I called Jim Trimble and went down to see him. Sam Etcheverry and I were pretty good friends. He called me and said they couldn't trade him without his consent.

"So I asked Gaudaur if it was an unconditional trade. He said it was. So what really happened was I went to Montreal, and Sam and I went to the hockey game together, which created a little furor in the press.

"We had a meeting with Leo Dandurand, who indicated that if Sam couldn't be traded without his consent, and if Sam didn't want to go to Hamilton but wanted to go to St. Louis, then there was no trade. That's exactly what happened.

"I was interviewed the next day and I just told them I wasn't interested in coming to Montreal. So the trade then went back as null and void with the exception that Patterson and Paquette were traded.

"Then I challenged Jake Gaudaur about his telling me it was an unconditional trade when it wasn't. I wound up back in Hamilton with a new contract."

Despite Gaudaur's rejection of him, Bernie Faloney was happy to stay in Hamilton. "I didn't want to leave. I didn't have any mixed emotions. I wanted to stay in Hamilton. I was making my home and business in Hamilton. I had my farm going, my work going, I had my two children. We were entrenched. Jim Trimble didn't want to make that trade—he told me that."

"I never did consult with Jim Trimble when I did the Etcheverry–Patterson trade," said Gaudaur, "because if that had leaked out in any way, I would never have been able to pull that one off."

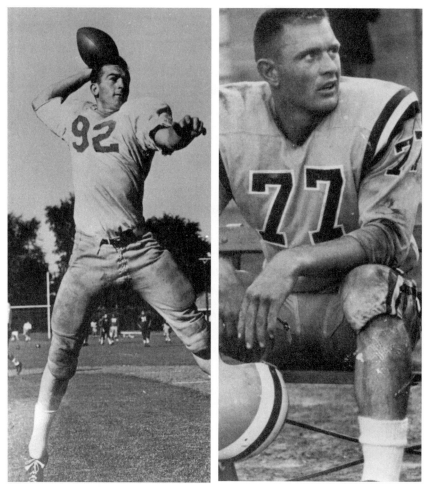

Sam "The Rifle" Etcheverry (left) and Hal Patterson, two of the greatest battery-mates in CFL history, were stunned when Montreal owner Ted Workman traded them to Hamilton in 1960.

Round Four

In 1961 the Ti-Cats returned to first place with their customary record of 10–4. The Argos had fallen from first to third but hammered second-place Ottawa 43–19 in the semifinal. They then routed the Ti-Cats 25–7 at CNE, carrying an 18-point advantage into the second game in Hamilton.

Overtime would be the word of the day in 1961 postseason play. The Cats tied Toronto at the end of regulation time and won the right to advance to the

Grey Cup against Winnipeg by scoring four touchdowns in 20 minutes of extra play.

They weren't so fortunate a week later against the Blue Bombers for the Cup. The only scoring in the first half came on a Bomber single by Jack Delveaux and a touchdown pass from Faloney to Paul Dekker. In the third quarter Faloney and Ralph Goldston teamed up for a major, answered by two Gerry James' field goals. James added a touchdown in the fourth to send the game into overtime.

According to Frank Rigney, Winnipeg dominated Hamilton in the fourth quarter. "That was one time we did handle them reasonably well. We had a pretty good offensive team in terms of controlling the football because Leo Lewis was such an outstanding back. So was Charlie Shepherd."

Steve Patrick had a theory to explain why Winnipeg dominated late in the game. "We thought they would whip us in no time because we were a much lighter team. They were a big, heavy team. But I think they tired more quickly than we did. It seemed that toward the end of the game we had more energy than they did."

For Winnipeg coach Bud Grant, the day began in a most unusual way. "We were staying at the Westbury Hotel. We went to leave for the game on the bus, and the elevators were all messed up. We were staying on the top floor to kind of get away from everything.

"We were always sticklers to leave right on time, and everybody had to be there because we didn't want to be at the stadium too long, sitting in the dressing room. We had it timed out pretty good.

"Some of the players got stuck up on the top floor. They had to walk down. Others were stuck in the elevators. We left about 15 minutes late, so the ride to the stadium was just like we were in a pressure cooker. The players were just ready to burst.

"There wasn't a word spoken when we got off the bus. We had to change and get on the field in about 20 minutes. I thought we were going to explode when we got there."

"By the time we got out there, we were ready," Leo Lewis said with a chuckle.

Both teams played such tenacious defense that the game had to go into a second overtime period. With the ball on the Ti-Cat 18, Kenny Ploen stepped back to pass. Hamilton defenders dropped back to cover so Ploen took advan-

Kenny Ploen leads the way in the only overtime Grey Cup game, 1961.

tage of a gaping hole and ran for the winning touchdown. Winnipeg won 21–14 in the only Grey Cup in history to go into overtime.

Ploen explained what happened. "It was a pass play to Farrell Funston, but he got wrapped up and knocked down going over the middle. That kept me chugging around. It was just one of those instinctive things. The pressure starts coming, there's a little opening, you feel something, you start running to the right. The first thing you know you pick up a couple of good blocks, get a couple of breaks and you're in the end zone.

"Scoring the overtime touchdown was a great thrill. We were down 14–7 before we tied it up. We almost won in regulation. We kept on coming in the overtime. Hamilton and Winnipeg had some great Grey Cups."

Round Five

Winnipeg and Hamilton were back in 1962 for the famous Fog Bowl. Visibility was good when the game began, but the fog arrived early in the second quarter. Several times Commissioner Sydney Halter went down to the sidelines and found that visibility at field level was good. Because the fog seemed to be getting thicker, Halter ordered half time cut by five minutes. By the fourth quarter the players could barely see one another, and Halter called the game with 9:29 remaining. Trailing the Bombers 28–27, Hamilton had the ball in Winnipeg territory. Hostilities resumed the following day.

The fog that day prevented fans who paid their way into CNE Stadium from witnessing brilliant performances by Ti-Cat Garney Henley and Blue Bomber Leo Lewis. Lewis, the game's Most Valuable Player, scored two touchdowns, threw for another, rushed 41 yards and caught seven passes for 77 yards. Henley was even better with two majors, 100 yards rushing and 119 yards on pass receptions.

Henley opened the scoring by running 74 yards for a touchdown, the second longest romp in Grey Cup history. Don Sutherin missed the convert. In the second quarter Garney Henley ran 18 yards to pay dirt. Again the convert was missed. Bob Kuntz rounded out Ti-Cat scoring in the first quarter with a 2-yard plunge for a touchdown. Leo Lewis replied twice for the Bombers and threw for a third to Charlie Shephard. At half time Winnipeg led 21–19.

Scoring was completed in the third quarter when Dave Viti and Shephard exchanged majors and Sutherin picked up a single on a missed field goal. The Fog Bowl was the only Grey Cup played over two days, won by Winnipeg 28–27. For the players it was their strangest football experience.

"At field level it wasn't that bad," remembered Bernie Faloney. "For 10 or 15 yards you could see very well. It wasn't as bad as a lot of people made it out to be, but it got pretty bad in the fourth quarter.

"When it opened up next day with about nine minutes left, we had the chance to move the ball in. I believe it was third down, and Joe Zuger threw a real fine pass from punt formation to Dick Easterly, who dropped the ball. That would have put us on about the 30-yard line going in. Even if we didn't score the touchdown, a field goal would have the won the game for us."

Hamilton's John Barrow didn't think their chance to move the ball in amounted to much. "Instead of having a coin toss and a kickoff the next day, which would have been fair, we began on third down, which meant Winnipeg would have immediate possession. Winnipeg had all night to think about what they were going to do the next day."

As far as making the decision to carry on the next day exactly where they left off, Jake Gaudaur was in a difficult position. "I'll never forget the Fog Bowl because that year I was not only president and general manager of the team that was on the field and behind by one point, but I was also the president of the league and supposed to be thinking nationally. There was no doubt in my mind that I was thinking locally.

"We had the ball on the 40-yard line when Sydney Halter called the game. Syd was absolutely right. Technically the president is over the commissioner, but on game operations he had the authority to make the decision.

"I have to be honest and admit that at the time I didn't think calling the game seemed to make sense, but since we had possession on the 40-yard line I thought we could at least tie it.

"One of my favorite pictures shows us standing down on the field arguing about it. I'm convinced he did the right thing."

So was Kenny Ploen. "I think the officials made the right decision. I didn't think so the day they called it because down on the field at our level, it was still workable to do things. A punt would go out of sight, and if you threw a long, high pass you might lose a bit of it, but otherwise you could still see not too badly. Later, when I saw the replays of the game from the fans' viewpoint. I could understand. They couldn't see anything. It was only fair that they called it, I guess."

The decision to halt the game was actually made by referee Paul Dojack. "We knew ahead of time there was liable to be a fog coming in. Syd Halter kept pushing and pushing and telling me to run the game pretty fast. 'Keep it going, keep it going. We're liable to get a fog.' Sure enough, by the fourth quarter we were having difficulty.

"It was left up to me. We were communicating with the sidelines quite regularly. There were nine minutes to go in the quarter. From the far hash marks, I couldn't see the down markers. The fog was pretty low then. So we had a consultation. We said let's delay for a bit of time. Ultimately the two managers and Syd Halter got together and put it off for 24 hours. When we came back the next day, there was no further scoring. Strange."

Joe Zuger was a rookie in 1962, participating in the first of 10 Grey Cups as a Ti-Cat player or general manager. (In his debut as a starting quarterback, he set the still-standing record for most touchdown passes in a game—8—when Hamilton defeated Saskatchewan 67–21. After the game Roughrider Ray Purdin said, "Let's get on the bus before they score another one.")

Like most of his teammates, Zuger found defeat in that Grey Cup very difficult to take. "The most disappointing Grey Cup for me was the Fog Bowl, where we had to come back the next day and play the final nine minutes. I was a rookie, and we were really on a high for the game. Then we had to come back the next day.

"It was awfully strange throwing passes in the fog. I threw a touchdown pass to Dave Viti. I threw it up in the air into the fog. I don't know how he saw it coming down out of the fog.

"I hurt my left ankle during the game. All I did the next day was punt. We didn't get much sleep the night before the second day. We had to go to another hotel. It was an emergency thing. We just went in with our equipment on, took it off and went to bed, got up and put it on again. It wasn't a good night."

Blue Bomber Leo Lewis agreed. "That was an experience you wouldn't want to go through again—coming back the next day, after playing your heart out that one day and then having to come back the next day.

"Even though there were only 9 minutes and 29 seconds left, we had to go through the whole thing, getting dressed, getting warmed up and enthused. There were guys who played the day before who could not play the next day. Luckily we hung on. Hamilton didn't do much and neither did we."

Kenny Ploen remembered the difficulty of coming back the next day. "It was a most unusual thing in my mind (I guess only a football player can appreciate this) of playing the way we did on the Saturday and then having to come back the next morning and have a pregame meal, strap back up and go out and play that last nine minutes or so.

"You're so damn stiff. I'm sure it took everybody on both sides quite a while to get going. I know there were a couple of our players that didn't even go out onto the field. They tried, but they were black and blue or had a bruise and they just couldn't play."

Steve Patrick said, "You had an empty feeling. You didn't lose, you didn't win and there was something next morning that you had to do."

"There was a hell of a lot of pain in the dressing room the next day," recalled Rigney. "All your bumps and bruises come out the next day. There were a number of people being shot with Novocain so they could go out and play. And then not really much happened in those final minutes."

While the Ti-Cats went right to a hotel and hit the sack, Bud Grant approached things differently, as Kenny Ploen explained. "Bud didn't put a curfew on us. He said use your head, go on out, see what's going on out there, relax, you know you've got to play tomorrow. Everybody went out for a little while, but we were in bed pretty early. I can tell you that we were pretty tired."

Rigney appreciated Grant's approach. "Grant was always a great user of psychology. Instead of him dictating what we should or should not do, he just left it up to us. He said he thought we should have a meeting on our own, which, of course, put the decision in our lap.

"It was rather strange because we had a number of parties all set to go on that Saturday night, and, of course, they all got canceled. We decided we'd have a voluntary curfew. It was 11:00 P.M. as I recall. Most of the guys caught a movie."

According to Norm Rauhaus, not all rival Ti-Cats stayed in their hotel. "I can remember running into a few Hamilton guys. You talked to different people, and they would say, 'We should be ahead or you should be ahead.' It was a little different."

Angelo Mosca was one of the Ti-Cats who longed for some action on a Saturday night. "Bob Minihane and I said, 'Shucks, we can play nine minutes standing on our heads. We went downtown and flagged a cab. There's got to be 10,000 taxis in Toronto, but flag down one with our assistant coach, Ralph Sazio, in it!"

When analyzing the Fog Bowl, the Hamiltonians believed the damage had been done the previous day. Said Mosca, "We should have won the Grey Cup. Don Sutherin missed a convert. We came back, ran all over them and did everything except score a touchdown."

For Hall of Famer Don Sutherin, the Fog Bowl was a nightmare. Though he holds the record for most Grey Cup converts at 17, he missed a crucial kick and had a disputed field goal. Not only was it his third loss in three Grey Cup games, but he felt personally responsible for the defeat.

"There was a discrepancy over a field goal that I had kicked, and I missed an extra point that day. As a matter of fact it boiled down to where that was the point that cost us the ball game. You just don't miss extra points. I did and that was the deciding factor in that Grey Cup. It was a very disappointing afternoon.

"*Wide World of Sports* televised the game. It was so foggy that anything with any height—like a punt or a field goal—couldn't be seen at all. But the TV camera showed the ball hitting right in the middle of the top of the maple leaf that was situated in the center of the end zone. To do that, the ball had to go through the uprights."

Being on the receiving end of a kickoff or punt also was a problem. "Garney Henley and I were returning punts," Sutherin recalled. "You could hear the ball kicked, but you couldn't see it. All of a sudden you'd hear it hit the ground beside you. You'd run over to pick it up and you could see bodies coming at you, but you could only see them from the knees down. It was scary. You didn't know who was coming at you.

"They should have called the game a lot earlier than when they did. To play 9 minutes and 29 seconds the next day was horrible. We stayed in some little, crappy hotel on the lakeshore in Toronto. We didn't sleep well, and then we came back the next day and played those nine minutes."

"I think the biggest effect of the fog was in the kicking game," said Rigney. "When you went down to cover a punt, you had no idea where the hell you were going. You just had to search for the punt returner. He was going to lead you to the ball eventually."

Rauhaus was of the same opinion. "But the problems weren't that great for defensive backs. There were more problems for the offense. Say, for example, a guy ran a 15-yard pattern and the quarterback made an 8–10-yard drop. He would have trouble finding someone to throw to."

"We stopped throwing at the end of the third quarter," said Kenny Ploen. "I went over to defense in that game, and Hal Ledyard did a great job at quarterback. He brought us out of our end before the game was called."

The Bombers' Steve Patrick said, "It was the same as the year before. We were playing better than Hamilton, and they seemed to be getting tired. We were afraid that the next day they would come out refreshed and we would have a hard time.

The Fog Bowl was a great day in a losing cause for Garney Henley. Henley's magnificent career spanned 16 seasons, all with the Tiger-Cats. He appeared in seven Grey Cups, winning four. The diminutive defensive back and receiver from Haiti, South Dakota, was the last of the great two-way players.

Fifth in all-time interceptions with 59 (Sutherin is sixth), Henley caught passes through 16 consecutive seasons, a record that still stands. He was an All-Canadian defensive back nine straight seasons from 1963–1971. In 1972 he made All-Canadian as a receiver. That year he also won the Schenley Award for Most Outstanding Player, recognition of his two-way talents. Three years after retiring, he was inducted into the Football Hall of Fame. No one was elevated to that select company sooner after leaving the game. Of all his honors, that one means the most to him.

"That was the ultimate in my career," he said. "I never really thought about getting into the Hall of Fame until I retired. Then you start living on your past and thinking about what you did accomplish. It happened so fast I didn't have time to dwell on it. It means a lot to me now."

Henley's Grey Cup performances were outstanding. Besides the 74-yard run, he had 15 receptions for 267 yards and three interceptions. His 266 combined yards in the Fog Bowl are the second most in Grey Cup history. He is fifth in combined yardage with 448 and the third most productive punt returner in Grey Cup history.

Garney Henley may have been the most gifted individual to ever play in the Canadian Football League. Ironically basketball was his first love and baseball second. Football was both an afterthought and a third choice.

"Garney Henley was tremendous," said Ralph Sazio. "It's too bad he didn't go one way. We couldn't decide whether we should play him defensively or offensively, so we ended up dividing his time. He was a great receiver and a great defensive back. He had such great range."

The Player of the Game in the Fog Bowl was the Bombers' Leo Lewis, one of the greatest running backs in the history of Canadian football. A six-time All-Star, the Lincoln Locomotive scored 79 touchdowns during his 12-season career. Only George Reed, Johnny Bright, Normie Kwong and Mike Pringle surpassed his rushing total of 8,861 yards. Lewis also is second to Henry Williams in kickoff return and total yardage and is the Grey Cup leader in rushing and kickoff return yardage. He was the first member of those great Bomber teams to be inducted into the CFL Hall of Fame.

Yet Lewis never won a rushing title or a Schenley Award. Did such lack of recognition bother him? "It did, yes, but during the time I was playing, Jackie Parker was nominated seven times to represent the West in the Schenley Awards. I had a real good rookie year, but at that time the rookie award went just to a Canadian player. So I missed out on that." Saskatchewan's Harry Lunn won it.

"I came up when Edmonton had those great ballplayers. There was no doubt that Jackie Parker and Johnny Bright were outstanding. Any other time I might have had the opportunity to win an award."

Frank Rigney thought Lewis made him a better ballplayer by reading blocks. "I was fortunate enough to get out in front of Leo on quite a number of occasions," he remembered. "A good back can always make a blocker look good by setting the defender up. Leo had a great knack for that. You really didn't have to block the guy very much with Leo. Give him a little space and he was gone."

Lewis was another Iowa product who found his way to Winnipeg after attending Lincoln College in Missouri. It was somewhat of a lucky accident that he ended up in Winnipeg. Lewis explained. "I heard that my first contact was brought about because of a person who worked on the railroad that ran from St. Paul to Winnipeg. Even though my name was in the newspapers because I had made All-American, some of the individuals in an administrative capacity in Winnipeg did not really know about me. I heard that a waiter or a porter on the train had the opportunity to talk to an administrator on the Winnipeg team. He mentioned my name and showed him a press clipping about me.

"At the same time I was drafted by Baltimore in the NFL, and I had a choice of going to Winnipeg or Baltimore. At that time in the States we didn't know much about the Canadian Football League. We didn't know anything about the Grey Cup.

"Coming to Canada was high adventure for me. In the mid-1950s individuals from small black colleges did not have much of an opportunity to play pro ball. Even though some of us did good things, we weren't recognized. When I came to Winnipeg in 1955 there were only two of us, Tom Casey and me."

Racial problems were a reality for black ballplayers no matter where they went. "There were some negative experiences," Lewis recalled. "I think any racial problems we had with Canadian ballplayers were brought about because of Americans from the southern States. I do believe that. Generally speaking,

The "Lincoln Locomotive" Leo Lewis.

Winnipeg was a good town. There wasn't much racism that I could see. I think Canada was a great place. It was an adventure for me coming from a small school and having the opportunity to go to Winnipeg and play 10 full seasons."

Back at home, after their loss in the Fog Bowl, the Tiger-Cats regrouped for the 1963 season. In 1963, following 13 years as an assistant with Carl Voyles and Jim Trimble, Ralph Sazio became Hamilton's head coach. Trimble had compiled a record of 60–36–2. His teams finished first and went to the Grey Cup during five of his seven years. But after winning his Grey Cup debut, he lost four in a row.

Ralph Sazio said it was time for a change. "Sometimes a coach has to move on. Jim was very frustrated because his team had lost four straight Grey Cup games. Ted Workman wanted a guy like Jim. Jim was a very colorful guy, and he had a good background, having been Coach of the Year in the NFL."

Colorful often meant controversial. Prior to the 1962 Grey Cup, Trimble was drinking with a Toronto reporter in the bar of the Royal York Hotel. Taking exception to the reporter's prediction about the coming confrontation with the Blue Bombers, Trimble, it was alleged, dragged the scribe from the bar down to the waterfront where he wailed the tar out of him. As Sazio said, "Sometimes a coach has to move on."

Still, Sazio had a tough act to follow. "When I took over from Jim in 1963, it wasn't good enough just to go into the Grey Cup. The pressure was on us to win, which we did."

During Sazio's five years at the helm, he had a winning percentage of.707, fourth best in league history. Hamilton finished first four times and won three Grey Cups.

Cat Fight

In Ralph Sazio's inaugural campaign, the Ti-Cats won 10 games to finish first. They took the opener of the Eastern Final 45–0 and won the round 63–35. Winnipeg meanwhile had fallen on hard times, finishing fourth that year with a record of 7–9, so the 1963 Grey Cup was a battle of the cats in Vancouver.

The first quarter was scoreless. Early in the second frame Hamilton quarterback Faloney capped off a long drive by hitting Willie Bethea with a 4-yard pass for a touchdown. Minutes later, Art Baker went over from the one, putting the Easterners into a 14-point lead. Then, at the nine-minute mark of the second quarter, it happened.

The heart of the Lion attack was halfback Willie Fleming, who had picked up 1,234 yards that year. Fleming took the ball from quarterback Joe Kapp and headed around the end toward the sideline. Joe Zuger hit him and Fleming fell forward to the ground. In the meantime Angelo Mosca had been running hard toward the sideline, thinking that if he didn't cut Fleming off, he could score. Mosca hurled himself through the air. A second or two after Fleming hit the turf, Mosca landed on top of him in what was either a late hit (the Lions' story) or an unavoidable accident (the Ti-Cats' story). Mosca was penalized, but the Tiger-Cats went on to win 21–10.

The Lions were outraged, blaming their defeat on the fact that Fleming could not continue. Sazio was unimpressed. "That was a lot of crap. Instead of saying it was a well-played, hard-fought game and we won it, B.C. wanted to make excuses.

"If you look at the film, you'll see that Mosca made a great play. He was playing left tackle, and he came from that position past John Barrow, Eddie

The infamous Mosca–Fleming Incident, Grey Cup 1963. Mosca is wearing Number 68, Fleming Number 15. A great play or a late hit?

Bevan and Pete Neumann, past three or four guys to meet Fleming at that point. He showed great quickness. There was no controversy. As far as I'm concerned the Lions had their ass beat."

Don Sutherin was nearby. "I was about five steps from that incident. What happened was this: Joe Zuger was the guy that hit Fleming first. But he hit him in such a way that he bounced off. Mosca was coming in and thought that Fleming was still going to be standing when he got there. He dove, Joe slid off Fleming, Mosca was still in the air, and by the time Angie landed, Fleming was lying flat on his stomach on the ground. That was the incident. I heard the collision and the grunt, and it was history. It's pretty tough to stop a 285 pound man in midair."

Bernie Faloney had no doubt that the incident didn't affect the final outcome. "We played well that day even though the 21–10 score wasn't that great. Our passing attack was good, our ball control was good. Whether or not Willie had played wouldn't have made a damn bit of difference. We came out in the second half and Patterson caught that long pass for a touchdown. That just broke the Lions' spirit. Really, all we did in the fourth quarter was play defense and a little ball control. I think we thoroughly whipped them."

John Barrow thought Mosca got a bad rap because of his reputation as a tough guy. "Mosca may have been a little bit late, but we ran that film back 50 times, and I don't think it was a cheap shot. I wasn't more than five feet away from Angie when it occurred. I would not have called a penalty on it. The attitude of the crowd and the media afterward was uncalled for, although I can understand why. Mosca had built a reputation, and I think that hurt him, I really do.

Mosca pleaded innocence. "The situation was this: he was cutting up the sidelines. I came from 45 yards away to make that play. I was scared he was going to turn back up into the playing field, so I dove to cut off the angle, and as I did he put his head down.

"It was one of those things where I went over the top of him and caught the back of his head with my knee. It wasn't an intentional thing. If you see the play it looks like I deliberately did it, but I had already committed myself."

As far as his reputation hurting him, Mosca agreed. "I never got the recognition I deserved as a player because of my so-called reputation."

B.C. quarterback Joe Kapp saw the situation differently. "Old Angelo was never known as the most disciplined of football players. You might even say he was hard of hearing. I told him what I thought when it happened, and I talked to him again after the game. He knows what I said, but that is between him and me."

"Joe refused to shake hands with me after the game," said Mosca.

"Oh, Joe Kapp gave everybody hell," sneered Faloney. "Joe was always hollering at everybody."

Paul Dojack explained the call. "Mosca was an aggressive player. When you get to know players' tactics and methods, you police them accordingly. Fleming was out of bounds, Mosca's momentum was there, but there was no effort to let up a bit. Usually when I was around the play, I yelled at them to slow down or ease off. I got into the game just like a ballplayer and I tried to prevent penalties.

"On that particular incident the sideline official called a late hit out of bounds and the penalty was applied. Mosca wasn't disqualified—he was just given a penalty."

Dojack didn't share Ti-Cat opinion about Joe Kapp. "As a referee I really liked him because he was so competitive. He used to say, 'Dojack, never mind protecting me by giving me any quick whistles. You just let me go because I want to throw that ball. If I'm not on the ground and I'm not legally dead, don't you try to protect me.'

"Joe Kapp and I had quite a few sessions. I loved Kapp as a ballplayer and competitor. Often in talks and speeches he said I was the best official in North America. I appreciated that from him although I wasn't giving him any favors — no more than anyone else.

"In one game he came to talk to me and put his arm around my shoulder. I said, 'Joe, get your hands off me!' In fact a photographer took a picture and called it 'When a Fellow Needs a Friend' and there was big Joe Kapp with his arm around me as we were walking off the field at half time."

The injured Willie Fleming said, "I'm the last one to know what happened. The Hamilton players saw it one way, Joe Kapp saw it another way, and I was the one on the ground who was out cold and didn't see anything."

When the second half began, Hamilton led 14–3. Soon after, Faloney hit Hal Patterson for a 70-yard touchdown, and the game was essentially over. In the last quarter Mack Burton ran 5 yards for B.C.'s only major of the day.

Patterson's touchdown was his fifth in Grey Cup competition, a record that still stands. He also holds the records for most career Grey Cup receptions (29) and yards (580).

In 1964 the two teams hooked up again in the Grey Cup, this time in Toronto. Hamilton's offense was humming, running up 436 yards in total offense compared to B.C.'s 309. The Ti-Cats had 24 first downs, the Lions 16. Yet they trailed 34–8 at the end of the third quarter.

When the Lions were given a couple of lemons, they made lemonade. Joe Kapp worked the Lions down the field to the Hamilton 1-yard line early in the first quarter. Bob Swift scored the touchdown. In the second stanza the Leos lined up at the Ti-Cat 15 to try a field goal. Holder Pete Ohler dropped the ball. He calmly picked it up and threw to Jim Carphin in the end zone. Before the half ended, a determined Willie Fleming ran 46 yards for B.C.'s third touchdown. The score was 20–1 at the half.

Early in the third quarter, Hamilton scored their first touchdown when Faloney lateraled to Johnny Counts, who ran 58 yards to the end zone, the third longest run from scrimmage in Grey Cup history.

The mishandled snap wasn't the only "bad" break B.C. suffered in the game. Their starting fullback Bob Swift, who had picked up 1,054 yards rushing that year, injured his knee before the half and couldn't continue. Swift would return in 1965 and '66 as a running back and play 11 more years as an offensive lineman, making All-Canadian three times at center for Winnipeg. Bill Munsey replaced him and went to work like a man possessed.

In a performance reminiscent of Red Storey, Munsey demolished the Tiger-Cats in a mere three minutes and eight seconds. With the score 20–8, Munsey ran 18 yards for a touchdown. Three minutes later Faloney tried the lateral to Johnny Counts again, but it was low and Counts couldn't handle it. Munsey picked up the ball and went 71 yards for another major, the third longest fumble return in Grey Cup history.

Behind 34–8, a lesser team would have collapsed. Not Hamilton. Faloney threw touchdown passes to Tommy Grant and Stan Crisson. Don Sutherin added a convert, Joe Zuger a single and B.C. conceded a safety touch. The final score was 34–24. In their first win ever over Hamilton, the Lions had also won their first Grey Cup.

For Hamilton's Angelo Mosca 1964 was his most disappointing Grey Cup. "I thought we had a better ball club than in '63, when we won the Grey Cup. A couple of plays happened in that game against Vancouver. Bob Swift got hurt and Bill Munsey came in and just ran all over us. We'd have preferred to play against Swift because he was the slower back."

Ralph Sazio had another point of view. "There were a couple of plays that went against us, but I think they just wanted to win more than we did. Sure, Bob Swift got hurt and Bill Munsey went in and had a hell of a day. But we moved the ball exceptionally well. We were in the ball game all the way through."

For Faloney, making his last Grey Cup appearance, 1964 was a particularly disappointing loss. "There was the Pete Ohler play, where a field goal turned into a touchdown. That was strange. Another strange play was that fumble picked up by Munsey, who ran 70 some yards for a touchdown. That was 14 points and we didn't lose by 14. We were down 34–8, but we came back strong in the second half. I'd like to write those two plays out of that game, but you can't do that."

Round Six

Of all the forces of nature that can affect the outcome of a football game, none is harder to handle than wind. That is why the punting and place-kicking accomplishments of Bob Cameron and Dave Ridway are so remarkable because there are no windier places to play than Winnipeg and Regina.

The wind was so bad during the 1995 Grey Cup in Regina, for example, that fans sitting high up in the south end zone stands had to leave the game by half time because of debris blowing into their eyes. One writer stepped outside the press box to see what it was like and was almost blown over the railing into the seats.

Breezy Grey Cups happened in '75, '88 and '95, but only one has been called the Wind Bowl. That was 1965, the last of the great match-ups between the Bombers of Bud Grant and the Trimble–Sazio Tiger-Cats. The temperature at game time was 4°C, but the wind was gusting to 85 kilometers per hour. Under normal circumstances the Bombers likely would have won. Winnipeg had 15 first downs to Hamilton's 8. They recovered five Hamilton fumbles. Usually the team that makes the fewest mistakes wins. But not on this day, unless you include errors in judgment by the coaching staff.

Don Sutherin opened the scoring by driving the kickoff into the end zone, where Dave Raimey gave up a single. The Bombers could go nowhere on their possession and the punt barely made it over the line of scrimmage. Dick Cohee ran 32 yards to the Bomber 7 and then went over for the touchdown. A couple of minutes later Hamilton increased their lead to 10–0 when Kenny Ploen conceded the first of three safety touches.

The second quarter and wind belonged to Winnipeg. Art Perkins scored an 8-yard touchdown after being set up by Leo Lewis. Later Dave Raimey set up Lewis for his 5-yard major. One convert was good, so Winnipeg led at the half by 3 points.

Hamilton scored 8 points with the wind in the third quarter, a 69-yard Joe Zuger to Willie Bethea pass and run touchdown and a single that Zuger kicked on the run. Winnipeg conceded two more safety touches, confident they could pull the game out of the fire in the fourth quarter, when they would have the wind.

It was not to be. The staunch Ti-Cat defense held the Bombers to a field goal, and Hamilton won 22–16.

Ralph Sazio praised his Ti-Cat defenders. "We were leading near the end with two or three minutes left, and Winnipeg had the ball. They must have gambled at least three times on third and three and third and four. Their big fullback Art Perkins hit in there time and time again, and it looked like they might score a touchdown and beat us.

"But Herb Paterra was our linebacker, and on their third gamble, Herb stuck him right in the hole and ran the clock out. We hadn't beaten the Blue Bombers of Bud Grant in four previous tries, so this was a big one."

The Bombers contended that Perkins made that yard, and if Paul Dojack had spotted the ball properly, Winnipeg would have gone on to win. Dojack conceded that spotting the ball is an official's most difficult call. "If you're not right there with the ballcarrier, and he's moving forward and then gets knocked back, spotting the ball is difficult. Sometimes you just can't do it accurately because you can't see where the ball is."

Although Ploen was convinced Perkins made the first down, he wasn't critical of Dojack. "I can appreciate how difficult it is. Let's face it. Over a career or even a game you get some good spots and bad ones. I think it all averages out. The game's too long, you've got too many opportunities. To blame the official is nothing but an alibi. We had our opportunities in that game. We just couldn't take advantage of them."

Rigney also sympathized with the referee. "There is a mass of humanity out there, and it is very difficult to see where the farthest advance did occur. I think officials spot it somewhere within a yard or two of where it should be."

Whatever the call, Dojack made it quickly and decisively. "I didn't like too many penalties. I thought we should cut down on the penalties and run a fast game. Syd Halter's instructions were to keep the game down to two hours. Don't let it drag. Don't have conferences out there. Make your decision and that's it. With his backing on that approach, I did it.

"I hustled the players quite a lot. I'd say, 'Come on, come on, come on. You're getting close to 20 seconds.' One time a player said, 'What's the matter, Dojack, you gonna be late for your eye appointment?'

"I was very definite and decisive. I worked very hard during the course of a game. I was very concentrated."

Despite the obvious importance of officials to the game, their contributions to the success of Grey Cups isn't acknowledged in even the simplest ways. "Why," wondered Dojack, "doesn't the league list the officials for the Grey Cup in the program? They've got every player, manager, coach and mascot listed, but they never mention the referees. It would be a simple matter to add five more names to the program."

Sazio described what it was like to coach in such windy conditions. "You pretty much throw the game plan out the window and improvise. You play it a little tighter and eliminate as many mistakes as possible. You eliminate mistakes by not making things too difficult."

Did Sazio out-coach Bud Grant in the Wind Bowl? "Yes," said Sazio. "Bud conceded three 2-pointers to me when the wind was against him and that was the difference in the ball game. We refused to concede points. I preferred to take our chances rather than give up those points."

Rigney conceded that Hamilton handled the wind better than they did. "They shut our running game down," he conceded. "And there wasn't much else we could do. Obviously, when it came to kicking, you couldn't advance it very much. That's why we conceded the safeties. I never really had any regrets or second thoughts about the safeties."

Neither did Ploen. "Much was made of the safeties because six points was the differential in the game, but under the circumstances, had we not done that we may have been down a hell of a lot more than six points."

Winnipeg's Norm Rauhaus concurred. "All the ball did was hang up there. At the very least you were going to give them 3 points and probably 7. By conceding the safety at least you've got field position and you've got a chance."

Although John Barrow was the Most Valuable Player, the only defensive lineman to ever win that award, Angelo Mosca thought Joe Zuger was the unsung hero that day. "Winnipeg gave up three safeties and we won by six points. We didn't have to concede points because Joe Zuger had a great day punting into and with the wind. He kicked very low into the wind and then got it up high when he had it at his back. He could kick with either foot, too."

Ploen was of the same opinion. "Nothing against Ed Ulmer, our punter, but they had Zuger kicking the ball. He was probably one of the best wind-kickers in the league. He could keep that ball low with the point down. I can remember Ulmer hitting one. It went high into the wind and went nowhere. The officials had to call it dead. Punting into the wind is an art, and Zuger was the best."

With the Hamilton win in the 1965 Wind Bowl, one of the great rivalries in Canadian sports had come to an end. Hamilton and Winnipeg wouldn't contest another Grey Cup until 1984. Often, when teams play each other so often for the national championship, bitter feelings result. Such was not the case with Winnipeg and Hamilton.

"They were great guys," Bernie Faloney said. "I enjoyed playing against Winnipeg. They were tough, good football people."

Angelo Mosca echoed the sentiment. "There was a good rapport between the two teams. There wasn't a hate thing, just a really competitive attitude. I thought it was part of our schedule to play Winnipeg at the end of the season."

John Barrow said, "I've got some fond memories of those games. Ken Ploen is a dear friend. So are Frank Rigney and Herb Gray. I suppose the people I related to most were the guys I played across from, like Rigney."

The Defense Rests

In 1966 Hamilton finished second and beat the Alouettes 24–14 in the semifinal. They lost the final round 72–17 to Ottawa, the worst drubbing in Eastern play-off history. But the following year the Cats were back in their customary position in first place with their usual 10–4 record. They won the play-off round over Ottawa 36–3.

Hamilton gave up only 195 points in 1967 and didn't surrender a touchdown during the last six games of the season. In fact, opponents scored a measly 17 points over that period. The 1967 Tiger-Cats were one of the greatest defensive teams in CFL history. Their offense wasn't that bad either.

The defending champion Saskatchewan Roughriders never stood a chance when they faced the Ti-Cats in the Grey Cup. To make matters worse, they were beat up following a tough three-game final against Calgary.

Hamilton opened the scoring when Joe Zuger capped off an 85-yard drive with a 2-yard plunge for a touchdown. Saskatchewan's Alan Ford made the score 7–1 by kicking a still-standing record 87-yard single.

Ralph Sazio remembered the play that broke the game wide open. "Joe Zuger hit the kid I got from Ottawa, Ted Watkins, at the start of the second quarter. Saskatchewan was in a blitz, but Joe hit him quickly and he went 72 yards for a touchdown."

Watkins would later come to a tragic end. "Ted Watkins was later shot and killed when he went into a store. They thought he was going to rob it. I think the guy panicked a bit.

"I appeared as a witness on behalf of Ted's family. I remember I was asked if he had phoned me and asked me for a couple of thousand bucks. I said he had and that I would have sent it to him because he was that valuable to our team."

Tommy Joe Coffey converted both touchdowns and scored a single on a missed field goal. Zuger had two singles. The only other scoring was another Zuger single and a major by Billy Ray Locklin, who picked up a Saskatchewan fumble and went 43 yards for the score.

The win was the highlight of Zuger's career. "We had been ridiculed all year. They said we didn't have any offense, that we played boring football. So it was gratifying to score 24 points and win the Grey Cup.

"The weather was really brutal. We had to change shoes three different times. We started with broom-ball shoes but we tore the soles off them. The field was so hard it was like playing in the street."

Although 24 points were scored on the Riders, the Saskatchewan defense was tough. Joe Zuger punted a record-tying 17 times for a second-best all-time total of 760 yards. Zuger always contributed significantly to his team's success. It would be natural to assume he was one of Steeltown's favorite sons, but that was not the case. "The fans got on my back quite a lot," he admitted. "That bothered me personally, but the coaches believed in me and were behind me. That was the main thing. Those were the guys I had to answer to."

Still, the day belonged to the defense. "It was unbelievable," enthused Coach Sazio. "We went the last four games of the regular season, the play-off and the Grey Cup without giving up a touchdown.

"We had the game pretty well won in the last quarter. I always felt I should put the young Canadians in there to give them the experience of playing in a Grey Cup game, so I started substituting pretty freely. I had a guy by the name of Ted Page, a tough little defensive back. I took him out. He came over to me, and, boy, I'll tell you he had fire in his eyes.

"He said, 'Why are you taking me out?'

"I said, 'Let's give these guys a chance to play.'

"He said, 'We haven't been scored on the last six games, and I don't want to get scored on today.' I sent him back in. The Riders got a single but no touchdowns."

Bud Grant believed the importance of the Grey Cup made coaching simpler in some ways. "We didn't have to do emotional preparation. It meant so much to our Canadian kids that anybody who didn't know about it as an American coming up really got caught up in it. And, oh, the hoopla! In Winnipeg we had some very clever radio announcers who wrote a lot of words to a lot of songs, and they played them constantly. You'd have to be blind or deaf not to get caught up with all the hysteria that was involved in the game."

Winnipeg's Grant didn't isolate his players from the hoopla. "We encouraged them to take part in it. I remember the nights before the games when we were staying downtown. We let the players get out to get a feel for the Grey Cup. They didn't stay out all night, of course, but at least they took part in some of what was going on. It was probably better that they got out and got a feel for what the game meant to so many people."

The Ti-Cats' Sazio agreed. "We always felt the fans and the pregame cele-bration worked in your favor because it proved to the players that this was a very meaningful game. But we always tried to stress the fact that we were there to do a job. This was our business, our work.

"You just keep stressing to them that you don't blow a Grey Cup game. You play 16 regular season games, you play two play-off games, and if things happen they are forgotten. But if anything happens in a Grey Cup game—like you make a mistake and lose it—you'll never be given a chance to forget it. It goes into his-tory. That's how meaningful the Grey Cup is."

Bud Grant and Ralph Sazio

At the 1993 Grey Cup in Calgary, Bud Grant was chosen the coach of the all-time Grey Cup All-Star team. Minnesota's Athlete of the Half Century had joined the Bombers as a player in 1953 and had performed at end and defensive halfback through the 1956 season. When Allie Sherman left for the New York Giants, Grant succeeded him as coach. It was an inspired choice.

In addition to his seven Grey Cup appearances, Grant played for the 1950 NFL champion Philadelphia Eagles and coached the Minnesota Vikings to four berths in the Super Bowl. He compared the championships of the two leagues. "The Super Bowl was such a media event that it wasn't the fans or the celebra-tion that bothered you, it was the crush of the media that wore you out. The Super Bowl is a big public relations event. The media crush is a real distraction to the coaches and players because there is so much of it. That is the toughest part to handle. You can handle the enthusiasm of the fans, but the media crush was heavy and constant. The Grey Cup was more fun."

Ranked sixth all-time in winning percentage, Grant had a record of 122–67–3. He won four out of six Grey Cups. He went on to an impressive record in the NFL.

Recalling the 1963–64 seasons when the Bombers missed the play-offs, Grant dismissed the accolades about his abilities. "The longer you are in coach-ing the more humble you become. You find out there are no geniuses in the coaching profession and certainly not yourself. The team that will win is gener-ally the team with the best players, not the best coaches.

"In 1964 we lost nine players who went out for the season at various times. We started with a record of 1–1–1 and then we proceeded to lose 13 in a row. The next season, when seven of those nine players came back from their injuries and played the whole year, we went to the Grey Cup. So any ideas I ever had about being a genius coach were dispelled right there.

"You get the best players, that's the big hurdle. There are some coaches who can mess up with the best players, but there are no coaches who can win championships with the poorest players."

According to Buddy Tinsley, Grant also picked outstanding assistants. "He was very shrewd and he had a lot of good people around him. He brought in coaches like Jerry Burns, Joe Zaleski and John Michaels to help him. He had a good staff who put it all together in a very scientific manner. They knew what was going on at the time it was going on. We were well coached."

Norm Rauhaus said, "In my rookie year in training camp, I'd see a guy out there in a baseball cap kind of going through the motions when the hitting drills started or in calisthenics. Then, bang, the next year he's the head coach and I'm thinking, 'What happened to him?' We were lucky to get through calisthenics, and some of the physical drills he put us through were unbelievable. But he could really pick football players. That was Grant's greatest talent."

Steve Patrick agreed. "He was an unbelievable judge of personnel. We had a guy named John Varonne, an All-American, a great football player, who played in the 1958 Grey Cup. He had a big year. In 1959 Grant cut John and brought in Jack Delveaux. "It was like a wake at practice. We said, 'What's going on? How could he do this?' After about four games that Jack played, we said, 'This guy knows what he's doing.' Jack became one of the best linebackers I've ever seen. If you talked to any ballcarrier, he'd say he didn't want to get hit by Jack Delveaux.

"You always knew you'd get a fair shake from Bud Grant. I remember one time he had to cut a player he had gone to school with. You would have never expected him to cut somebody he went hunting with and everything else because when you get two players that are pretty close, naturally you expect some favoritism. But you knew from Bud you wouldn't get that. You had to respect him for that."

Bud Tinsley commented, "Jack Matheson said about Grant one time that if he could find someone who would keep house better he'd fire his wife or trade her."

Bud Grant conceded, "A good coach needs a patient wife, a loyal dog and a great quarterback—but not necessarily in that order."

The public often missed the twinkle in his steely blue eyes and concluded that he was a cold man who was all business. Nothing could be further from the truth. When he was asked if his Grey Cup experience helped him in preparing for Super Bowls, he replied, "Well, the record wouldn't show that."

He was equally proud of taking part in the Grey Cup and Super Bowl. "All you can do is do the best you can do in your field. The Grey Cup is the pinnacle in Canadian football, what you are striving for, just as the Super Bowl is here. As far as comparing the two, one is no more important than the other."

Still the Grey Cup had a special meaning for Grant. "There was a little bit more separation between East and West in those days. There wasn't the coverage—television, for example—that you have today. We knew how rabid the Western fans were with their football. When we played in Toronto, where the Grey Cup was traditionally held, it was a big event.

"Those were the years when Calgary used to make the big trek east with all their horses and wagons, white hats and boots. They used to have Grey Cup trains. They'd party all the way there, have three days in Toronto and then head back. Toronto really came apart at the seams in those days.

"I remember in B.C. when they had police dogs on the streets to try to control the crowds the night before. It was an event that everyone went to or was interested in. John Diefenbaker said the Grey Cup was the greatest unifying force in Canada in bringing East and West together."

Why were those Bud Grant Blue Bomber teams so good? "We put the emphasis on team," said Ploen. "There was that chemistry, or camaraderie, a group of guys wanting to win. The right combination was there. Bud Grant was part of that in the way he coached and in his attitude toward the game. We had a good mix of Americans and Canadians who got along well and wanted to win.

"If you look at other teams, they had Schenley Award winners coming out their ears and all those great superstars. I think in our era Frank Rigney, Herb Gray and Gerry James won Schenleys, but other than those there wasn't anybody. All we won was championships. Nobody really gave a damn about awards."

The Bombers had a great offensive line, anchored by Frank Rigney, who said, "We played together for an awful long time—George Druxman, Cornell Piper, Ed Kotowich and me. Four out of the five offensive linemen were together throughout my career."

Rigney felt consistency of personnel produced another important ingredient: leadership. "I think that comes with a veteran group. We changed a fair number of guys every year, but we had a core of maybe 20 that played together for an awfully long time. That was part of it.

"The other part of it was Grant was that kind of coach. He was very adroit at letting you talk yourself into what he wanted you to do rather than telling you what to do. But I think Grant's number one attribute was his ability to recognize talent. We won because of a combination of Grant and a nucleus of pretty good football players who played together for a long time.

"A key element in any winning team is that you've got to have fun together in order to win together. That's one of the disappointments, I think, about pro sports these days. Guys jump all over the place. There's just no such thing as loyalty anymore. It's all bucks. I don't blame them for going for the bucks, but there is no sense of team or community anymore. When I went to Winnipeg, I stayed there."

Norm Rauhaus agreed that the team that stayed together won together. "When you play with a winning team you gain a certain confidence in what you can do and what you can get away with. When a good team gets down, there is a sense that this is no problem, the game's not over.

"You look around when you are dressing before a game and, boy, you see some winners, and it makes a difference. You get enough winners and they pull the people who don't know they are winners over the line. Then they become more confident."

Steve Patrick singled out Herb Gray as an important contributor to Winnipeg's success. "He provided great leadership by the way he played. He played the first play of the game full blast and the last play of the game full blast. The rest of us asked, "Where does he get his stamina?'"

Why did Patrick think those Bomber teams were so good? "Because there were no great stand-outs. We were all the same. That was what Grant would instill in us. You have to play as a unit, you've got to be friends together—no cliques.

"He had the colored kids rooming with the white kids. There was no such thing as Canadians or Americans. It was a team. It was the players. We were friends. We got together with the wives or girlfriends for sandwiches and so forth at a hotel after the game."

Norm Rauhaus had another explanation for why those Winnipeg teams were so good. "Good Canadians. You can always buy an American. You take a look at the Grey Cup teams of Edmonton, Hamilton and ours, and you find out our Canadians were far better than those of the competition. Although there were the Parkers, the Ploens, the Rigneys, the Grays and the Faloneys, I really think the main difference on those teams was that they had better Canadians than the other teams."

Grant left the Bombers for the Minnesota Vikings after the 1966 season. A year later Ralph Sazio stepped down as head coach of the Ti-Cats. Jake Gaudaur became league commissioner, and Sazio succeeded him as general manager. "Even though I enjoyed coaching tremendously," he said, "I just felt it was the right time to make a move into another bracket. It was another step up."

Why were those Hamilton teams of the '50s and '60s so successful? According to Ralph Sazio, leadership in the dressing room was the key. "You need players who take on some responsibility," explained Sazio. "As a coach, you put me in one hell of a spot if there is something going on I just can't let go by. You need a player to say to a guy who is out of line, 'You'd better smarten up because if the coach finds out, you're gone.' John Barrow and Bernie Faloney played that role in Hamilton."

There was continuity. "Carl Voyles in 1950 established how the club was going to be run. After practice during the season the club provided meals for the players because we used to practice at 5:00 P.M. He kept them together. He built a sense of comradeship. He felt that the football team could not have too much outside influence. Even though it was a community-run club at that time, the president and other executive members were kept at arm's length from the team. He started that.

"Jake Gaudaur was one of the players under Carl. When Jake took over as manager, he continued the same pattern, and when I took over from Jake, it was just a continuation."

Sazio was a good general manager because, he said, "I had a pretty good business background and training. You have to have the business situation under control. I think I knew personnel. If you can combine that, you should have a reasonable amount of success."

Jake Gaudaur agreed. "In the final analysis, the difference between winning and losing is players and coaching, and I've always believed mainly players. A mediocre coach can get by with outstanding players but an outstanding coach can't get by with mediocre players.

"I had read somewhere that an athlete would be at his peak at the age of 27, so I strove to try to have an average age. I always felt that two-thirds of your team should be comprised of veterans of at least four years."

When Sazio moved upstairs, he hired Joe Restic from Harvard University to replace him. Hamilton finished third twice and first in 1970 but lost the Eastern Final to upstart Montreal. In 1971 Al Dorow led the team to second place before bowing to the Argos in the Eastern Final.

Peach-Fuzz Versus the Vets

Sazio then hired Jerry Williams, who had enjoyed considerable success in Calgary before taking over the Philadelphia Eagles. With a retooled Tiger-Cat team in 1972, Williams got to the Grey Cup in his very first year. Saskatchewan represented the West.

The Ti-Cats had a rookie quarterback in Chuck Ealey and an 18-year-old place-kicker, Ian Sunter. They faced a Roughrider squad loaded with grizzled Grey Cup veterans.

It was Sazio who brought Chuck Ealey to Canada. "They used to have an American–Canadian All-Star type of game. I was looking for a running quarterback. I was trying to replace Zuger.

"Chuck impressed me because he never lost a game while he was in high school or college. Anybody who had that kind of winning attitude has to be pretty good. I recruited him pretty hard. He was at a small school in Ohio."

In the 1972 Grey Cup, Ealey completed 18 of 29 passes for 291 yards and a touchdown. Ron Lancaster was good on 20 of 29 for 239 yards and a touchdown. Both touchdowns were controversial.

In the first quarter Hamilton's Al Brenner picked off an errant Lancaster pass, and Ealey directed his team 52 yards for the opening touchdown, a 16-yard pass to Dave Fleming in the end zone. The Riders argued vehemently that Fleming had gone up for the ball and came down out of bounds.

Not so, said Sazio. "It was not out of the end zone. They had pictures that showed everything. Fleming just made a great play."

When informed that a Rider had said Hamilton was lucky to win because of the Fleming play, Angelo Mosca sneered, "Isn't that too bad? There are always gripers and complainers. There were years *we* should have won but didn't."

The Roughriders replied with a 75-yard drive, capped by an 8-yard touchdown strike to Tom Campana. The Ti-Cats argued that defensive back Gerry Sternberg had been the victim of an illegal Bob Pearce pick.

Ian Sunter kicked a field goal in the first quarter. Saskatchewan's Jack

Abendshan replied in the second. The teams remained deadlocked at 10 until the dying moments of the final frame. Then Chuck Ealey went to work. With 1:51 left in regulation time, Hamilton scrimmaged on their 15-yard line. Although he had done nothing throughout the game, second-year Canadian Tony Gabriel was on the receiving end of three consecutive Ealey passes of 27, 12 and 15 yards.

"I was really fortunate to be part of that game," said Gabriel. "It was only my second season. In the last minute Chuck Ealey threw three passes to me to bring us into range so Ian Sunter could kick the winning field goal."

The three completions brought the Cats to the Roughrider 41. Ealey ran for two and threw to Garney Henley for 12. The ball was on the 27. Sunter took to the field.

Henley told the kid to keep his head down. He did, and with 13 seconds left, he kicked it cleanly through the uprights. Final score: Hamilton 13, Saskatchewan 10. It was the first time in 20 years the home team had won the Cup.

Ian Sunter was named player of the game despite the special-team heroics of Bob Krouse, who blocked a punt, partially blocked another one and fell on the ball when John Williams blocked a third. Those blocked kicks were the difference in the ball game.

The win capped a spectacular first year for Chuck Ealey. He made the Eastern All-Star team and won the Schenley Award for Outstanding Rookie. Unfortunately his blaze of glory was short-lived for his first season was his best. Less than two years later Ralph Sazio dealt him to Winnipeg. "He got dinged a couple of times and we traded him," said Sazio.

Sixteen players left after the 1972 season, including All-Canadian running back Dave Buchanan, Tommy Joe Coffey and Anglo Mosca. The defense was hit particularly hard.

Hamilton missed the play-offs in 1973 and finished tied for second and third the next two years. Sazio then appointed Bob Shaw as general manager, who in turn hired George Dickson to coach. Shaw fired Dickson halfway through the season and assumed the position himself. The team went 8–8. The following year, after finishing last, Shaw replaced himself with Tom Dimitroff. Then, in one of the strangest moves in CFL history, he fired Dimitroff at the end of the preseason in favor of John Payne, who didn't have a winning season until 1980, when the club finished first in the East with a mark of 8–7–1 and advanced to a humiliating 48–10 defeat in the Grey Cup at the hands of the Edmonton Eskimos. Shortly afterward he was gone.

A Decade of Disappointment

Winnipeg also had a good year in 1972. With All-Canadian quarterback Don Jonas at the helm and the spectacular playmaking of Mack Herron and Jim Thorpe, the Bombers finished first and awaited the third-place Roughriders in the Western Final, a sudden-death affair for the first time since 1949.

After 30 minutes the Bombers were leading 21–0 and making plans to go to Toronto. But in the second half Ron Lancaster engineered one of his patented comebacks, pulling his Roughriders into a 24–24 tie going into the final minute of the game.

On the last play of the fourth quarter, the Riders' Jack Abendshan was wide on his field-goal attempt. Paul Williams and Ron Lancaster exchanged punts twice before Winnipeg was called for no yards. Abendshan had another chance. He kicked the Riders into their fourth Grey Cup appearance in seven years.

In addition to Jonas, four Bombers made All-Canadian on offense that year, including three of the five linemen, center Bob Swift, tackle Bill Frank and guard Bob Lueck, as well as running back "Mini" Mack Herron. The future looked bright.

It was not to be. Herron and Thorpe were arrested on drug charges, and General Manager Earl Lunsford got rid of them before they could enter a plea. Head Coach Jim Spavital didn't agree with the general manager's draconian approach. "Earl cut them right away. I didn't have anything to say about it at all. At the time I felt he should have waited until they were proven guilty. I don't have any use for drugs whatsoever. When they were proven guilty I would have been the first to send them on their way. But I always felt a person is innocent until proven guilty."

After the 1972 season the Bombers went downhill, and Spavital was help-less to do anything about it. "Herron and Thorpe weren't the whole problem," he explained. "Those two were outstanding players, and we didn't fill those spots. But I didn't have much to do with personnel in Winnipeg. Earl Lunsford was just getting started in the business, and he made a lot of deals with a lot of people.

"For example, when Jerry Keeling became available, I needed another quarterback, but Lunsford wouldn't pick him up because he'd made a deal with Calgary GM Rogers Lehew that he was going to get Lehew out of the West so they wouldn't have to play against him."

In his four years with the Bombers, ending in 1973, Spavital's record was

23–39–2. He went on to coach the Chicago Fire of the World Football League and then coached running backs in San Francisco before joining Jack Gotta in Calgary. In 1980 he became Saskatchewan's GM and was building a contender despite the team's chronic shortage of money. Spavital commented wryly, "If it costs a nickel to go around the world, we can't get out of sight."

With Roughrider fortunes on the rise, he had to resign after the 1982 season because of blindness. One of the finest and unluckiest men the game has known, he died a few years later.

Back in Winnipeg, Lunsford replaced Spavital with Bud Riley, who compiled a four-season record of 34–28–2, including three play-off appearances.

In 1978 Ray Jauch, bored with his front office job in Edmonton, decided to accept Lunsford's offer to return to the sidelines. During Jauch's five-year tenure, the Bombers were 47–35. Characteristically his team finished third in the first year and then missed the play-offs while he tore the team down and began to rebuild. The Bombers finished second to the mighty Eskimos three years running, tying Edmonton for first in 1982 with 22 points. In the process Jauch revolutionized the game by introducing the twin slotback system, something that happened by accident.

"When I went to Winnipeg, I had two ends," explained Jauch. "One was Gord Paterson. Tommy Scott went to Edmonton, and we got Joe Poplawski. I also had Rick House. Paterson was the only guy I ever ran off the field during a game. He was one of those guys who, no matter how hard you try, you just can't like the guy because he won't let you. I had just had enough of him.

"We were playing a tough game against Edmonton, and he came off the field in the second quarter yelling and screaming. I said, 'Get out of here, get out of here.' He looked at me and I said, 'Get to the locker room. Get out of here. I don't want to see you anymore.'

"I didn't have another end to replace him with so I went with Rick House and Joe Poplawski as twin slotbacks."

Jauch had an explosive offense led by Dieter Brock, the leading passer in Bomber history. Brock was All-Canadian in 1980–81, winning the Schenley in both years, one of only three to accomplish the feat. Called the Mad Bomber before Jauch got there, Brock was sold by his new coach on the advantages of a short passing game.

Winnipeg's emphasis on offense came from General Manager Earl Lunsford. "Some people believe that when you rebuild, you start with the defense," he said in 1985. "I've always believed the quarterback is most important. Without him, you won't win games or put people in the seats."

Jauch, on the other hand, never entirely agreed and was critical in the early going of Winnipeg's approach to personnel. After the 1982 season Jauch left to coach the Washington Federals of the United States Football League. Earl Lunsford also was on his way out. Tired of always being a bridesmaid but never a bride, the Bomber executive were impatient to get to the altar. To that end they brought in former Bomber player and Winnipeg native Paul Robson as general manager and Cal Murphy as head coach.

Hogtown Harold Saves Hamilton

The most important change that took place in Hamilton during the late 1970s was new ownership. The team was purchased by the hated Hogtowner Harold Ballard because, he said, "I had nothing to do during the summer and wasn't prepared to sit around and watch the sky stay up."

Ballard was never accepted in Hamilton even though it is unlikely the Ti-Cats would have survived the lean years of the 1980s without him. During his 11-year tenure, average per game attendance dropped from 25,560 in 1978 to 14,756 in 1988, even though Hamilton appeared in the Grey Cup three straight years.

Various reasons were advanced for the decline of football fever in one of the bedrock franchises of the CFL. Stelco wasn't doing well, the Blue Jays arrived in Toronto, the Buffalo Bills siphoned off five or six thousand would-be season ticket holders to the NFL. And despite making the play-offs every year, the team lost more games than they won. Knowledgeable football fans weren't fooled by the product on the field.

"They can tell the difference," said Coach Al Bruno. "It may be exciting to be in the play-offs and go the Grey Cup, but if you keep having 5–11 seasons, the fans will stay away."

Despite very legitimate reasons for the decline of the franchise, many Hamiltonians blamed Ballard. Ralph Sazio thought that was unfair. "Ballard certainly didn't put any stops on things. He was willing to spend the money to do it. However, the whole hometown ownership image hurt him. Ballard was never accepted by people in Hamilton."

Sazio decided to leave his post as Ti-Cat general manager halfway through the 1981 season and move down the Queen E to Toronto. He stressed that he didn't leave because of Ballard.

Ballard's coach for most of his ownership years was Al Bruno, who had fond memories of his irascible boss. "I loved the man. Ballard didn't stick his nose in like he did with his hockey team. If you did well, he rewarded you well. We won the Grey Cup in 1986. Our guys really played well against Edmonton and upset them. Matter of fact we beat the hell out of them. After that he gave me a three-year contract. He made us feel like we were somebody. They should have appreciated that man because he kept football going in Hamilton."

Ballard's efforts were recognized by his 1987 induction as a builder into the Canadian Football Hall of Fame. But Ballard would have rather owned the Argonauts, a fact he admitted in 1981. "I would very much have preferred to own the Argos, but I couldn't. John Bassett said he wouldn't sell to a Ballard. I sent a check down for $25,000 to start negotiations, and he sent it back saying he wouldn't sell to me. You know, I wouldn't want him as a partner now, but we could have got along pretty well together. I could have run it, and I know I'd have been very successful."

Ballard's secret to success was simple. "Listen, there's no substitute for hard work. If you work at something and work hard, you're going to win. I don't care what you do—if you work at it, you're going to get promoted, you're going to get results."

Asked if he was involved with the Ti-Cats to the same degree as the Maple Leafs, he was characteristically blunt. "Pretty well, yes. Listen, it's my money."

Ballard preferred tough guys, so in 1981 he hired Frank Kush as coach, a man who made Simon Legree look like Mother Teresa. After a 26–6 July 17 loss in Calgary, the team got back to Hamilton at 7:00 A.M. Kush ordered them to the practice field, where he worked them into exhaustion.

"I think Frank Kush is one of the greatest things that ever hit Hamilton," enthused Ballard at the time. "A player was crabbing about Kush scrimmaging seven days a week. I said, 'What the hell are you talking about? You go to work seven days a week. Everybody works. The guy who works on the road from eight in the morning until five at night with a sledge hammer and a pick, he's not crying and you're getting yourself $100,000 for doing nothing.'"

Ballard maintained that he was willing to pay for success. "I don't mind signing a check for a guy who's playing well. I know that if I pay him too much it's my fault. But if he earns what I agreed to pay him, I'm very happy to sign the check. I've had situations where I've signed guys who are doing well and who want to renegotiate their contracts. Sure, I'll renegotiate it. But it seems to me they don't appreciate the fact that when you do renegotiate with them, before the ink's dry, the bastards aren't doing anything. They've got their ass in a tub of butter. But I'm not doing that anymore. I'm not renegotiating. I'm getting a little tougher."

No more Mr. Nice Guy. When reminded that he was in his 70s, Ballard replied, "Getting old is all in your head. If you want to get old, you can get old. It amazes me when I hear of people 60 and 65 going on the pogey and waiting for their old age pension. They ought to cut that old age pension out and make people work.

"How many people do you know that quit or were pushed out of their job at 65 and within two years they're in a box? They've got a pain in their finger, a pain in their toe, a pain in their ear or some goddamned place, and the first thing you know you're reading an obituary about them.

"I don't smoke or drink. But I know guys who do and are hearty, but they work like a son of a bitch. I'll never retire. They'll carry me out of here."

How did he want to be remembered? "I don't want anybody to remember me. I just do it myself while I'm here and remember myself."

The mutual admiration society of Ballard and Kush didn't last long. Despite leading the team to first place with a record of 11–4–1, Hamilton's best record in 10 years, Kush was fired after losing the Eastern Final to the 5–11 Ottawa Rough Riders.

He was replaced by former Bomber coach Bud Riley. Under his direction the Cats finished second to Toronto with an 8–7–1 record. The following year the team hit the doldrums, and, with a mark of 3–9, Riley was replaced by Al Bruno.

Bruno had played his college football at Kentucky under Bear Bryant. He explained how he ended up in Hamilton. "I was drafted in the third round by the Philadelphia Eagles in 1951. When I was let go, I went back to finish my education. Frank Clair, who was coaching Toronto at the time, came by to check on Ken McKenzie, one of the tackles on our team. Clair asked Coach Bryant if he had any receivers and he mentioned my name. The year I went up, 1952, I was the leading receiver in the league, and I was in the Grey Cup my first year."

He won it, too, after another year in Toronto, Bruno moved on to Ottawa and then to Winnipeg. After the 1956 season Bruno, now the father of twins, returned to Toronto to teach high school. He then replaced Indian Jack Jacobs as head coach of the London Lords and taught at London Catholic Central as well. When the Ontario Rugby Football Union folded in 1960, he went home to Pennsylvania.

"Then Frank Clair hired me as offensive coordinator of the Rough Riders in 1966," Bruno explained. "Just as in my first season as a player, in my first season as a coach, we went to the Grey Cup, but we lost it.

"I coached in Hamilton for three years from 1969–71 with Joe Restic. Joe got a job at Harvard University. I applied for the job in Hamilton, but Sazio opted for Al Dorow from Michigan State, so I went to Harvard with Joe for 11 years. We won three Ivy League championships. I was trying to get a head job down there in the Ivy League, but things didn't work out for me. I don't know why.

"Then Joe Zuger became GM in Hamilton and Frank Kush left. I applied for the job, but Zuger instead offered me the job of personnel director under Bud Riley. So I came to Hamilton again in 1982. In '83 things went haywire. Zuger and Harold Ballard then gave me a chance to coach."

Bruno's initial appearance in the Grey Cup as a head coach came in 1984. The Ti-Cats had tied Montreal for second and beat the Argos 14–13 in overtime in the Eastern Final, but they had managed only one touchdown in the two postseason games.

Despite Hamilton's on-field success, only Montreal had worse attendance. Those who did show up at Ivor Wynn Stadium did so mainly to boo. It got so bad in Steel City that the players said they preferred to play on the road, and Ballard threatened to move the team to Toronto.

Under the pressure of criticism, the Ti-Cats dug their claws into each other early in September. Defensive stalwart Ben Zambiasi offered the opinion that his coaches couldn't coach a high school team. Before the team left to play Saskatchewan in early October, Ballard labeled his players a bunch of overpaid bums. He also announced that Bruno would only be retained if the team made the play-offs.

The Cal Murphy Era

For the eleventh and last time in 1984, Hamilton's opponent in the first Grey Cup played in Edmonton was Winnipeg. Making the match-up more interesting were the number of personal scores that begged to be settled.

In 1983 Bomber quarterback Dieter Brock had gone on strike to force the team to release him from his $1 million contract so he could finish his career in the States. While admitting that the Bombers treated him well over the years, his family had to come first, he explained at the time. "The reason I want to leave Winnipeg is my family, to get back down here in the States. We've been moving back and forth for nine years. We just feel we want to make our living down here. I feel I've got to make the first move now."

General Manager Paul Robson wouldn't void the contract and traded him to Hamilton in September for Tom Clements. Ballard agreed to a deal that would allow Brock to leave after the 1984 season.

Safety Paul Bennett had won the 1983 Schenley Award for Best Canadian as a member of the Blue Bombers. He was then traded to Toronto, cut by the Argos, picked up and released by Edmonton and went on to star with Hamilton.

Brock was upset on offense, Bennett on defense. That left the special teams. Kicker Bernie Ruoff had been convicted of possession of marijuana while a Bomber in 1979. He was promptly cut and was picked up by Hamilton.

In 1984 Winnipeg didn't miss a beat with Tom Clements at the helm, scoring 61 touchdowns, 21 more than in 1983. They led the league in points, touchdowns and total offense. Willard Reaves picked up 1,733 yards rushing, winning the Schenley Award for Most Outstanding Player. John Bonk won for Offensive Lineman. Clements, Bonk, Reaves, Poplawski, Walby and Bastaja made All-Canadian.

The biggest area of improvement was defense. The Blue Bombers reduced their points allowed from 402 to 309, second best in the league, and intercepted more passes, forced more fumbles and gave the offense better field position than had been the case in many years.

There were three keys to the rejuvenated defense. Scott Flagel, a Winnipeg native, developed into such a promising safety that Cal Murphy was able to trade Paul Bennett to Toronto for standout defensive back Donovan Rose. He was then able to trade defensive back Ken Ciancone to Montreal for import linebacker Delbert Fowler.

About the same time, Saskatchewan cut Frank Robinson adrift. He joined Fowler, Aaron Brown and Tyrone Jones as a fearsome foursome of linebackers.

In the Grey Cup's early going, it looked like underdog Hamilton had solved the Blue Bomber defense when they jumped into a 17–3 lead. By the end of the game, 44 more points were scored, but unfortunately for the Ti-Cats, all were scored by Winnipeg.

But in the first quarter the underdog Ti-Cats looked like world-beaters.

Dieter Brock marched his team smartly downfield to the enemy 15-yard line. He dropped back to pass, found no one open and scampered up the middle for a touchdown. Later in the quarter Brock hit Rocky DiPietro in the end zone for a 7-yard touchdown. Trever Kennard and Bernie Ruoff traded field goals.

Then fate intervened. The Bombers' Tom Clements was having a lot of trouble moving the ball. Early in the second quarter he lost a contact lens and had to leave the field, replaced by John Hufnagel. Hufnagel explained what happened. "At that point I had been in the league for quite a while and understood the defenses. That helped my playing because once I got on the field I knew 100 percent what I wanted to do.

"Basically we had put in a play, just an easy play, where we would release the back in the flat. In our preparation it looked like the back would be open, and he was. I just ran it a couple of times, dumping the ball. I think what it showed was that if you're patient and make some decisions, you'll start moving the football. Once Tom got back on the field (whether I helped him or not, I don't know) we moved the ball awfully well."

Cal Murphy recognized Hufnagel's contribution. "I can remember saying on the sideline, 'If we can just get this offense going, we'll be all right' because I really thought we'd be able to move the football.

"Huf started to do the things we thought could go. Then Tom got another lens, and I was betwixt and between as to whether I'd send him back in. I thought, 'Heck, he's the guy, and so that's where we're going.'

"I remember talking to Huf a few years ago. I said to him, 'Huf, you've probably often wondered why I did it. He said, 'Yeah, I did, but now that I've been coaching, I'd have done the same thing you did.'"

Eleven years later, Hufnagel faced the same decision. As Calgary's offensive coordinator he had to decide whether to start Jeff Garcia, who had gone 8–1, or Doug Flutie, returning from the injury list. He chose Flutie to start the 1995 Grey Cup game against Baltimore.

"I told Jeff Garcia before the 1995 game that there would be a point in time when that decision will go his way," said Hufnagel. You pay your dues in any professional sport and with that comes some privileges. I truly believe it was the right decision by Cal, and I believe going with Flutie was the right decision for us."

Hufnagel and Clements went back along way. "I enjoyed Tom," Hufnagel said. "Tom and I grew up together in the same neighborhood in Pittsburgh.

We've known each other for a long time. We're quite good friends. I enjoyed competing and playing with him."

Hufnagel was an All-American at Penn State while Clements was rated the best Notre Dame quarterback since the Second World War.

Before losing the lens Clements had managed only one first down. Hufnagel came in for three plays. The ball was on the Hamilton 54. He took them to the 18 and retired to the sidelines. A couple of plays later Willard Reaves ran it into the end zone.

Good defense continued the revival. "I still remember the big hit Tyrone Jones made on Dieter Brock," Murphy said. "Stan Mikawas picked up the ball and ran for his only career touchdown. You look at the interception that David Shaw made. It was plays like that I really believe turned the game around."

For Winnipeg native and defensive lineman Stan Mikawas it was a dream come true. "I saw Tyrone Jones from the corner of my eye come in on a blitz and hit Brock, causing him to fumble. As I was rushing Dieter, the ball bounced, I scooped it up and ran 22 yards for a touchdown. That was a key point in the game because we were down to Hamilton, and that touchdown gave us a spark of new life and we went on to win the game."

After the Shaw interception, Winnipeg pivot Clements and Poplwaski combined for a 12-yard touchdown. Kennard added two more field goals. The score at half time was 30–17. Winnipeg's 27 second-quarter points was a record until 1990, when the Bombers scored 28 against Edmonton.

Kennard kicked a 16-yard field goal in the third quarter. Reaves plunged over from 3 yards out in the fourth, and Hufnagel threw a 4-yard touchdown pass to Jeff Boyd. The final score was 47–17. Winnipeg had won their first Grey Cup in 22 years.

Hamilton's Al Bruno bemoaned his fate. "We were going pretty well. Dieter was hot, hitting passes. We ran the ball fairly well. We went ahead in that game, but, darn it, we couldn't cover that damn swing pass. We were slipping and sliding. Bernie Ruoff had a really bad day trying to maintain his footing. Clements went out, and when he came back in he got hot. We had too many turnovers and that just kills you. I mean, a lineman picked up a fumble and went for a touchdown. It wasn't a good day for us. They had a good ball club, but it wasn't really our day to play."

In 1985 Hamilton was back in the Grey Cup, this time against B.C. at the Big O in Montreal. That wasn't their day either. The Leos turned potential disasters into triumphs and won 37–24, their first Grey Cup in 21 years.

Paul Osbaldiston,
all-time leading Grey
Cup scorer among
active players.

But every cat has his day. For Bruno that glorious moment came November 30, 1986, at B.C. Place. Undisputed underdogs, the upstart Steeltowners thrashed Edmonton 39–15. Edmonton's total offense at the end of the half was minus 1 yard!

Bruno described his defense. "We had a good veteran ball club. We kept them around. It took three years for them to really gel—Grover Covington, Mike Walker, Ben Zambiasi. We picked up Leo Ezerins and Frank Robinson from the Bombers—really experienced linebackers—and they played well together. I didn't give a damn how old they were. They played their asses off.

"In the secondary we kept the young kids around, and they gained experience. Guys like Howard Fields, Mark Streeter and Less Browne. We picked up Paul Bennett. We really got it together in the third year."

To get to the Grey Cup Hamilton had to overcome considerable adversity. After finishing second with a record of 9–8–1, they dropped the first game of the Eastern Final 31–17 in Hamilton. They fell behind 10 more points in the second game at Toronto before coming back to defeat the Argos 42–15 and win the round 59–56. Kerrigan completed 58 passes for 633 yards and picked up an additional 304 yards on 15 catches against Edmonton. He won the Grey Cup Outstanding Player Award and was the Eastern All-Star quarterback, an honor he won again in 1989. Despite those good years, Kerrigan was inconsistent and never truly fulfilled his promise.

His coach was mystified by the problem. "Kerrigan was hot and cold. I can't explain it. He was nonchalant. Nothing bothered him. Whether he was picked off or threw a touchdown pass, he was in the same mood. When he was down he didn't give up. But it was strange. He was up one game and down the next."

Bruno discounted Edmonton's offensive line problem as a determining factor in the outcome. "I was aware they had lost an offensive guard, but we'd have kicked the hell out of them anyway. They only lost one lineman.

"In that two-game total point series against Toronto, we lost two starters at the beginning of the game, a big offensive tackle and Less Browne on the kick-off return. I don't think one guy could mean that much unless it's a quarterback."

Matt Dunigan claimed Edmonton did not take Hamilton lightly. "You respect everyone, especially in the Grey Cup. We just got beat by a better football club."

The pinnacle of Bruno's coaching career came in 1986. Not only did he win the Grey Cup but he was chosen Coach of the Year. The following year he suffered a heart attack. The team was 6–6 at that point and finished the regular season 7–11, good for third place. Bruno resumed his duties for the semifinal, a 29–13 loss to the Argonauts.

In 1988 the Cats tied Winnipeg, now in the Eastern Division, for second place with a 9–9 record but lost the play-off game at home 35–28. In 1989 Harold Ballard sold the club to David Braley. Braley's first year was a happy one as the Ti-Cats finished first with a record of 12–6, the best in club history. They then beat the Bombers in the Eastern Final 14–10 before losing 43–40 to the Saskatchewan Roughriders in one of the most exciting Grey Cups ever played.

After that the team entered an era of uncertainty and failure that almost brought the franchise to an end. When on September 22, 1990, with a record of 4–7, the Ti-Cats were bombed at home 34–4 by the bedraggled Lions, Al Bruno was fired, despite having made the play-offs every year and going to the Grey Cup four times.

Since then the Tiger-Cats have been coached by Dave Beckman, John Gregory, Don Sutherin and Urban Bowman. Dave Braley sold the team to a community group headed by David MacDonald. Full of hope when they signed Matt Dunigan in 1996, the team's chances ended early in the season when he suffered a concussion. The following year's record of 2–16 was the worst in franchise history.

To turn the team around, Ron Lancaster was enticed into the Ti-Cat den for the 1998 campaign. He took them from last to first and a Grey Cup appearance against Calgary.

Problems also dogged the Winnipeg Blue Bombers in the mid-1980s. After winning it all in 1984, the Bombers didn't return to the Grey Cup until 1988. Stan Mikawas tried to explain why. "We did have some good teams in between, but there are a lot of factors. When you get down to the big game, you've got to want to win. We had some teams, I guess, that didn't want it bad enough."

Coach Cal Murphy knew defending the title in 1985 would be difficult. "Our biggest problem was replacing the four starters we lost: Rick House, Doug McIvor, Aaron Brown and Delbert Fowler. The two linebackers we lost were excellent. If you even took one guy out of B.C. like Tyrone Crews, they would be a different football team. We lost two."

From 1984–92 a Bomber linebacker made All-Canadian every year but two, with Tyrone Jones being picked four years in a row, 1984–87. From 1984–91, Bomber linebackers won three Outstanding Defensive Player Awards and were runners-up twice.

After failing to return to the Grey Cup for two years, GM Paul Robson was fired, replaced by Cal Murphy, who left the sideline in favor of 35-year-old Mike Riley, son of Bud. Cynics suggested Murphy hired a young man with no head coaching experience because he wanted to maintain complete control, a charge the new general manager denied. "According to the media here, I throw my voice from the office to the field, but I don't. We have a good relationship. We do talk about different things. We both find it very easy that way."

Why did Murphy give up coaching and why did he hire Mike Riley? "I had been thinking about Mike for a long time. When he was here before, I spent a lot of time with him after practice, just sitting watching film, talking about personnel and ideas. I felt he had a better handle on personnel and what was needed than anyone else on the staff, and that's basically why I went with him."

Said Stan Mikawas, "Mike was a player's coach. He got a lot of respect from the players. He knew the game inside and out. He knew the position where every guy should go. He treated you like a professional."

Tyrone Jones, great Winnipeg linebacker of Grey Cups in '84, '88 and '90.

In his four years at the helm, Riley's teams finished first twice, second and third once. He won Grey Cups and Coach of the Year awards in 1988 and '90. After the 1990 season Riley joined the staff at Stanford University. In December 1996 he became head coach at Oregon State and in 1999 took over the NFL San Diego Chargers.

Riley's Bombers played well for most of the 1987 season before fading away and losing to the Argonauts. Given that Murphy's Law was in full effect in 1988, no one in his right mind would have picked the Bombers to win the Grey Cup. They had lost five All-Canadians including Tom Clements, Willard Reaves, Tyrone Jones, Roy Bennett and Scott Flagel. Murphy signed veteran B.C. pivot Roy Dewalt, but he proved ineffective and second-stringer Tom Muecke got hurt. That left the quarterbacking duties in the hands of rookie Sean Salisbury. Just before the play-offs Chris Walby and Greg Battle went down.

Although the Bombers had finished in second place, 10 points behind the Argos, they handled them easily in the final, advancing to the Grey Cup against the Lions, who had finished third but won the semifinal in Regina and then become the first visiting team to win a play-off game at Edmonton's Commonwealth Stadium. The Lions won seven of their last eight games and were heavily favored because quarterback Dunigan was a veteran and Winnipeg's quarterback Sean Salisbury was a rookie.

But being the underdog can be a blessing in disguise, according to Cal Murphy. "I think back to when I was with Edmonton, when we were playing Ottawa in the Grey Cup in 1981. What did they win—five games all year? By the grace of God and whatever we won that football game.

"All week long I can remember our guys saying, 'We won't get overconfident. You can't help but hear it, and I think it may sting the underdog a little more. That would help you if you're the underdog, but if you're the favorite I think it works to your disadvantage."

Why They Call It Football

The 1998 Grey Cup game was played in Ottawa. Despite the usual fears the weatherman was in a good mood that week and the Bytowners staged a tremendous festival. The full stands at Lansdowne Park were a sight for sore CFL eyes.

Grey Cup day dawned sunny, warm and one of the windiest days in Grey Cup history. At game time the temperature was 14°c with the wind at 40 kilometers out of the south.

Although the team from windy Winnipeg handled the breeze better than B.C., coaching mistakes proved to be the difference in the ball game. Winnipeg opened the scoring with a Bob Cameron single, set up by a 40-yard Sean Salisbury pass to James Murphy.

Starting on their 35, Vancouver's Matt Dunigan threw to Jan Carinci. Anthony Parker ran for a first down and Dunigan scrambled 19 yards to the enemy 37. When Scott Lecky caught a pass for 9 yards, the Bombers were called for rough play. That moved the ball to the 14-yard line. From there Tony Cherry ran it into the end zone.

Near the end of the opening quarter, Salisbury and Murphy teamed up for a beautiful, dipsy-doodle 71-yard pass and run play that brought the ball to the Lion 6. Two incomplete passes later, Trevor Kennard kicked a 13-yard field goal. The Lions led 7–4 at the quarter.

Early in the second, Kennard tied the game with a 43-yard field goal.

Dunigan came back, running the ball to the Bomber 36. After a 10-yard pickup, Benny Thompson blitzed, Dunigan read it and hit Schenley Award winner David Williams in the end zone.

Winnipeg struck back. Scrimmaging at the Lions' 35, Salisbury teamed up with Murphy for a touchdown that tied the game at 14. Lui Passaglia completed the first half by scoring a single. The Lions went to the dressing room leading 15–14. So far the wind had not been a factor.

The Lions' Anthony Drawhorn opened the second half with a long kickoff return. After a pass to Carinci and run by Lecky plus a face mask and roughing, the Lions had the ball on the Winnipeg 10. Again the defense came up big, and B.C. had to settle for a field goal.

Winnipeg couldn't move the ball, but Bob Cameron punted the Lions in deep. Two plays later it was third and one on the B.C. 18. The Lions had the wind, enabling them to send the Bombers reeling toward their goal line. Instead Coach Larry Donovan called for a quarterback sneak.

The Bombers stopped them cold. "They were third down in their end of the field," said Mikawas. "That was the biggest turning point right there. If they had kicked it and maybe held us down in our end, it would have been a different game. But we stopped them, and at that point momentum swung our way."

Dunigan contended, "I don't think anybody in our huddle would have called that play."

The Lions' offensive coordinator was Adam Rita. "It was on the 18-yard line on the right hash with the wind behind us, third down and one and half. The head coach asked me what I wanted to do. I said, 'Punt it.'

"Our defense was playing well. Winnipeg was minus 14 yards rushing and only had one first down. So all we had to do, really, was play field position and we would have had our chances. The field is 110 yards long, you've only got three downs, and so the wind is a big factor. But, you know, it was his first year as a head coach in the CFL."

But B.C.'s defense rose to the occasion, and Winnipeg had to settle for a 21-yard field goal. The Leos led by a point.

The next Lion drive stalled on the Bomber 36. Willie Fears broke through to block a 43-yard field-goal try, another big play according to Stan Mikawas. "With Willie we had a good chance to block it because he was such a big guy. So we would double team the guard, and I'd pull the guard away, leaving a big enough gap for him to squeeze through, which he did. He got his hand up and blocked the field goal."

Shortly after, Rod Hill picked off a Dunigan pass and returned it to the 26. Going nowhere, Trevor Kennard missed a 33-yarder but picked up a single to tie the game.

On the next series Lui Passalia replied with an 84-yard single. The Lion lead was short-lived. Dan Wicklum recovered a fumble on a punt return, setting up Cameron's single to end the third quarter in a tie at 19.

Both defenses were magnificent throughout the final 15 minutes. It wasn't until just over 12 minutes had elapsed that Winnipeg was able to use the wind to their advantage. Kennard kicked a field goal set up by a Passaglia punt and a no yards penalty. According to Passaglia, "I hit that punt maybe 35 yards downfield, which wasn't a bad kick against that wind. I remember our guys running down, and it bounced back right over their heads. I think it netted around 20 yards. The way our defense was playing, that extra 15 yards would have put them out of field-goal range. But they did kick a field goal. If there was one punt I'd like to have back, it would probably be that one."

With Winnipeg leading by 3, the Lions took the ball at their 35. Tony Cherry swept around the end on an electrifying 52-yard run, bringing the ball to the Bomber 23. After an off side, Cherry ran to the 10, picking up a first down, and then to the 7. The Lions had gone 68 yards on the ground in three plays and were squarely in front of the goalposts. Passaglia waited to tie the game.

At that point Dunigan went back to pass. Although Jan Carinci was wide open in a corner of the end zone, Dunigan was looking straight ahead. He released the ball. Winnipeg's Delbert Fowler deflected it up in the air. Michael Gray made the interception. A few seconds later Bob Cameron conceded a safety touch. Winnipeg won their tenth Grey Cup 22–21.

Bomber assistant coach Gene Gaines described what happened. "Our cornerback, James Jefferson, had slipped down and his man was wide open. But Dunigan had decided where he wanted to throw the ball and he did. Delbert Fowler batted the ball up in the air and the next thing I knew, Michael Gray had it."

Said General Manager Murphy, "Dunigan threw one up the middle though he had a guy wide open in the corner. He wanted very much to throw it inside, but it got deflected and Gray made the interception on about the 2- or 3-yard line."

Stan Mikawas also recalled Dunigan's single-mindedness of purpose. "Matt could have thrown it to a number of guys who were open in the end zone, but he had tunnel vision. He was trying to get it to that one receiver even though there were two or three guys in the way."

"I had called a play called 54 Yankee," explained Dunigan. "I had Jan Carinci coming over the middle. He was open, but the ball got tipped at the line of scrimmage and went about 30 feet up in the air. Michael Gray, of all people, caught it about 6 yards downfield. What he was doing 6 yards downfield was news to me, but he came up with the key interception.

"If you look at the film you'll see David Williams worked the defensive back so bad he made him fall down and was open in the corner of the end zone. But my read took me to Jan Carinci."

"Talk about the Argo bounce," groaned Lui Passaglia. "That was the Bomber bounce there. Talk about fate not being in your corner. I mean, a defensive lineman starts running backward and the ball ends up in his hands for an interception."

Rita made no apologies for the call. "What happened was Jan Carinci had come off the field at a time-out and said he could get open on the guy because he was playing so far outside. He could run a 54 Yankee across the field. And he was open, except we had blocked Delbert Fowler fairly well. He came off the ground. Matt didn't see him because you see a lane and throw the ball. Fowler tipped it, the ball was up in the air and Michael Gray caught it.

"Fowler had a knack of being in the right place at the right time. He's done that several times. It is just that our guy probably blocked him too well. I think what he had done was cut him and he came off the ground and tipped the ball.

"It was exactly what we wanted, and it was there. Larry Donovan told me he never would have called a play like that. I said, 'That's the play that brought you to the Grey Cup.' It did work, except Michael Gray makes a play. That stuff happens."

Why didn't Dunigan go for the tie? "It is the competitive instinct to put the nail in the coffin, to put the game away," he explained. "It was second and 7. I felt it was a very secure play, a very confident play, a play we had set up and not used up to that point. We had saved it for the right opportunity, and it was one of those things where a guy got his hand up and tipped the ball. If not, it's a touchdown. Nobody talks about it. It's a great win for us. But it didn't work out that way.

"You can call it luck or you can call it fate or you can call it ability. Winnipeg created their own luck. You've got to give them credit as well.

"I think they had one first down offensively in the second half. They were playing with a quarterback who I certainly felt was suspect in our league. To have one first down and come away with the victory is a credit to their defense and organization.

"It was tough to swallow, as far as we were concerned, because we were on a roll. We felt we had the upper hand. To come short like that was difficult."

Dunigan's thoughts were echoed by Adam Rita. "The thing that disappointed me was that basically we got beat because we didn't make the right decision in the third quarter. The right decision was to punt. I had never heard of anybody going for it at a time when you have the wind at your back and it is just before the fourth quarter. That one baffled me."

Did the players question the decision to throw? "Not so much that one," said Passaglia. "Earlier on in the game we had a third and one with the wind. I was probably punting 55 or 60 yards with the wind. If we'd punted they would have been in a hole trying to do something against the wind.

"Instead we went for it and didn't make it. They kicked a field goal against the wind. Without that field goal it would have been a different story near the end. We wouldn't have had to score a touchdown to win, so Dunigan wouldn't have had to throw the ball. That play stands out because they came out of it with 3 points. I had an 84-yarder that day. We should have punted."

James Murphy won the offense award, Bob Cameron top Canadian and Michael Gray defense although Benny Thompson had a better day. Murphy's 165 yards on five catches was the third-best performance in Grey Cup history. Over his eight-year career with the Bombers, he picked up three Grey Cup rings, a Schenley Award and four All-Star selections. Because Winnipeg only picked up two first downs in the entire second half, Bob Cameron's punting was essential to victory.

"Salisbury completed two passes in the second half," recalled Cal Murphy. "I think it was 2 for 21 to be exact, but Cameron just popped the ball the whole second half. Bob's kicking into the wind was the deciding factor in that football game.

"To me Cameron is like a coach on the field. Most of the time I just go to him before the game and say, 'What do you think?' When Tom Clements was quarterback I used to go to him and say, 'I think I'll take the wind in the second quarter,' and he'd say that it didn't matter to him.

"Very often I let Bob make the decision on the wind. We'd talk it over, and I'd say whatever you feel is right, do it. Bob kicks the ball consistently, the same all the time, and when it's windy he can really pop it. The one thing I will say about Bob is that the bigger the game the better he is."

Cameron recalled that great day in a distinguished career. "I was fortunate enough to win the Outstanding Canadian Award. That was an incredible win for our team because no one gave us much of a chance to win. Everything we needed to happen did happen.

"We needed a big wind. A windy day gave us the advantage because we had a good running game. We had a tough defense. Our offense usually just scored enough points to win. We had excellent special teams and our coverage was phenomenal. Our net was around 40 yards a punt, which is really unheard of.

"Another factor in that game was the temporary stands in the end zone. The wind went up over the fans. If you could keep your punts beneath the wind, you got good distance. If you had to kick from the opposite end zone, it was ugly. Lui Passaglia had to punt three or four times from there. There was a lull in the wind on both of mine from there, and I got good distance."

It is a testament to his persistence that Cameron had any career at all. Cameron was drafted out of Acadia by Edmonton in 1977. "After I didn't make it in 1977 with Edmonton, I tried out for Calgary," he recalled. "Jack Gotta called me into his office after four days and said, 'Bob, you are the best punter we've got, but you can't play another position except quarterback so, sorry, we don't need you. He really had no idea about kicking. To him it was just a necessary evil, which he never really took seriously.

"I went back to university. In 1978 I tried out for the Philadelphia Eagles, Ottawa, Hamilton and Toronto. I went back to university again in 1978 and won the MVP Award in the Can-Am Bowl. I signed with the Buffalo Bills and went all the way through their training camp in '79 before I was cut. At that point I decided that I had given it a pretty damn good shot and I gave up."

But not for long. "I was driving from Red Deer to Calgary on a day off from my job and I heard over the radio that Bernie Ruoff got hit with a drug charge. Winnipeg assistant Bob Vespaziani had been my coach at Acadia for five years, and I knew he would put in a good word for me. Two weeks later Paul Robson phoned me and asked if I wanted to give it one more try. I said, 'Sure, I'll quit my job and be up there this spring.' And that was it.

"But I'll tell you what. I tried out for a couple of teams where I know I was the better punter than the guy they kept. One was Ottawa. I went through their entire training camp and out-punted their other guy by a yard and half each time. When I was cut I went into George Brancato's office and pleaded with him. 'Look,' I said, 'how can you possibly keep this guy over me? I'm five years younger, I can only get better and I outkicked him.'

"Brancato told me that one of his assistants had been a punter in the NFL in the '50s, and he said I dropped the ball with one hand and the other guy with two, so he would be more consistent. I just looked at him and said, 'I'm more consistent already. How the hell can you make this move?'

"That showed me one thing. If you ever get your foot in the door—in that you make a professional football team—coaches are so stupid that even if a guy comes in who is better than you are, they are going to say, 'Oh, well, he's the incumbent kicker, we sort of like the guy, so I think we'll keep him.'

"When I look back I think there were guys as good or better than me who have come through Winnipeg, but because I've done a half-decent job, they don't really get a serious look."

Cameron maintained that he was essentially self-taught. "I used to watch all the best punters in the CFL and NFL. I would critique them down to their stance, how they held the ball, everything they did. Then I incorporated those things into my style and worked like crazy. I always figured I worked harder and spent more time punting than any sane human being would to develop my skills so I could make it as a pro and hold on to my job because I never had a super powerful leg like Hank Ilesic. My forte has been consistency and not screwing up in pressure situations—although I did in the 1993 Grey Cup."

As in place-kicking, the center is crucial to a punter's success. "One year in university I had a center who was unbelievable. He would just rifle it back to me, and I had all day to get the ball off. I had a 45.8-yard average. The next year with a different center I had a 41-yard average. If your center rifles the ball back and consistently puts it on your hip, you've got an extra tenth of a second. The center is the key to punting well."

So is the wind factor. "We were playing in Regina on Labor Day in my rookie year, 1980, and I was under a lot of pressure to hold on to my job. It was the biggest wind I had ever seen. My first punt was from the 20-yard line. The Riders gave me a big rush, the ball went off the side of my foot, landed 15 yards downfield and started bouncing back.

"I was trying to draw a roughing-the-kicker penalty, so I was on my back. I looked up and saw the ball bounce by me and out of bounds at the 12. It counted on my average as a minus 8 punt."

Cameron and company made history that year. The Winnipeg Blue Bombers of 1935 had become the first team to win the Cup for the West. In 1988 the Bombers became the first western team to win the Cup for the East. But by 1989 the Bombers slipped to 7–11. Only Toronto was worse offensively. However, they blasted the Argos at SkyDome 30–7 in the semifinal before bowing 14–10 to Hamilton in the final.

The following year Murphy and Riley retooled. There were eight new faces on defense, three defensive backs, four new linebackers and one lineman. Seven changes were made on offense, including three receivers, the entire backfield and one lineman.

The most important change was quarterback Tom Burgess came over from Saskatchewan to replace Sean Salisbury, who returned to the States. Burgess had lost the starting job to Kent Austin. Under Mike Riley, Burgess had the best year of his career, completing 330 out of 574 for 3,958 yards and 25 touchdowns, 27 interceptions and a percentage completion of 57.5. His totals were second only to Kent Austin.

Still, Winnipeg was last in points scored and sixth in total offense. The Eskimos were number one. Defensively the Bombers were the best in the league, led again by magnificent linebackers Tyrone Jones, Greg Battle, Paul Randolph and Albert Williams. James West was a backup.

Winnipeg finished atop their division with a record of 12–6. They overcame a stubborn Toronto team to advance to the Grey Cup. There, they handed the Eskimos their worst drubbing in Grey Cup history, 50–11.

Greg Battle's Finest Hour

Stan Mikawos took pride in the performance of the defense during the 1990 Grey Cup. "It was a great defensive performance. With his two interceptions, Greg Battle had the best game of his life. Edmonton couldn't get anything on us. Every time they started to move the ball, they would cough it up. It was a lopsided game, but everyone on our defense played well."

Still, Winnipeg was only up 10–4 at the half. Mikawos wasn't worried. "After the first half we had confidence going into the second half because of the way our defense was playing, even though our offense was basically sputtering. We knew we were going to win the game."

Greg Battle wasn't so sure. "I think we felt pretty fortunate because if you take the beginning of the game, the Eskimos had a 10-play drive and, as defensive players, we were back on our heels, second-guessing ourselves. It wasn't only in our call-making but also in our minds. We thought that they were running right through us, that we were not able to stop them. I came up with the interception, and I think that helped us. It didn't turn the tide, but it evened the tide, especially in field position."

Battle described what happened. "I could see Tracy Ham, but I know he couldn't see me because generally you don't have a deep player coming from where I was coming from. I give all the accolades to the coaching staff because they came up with that scheme where we brought down the safety. If the quarterback is reading properly, when the safety disappears you throw into the middle. But I showed up.

"If Ham had had a clear throwing lane, he probably wouldn't have thrown it because he probably would have seen me. He knew the free safety wasn't there, and he caught the receiver in the early part of his pattern, but the defensive front was bringing so much pressure that I think he basically threw the ball to the area, hoping the receiver would get it.

"The reason we were bringing up the safety was because they were running five bona fide receivers, so instead of asking one of the linebackers to come out and cover one of the receivers we brought the free safety up and therefore had two free linebackers, the short linebacker Paul Randolph and the deep linebacker, me."

Battle described the touchdown interception. "I have to give all the credit to the defensive line. We had a five-man rush, and we were playing man coverage behind it. I slackened off on the pass pattern, but generally if you can't find someone to block you sneak out and that was my man.

"When Tracy went to throw, Albert Williams put his hands up. Tracy ducked under him and basically threw a bad pass. I believe he was throwing it away.

"Michael Soles was looking downfield—I don't know what at—but I was right on his back. Tracy threw the ball right over his head. I just jumped up and grabbed it, and he didn't even see me. I had run maybe 4 or 5 yards before he noticed I had the ball and I was only around 30 yards from the end zone. It was an easy score."

It was the greatest week of Battle's football career. "My wife was up, my grandfather was up, I was up for an award. I was doing all those banquets. After practice I was spending time with my granddad and my wife and having a great time.

"In my football career, nothing will ever top that Grey Cup week. Not only the awards but having my granddad and my wife there to share everything with me. Everything was perfect. Playing the game was almost secondary."

Battle won the Outstanding Defensive Player Award that year and was named Outstanding Defensive Player in the Grey Cup.

Winnipeg head coach Cal Murphy wasn't expecting the margin of victory. "I was surprised at the final outcome," he said. "By the end of the first half, Ham had run around so much that I was afraid our defensive people were tuckered out from chasing him.

"I felt we had so many opportunities in the first half and didn't capitalize. I can remember saying at half time that I just hoped we hadn't gassed ourselves because I've seen that happen. To come out in the second half and totally annihilate them—you don't often see that. Greg Battle made some great plays. We scored 28 points in the third quarter, the most ever.

"In 1990 I thought we were a darn good football team. I really thought we were very good, very aggressive. But I also knew we were on the verge of difficulties. It had to get done."

In 1991 Cal Murphy returned to the bench after Mike Riley went to the States. The Bombers led the league in defense, the East in total offense, but were seventh in points scored. They finished second at 9–9, beat Ottawa 26–8 in the semifinal, but lost the final to Toronto 42–3.

In preparation for the 1992 campaign, the Bombers added three new defensive backs, a linebacker and a down lineman. On offense Tom Burgess was replaced by Matt Dunigan. All the receivers were new as was running back Michael Richardson. Trevor Kennard was replaced by Troy Westwood. Kennard had kicked for 1,840 points in 12 seasons with Winnipeg, making him the CFL's sixth leading scorer of all time. No Blue Bomber has scored more.

For the Bombers 1992 was a year of tragedy, triumph and disappointment. Early in July, Cal Murphy was admitted to the University Hospital in London, Ontario, to await a heart transplant. Without it he would surely die. A devout Catholic, Murphy's prayers were answered and he received a new heart quickly.

Interim head coach Urban Bowman coached the team to 11 wins, 7 losses and a first-place tie with Hamilton. The Bombers crushed the Ti-Cats 59–11 and moved into the Grey Cup against Calgary.

The Stampeders led 11–0 at the end of the first quarter on the strength of a field goal and single by Mark McLoughlin and a 25-yard Doug Flutie to Dave

Sapunjis touchdown pass. McLoughlin added 6 more points by the half. No scoring occurred in the third quarter. At 2:36 of the final frame, Calgary increased their lead to 24–0 when Allen Pitts caught a 15-yarder for a major.

With 6:37 left in the game Troy Westwood finally got the Bombers on the scoreboard with a field goal. At 12:39 reliever Danny McManus hit Gerald Alphin for a touchdown. The final score was Calgary 24, Winnipeg 10. The score flattered Winnipeg. Flutie was good on 33 of 49 passes for 480 yards, Dunigan only 6 of 19 for 47 yards. McManus fared better at 7 of 18 for 155 yards and a touchdown. Calgary had 528 yards total offense, Winnipeg 238. Bob Cameron was the only bright spot for the losers, out-punting Tony Martino 43.7 yards to 34.4.

When it was suggested to Murphy that Calgary dominated on both sides of the ball, he laughed and replied, "You're being kind. We were never in it. It was Flutie, Flutie and more Flutie."

Mikawos agreed. "Flutie did a number on us. He is very fast with his release and his speed. We just couldn't stop him, and our offense couldn't get anything on the board. It was exactly opposite to what we did to Edmonton in 1990."

Greg Battle felt Winnipeg had been out-coached. "Their scheme was such that we were put in bad situations. Several times I had to go out and cover Derrick Crawford. He was one of the slotbacks then, and that's definitely a mismatch. Now, if Flutie was running the ball up the middle that would be my forte, and I'd have an advantage. They were running a package that caught us off guard and we didn't make any adjustments."

Although some questioned Urban Bowman's game plan, Dunigan wasn't one of them. "We had opportunities early, but we were just missing. It was just a matter of inches. If we had made some of those plays, it would have given the game a totally different complexion. You hear often that football is a game of inches. In that game I believe it was. We were maybe an inch away offensively from making it happen. A receiver would stumble or let up. We did not make the plays. Calgary did, so you take your hat off to them and move on."

Although he is presently the second-ranked passing quarterback of all time, Dunigan has been injury prone, missing parts of four of his first seven seasons. In 1990 he only played eight games, the same in 1991 although he did manage to make it back for the Grey Cup.

Before he came to Winnipeg, because of his hefty price tag and inability to survive an entire season, Mike McCarthy and the Argos would only renew

Dunigan's contract on a per-game basis. He refused and signed with Winnipeg. He made it through the entire 1992 season, including the Grey Cup, as well as the first 16 games in 1993.

According to Winnipeg coach Cal Murphy, that was no accident. "When we brought him in that was one of the things we said we were going to do. When we talked to his agent, I guaranteed him that we would have one or two backs in there to protect him. We weren't going to empty the backfield and let people take a shot at him."

On August 13 Dunigan scored three touchdowns himself and threw for three others as the Bombers routed the Eskimos 53–11. On September 26 in Edmonton, the Bombers trounced the Eskimos again, this time 52–14. The only team to beat Winnipeg decisively was Calgary, and they didn't make it to the Grey Cup.

With two games left on the 1993 schedule, Dunigan blew his Achilles tendon. Without him Winnipeg barely scraped by Hamilton 20–19 in the Eastern Final. Although Sammy Garza played well in the Grey Cup, the Bombers weren't the same team without Dunigan. The Bombers are certain the outcome would have been different had their best player not been hurt.

The game's outcome, however, was decided more by mistakes. The team that made the least mistakes won. Winnipeg center Nick Benjamin snapped the ball over Bob Cameron's head. The veteran punter should have run to the end zone and conceded a safety touch. Instead he tried to kick the ball, it was blocked and Edmonton recovered on the 4-yard line. Lucius Floyd scored on the next play.

Blaise Bryant fumbled the ensuing kickoff. Damon Allen hit Jim Sandusky in the end zone. On Winnipeg's next possession, Garza was intercepted by Dan Murphy. Sean Fleming then connected on the first of a record six field goals. Fleming scored 4 more points before Winnipeg got on the board with a Michael Richardson touchdown.

By dropping behind so far so early, the Bombers were forced out of their game plan to control the ball with Richardson's running. Instead they had to go to the air and play catch-up football. Garza passed admirably, but he had to climb out of too deep a hole.

Winnipeg's defense played heroically. Edmonton's two touchdowns came after drives that started on the enemy 4- and 26-yard lines. Other than that, they were held to field goals and a single. Offensively, after spotting the Eskimos 21 points, the Bombers outscored Edmonton 23–12 the rest of the way. Final score: Edmonton 33, Winnipeg 23.

In 1994 Baltimore and Shreveport were added to the Eastern division, neither team having to employ Canadians. Winnipeg didn't miss a beat, finishing atop the standings with a 13–5 record, two points ahead of Don Matthews' powerful Baltimore CFLers. Winnipeg beat Ottawa 26–16 in the semifinal but lost the final to Baltimore, 14–12.

The following year was one of crisis for the Bombers, who had to undergo a major rebuilding. Dunigan left for the Birmingham Barracudas, and Murphy went through five quarterbacks before settling on Reggie Slack. They averaged 19 points per game for the first half of the season while surrendering 34. But during the second half of the season, they scored an average of 26 points while giving up 38 and made the play-offs.

Poor play resulted in poorer attendance. The Blue Bombers were staggering under a crushing load of debt brought on largely by the need to prop up ailing franchises like Ottawa. The club almost went bankrupt. Perhaps frightened by the loss of their National Hockey League franchise, the people of Winnipeg rallied behind the Bombers and provided the team with a solid season ticket base and operating capital.

Cal Murphy and the Blue Bombers survived the toughest test of all. Murphy managed the purse strings so well that Winnipeg was the only team that made money. Despite an injury-riddled season, including at times both starting quarterbacks Kent Austin and Reggie Slack, the Bombers made the play-offs for the seventeenth straight year. Only Edmonton has done better.

Murphy's reward? After losing the semifinal 68–7 to the Eskimos, he was fired. He was succeeded by the flamboyant B.C. assistant Jeff Reinebold. Although his only head coaching experience had been one year at Rocky Mountain College, the Bomber executive turned the whole operation over to the University of Maine alumnus, making him director of football operations and head coach. The Bombers went 4–14 in 1997, attributable, it was said, to the fact it would take a year to clean up Cal Murphy's mess and bring in players of Reinebold's choosing.

The facts indicate otherwise. Murphy was fired in December 1996, so Reinebold had lots of time to recruit. In his first year he replaced 11 starters on defense and 9 on offense. The following year he cleaned house again, replacing 10 first-stringers on defense, 8 on offense. The new bunch was no better.

Halfway through the 1998 season offensive coordinator Joe Paopao resigned. In October, with a mark of 2–12, Reinebold was fired, the first time in team history the Bombers had fired a coach during the season. The players swore to win one for Jeff. Instead they lost at home to the Eskimos 40–20. With friends like that who needs enemies? Gary Hoffman took over, going 1–3. He was replaced by Dave Ritchie.

Cal Murphy moved to Regina as special teams coach, helping the Roughriders get to the Grey Cup, a 47–23 loss to Toronto. When Jim Daley was fired after the 1998 campaign, Murphy became Saskatchewan's head coach and director of football operations.

The great Winnipeg–Hamilton rivalry will, unfortunately, remain a thing of the past as long as the Blue Bombers are in the Eastern division. Despite the Eastern play-off battles between the Bombers and Hamilton and Toronto, no real sense of rivalry has developed. The biggest dates in the Blue Bomber calendar are against Saskatchewan, a natural rival geographically. Fans everywhere in the country will be pleased when Ottawa returns to the CFL, probably in 2001, and Winnipeg goes back to its natural home in the Western division.

Edmonton and Winnipeg have been the stablest franchises in the CFL. While Saskatchewan is praised for their fan support, no cities can match Edmonton and Winnipeg for gate receipts when the going gets really tough. With Dave Ritchie at the helm, the Bombers will fly into the third millennium on a winning note.

Things are not so rosy in Hamilton, traditionally one of the bedrock franchises in the CFL. Hamilton struggled throughout most of the 1990s partly because of an economic downturn plus competition from the NFL and the Toronto Blue Jays. It's strange the dislike Steeltowners have for Hogtowners doesn't keep them from supporting the Blue Jays and Maple Leafs. Now that ownership has stabilized and Ron Lancaster has turned the team around on the field, one of the real bedrock franchises of Canadian football can also look to the future with confidence.

CHAPTER 3

Toronto

Arrrr—Go!

It was raining cats and dogs the day before the 1976 Grey Cup game when members of the media were assembled in their favorite watering hole, the Schenley hospitality suite at the Royal York Hotel, hosted by the amiable *Calgary Herald* sports editor Hal Walker and his charming wife, Betty.

Someone phoned the desk to have them activate the adult movie on the television set. In one scene a beautiful young woman disrobed and threw a reluctant man down on the bed. At the same moment a voice then boomed from a dark corner of the hotel room, "But I don't want to coach the Argonauts!"

Small wonder. After winning the first Grey Cup in 1909 with stars such as Hugh Gall and then dominating the league until 1952, the team had appeared in the Grey Cup only three times in the modern era. Russ Jackson, the latest big-name savior, had just been fired as head coach and was licking his wounds at the Florida retreat of the man who swung the ax, owner Bill Hodgson.

Until Ralph Sazio moved down the Queen E from hated Hamilton to restore Toronto fortunes in the early 1980s, the Argos led the league in spending, were number one in self-proclaimed saviors and superstars, first in attendance and last in the Eastern Conference 18 times. Seldom in the history of sports had so many spent so much to achieve so little.

Hugh Gall starred for the University of Toronto.

Before the 1980s management was always after the quick fix, be it Ronnie Knox, Tobin Rote, Jackie Parker, Greg Barton or Anthony Davis. Players like Peter Liske and Tom Wilkinson, who would go on to greatness, were traded away because they didn't fit the Argo mold. In the 31 years between Grey Cup victories, 1952–83, the Argos had only eight winning seasons. Leo Cahill coached six of them and was fired twice.

The Argonauts' problem was bad management. It wasn't always that way. Between 1933 and 1952, the Argos won eight Grey Cups in as many tries. They became the first postwar team to win three Cups in a row (1945–47) and the last totally Canadian team to win the national championship in 1947. Among the stars of those teams were Frank Morris and Joe Krol.

Joe Krol

Quarterback Joe Krol won championships at Kennedy Collegiate in Windsor and at the University of Western Ontario. He won Grey Cups punting, throwing, running, catching and intercepting passes. The late Gordon Walker wrote in his book *Grey Cup Tradition:* "Even dictionaries have trouble providing the right kind of words to describe how great was the young man who burst onto the Canadian football scene in 1943. Boiled down to basics, Joe Krol was a winner, maybe the best-ever in Canada when the chips were down. The more challenging the situation, the better he resolved it."

In 1943 Krol joined the Hamilton Flying Wildcats, leading them to the Grey Cup in his rookie year. The following year marked the last time the national championship was played without a Western representative. It was also the only time Joe Krol lost a Grey Cup, when his Wildcats were defeated by HMCS Donnacona of St. Hyacinthe, Quebec, 7–6. Although Donnacona won the Grey Cup, they weren't the navy champions. HMCS York, coached by Ted Morris, defeated Donnacona for that title. When the war ended, Ted Morris took over the helm of the good ship Argonaut, bringing several stars with him.

Offensive guard Frank Morris was a member of the All-Canadian Argo team that won those three straight Grey Cups as well as part of the three-peat Edmonton Eskimos of 1954–56. He later became Edmonton's super scout, playing a major role in building the great Eskimo teams of the 1970s and '80s.

A Toronto native, Morris grew up playing a variety of sports but not football. "I had never played football before," he said. "I joined the navy in 1942 and played fastball. We had a good fastball club, representing Canada at the World Championships in Detroit. A number of guys on that fastball team had played with the Argos. They decided they were going to put a navy football team together. They felt I was big enough to come out and give it a shot. That was my introduction to football."

Morris joined the Argos in 1945, the same year Joe Krol signed with the Detroit Lions. Around Thanksgiving Krol was released. A week later he and the Argos agreed to a contract over the phone. The next day his old team, the Wildcats, looked him up, but it was too late.

On October 27, 1945, Krol played his first game for the double blue in Montreal, throwing five touchdown passes in a 31–6 victory. Four of the passes were to Royal Copeland. From then on they were dubbed the Gold Dust Twins, and their impact on the Grey Cup was immediate. In their first of three straight wins over Winnipeg, the Argos crushed the Bombers 35–0. Krol and Copeland each scored a touchdown, Krol on a 50-yard interception return. Krol also threw two touchdown passes.

The 1945 game was the last Cup played by teams made up entirely of Canadians. The following year Winnipeg added imports, but the Argos remained All-Canadian until 1948.

The Gold Dust Twins were at it again in 1946. In the course of their 28–6 Grey Cup romp over Winnipeg, Krol threw a touchdown pass to Copeland, who later returned the favor after Krol intercepted a pass on the Bomber 45-yard line. Krol also connected in the end zone with Rod Smylie and Boris Tipoff. The fifth Argo major, a 1-yard run by Byron Karrys, was set up by one of the most spectacular plays in Grey Cup history.

In those days teams would often put a speedy receiver out on the flank and slightly behind the punter because a player behind a kicker was eligible to recover the ball. Joe Krol punted the ball toward the sideline. Royal Copeland raced down the field and caught it over the heads of the Winnipeg defenders and made it to the 1-yard line.

The next year, 1947, saw the third straight match-up between Toronto and Winnipeg. The Argos never lost a Grey Cup to Winnipeg, but they came close that year.

Sculler coach Teddy Morris refused to use imports. The Blue Bombers, determined to improve after being outscored 63–8 in the title games of the two previous years, used five, including their Minnesota quarterback Bob Sandberg, who almost beat the Argos single-handedly.

Sandberg led the Bombers to a 9–1 lead at the end of the half. But the Gold Dust Twins sang their old familiar song when Frankie Morris recovered a fumble and Krol promptly hit Copeland with a pass for a touchdown, making Copeland the only player to score a touchdown in three consecutive Grey Cups.

Near the end of the game, Krol scored a single on a missed field goal, and with less than two minutes to go, Krol kicked a single to tie. With seconds remaining, Winnipeg, wanting to retain possession, gambled on third and 2. The Argos stopped the exhausted Sandberg dead in his tracks. On the last play of the game, Krol punted the ball into the end zone and out of bounds. Toronto won 10–9.

Frankie Morris's play was instrumental in the victory. "It was third down and they had the ball on the 30-yard line," he recalled. "The Bombers lined up in punt formation. I knew that at times, instead of centering the ball back to the punter, they would give it to Bert Iannoni, a guard. They had a guard sneak play.

"When the center turned the ball, I knew he wasn't going to make the long snap, and I damn near took the hand-off myself when I made the tackle. We took possession of the ball because Winnipeg lost yards on the play. The funny part of it is, when we got into the huddle and Joe Krol started to call a play, our team captain, Steve Levantis, said, 'To hell with the running play. Kick it.' Krol kicked it into the end zone for the winning point. If we had run a play we could have been in overtime."

The 1947 Grey Cup was the most memorable for Krol. "That was quite a game. We beat the Bombers on the last play. I kicked a single on a quick kick to tie the game and another one to win it. That one took a bounce over the goal line and rolled out of bounds.

"The Blue Bombers' Bob Sandberg played one of the greatest games I've ever seen. He was a team in himself. We knew he was going to carry the ball, and we still couldn't stop him. I don't think he ever played a game like that before or since."

The most bizarre Grey Cup for Krol was the 1950 Mud Bowl, a 13–0 shutout of the Bombers. Winnipeg couldn't run in the slop, and Indian Jack Jacobs, a superb passer on dry land, couldn't handle the slippery pigskin. Onlookers were surprised that Toronto didn't have the same problem. Krol explained why. "Our quarterback Al Dekdebrun had thumbtacks taped to his fingers with just enough of the points sticking out to grip the ball. It turned out to be a heck of a gimmick."

When asked about the thumbtacks, Argo coach Frank Clair first feigned ignorance. "Well, I was only told about it afterward," he said carefully, "and all I can say is I don't know. But if Dekdebrun used thumbtacks, it was a good idea."

Then he changed his tune. "Actually, the thumbtacks were cut down to about a thirty-second of an inch so they wouldn't hurt anybody. It was a pretty good idea on that day because it was so muddy you could barely hold the ball."

The myth persists that field conditions during the Mud Bowl were so bad that Buddy Tinsley would have drowned had it not been for the quick thinking of referee Hec Creighton. If the event did happen, it escaped Krol's notice. "I suppose it was possible," he commented, "because I know the slush was ankle deep. It is quite possible if he was laying there for any length of time that he could have hurt himself."

Even Tinsley got a kick out of the story. "I wasn't drowning," he insisted. "But the conditions were atrocious that day. There was water floating on the field and pieces of ice. I had hurt my knee in the play-offs. They taped my knee and my quadriceps so tight that the muscles wouldn't move. I happened to get hit right on the thigh real hard. That paralyzed my leg and I fell forward. I was lying there with my head on my arm very unhappy because I had got hurt. I was just laying there because I couldn't move my leg. A couple of guys came over and helped me up. I don't know how that story got started. I think people in the stands thought I was drowning because of the conditions."

It is a sore point with Krol that he didn't see much action in his last two Grey Cups. "The last couple I was involved in, '50 and '52, were disappointing in that I didn't play very much. Prior to that I played most of the games. All I did was kick while Frank Clair was here."

Did Clair have something against Canadian ballplayers? "He won't admit it, but I think he did," Krol commented. "But not only Clair. Ninety-five percent of American coaches that came up here initially didn't have much faith in Canadian ballplayers. I've seen American coaches play Americans that were only able to perform at 50 percent of their abilities due to an injury. But they'd rather play an American who was going 50 percent than put in a 100 percent Canadian. I think Frank learned his lesson after he went to Ottawa and realized Canadian boys could play the game. He ended up with Russ Jackson and a bunch of championship teams."

Maybe Krol was right about Clair. When asked about great Grey Cup performers he coached, Clair replied, "Russ Jackson and Ronnie Stewart were standouts. Although they *were* Canadians, those two alone were the kingpins of our club."

Although there was very little hoopla associated with the Grey Cup during Krol's salad days, this remarkable athlete believed the event was of great importance. "At the time it was the only sport where you played teams representing all parts of Canada. I don't think anything could compare to it. We didn't have major league baseball then, and there were no Western NHL teams. Football was the only nationwide sport, and it did bring East and West together."

One thing that hadn't changed over the years was the fact Grey Cup champions didn't make much money winning the title. "We just worked on a game-to-game basis," Krol said. "The most I ever made in one year—and that included the Grey Cup—was $6,400."

The legendary Lew Hayman had a perfect Grey Cup coaching record: five wins, no losses.

Frank Clair, the "Old Professor," coached Toronto and Ottawa to five Grey Cup victories.

Notwithstanding Krol's memories of the '50 and '52 Grey Cups, when Head Coach Frank Clair led the team into the second half of the century with two Cups in three years, the future for the double blue looked bright.

Then Harry Sonshine took over and the fortunes of the club took a turn for the worse. Sonshine had used his friendship with Frank Clair to wheedle his way into Argo management circles. Clair supported Sonshine's bid to become a director because he wanted someone on the board who would advance his point of view on player recruitment. Soon after, Sonshine was calling the shots. Clair quit in disgust, landing in Ottawa as head coach.

Among Sonshine's shenanigans was cutting all his imports except Al Pheifer and Dick Shatto, replacing them with eight stars from the NFL. The Big Four ruled that players under contract to NFL teams were ineligible. Later they let him keep four players, including quarterback Tom Dublinski, who threw a still-standing record 34 interceptions in his inaugural season in 1955.

In 1872 Harry O'Brien started the Argonaut Rowing Club, named after the crew of the legendary Greek hero Jason, who sailed the good ship Argo in search of the Golden Fleece. In honor of the two contestants in the Henley Regatta, Oxford and Cambridge, he chose their light and dark blues as the colors of the rowing club. The Argonauts have been wearing the double blue ever since.

The Toronto Argonaut Rowing Club fielded a football team one year later. Despite the great success of the gridiron group over the years, the major preoccupation of the club was rowing. In 1957 they sold the team to John Bassett, Charley Burns, Eric Cradock, Bob Moran and Joe Wright. Sonshine was out.

Cradock, Leo Dandurand and Lew Hayman had started the Alouettes in 1946. Hayman left the Larks in 1954, and, at the urging of Cradock, was hired as managing director of the Argos in 1957.

During Hayman's 10 years at the helm, the Argos went through four coaches —Hampton Pool, Lou Agase, Nobby Wirkowski and Bob Shaw—finishing last eight times. With former Detroit Lion Tobin Rote at quarterback in 1960, Toronto finished first but lost the final to Ottawa. Rote set several records, since eclipsed, including throwing seven touchdown passes twice in the same month.

In 1961 the Argos waxed the second-place Ottawa Rough Riders 43–19 in the semifinal before hammering Hamilton 25–7 in the first game of the Conference Final. In the rematch the Ti-Cats tied it up at the end of regulation time and then scored four unanswered touchdowns in overtime, a grim harbinger of things to come. The Argos finished last the next five years in a row.

When the double blue lost their first three games in 1962, Hayman fired Agase despite a record of 17–10–1 and two straight appearances in the Eastern Final. Former Sculler quarterback Nobby Wirkowski took over, losing 7 games that year and 21 more over the next two seasons. In 1963 Hayman traded five players to Edmonton for Jackie Parker, who won 10 games in three years.

At the end of the 1964 season, Hayman fired Wirkowski and hired Bob Shaw away from Saskatchewan. Despite going 8 for 22, Shaw was not fired. He quit after losing a power struggle with Hayman.

The Luck of the Irish

Even a blind squirrel finds an occasional nut, and in 1967 Hayman hired Leo Cahill away from the Toronto Rifles of the Continental League. He ended the five-year play-off drought in his first year, going 5–8–1 and finishing third. Ottawa beat the Argos 38–22 in the semifinal.

Cahill brought quarterback Tom Wilkinson with him from the Rifles to go with Wally Gabler. He had a solid receiving corps with Mike Eben, Bobby Taylor, Jim Thorpe and Mel Profit. In 1968 Gabler and Taylor led the East in passing and receiving.

An afterthought in a trade with B.C., Bill Symons gave the Argos a ground game. In 1968 he led the Eastern Conference in rushing with 1,107 yards and won the Schenley Award over George Reed, who had 115 yards more.

The fans appreciated Cahill's efforts. In two seasons, average per-game attendance went from 23,654 to 32,373. In 1968 the Argos finished second with a 9–5 record, two points behind the powerful Rough Riders. It was Toronto's first winning record in seven years.

The Argos rolled over Hamilton 33–21 in the semifinal and then edged Ottawa 13–11 in the first game of the Eastern Final at CNE. Back at Lansdowne, Toronto's Grey Cup hopes were dashed when they lost 36–14.

The next season the Argos again finished second, two points behind Ottawa. Again they eliminated Hamilton in the semifinal and beat Ottawa in the first game of the Conference Final, this time 22–14. Up by 8 points, the flamboyant Cahill was so convinced the good ship Argonaut was about to come in that he proclaimed, "Only an act of God can stop us from winning the game." They lost 32–3.

As far as Cahill was concerned, he wasn't boasting idly but merely stating a fact. "I'm a Midwest kid from Illinois," he said. "One of the things they have in the farm country is the act of God thing. If the crops get ruined by a storm or frost or anything else, it is called an act of God. I was referring to the weather.

"What happened was we went over there, and it was icy. They wore broomball shoes and we didn't, and they beat the hell out of us."

The players weren't bothered by their coach's outrageous statements. "That kept Leo flying," said receiver Mike Eben, "and it sort of kept us with a bemused look on our faces. What goes around comes around, and some of Leo's statements came around and stabbed him sometimes.

"In 1969 we had a very fine team, but we lost to Ottawa in the Eastern Final. That was the year Leo made his act of God statement, and, of course, the press jumped on that. I always maintained that God came out of his seat with all his converts and picked on our game and zapped us."

Eben credited the dynamic Cahill with much of the Argos' success. Life with Leo was, in a word, "Hectic—always something up his sleeve and buzzing around. He was a good estimator of personnel. He was a good recruiter who had the wit and the wisdom to keep the good veterans together, and that is always key on a team.

"It was actually after he was unceremoniously fired that other people came into coach who weren't always so sensitive to the nature of the Canadian game and the importance of keeping Canadian veterans on the team. That's when the Argonauts went into a tailspin for a number of years."

Eben was one of the more interesting individuals on a team loaded with them. Not only an All-Star football player, he was also a scholar. "I was drafted by B.C. in 1968 out of the University of Toronto. I was planning to do my graduate work in Toronto so I didn't want to go out to B.C. After long negotiations between B.C. and Toronto, they finally made a trade for me, so I did end up beginning my career with the Argonauts in 1968.

"After two years I was loaned out to the Eskimos for a season. That was kind of a lend-lease thing between me and the general managers of the two teams. The coaches didn't seem to know.

"At the end of the 1970 season, which was actually a very happy one for me, the bargain had been that I was to come back to the Argonauts, which I did with some misgivings because I enjoyed my year in Edmonton.

"But I was still working on my doctoral studies, and I needed to be in Toronto for that. So that's what, in a weird way, got me back to Toronto again.

"I finished the doctorate in 1975. I was a professor for 12 years at York University, but in 1987 I moved to become a teaching master at Upper Canada College, a private boys' school in Toronto. I've been there ever since."

If the 1968–69 seasons were two steps forward to the Grey Cup, 1970 was one step back. With Ottawa decimated by retirements, the Eastern Conference was up for grabs. The order of finish was Hamilton, Toronto, Montreal and Ottawa.

The Alouettes upset Toronto in the semifinal 16–7. Owner John Bassett demanded changes. Because Bassett didn't think Tom Wilkinson looked like a quarterback, he was sent to B.C. He didn't like their other quarterback either, so Don Jonas and receiver Jim Thorpe were dealt to the Bombers. Both quarterbacks were to go on to win Schenley awards.

Coach Cahill faced 1971 without a quarterback. He signed a rookie and a veteran. The vet was Greg Barton, who had been warming the bench for a couple of years in Detroit. Because he was playing out his option, the Lions had traded him to Philadelphia. Barton refused to report, signing with the Argos instead. The rookie was Joe Theismann of Notre Dame, the 1970 runner-up to Heisman Trophy winner Jim Plunkett. After three years in Toronto he would go on to the Washington Redskins, where he established himself as an NFL star.

Cahill was a great recruiter. "A lot of people thought it was just money," he said, but "Joe Theismann, Tim Anderson and Jim Stillwagon were offered $23,000–24,000, which wasn't big money then. It was a matter of being in the right place at the right time, getting some good information from capable people, plus a little Irish luck and Irish blarney.

"We had a couple of our coaches stop at Notre Dame's spring practice. They called me and told me there was a kid by name of Theismann, kind of a skinny kid, who looked like he'd be a great prospect for Canadian football. I told them to give him a good look. I went down to South Bend to talk to him, and then he came up here on a couple of occasions.

"After all of this he finally made up his mind that he was going to sign with the Miami Dolphins. He went down to Florida, and they had a press conference. He came back to South Bend and I gave him a call. I said, 'Joe, I just want to let you know that I appreciated meeting you. You're a very competitive guy, and I'm sure you are going to be successful. I just want to wish you and Sherri a lot of luck.'

"And he said, 'I really appreciate it, coach, but you know I haven't signed the contract yet. I've got it in my back pocket. I want to speak to Ara Paraseigan (the coach at Notre Dame at the time) about a couple of things in the contract before I sign.'

"I said, 'Well, Joe, if you haven't signed it yet, you owe it to yourself and your wife to come back up here and take another look at Toronto. I think it's really important that you have a clear mind about this thing.'

"So he came back up here and we signed him. Bill Stevenson, who ended up playing several years for Edmonton, was a fifth-round draft choice for Miami, and we signed him in the World Football League, along with Larry Csonka and Paul Warfield of the Dolphins. That's why I didn't get any Christmas cards from Miami Coach Don Shula."

Although pundits predicted Barton would lead the Argos, the rookie stepped up instead. Theismann led the Big Four in passing and was named to the Eastern All-Star team. More importantly the Argos beat Hamilton in the Eastern Final and headed to Vancouver to face Calgary in their first Grey Cup encounter since 1952.

Mike Eban had a lot on his mind that year. "I was doing my doctoral defense a couple of weeks after, so I had to be studying out there," he recalled. "I went out a tiny bit, but I was really stuck in my hotel room, studying.

"We stayed downtown, so we were in the midst of all the hubbub. We had a lively bunch of guys on the team, so there was always something happening or about to burst.

"We had a pretty confident team. We had strength at a lot of positions, and we had beaten Calgary during the regular season. Practices that week were pretty loosey-goosey."

It poured before and during the Grey Cup. The Stampeders struck first with a 13-yard touchdown pass from Jerry Keeling to Herm Harrison. Ivan MacMillan replied in the second quarter with a field goal. Jesse Mims gave the Westerners a 14–3 half-time lead, running the ball in from 6 yards out.

A lineman's dream came true when Roger Scales scored Toronto's only touchdown of the day. When Jim Silye fumbled a Zenon Andrusyshyn punt, it was recovered by Joe Vijuk, who lateraled to Scales, who lumbered 36 yards to the end zone.

The Argos' MacMillan picked up a single on a missed 31-yard field goal in the third quarter, making the score 14–11.

Late in the fourth quarter, the Argos' All-Star defensive back Dick Thornton picked off a Keeling pass at the Argos' 42-yard line and returned it 54 yards to the Stampeder 14, a record that stood until 1977.

On the first down Bill Symons hit the middle for 3 yards. Leo Cahill then called for a left sweep to get in front of the goalposts. Chuck Hunsinger would have had mixed feelings about what happened next. On the one hand he would feel sorry for the star-crossed Leon McQuay. On the other hand he would be relieved there was a new Grey Cup goat for people to talk about. Maybe they'd forget about him.

At any rate the Argo back took the hand-off and moved to the left. When he tried to make his cut to turn upfield, he slipped, fell and the ball popped loose. The Stampeders' Reggie Holmes fell on it at the 10.

The game wasn't over. Calgary couldn't pick up a first down and had to punt. Toronto would get another opportunity to move into field-goal range. But Harry Abofs mishandled the ball and kicked it out of bounds, thinking the last team to touch it retained possession. Not so. In that situation the kicking team took over. The Stamps ran out the clock. The term *Argo bounce* took on new meaning.

Leon McQuay's fumble was uncharacteristic for the rookie who had had the kind of year in 1971 that players only dream about. He led the Eastern Conference in rushing with 977 yards. His average per carry of 7.1 yards and per-kickoff return of 26.7 yards were among the best in CFL history. He fumbled only once during the regular season.

Leo Cahill didn't blame McQuay for the loss. "He had a sensational season. In the first 12 games he had amassed 950 yards. He missed a couple of games at the end of the season before the Grey Cup. We kind of held him out. He was coming back from an injury. I don't think he was 100 percent for that game."

Cahill also disputed the referee's call. "I don't think it was a fumble by the rules then. The rule then was that the ground couldn't make you fumble. We were on the right hash mark, and he ran to the left. I had sent in the word to get into the middle of the field so we could kick an easy chip shot for a field goal in case the play didn't work.

"So he ran to the left. The off-tackle play opened up. When he planted his outside foot to make the cut, it just gave way. He fell on his elbow, and when he hit the ground, the ball came out. Calgary recovered it. That was the end of the story. Leon slipped and I fell."

"Poor Leon didn't fumble the ball," Mike Eben recalled. "That ball was gang-tackled. I had a good view of the play, and I saw how it unfolded. He just didn't let the ball drop out of his hands. It was Larry Robinson's helmet on the ball that popped it free. Poor Leon was touched by that forever, it seems. They were going after and gang-tackling the ball. I thought it was a very strong, aggressive play on their part."

"That's exactly right," said Calgary's Herm Harrison. "What the coaches said to us was that, because of the conditions, we've got to go after the ball. And that's what we were doing. We were slapping at it, we were doing everything to knock it loose. Reggie Holmes said he was going after the ball when he went after Leon, but when he was heading at him and saw the ball drop, he just dove on it."

But if McQuay hadn't fumbled and Toronto had kicked the field goal, that would just have tied the game. He did not cost Toronto the Grey Cup. He cost them an opportunity to win the Grey Cup in overtime. To a lesser degree, so did Harry Abofs, when he kicked the ball out of bounds.

Again, everyone was forgiving. Eben said, "I never blamed Harry for that whatsoever. I believe he was thinking it was the safest thing to do, and I gave him full marks for it. Nobody and his brother knew that rule at all."

Herm Harrison agreed, "I don't think anyone knew the rule. When Harry Abofs kicked it out of bounds and the official said, 'Calgary ball,' I thought he had made a terrible mistake."

Cahill analyzed what happened. "Poor Harry Abofs was trying to save time on the clock. The ball was bouncing along the sidelines. He kind of touched it and kicked it out of bounds to stop the clock. He forgot that the rule was that if the ball hits you below the knee and you're on the defensive team, the ball is awarded to the offense. In all the time I coached in Canada, I never saw it happen to anybody else, but it happened to me twice."

The 1971 Grey Cup was the first to be played on artificial turf but the drainage system at Empire Stadium was poor and the surface was like cement. Eben believed the weather and field affected the outcome. "I felt inhibited by that horrible, rainy day and the Astroturf, which certainly wasn't the best. It didn't allow good cuts and pass routes.

"Calgary had a fine team and a good defense, but we had a pretty explosive team, and the turf just seemed to inhibit us a lot that day with the slipping and sliding.

"In those days, when there was water on Astroturf, it became very slick. I like to know when I go down and plant hard to break off the planting foot that I can do it, but I didn't feel that. Since then they've refined turf so much that they're probably going to go away from it because it is so injurious."

Herm Harrison agreed with his fellow receiver. "You felt like you were hydroplaning. You just could not get the footing. It was terrible.

"But it was tough for the defense to cover you. The offense had the better chance of getting open because once you made your move you knew where you were going. The defense was struggling to make their move to get to you."

"I don't think there is any question that field conditions had an effect," said Leo Cahill. "I think it really bothered our running backs. It happened on both sides, but defensively speaking, they only had one first down in the second half. Neither team played very well offensively."

Calgary middle linebacker Wayne Harris was named the star of the game. He almost single-handedly prevented Toronto from taking advantage of turnovers and kept them out of the end zone. Toronto's only touchdown was scored by the defense when he wasn't on the field.

An example of Number 55's brilliant play came when the Argos were zero-ing in on the Stampeder goal line early in the second quarter. Expecting the usual man-to-man coverage at the 15-yard line, Theismann called two out patterns that had worked for a touchdown in the Eastern Final. Harris kept Calgary in zone and held the Argos to a field goal.

"That's right," recalled Eben. "When you get in around the 20-yard line, teams should in some commonsense way go into man-to-man coverage because that always allows people, particularly the linebackers, to pick up on otherwise free running backs. It also frees up a linebacker to put added pressure on the quarterback by blitzing."

Eben's recollections of Calgary's Wayne Harris were of a highly personal nature. "I remember getting some deep curls and, despite the depth of the curls, getting really rocked a few times by Wayne Harris. In fact I needed smelling salts one time.

"Come to think of it, he cracked me twice. I figured at that point I would have established a little bit of a record, being the only Czech football player who had been knocked out and revived by smelling salts twice in a Grey Cup game. I figured if I got enough variables in there, it would be a record.

"I was trying to stay behind the linebackers, but Wayne was a very fine player, and he could get back into the drop zones for the center curls. And he got me all right."

Calgary's defense sacked Argo pivot Theismann six times and broke his nose. But even in the face of that kind of pass rush, he uncharacteristically, as Mike Eben explained, didn't throw a single interception that day. "Joe, in his own mind, was utterly invincible. And that's why he threw 900 interceptions that year. I used to know, of course, the defensive backs on the opposition pretty well, and I remember they used to lick their chops when Joe was coming to town.

"But Joe could make things happen. He was a good athlete, but he hadn't come to grips yet with the five defensive backs, the bigger, wider field and the free safety or the middle rover that the Canadian league had.

The 1971 game was the Argo's first Grey Cup defeat since losing to the University of Toronto in 1920. Their last win had been 1952, after which they fell apart. They would fall apart again in 1972 and, after winning the Grey Cup in 1991, they would—to no one's real surprise—fall apart again. The word just *dynasty* wasn't in their vocabulary.

Back to the Wilderness

Over the next 10 years after their Grey Cup defeat the Argos finished last eight times with a record of 51–100–5. They went through 10 head coaches, including Leo Cahill twice. Only seven Argos made All-Canadian during that time. Sam Cvijanovich won the Most Outstanding Rookie Award in 1974 and Jim Corrigal the Outstanding Defensive Player in 1975.

The 1972 season was a nightmare for Cahill. "I felt we had a real chance. But that's when we had all the injuries. Joe Theismann broke his leg in the first game against Montreal. Jimmy Corrigal broke his leg. He was a second-round draft choice of the St. Louis Cardinals. Timmy Anderson broke his leg, and he was the first-round draft choice of the San Francisco 49ers. Three superstars, three broken legs.

"In 1971 I was the Coach of the Year and we went to the Grey Cup, losing by three points when Leon had his fumble. In 1972 I was fired. It was probably the most unfair firing in the history of football because I had taken that team from 13,000 to 31,000 season tickets. We made the play-offs five out of six years and went to the Grey Cup. It just wasn't those three guys who were hurt. We had six regulars out for most of the season.

"Management didn't even give me a chance to turn it around. Hamilton beat us in the final game of the year, knocking us out of the play-offs."

Cahill described how the dastardly deed was done. "I was called into the office at the *Telegram*. John Bassett was the one that finally gave me the ultimate word that I was fired. He acted like he was very upset about it and that it was a very difficult decision that he had to make, but it was really only difficult for me."

He would be back. Cahill was replaced by John Rauch, who, as coach of the Buffalo Bills, used O.J. Simpson as a decoy instead of a running back. Relatively injury free, the Argos challenged Ottawa for first place, settling for second in late October by losing to the Riders 20–19. They then lost the semifinal 32–10 in overtime to Montreal.

By the end of the 1973 season, 24 members of the 1971 team were gone, including Tim Anderson, Charlie Bray, Paul Desjardins, Marv Luster, Leon McQuay, Mel Profit, Joe Theismann, Dick Thornton and Jim Tomlin. Jim Still-wagon left in 1975.

John Rauch was fired after Labour Day in 1974, when the team was 3–4. His replacement, Joe Moss, went 3–5–1 and was also dismissed.

In 1974 Bill Hodgson bought the team from Bassett. The Argos hired the legendary quarterback Russ Jackson as head coach in 1975, signing him to a five-year contract. He lasted two. Jackson's Argos had a record of 5–10–1 in 1975. The following year the team was 7–8–1, the same as Montreal, who got the play-off spot on the basis of a better record against Toronto. Still they were just one point out of second, four out of first. The Alouettes didn't fire Marv Levy when he slipped from 9–7 to 7–8–1, and they won the Grey Cup the next year.

"When I took the job I realized it was a terrific challenge because of the unsuccessful atmosphere that surrounded the organization," Jackson commented in 1976. "That is why I demanded a five-year contract. I wanted time to do something. You can't do it overnight. That's one of the things we kept reminding ourselves: we're not going to turn this thing around overnight.

"A great deal of the Argonaut situation is mental. They used to be thinking, 'How are we going to lose?' rather than 'How are we going to win?' Turning it around is basically a matter of changing the players' attitude to thinking positively about winning.

"I'm a very positive person," Jackson explained. "I've always felt that what I'm doing is the right thing. People have criticized me as a coach. It bothers me. I hate to be criticized, the same as everyone else. I feel that in the long run if we don't do the job, the criticism will be justified. But I hope that when we turn it around, those same people will say we did the right things and turned it around."

He quoted a favorite line of verse: "Too soon we rest the tape, too late we realize the fun was in the running." Jackson smiled and said, "I want to enjoy this running."

He didn't. One of the major distractions for Jackson was the University of California's All-American running back Anthony Davis, another typical Argo big fix, another typical Argo bust. Davis rushed for 417 yards on 104 carries, 196 yards less than Toronto's quarterback Chuck Ealey. He also caught 37 passes for 408 yards and had 701 yards on kickoff returns.

Despite his mediocre performance, Davis insisted on being treated like a superstar. Contrary to the advice of Russ Jackson, management granted his every wish, including his own private trailer for a dressing room.

Jackson was placed in an intolerable position. "Part of what led to Jackson's demise," explained Mike Eben, "was the way the management controlled the Anthony Davis thing. Russ had very little control over that.

"Giving Davis his own trailer? That was a bit overblown, but there was still too much pandering to him. I guess Anthony at the time wasn't mature enough to realize that his behavior was driving a wedge between him and the team. I remember trying to talk to him a little bit about that, but it seemed to fall on deaf ears."

Eben thought Jackson got a raw deal from incompetent management. "Russ knew the nature of the game. He had a good sense of what he was doing, but he just had too much interference from the head office, from Dick Shatto and J.I. Albrecht. Bill Hodgson was an exuberant, enthusiastic owner who should have kept his nose out of it. He didn't know what he was talking about when it came to football.

"I thought Russ got the short end of the stick. After that it was a horror show because management had interference all over the place. They were trading Canadians away—good Canadians like Larry Uteck, Barry Finlay, Wayne Allison, Al Charuk and me.

"It was stupid. They really went nuts then. Part of the reason I got traded to Ottawa was because basically I told J.I. and Shatto that they were fools. The rest of the league was licking its chops as they picked them all up. Ach!" he concluded in disgust. "It was very tiresome."

Still Eben enjoyed his football career. "Being a receiver, you take your licks, but practice was always fun for me. I always enjoyed catching the ball and running patterns.

"The only frustrating times were when we had so many quarterbacks. After Joe left we went through a whole raft of quarterbacks until 1978, when I was finished.

"I always enjoyed it. I had a few injuries but not, in the grand scheme of things, debilitating injuries. I've been able to do a lot of sports since I retired, particularly basketball and tennis."

Leo Cahill returned to the Argos in 1977, picking off the last play-off spot before losing to Ottawa 21–16. The Argos got off to a good start in 1978, winning three of their first four games before losing five straight. After losing 27–2 to Montreal on September 10, Cahill was fired. He would be back. He holds the Argo record for most coaching victories and defeats: 54 each.

Cahill was replaced by Bud Riley, who won one game the rest of the way and was fired. Looking for the big name, the Argos hired two Green Bay Packer greats from the Vince Lombardi era, Forrest Gregg, who went 6–10 in 1979 before returning to the NFL, and then Willie Wood, who was 6–10 in 1980 and 0–10 in the following year when he was dismissed in favor of Tommy Hudspeth, who compiled a record of 2–4 and was not invited back.

Sazio Saves the Day

Carling O'Keefe Breweries, which had bought the Argos in 1979, were fed up with the team's spectacular ineptitude. To fix the problem they looked to hated Hamilton and hired one of the best football brains in the game.

Enter Ralph Sazio. Sazio had been brought to Hamilton as an assistant coach and player in 1950 by his coach at William and Mary, Carl Voyles. Thirteen years later he became head coach, making the play-offs every year and winning three of four Grey Cups. He was the general manager or president of the Ti-Cats from 1968 until six games into the 1981 season, missing the play-offs only twice by a grand total of three points.

He left one of the bulwarks of the CFL to assume command of the Titanic, but he had his reasons. "At that time there was a strong anti-Ballard feeling despite the fact that I felt Mr. Ballard would be the man to give Hamilton whatever their sporting needs were. They were talking about having a new arena and getting a NHL club there, and who could do more for them, in getting the whole thing set up, than Mr. Ballard? That's his franchise area.

"All he was saying was, 'Look, there's a value to this franchise area, and I don't want you to pay me for it, just put the money into a better facility for the football team.'

"That never came about. I was sort of the guy in the middle. I felt a change would be beneficial."

So he didn't leave because of Harold Ballard? "No way. I liked the man. We were good friends. I liked the challenge in Toronto. I was always close by but never knew what the hell went on. As it turned out, it was a mess.

"The whole concept of what the organization was about had to be changed. A football organization should be dedicated to putting a good football team on the field. That should be its number one goal, and everything should be pointed in that direction. But I got the feeling it was the other way around. Other things like social aspects were being stressed more than the football end of it.

"It was funny. Everybody had their own little empire, but no one took any responsibility. So whose fault was it that the team wasn't doing well on the field? That was the least of their worries."

He quickly decided a coaching change had to be made and turned to Bob O'Billovich. "Willie Wood had the great name. He was a nice guy but not the kind of guy who could handle that team. With Bob we wanted a whole new feeling, and it turned out fine.

"I interviewed a hell of a lot of people, most of them more eye-catching than Bob. You'd be surprised at some of the people that I talked to about the head coaching job. But I thought I'd have to get a guy who had a background in the Canadian game.

"Bob approached me directly. He wanted to meet with me face to face and showed enough initiative for me to go ahead and meet with him. We sat down and chitchatted for what seemed like half an hour, but it was actually three and a half hours. He understood the issues I felt were important, and all of a sudden he went up in my estimation.

"I didn't make up my mind right away because Bob's not the most impressive guy when you first see him. But when you get to talking to him, you find out that this guy's head is screwed on right.

"I finally cut the shortlist down to five people. I brought O'Billovich back and met with him a final time. We had too much to do in Toronto not to go after a guy who had his experience as a player and coach in this league. As it was, we were going to have so many new people. I had to bring in new coaches, a new office staff and new players. I was in a tough position.

"Bob's ideas, Bob's value of Canadian players — things like that made us hit it off together. I felt I could work with him, and he was willing to work with me, which was important.

"We made a lot of changes, we cleaned house."

Bob O'Billovich explained why he thought he got the top job. "They had been hiring high-profile American guys. It used to take American coaches a year or two to understand our game, and by that time management would either trade away the Argos' draft picks or cut good Canadians that they should have kept. That and my background in the league were the kind of things that sold him.

"But what happened was that when I finally went down and interviewed with him, he told me he would call me after Christmas and let me know definitely one way or the other. From what we had discussed, it looked pretty promising and he just had one more guy to interview before he would get back to me. He called me a day earlier than I thought he would.

"When I answered the phone that day, he said, 'Well, you've got the job.' I thought it was one of my buddies, so I said, 'Stop screwing around.' And he said, 'Do you want the job or not?' I said, 'Yes, I sure do want the job.' And he said, 'Well, it's yours if you want it.' I said, 'Okay, I'll be there.'"

O'Billovich enjoyed working with Sazio. "We were both very disciplined and organized guys. We were both very competitive. We hated to lose. Once we got to become partners, I think we complemented each other. He was a great resource guy for me as a young head coach because he had been in the league as a head coach and knew the league as well as he did."

Fixing the Argonauts was a task akin to cleaning out the Augean stables. The team had missed the play-offs four years in a row. They were 2–14 in 1981, averaging 15 points per game on offense while giving up 31.6. They were last in total offense, despite talented players like Condredge Holloway, Cedric Minter, Paul Pearson, Peter Muller, Jan Carinci and Terry Greer. Defensively they also were a disaster, giving up the most points and yards while having the fewest interceptions and the second lowest number of quarterback sacks. The good news was that the rest of the Eastern Conference was just about as bad.

O'Billovich said, "I felt we really had to improve our Canadian content. Toronto had given up a lot of good players over the years, or the rights to them, with trades.

"I was fortunate the year I went in there. Toronto had four first-round picks from previous deals. That first draft was one of the key things that helped us rebuild our Canadian content. We had our two protected players and four first-rounders. I think of all those guys we picked in that draft, only one guy didn't pan out.

"We protected Steve Del Col, who was a defensive end, and Geoff Townsend. Then we drafted Greg Holmes, Tony Antunovic and Mike Kirkland. Our last first-round pick was Chris Schultz. It was a heck of a draft for us. Then we acquired Don Moen in a trade with B.C."

O'Billovich learned from a legend. "Frank Clair used to always say that you had to get a quarterback first and then build your defense and fill in around those two things to get your team solid. We had Holloway, but we felt we needed two quarterbacks, so we made the trade with Saskatchewan for Joe Barnes.

"It was a funny situation because our whole defense had to be rebuilt. When we evaluated our defense, Dennis Meyer, our secondary coach, rated Marcellus Greene as our best defensive back. Out of all the defensive guys we had, he was the only one we would have kept. So Dennis came in and gave me his report and I said, 'You don't have to worry about Green anymore because I just sent him to Saskatchewan.'"

Another key addition was Darrell "Mouse" Davis as offensive coordinator. He had introduced the run-and-shoot offense to the CFL. Veteran coach and scout Bud Riley explained how it works. "The quarterback has different reads on the defenses. Overloading is really what happens when receivers have optional routes to run on the offense. It depends on what they and the quarterback read. Essentially the offense is trying to overload or flood an area all the time."

The run-and-shoot allowed O'Billovich to make the best use of his personnel and overcome the lack of experience on his offensive line. In 1982 the Argos went from last place to first. They defeated Ottawa 44–7 in the Eastern Final before losing to Edmonton in the Grey Cup 32–16. Condredge Holloway won the Most Outstanding Player Award and O'Billovich was named Coach of the Year.

The Argos led the East in points with 426 and were second only to Edmonton in total offense. They gave up the fewest sacks in the league.

Even O'Billovich was surprised. "It wasn't something that ordinarily happens. We went from the worst record in the league to first place in the East and into the Grey Cup in that first year. I think we utilized the people we had really well. For example, we made Holloway a better quarterback by the kind of offense we instituted. We better utilized guys like Terry Greer and Paul Pearson. We really got a lot out of Cedric Minter although he was the Eastern Finalist for the rookie award the year before."

The Grey Cup challenge facing the upstart Argos in 1982 was insurmountable. Still Toronto scored the first touchdown of the game when Condredge Holloway hit Emanuel Tolbert for an 84-yard pass and run. It was the first offensive Grey Cup major the Argos had scored in 30 years.

Hogtown hopes were raised when Holloway threw to Terry Greer for a 10-yard touchdown, giving the locals a 14–10 lead. All they could muster thereafter was a safety touch.

O'Billovich explained the loss. "The Eskimos were a better football team, but we played them pretty even the first half. The weather did come into play in the second half. They had a much better offensive line, and they could run the ball with Germany and Lumsden better than we could at that time. When the weather got bad, that, along with Warren Moon's ability to run, made them tougher.

"There was a big controversial play in the second half, when Cedric Minter had caught a ball out in the flat and was running up the field. He got hit, the ball came out and the officials called it a fumble. Whatever it was, Edmonton got the turnover. We didn't think it was a fumble.

"That was it. We were moving the ball and they got it. From that point on, we never seemed to be able to get back into the game."

Delighted to be taking part in a Grey Cup game was a hometown boy, second-year Sculler Dan Ferrone. Offensive lineman Ferrone played his college football at Simon Fraser, but was a Toronto territorial draft exemption in 1981. He played for the Argos from 1981–88, for Calgary in 1989 and again for Toronto from 1990–92. He went on to become the president of the CFL Players' Association.

During his distinguished career he was All-Canadian five times and a Conference All-Star nine times. He was Toronto's nominee for Outstanding Offensive Lineman on eight occasions and came second in Schenley voting twice.

Playing in his first Grey Cup at home was an unforgettable experience. "We went from the worst record ever in the history of the Toronto Argonauts, 2–14, and the next year we were going into the Grey Cup against the four-time Grey Cup champion Edmonton Eskimos. I remember the beginning of the game with the jets going over. I remember the place being jam-packed. I also remember it was cold, wet, rainy.

"I think weather has an impact on the team, depending on whether you're winning or losing. When I would reminisce about the '82 Grey Cup, I would mention how cold and wet it was, but when I talked to the Edmonton guys we played against, they didn't remember it at all.

"In 1991 in Winnipeg I remember the drinks freezing up. I remember having to cut my visor off because it was so fogged up from ice on the inside. That was how cold it was. They said it hit minus 27 degrees or something like that.

"But the day after, when people would say how cold it was, I said, 'Well, you know, it wasn't too bad actually.' But if you talked to anybody who was on Calgary, they were saying, 'Man, it was the coldest day ever.' I think weather takes its toll on you when you're not doing well and everyone seems to be down on you."

Hammerin' Hank

Although the Argo's offense had shown dramatic improvement by 1982, defense was another matter. "We didn't sit still," said Ralph Sazio. "We didn't say, 'Okay, we had a good year, we surprised a lot of people, so consequently let's stand pat.' We made changes in the area we felt we needed to, and that was defense. Our offense remained intact, but when you score 426 points and have 426 points against you, you'd better smarten up."

And smarten up they did, taking advantage of errors in judgment by other teams. O'Billovich and Sazio replaced 9 of the 12 defensive starters at the end of the 1982 season. O'Billovich reacquired Marcellus Greene from Saskatchewan as well as Roughrider defensive back Ken McEachern. He picked up linebacker Bill Mitchell from Ottawa, who mistakenly put him on waivers twice. Defensive linemen Franklin King had been cut by Calgary, James Curry by B.C. and Matthew Teague and Carl Brazely by Ottawa. Rookie middle linebacker Darrell Nicholson played so well he made the All-Star team.

Sazio made one more important acquisition. "What we missed most in 1982 was a good punter. That's when I got hold of Norm Kimball. Kimball was trying to move Hank Ilesic, and we paid the price of a pretty good back to get him. He made the difference in the 1983 Grey Cup. Time and again he took us out of trouble. He had a hell of a punting average. I mean, it wasn't 5 or 10 yards, it was 20–30 yards difference on punting exchanges."

Although only 23 years old, Ilesic was a six-year veteran when he joined the Argos. He had been All-Canadian four years in a row. "I was 17 years old when I began my career with the Eskimos while at the same time attending St. Joesph's Composite High School," he explained.

His youth, however, did not present problems fitting into the team. "I had a lot of idols on that club. They were very patient and good with me. Possibly with another team it would have been difficult. If there are a lot of people uptight or insecure about their positions, they don't have time to try to bring you along or teach you the right ways. With Edmonton being a veteran ball club, that didn't happen. The players went out of their way to make me feel a part of the team."

In 1982 Ilesic and Norm Kimball had a falling out. "I had a difficult time in Edmonton with my contract situation. It got to be pretty dirty. By coming to Toronto I could start all over again. I was very fortunate that, because of my age, I had a second chance."

Every time the Argos played in his hometown, he was unmercifully booed. "It is something you learn to accept, but the more they booed the more pumped up I got," he concluded.

As an Argo, Ilesic was All-Canadian another four times. He holds Grey Cup records for most punts and punting yardage and is tied with five others for most games played—nine. He holds every Argo punting record but two.

The Argos breezed through the 1983 regular season with 12 wins, a surprising record considering that Mouse Davis quit during training camp, Holloway injured his hand twice, Cedric Minter missed two games and superb blocking back Bob Bronk sustained a season-ending injury in August.

No Eastern team had ever won 12 games before. Toronto's consecutive first-place finishes were the first for the club since 1937–38 and the first back-to-back Grey Cup appearances since the 1950s. But their best season ever was almost ruined by 5–10–1 Hamilton, who advanced to the Eastern Final with a narrow 33–31 win over Ottawa. Trailing by 10 points going into the fourth quarter, the Argos pulled it out with only 27 seconds left, when Cedric Minter scored the winning touchdown. The final score was 41–36.

Toronto's opponent in the Grey Cup would be the Lions, playing at home in their brand new dome, B.C. Place, referred to by Jack Gotta as the Big Tent. The Leos, led by Don Matthews in his first year of an illustrious career as a head coach, were the best in the West in points for and against, percentage completion and sacks. Defensively they surrendered the fewest points and yards in the league. They had one less win than the Argos.

Both teams were hungry. Toronto hadn't won since 1952, B.C. since 1964. The Argos had won both regular season match-ups. Dan Ferrone recalled that you could cut the tension in the Argo camp with a knife. "The day before, in our last practice, I thought maybe we had a chance to win it. But we were fighting like crazy. It was ridiculous. Earl Wilson, a defensive lineman, and our fullback, John Palazeti, had a big fight. Everybody was fighting. Cedric Minter was fighting. Everyone was fighting Wilson. James Curry was there. I remember getting into a fight with him.

"After the practice we pulled everybody into the middle of the field. All the coaches were told to leave, and we talked about what we had to do: quit fighting each other and get ready to fight the other team. It was getting ugly. Everybody was really on edge."

How Sweet It Is

The next day the Argos found themselves down 17–7 at the half. Merv Fernandez and John Henry White tallied majors for the Lions with Passaglia adding converts and a field goal.

The Argos only scoring occurred when Jan Carinci took a pass from Holloway and worked his way 14 yards to the end zone. Hank Ilesic missed three field goals. Coach O'Billovich was not amused. "I finally said to Ilesic after he missed the third one, 'Hank, you've got to start making some of those. We're going to need those points.' He said, 'Don't worry, coach. I'll make it when it counts.'

"Sure enough, late in the fourth quarter he made a 44-yarder that was the key kick. If he had made the ones he should have made, the game never would have been that close."

Ferrone also talked to the young Argo kicker. "He was feeling bad. I wanted to cheer him up. There were a lot of Shank jokes told afterward. If we had lost he would have felt a lot worse even though I'm sure he recognized that we don't win or lose because of him and it's definitely a 60-minute game."

Ferrone recalled what happened in the dressing room at half time. "I remember being so tired. I couldn't breathe. There's no oxygen in that damn place when it's full. I was trying to stay cool.

"We had missed so many chances that we didn't feel we were out of the game. We were more frustrated with what *we* had done more than with what the Lions were doing.

"Coach Obie always made sure everybody focused just before we went out. He gave you time to do whatever you had to do and then just before we were going out, he would talk to everybody and go through the drill about what we had to accomplish, what we had to execute, and we'd just go like that."

O'Billovich changed quarterbacks for the second half. "B.C. had done a great job of defensing us in the first half," he said. "They were doing some overloads, and they were keying the flow of our fullback. They were well prepared for our offense and the stuff that Holloway did really well.

"In the second half we went to the more conventional stuff, more misdirectional stuff, bootlegs and sprint-outs that Joe Barnes was good at. We ran the ball a little more. Those adjustments got our offense into gear in the second half. Joe came in and got us going."

Ferrone had another explanation for the change. "Condredge was sick. A lot of people were sick going into that 1983 Grey Cup. Joe and Condredge were always a good pair. One's strengths were the other's weaknesses and vice-versa. The way the Lions were playing, and the way Connie was feeling, he wasn't able to get things going.

"Joe was running more straight drop-back stuff, and the Lions were still waiting for our quarterback to roll one way or another. That started opening up our running game for Cedric Minter, and suddenly everything started to come together.

"By the same token the whole time Connie was in there, we had moved the ball quite a bit, but Hank Ilesic missed three field goals. That had an impact on Condredge as well. We were coming away with no points when we were going for field goals with the Shank."

In the second half Ilesic closed the gap to five points with a field goal and two singles. With four minutes remaining in regulation time, Toronto was second and 6 at the B.C. 53. Barnes threw to Paul Pearson over the middle. When he was tackled the ball flew out of his hands. The Argos' Emanuel Tolbert picked it off without missing a beat. Three passes later Barnes hit Cedric Minter for a 3-yard touchdown.

The 2-point conversion attempt failed, but the defense held for the last 2 minutes and 45 seconds. Final score: Toronto 18, B.C. 17. The 31-year drought was over.

Joe Barnes won the Player of the Game Award, but in reality either the defense or Hank Ilesic deserved the credit for the Argo's eleventh Grey Cup. The defense shut the Lions out in the second half. Adam Rita, a Lions' assistant coach, explained how that happened. "They played more deep zone. We were a deep-ball team, and they did a good job against us. Our defense played well, too, but it became a kicking duel. They kept us pinned down with Hank's kicks, and we were having difficulty moving the football."

"A score of 18–17 doesn't say a whole lot for either offense," said O'Billovich. "Both defenses were paramount. They both controlled the game. The key thing that contributed to our defense being so good was the punting of Ilesic in the second half. That helped give our defense really good field position and kept the Lions in their end."

Obie also singled out defensive back Carl Brazely for special praise. "He was picked the defensive player of the game. He was one of the better people I've ever coached. I had recruited Carl when I was in Ottawa in '81, when we needed a corner. He had been with Montreal but had left their camp. He got disenchanted with things when they brought in Ferragamo and all those guys. Carl was doing everything: returning punts, kickoffs, starting at DB. He just got turned off, and they ended up letting him go. So I talked him into coming to

Ottawa. He left Ottawa in '83 and tried out with San Diego and didn't make it. I got him to come to Toronto."

In the Grey Cup, Brazely returned nine punts for 58 yards, three kickoffs for 82 yards, made six tackles, recovered a fumble and intercepted a pass. When, in 1994, O'Billovich was asked to pick an all-time Argo team, Brazely was one of the defensive backs.

Though the Argos won the game, the tremendous noise inside B.C. Place gave new meaning to the term *home-field advantage*. O'Billovich came up with an ingenious solution to the problem. "I had our marketing guy, Dave Watkins, make a tape of crowd noise. Whenever we were getting ready to play B.C., I'd play that crowd noise tape so our players were used to signaling and to the quarterbacks yelling out the plays and the audibles so when we went out to Vancouver it wasn't that big a deal.

"The noise in '83 was more of a factor than in '87 because B.C. was the home team and they had Crazy George. They used to get pumped up. The only way to keep that crowd out of it was to quiet them down early by getting some points."

Tackle Dan Ferrone agreed. "Obie used to drive us crazy with it. He used to put us into Lamport Stadium and play this grinding sound through speakers. You had to do your cadences in that noise.

"We didn't hear the quarterback calling the cadence or anything. We'd go the same as the defense was going. On the movement of the ball, everybody would go. The noise has a big impact in B.C. Place."

Said Danny Bass, "You learn to play with the noise. We did certain things like going to Clarke Stadium and turning on speakers. You use different hand signals. It's good to prepare for crowd noise because it is amazing how much it takes out of you when you have to yell up and down the line of scrimmage, how much energy that takes, and even then some guys just don't hear."

The win in 1983 was extra special for Ferrone because, he said, "Doug Mitchell was the commissioner. I'm coming off the field and saw Ralph Sazio and Mitchell. Out of the blue I hear Mitchell say, 'Who do you want me to present the Cup to?' Ralph just looks up and says, 'Give it to Ferrone, right there.' I go, 'What?'

"So they presented me with the trophy. I only held it for like two seconds before Curry had climbed on the platform and took it for the rest of the evening, which was great. Ralph always had a soft spot for me, I thought. Twice we won the Grey Cup; twice I was presented with it. That was phenomenal."

The Beginning of the End

The 1983 Grey Cup recaptured the national imagination. Canadians from every part of the country pouring into Vancouver to revel long into the night, to watch a match-up between two entertaining football teams and to see the eighth wonder of the world, B.C. Place.

It rained buckets Thursday of Grey Cup week and again Saturday. Despite the rain the hordes of visitors celebrated unabated. On Friday evening thousands jammed Georgia Street near the hotel of the same name and the stately Hotel Vancouver. Singing the B.C. Lion fight song or shouting "ARRR–GOS," the fans good-naturedly roamed the streets, packed the bars but generally behaved themselves.

Hospitality suites for media, corporate sponsors and fans were an attractive part of Grey Cup week. Each team had a suite, as did the Schenley Corporation. The highlight of the week was the party in the Schenley suite on awards night. Football and media people from all over the country joined the Schenley trustees along with the hosts, Ray Boucher and Gordie Walker, in celebration. One of the most popular was the hospitality suite of IPSCO, the Interprovincial Steel Company, hosted by legends Eagle Keys and Jackie Parker. Great Grey Cup tales were told into the small hours of the morning.

The 1983 Grey Cup was the beginning of the end of the Grey Cup festival in Canada's largest cities. The celebration that year was so great because the six-year Western Conference reign of the Edmonton Eskimos was over. People from the other Western cities had grown tired of the Eskimos consistently being in the Grey Cup and had stopped going to the big game in November. Now they were excited about B.C. competing against Toronto and didn't want to miss the festivities.

Two years later, when the game was played for the last time in Montreal, the city was indifferent to the whole affair. Vancouver in 1986 was no better, partly because of the hostility of the locals to the Eskimos.

The mid-1980s saw the dawn break on the darkest period in the history of the Canadian Football League. The Calgary Stampeders almost went under while the Alouettes did. Mirroring the economic distress every other sector of the Canadian economy was experiencing, all CFL franchises fell on hard times. The team hospitality suites were closed. IPSCO was no more when Jackie Parker took over the reins of the Eskimos and Eagle Keys retired. Schenley dropped the awards.

But the game's the thing. And when Toronto returned to the national classic four years later, the CFL was in desperate need of a marvelous performance. They got it.

When the Alouettes folded, they were replaced in the Eastern division by the Winnipeg Blue Bombers. The Boatmen and Bombers battled to the regular season wire with the Westerners finishing first in the East with a record of 12–6, one point ahead of the 11–5–1 Argonauts.

After polishing off the Ti-Cats 29–13, the Argos went to Winnipeg Stadium for the Eastern Final. The Bombers had lost a grand total of three home games in four years, but they were no match for the Argos that day, losing 19–3.

Argo coach O'Billovich was proud. "I think our '87 win in Winnipeg in the Eastern Final was one of the best wins we ever had against a heck of a football team. They had Tom Clements, Willard Reaves and James Murphy on offense and a great defense. We beat them in their own backyard. They didn't even score a touchdown on us.

"We went into Winnipeg that year, and Delbert Fowler, James West and Tyrone Jones were so mouthy. I used to call them the three magpies. They were mouthing off going into the game that our linebackers couldn't hold a candle to any of theirs. We had Doug Landry, Willie Pless and Donny Moen. When those guys from Winnipeg made that statement, that just added fuel to our fire. Doug Landry played probably the best game of any person on the field that day and, boy, they had to eat their words, I'll tell you."

Going into the 1987 Grey Cup, the Eskimos were favored despite O'Billovich's three first-place finishes, two Grey Cup berths and the Argos' only national championship since 1952. His record of 57–40–3 was the best in Argo history. Going into the game in Vancouver, Obie's Argos had won eight of their last nine games.

The Argos' record was remarkable considering that they started the year with no real experience at quarterback. New General Manager Leo Cahill traded for Gilbert Renfroe of Ottawa to go with rookie John Congemi and Danny Barrett, who rendered yeoman service when the other two were injured. Also, there were eight newcomers each on offense and defense.

Running back Gill Fenerty won the Rookie of the Year Award and Ian Beckstead was runner-up for Outstanding Offensive Lineman. O'Billovich won his second Coach of the Year Award. The Argos had a lot going for them in that 1987 Grey Cup game. What they didn't have was luck.

The 1983 Argos were able to overcome three missed field goals and win by a single point. This time Lance Chomyc missed three field goals and the Argos lost by two. Not only would the field goals have meant nine more points for the Scullers, the most dramatic play of the game, a 115-yard Henry Williams return for a touchdown, wouldn't have happened.

O'Billovich groaned when he recalled what happened. "Chomyc missed that field goal by about two inches. It was so close to being good it wasn't even funny. I hate a long field-goal attempt because it is the toughest thing in the world to cover. When you kick one and miss, you hold your breath because you just don't have a lot of guys getting down there to cover, and in most cases a lot of those guys are offensive linemen who aren't really good tacklers. You usually put some defensive guys on the line to have better coverage going down.

"Donny Moen was the only guy who really had a shot at Gizmo at about the 5-yard line, when Gizmo made a quick cut. Donny lunged at him but couldn't get him. Gill Fenerty didn't get his outside containment, which didn't help the situation. The holder, Danny Barrett, just didn't get over with our safety guys.

"Actually Chomyc chased Williams all the way to the other end and did tackle him as he crossed the goal line. That said a lot for Lance's effort. Gizmo's not the easiest guy in the world to catch, but he'd run 115 yards and was a little tired by then."

Faster than a speeding bullet? A fair description of Gizmo according to Dan Ferrone. "He slipped by me so fast I didn't even see him. The kick went wide and maybe 5–10 yards in the end zone. We didn't think he was going to run it out. I think everybody just casually started walking away, thinking he was going to give up the single point.

"But once he got started, he kept going. I remember him starting to go to the right side of the field, and I tried to pick an angle of pursuit. I should have intercepted him within 10 yards, but I missed him by 20. He just ran by and went pretty much untouched. I think it was partly a case of us forgetting who was back there catching the ball."

No blocks were thrown explained Edmonton's Danny Bass. "You don't want to take a chance on making a block because when you do, sometimes you'll clip a guy. With Gizmo's speed and talent, you try to help him out as much as you can without hurting him, and then you let him do the rest.

"When a team attempts a field goal, that is the best situation for the defense because they've got offensive linemen out there and they just don't cover the field as well. They're not used to being in that range, not used to spreading out. If you're prepared you have a chance for a big return. Gizmo was, and he took it all the way."

Early in the second quarter, with the score 10–3, the Argos' Gilbert Renfroe teamed up with Gill Fenerty on a sensational 61-yard pass and run for a touchdown to even the score. Fenerty gave Ferrone cause for concern. "Fenerty won the Rookie of the Year Award. We were telling him about Terry Greer winning the Schenley in '82 and how we lost the Grey Cup, the omen being that if Fenerty loses we could win the Grey Cup again, but he won.

"Not that I'm superstitious, but the next morning I thought, 'Oh no, here we go. He's probably going to have a bad game or something like that.' Well, I think it was the second or third play and this guy broke one right away. Bang, he's 40 or 50 yards down the field. I thought, 'All right! Here we go!' He was running the ball great. Fenerty did a tremendous job. Then we started to move away from running the ball to passing it."

A few minutes later Fenerty scored again, set up by a Darnell Clash interception. Shortly after, Glen Kulka knocked the ball loose from Dunigan, Landry picked it up and went 54 yards for a touchdown. With the first half nearly over, the Argos were firmly in command, leading 24–10 with Mr. Momentum wearing the double blue.

Unfortunately for the Argonauts, Lady Luck was dressed in green and gold. Stanley Blair blocked an Ilesic punt. Edmonton moved 40 yards to the end zone in three plays. "Hank Ilesic dropped the goldang ball right before the half," Obie moaned. "We were punting from about our own 40. If he had kicked the ball, we would have gone into half time with a two-touchdown lead. I always said offense sells tickets, defense wins games and special teams win championships. That game was a good example."

The Eskimo touchdown near the end of the half was engineered by Damon Allen, a sign of things to come. Before Matt Dunigan was knocked out of the game, he had been ineffective. The injury to the Edmonton quarterback was, in reality, a break for the Eskimos.

On the other hand, Gilbert Renfroe was playing very well, but he went down in the third quarter. "When Dunigan was knocked out of the game, he wasn't playing very well against us," said O'Billovich. "We had complete control of the ball game. Gilbert Renfroe was having a heck of a game for us, and then he got hurt early in the third quarter. Actually our own guy fell on his knee. We then had a drop-off. When Danny Barrett came in, he didn't play all that badly, but Gilbert had had such a hot hand that we were really clicking."

Argo linebacker Willie Pless disagreed. "It didn't really hurt us because Danny Barrett came in and picked up exactly where Renfroe left off. He did an outstanding job and got some points on the board. He moved the ball. We just came up short."

Said Ferrone, "Dunigan was having a bad game. That was a thing chasing Dunigan then—that he couldn't win the big one. Damon Allen changed the play of the game. He was breaking outside all the time. They were starting to move the ball and control it, which they hadn't done all game long.

"I remember Allen running out of bounds, running out of bounds. They were always going to the left, Allen and Milson Jones. They had one of the best games I've ever seen them play. Those two gave them the momentum, and they took it from that point on."

O'Billovich agreed on the importance of Milson Jones. "The guy who made the big play for Edmonton was Milson Jones. We had him tackled behind the line of scrimmage on a screen pass, and Don Moen and Doug Landry knocked each other off. They both hit Milson. He had strong legs, broke their tackle and got Edmonton into position to kick the field goal. Otherwise they would have been back on their side of the field. They would have had to decide to gamble on third and 10 or punt. With so little time left, they probably would have gone for it. That was the big play of the game. Jones played really well."

Even after Jerry Kauric kicked the go-ahead field goal, the Argos still had a chance. This time, Obie recalled, mistakes, not Lady Luck, did them in. "After Edmonton kicked that 50-yarder to take the lead, there were 25 seconds to go. They kicked off to us, Dwight Edwards returned it and all he had to do was step out of bounds at the 45 to conserve some time. Instead he got over to the sideline right by us and then reversed his field to try to get across to the other side and make a play. All he did was run off about 8 or 9 more seconds on the clock.

"On that last series Danny Barrett hit Paul Pearson right in the chest, and he couldn't hold on to it on a third-down play that would have given us a first down on Edmonton's side of the field. If we had kept that going, we would have had a chance at a field goal."

The loss was Dan Ferrone's toughest. "We just annihilated the teams going into the play-offs, and then in the Grey Cup we took control early. We were scoring, and we led for most of the game. And then for Kauric to kick that far—I just didn't think he was going to do it. He was gone right after. I hold that against him. If he had gone on to have a great career, you could understand, but the one time he had to have a great game, it was that one."

O'Billovich agreed that Kaurich didn't do much after the Grey Cup defeat. "No, but that was enough," he said. "He took a ring away from us."

Cahill and Obie Take Their Leave

The Argos had their best record ever in 1988, finishing first at 14–4. They led the league in points with 571 and surrendered the least at 326. They were number one in first downs, total offense, passing yards, percentage completion, punting and the giveaway–takeaway category.

Six Boatmen made All-Canadian, 11 made All-Eastern. Gilbert Renfroe led the CFL in passing. Playing only 12 games, Gill Fenerty was still second in rushing and an All-Canadian. But turnabout is fair play, and Winnipeg defeated Toronto 27–11 and went on to win the Grey Cup.

Toward the end of the season, Carling O'Keefe sold the Argos to Harry Ornest. A casualty of the ownership change was Leo Cahill. Ralph Sazio fired him. "Sazio was really something with me," spat Cahill. "They brought me there as general manager. I thought it would be very difficult ever being associated with them again, but I happened to have breakfast with him one morning, and he presented me with the idea of being the general manager of the Argonauts.

"They brought me there as general manager, and I thought that I'd earned the right to finally be the general manager and finish my career in Toronto. Then Harry Ornest came in there and bought the team for a gum wrapper. The first thing Sazio did was talk Harry Ornest into not rehiring me. Sazio never wanted me there in the first place. He was very insincere with me. He was forced to hire me by Carling. Johnny Bassett, God rest his soul, told me about a month before I got hired back with the Argonauts that when the CEO of Carling O'Keefe called and said, 'Johnny, what about bringing Leo back to the Argonauts?' he said, 'I told him he'd save your season tickets.' And he said, 'Well, that's good enough for us.'

"And so about a week or 10 days later I got a call from Sazio saying that it was his idea to bring me back, that he wanted me there and that I was going to take over for him because he was going to retire and all that kind of stuff.

"I wasn't there one month when we had some kind of disagreement on a personnel situation and he turned to me and said, 'Why don't you quit?' He didn't want me there."

During Cahill's tenure in the front office, the Argos were 25–10–1 with a Grey Cup appearance and first-place finish. He wouldn't be back.

The injury bug hit in 1989, the Argos fell to 7–11 and Bob O'Billovich lost his job. Fenerty, Renfroe and Pless left. Tank Landry was traded to Calgary in 1988. He starred there in 1989 before finishing his CFL career with the Lions in 1990.

The Pinball

O'Billovich was replaced in Toronto by Don Matthews. The Argos went from 7–11 to 10–8 and second place. They knocked off Ottawa 35–24 in the semifinal before bowing to the Blue Bombers 20–17. They scored a record 689 points, finishing second in total offense. Michael "Pinball" Clemons gained an amazing 44 percent of it, 3,300 yards, setting a CFL record for most combined yards in a season. A multitalented athlete, Clemons had 519 yards rushing, 905 receiving, 1,045 on punt returns and 831 yards on kickoff returns, a true triple-threat running back. The 5'6" 170-pound phenom was named the 1990 CFL Most Outstanding Player.

Were it not for a quarterback's wonky knee, the Pinball would have been a Stampeder. "I was supposed to go to Calgary in 1989," he explained. "They had my rights. For some reason I wasn't coming to training camp on time. The day before they had scrimmaged and quarterback Erik Kramer had torn up his knee.

"They called me and said they wouldn't be able to bring me in because they were going to have to sign another quarterback. When I went over the waiver wire, Ralph Sazio picked me up. He was a graduate of William and Mary, just as I am, and he knew about me."

Clemons was so good that in just nine seasons he became the CFL's all-time combined yardage leader with 21,266 yards. "You can't really predict a season like 1990, but it didn't come as a surprise," Clemons said. "I've always been an all-purpose type back. When I'm allowed to do several things, it suits my style."

Clemons flourished under the coaching of Don Matthews and Adam Rita. "Don and I saw him on film and we really liked his quickness," said Matthews. "We liked him better than Gill Fenerty in other areas, so basically we decided he was going to be our guy. Anybody who came to camp had to beat him out.

"The hardest thing in the CFL is to find out what talent you have. Given the guys you choose, what can they do? The quicker you can find their talents, the quicker you stay away from the things they can't do.

"With Pinball at 5'6" and 170 pounds, I wasn't about to have him stay in the backfield to block. We used him out of the backfield, and he set all kinds of records. He was an excellent player, and I wasn't about to stop him playing because he didn't have the size. He offered us too much in other areas. Even though he had never been a starter, we made him a starter."

Clemon's greatest satisfaction is being part of a group pulling together to achieve a goal. "The team concept is a microcosm of society," he said. "None of us is perfect. There has never been a perfect game played. What makes football so great is that you take something that is so imperfect and make it work to a successful outcome. You know you and your buddies aren't going to do everything right, but if you work together and have that *esprit de corps*, you can reach your goal. That is the beauty of the game."

Because of a disagreement with General Manager Mike McCarthy, Don Matthews left the Argos after only one season to coach Orlando in the World League of American Football. He was succeeded by assistant Adam Rita.

Magic Moments

Matthews left a team on the verge of winning it all. His most important acquisition had been quarterback Matt Dunigan, acquired in a six-for-one deal with the Lions. Dunigan came east in exchange for DT Jerald Baylis, LB Willie Pless, QB Rick Johnson, LB Tony Visco, SB Emanuel Tolbert and DB Todd Wiseman.

Dunigan was both shocked and relieved. "That trade totally caught me off guard," he said. "I thought I was going to be in B.C. for the duration of my career. When Kuharich and Kapp came in, it was a very volatile, ugly situation that I was pleased to get out of."

The most exciting off-season news in Argo history came in February 1991 when it was announced that Bruce McNall, Wayne Gretzky and John Candy had bought the team. News coverage of the Argos went from the lingerie ads to the front page overnight.

The new owners possessed a deft marketing touch, something the tight-fisted Harry Ornest didn't believe in. Soon after buying the club, McNall negotiated a cable TV deal in the United States. John Candy toured all CFL training camps to promote the league and made most Argo road trips. His sideline presence sold thousands of tickets in every stadium in the league.

Understanding Torontonian's hunger for big league status, the new owners signed the NFL's projected top draft pick, Notre Dame's Raghib "Rocket" Ismail to a contract estimated at between $18 and $26 million. When the Argos opened their 1991 rookie training camp, a large tent was erected for a press conference with Gretzky, Candy, McNall and the Rocket. The setting was appropriate to kickoff a year-long three-ring circus that was just the tonic a weary league needed to revive its sagging fortunes. Their pizzazz was also vital to Toronto because winning wasn't enough to attract fans to SkyDome. Bob O'Billovich and Ralph Sazio had restored the Argo winning tradition, but the crowds continued to dwindle.

Over 41,000 fans turned up at SkyDome on July 18 to see a glittering array of Hollywood personalities and the launching of the Rocket. He didn't disappoint, picking up 213 yards overall as Toronto won their home-opener over Hamilton 41–18. They wouldn't taste defeat under the Dome for another 370 days.

The 1991 edition of the Toronto Argos finished first with a record of 13–5, despite the fact that quarterback Matt Dunigan was hurt in the home-opener and missed 10 games. Clemons missed seven.

With backup Rickey Foggie at the controls for most of the season, the Argos were second to Edmonton in scoring with 647 points but only fifth in total offense. Because of their dazzling special teams, they didn't have to go far to score.

The Rocket Man picked up 3,049 all-purpose yards, the third highest total in CFL history, including 1,300 yards on 64 pass receptions. He made All-Canadian but lost the Outstanding Rookie Award to B.C.'s Jon Volpe, who picked up 1,077 fewer yards.

Given that Michael Clemons had just won the Outstanding Player Award, it would have only been natural for him to resent rookie Pinball Clemons' instant star status and hefty paycheck. Such was not the case. "The Rocket is a great guy, a great talent," enthused the Pinball. "He adds so much to our team not only in publicity but in the spark he provides. He is a quality athlete. Rocket is a great person, a magnetic personality who is fun to be around."

Head Coach Adam Rita rated the Rocket. "He was great. Rocket was only the third person in football history to gain over 3,000 yards in one season. If you measure production, there are only two other people, Pinball and Rufus Craw-ford, who did what he did.

"We did a lot of things with him. He played running back, quarterback and receiver. He was on the punt return team, block team, kickoff return team. I loved working with him. He was a fun guy. He worked hard when he was out there on the field. That was his only refuge from all the bull crap around him."

But Team Captain Dan Ferrone saw things differently. "We had a lot of problems with the Rocket. I tried to talk to him, telling him that he couldn't miss practices like he did, but the coaches would come down and say that's not your job, leave it alone.

"Well, okay, if it's not one of the player's jobs, then it is your job as a coach and you aren't doing anything. This guy is wreaking havoc on the team by not showing up. We are trying to develop a whole offense around him, but he's not there for practices. Come on. Where do you get off doing this? People started to take sides as far as management and Rocket and the players were concerned. Those things created problems.

"In most cases, as the captain, it's expected of you to go and talk to guys who get out of line. There is an expectation that you try to see what you can do.

"I was very disappointed in the attitude the Rocket would take. But when you're told that is none of your business, then you go off and say okay. But that takes a further toll on the athlete in his relationship with the rest of the team."

Apart from problems with the Rocket, the Argos had a tough pass defense, giving up the fewest yards and making the most interceptions. They surrendered the fewest touchdown passes. A mainstay was Canadian linebacker Don Moen.

Moen came to the Argos in 1982. He logged 198 straight regular season con-tests before getting hurt in the tenth game of the 1993 season. He appeared in 12 play-off games and four Grey Cups. Although an Eastern All-Star only once, he was honored in his own land: Moen was the Argo nominee for Outstanding Canadian six times.

Moen starred in an Argo uniform because of a typical B.C. error in judg-ment. "I was born in Swift Current, Saskatchewan, but left when I was four," he explained. "I played my high school football in Kamloops, B.C., and I attended UBC. I was drafted in the second round by B.C. in 1982 and played four presea-son games. Coach Vic Rapp wanted me to go back to college, but I didn't want to. Next day I was a Toronto Argonaut."

Moen considered making it to the pros and starring for 12 years quite remarkable. "It was always a dream to play professionally, but I never thought it would be a reality. I was a late bloomer. I wasn't like other players who starred in high school and university. I was a high school quarterback who lasted about two days at that position in university before they made me a defensive back. I never truly started at university until my fourth year."

The Argos started the 1991 season on an ominous note when Dunigan went down early in the first quarter of the home-opener, but he returned to lead his team to a win over the Lions on August 27. On September 15 in Calgary, Dunigan was injured again, breaking his collar bone in several places.

Dunigan returned for the last game of the regular season. During the course of a 42–3 romp over the Bombers in the Conference Final, Dunigan reinjured himself. During Grey Cup week in Winnipeg, with his arm in a sling, it looked for certain that he would be watching the game from the sidelines.

Not so. The day before the game, he was working out in a hotel ballroom. "I had my shoulder shot up to see if I could throw a football," he confirmed. "They shot it up with the medication and gave me a few minutes and I was throwing the rock to Mike McCarthy. We were trying to get it right. I said, 'Hey, this is pretty good.' That's what happened."

This wasn't just a ploy to fool the opposition Calgary Stampeders? Hadn't the Argos planned all along that he would play? "No," Dunigan replied, "not until that point on Saturday when I sat down with Dr. Jackson, our trainer, Adam Rita and Mike McCarthy. At that point it was a joint decision among five people. There was a discussion for a lengthy period of time to weigh all the different scenarios: team, personal, career. What it came down to was can you or can't you? We had to figure that out.

"So the doctor got a couple of needles and shot the shoulder up, gave it time to take effect, and I threw the rock and decided it felt pretty good. So we decided to go ahead and give it a shot tomorrow.

Adam Rita agreed. "Basically it was a decision made the night before the game. I had been told all week he wasn't going to play, so we had prepared Rickey Foggie.

"I talked to his parents, I talked to Matt. He talked to his wife. I talked to his doctor, who said there was no further damage that could be done. I talked to Foggie and Matt and decided to go that way. He hadn't practiced for two weeks."

Dan Ferrone remembered things differently. "Actually we knew all along he was going to play. They just played it that way for the media and stuff like that, but we knew all along he was going to play. He had a sore shoulder, but they were going to freeze it. It reached the point that he wasn't going to miss the game no matter what. So as far as the players were concerned, we knew all along, so it was something we were prepared for.

"At the same time Rickey Foggie had played the last nine games and won eight of them, so he was a pretty dominating quarterback. To tell you the truth, when Dunigan couldn't get things going until the third quarter (it was the defense that kept us in there) we were kind of surprised the coaches weren't going to Foggie because we knew Matt was hurt."

Ferrone held Dunigan in the highest regard. "He certainly sucked it up. He was tough, very focused, a winner. He brought a lot of qualities, definitely leadership skills. When he left after the 1991 season, we missed him.

"Foggie had just as good a record the year before, and he was a pretty good quarterback who had all the tools, but he couldn't contain the personalities we had on the field: the Rocket, Darrell K. Smith. Those guys were creating so much havoc for Foggie because Foggie was a little bit too easy going.

"But they didn't get away with things when Dunigan was there. He was very demanding as a quarterback in terms of what he wanted to get done."

According to Dunigan, getting to the Grey Cup is partly the survival of the fittest. "As the season wears on you get physically and mentally drained. It is such a chore, such a constant struggle to continually monitor yourself physically and mentally to make sure you are in the best condition possible. That's so important.

"Coaches monitor that daily and make adjustments accordingly. Are we going to go 15 plays or 20? Are we going to run some extra here, some extra there? Are we going to give the players days off or not? Understanding what the players are going through is an important part of a coach's ability. That's why a Jackie Parker and a Don Sutherin are successful."

November 24, 1991, was the first time the big game had been played in Winnipeg. It was the coldest Grey Cup ever. The temperature at kickoff was –19°C, and with the wind chill factored in, it was about –30°. Despite the conditions the week was a huge success. Visitors had a wonderful time.

The game itself would be not just Toronto against Calgary but the Rocket against the Little Engine that Could, the Hollywood All-Stars versus the No Name Nobodies. The odds makers gave the Argos the edge.

The Stampeders hadn't appeared in a Grey Cup since their 1971 win over Toronto. The two teams had split their regular season games, both winning at home. The Argo victory was sewed up by a scintillating Rocket Ismail punt return for a touchdown in the final minute of play, assisted by at least three illegal blocks.

It would be Calgary's outstanding six-pack receiving corps of Allen Pitts, Carl Bland, Shawn Beals, Pee Wee Smith, Dave Sapunjis and Derrick Crawford against a strong Toronto secondary featuring Reggie Pleasant, Carl Brazely, Dave Bovell, Don Wilson and Ed Berry. Bovell was only in his second year. The rest had 16 All-Star selections among them.

The Argos had great speed offensively with Dave Williams and Rocket Ismail, the wide-outs, and Paul Masotti and D.K. Smith in the slots. And, of course, Pinball.

Attempting to shut down the Argos' air attack were Junior Thurman, Darryl Hall, Greg Peterson, Karl Anthony and Errol Tucker. Thurman and Hall were All-Canadian. So was defensive end Will Johnson, a unanimous choice.

The Stamps were led by Danny Barrett obtained in a 1989 trade with Toronto, an unspectacular but steady quarterback. His passing totals were average except for one remarkable statistic. He had thrown only five interceptions all year, one every 87 times he put the ball in the air. The unanimous choice for All-Canadian quarterback was Doug Flutie of B.C., who was picked off every 30 times he threw the ball.

One of the oldest clichés in sport is that the team that makes the fewest mistakes will win. Throughout the season Calgary was the team that made the least mistakes with 18 fewer turnovers than Toronto. But come game time, that meant nothing as Barrett was intercepted three times.

Toronto had the first possession at their 37. Dunigan threw two incompletions and Ilesic punted.

On Calgary's very first play at the 44, Danny Barrett was picked off by Ed Berry, who returned it 51 yards for a touchdown. "I can't remember the last time I threw an interception for a touchdown," moaned the disconsolate Stampeder quarterback.

Stampeder receiver Dave Sapunjis explained what happened. "Our offense, our whole team, was flying high. Emotions were up. Danny was a little nervous, threw a bad ball and the receiver didn't do anything to knock it down."

Return man Pee Wee Smith also had the jitters, fumbling the ensuing kickoff at the 30-yard line. Kevin Smellie was held to no gain and Dunigan over-threw his receiver. Lance Chomyc's field-goal attempt went wide for a single. Two plays later Barrett was sacked by Brian Warren.

Sapunjis described the mood on the Calgary bench. "You are quickly hum-bled. It is obviously discouraging when you go out in a big game and you don't start off well. So we had to kind of gather our thoughts, calm each other down and go out there and start doing what we had to do—start to play a little better."

The Stamps started at their 33. On first down Barrett threw to Sapunjis for 11 yards, Calgary's first gain of the ball game. "It was sort of an out," Sapunjis recalled, "a read play for me. I remember it clearly. Danny saw me and threw me a nice ball. That started our offensive scheme the way we wanted it."

Nine plays later Barrett plunged over from the one. The play had been set up by an end-zone interference call on Carl Brazely.

In the second quarter the teams traded field goals, making the score at the half 11–10 in favor of Toronto.

The Rocket opened the third quarter with a blazing 43-yard kickoff return to the enemy 35. After completions to D.K. Smith and David Williams had brought the ball to the 22, Dunigan went incomplete and was hit by Will John-son. "I hit Dunigan a couple of times," Johnson said. "That one time I hit him he coughed the ball into the air and Tim Cofield caught it and got a few yards before an offensive lineman grabbed him."

The Stamps drove to the Argo 35, where Mark McLoughlin scored a single on a 42-yard field-goal attempt. Four minutes later McLoughlin connected from 27 yards to put his team into the lead for the first and last time, 14–11.

The name of the game in football is field position. For most of the game, Toronto had it. Their advantage in field position was attributable to the Rocket as well as the abysmal performance of Calgary punter Jerry Kauric, the worst in modern Grey Cup history. His average was 28 yards, his net punting average a dismal 19 yards. Late in the third quarter Kauric kicked from his 38-yard line. Toronto scrimmaged from the Calgary 48 without benefit of a return. On the very next play Dunigan threw to Darrell Smith for a touchdown.

On the opening play of the fourth quarter, Barrett was intercepted a second time by Reggie Pleasant at the Stampeder 40-yard line. Pleasant returned it to the 12. Again the defense came up big and forced the Argos to settle for a field goal. Argos 22, Calgary 14.

On the next possession Kauric got away a good punt, pinning the Argos at their 6-yard line. After throwing incomplete, Dunigan ran for eight and Ilesic got off a 16-yard punt, probably the worst punt of his Grey Cup career. Two plays later Barrett isolated Allen Pitts on Carl Brazely and threw to him for a touchdown. The Stampeders trailed by one, but Mr. Momentum seemed to be on their side.

Not for long. Mark McLoughlin kicked off to Raghib "Rocket" Ismail, who streaked 87 yards to the Calgary end zone, setting two Grey Cup records for longest return and most kickoff return yardage.

Toronto was ahead by eight points with 10:26 remaining, hardly an insurmountable lead. But then Keyvan Jenkins allowed the kickoff to bounce off his foot, and Keith Costello recovered his second fumble of the game for Toronto at the 36. Dunigan promptly hit Paul Masotti in the end zone for a touchdown. At the 5:19 mark of the final frame the scoreboard read Toronto 36, Calgary 21. In 58 seconds Calgary's hopes and dreams of two decades were shattered.

According to Argo coach Adam Rita, the turnovers on kickoffs were no accident. "Because of the wind we decided to sky-kick the ball, but so many things have to go right. The kick has to be right, the guy running down the field has to have a free shot at the ball—he can't get bumped on blocks—and that's exactly what happened."

And some things happened by accident, as Rita explained about Masotti's touchdown. "That play was designed to go to David Williams, but the ball was underthrown because of the wind. Masotti just decided to cut across because he didn't think the other receiver had seen it. He cut across, caught the ball and fell in the end zone."

The Stampeders had a chance to get back in the game when they marched from their 31 to the Argo 2-yard line. Instead of running they chose to throw. The first was incomplete, Barrett was sacked for a 9-yard loss on the second and the third-down gamble failed. The Argos won their twelfth Grey Cup 36–21.

Statistically the Stampeders had the edge throughout the game. While Toronto's Dunigan was 12 of 29 for 142 yards and 2 touchdowns, Calgary's Barrett 34 of 56 for 377 yards, 1 touchdown and 3 interceptions. No quarterback has ever thrown over 50 passes and won a Grey Cup.

But, oh, those special teams. The Rocket, Pinball and D.K. Smith ran six kickoffs back for 244 yards, the second best Grey Cup total in history. Toronto averaged 40.7 yards per return, Calgary 13. Special teams made the difference. The Rocket showed up a lot of people who questioned his commitment and courage. Matt Dunigan's statistics weren't impressive, but he shook off the Grey Cup jinx and finally won the big one. The Easterners made the most of their opportunities, the Westerners did not.

Said Calgary's offensive coordinator John Hufnagel, "We gave it away."

Toronto coach Adam Rita didn't think so. "I went into the game knowing we were going to win it. I haven't been in a Grey Cup we've won that I didn't think we were going to win before the game. All we had to do was be patient and not panic. Somebody would pick up the slack. All we had to do was take advantage of the field position we had, kick field goals or score a touchdown and we would win the game. We didn't screw up too many times. Masotti had a good game and we were able to make plays off what Keith Costello and the kickoff team were able to do."

In Rita's opinion the offense could have done better if Dunigan hadn't been so stubborn. "We had to warm up Foggie a couple of times to get Matt cranked up to do a couple of things I wanted him to do, which he did with great, great reluctance.

"He was so pissed off at me because I had asked Foggie to warm up that he said, 'I'll call that play,' and he threw a touchdown. It was the 1–41 Play Action Pass to Smith. On offense we didn't have to do anymore than what we did. The defense did everything they knew they were supposed to do, and the kicking game was above and beyond our expectations."

Offensive lineman Dan Ferrone also saluted the defense and special teams. "Defense dominated the whole game for us. They were the ones who kept us in. When I talked to them afterward, they talked about how some of the play-calling was terrible, really bad. Rocket won it. There is no question, that was his game. He had two big runbacks off a punt and a kickoff."

Was it tough to play that day because of the cold? "Yes, it was," Dunigan replied. "Regardless of whether you are hurt or not, those are difficult conditions to play in. The ball is certainly a lot harder. There's no give. It's like throwing or catching a brick. There's no feel for it. But what makes the CFL so grand, so unique, are the conditions football is played in, year in and year out. It gives the game a lot of color."

The 1991 season was special for Don Moen. "I was very fortunate when I came into the league in 1982. We went to the Grey Cup and we came back in 1983 and won it. I was young and I figured that was just the way it was.

"Then in 1987 we had that devastating loss to Edmonton on a last-play field goal and we didn't get back until 1991. The fact that there was a spread between the two and we had a great bunch of guys and great ownership made the game very exciting. The fact that I was getting older made me cherish winning the Cup a lot more."

What Have You Done for Us Lately?

While Argo ownership may have been great, management wasn't. A year later the Argos finished last. Coach of the Year Adam Rita was fired. "Sometimes that Coach of the Year Award is the kiss of death," Rita said ruefully, being one of 14 recipients who were later fired by the club with which they won the award.

He explained what went wrong in 1992. "Several things happened, but basically we couldn't re-sign Matt Dunigan. In 1991 we had very few injuries, and we had the backup to step in. But we were beyond backups in 1992. We had guys coming in off the street playing.

"The McNall group was having problems with money. Promises were made after the Grey Cup that weren't kept."

Ferrone also pointed to the loss of Dunigan as the major cause of the team's demise. "We went from the penthouse to the outhouse really quickly because Dunigan wasn't there. Dunigan controlled the guys. He was very demanding. The year after we won the Grey Cup, these guys thought they were invincible. Some of them had an attitude that was creating problems for us as a team. High expectations were there because the team was completely intact except for Dunigan. When we didn't start winning right away, suddenly things were going all sorts of ways and it became a very difficult year."

Don Moen agreed. "The one big thing that really hurt us was the loss of Matt Dunigan. We had too many free spirits on our offense that needed his leadership to get things done. Even though he was hurt a lot, his influence was very positive."

What about the injury factor? "You're always going to have injuries," said Ferrone. "How much impact those injuries have is always a sign of the times. If you're not doing well, an injury has a big impact on you, and if you're doing well sometimes an injury has no impact at all."

Dunigan had another explanation for the Argos rapid descent. "The biggest mistake was the fact that they fired Adam Rita. He was our leader. But there were going to be a lot of changes regardless because of contracts and management."

Dunigan was one of them, refusing to sign because Mike McCarthy wanted to put him on a plan whereby Dunigan would play for pay. "Pay for play?" exclaimed Dunigan. "Hello, this is a violent contact sport here. Wake up and smell the coffee, pal. It's unprecedented. Everybody is jeopardized play in, play out. So to sign a contract like that you'd be absolutely crazy."

The free fall continued in 1993. Desperate for a big-name quarterback, the Argos sent Rickey Foggie, Darrell K. Smith, Don Wilson, Ed Berry, Bruce Dickson, Eddie Brown, J.P. Izquierdo and Len Johnson to Edmonton for Tracy Ham, Craig Ellis, Enis Jackson, Travis Oliver, John Davis, Ken Winey, Chris Johnstone and Cam Brousseau. The Argos went 3–15, the most regular season losses in franchise history. Edmonton won the Grey Cup.

Rita's replacement, defensive coordinator Dennis Meyer, put run-and-shoot guru Darrel "Mouse" Davis in charge of the offense. His system demanded a quarterback who was adept at quickly reading defenses, Tracy Ham's Achilles heel. The result was predictably disastrous. After losing 9 of his first 10 ball games, Meyer was fired, replaced by Bob O'Billovich, who became both coach and general manager.

Dan Ferrone was glad to see Obie back. "I had a lot of respect, and I gained even more respect for Obie when I left him and saw other coaches. It is a tough job in pro sports having to treat everybody equally, but he did it. He had a tremendous record. He got a tremendous number of wins. He had a winning attitude and a winning system."

What O'Billovich didn't have in 1993–94 was talent. He was 2–6 finishing Meyer's term and 7–11 the following year. The Argos made the play-offs but lost the semifinal to Baltimore. Obie relinquished his coaching responsibilities, picking Mike Faragalli, son of Joe, to succeed him.

On May 5, 1994, TSN Enterprises bought the Argos. Paul Beeston, CEO of the Blue Jays, became CEO of the Argos. Promotion of the team improved dramatically, but unfortunately O'Billovich had picked the wrong head coach. Mike Faragalli was a disaster. After starting the 1995 campaign at 2–3, including one loss by one point and another loss in overtime, the Argos dropped four in a row. They finished near the bottom in most offensive and defensive categories even though Michael Clemons led the league with 2,588 all-purpose yards. He didn't make the All-Star team, divisional or league.

Averaging only 17,214 fans a game, O'Billovich fired Faragalli and returned to the sidelines. When Obie matched Faragalli's record, he, too, was fired.

Don Matthews Returns

Soon after, Toronto was able to benefit from the misfortunes of others. Cleveland Browns owner Art Modell moved his team to Baltimore, thus ending the life of the Baltimore Colts, the one bright spot in CFL expansion south. Jim Speros moved the team to Montreal, but Coach Don Matthews couldn't see much of a future in Montreal and signed with Toronto.

Going into the 1999 season, Matthews ranked first in all-time wins with 157. He had coached in the Grey Cup 12 of 19 years. With a winning percentage of.670, Matthews' teams won two out of every three games they played.

In the West, Calgary Stampeder owner Larry Ryckman was bankrupt. He hadn't paid Doug Flutie all year, rendering his contract null and void. When Flutie missed most of the 1995 season due to injury, his successor, Jeff Garcia, filled the void by leading the team to a Grey Cup appearance against Baltimore. Not only was Garcia successful, he played for over $900,000 less.

Flutie was available, wanted to be closer to his Massachusetts home and wanted the big bucks. He signed with Toronto. Matthews again chose Adam Rita to be his offensive coordinator. Rita explained why he liked working with Don Matthews. "My philosophy jives with his philosophy, so there is very little conflict. Don't get me wrong, there have been times Don and I have gone toe to toe on some ideas. But we're friends.

"But the one thing about him is that if I can sell him on something, when he goes on the field, it is *our* idea and he accepts responsibility if it doesn't work. All you have to do is explain to him why you want to do it. Sometimes you don't even have to do that. He'll say, 'You know what you're doing—go for it.'"

Both men believe in assembling a team the same way. "You build down the middle," Rita said. "You start with your quarterback, your center, your tailback, your middle linebacker, free safety, strong side tackle and rush end, the short-side end, the halfbacks and the corners."

Down the middle for Toronto meant Mike Kiselak, the 1995 All-Canadian center from San Antonio. The quarterback, of course, was Doug Flutie, who went on to win his fifth Most Outstanding Player Award. When former Rookie of the Year and Ti-Cat Michael O'Shea was cut by Detroit, Matthews was quick to make him his middle linebacker. The safety, Lester Smith, had been with Matthews in Baltimore and came over to Toronto when released by Montreal. The Smith gang dominated the secondary. In addition to Lester, Adrian and Donald manned the corners.

Matthews had nine newcomers on defense, including one rookie, Cooper Harris. The holdovers were linebackers Don Wilson, Ken Benson and Ed Berry. The front four were all veteran newcomers, Demetrious Maxie, Andrew Stewart, Rob Waldrop and Reggie Givens.

There were three newcomers to the O-line, including Mike Kiselak, Chris Perez and Vic Stevenson. Slotback Tyrone Williams was obtained from Calgary in exchange for the negotiating rights to University of Montana quarterback Dave Dickenson. The other slotback, Duane Dmytryshyn, was signed after the Stampeders cut him. Former Stallion Robert Drummond was the fullback. The holdovers on offense were Paul Masotti, Jimmy "The Jet" Cunningham and Pinball Clemons. The punter–place-kicker was rookie Mike Vanderjagt. Seventeen of the starting 25 were new to Toronto. The fit was perfect.

The offense was spectacular with Cunningham leading the league with 2,638 all-purpose yards. Second in that category was Michael Clemons, 12 behind the Jet with 2,626, moving him into fifth place on the all-time list. Clemons led the league with 116 receptions, fourth-best ever, but he did not make the All-Star team.

Adam Rita put together a devastating offensive package using his running backs as receivers. Clemons and Drummond together caught 188 passes for 2,066 yards and scored 26 touchdowns. Paul Masotti recorded his third straight season of over 1,000 receiving yards, 1,023 on 73 receptions.

And there was Flutie. Completing 434 of 677 passes for 5,720 yards and 29 touchdowns, Flutie, in only seven seasons, moved into fourth place on the all-time list behind Ron Lancaster, Matt Dunigan and Tom Clements. He is the all-time leader in completions with a 60.8 percent rate. His six selections as All-Canadian quarterback are the most ever. Ron Lancaster is next at four.

Edmonton would face Toronto for the 1996 Grey Cup, which was hosted by Hamilton for the first time since 1972. The CFL was now using the Grey Cup to bail out ailing franchises. The 1995 game in Regina moved the Roughriders into the black for the first time in many years, and the Eskimos turned a profit with the 1997 championship.

Alas for the Tiger-Cats, Hamilton was the only host to lose money on the Grey Cup. Capacity at Ivor Wynne was 40,400, and 38,595 tickets were sold, including 4,500 end-zone seats bought by Tim Horton's the day before the game. They sold these $100 tickets at their Hamilton area stores for $25.

In spite of Hamilton's proximity to Hogtown and the good weather that week, fewer than 6,000 tickets were sold in Toronto. The poor ticket sales may have been partially accounted for by the traditional animosity displayed by the locals for Toronto.

At Sunday morning Mass at St. Patrick's in Hamilton the priest called the little children up to receive their blessing before going off to Sunday School. He asked them if they knew what Sunday it was. Blank little faces. After informing them it was Grey Cup Sunday, he asked if they knew who was going to win. More blank faces. "Can you say Edmonton Eskimos?" he asked.

While it was true some Westerners were cheering for the Argos, it was essentially good-natured, just as the Edmonton–Calgary rivalry is basically good-natured. In Hamilton the most common button displayed read Argos Suck. Doug Flutie was offended by it, especially when asked for an autograph by a "fan" sporting the button.

The Argos Suck attitude had a double-barreled effect on ticket sales. Torontonians were loathe to come to Hamilton, and many Hamiltonians were loathe to fork over $100 plus to watch the Argos. Perhaps if Edmonton had been favored to win, more tickets would have been sold locally.

The Argonauts were favored to win. Edmonton had averaged 25.5 points per game, Toronto 30.9. Toronto had 97 more first downs. Toronto was first in passing, Edmonton eighth. The Argos outrushed Edmonton 2,075 yards to 1,467.

Defensively the teams were much closer. Toronto surrendered 359 points, Edmonton 354. The Argos gave up 5,636 yards to Edmonton's 5,046, a difference of about 8 yards per quarter. The Eskimos had the better pass defense. They were great at pressuring the quarterback, recording a league-high 70 sacks though none came against the Argonauts. Toronto was third with 44.

Despite the presence of Henry "Gizmo" Williams, the greatest punt returner of all-time, Toronto had the edge on special teams with Cunningham and Clemons. Edmonton had the advantage in the kicking department with veterans Sean Fleming and Glenn Harper against Toronto's 26-year-old rookie Mike Vanderjagt.

The Grey Cup game turned out to be typically atypical. The Eskimos outperformed Toronto offensively, the Argo defense was better than Edmonton's and the kicking game was won by the rookie.

On game day it began to snow about 11:00 A.M. As the day wore on, the wind came up. By kickoff at 6:30 P.M. the temperature was –3°C. with a wind of 35–40 kph. The first snowstorm of the winter blew in, deepening the depression of all who cared about the survival of the CFL. They needn't have worried. Despite the elements the Argos and Eskimos put on one of the most entertaining Grey Cups ever.

It was perfect Eskimo weather. Not only did the Esks play well in the white stuff, their old nemesis Doug Flutie did not. Let it snow, let it snow, let it snow!

In the first quarter, Toronto looked anything but like a 15–3 team. On their first play Paul Masotti dropped a Flutie pass. With Derek MacCready in his face, Flutie threw the next one away.

On Edmonton's first possession at their 47, Danny McManus completed a hitch screen to Eddie Brown for 5 and a 16-yarder to Darren Flutie. Eric Blount ran for 2 and Toronto was penalized 10 yards for objectionable conduct. After two incompletions Sean Fleming missed a 37-yard field-goal try. Cunningham returned the ball to the 19.

On first down All-Star center Mike Kiselak snapped the ball over his quarterback's head. Flutie conceded a safety touch. Edmonton 2, Toronto 0.

Eight minutes later Eskimo quarterback McManus dropped back to pass from his 46-yard line. Given great protection he hooked up with Downtown Eddie Brown for a 64-yard pass and run for a touchdown. Streaking toward the post, Brown caught the ball at his knees, somehow managing to maintain his balance on the slippery field. "It was just a go route on his part," explained McManus. "I just threw it up high and as far as I could. I really didn't see how he caught the ball until we watched the game film afterward. I saw it kicked off his heel.

"Eddie said he could run past the guy, and when I got single coverage on that side, I just threw it up and he made a great catch." Edmonton 9, Toronto 0.

When the opening stanza ended, Flutie had the Argos on the Edmonton 15-yard line. After a holding call and a Derek MacCready sack, Mike Vanderjagt kicked a 37-yard field goal.

Then the fireworks began. Through the next 13 minutes and 25 seconds in driving snow, the teams tallied 38 points.

After the field goal, Edmonton scrimmaged at the 35. Two plays later, the Eskimos' Glenn Harper outkicked the coverage. Jimmy "The Jet" Cunningham ignited the explosion when he took the ball on his 30. He got a devastating block from Donald Smith, burst up the middle and outraced the rest to the end zone. Toronto 10, Edmonton 9.

On their next possession at their 48, Flutie scrambled 14 yards to the

Edmonton 48. He threw to Cunningham for 20 and tossed to Masotti for 3. Vanderjagt kicked a 32-yard field goal. Toronto 13, Edmonton 9.

Edmonton quickly regained the lead. Danny McManus found a wide-open Jim Sandusky at the Argo 50-yard line. The great veteran went the rest of the way to the end zone. McManus described the play. "That was kind of a coverage mess-up on their part. We were running some schemes between Jimmy and Darren Flutie, and on this occasion the Argos jumped really hard on Darren and let Jimmy through the middle. I snuck one in there, and then the two guys ran into each other." Edmonton 16, Toronto 13.

In 4 minutes and 18 seconds Flutie marched the Argos 65 yards on 6 plays to the end zone. The key was Canadian receiver Paul Masotti, who picked up 64 of his 100 yards on that drive.

On second and 8 at the Toronto 37, Flutie connected with Masotti for 29 yards to the Eskimo 44. On the next play Derek MacCready dropped Flutie for a 10-yard loss. Flutie came right back to Masotti for 35 yards, Cunningham for 15. On first and goal at the 4, Robert Drummond ran it in for the touchdown. Toronto 20, Edmonton 16.

The lead lasted 15 seconds. Fielding the kickoff at his 19, Henry "Gizmo" Williams electrified the crowd with a 91-yard return, the longest in Grey Cup history. Although Gizmo has returned 25 punts for touchdowns, that was only his second score from a kickoff. Edmonton 23, Toronto 20.

Gizmo's touchdown return did not demoralize the opposition. Toronto came right back with Pinball Clemons returning the ensuing kickoff 30 yards to the Argo 48. The next sequence of plays was pivotal. On first down Flutie threw toward Clemons in the flat. The Eskimos' Darian Hagan got his hands on it and should have picked it off. Instead it went incomplete. On the next play Flutie was trapped but pitched the ball forward between two defenders to Clemons, who ran 16 yards into enemy territory.

Drummond ran for 11, Flutie for 10 and Drummond for another 10. After an incompletion, Flutie scampered 10 yards into the end zone. The drive took 1 minute and 49 seconds off the clock. Toronto 27, Edmonton 23.

Edmonton had an opportunity to close the gap, but Sean Fleming missed a 47-yard field goal to end the half. In terrible weather the teams had put 50 points on the board in a single half of football. Incredibly there were no turnovers.

Equally incredibly, the form chart could be thrown out the window. McManus was 10 of 16 for 227 yards and two touchdowns, Flutie was 12 of 21 for

190 yards and no touchdowns. Toronto had 17 first downs to Edmonton's 8 but had 32 fewer yards. Veteran Glenn Harper was averaging 31 yards per punt, the rookie Vanderjagt 41.5. Vanderjagt made both his field goals while Fleming went 0–2. Edmonton sacked Flutie twice for 35 yards. The relatively immobile McManus was unscathed.

The 41 points in the second quarter were followed by just 3 in the third. Vanderjagt made it 30–23 at the 4:22 mark from 16 yards out. On the next sequence, Sean Fleming missed from the 37. The Argos returned all three misses into workable field position.

What was wrong with Sean Fleming? Coach Lancaster explained. "He got hurt in the Western Final making a tackle, which probably preserved our win against Calgary, to tell you the truth. On the one field goal he missed, the guy came out, he made the tackle and hurt his leg. We missed three field goals in a Grey Cup. Sean's not going to do that. But he had the bad leg."

Calgary's Wally Buono's sympathy was restrained. "On the missed field goal late in the Western Final, there should have been a penalty. Marv Coleman's running the kick-out—he's going to score. If Sean Fleming doesn't stick his leg out and trip him, Coleman scores. Guess who wins?

"But now it's late in the game. We punt, we get a no yards and they kick a field goal and win. If we'd been up by 7, they would have had to score a touchdown, which they hadn't done in two Western Finals. They hadn't moved the football all game."

By the end of the third quarter, the Argo offensive line was winning the battle in the trenches. Still, the Eskimo defense stopped an enemy drive at the 21, forcing the Argos to settle for another field goal. They retaliated with a 65-yard march of their own with Danny McManus throwing twice to Marc Tobert and Eddie Brown, once each to Eric Blount and Tony Burse. Blount ran it in from the 5. The Westerners trailed by 3 with 6:57 left to go, an eternity in the CFL.

Especially with Flutie at the controls. The little guy engineered a brilliant 71-yard, 13-play drive for a field goal that used up 5 minutes and 23 seconds. The drive was kept alive by a controversial call at the Edmonton 24-yard line. On first down at the 33, Flutie ran for 9 yards. Robert Drummond was stopped dead in his tracks. Flutie called a quarterback sneak on third and 1. As soon as he took the snap, Flutie was hammered by Willie Pless. Flutie appeared to drop the ball, but before Edmonton could recover, the play was whistled dead, giving the Argos a first down.

The Eskimos' Pless was philosophical about it. "The ref called it and that's the way it is. What I or anyone else thinks isn't going to change anything. It was called dead and we continued on. But the ball was already gone when I hit him. It was already out of his hands."

So Flutie dropped it? "Well, the referee said he didn't drop it."

"All I can tell you is what I saw on television afterward," said head referee Jake Ireland. "What I saw on television afterward is that clearly he fumbled the ball before his forward progress was stopped. However, an official on the field blew the whistle and marked the forward progress. That was the end of that. There was nothing I could do about it."

"Jake said that?" asked Edmonton's Rod Connop. "My screensaver says, 'Jake Ireland Sucks.' I can take that off my computer now?

"I don't think he could say anything else. Anybody who looked at the replay and continued to argue that it was the right call is in need of glasses. That thing was just blatantly obvious—even by the reaction of the Argos who would know, Flutie and Drummond. I think they fully realized it was a fumble. That's the way it goes."

When Toronto's Vanderjagt kicked a field goal with only 1 minute and 33 seconds remaining, and the Argos scored another touchdown, many felt that the official's mistake didn't affect the game's outcome. But Rod Connop begged to differ. "It wasn't just a fumble," he commented. "It was going to be a fumble for a touchdown because we had a convoy gathering steam, and the only person who had a chance to get that ball was Robert Drummond. If you watch the replay you'll see he dives, he misses the ball and it's behind him. It's behind his back and *Singor* Mobley from our team is in the process when it is blown dead. There is going to be a convoy of three or four guys that are going to take him 75 yards the other way.

"When it was all over and done with, that fumble was the key play of the game. It doesn't necessarily mean the outcome of the game would have been any different, but the score would have been different. We have to live with it."

Eskimo coach Ron Lancaster was so incensed at the call that he ran on to the field, screaming at the officials. After Mike Vanderjagt increased the lead to 6, Lancaster took to the field again and slipped and fell. Embarrassed and angry, he returned to the bench. Just over a minute and a half remained.

Months later he looked back on the fumble that wasn't. "You know what? It probably wasn't that important," he said. "Things happen in any athletic event at a certain time, and they seem like they're life and death, but in the overall picture, they weren't really that important. We had places where we could have done a little better and won—offensively, defensively and special teams. It's just that when things happen at a particular time, you are so involved in the game that they become probably more important than they really are."

As to Jake Ireland's comment, the ever-gracious Lancaster replied, "That's okay. I really believe the referees make far fewer mistakes in a game than either team."

Scrimmaging at the 39, MacManus, looking for Darren Flutie, threw the ball low toward the sideline. The ball bounced off Flutie's chest into the arms of Adrian Smith, who ran 49 yards to the end zone. Toronto 43, Edmonton 30. Fifty-eight minutes and 38 seconds had gone by before the first and only turnover of the game.

Characteristically the Eskimos weren't finished. On third and 5 at their 45, McManus hit Darren Flutie for 20 yards and Tobert for 9 and 26. After an incompletion McManus found Tobert in the end zone for a 7-yard touchdown to end the scoring. The final score was 43–37, the second-highest total in Grey Cup history. (Tops was 83 points in the Saskatchewan versus Hamilton game of 1989.)

Ron Lancaster's reason for the Toronto win was simple: Flutie. "At certain times Flutie would run with the football and make a first down. The Argos would run that shovel pass and the guy would make the first down. Instead of having a third and 5, Flutie would make the 5, just getting to the first-down marker. Playing against him is very, very difficult. You have to control him because if you don't, he'll figure a way to beat you. That was the difference in the game."

McManus agreed. "One guy's performance is not going to win or lose a game, but I think Flutie did a great job of putting his team in position to move the chains and keep scoring points. That's all a quarterback is supposed to do, and Doug did an excellent job of that."

Because of play-off losses in 1994–94 on snow-covered fields in Calgary, Flutie was labeled the quarterback who froze in the cold, who had to have ideal conditions to win. The ridiculous charge bothered Flutie immensely, and he felt vindicated after his win. "There's one in the critic's face," he said without a trace of anger in his voice. "It's like, 'Shut up and let's move on.' This should dispel all myths."

When analyzing Edmonton's strengths, few saw McManus as one of them, yet he played very well. But he didn't feel the same sense of vindication. "If we had scored 7 more points it would have been great," he commented. "It was a great team effort. The guys up front did a super job against their defense as far as giving me time. We played a good game. We just didn't play quite well enough to win."

Flutie carried 13 times for 98 yards, including a touchdown. Five times he ran for first downs that kept drives alive. Under Don Matthews' system, Flutie could be at his creative best. The coach explained. "Flutie has total control while he's out there, so he calls what he is comfortable with. I think he completed about 65 percent of his passes in 1996. If he hadn't had more drops than normal that year, he might have been over 70 percent. His performance was just remarkable.

"Flutie is a master of the ad lib," Matthews continued. "No matter how much you prepare against him, he just ad libs. If everything breaks down around him, he just makes things happen. He's the best I've ever been around. He did some things in the Grey Cup I've never seen anybody do—in the snow."

Flutie turned the ice and snow to his advantage, twirling like a matador to elude the rush, pitching the ball forward to Robert Drummond or the Pinball.

"We thought we could run the shovel pass against them because we had been running it all year," said Rita. "It's called a Draw Trap. Because of the balanced defense Edmonton played, they didn't give up much up field, so we wanted to work underneath them a lot. We were able to do that most of the game.

Said Edmonton linebacker Willie Pless, "What the Argos did was use the whole field, spread us out pretty good. When they send men out that wide, we've got to respect that, got to go with them. Once we did they'd come back the other way."

The Argos insisted they didn't make any last-minute adjustments because of the weather. "No, we didn't," Matthews said ruefully. "In fact we didn't know exactly what to do and our offense looked like it. We didn't know what would be successful. Doug was sort of probing around to find out what we could do. He had a great feel for the field and the skills of the players in that kind of weather. He adjusted his game-calling accordingly."

Adam Rita welcomed the bad weather and poor field conditions. "We wanted to prove that Doug could play in those kinds of conditions. Doug more than anybody wanted to prove that. If you look at Doug's track record in the past, except for that game in 1993, he averaged 33 points per game in bad weather. But all blame goes on the quarterback, as well as the glory, so he took that 1993 loss quite personally. In 1996 the harder it snowed the more focused we got."

Edmonton felt the same way. "When it started to snow on Sunday afternoon, I thought, 'Perfect!'" said Rod Connop. "We knew how we would play in that weather. But we didn't assume that Toronto would fold up in that weather—they've got too many good players.

"As long as I've been with the Eskimos, our feeling going into winter weather games is that we will play better in this weather than the other team," Connop continued. "The other team may play as good as us in many cases, but they won't play better than us. Maybe it's because we practice in the snow and live in Edmonton."

McManus concurred. "As the snow came down, our confidence level went up. After the first two games we had just played to get to the Grey Cup, we figured the weather would be an excellent equalizer."

Toronto head coach Matthews wasn't concerned when they were down 9–0. "I had confidence our players would find a way. They did all year and they certainly did in that game. We as coaches didn't have to do very much. We have a saying that players have to find a way to win. In fact they put that saying on their Grey Cup ring.

"Players during the game are responsible, each and every one, to find a way to win. If someone starts hurting you, you've got to have an answer for it. Flutie and Drummond were the second-half answer. Pinball, Masotti and Jimmy the Jet were the first-half answer. Flutie had a great feel and called a great game. I would think he's put all his critics to rest now."

Willie Pless didn't have to be convinced. "Flutie could be playing marbles and he'd be hard to beat. It doesn't really matter what team he's playing for, he's going to be tough. He's definitely going to be on the mind of every defensive player. He is the main person you have to slow down. I say slow down because there's no way to stop him."

Edmonton coach Lancaster praised his quarterback in spite of the loss. "Danny McManus played a great game. He threw a couple of balls that I have no idea how they got there or where they had to go, but they got there.

"Danny is an excellent leader. He's the kind of guy that if you know him, you like him. He's a very good person. He gets things done without being a screamer. He just goes about his business. He exudes an air of confidence. People buy into that. It took awhile for that to happen but that's what finally got us over the hump. Everybody started to believe in him."

Less Browne, McManus's teammate in B.C., wasn't surprised at the quarterback's success. "In my first year with TSN I kept telling everybody, just wait and see, this kid's good, he's real good. He does just enough to get by. He does just enough to win. He knows how to win.

"I remember after the 1996 Grey Cup, after everybody left, Ron Lancaster said to me, 'I want to thank you for sticking up for Danny Mac the whole year while everybody was trying to tear him down and crucify him.

"I said, 'Well, you know, I did it through experience. I've been with him for a while. I know what he can do. I've seen him come off the bench and control the game.'"

McManus came to Canada in 1990, backing up Tom Burgess and Matt Dunigan in Winnipeg before signing with the Lions, where he played second fiddle to Danny Barrett and Kent Austin. After leading the Lions into a successful 1994 Grey Cup appearance and a solid 1995 season as the starter, the Leos went in a fruitless pursuit of Matt Dunigan and gave McManus his release. In 1998 Edmonton preferred David Archer, so MacManus joined Lancaster in Hamilton.

In all Grey Cups there is an unsung hero who goes unnoticed by press and fans. Adam Rita thought Drummond played a great game and that the Argos' offensive line did a good job. "Edmonton was the number one sack team in the league, and they only got to Flutie twice," he said.

Matthews mentioned something else. "We had a bunch of guys hurt. Nobody seems to remember that. Andrew Stewart didn't play at all. He had a hamstring. He was one starter that was out. Paul Masotti was hurt most of the game and was in and out. Donald Smith was hurt and went out in the second quarter. His replacement, Marcello Simmons, pulled his hamstring and was all taped up, trying to help us get through the day. We were playing four guys short most of the game.

"Our players had injuries all year and never once complained about it. We never felt that injuries were a reason not to perform well. Find a way to win was always the answer."

In addition to a tough team of Eskimos, the Argos had to cope with a hostile crowd. Matthews was used to it. "The fans made it a difficult field to play on because of the noise factor. They tried to disrupt our game. I've been in the last four Grey Cups, and they've all been on hostile fields: in Vancouver against the Lions, certainly against Baltimore in Saskatchewan, when we were the Americans playing the Canadians, and then in Hamilton and Edmonton.

"The rivalry between Hamilton and Toronto is so fierce that no Hamilton fan would ever be caught dead rooting for Toronto," Matthews continued. "Most of the fans there were from Hamilton, so Edmonton automatically got their fan support. Players don't get disheartened by it. It just makes it a more difficult field to play on."

If Flutie's winning the Grey Cup Most Valuable Player Award was predictable, the success of Mike Vanderjagt was not. The 27-year-old rookie made all five field goals he tried and added four converts. This unlikely Grey Cup hero personified grit and determination. Drafted out of West Virginia by Saskatchewan in 1992, the Oakville, Ontario, native reported to Regina the following year and was cut. He tried out for the Argos in 1994 and was cut. Down the road in Hamilton was the same. Back in Toronto in 1995, he was cut again. From there he was off to Ray Jauch's Minnesota Fighting Pike of the Arena Football League and then back to Toronto, where he finally made the team.

During the pregame warm-up, Vanderjagt couldn't get solid footing and was so tentative that he was missing most of his kicks. When he returned to the dressing room, he mentioned the problem to equipment man Danny Webb. Prepared for anything, Webb dug out a pair of cleats that hadn't been worn since the Grey Cup of 1991 in Winnipeg. Vanderjagt put them on and the rest, as they say, is   history.

Losing a Grey Cup in the last couple of minutes is usually pretty tough to take. For the Esks' Rod Connop, strangely, that wasn't the case. "Actually it was the opposite," he said. "It was the easiest to take. If you'd asked me before I would have thought, 'Well, losing big, at least you know well into the game, but being embarrassed in a Grey Cup game hurts more than playing well and losing to another good team.' I wouldn't have been able to say that before because I wouldn't have known that was the way I was going to feel.

"But when it was all over and I got in that locker room (for all I knew it was my last game ever), I just sort of felt good about it. A couple of things really bothered me, but I thought it was a good, hard-fought game. The Argos won, they're a good team, but we pushed them right to the limit, and it could have gone either way.

"Then about a week later I saw the replays and I started dwelling on that a

little bit. It was so close—what could have been—it was so close. But . . . it does-
n't matter now."

Pless took the more traditional approach. "I don't care if it's a regular season, play-off or Grey Cup game. When you lose it's a loss, and we want to win
every chance we get. With the Grey Cup game, it doesn't matter which one it
was if it was a loss. It is disappointing, but we'll live and learn with it."

Ron Lancaster sided with Connop. "That was such a well-played game, and
everybody should walk away from it happy. It never happens that way because
somebody's going to lose. But as far as a showcase for playing in tough conditions, that was a good one."

What a year 1996 was. The Argos had gone from 4–14 and twelfth in a 13-
team league the previous year to 15–3 and a Grey Cup. "If this isn't the best Argo
team of all-time," summed up Paul Masotti, "you tell me why it isn't."

The Icing on the Cake

It wasn't because the 1997 Argos were even better. They swept through the
regular season and then demolished Montreal in the Eastern Final. In the
Grey Cup they lined up against the Cinderella Saskatchewan Roughriders,
one of only three teams to beat them during the year. Because Matthews had
coached in Regina, he knew how hard they would play. Because the Riders had
vanquished both the Stampeders and Eskimos, he wasn't about to take them
lightly.

Odds makers heavily favored the double blue. For Saskatchewan to win
they would have to play the game of their lives while Toronto would have an off
day. Unfortunately for the 60,000 Saskatchewan fans who descended on
Edmonton, as well as at least one million watching on TV, Toronto, one of the
great teams of all time, played to the very best of their ability, staging a flawless
performance.

Temperature at game time was a bearable –7°C with very little wind. The
stands were full, mostly with those hoping for an upset. Their spirits soared
when Shannon Baker returned the opening kickoff 74 yards to the Toronto 34.
Kicker Mike Vanderjagt made the saving tackle. Reggie Slack threw 7 yards to
Don Narcisse, 4 to Mike Saunders. Shawn Daniels ran for 3 but that was it. Paul
McCallum kicked a 28-yard field goal at 2 minutes and 8 seconds to give the
underdogs a 3–0 lead.

Starting at his 27, Flutie marched the Argos to the Rider 30, the big play being a 34-yard strike to Paul Masotti. Rider hopes rose again when Bryce Bevill stepped in front of Robert Drummond at the 14 and picked off a pass. Shortly thereafter Lester Smith intercepted Reggie Slack. As in the previous Grey Cup, the Smith gang was making their presence felt.

Two plays later Bobby Jurasin sacked Flutie for a 17-yard loss. Vanderjagt punted to the Rider 39. After two incompletions Paul McCallum went back to punt. Donald Smith raced in from the right side and got a finger on the ball, deflecting it over the line. Saskatchewan was called for no yards. Toronto scrimmaged at the 32.

Drummond ran for 9 and 3 before Flutie hit Derrell Mitchell in the end zone for the touchdown. Toronto 7, Saskatchewan 3.

On the last play of the first quarter, Toronto started out at their 45 with a 5-yard run by Drummond. Masotti caught two passes for 12 and 7 yards. After Drummond picked up 5 yards on 2 carries, Flutie completed a 31-yard pass and run to him for a major. Toronto 14, Saskatchewan 3. The feeling running through the crowd was that it was over.

On their next possession the Argos went from their 51 to the Saskatchewan 15 but had to settle for a field goal. Trailing 17–3, Reggie Slack finally got the Westerners rolling, completing passes of 22 yards to Saunders, 15 to Dan Farthing and 13 to Curtis Mayfield. Mike Saunders ran 9 yards to the 3. Shawn Daniels took it in for the touchdown. Kevin Mason and Paul McCallum botched the 2-point conversion. Toronto 17, Saskatchewan 9.

With only 41 seconds remaining in the half, Saskatchewan went into the prevent defense. Flutie completed three passes totaling 42 yards, taking them to the Roughrider 5-yard line. On the last play of the half, Vanderjagt increased Toronto's lead to 20–9.

The Argos were out of the dressing room early, anxious to get the third quarter under way. For Saskatchewan to have a chance, it was imperative that they got off to a good start in the third quarter. Instead the Argos ran a reverse on the opening kickoff and Adrian Smith ran it 95 yards for the winning touchdown. Game, set, match: Toronto 27, Saskatchewan 9.

On their next possession the Argos went 73 yards in five plays for another touchdown. Three plays later the Smith gang was at it again with Lester intercepting Reggie Slack and returning it to the Rider 44. Five plays later, Flutie hooked up with Pinball Clemons for the score. At the end of the third quarter the score was Toronto 41, Saskatchewan 9.

In the final 15 minutes Toronto added two field goals, the Riders two touchdowns. The final score was Toronto 47, Saskatchewan 23, but it wasn't that close.

Flutie was in fine form for the postgame interviews. "I'm sorry we're from Toronto, but we're from Toronto," he said with a grin, knowing their win was unpopular. "Everybody hates you. It would have been nice to have 50,000 people cheering for us and enjoying the game instead of being disappointed at the outcome. But it was a great atmosphere and Edmonton's thrown a great party all week long. The activities were well-attended. You walked down the street and everybody was talking Grey Cup, and that's a great feeling. This league has made so much progress over the last couple of years. This year has been a very, very positive year for the league."

Flutie was proud of his back-to-back Grey Cup wins. "For those who were there last year and this year, it is something extra special because it puts you into an elite group. Now you start working toward next year."

He paused. "I don't enjoy wins enough. I really don't know how to celebrate. It's a feeling of satisfaction to me, kind of a relief, it's off my chest, it's done. I can enjoy my off-season now and relax."

Don Matthews talked about the big plays. "The return just before the half, where we got points going in, and then the return to start the second half. That's 10 points and all of a sudden our lead grows."

As for Adrian Smith's return, he said, "If I had known what he could do, I'd have put him back there sooner. He was back there because Derrell Mitchell wonked his knee a little bit. Mitchell was supposed to be the guy.

"Daryl Edralin, who was the coach during the week, found that the wide-field return was going to be effective, and we put it in for Derrell Mitchell. When he hurt his knee, we just made the change to Adrian and faked the reverse to a high-profile guy named Pinball, who sucked a bunch of people with him, and Adrian took it to the house. This is all group effort though. It always is."

Adrian Smith's contribution didn't surprise Flutie. "Adrian's been making big plays for us the last two years. This was just a unique situation in that it was a kick return. Adrian may be the fastest guy on the team. I was hoping to take the ball and march it down the field, put a nice drive together and try to break their back. The drive ended up being one play, a kick return."

Matthews summed up 1997. "This is the best team I think I've ever been on because of Doug Flutie. Has anybody ever thrown 47 touchdown passes? The year before 48? 5,500 yards? Our defense? To me what this team has accomplished is unparalleled. The numbers say that. Today they went out and played. They do the things necessary to win. They care about each other. They are really a fine football team."

Was the 1997 Argo team the best? Said Paul Masotti, "I think it was because we had our starting unit go through training camp. We had a lot of late additions the year before, guys like Johnny Harris, Mike O'Shea. I mean our offensive line picked up where we left off last year with Willie Williams, with the addition of Dan Payne moving in for Vic Stevenson, and Chris Perez. We're well coached, we're very driven, we're dedicated to what we do and I think we've proved it two years in a row."

Keeping this great team together proved an impossible task. Robert Drummond, Jimmy Cunningham, Dan Payne and Noah Cantor defected to B.C., Andrew Stewart and Ken Bensen to Saskatchewan, Most Outstanding Lineman Mike Kiselak to Dallas, Mike Vanderjagt to Indianapolis and Most Outstanding Player Doug Flutie to Buffalo. Don Matthews had to replace 15 players.

His new quarterback was Kerwin Bell, who had previous stops in Sacramento, Edmonton, Atlanta, Tampa Bay and Indianapolis. Bell was Matthews' quarterback with Orlando of the World League of American Football. Although considered a mediocre journeyman, Bell, under Matthews' tutelage, led the league in completions, percentage completions, yardage and passing efficiency at 100.3. Toronto finished at 9–9 in third place, losing the semifinal to Montreal. Citing uncertainty over Argo ownership, Matthews signed with the Eskimos on January 11, 1999. He was replaced by his assistant Jim Barker.

As the millennium draws to a close, the Argos are in the hunt for a play-off spot even though they have traded sophomore sensation quarterback Nealon Greene to—who else?—Edmonton for Jimmy Kemp. When team owner Interbrew, a Belgian company, announced in August 1999 that the Argos and Blue Jays were for sale, the resignation of the dynamic president of the club, Bob Nicholson, soon followed.

Toronto has appeared in 34 of the 86 Grey Cups played, winning 21, making them the unofficial Grey Cup champions of the twentieth century. Given that proud tradition, it is difficult to imagine Canada's largest city without the Argonauts. But with ownership uncertainty and the never-ending efforts of some Hogtowners to bring NFL football to the shores of Lake Ontario, the long-term prospects for survival are in doubt.

CHAPTER 4

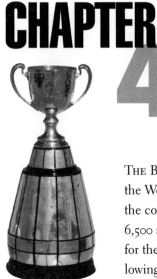

British Columbia
Roar You Lions Roar!

THE BRITISH COLUMBIA LIONS WERE ADMITTED TO the Western Interprovincial Football Union in 1953, the conditions being a 15,000 seat stadium, the sale of 6,500 season tickets and guaranteed travel expenses for the visiting teams. The team began play the following year. So began the story of one of the truly wonderful and wacky franchises in the history of Canadian sport. What other team was afraid of their playing field because they thought they might get lockjaw? Is there another franchise from whose ranks you could pick an all-time prison team like Vancouver columnist Jim Taylor did? What other team was kept out of the Grey Cup for 13 years, some believed, by a mother's curse? What other team would fire a coach who never had a losing season and who had won the Grey Cup?

Allan McEachern, former Lions director and president, CFL President and Acting Commissioner, and now Chief Justice of the B.C. Supreme Court, was present at the creation although not directly involved. "There are always a lot of myths and mystery about those things," he said. "I can't tell you who had the actual inspiration, but a lot of people think it was Ken Stauffer and Vic Spencer, some of their friends and a fellow called Bill Clancy.

"Stauffer owned a well-frequented nightclub called the Arctic Club. That's where a lot of the beautiful people gathered. That's the myth everybody generally accepts, and I think it's true.

"They got other people to join the group, and eventually they made a proposal. The timing was right because in 1954 we hosted the British Empire Games, and they were building a new stadium at Exhibition Park, Empire Stadium. These people put the idea together and hired Annis Stukus to promote it.

"He was going to be the coach, general manager and head salesman. He did a first-class job of stirring up interest. He wasn't known as the Loquacious Lithuanian for nothing."

Stuke

Annis Stukus at first resisted the siren song from Lotus Land. After founding the Edmonton Eskimos, Stukus had returned to Toronto. But the Lion directors kept after him to come out to the West Coast, and, he said, "I came out here to tell them to leave me alone. I gave them about a seven-to-eight-page single-spaced history on legal pad paper of how to start a football team from scratch: the pitfalls, the things to do, how to raise the money, the whole damn thing. I gave it to them for nothing. It was worth $25,000–50,000. It would have been a hell of a book.

"They'd have a meeting that ended at 11:00 P.M. Vancouver time and they'd phone me at 2:00 A.M. Toronto time and say, 'We don't understand page three, paragraph four.'

"I told them, 'I have a good notion to go out there and straighten you guys out once and for all. I want you to leave me alone!'

"I went out there in the middle of February. The sun was shining, the crocuses were blooming, the daffodils were up. They drove me through Stanley Park and put me up at the Sylvia Hotel on the waterfront.

"I phoned my wife that night and said I found out why they built the Rocky Mountains: so we Easterners wouldn't find out about British Columbia. But I told her I wasn't taking the job. Famous last words.

"Just so they'd leave me alone I asked for a three-year contract. They said they couldn't afford to pay that kind of money, that's more than the NFL pays. They said they expected to lose $100,000 per year for the next two or three years.

"Knowing they wouldn't do it, I said, 'You give me a three-year contract at X dollars and give me 25 percent of the profits. I'll gamble with you.' They had a meeting and agreed to pay me what I originally asked. That 25 percent of the profits cost me $53,000 over the next two years."

Stukus was a bargain. "I did everything," he recalled. I was a one-man staff.

I had a business manager, but I ran the operation. Period! Coach, publicity, ticket sales, the whole damn schmear."

The team went into their inaugural season with the slogan "The Lions will Roar in '54."

"We roared," Stukus grimaced, "mainly in pain. We won one game but broke every attendance record in the CFL. We beat Calgary—a 9–4 one-sided win—and as a result of it, they missed the play-offs. They've been mad at us ever since."

When Stukus started the Eskimos, he was able to raid other teams and put a winner on the field his second year. Building a ball club was a lot tougher in B.C. "By the time B.C. got into it, all the doors were closed. The only negotiation list they gave me was a copy of the other teams' so that I wouldn't touch any of their players. So they made it very difficult. Getting the Canadians was the toughest part. We had to develop our own—no more stealing, no more borrowing. The league hadn't come up with free agency yet. I was lucky I was able to pick out talent."

A recruiting coup for Stukus was NFL star offensive tackle Arnie Weinmeister. "I was able to get him for one reason: he was tied up with the Teamsters Union in Seattle. When Saskatchewan took him off their negotiation list, I jumped into my car and drove down to Seattle to see him. Crossing my fingers, I said, 'Arnie, what would it take to get you to come and play in Vancouver for two years?'

"He said, 'Give me a two-year, no-cut contract at $15,000 a year (I was figuring $25,000). Plus, after we play on Monday, I want to go down to Seattle for a couple of days and keep my contacts with the Teamsters Union going.'

"That's what we did. That was the reason we got him. Arnie Weinmeister turned out to be the number three man in the entire union. Weinmeister had been the highest paid lineman in the NFL at $10,000 a year."

In 1954 the Western Interprovincial Football Union quarterbacks were Bernie Faloney, Frank Tripuka, Indian Jack Jacobs and Eddie LeBaron. Stuke had a guy named Johnny Mazur, late of Notre Dame. When he started for the Fighting Irish, rosary sales went up considerably.

"I found out later he was the only college senior that ever got beat out by a sophomore," Stukus recalled. "After a couple of games I could see why. Johnny would freeze. I told him once when we were pinned down inside our 15-yard line, 'Johnny, I want you to throw the ball.' 'Yeah, yeah,' he said. Two running plays and a kick. I said, 'I told you to throw the damn thing.' Two running plays and a kick. I finally pulled him out. 'What the hell's going on here? I told you what to do.' He said, 'My college coach doesn't let you pass inside your 25-yard line. No goddamn Canadian coach is going to make me do it.'

"I said, 'Well, *this* guy will. Now you get the hell out there and throw the ball or I put on the pads at my age and show you how.' He went out there and threw a pass, hauled off and just threw it 80 yards to make sure it wasn't intercepted—or caught.

"Every once in a while the fog would clear, and he'd take the team up the field like there was nothing to it. He could have been a hell of a quarterback, but he was too American footballized."

It rained so much in the Lions' inaugural season that the field at Empire Stadium resembled a swamp. The players were seriously afraid of getting lockjaw. "Our gang took tetanus shots," Stukus said. "They put the wrong kind of grass in there, plus we had eight home games and it rained—and I'm talking about rain—for six of them. The field was a quagmire. I was afraid they were going to make us play somewhere else."

The slogan for the following year was "The Lions will Survive in '55." Which they did, winning five games. Stukus had a quarterback, Arnie Galiffa from the NFL. "I got him for about $12,000," Stukus recalled. "He had been with the 49ers and Giants. Arnie Galiffa was the kind of guy I was looking for. He had earned the most letters of any athlete in the history of West Point. He was an All-American basketball player, an All-American football player. He could have been an All-American baseball player because he hit.380. He won two medals in Korea for leadership and bravery.

"We won five games in 1955. We came awfully close because by now I had some football players. We had a 4-point game that cost us a chance for the play-offs. Some of my Canadians had developed. And I had Galiffa, so I knew I was okay."

When Stukus left at the end of the season, Galiffa also was gone. But thanks to Stukus the Lions were a big hit at the box office. He described his approach. "I gave my directors the budget that was the highest in the West and told them, 'Right now there is no chance of us winning a game. I haven't got a quarterback.'

"Two weeks later I went back to them. I said, 'I forgot. I need $40,000 more.' They said, 'Oh, no! What for?'

"I said, 'Most of the teams spend $5,000 for the entire year on pregame and half-time entertainment. I'm going to spend $5,000 a game to disguise the fact that there are nights when there is not much of a football game going on. I'm going to hook the women.'"

"I would say that when we were breaking attendance records we had the highest concentration of women at a sports event anywhere in the world except maybe Wimbledon tennis. We sold the game to the gals."

As it turned out, Stukus was too successful for his own good. From the beginning he had to cope with a meddlesome board of directors, some of whom, in his opinion, were conspiring to put an end to community ownership by purchasing the team themselves. Stukus would have none of it.

"The whole problem," he explained, "was we had made so much money with only six wins—one in '54 and five in '55. I left them with $210,000 cold cash in the bank.

"But then I began to get little feelers. 'Stuke, what do you think of private ownership?'

'Oh, one day, when we've got the damn thing settled away,' I'd say, 'and it's going by itself, where we can let the secretary run the operation, yeah, not a bad idea. A couple of young millionaires pick up the team for a Cadillac or a boat and put the rest back in the football operation where it belongs.' But any five-man syndicate that's going to pick up a fast $25,000 a year—over my dead body.'

"So they arranged it."

Stuke called a confidence meeting of the board of directors. "I had heard rumors that there was some sabotage going on," he said. "I figured I'd had enough of this. Three bloody years of sticking my neck out, busting my ass 20 hours a day—for what? It was for them, not for me!

"Teddy Reeve and Jim Coleman had warned me about it. 'Stuke, not even you can sell football to those fish-eaters.' My ears went up."

Stuke laid his cards on the table and asked for the directors' continued support. "I lost 15–13," he recalled. "They were supposed to offer me another job, but Hal Strait of the *Vancouver Sun* had been after me for a couple of years. He had told me before going to the coast, 'Stuke, this isn't like Edmonton. You think that bunch in Edmonton were nuts? Wait'll you meet these guys.' He was right.

"We had another meeting, and the directors said they would like to talk over the situation. I said, 'Too late, fellows, I just signed a contract with the *Vancouver Sun* to be their football editor.'"

Feline Follies

For the rest of the decade the Lions were a good example of how too many cooks spoil the broth. Continual interference by directors resulted in terrible decision-making.

Stukus was succeeded by Clem Crowe, who had coached Ottawa to a Grey Cup in 1951. The Lions won 10 games over the 1956–57 seasons. The fans would chant "Crowe must go," and after starting the 1958 season with five straight losses, they got their wish. He was followed by former player Danny Edwards, who won three games the rest of the way.

In 1957 Lion president Bill McMahon hired Kelowna whiz kid Herb Capozzi as general manager. Bob Ackles, who would build a Grey Cup champion in Vancouver, a Super Bowl champion in Dallas and is now doing the same with the Miami Dolphins, remembered Capozzi well. "Herb had always done a good job. The only time there had been a hint of a problem was when he wanted to get too much involved in the coaching. That's always what it seems to be in our business when someone wants more credit.

"Herb Capozzi became the general manager in his late 20s. He had a lot of good ideas and did a lot of good things for the CFL at that time. I always felt he missed his calling because he was a very bright guy and well spoken. He speaks five or six languages. He wasn't a Rhodes Scholar, but he was that kind of student.

"After he got out of football, he got into politics. He got beaten there after about six years, and he never really did anything with his life."

After the disastrous 1958 season, Capozzzi plucked Wayne Robinson from Bud Grant's staff in Winnipeg. Robinson was a drill sergeant type of coach whom Dale Carnegie would have punched in the mouth.

With number one NFL draft pick Randy Duncan at quarterback and Willie Fleming at halfback, Wayne Robinson's 1959 Lions recorded their first winning record—9–7—and their first appearance in postseason play. Although they lost to the Eskimos 61–15 in the two-game total-point semifinal series, things were looking up on Canada's West Coast.

It was a mirage. The following year the Lions were 5–9–2 and back in fourth place. In 1961 Wayne Robinson recruited Minnesota All-American middle linebacker Tom Brown and halfway through the season traded quarterback Jim Walden, tight-end Bruce Claridge, defensive end Ed O'Bradovich and guard Bill Crawford to Calgary for quarterback Joe Kapp. The Lions won but a single game that year. Robinson was fired in September, replaced by assistant Dave Skrein.

Because of continued mismanagement and executive interference, the Lions were going nowhere. In 1961 the board of directors asked for an investigation, the recommendations from which would serve to guide the future of the franchise. One of those asked to take part was Allan McEachern. "The team hadn't done well on the field although it was a great success financially," he said. "There was a lot of dissension. The annual meetings were just a riot, and the election of directors was a popularity contest. Everybody was quite unhappy with the way the team was performing.

"It was recognized that there was a problem of management. There were groups out there trying to buy the club. So they invited Frank McMahon, who had been involved with the Stampeders, Al Anderson from the Eskimos and Don McPherson from Regina to take a look at the situation."

Why was the investigative team necessary? Bob Ackles explained, "I think it was because of all the squabbling. We had 25 members on the board of directors. They were always having these great meetings where someone was going to take over the team, that type of thing.

"Kenny MacKenzie and that group went to Commissioner Sydney Halter and said we needed some help. They recommended that the board of directors be reduced to nine and that there be a three-year maximum term.

"They came up with a president, Slim Delbridge, who was a strong, business-minded type of guy. When Slim came in with that nine man board, Al McEachern was there, and they became a strong, no-nonsense group.

"Slim had the final say, and nobody would ever argue with Slim Delbridge because of the kind of guy he was."

Said Allan McEachern, "I was one of the three-year appointees on the first round. Slim Delbridge was one of the directors. He was the natural president because he had the time. He was a businessman. He published the local newspaper. He turned out to be a very strong president."

The Lions Roar in '63 and '64

Coming into the 1960s the Lions had the nucleus of a good football team anchored by linebacker–defensive end Norm Fieldgate and fullback By Bailey, who had been with the team from the beginning.

Fieldgate went from Regina's Scott Collegiate to the CFL Hall of Fame.

Although he couldn't make his hometown Roughriders, he played 14 years for the Lions, appearing in two Grey Cups. He was a co-founder of the CFL Players Association. His sweater was retired, and the trophy for Outstanding Defensive Lineman in the Western Conference was named for him. He was four times an All-Star. He retired after the 1967 season, and in 1994 as a B.C. Lions executive, Fieldgate was honored for his contributions to the game with the Commissioner's Award.

How did the boy from Regina with the nickname "Mouse" end up with the B.C. Lions? "I played junior football in Regina," he explained. "A couple of the pals I went to school with moved to Vancouver, so after I tried out in Saskatchewan and didn't make it. I thought I can't stop there, so I went to B.C., where my friends were. I stayed with the team 14 years and got established."

After six years of doing the wrong thing, Fieldgate explained what turned the Lions around. "The players stayed together. The coaches didn't make too many changes. We didn't have too many injuries in '63 and '64, so they weren't replacing players in the middle of the season. Willie Fleming came into his own. We got Tom Brown. He was probably our biggest asset at the time. His ability and leadership had a lot to do with our success. Joe Kapp's leadership was also very important."

After the Lions' 1–13–2 1961 season, Dave Skrein coached the club to 7–9, good enough for fourth place. In 1963 the Lions finished first with a mark of 12–4, defeated Saskatchewan in the Western Final and prepared to host the Grey Cup against Hamilton.

The Lions' offense was led by quarterback Joe Kapp and halfback Willie Fleming. Pat Claridge, Jerry Janes, Mack Burton and Sonny Homer were the receivers. Lonie Dennis, Tom Hinton, Steve Cotter and Gary Schwertfegert anchored the line. Nub Beamer and Bill Munsey were in the backfield with Fleming.

Dick Fouts, Mike Cacic, Mike Martin and Greg Findlay were on the defensive line with Tom Brown, Norm Fieldgate and either Walt Bilicki or Paul Seale at linebacker. The stars of the secondary were Bill Lasseter, Ron Morris, Neal Beaumont, Steve Schafer and By Bailey, who led the team with eight interceptions.

Seven Lions made All-Canadian in 1963, Dave Skrein was Coach of the Year and Tom Brown won the Schenley Award for Most Outstanding Lineman.

The Lions won the awards, Hamilton the Grey Cup. On Grey Cup day,

Saturday, November 30, the sky was clear and the temperature was 7°C. This was the fourth Grey Cup held in Vancouver, but despite the presence of the hometown team and good weather, the game drew the smallest crowd at 35,545.

Before the half Hamilton's Bernie Faloney threw a 4-yard touchdown pass to Willie Bethea. Art Baker scored from the 1. Peter Kempf replied for the Lions with a field goal.

Hamilton added to their 14–3 lead in the third quarter when Faloney and Hal Patterson combined on a 70-yard pass and run for a touchdown, making the score 21–3. Mack Burton scored the Lion's lone major in the fourth quarter. The final score was Hamilton 21, B.C. 10.

The 1963 Grey Cup is remembered for the Willie Fleming incident, when an Angelo Mosca hit knocked Fleming out cold and out of the game. The event obscured the fact that Hamilton was a fine football team that beat the best defense in the country.

How big a factor was the loss of Willie Fleming? "The odds were against us after Willie was hurt although we were respectable," observed Norm Fieldgate. "I guess the play itself wasn't that bad, except Mosca did catch him with his knee. He got a 15-yard penalty, which isn't much to sacrifice for losing a player. I don't think there was any intent to harm. That was just the way Mosca played. But Willie got hit on the head and was dizzy, so it was hard to put him back in."

Bob Ackles looked back at the Fleming incident. "I think it was blown out of proportion. Here's the home team getting beat, and Angelo Mosca is a guy everyone loves to hate. Yeah, it was kind of a late hit on the sidelines, but it wasn't as bad as it was built up to be. But here's your star player going out, the only hope you thought you had at that time of winning the game, and Mosca puts him out for the remainder of the game.

"Those things happen all the time. It's just that it happened in Vancouver. At the time it really got everyone up in arms against the dirty *Easterners*."

The Ti-Cats claim they would have won anyway. "Yeah, I don't question that," Vancouver's Ackles allowed. "They were a better team at that time, and they'd been to Grey Cups. They were a more mature team."

When Fleming got hurt nine minutes into the second quarter, he had 12 yards on 5 carries and no receptions. The Ti-Cats were ready for him. But Fleming had had an excellent season, rushing for 1,234 yards and averaging 9.7 yards per carry, the best in Canadian football history. His 7.05 career average has been exceeded only by Tracy Ham and Damon Allen.

Although they lost at home 21–10, the Lions' Norm Fieldgate had few regrets. "It may be a little different getting into a Grey Cup when you are 21 years old versus when you are in your 30s. I had been through enough of the losses that just getting there was a great thrill. Playing in Vancouver in front of our fans was great, and then having a chance to go back the next year and play the same team made it all that much sweeter to beat them in Toronto 34–24."

That year was 1964. The Lions beat Calgary in the Conference Final after finishing first again with a record of 11–2–3. The Lions placed six players on the All-Canadian team, Hamilton nine. The Ti-Cats' Ralph Sazio was the Coach of the Year. Tom Brown repeated as the winner of the Schenley Award for Outstanding Lineman. Tommy Grant of Hamilton won the Schenley for best Canadian.

This time Hamilton won the awards, B.C. the Grey Cup.

Early in the first quarter Joe Kapp worked the Lions down the field to the Hamilton 1-yard line. Bob Swift went over. B.C. 7, Hamilton 0.

In the second stanza the Leos lined up at the Ti-Cat 15-yard line to try a field goal. Backup quarterback and holder Pete Ohler dropped the ball. He calmly picked it up and threw to Jim Carphin in the end zone. They missed the convert.

Willie Fleming recalled the play. "An accident? Not really. We had *thinking* ballplayers. Jim really had to be thinking to get up, see it was a broken play and get out there for a pass. We turned misfortune into victory."

Before the half Fleming ran 46 yards for B.C.'s third touchdown. The score was 20–1 after 30 minutes of play.

The mishandled snap wasn't the only "bad" break B.C. suffered in the second quarter. For the second year in a row, the Lions lost their leading rusher, this time fullback Bob Swift, who tore up his knee and couldn't return to battle. He had led the Lions with 1,054 yards rushing that year. Swift was replaced by second-year man Bill Munsey, an All-Canadian defensive back with nine interceptions.

Before that Hamilton scored their first touchdown. Bernie Faloney ran a yard beyond the line of scrimmage before pitching out to Johnny Counts, who went 58 yards to the end zone, the third longest run in Grey Cup history.

Then Bill Munsey went to work.

In a performance reminiscent of Red Storey in 1938, Munsey demolished the Ti-Cats in a mere 3 minutes and 8 seconds. He was devastating on both sides of the ball. With the score 20–8, Munsey ran 18 yards for a touchdown. Three minutes later Falony tried the lateral to Johnny Counts again, but it was low and Counts couldn't handle it. Munsey picked up the ball and went 71 yards for the touchdown, the third longest in Grey Cup history. At the end of the third quarter, B.C. led 34–8.

In the final frame, Faloney threw touchdown passes to Tommy Grant and Stan Crisson. Don Sutherin added a convert, Zuger his second single and the Lions conceded a safety touch. The final score was 34–24. In their first win ever over Hamilton, the Lions had also won their first Grey Cup.

Joe Kapp compared the two Grey Cup games. "The difference between winning and losing in those years was our health and our growth from one year to the next. We had terrible injuries in 1963. Several of our guys didn't play, and Willie Fleming didn't finish the game because he got hurt. In 1964 I knew we were going to win. We were healthy, we had grown as a team and we had no trouble winning."

Kapp also played in the 1959 Rose Bowl and 1970 Super Bowl. "I wasn't able to be on the winning side in the Rose Bowl or Super Bowl. We won the Grey Cup, so naturally I have a very special feeling when I think of it. The Grey Cup is special because there is a lot of national pride involved."

"I think it was just a case of growing up in 1964," said Willie Fleming. "We were kind of excited the first time in '63. In '64 we knew what to look for. We had a lot of good ballplayers and everybody contributed. We really pulled together. We had a good team that had been together for four or five years."

While Kapp and Fleming were great ballplayers, the real reason for Leo success, contended Norm Fieldgate, was an exceptional defense. "Having a middle linebacker like Tom Brown was like having an extra guy on the field most of the time," he contended. "Dick Fouts made a great contribution at defensive end. We never had any real superstars on defense, but we played as a unit. We held many teams to under 100 yards per game."

Bob Ackles fondly remembered November 29, 1964. "I think we just kicked their ass. Hamilton had big, tough guys, and they were playing pretty close to home, but we beat their butts pretty damn good."

The Chief Justice also remembered that day. "Oh, gosh, yes," he enthused. "Oh, boy, do I ever. We were underdogs and just had an outstanding Grey Cup game. Kapp, Fleming and Bill Munsey had the greatest game of their lives. That's what did it.

The B.C. Lions on their way to their first Grey Cup win in 1964.

"I was with the team in Toronto and it was just a great experience. Every-one wanted to be in the dressing room of a championship team. It was a great moment. You don't forget those."

Ackles described the scene upon the team's return to Vancouver. "Wild. We arrived home late, about nine or ten o'clock. There were about 20,000 people at the airport all standing in the pouring rain. It was quite a sight."

Many thought a dynasty was in the making, but the Lions wouldn't win another Grey Cup for 21 years. "In 1965 we lost several games by a point," explained Fieldgate. "The difference between winning and losing isn't very great. Once you start to lose, things start to break up. Guys are cut, new guys are brought in. Tom Brown got hurt. In 1967 Kapp went to Minnesota and Willie left. There was no one to replace them."

How good was Tom Brown? He made the Hall of Fame on the basis of only three seasons, 1962–64. In 1965 Brown injured his neck, playing very little his last two years. The tragedy of Tom Brown is that he was probably the greatest linebacker of all time in the CFL, but his career was cut short because of an injury.

Feline Follies: The Sequel

After winning the Grey Cup, the Lions missed the play-offs seven of the next eight years. Denny Veitch replaced Herb Capozzi as general manager in 1967, and when the Lions started off 0–3, he fired Coach Dave Skrein, replacing him with his assistant, Jim Champion.

Under Champion the Lions won eight games. When they went 1–10 in 1969, Champion was replaced by Jackie Parker. He inspired the Lions to win four of their last five games and finish in third place. The next year the Lions dropped to fourth place with a 6–10 record.

Jackie Parker replaced Denny Veitch in the front office. He brought in his old buddy Eagle Keys to turn the franchise around. Center Al Wilson, an All-Canadian seven straight years (a feat equaled only by Jerry Campbell and surpassed by Garney Henley), thought the world of the Big Bird from Turkey Neck Bend. "He was great. I was very young when I got Eagle," recalled Wilson. "He was probably one of the last old-school coaches who loved the running game and understood it immensely. We only passed when it was time to pass. He knew the game well.

"Eagle Keys was charged with rebuilding a team," Wilson continued, "He had come from the great Saskatchewan teams, and it was a little rough for him on the West Coast. The West Coast boys weren't quite up to what the farm boys of Regina were doing."

With players like Jim Young, Don Moorhead, Rocky Long, Al Wilson, Johnny Musso, Ray Nettles and Monroe Eley, Keys began to build another Lion contender. Jim Young became the first Lion to win a Schenley, the Outstanding Canadian Award in 1970, which he won again in 1972. Ray Nettles and Young were All-Canadians.

In 1971 the Lions finished fourth with a record of 6–9–1. The following year was worse at 5–11 and a fifth-place finish. They made third place and the play-offs in 1973. Come Thanksgiving of 1974, the Lions were 8–4, in first place and ready to play a home-and-home series with the Saskatchewan Roughriders. They lost both games.

Then B.C.'s old nemesis struck again: things off the field started to influence things on the field. Al Wilson explained what happened. "We're 8–4. We're in first place. We go down to a nightclub, The Breakers. Don Moorhead gets into a fight, punches some guy and breaks his throwing hand. We go 8–8, wind up third and lose a play-off game 24–10 in Regina."

Problems continued into the off-season, when defensive linemen Garrett Hunsperger and Bud Magrum were charged and convicted of assault and willful damage. They were fined thousands of dollars. Assistant General Manager Bob Ackles talked about the incident. "The Hunsperger thing was one of the toughest things that ever happened to that football club. At that time the club was down. We hadn't been winning. We'd been almost begging people to attend the games. And then the Hunsperger thing.

"I brought Hunsperger and Bud Magrum into Eagle's office and said, 'Coach, here's what we can do.' They both had received a summons from the court. I had the summons in my hand for each of them. The events had happened in Prince George and on Vancouver Island.

"I had this lawyer lined up on Vancouver Island, and he said, 'I need $100 each from the players. I don't want it from the club—it's got to be from the players so they understand that it's going to cost them some money.'

"So I said, 'Eagle, we've got to get these guys to give us a check for $100 each, and I'm going to send it overnight to this lawyer, and they'll get their day in court.'

"In front of Eagle, they said, 'Yeah, okay, we're going to do it,' but then the bastards never did anything. It just blew up. If you don't reply to a summons, it's almost like telling the judge to go screw himself.

"It caused an awful lot of problems. It just killed us in the press. They hammered us on a daily basis for nearly two weeks on that thing. We had more season ticket cancellations over that situation than having a losing season. It set the club back a long way, and it took a long time to get over it. In fact it took probably to the 1977 season before we began to come back from those problems.

"Then we got into a hassle over the sale of the club that lasted two and one-half months, and that was in the press on an almost daily basis. We had a constant state of disruption since dropping that game to Saskatchewan in October of '74 and it just kept building, building, building."

The team's fortunes in 1975 were no better. By August 27 the Leos were 1–5. Attendance was down, the club was facing a financial crunch, and Jackie Parker and Eagle Keys were fired. Al Wilson commented, "The directors felt they had to make a change. I don't think it had anything to do with Eagle Keys, quite frankly. It was totally political. It had nothing to do with ability."

Parker and Keys were replaced by Canadians Cal Murphy and Bob Ackles. For Ackles, becoming general manager marked the final step in a career that had begun as waterboy. Ackles explained how he came to work for the B.C. Lions. "I moved from Ontario with my family in 1952. I was just turning 13, and in 1953 the Lions were accepted into the WIFU for the 1954 season. As soon as there was an announcement made, I went down to 411 West Hastings Street and applied to Annis Stukus to be the first waterboy for the B.C. Lions.

"And, of course, I didn't hear from them, but I kept watching the papers. Then within, I'd say, two or three months, there was a notice in the paper that they were going to have a tryout. I cornered Stukus again and he put me to work with Tiger Kozak, who was the first equipment manager. I actually watched the first practice they ever held and was an employee at the end of the first practice.

"I had some great times. Tiger Kozak was a Damon Runyan type character. I traveled with the team on a couple of occasions and roomed with Tiger, which was quite interesting for a 16-year-old."

He described the situation when he took over as GM. "Well," he chuckled, "I didn't really know that the club was near bankruptcy even though I was the assistant general manager. We were down to maybe 10,000 season ticket holders. I was brought into a board meeting at noon one day and told that they were firing Jackie Parker and that they wanted me to take over as interim general manager. After a discussion with them, I did.

"And they said, 'Now we're going to fire Eagle Keys. Who of the assistants do you want as your head coach?' I said, 'Cal Murphy.'

"I went out with Tom Hinton to the stadium and talked to Eagle. Then I had to talk to Cal. Of course, assistants, when they first find out the head coach has been fired, are all up in arms—you know, *grrr, grrr, grrr*. I had to talk to Cal. It was tough. It was really the darkest day of my career with the B.C. Lions, firing two good friends, guys I'd worked with for five or six years.

"And then we weren't a very good football team, but we went on to win the next three games, two against Winnipeg, one at home, one on the road. Then we beat Toronto. We started to get a little excitement going and get a few more people in the park. Then the thing collapsed.

"I don't think anyone expected me to be there more than that season," Ackles continued. "People thought when I got this job, 'What are they doing now, getting the waterboy to run the club?' Things were difficult, but I was tougher than a lot of people thought I could be."

At the end of the 1976 campaign Ackles fired Cal Murphy, another friend of long standing. Murphy was hurt and disappointed, and the myth persists that for several years they didn't speak. Murphy said, "I ran into Bobby at the coaches convention in the Fort Lauderdale–Miami area a few weeks after he fired me and we had a drink together. He was buying." (After Donald Crump resigned as CFL commissioner in 1991, Murphy campaigned on Ackles' behalf for the job. Larry Smith got it.)

The new coach was Vic Rapp, a Ray Jauch assistant from Edmonton. He wasn't the Lions' first choice. B.C. had actually hired Leo Cahill, but Leo asked to be released from his agreement when Bill Hodgson called from Toronto.

Rapp put his stamp on the team immediately, cutting All-Star defensive end Wayne Smith for showing up late for training camp and trading All-Star Ray Nettles to Toronto. Making Simon Legree look like a choirboy, Rapp ran the toughest training camp in the country. By opening day the team was in superb shape and ready to rumble.

Led by former Green Bay quarterback Jerry Tagge, the Lions went 10–6, finishing in a first-place tie with Edmonton and Winnipeg. The Lions got second. In their first play-off game at home since 1964, the Lions squeaked by Winnipeg 33–32 before being lambasted by the Eskimos 38–1.

Receiver Leon Bright won the Schenley for Outstanding Rookie and Al Wilson the award for Outstanding Lineman. Tagge was runner-up for the Most Outstanding Player Award. Vic Rapp was Coach of the Year.

Plagued by inconsistency, the Lions never fulfilled their promise under Vic Rapp. After finishing second in 1977, they made the play-offs in alternating years. When they finished fourth in 1982, Rapp was fired.

A Mother's Curse

Perhaps the reason the Lions didn't win a Grey Cup between the Skrien and Matthews eras had nothing to do with the coach. Perhaps they were unsuccessful in their quest because Jimmy Young was in their lineup.

In 1965–66 Young had been busy ruining the chances of the Minnesota Vikings. Many believe it was the arrival in the Twin Cities of Bud Grant in 1967 that turned the expansion Vikes from doormat to perennial contender. Not so. In 1967 Young was traded to the Lions for Joe Kapp. From that point on Minnesota couldn't lose (except Super Bowls) and B.C. couldn't win.

The story began in Hamilton, where, according to a Toronto proverb, formal dinner means bringing a black lunch pail. In the late 1950s Jim Young was an all-around athlete, a conscientious young man, an excellent student and a pride and joy to his parents, whose lives revolved around the Brethren Church.

Jim wanted to play football. Because of the pacifist beliefs of their Quaker-like church, his mother was opposed. When Jim's dad finally got his wife to attend a high school game, the favorite son was injured and carried off the field. Her worst fears were confirmed. Although Young's father was a football fan who attended most of Jim's games at Queen's, his mother would never be convinced.

After the shy, God-fearing Young left the cocoon to attend university, he became the outstanding college player in Canada. When he acquired the nickname "Dirty 30" as a pro, his mother went from afraid to appalled.

Although Young was a member of Athletes In Action, a group devoted to Christianity, he never returned to the church within which he was raised. Because of that his mother told him he had become a Jonah and his teams would never win. His mother's curse held. They didn't. In Lotus Land anything is possible.

When Young had left Queen's, the Argos drafted him but made no attempt to sign him. Joe Thomas, the man who built both Minnesota and Miami into champions, made him an excellent offer. Preferring to stay in Canada, Young apprised Argo GM Bob Shaw of the Viking offer. Refusing to take Young seriously, Shaw told him to sign with them. He did.

At the Viking training camp Young was surprised to realize that the Americans weren't any better than he was. He made the team but saw limited action due to injuries. At the end of the 1966 season, the Vikings decided that because of a wonky knee, Young was too much of a risk.

A measure of Young's ability was the maneuvering that followed to get him. First of all, B.C. traded three-time All-Canadian defensive end Dick Fouts and halfback Bill Symons to Toronto for his rights. The Lions then traded Joe Kapp to Minnesota for Young.

The Lions continued to lose after Young retired in 1979. The curse no longer in effect, Vic Rapp was quite capable of losing on his own.

Al Wilson described the Rapp regime. "We didn't have any true leadership on the teams at that time. There was no team consistency. When Vic Rapp came in, we played some great football, but Vic's problem was he never knew when to let up on us. He used to wear us out. We never let up during the second half of the season—never let up. It was like playing two games during the week.

"Rapp was a classic. Let's just put it that way. He was a classic. He was so hot-headed at times that he should have been on Valium. He knew his football, but, boy, he couldn't handle it. He was Vic against the world. He would take on anything or anybody at the drop of a hat. He never knew how to smooth out any situation."

Return to Greatness

Ackles again raided the Eskimo coaching staff for Rapp's successor, Don Matthews. In his first year at the helm, Matthews took the Lions to the Grey Cup, his seventh consecutive appearance.

Ackles thought Matthews was the key to success. "Hiring Don Matthews was the major move. We had a pretty good football team. Next to Jimmy Johnson, Don Matthews is the best I've ever worked with. Some people don't particularly like Don, but Don knows how to win football games. He knows talent, he knows how to select talent, he knows coaches, he knows how to hire coaches and he knows how to let them work. So I think the hiring of Don Matthews was key because he took a decent football team and put it into the Grey Cup in his first year.

"We would have been in the Grey Cup the next year, but we lost our starting quarterback, Roy DeWalt late in the season," Ackles continued. "We still finished first in 1984 but lost in the Western Final, and then in '85 we finished first and won it all. In '86, the year I left, Matthews lost in the Western Final, and the next year he got fired by Joe Galat because he lost three games. How dumb is that?"

For Al Wilson, the key to the club's change in fortune in 1983 also was Don Matthews. "He didn't make a lot of changes to the team, he just managed it differently. He managed his veterans very well. He didn't overwork them. He knew it was a long season. It was a completely different type of coaching approach, and it worked.

"And there we were in the Grey Cup, the first year that the man came. It was like we were walking on water. It was incredible that we actually got there."

Running back John Henry White also appreciated the Matthews approach at that time. "The main thing is the situation now is more relaxed," he explained at the time. "The players are not as tense. We can go out there and enjoy ourselves. The biggest thing is that we are on the same emotional level all the time instead of being really up for one game and down for the next."

Matthews explained his minimal contact approach to coaching. "The purpose of my training camp is to teach the system and evaluate players. We use the preseason games to scrimmage and make the final decisions. We used a similar system in Edmonton, and it seemed to be effective."

Matthews disagreed with Vic Rapp in other important ways. "Vic Rapp believed in running to set up the pass," said Matthews. "Our philosophy is just the opposite," said Matthews. "We're going to throw the ball first and then set up the run with the pass.

"The approach they used on defense was a bend-but-don't-break zone type of philosophy. I like to play a more aggressive style of defense. I want to put pressure on the opposition. When you try to put pressure on, you are assuming a lot of risk, but I'm willing to assume that risk for the result."

His approach was justified. The 1983 Lions finished first, scored the most points and surrendered the least. Defensively they led the CFL in almost every category. And if you build it they will come. A record 448,857 paying customers filled beautiful new B.C. Place Stadium.

The Lions had an outstanding offensive line with Al Wilson, Gerald Roper, Glenn Leonhard, John Blain and Don Swafford. The wide receivers were Merv Fernandez and Mark de Brueys. Jacques Chapdelaine and John Pankratz were the slots. Ron Dewalt was the quarterback with Ray Strong and John Henry White in the backfield.

Defensively Brent Racette, Mack Moore, Ruben Vaughan and Rick Klassen were the front four. The linebackers were Glen Jackson, Dave McNeel and Kevin Konar. The secondary had Jo Jo Heath and Kerry Parker on the corners, Melvin Byrd and Larry Crawford at half with Nelson Martin at safety. Lui Passaglia, already an eight-year veteran, was the kicker.

The 1983 Western Final against Winnipeg was a showcase for the talents of "Swervin'" Mervyn Fernandez. He was dynamite, hooking up with Roy Dewalt for three touchdowns on plays of 61, 27 and 71 yards. The final score was 39–21. The Lions were returning to the Grey Cup for the first time in 19 years. For the second time the Lions would play a Grey Cup at home. For the second time they would lose, this time 18–17 to the Argonauts.

The Lions won the first half, Toronto the second. Fernandez continued his sizzling play with 130 yards. He scored on a 45-yard pass and run in the first quarter. John Henry White took a pass 20 yards for a touchdown in the second stanza. Lui Pasaglia kicked a field goal. Jan Carinci replied for the Argos. The home team led at the half 17–7.

The Lions didn't score another point. Joe Barnes came on in relief of Condredge Holloway and led the Argos to a field goal and touchdown. "I remember at half time," said Wilson, "there was almost a festive atmosphere. I looked around and I couldn't believe it. We were all excited. It wasn't the same way we approached a game during the season or the play-offs. We all knew there were 60 minutes to play. It wasn't that we thought we had won it, but we certainly weren't in the same frame of mind that we usually were.

"And then a couple of things went wrong for us and a couple of plays never materialized. There was a fumble (it wasn't even a fumble). Carl Brazely came and stripped the ball right out of Ray Crouse's hands as he was going for a first down in open field. And then Jacques Chapedelaine doesn't pull one in.

"We had one of the best offenses in the entire league, and we couldn't muster a single point in the second half," Wilson continued. "Think about that. A couple of things went Toronto's way and that's all it took."

"The thing that hurt us," recalled GM Ackles, "was not having our receiver Ned Armour. We went with a rookie, Jacques Chapdelaine, and the poor kid dropped a ball that would have put us in field-goal range. That could have won us the game.

"Hank Ilesic had a hell of a day booming the ball, but both kickers had a good day. Lui was at his peak, too."

"I don't think the Argo bounce beat us," conceded Passaglia. "Toronto outplayed us. We had a good first half, but we didn't do anything the second half. I know Ilesic went one for five that day. If he had had a decent day field-goal kicking we wouldn't even have been in it near the end. I think Toronto was probably overall the better team, offensively anyhow. We had a chance near the end, when we threw a long pass. Jacques Chapdelaine got behind them, but the ball went right through his arms because it was a little bit short. That would have put us in field-goal range to win it. You've got to take those breaks and make something out of them. We never did. They did and they won it."

Al Wilson felt home-field advantage sometimes is a disadvantage. "We had a long drought," he concluded, "and we finally got in the Grey Cup. Everywhere you turned people were totally excited. When I look back on it, getting to play in front of our home fans was not the best thing to happen on our first Grey Cup because there were too many distractions.

"I probably didn't really know how to handle it—everybody congratulating you, wishing you well. It was constant, 24 hours a day. Maybe it took away a little of the focus. Forty-eight hours before the game you should almost go into isolation and concentrate totally on the task at hand. There is lots of time for partying afterward.

"It was a lot easier in 1985 when we practiced and played the game and only had a few functions to go to. When you actually had the game in your hometown, there was too much of a party atmosphere."

"What hurt us was Hank Ilesic's punting," Coach Don Matthews concluded. "The whole second half we were almost entirely in the shadow of our own goalpost. We were punting the ball back to them and they were getting it close to midfield.

"The Argos weren't moving and kept kicking it back in there. Our starting position was just horrible. Twice we moved it out and got close to scoring position. Once Roy got picked off and another time our running back got stripped of the ball after he caught a flair pass. Those two times Toronto took the ball away from us."

Al Wilson disagreed with the coach's assessment of the loss. "We didn't do the things on offense we did all year. I'm not talking about being spectacular. I'm talking about grinding it out for first downs, getting the field position whether we scored or not. We always had the capability of moving the ball whether we took it over on our own 10 or wherever. But we never did anything. We were so inept in the second half of that Grey Cup."

Losing at home was particularly hard on Vancouver native Lui Passaglia. "That was the hardest Grey Cup game to swallow because we waited so long to be in it. We had a great defense and a great coaching staff. The team was well run, but we just couldn't get the job done. And to play in front of 60,000 fans the first year in B.C. Place. I recall after the game a lot of tears from professional athletes. A lot of the guys were there for seven or eight years. To take that long to get a taste of it, and then to blow it away by a point! When it comes to championships and anything in life, whatever you are doing, when you get that one shot at it, you've got to take it and grasp it."

The 1983 Grey Cup was one of heartbreak and tragedy for Don Matthews. "I don't remember a lot of that game. My children got in a very bad car accident the day before the game, and I spent the entire night before the game at the hospital. Two of them broke their backs. In fact I told my coaches at the start of the game, 'I can't help you, my mind's not even here. All I can tell you is just try to stay aggressive.' I was there, but I didn't have any input into the game. I was completely ineffective as a football coach.

"My children were in the hospital for over two weeks. When they finally got out they had to wear back braces for over six months. They both healed perfectly and went on to play high school and college football, which was great. At the time, though, the doctors couldn't tell us if they were ever going to walk again. It was a major traumatic time in my life, so I remember bits and pieces, but I really wasn't into that game."

In 1984 the Bombers and Lions once again raced to the wire with B.C. taking first place on the last game of the season with a victory over Winnipeg in Vancouver. But the Bombers got hot, knocking off Edmonton 55–20 in the semifinal and the Lions 31–14 in the final. Al Wilson had a simple explanation for this turn of events. "Winnipeg played better than us."

Winnipeg pivot Tom Clements was sensational in the game. In 1984 postseason play, including the Grey Cup, Clements completed 61 of 86 passes for 933 yards and 8 touchdowns. Roy Dewalt couldn't play due to injury, placing B.C. at a considerable disadvantage.

Roy DeWalt

Additions to the 1985 Lions included Darnell Clash and Keith Gooch in the secondary, Tyrone Crews at middle linebacker, D-line guy Michael Gray, O-lineman Brian Illebrun and running back Freddie Sims. Nick Hebler assumed a starting role on the defensive line. Receivers Jim Sandusky and Ron Robinson were in their second season. The Lions of 1985 were a veteran football team.

The Lion leader was quarterback Roy DeWalt, who ranks seventh all-time in percentage completions. Near the end of his career he was third all-time in completions and in the top 10 for all-time passing yardage. He was, however, never an All-Star or the West's candidate for the Most Outstanding Player Award. In Vancouver he was the object of abuse from fans and media alike. "You would like to be recognized for some of the things you have done," he said in 1987. "I felt that particularly in 1985 I had an opportunity to be an All-Star, but that didn't happen even though I led the league in every passing category and had the fewest interceptions per passes attempted."

Despite ranking fifth in passing, Matt Dunigan was the 1985 All-Canadian quarterback. In 1986 one-year wonder Rick Johnson got the nod.

Dewalt soldiered on. "You just keep trying to pull yourself up by the bootstraps and keep going out there," he concluded. "I guess the biggest consolation

I get out of it is Warren Moon. His last three years Moon was the best in the CFL, but he didn't get Schenley or All-Star recognition until his last year here. I find great consolation in that he was honored only once and was the best before that. Maybe there is hope for me yet."

Unfortunately, no.

Dewalt seldom put the ball at risk. When no one was open he would take the sack rather than put the ball up for grabs. His drop was so short that he lost very few yards when he was sacked. He was roundly criticized for eating the ball. "Roy was probably the most under-estimated quarterback the league has ever seen," said Al Wilson. "Everybody was giving him heck. When he came in, everybody thought he was a running quarterback, but he got the pin in his ankle and turf toe, and he couldn't run anymore, so he had to stay in the pocket. And he still won. He became a classic dropback throwing quarterback. He adapted. He learned a new style.

"Doug Flutie is an excellent quarterback. I'm not ever going to take any-thing away from Doug," Wilson continued. "But he gets himself out of a lot of jams just with his scatback ability. Guys like Ron Lancaster and Roy, who could-n't run a lick, did it all with their brains and arm. Not enough people gave Roy Dewalt the credit that he deserved. There were slams on his playing ability, his play-calling and everything else, but he was an excellent quarterback. I don't think Roy was ever intercepted for a touchdown."

Dewalt was the 1985 Grey Cup Most Valuable Player for offense, the only formal recognition he ever got. Said Adam Rita, "His first year he played 18 games with a broken ankle. He had a stress fracture in his ankle, but there was no swelling—just pain. Dewalt wouldn't even take an aspirin. That guy was tougher than nails. He played all season and what happened was the bone kept splitting. After the season they operated on it and put in screws. He didn't miss a beat.

"He was much maligned. He was not a very popular quarterback in B.C. yet all he did was win."

His opponents admired him, too. "Roy Dewalt was one hell of a quarter-back," said Tiger-Cat defensive back Less Browne. "He had a very strong arm. He didn't throw the ball in such a way that any defensive back had a chance of getting at it. He knew how to throw the ball and lead the guy just enough to get him there."

The Lions went into the 1985 Western Final without the injured Schenley winner Mervyn Fernandez and All-Canadian running back Keyvan Jenkins. Winnpeg's Tom Clements was hurt, and their coach, Cal Murphy, had earlier suffered a heart attack. For the play-off game at B.C. Place, Murphy wanted an extra headset for his use in the press box. Genreal Manager Ackles refused.

"I'll get the little weasel," thundered Murphy and told Ackles exactly what he thought of him. Fifteen minutes later they were friends again. When Murphy was with Saskatchewan in 1997, the Roughriders opened the season in Vancouver. Ackles was there visiting. When they met, Murphy said, "Hello, you little weasel," and Ackles replied, "You're still not getting an extra headset." They laughed and wished each other well.

The Lions won 42–22 and went on to Montreal for another Grey Cup match-up against the Tiger-Cats.

Grey Cup 1985

The Lions jumped into a 13–0 lead when Dewalt hit Ned Armour down the sideline. Less Browne and the receiver arrived at the same time, but Armour wrestled the ball away and headed for the end zone. Lui Passaglia kicked the convert and added two field goals.

The Ti-Cats replied with Ken Hobart throwing to Ron Ingram for 6 points and then engineering a drive culminating in a Johnny Shepherd 1-yard plunge for a touchdown. The Ti-Cats led 14–13.

Just as a broken kicking play was instrumental in B.C.'s first Grey Cup victory, a broken kicking play turned the 1985 game in their favor. Near the end of the second quarter, the Lions were forced to punt. After taking the snap and starting to move forward, Passaglia saw Mitchell Price coming at him. He pulled the ball down and took off around the end, picking up a first down at his 51. On the next play Dewalt hit Ned Armour for a touchdown, and on B.C.'s next possession Passaglia kicked a field goal.

Passaglia described the pivotal play. "The Ti-Cats were leading 14–13. They had to kick off, but they stopped us right away and had some momentum going. We were ready to punt from around our 40-yard line.

"Really, I had no choice but to do something because when I was ready to drop the ball I could see yellow and black jerseys—in fact, two of them—coming up the middle. If I had kicked it they would have blocked it.

"I think somebody just missed tripping me up by about an inch. I just happened to go outside and get the first down, and we scored on the very next play.

That turned the whole year around. We were heavy favorites, but at that point, if Hamilton had blocked the punt, they would have come back from a 13–0 deficit and got a touchdown and gone into half time leading 21–13.

Al Wilson remembered the broken play well. "The defensive end came free, and Lui knew it was going to be blocked, so he just pulled it down and took off for the first-down marker. Once he got past Price, he would have punted it if he had to, but he saw he had the opportunity to get the first down, so he went for it. It was just Lui's instincts."

Ti-Cat defensive back Less Browne recalled the play vividly. "I'm always the guy who goes for the block. I'm not a big man so they don't put me on some-body to block. I remember going in and I thought, 'Oh, man, I'm going to get this, I'm going to get this.' And then all of a sudden—damn. I mean there must have been a huge hole right up the middle. And Passaglia just took off and ran right up the middle, right past Mitch Price, who had his fingertips on him. That's when they say it's a game of inches. Mitch had his fingertips, I would swear, right on Passaglia's jersey. I kept thinking, 'Just grab him, Mitch, just grab him!' He couldn't and B.C. ended up getting that first down, which kept their drive alive."

The Lions went into the dressing room leading 23–14 and maintained their momentum in the second half. Jim Sandusky scored a touchdown and Passaglia added two field goals and a single. Hamilton rounded out their scoring with a Steve Stapler touchdown and Paul Osbaldiston field goal in the fourth quarter. B.C. had won their second Grey Cup 37–24.

The win was special for Don Matthews. "That year was my first win as a head coach," he said. "That win over Hamilton was the result of a great effort by a lot of people. We'd lost Keyvan Jenkins and Merv Fernandez. Ned Armour replaced Mervyn and caught two touchdown passes. Jim Sandusky had one. Lui Passaglia kicked five field goals. Roy Dewalt was the player of the game on offense and James Parker on defense.

Mervyn Fernandez had led the league in 1985 in receiving yardage with 1,727. His loss could have been devastating had Ned Armour not stepped in and scored two brilliant touchdowns. "Ned Armour had remarkable speed," said Matthews. "He hadn't played very much, and I don't think a lot of people knew how good he was. He had a different kind of speed than Merv did, and it prob-ably caught Hamilton by surprise."

"We scored early on a long bomb that Armour stole right out of Less

Browne's hands," recalled Passaglia. "They both had it, and he pulled it away and kept on running. That gave us confidence, knowing that we could go deep. Mervyn had been our deep guy all year long, but Ned caught two bombs that day and a couple of long balls in the Western Final, too. So we knew with Ned and Jim Sandusky we could go deep, and that kind of opened it up for us.

"The catch probably gave Roy Dewalt some more confidence, too, that with Freddie Sims at running back with John Henry White, we could run and throw during the course of the game pretty well at our discretion."

Although Matthews singled out Passaglia's heads-up play, Lui disagreed. "I think about the play right afterward, when we had Ned going down our left side-line for a touchdown. All of a sudden the enthusiasm and the joy of the game came rushing back.

"You've got the adrenaline of the punt run, which rarely happens, and that gives you a little bit of momentum—but to strike so quickly? That was probably the play of the game, the Ned Armour touchdown right afterward."

"I think it was hard for Hamilton to play against a guy that's a different type of receiver than Merv," said Adam Rita. "Ned was a flat-out speed guy, and he was a lot stronger and more explosive than people gave him credit for. He was fifth in the world in the long jump at one time.

"Just after the Ned Armour touchdown, Jim Sandusky said that he could get behind Paul Bennett on a 54 Yankee, that all he had to do was pop the over-route. Roy threw the ball over the defensive back, and Jim was able to go in for a touchdown."

If Armour, Sandusky, Dewalt and Passaglia were the heroes of the game, Ti-Cat coach Al Bruno thought Less Browne was the goat. "We felt we could beat British Columbia," he said. "Then we almost had that damn punt blocked and Passaglia ran for a first down. We were coming back. Then Ken Hobart threw the ball to Rocky DiPietro and hit the crossbar. Hobart injured his shoulder early in the game, which hampered him.

"But Less Browne got beaten two or three times on long touchdown passes. On the first one Less tried to pick it off. He had fairly good coverage, but I don't think he realized how quick and fast that kid Armour was. On the other one, it was just one of those things. Dewalt made a hell of a throw and Armour made a hell of a catch right over his shoulder. It was a smart play on B.C.'s part after that Passaglia play to hit us with a long one."

The Lions' Adam Rita came to Browne's defense. "Less was a great defensive back all his career, and he was great then. The problem was that there was a different kind of coverage they were playing at the time. Less was all alone with Ned with no help. He was on an island."

"As for Armour fighting Browne for the ball, Rita said, "Every training camp I'd ask Merv, 'What happens when the ball is in the air?' He'd say, 'It's my ball, nobody else's ball.' That's what he and Ned and the other receivers used to say.

"That's what I always told the guys—when the ball is in the air basically even if you have to cause offensive pass interference, you fight for it just to protect the quarterback. If you protect the quarterback from an interception that way, the quarterback will take more chances with you as a receiver. Merv was very good at that. So was Ned."

The Ti-Cats' Less Browne came to his own defense. "I was step for step with Ned and we both caught that ball at the same time. My mistake was, I guess, going for the interception, which is 50–50. If I had to do it all over again in a big game, I would probably have just knocked it down. But heck, the way I was taught by Rich Stubler, if you're there, go for it. Who says defensive backs can't catch the ball?

"While Ned and I were fighting for the ball, we both had it in our hands for at least 2 yards. I tripped and fell down, and he didn't. He still had the ball in his hands while he was running in the end zone.

"The second touchdown wasn't on me at all. We were in a three-deep zone. Ned Armour ran a post, which means that when he leaves my area to catch the ball in the middle of the field, there ought to be somebody there.

"I took the blame for that in the locker room when I was asked about it, and the guy I took the blame for came up to me afterward and said, 'I just want to thank you because most guys would probably sit there and point the finger and say whose man it really was.' And I didn't. I felt good about that, too, even though the headlines read that I got beat for two touchdowns."

When asked later if Paul Bennett, the safety, was playing too low, as Don Matthews had said, Browne replied, "That's who was supposed to be there."

Whatever the final reason for the Lions' 1985 Grey Cup win, Al Wilson was impressed by the way Coach Matthews prepared the team. "He was cagey. He was less gung ho about the Grey Cup," Wilson said. "He used to say the Grey Cup will look after itself. I can still remember him saying the game will go faster than any game you've ever played in. Just go out and play as a team. And that's what we did.

"He was more of a settle-you-down type rather than a hype-you-up type. For all the detractors of Don Matthews, his style works. He's figured it out."

Still Wilson wasn't settled down. "I was scared stiff going into that '85 Cup because I knew it was probably my last one. I was confident, but I didn't feel the whole game that we were going to win. Hamilton was tough. It wasn't until there were 30 seconds left and we had a 13-point lead that I would kiss my wife, who was leaning over the railing in the stands. We knew we had won the game at that point. One of the attitudes of the B.C. Lions going into the game was that this might be the last time we pass this way together. That was right. We never did pass another Grey Cup together, and a lot of guys started retiring after that."

The 1985 season was the greatest in B.C. Lion history. In addition to winning the Grey Cup, Mervyn Fernandez won the Schenley Award for Most Outstanding Player, Michael Gray for rookie. Fernandez, Gray, Keyvan Jenkins, John Blain, James Parker, Kevin Konar and Darnell Clash made All-Canadian. Matthews won his first Coach of the Year Award.

The 1985 Grey Cup would be General Manager Bob Ackles' last hurrah as a B.C. Lion. The following year he shocked Canadian football by ending his association with the team that had been his life. "I got a call out of the blue. I was driving to training camp in May 1986. When I got there, there was a message to call Tex Schramm. When I returned the call the next day, he offered me a job with the Dallas Cowboys as the vice president of pro personnel.

"I still had two years to go on my contract, so I called our president, Woody McLaren, and told him. He said, 'Let me get back to you.'

"I was supposed to go to a league meeting in Toronto with Woody. It was Memorial Day weekend in the States, and he said, 'Why don't you go down and talk to them and see if that is what you'd like to do, but don't do anything. In the meantime I'll go to the meeting in Toronto and talk to the board of directors. When you get back we can talk about it.'

"Which I did. I left Kelowna, went to Vancouver, picked up my wife and we went to Dallas. Tex and his wife, Marty, picked us up at the airport. We weren't even to the hotel and he said, 'Well, are you going to take the job?' I said, 'Tex, I've got two years on a contract, I'd love to be here — it's a great honor to be asked.'

"When I got back to training camp in Kelowna, Woody arrived. By this time there had been some media attention. Something had leaked from somewhere. I'm sure Tex had leaked it because that's the way he operated.

"So I talked to Woody. Because I had spent thirty-four and a half years of my life as a B.C. Lion, the board felt it would be appropriate to let me out of my contract if that is what I wanted to do.

"B.C. was a challenge. It was an opportunity. And you know, when I left there in 1986, we had just nudged our season tickets over 30,000. We'd just won a championship. Basically all the players were under contract—the ones we really wanted to be under contract. We'd paid off most of the debt. Things were in good shape, so I felt good about leaving."

After playing a pivotal role in building a Super Bowl winner in Dallas, Ackles moved on to Arizona and Philadelphia before answering Jimmy Johnson's call to join the Miami Dolphins.

Feline Follies: The Never-Ending Story

When Ackles left the Lions, the chemistry went with him. Don Matthews wanted the GM's job, saying, "There is another challenge coming up with Bob Ackles leaving. That is certainly an avenue in which I would like to expand my responsibilities."

Ackles agreed. "What they probably should have done when I left was go through the year with Don running the football and Roger Upton, who was the marketing guy, running the front office, with the treasurer just keeping a close eye on it, rather than going out and hiring someone outside."

Instead the Lions hired Joe Galat, the coach and director of football operations of the Montreal Concorde, a man who could charm the stripes off a tiger. Because of his self-deprecating humor and reputation for honesty, he was a media darling.

The Lions failed to defend their title in 1986, finishing second to the Eskimos. After knocking off the Bombers in the semifinal, they were humiliated in the Igloo 41–5. At the end of the 1986 season, Matthews lost Defensive Player Schenley Winner James Parker along with Mervyn Fernandez, Al Wilson, Michael Gray and Glenn Leonhard. He said, "Because there are going to be so many changes on our veteran football team, it is going to be interesting to see how the personality of the team changes."

Change was the order of the day during the 1987 season as John Henry White, Roy Dewalt, Glen Jackson, Kevin Konar, Bernie Glier, Jan Carinci and Jamie Buis missed considerable time with injuries. Matthews had to do an incredible patching job.

He hit a rough spot in October, losing three games in a row. Still he was only two points out of first place. Then, in a move that outraged B.C. football fans, Joe Galat fired him.

Relations between Galat and Matthews had always been uneasy. They were aggravated that year when Matthews refused to re-sign middle linebacker Tyrone Crews or play Condredge Holloway, whom Galat had acquired as back-up insurance to Roy Dewalt. Matthews preferred to go with Greg Vavra, who had paid his dues as a Lion. During the three-game tailspin, Galat felt that by not using Holloway, Matthews was letting his personal feelings overrule sound football judgment.

When the CFL had announced a salary cap that year, Galat at first refused to go along. Facing declining attendance and revenues in September, Galat clumsily imposed a salary cut on everybody. Because of the unilateral salary cuts, the players were furious with Galat, who believed Matthews aided and abetted the fury by taking the players' side. He saw Matthews as the central figure in a potential player revolt. "We had a lack of motivation," said Joe Galat. "We had players making decisions on the field such as not letting the punt team come on the field. Things were in disarray.

"We had a tough time with pay cuts," he continued. "Remember when Edmonton players agreed to a 10 percent pay cut? Our players had a totally different attitude about it. I think the coach was part of that attitude. It wasn't a team effort in making the cuts. We had to be a team. We had to acknowledge the fact that the league was going through a tough time."

Before the start of the 1987 season Matthews had said, "My wife and I are building a house here in White Rock. We enjoy being here very much. My plan is to stay right here and live happily ever after."

Assistant Larry Donovan replaced Matthews. The team came on strong at the end while Edmonton slumped. The Lions finished first by two points but lost the final 41–7 to the Eskimos, who were cheered in B.C. Place when they met Toronto for the Grey Cup.

In 1988 Galat swung the trade with Edmonton that brought Matt Dunigan to the Lions. It was an audacious move that looked like a mistake when the Lions finished third behind Edmonton and Saskatchewan. However, they defeated both before losing the ill-fated Grey Cup to Winnipeg 22–21.

Although the trade for Dunigan got them to the Cup in 1988, Galat gave up too much to get him. When the Leos lost their first four games in 1989, Galat fired Donovan, assuming the coaching reins himself. The team finished the year in the cellar with a record of 7–11. At the end of the season Galat, who had wielded the knife had it used against him. He was gone.

Leo Loonies

For a franchise used to the wild and wacky, the worst was yet to come. The Lions, under the ownership of razzle-dazzle stock promoter Murray Pezim, brought back the legendary Joe Kapp as general manager. He hired Lary Kuharich, late of the Calgary Stampeders. Kuharich had been nicknamed Coach Q in Calgary, which could have stood for Quixote. Hands down the most bizarre individual to ever coach a CFL team, Kuharich was known for his fits of rage. Stampeder General Manager Normie Kwong showed the restraint of a saint in putting up with him. He found out his coach had gone to B.C. when he discovered that Kuharich had cleaned out his office in the middle of the night and left town.

Kapp had been coaching the University of California, wearing out his welcome when he had mooned the crowd. During the 1989 semifinal at McMahon Stadium against Saskatchewan, Kuharich gave the crowd the finger. Kapp and Kuharich were meant for each other.

Joe Galat had acquired Matt Dunigan to put fans in the stands with entertaining offense, sacrificing defense to get him. Joe Kapp then traded Dunigan to Toronto for defense, getting DT Jerald Baylis, LB Willie Pless, LB Tony Visco and DB Todd Wiseman. The Lions also picked up receiver Emanuel Tolbert and quarterback Rick Johnson, who didn't report.

Jerald Baylis sat out the 1990 season with an injury. The Lions cut him in 1991. He was All-Canadian three of the next four years, twice as a Saskatchewan Roughrider, once as a Baltimore Stallion, and won the award for Most Outstanding Defensive Player in 1993. Pless played one year in Leo livery before signing with Edmonton, where he won five Outstanding Defensive Player Awards.

In fact, former Lions won the Outstanding Defensive Player Award five of the first seven years of the decade.

Before the start of the 1990 regular season, Kuharich's defensive coordinator, Charlie West, quit after a shouting match with him. Backfield coach Larry Dauterive broke down under the stress and left. The security chief, marketing director, public relations director and a secretary also quit.

In Calgary, Kuharich's wild mood swings had been offset somewhat by

General Manager Kwong's stature in the community and his gentle, forgiving nature. In B.C., General Manager Kapp and owner Pezim were as flamboyant, unpredictable and volatile as Kuharich himself.

Kapp signed ex-New York Jet Mark Gastineau, who quit after embarrassing himself through four games. Lacking faith in quarterback Rickey Foggie, Kapp signed All-American Major Harris. He lasted eight games, replaced by Doug Flutie, whom Kuharich didn't know how to use.

In September the Lions lost a home-and-home series to Toronto by scores of 68–43 and 49–19. With a mark of 2–9, Pezim fired Kapp *and* Kuharich, replacing them with Jim Young and Bob O'Billovich. With Flutie at the controls the Lions were 4–3 the rest of the way.

Flutie had played for Donald Trump's New Jersey Generals of the United States Football League and the NFL Rams, Bears and Patriots. He compared quarterbacking in the NFL and CFL. "Down there, you're definitely a robot. Everything is signaled in from the sidelines. Everything is predetermined. Up here you have a lot more responsibility. You are in total control. Because it is a passing game, the ball is in your hands a lot more. I enjoy playing up here a lot more."

Asked about his greatest strength as a quarterback, he replied, "Just making the right reads and doing the right thing at the right time."

With Flutie the 1991 Lions went 11–7, tying Calgary for second place, two points behind the Eskimos. They scored 661 points, the second-highest total ever except for Edmonton's 671 of the same year. They lost the semifinal in Calgary 43–41, the second-highest single game play-off total in CFL history.

And then typical of the Lions, just when it was dynasty time, disaster struck. Murray Pezim didn't have the kind of money people thought he had. He couldn't afford to keep Doug Flutie, who signed with Pezim's kindred spirit and fellow snake-oil salesman Larry Ryckman of the Stampeders. Ryckman then traded veteran Danny Barrett to the Lions for Rocco Romano.

O'Billovich prepared optimistically for the new season. It didn't happen. The Lions went 0–8 before putting together a three-game winning streak. They then lost their last seven games. The seventh game symbolized B.C.'s season. Playing in Calgary on August 21, the Lions lost in a snowstorm. Snowed under literally and figuratively, Pezim declared bankruptcy and walked away from the club, saying, "The team let me down. I don't enjoy it anymore." After a period of CFL control, Bill Comrie, owner of the Brick Furniture chain, bought the club.

Seraphim in the Secondary

At the end of the season Comrie fired O'Billovich and installed Eric Tillman as general manager. Tillman hired Dave Ritchie, formerly an assistant with Montreal, Winnipeg and Ottawa. Ritchie's Lions went 10–8 in 1993, losing the semifinal 17–9 to Calgary.

The theme song in 1994 would be "Do You Believe in Miracles?" When training camp opened, the Lions looked good offensively. Kent Austin was the quarterback, fifth all-time in completions and yardage, backed up by Danny MacManus. True, Jon Volpe defected to the Pittsburgh Steelers, but Sean Millington and Cory Philpot were more than adequate replacements.

The receiving corps of Mike Trevathan, Matt Clark, Ray Alexander and Darren Flutie was outstanding. So was the offensive line of tackles Rob Smith and Vic Stevenson, guards Denny Chronopoulos and Jamie Taras, and center Ian Sinclair.

Defense was another matter. Ritchie lost three starting linebackers— Tyrone Jones, James West and O.J. Brigance—as well as left corner Andre Francis. Ritchie picked up Angelo Snipes from Ottawa to go with rookies Tyrone Chatman, Henry Newby and Virgil Robertson.

The front three were second-year men David Chaytors and Andrew Stewart, and rookie Doug Peterson. The secondary was the real question mark. Ritchie loaded up with old veterans. Did they have another season in them? After all, Less Browne, the CFL's all-time interception leader, was 35. James Jefferson had just turned 31, as had Enis Jackson, and Barry Wilburn would soon do so. The babies were 26-year-old Charles Gordon and Tom Europe, 24. Kicker Lui Passaglia was 40.

The gamble paid off with B.C. having the second-best defense in the league. Less Browne was the CFL interception leader with 11.

Secure at quarterback for the first time since the departure of Flutie, the Lions were second in the West to Calgary in total offense. Austin was third in passing, Darren Flutie second in receptions with 111. Cory Philpot was second in rushing yards with 1,451.

The success of the rebuilt defense was a tribute to the recruiting skills of personnel man Bill Quinter and the coaching ability of 56-year-old Dave Ritchie, who was rumored on his way out in favor of Comrie's friend Tom Wilkinson. In fact Ritchie had a clause automatically adding a year to his contract if he had a winning season. The Lions were third at 11–6–1.

Although the 1994 Grey Cup would be played in Vancouver, the Lions faced the impossible task of winning two on the road in Alberta to get there. The Lions were the undisputed underdogs. But they fashioned a dramatic comeback in the fourth quarter to knock off the defending Grey Cup champions 24–23. Charles Gordon killed an Edmonton drive by intercepting in the end zone, and Passaglia kicked the game-winning field goal with 30 seconds left on the clock. On to Calgary.

Calgary hadn't lost a play-off game to B.C. in 30 years. To make matters worse the Lions were in no shape to play anybody, let alone the powerful Stampeders. Kent Austin had a separated shoulder. Danny McManus had torn a muscle against Edmonton. Less Browne had a cartilage injury, Barry Wilburn a broken rib.

So the Lions borrowed a secret weapon from the Vancouver Canucks, an oxygen chamber called a hyperbaric machine. Less Browne described what happened to him in the semifinal, as well as in the subsequent treatment. "My knee locked up on me, the same knee I blew out in 1986. It was the first time I ever thought for sure my career was done right then and there.

"On the plane ride home to B.C. that night it unlocked. When we got back they sent me to that oxygen chamber the Canucks have. There were three or four of us who were in there that week. Man, it seemed to be a miracle machine because it worked miracles on me and a lot of other people. I kind of enjoyed that.

"They bolt you in there. The pressure inside the tank is like you're going 30 feet below sea level. You ears start to pop and it takes awhile to come back out, too.

"Going to Calgary," he continued, "no one believed in us anyway. I think that benefits a team, knowing that you are the big, true underdog, that you're going just to be a body on the field. That makes people play above their abilities. I think we all did that."

Calgary was leading the final 36–31 with about a minute to play, when they drove into B.C.'s end and set up for a field goal. It was blocked. Stampeder kicker Mark McLoughlin explained what happened. "Apparently Ray Alexander pyramided. He made a great play. The ball was hit well, but it was just a great play on the Lions' part." It was the first time in McLoughlin's CFL career he'd had a kick blocked.

Not to worry. With less than a minute to play, the Lions would have to move the ball 64 yards and score a touchdown to win. With Austin on the sideline, the fate of the Lions was in the hands of Danny McManus. He barely missed one to Ray Alexander. Then he connected in the flat to Matt Clark and Yo Murphy. A completion to Darren Flutie got the Lions to the Calgary 4. McManus to Flutie. Touchdown. Final score underdogs 37, overdogs 36.

"Darren was supposed to go to the back corner of the end zone," McManus recalled, "but as he does frequently, he just saw the open space. It was weird. He and I sort of made eye contact, and I had an idea he was just going to sit there. I got lucky and put the ball between two guys, and he was able to catch it."

Calgary's coverage on the play was soft, to say the least. "I could see they were playing off," said McManus, "and I was just trying to get stuff underneath. Basically they gave us anything underneath that we wanted."

Calgary's Less Browne said, "If I was a coach, there would never be a prevent defense in my vocabulary. I would never go into it. It prevents you from winning. They play back, they sit back and let guys catch the ball on them and march down the field. Hell, in the CFL, if there's a minute left on the clock, you can score two touchdowns.

"That's what the Lions did. I believe it was the coach up in the booth who was telling our players to get back and play loose, and that's what they were doing."

Said B.C.'s Kent Austin, "Defensively Calgary was playing so passive. I mean their secondary was just so soft during that last drive. They didn't want to get beat for a big play or whatever. But Danny was hot, and I knew that with our quick little receivers we were going to be able to move the ball down there. After the first two completions, the big corner route that Darren Flutie caught, I find it hard to believe the Stampeders were so passive. You've got to play every play. One play can beat you."

Dave Ritchie described the winning touchdown. "With that particular play we had scored a couple of touchdowns by sending Darren to the corner of the end zone. But the defensive backs did not let our middle guy on the trips rub him off so Darren could get to the corner. They jammed him up real hard, and Darren did the next thing: he spun back inside, between the linebacker and a DB. Danny got it into him. It was just amazing. Every time I look back at it I shudder.

"When Danny had the ball with about a minute to go, Kent Austin said on the sideline, 'He knows what he's doing. He's going to take them down.' But you know what the most important thing is? We didn't leave Doug Flutie any time with the ball. That guy could bring them back down the field. After the blocked field goal our guys on the sideline were so jacked up it was unbelievable."

Less Browne praised his coach. "Dave is one of those coaches who is a good motivator by his voice, just lifting his voice, the way he talks to people, sort of like a good preacher when you go to church, especially Baptist churches, where you hear the preacher raise that tone and get people all excited. He's kind of like that in a way, getting people excited and getting people to believe in themselves. I learned a lot by being with him and Mike Riley. If the coach shows that he believes in you, you can do things that your talent wouldn't otherwise permit you to do.

"We had a defensive back, Derek Grier, and I remember how at one point the coaches didn't have any faith in him. But he was a good defensive back. He had good speed, good feet and could cover people well. But because the coaching staff didn't believe in him, he played poorly. When he got with Coach Ritchie, he seemed to lift up his game a bit.

"The same thing with Charles Gordon. He was in Ottawa, and the coaches there didn't believe in him. They let him go. He came to the Lions and once he got with Coach Ritchie he made all-pro two years in a row."

Perhaps Edmonton and Calgary took the Lions lightly. "I don't know why Edmonton would," said Kent Austin. "We went there during the regular season and beat them. But Calgary may have."

Calgary's Mark McLoughlin had a simple explanation for losing the 1994 Western Final. "No matter how you look at it, everything strange that could happen in the fourth quarter did happen."

"Anything You Can Do, We Can Do Better"

Because national pride was at stake the 1994 Grey Cup was unique. It was Canada versus the United States. The Lions were determined to prove Canadians were just as good as Americans. It was up to a battered bunch of B.C. Lions to prevent the Holy Grail of Canadian football from being taken to the States.

Even the Americans on the team were caught up in the nationalistic fervor. "I believe that you had to," recalled Less Browne, "because you were playing on the Canadian team. That meant that Canadians all across the country were cheering for you. The whole country would be going nuts because it was the first time the U.S. and Canada were playing against each other. The Canadian players were hyped because they had always said, 'We can compete with them.'"

Danny McManus, an American citizen, said, "I don't know if it was confidence or what, but we just had a feeling that we needed to represent Canada in the right way and keep the Grey Cup in Canada. We didn't want to be the first team to let the Grey Cup go south of the border."

B.C. Coach Dave Ritchie agreed. "All week I'd been telling them that they did not want to be the answer to the trivia question 'Which Canadian team lost the first Grey Cup to which American team?'"

Canadian Lui Passaglia wasn't quite as pumped as his American colleagues. "I didn't look at it as a Canadian–American thing until afterward. But when they played the national anthem of both countries before the game, you could see it in some of the players' eyes, in their reaction to the anthems, that this was a little bit more than a Grey Cup game. There was an extra incentive to go out there and play harder than you normally would."

Baltimore was the jewel in the expansion crown. Don Matthews had built his team around Americans who had enjoyed outstanding careers in the CFL. Baltimore had finished second to Winnipeg in the Eastern division with a 12–6 record. They were fourth in total offense, first in rushing, fifth in passing and third overall in team defense.

Mike Pringle had set records for rushing with 1,972 yards and 2,414 total yards from scrimmage. He lost the Most Outstanding Player Award to Doug Flutie. Tackle Shar Pourdanesh had won the Offensive Lineman Award, and linebacker Matt Goodwin had been named top rookie. Coach Matthews had won his second Stukus Trophy.

Baltimore's offensive line of Pourdanesh, Guy Earle, John Earle, Nick Subis and Neal Fort averaged a whopping 306 pounds. They would face three Canadians—Doug Peterson, Dave Chaytors and Andrew Stewart—who averaged 35 pounds less.

If football games are won in the trenches, clearly Baltimore was favored. They also had an outstanding quarterback in Tracy Ham, at the top of his game because Matthews believed in him and knew how to use him.

Defensively the Colts' front four was O.J. Brigance, Robert Presbury, the great Jerald Baylis and fourth-year CFL star Elfid Payton. The linebackers were Goodwin, Tracey Gravely and Alvin Walton. Brigance and Gravely had both played for the Lions.

Former Stampeders Karl Anthony and Ken Watson and Roughrider Charles Anthony were in the secondary. Michael Brooks and Irvin Smith were rookies.

A formidable foe entered the Lion's den. A total of 55,097 fans filled B.C. Place, many carrying Canadian flags. They kept up a steady roar from opening kickoff to the thrilling end. It was one of the best Grey Cups ever played, again a vital source of energy and renewal for the Canadian Football League.

The home team struck first. After returning the opening kickoff to their 32-yard line, Kent Austin, playing with a third degree shoulder separation, completed a 10-yard pass to Matt Clark and a 25-yarder to Ray Alexander. When the drive stalled on the Baltimore 40, Lui Passaglia kicked a 47-yard field goal.

On Baltimore's first play of the game, Tracy Ham was picked off by James Jefferson. Explained the Lions' Dave Ritchie, "When we played them down in Baltimore, on the very first play they threw a pass over by James Jefferson, and they completed it. On their first play in the Grey Cup, they threw the same pass, and James Jefferson intercepted it. Right then I knew they came to play."

Returning the favor, Austin was intercepted three plays later by Karl Anthony. The ball changed hands five times before the opening quarter came to an end with B.C. leading 3–0.

The fireworks began with less than seven minutes left in the half. With second down at his 51, Tracy Ham threw 13 yards to Chris Armstrong and 35 to Walter Wilson to bring the Colts to B.C.'s 11. Pringle ran for 5 yards, and when Ham threw into the end zone for Armstrong, but the Lions were called for interference.

Less Browne remembered the play well. "It was just a terribly bad call on Barry Wilburn. I mean, Barry had great coverage on the guy. We're very talkative. We're very aggressive. We play a one-on-one, in-your-face style that intimidates not only the players but the referees. The interference call in the end zone put the ball on the 1-yard line, first down, which gave them their first touchdown."

Ham took it in. Baltimore 7, B.C. 3.

The Lions returned the kickoff to the 35. Austin was picked off by Ken Watson, who lateraled to Karl Anthony, who ran 36 yards for a touchdown. Baltimore 14, B.C. 3. In the space of 35 seconds, the Lions went from a 3–0 lead to being down by 11.

For Ritchie it was steady as she goes. "We stayed right with our game plan. You just have to go out and keep doing the things you do best and not worry about what they've just done. You've got to fight your way back into the game. That's exactly what we did."

Again B.C. scrimmaged from the 35. Austin moved them to the Baltimore 46, where the drive stalled. Passaglia launched a beautiful punt, pinning the enemy at the 7.

Pringle ran for one. Ham then put the ball in the air and was intercepted by Charles Gordon, who ran 17 yards to the end zone. Baltimore 14, B.C. 10.

Browne described the play. "We had an all-out blitz. Dave sent everybody—the whole house. There was a play we had seen earlier, where Ham was going to Armstrong. Charlie and I both knew it, and Charlie just happened to step right in front of it. I don't think Tracy even saw him because all four of our linebackers were getting ready to hit him at one time. He just got rid of it. He didn't want to take the hit since it might have resulted in a safety or would have left them on the 1- or 2-yard line."

With 52 seconds left in the half, Donald Igwebuike gave the visitors a 7-point lead on a 17-yard field goal.

On first down at the B.C. 35, Austin's shoulder injury caught up with him, and he was picked off by Ken Watson. "I had pressure," said Austin. "That was one I probably shouldn't have thrown. I couldn't step into the ball because I was getting hit on the play. But that's the way it goes. That's football.

"I wanted to help the team, and Dave wanted to go with me, but if it had been anything but the Grey Cup, I wouldn't have been playing, I'm sure."

Baltimore had the ball on the Lions' 34, poised to score and go into the dressing room 14 points up. But the secondary rose to the occasion, blanketing the receivers and forcing Ham to intentionally ground the ball. On the final play of the half, Igwebuike missed a 47-yard field-goal attempt. The score remained 14–10 for Baltimore.

The Americans had reason to be optimistic going into the second half. They were getting lots of opportunities, and the Lions had lost their starting quarterback.

But into the breach stepped Danny McManus. "He's a winner," said Dave Ritchie. "His emotional pulse rate stays the same, so you can count on him all the time. He's just a winner. I love the guy. All the quarterbacks I've had up here—Danny Barrett, Kent Austin, Danny Mac, Tracy Ham—have all been winners. They do the things they have to do to win."

Despite McManus having engineered the last-minute drive that got the Lions into the Grey Cup, Ritchie had started Austin, a decision that bothered McManus not one bit. "Coach Ritchie told us right away what he was thinking.

If Kent was healthy enough to start the game, he would start it. That was not a problem for me at all.

"We were both pretty banged up, so I guess whoever was able to answer the bell first would get the nod. He had a shoulder separation and I had—I'm not sure what you would call it—but there was something from the knee all the way up the thigh. We were both going into that hyperbaric chamber early in the morning during Grey Cup week. I don't know if it helped physically, but it helped mentally.

"All through the play-offs neither of us finished a game. I started against Edmonton in the semifinal and Kent came in. He started against Calgary in the Western Final and I came in. So we were both ready to go. We were both getting equal reps during practice."

The third quarter opened with a nine-play drive for a Baltimore field goal that ran 4 minutes and 34 seconds off the clock. Baltimore 20, B.C. 10. It was then that the Lions began to implement their strategy, which was, as Dave Ritchie explained, a running game. "We wanted to run the football. We felt we could run the football."

First down at their 35, Cory Philpot ran for 10 and 8 yards. Sean Millington rambled 32 yards to the Baltimore 25. Philpot picked up 2. The Colts' Brigance then sacked McManus, and B.C. was third down at the Baltimore 27. Passaglia came on for a 34-yard field-goal try.

It was a fake! Holder Darren Flutie raced around the right end for 18 crucial yards. First down at the 9, Philpot ran for 6, Millington for 2 before McManus took it around the end for a touchdown. The drive took 5 minutes and 5 seconds. Baltimore 20, B.C. 17.

Said Dave Ritchie, "We worked on that field-goal fake. We had noticed that they brought seven guys off the edge on the one side wherever they lined up. So we wanted to run a field-goal fake and Jody Allen, the special teams coach, came up to me and said, 'Do you think this'll be the time?' I said, 'Let's do it.'

"And Darren took it and ran almost down to their goal line," Ritchie continued. "A couple of plays later Danny went in with the football. I think that changed things around for us, really changed the momentum."

McManus agreed. "It was a designed play, and the Baltimore guys bit on it really hard. It came at the right time because it was something we needed. "

On B.C.'s next possession, after running on every first down in the quarter, McManus threw to Ray Alexander for 42 yards. Philpot carried to the Baltimore

35. After an incompletion, Passaglia kicked a 42-yard field goal. When the third quarter ended 52 seconds later, the teams were deadlocked at 20.

The Lions took over in the fourth quarter. Millington ran for 17, Philpot 13, Millington 2. Passaglia scored a 27-yard field goal. B.C. 23, Baltimore 20.

But the Americans weren't done. Tracy Ham hit Joe Washington on a 55-yarder to get the ball to the B.C. 10. After an incompletion Ham headed for the end zone. At the 1-yard line he reached out with the ball to get it over the goal line. Tony Collier thanked him kindly and relieved him of the prize. With a face mask penalty tacked on, the Lions scrimmaged at their 23.

B.C. Assistant Coach Gene Gaines thought that was the play of the game. "Ham extended his arm across the goal line with the ball, but he allowed the ball to be exposed, and Tony Collier stripped him of it and scooped it up. That swung the momentum in our favor and gave us the advantage."

On Baltimore's next possession, aided by a great punt return and a 21-yard run by Ham, the Colts evened the scored again with a 29-yard field goal.

The ball changed hands four times before the Lions started off from their 37 with 1:40 left in regulation time. Again the big play was a pass to Ray Alexander, this time for 34 yards, bringing the ball to the Baltimore 36. Millington lost 2, Philpot gained 8. With third and 4 from the 30, Passaglia uncharacteristically missed one from 37 yards out.

Baltimore coach Matthews likes to run the ball out. In 1996 the strategy helped him win the Grey Cup. In 1994 it proved disastrous. Baltimore only got it out to the 2. Pringle picked up a couple, a pass was incomplete and Baltimore had to punt. With 28 seconds left, B.C. had a first down and a second chance on the Baltimore 34. McManus prepared to take to the field for one last drive. "All we did was try to run the clock down and let Lui come on for the last play. I knew Passaglia wouldn't miss two in a row," he said.

With no time left on the clock and the crowd in a frenzy, hometown hero Lui Passaglia drilled it through the uprights from 38 yards out to give B.C. a 26–23 victory and their third Grey Cup.

Was the first miss a blessing in disguise? "Oh, it was for sure," said Less Browne, "because it took all the time and gave us a second chance. Tracy got hurt toward the end, and they had to bring in their backup, John Congemi, and we knew we couldn't give them a first down. We knew if we held them, Lui would get another shot at it—even closer probably—if we got a good runback on the punt return. All those things worked out.

"When we stopped Congemi two and out, as I walked off the field, I walked right by Doug Flutie, who was standing on the sideline. He said, 'We've got this one won right now. It's over.' I just knew it in my heart right then and there that the game was over."

Kent Austin said, "I think what was more of a blessing in disguise was that Baltimore returned the missed field goal. I thought that was a bad decision. A field goal still would have beaten us even if they gave up the single. When I saw them returning it, I thought, 'Man, we're going to have a chance to pin them there.' And sure enough we pinned them on the 2. They couldn't get anything going, and winning the game was just nothing more than making sure we handled the punt."

Colt coach Don Matthews certainly saw Passaglia's miss as a blessing in disguise. "No question. That was one of those plays where we got caught up in the moment. We had a return call on, and Passaglia kicked it to the side of our return. When we do a field-goal return, we figure anything short of 40 yards means we didn't do a good enough job.

"Instead of us jamming their guys on the line of scrimmage, three of our guys on the side of the return turned to see if the kick was going to be good or not. Their guys, released free, made the play on the 1- or 2-yard line. Had they done their jobs, we would have got the ball out to the 30–35-yard line. Then we would have had a chance to use the last minute to score.

"But that was part of our problem. I use that example all the time now when I talk about field-goal returns and what your job is. Don't ever turn and see if the kick is good. Just assume it is going to be missed. Your job is not to try to block it—your job is to try to set the return. Had we done that correctly, we would have got the ball well out into the field.

"In the 1996 Grey Cup, we had brought three missed field goals out of the end zone against Edmonton, and those proved to be very big points. We had our returns on all the time. We got very good field position every time we brought it out and came very close to breaking it."

Some were surprised that the 1994 Grey Cup came down to a last-minute field goal, figuring Baltimore would have the game well in hand. Most observers were astonished at how the Canadians dominated the line play on both sides of the ball. Count Dave Ritchie among them. "I was surprised that we handled their offensive line so well," he said. "Danny probably only threw the ball seven times in the second half. The game was won in the line. Our Canadian kids—

men—stood tall. I tell you they stood tall. Our defensive line was as good that day as I've ever seen them play."

McManus also was surprised. "We got caught up in hearing about how the American players had better teaching and coaching. I think that's what fired up our Canadian offensive linemen. It was a real battle of pride for those guys. They just stepped up to the challenge."

"Once we started running," said McManus, "our team seemed to feed off putting a couple of runs together, and there was no reason for me to change the play. We were beating them off the line of scrimmage. As for Cory Philpot, it seems, the more times he gets the ball the better he gets. Sean Millington's blocking for him helped out quite a bit. We were able to keep the Colts' defense on the field and let our defense rest."

Could the heavily favored Americans have taken the Lions for granted? Less Browne didn't think so. "They weren't arrogant at all. They knew they were good. They had confidence that they were good. You saw what happened the very next year—they came back to the Grey Cup and won it. When you get a bunch of Americans on one team, I don't think it's arrogance, it's just confidence."

Browne paid tribute to his coaches. "Dave Ritchie and Gene Gaines are really smart when it comes to putting schemes together on top receivers and taking the quarterback's favorite out of the game. That was Armstrong, and after we took him out of the game, Tracy Ham was having a hard time finding everybody else. Basically he didn't have enough time to find them in the second half because we were putting a ton of pressure on him.

"We had excellent coverage all day against Baltimore. Playing indoors and on that carpet the advantage went to us. It favored our side all the way around but especially defensively. We contained their running back, Mike Pringle, who had over 200 yards against us in Baltimore."

Annis Stukus had a theory to explain the Lions' win. "With about 60,000 people at B.C. Place and no air conditioning, the oxygen gets eaten up pretty good, and it got hot in there. The linemen told me that by the fourth quarter those big 300-pounders were wheezing."

Less Browne thought Stuke was right. "When we went down to Baltimore, they kicked the crap out of us. We got beat 48–31. We played on grass, which benefited them. Being outside benefited their big 300-pound linemen. But the Grey Cup was in the Dome, where a lot of people have a hard time breathing. It was warm. After a while it is going to take its toll. And it did."

Passaglia scoffed at the notion the heat took its toll. "I don't think it comes down to size or whether it's hot in there. It comes down to talent. Everything comes down basically to talent. It doesn't matter if you're 350 pounds and 6'8" if you're no good."

Baltimore coach Don Matthews confirmed that the effect of the heat on his players was not a factor.

Usually, when a team wins the Grey Cup or any championship, the talk is about how they are fam–i–ly. According to Less Browne, the Lions were a dysfunctional family. There was a good deal of dissension in the dressing room. "We were never close to family, although I don't know, they say families fight," he laughed. "Families always have their little scuffles, too, especially if it's a big family. We had major problems in 1994 with off-the-field stuff and personalities clashing. I mean there was a ton of that all season long to the point where wide receivers and DBs [James Jefferson and Ray Alexander earlier in the season] were spatting between each other outside of practice.

"During the '94 Grey Cup, two days before the game, man, I remember Dave Ritchie being outside the locker room giving a press conference, while inside the locker room our team was in there just throwing down, having fights left and right. It was James Jefferson and basically every Jamaican who was on the team.

"Every Cup team I've been on except possibly 1986 fought. I remember in Winnipeg we fought between one another, too, during the week leading up to the game. It just seemed to make the team stronger for some reason. Everybody seemed to band together, thinking, 'We can beat up on each other, but no one else can beat up on us.' I think everybody took that kind of mentality into the game."

A question mark in training camp, the squabbling Lion secondary turned out to be one of the best in CFL history. "That was the strength of our team," said Less Browne, "because that allowed us to do a lot of things up front. Our linebackers could just have field days, and our defensive linemen could really play and put pressure on people because they believed we were going to do our jobs in the secondary.

"Basically we had four corners starting in the secondary with one safety, so we could cover anybody one on one, and Dave Ritchie took advantage of that. He did a lot of stunts and a lot of things in front that fired up those linemen and linebackers and gave other offenses hell."

Coach Ritchie talked about B.C.'s unsung heroes. "Vic Stevenson, Browne and Wilburn were hurt. Three of our linebackers were rookies. They played well. Near the end of the game Angelo Snipes was a highlight film. He sacked Tracy Ham and turned right around and sacked Congemi on the next play. He had a great, great game. Our coverage was really good."

Baltimore coach Don Matthews analyzed his team's defeat. "It was a very hostile stadium to play in with the crowd noise. We were a no-huddle offense, and the noise affected us. We couldn't do some of the things we should have. We missed some opportunities. There was one questionable catch that turned the game around, and that one as much as anything decided the outcome. But we had other chances to win that game. We didn't play our best football. We were an expansion team with only about 13 veterans on the whole team, and maybe some of our guys got caught up in the moment. Maybe I didn't do a good enough job of explaining what a championship game was all about.

"I had a very difficult time. It took me over six months before I was able to watch the film of that game. I was very, very disappointed that we had lost. I thought for sure we'd win that football game." Matthews has yet to win a Grey Cup in B.C. Place.

Some argued that the B.C. Lions weren't the best team at the end of the season, that they had just been lucky. Kent Austin objected. "I don't believe in luck in sports. I believe in hard preparation, hard work, and then, when it comes down to game time, the players make the plays. What happened to us is we made more plays than the teams we played against."

"Of all the things about that team," Ritchie concurred, "they overcame any adversity, and when they stepped between the lines, they were there to play. I think our guys came up notches and played above their capabilities. I don't think talent-wise, or however you want to look at it, that we were the best anytime until maybe for those three weeks in November. When we got beat by Calgary 24–23 the last game of the season, we were a pretty good football team. I think our players knew that when they walked off the field that day that it didn't matter who they were going to play. They knew they were going to hold their own and be okay. I think we had one of the greatest secondaries on any team ever. But I'll tell you one thing: from the standpoint of getting together and loving one another and wanting to fight to get the thing done, they were as good as anybody was in the CFL."

Less Browne said, "I don't think we were the best team at the end of the year, but we were a very progressive team. Every game we were always getting better. We had a lot of guys who had followed Dave Ritchie from Ottawa to B.C. A lot of guys had never been in a play-off game to get to the Grey Cup. There were a lot of guys who, because of age, would probably never see it if we didn't get there. And so those three games were fought with a lot of heart and desire."

The old veteran Lui Passaglia observed, "I think as far as a road to the championship, the dramatic endings of the last three games probably rank up there in the top 10 of all time in any sport. We won three key play-off championship games on virtually the last play of the game. That rarely happens. There's one thing about that team: it had guts and true grit in the last 30 seconds of a ball game."

Dave Ritchie had the last word. "That whole series was just through the grace of the Lord. How else would you win the last three games on either the last play or with not too much time on the clock?"

Instead of angels in the outfield were there seraphim in the secondary? Like always in B.C., winning didn't last. The following year the Lions played like mortals, finishing third with a 10–8 record, before bowing to the Eskimos in the play-offs 26–15.

At the end of the season, General Manager Erik Tillman resigned and Dave Ritchie was fired. "I don't know what happened," he said. "I came to grips with it last year. It was a nice place. I think we could have kept on winning.

"When I went to the Lions they were 3–15, and we did what we did. Last year they were 5–13, so the answer lies somewhere in between the 8 wins they had in two years and the 34 wins we had in the three years. That's what they've got to live with. I know we did the best we could."

In March 1996 Bill Comrie sold the team to 10 Vancouver businessmen led by Nelson Skalbania and Michael Jensen. Joe Paopao was head coach and Mike McCarthy president. The Lions went into receivership August 31 and were run by the league the rest of the season. They tied for last place.

On January 7, 1997, former Hamilton Ti-Cat owner David Braley bought the club and hired Adam Rita as head coach and director of football operations. Although the defense was green, Damon Allen was quarterback, and Sean Millington and Cory Philpot were in the backfield. The Lions were confident.

Halfway through the season B.C. was 6–3 in second place, 2 points behind the Eskimos. At the end of September they were tied for first with a mark of 8–6. They then lost four in a row, finishing last with a record of 8–10. In three of those losses they were outscored 130 to 19.

During the off-season, after losing Millington, Maurice Kelly, Joe Fleming, Alfred Jackson and Todd Furdyk to free agency, the Lions signed the Argos' Jimmy Cunningham and Robert Drummond and the Riders' Scott Hendrickson to shore up the offense and special teams. They really stocked up on defense, signing Troy Alexander and Dale Joseph from Saskatchewan, Glen Rogers and Bruce Dickson from Edmonton, Noah Cantor from Toronto, Jason Bryant from Montreal and Dwayne Knight and J. Borgella from Winnipeg. Adam Rita had assembled a veritable All-Star team.

Before the season started, Rita said, "We recruited guys with lots of pro experience. If they have the kind of work ethic and character I think they have, that should sustain us through the year. Hopefully we've kept the right guys from last year, and we've acquired some guys who will enhance the core of our team."

Rita never found out. The injury bug struck with a vengeance. Rita had to field a patchwork team all through the summer. At August's end the Lions were 3–6, their only victories at the expense of the lowly Bombers and Roughriders. On September 1, with his offense averaging 15 points per game, Rita stepped down as head coach. His place was taken by Dave Braley's assistant Greg Mohns, who, although once the boss at Ventura Junior College, had no professional coaching experience whatsoever.

But Mohns knew who to ask. He brought John Hufnagel, John Gregory and Joe Paopao in as consultants. They simplified the offense for Damon Allen. In addition, 1998 CFL Rookie of the Year, Steve Muhammed, solidified the secondary, and Eddie Brown, Rocky Henry, Rod Harris, Al Shipman and the returning Alfred Jackson came together as a receiving corps. Robert Drummond came back from the injury list to join rookie sensation Juan Johnson in the backfield. After losing three more games, the Lions reeled off six wins in a row, beating Calgary and Hamilton and making the play-offs before bowing to Edmonton in the semifinal.

Greg Mohns was rewarded with a new contract as head coach. By mid-August of his first full year in command, Mohns had the Lions in first place. With the Grey Cup slated for Vancouver in 1999, the B.C. Lions had a reasonable chance of being there.

CHAPTER 5

Saskatchewan and Ottawa

On Roughriders!

WHEN THE EXPANSION BALTIMORE COLTS WERE denied the use of that name, several wags suggested they call the team the Roughriders or the Rough Riders—take your pick of spellings. After all, in a league that already had two teams so named, what difference would a third make?

Unfortunately for the nation's capitol, soon after the end of the 1996 season, the Ottawa Rough Riders folded. Only months later the Saskatchewan Roughriders conducted a telethon to keep the team alive. They failed to reach the goal, but the storied franchise survived with money from the CFL's new relationship with the NFL. Saskatchewan without the Roughriders? Unthinkable.

People felt that way in Ottawa, too. When the 1997 kickoff took place around the league in June, Frank Clair Stadium sat beside the Rideau Canal resplendent in red, white and black, sparkling in the sun. Empty. No more the cheers of yesteryear, gone the gridiron greats. No Golab or Simpson, no Tucker or Atkins, no Vaughn and Racine, no Jackson and Stewart, no Clements and Gabriel. After 120 years, no Ottawa Rough Riders. Unthinkable.

The two franchises had more in common than their name. Until 1948 both teams wore black and red. That year the western entry switched to green and white to take advantage of a bargain. Rider executive Jack Fyffe found two sets of green and white jerseys on sale in a Chicago store. Because the price was so low Fyffe snapped them up, and the Kelly Green and White tradition so totally identified with the Wheat Province began. True to the Saskatchewan creed, a penny saved is a penny earned.

There is no agreement as to how the teams got their name. One account says there was a contingent of Canadian volunteers who fought with Teddy Roosevelt in the Spanish–American War. His troops were called the Roughriders. The unit's colors were red and black.

Some of those soldiers were with the Regina and Ottawa football teams and wanted the name. In 1924 the Ottawa Rough Riders changed their name to Senators, and the Regina football club promptly called themselves the Roughriders. Three years later Ottawa dropped Senators in favor of their old moniker.

Roosevelt's *Roughriders* is one word, not two, so it seems feasible that the Regina Roughriders were named after the heroes of the Spanish-American war. That leaves the Rough Riders to be named after the lumberjacks who rode logs down the Ottawa River.

In the last half of this century, Saskatchewan has appeared in eight Grey Cups, half of them against Ottawa. Saskatchewan won their first Cup against the Rough Riders in 1966. Ottawa inflicted the most bitter defeat in Saskatchewan football history a decade later.

Both teams had their glory years in the 1960s. When the decade began, Ottawa had quarterbacks Russ Jackson and Ron Lancaster. In 1963 Ottawa traded Lancaster to Saskatchewan. The two friendly enemy quarterbacks faced each other in two Grey Cups, each winning once.

The Ottawa Football Club was formed at the Russell Hotel September 18, 1876. In 1883 they became a charter member of the Ontario Rugby Football Union, losing the first championship game to the Toronto Argonauts 9–7. Twenty-four years later they entered the Big Four with Hamilton, Montreal and Toronto.

Ottawa won their first Grey Cup as the Senators in 1925, defeating the Winnipeg Tammany Tigers 24–1. They repeated as champions in 1926, beating the University of Toronto 10–7. Ten years later Ottawa returned to the national championship, losing to the Sarnia Imperials 26–20.

Beginning in 1939 Ottawa appeared in the Grey Cup game four times in three years (in the 1940 the Grey Cup was a two-game, total-point series). In the first one Ottawa was edged 8–7 by Winnipeg. The next year featured the two-game match-up against Balmy Beach. Ottawa won both games, 8–2 and

12–5. The Bombers were back in 1941, winning this time 18–16 against the Rough Riders.

In 1948 the Calgary Stampeders went East to challenge for the Grey Cup for the first time. Their opponent was the Ottawa Rough Riders. The Riders lost again, this time 12–7. The team was 0–3 in Grey Cups against Western opposition.

Ottawa had a powerhouse a year later, finishing the season at 11–1 but losing the final to Montreal. After a last-place finish in 1950, the Riders rebounded and tied Hamilton and Toronto for first. Ottawa won the coin toss and top spot. That year Hamilton edged Toronto in the semifinal, and they in turn lost the final round 28–16 to Ottawa, who prepared to meet their namesakes from the West.

The Saskatchewan Roughriders originally took form as the Regina Rugby Club at a December 1910 meeting held in the sports room at City Hall. Between 1911 and 1935, they finished first in the Western Rugby Union every year, playing in and losing seven Grey Cups. Their last appearance in the first half of the century took place in 1934. A Roughrider of that era was Harry Veiner from Dysart, Saskatchewan, a town about 80 kilometers northeast of Regina. Raised on a farm, Veiner moved on down the Empress line after the 1930 season and settled in Medicine Hat, where he became a millionaire in clay products, real estate, farms and ranches, and shopping centers. He could usually be found at his hangout on Third Street, Hat Hardware. As the mayor of Medicine Hat for over 20 years, Veiner put his city on the map. He clobbered Raul Castro in a cane cutting contest in Cuba, shipped a pig to Winston Churchill, kicked a soccer ball in Dundee, Scotland, and won other contests and events.

A man from Saskatchewan with a penchant for trying anything once would naturally find his way onto a football field. He explained how he became a Regina Roughrider. "I was brought in by Father Athol Murray. I was a country hick who played soccer football. I used to run on the first of July, and then I'd play soccer for McGowan's Hill Football Club. But I was brought up in the country, and what the heck did I know about football? We never played that kind of football in Dysart."

The priest from Notre Dame at Wilcox recognized genuine athletic talent when he saw it. "I was a good soccer kicker," continued Veiner, "and Father Murray and Al Ritchie said to me, 'By Joe, you come down and try out for the Roughriders. By Joe, you're going to make a football player.' I was 25 years old when I started. I used to drive in from Dysart for practices because I was still farming then."

In those days, before a game, the players would throw a few dollars into a pot and the first one who drew blood got the money. They were a tough bunch and determined to give the rookie Veiner a trial by ordeal.

"When I got to Regina I was put in the line, and what they did was try to test me. They made up plays and came at me and just about killed me. But I wouldn't give in. When I came off the field, I was black and blue. My cousin Saul Bloomfield (the first Roughrider to ever score a point in a Grey Cup in 1929) comes up to me and says, 'You darn fool, they'll kill you if you try to take all that.' I never let on I was black and blue, and next day I came back even though I could hardly move.

"They put me in the line again. But Father Murray saved me. 'I'm not going to let those fellows kill you,' he said. 'They're just trying to test you. You've had enough of that.' So I survived.

"I was a roughneck. If they wanted any dirty plays in the line they'd send me in. There were lots of injuries. I had my leg broken. I think on the line we were a lot tougher because everything meant the line. In those days it was hit the line all the time. They didn't really start the forward pass until the '30s.

"We also didn't have the equipment then that they do now. We wore shoulder pads and a helmet that looked like an old flyer's hat. The odd man would play without a helmet."

The Roughriders played Winnipeg, Saskatoon, Moose Jaw and Calgary. They drove their own cars to the Saskatoon and Moose Jaw encounters, getting paid for their mileage. Financially that's all Veiner ever got out of football. "They didn't pay me a damn cent," he recalled.

Although the game was tough, it wasn't complicated. "We'd go into the Balmoral Café with Al Ritchie and make up all the plays, and I'd listen to him. But it was all Greek to me at the start. It took me a little time to catch on to what all those plays were because I was a pretty green fellow. But those days it was hit the line and kick most of the time. Al Ritchie's basic play was to get in there and get him."

When Veiner played for the Riders, Taylor Field was being built. "We played at the Exhibition Grounds. But in the fall we went to train at the RCMP barracks, where they had the horses. We had to pull the boys out of that stuff, too. When you went to tackle someone, you came up with a mouthful. It wasn't the real stuff, it was shavings and things, but it seemed like the real stuff."

Veiner was with the team in 1929 but didn't get into the Rider's Grey Cup loss to Hamilton. In 1930, however, he took the field against Balmy Beach. "Certainly I got excited about playing in the Grey Cup. But don't forget that I never had the confidence of imports like Curt Shave, and I didn't know what the heck would happen or what I was doing wrong. We never won the Grey Cup. We weren't a finished team."

Dobberville

In the 1940s the Roughriders fell on hard times with only two winning seasons. In 1948, when Moose Jaw and Saskatoon dropped out, the Regina Roughriders became the Saskatchewan Roughriders. The legendary love affair between fans and football team began in 1951 when a tall Tulsan, Glen Dobbs, arrived in Regina to quarterback the Roughriders. Dobbs took Saskatchewan by storm.

License plates with "Dobberville" adorned cars from one end of the province to the other. At recess Dobbs' son was followed all over the school grounds by children anxious to bask in his reflected glory. Everywhere he went Glen Dobbs was mobbed by hordes of adoring fans. It would not be hyperbole to suggest the coming of Glen Dobbs was the greatest thing to ever hit Saskatchewan's Queen City.

"I didn't play football until I was a senior in high school," Dobbs recalled, "because I was too little. I was 5'8" and 128 pounds in the eleventh grade. I played the trumpet in the band. I was 6'1", 165 pounds the next year and 6'4", 185 pounds the year after that."

Dobbs attended his hometown Tulsa University, where he made All-American. "Yes, sir, I was the first one that they had—also the first one in the College Football Hall of Fame. I've been very fortunate to be in a lot of places where they had real good coaches."

He explained how he ended up in Regina. "I had retired from football after four years in the All-America Conference, and I came home to settle down in Tulsa. We had a small stock farm south of town with 280 head of cattle. I thought, 'Well, this is it.'

"Then a friend of mine got me hooked up with Senator Kerr, who had opened a radio station here in Tulsa. This friend of mine called down there and told him I was in town and that I should become their sports director on the radio. They okayed it and I went to work at the radio station.

"We signed a contract to broadcast the Oklahoma State football games for the 1950 season. My friend was going to do the color. So we were representing the City of Tulsa and Radio KRMG and doing the broadcasts from Stillwater and on the road.

"Somehow or other Mr. Bob Kramer, who was one of the most wonderful men I've ever met in sports, found out I was available. They were hunting for somebody to come up to Saskatchewan and play football. He and his wife came down to Tulsa. He called and invited me to come and visit with him. He wanted me to come and play quarterback that year, 1950.

"I told Mr. Kramer I would be interested, but I had signed a contract to do the broadcasts for Oklahoma State, and so I wouldn't be available for the 1950 season.

"He was so nice and kind that I just tried to talk as nice as I could, and yet I had to be firm because I had signed a contract with the radio station. Back in our day when you gave your word or signed a contract it meant something.

"He said, 'Well, I've got to get your name on a contract. If you play, will you play with us?' I said, 'All things being equal, yes.' And I signed a contract to that effect.

"I liked Mr. Kramer and his ideas and how hard they worked. It was kind of a Green Bay operation. The whole province owned the team.

"I decided the next year I would play for Bob Kramer. I belonged to the Bears by this time. I had been the number one choice of the Chicago Cardinals, and then the next year George Halas made a deal for me. I called and told him I was going to play again. He made me an offer. I said, 'Sir, that's nowhere near what I made in the American league.' He did the usual Halas thing.

"Saskatchewan made me an offer. I called Mr. Halas and told him what the offer was. All he had to do was match it. He passed. That's how I became a Roughrider."

Living in Saskatchewan was like never leaving Oklahoma, he recalled. "I was raised in Fredericks, a small town of about 4,500 people. Everybody knew everybody and were friends. We were just normal, everyday, southwest people. We all enjoyed our friends, and the people in Saskatchewan were the same to us. We went to church with them, we went to parties with them. We knew about their babies, when they were born. We'd go up to the lake when we had some free time and fish with different groups of people. We really enjoyed it. We just felt right at home.

"In fact, a lady moved in with her relatives and let us lease her house in 1952. Our first year we stayed at Sam Taylor's house (a Rider executive). He gave us his brand new home the first year.

"Fans came out in the cold and snow to the Quarterback Club meeting, where they introduced me. The theater was full. It was wonderful.

"We loved Saskatchewan, and it was a mutual thing. I felt like I was back in Oklahoma playing in front of the home folks. We felt bad when we'd lose a game, but the next day on the street the people would say, 'Don't worry about it—you've done all you could do.'"

Did his teammates resent all the attention he got from his adoring public? After all, football is a team game. "No, not at all," replied Rider veteran Ken Charlton. "He was a super guy. I don't think anybody on the team resented him for the publicity he got."

In 1951 the Western Conference, like the East, ended with a three-way tie for first. Saskatchewan, Edmonton and Winnipeg were 8–6. Saskatchewan got the bye. Annis Stukus kicked a field goal to give Edmonton a 4–1 win in the semifinal.

The first game of the Conference Final was played at Taylor Field on an overcast Saturday afternoon. In the dying minutes Jim Chambers streaked down the fan-laden sideline for a touchdown, giving the visitors a 15–11 victory. The Riders won the second game 12–5 in Edmonton and then advanced to the Grey Cup by winning a thriller 19–18 back in Regina.

Grey Cup 1951

Two days after winning the West, the Roughriders embarked by train for Toronto. Aboard were Mr. and Mrs. Ken Charlton. Charlton was a Regina native who went to Central Collegiate and played for the Regina Junior Dales. He began his career with the Riders in 1941. In 1942 he played for the Winnipeg RCAF Bombers, losing the Grey Cup to the Toronto RCAF Hurricanes 8–5. In 1943 he was with the All-Services Roughriders. After his discharge in 1945, he spurned an offer from the Cleveland Rams to sign with Ottawa. After three years there, Charlton returned to Regina, where he played until his retirement in 1954. An All-Star five times, Charlton was inducted into the CFL Hall of Fame October 24, 1992.

He loved the train trip to Toronto. "It was super," he recalled. "The train was loaded with people. It was like a big party all the way down."

Mrs. Charlton agreed. "It was absolutely beautiful, but the players didn't party. A porter came through the car and said, 'Shh, these are all the players' wives. They're a bunch of nuns.' The players were in another car. We were all at the back and it was just a ball. I rode on the bread truck in the parade." (Those on the Saskatchewan float in the Grey Cup parade threw little loaves of bread to the crowd.)

Dobbs described the 1951 Roughriders. "We were not an overwhelming team. We were only allowed five Americans and, darn, Jack Russell, the big end got hurt and we had trouble at center when Red Ettinger got hurt. We had to get my old friend Bob Nelson to come up from the Detroit Lions and play center for us. We got the big fullback Bob Sandberg, who was an architect over in Minnesota. He had played in Canada before and came up to help us out in the last part of the season.

"Some of our Canadians were older. Toar Springstein was in his second-last year. Ken Charlton, the perennial halfback, was close to the end of the line, just like a lot of us were. Kenny was a hardworking dude. We were all the same kind of guys. We knew we didn't have all the ability, so we worked hard."

Going into the Grey Cup, said Charlton, "We had a lot of injuries, but except for Jack Russell they all played, but not as well as they could have."

Getting ready to meet the Western invasion was Ottawa receiver Bob Simpson, a native of Windsor who had played one year of high school ball and one year with the hometown Rockets of the Ontario Rugby Football Union before joining the Rough Riders in 1950. Mr. Versatility, Simpson was an All-Star at end in '51, '56 and '59, flying wing in '52 and '53, running back in '57 and defensive back in '57 and '58. He scored 70 touchdowns, 65 receiving, tying him for twelfth all-time with Jim Young. He had the second-highest average gain per pass reception at 22 yards (Whit Tucker had 22.4) and the second-highest average gain per pass reception in a regular season game, 3 for 196 yards, when Ottawa played Toronto on September 17, 1955.

Simpson's coach in 1951 was Clem Crowe. "Clem didn't think Canadians could play football, so he didn't give much credit to them. If you weren't an American, you couldn't play well, which was really the way he expressed it. Obviously he and I didn't get along too well."

Fellow Windsorite and Argo Joe Krol felt the same way about Frank Clair, who later coached Simpson in Ottawa. "At the beginning Clair felt the same as Crowe, but when he got here in 1956," recalled Simpson, "he was much more

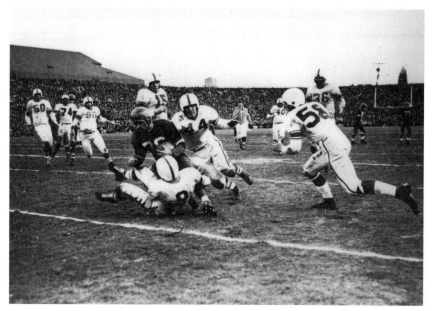

It was Ottawa over Saskatchewan in the 1951 Grey Cup.

mellow. He realized you couldn't win the Grey Cup without Canadians. He treated me a thousand percent. I had no complaints about my treatment from him at all."

Come Grey Cup week, the Ottawa Rough Riders were all business. "We arrived in Toronto on Tuesday and stayed at the King Edward Hotel," said Simpson. "We didn't really want to be part of the festivities. We had a job to do.

"You have to trust your athlete. He knows the job that's at hand. Sure he'll go out and have a couple of beers on Wednesday and Thursday night, but he is certainly not going to be walking the streets looking for trouble or anything."

In the 1951 Grey Cup game, near the end of the first quarter, Dobbs put Saskatchewan into the lead with two singles. Simpson is still in awe of the punting prowess of the Tulsa All-American. "I was catching punts at the time," he recalled. "There was quite a wind that day. On Dobbs' first punt he was standing on his own 40-yard line. I was standing on my 15-yard line and I never moved. The ball was going up when it went over my head. It went through the end zone and landed 12 rows up in the bleachers. I had never seen a kick like that before in my life."

That's all the scoring the Westerners could muster until the fourth quarter. Ottawa scored three touchdowns and a single, leading 19–2 after 45 minutes.

"Regina had the ball with the wind in the first quarter," recalled Simpson. "Once we changed ends for the second quarter, Dobbs still kicked the ball very, very high, but against that wind it didn't go very far. We took advantage of that situation. Benny MacDonell scored against the wind, and then Alton Baldwin scored with the wind. Then we had the wind when Pete Karpuk scored.

"On Benny's touchdown, Saskatchewan's Martin Ruby was playing defensive tackle on my inside. We had a double team on him, and Howie Turner took the ball 55 or 60 yards to the 1-yard line. MacDonell went in from there.

"The most important catch was Pete's. It was a streak pattern. Pete had good speed and he headed down the sideline. He outran their defensive back, who was a little banged up. Tom O'Malley threw an absolutely perfect pass. Pete caught up with it about the 12-yard line and went in for the touchdown. That put us up 21–7."

The Green Riders didn't give up. Trailing 20–2 early in the fourth, Dobbs completed a touchdown pass to Jack Nix while Regina fullback Sully Glasser scored another. But that was it. Ottawa won 21–14 in the two teams' first Grey Cup encounter.

"We made a tactical mistake," Dobbs explained. "The main problem was Jack Russell being hurt. For some reason the coach, Harry Smith, decided on game day that Jack Russell wasn't going to play. So they took the left end, Jack Nix, and moved him to right end and took a fellow off the bench, Johnny Bell, and put him at left end. Instead of having a new man in one spot, we had two ends in new spots. That, to me, was the biggest problem we had.

"Mr. Kramer wanted to play the fullback, Sandberg, as an import. For some reason Harry just refused to play him. Sandberg must have weighed 220. He was a big, husky guy.

"So we wound up with three positions that were quite undermanned. That was the biggest problem we had because there wasn't that much difference between the teams."

Simpson didn't earn a bonus for his Grey Cup win. "I was only 21, and I didn't have any bonuses in my contract," he explained. "I finally found out that was the only way to make any money. Then I put it in the contract. My first year I made $1,800 for 12 games and the next year $3,000 for 12 games. My top salary after 13 years was $9,750.

"You lived off your regular job. Football gave you a little bit extra, maybe a new car every two years. We bought a house in 1954 for $1,400. I ended up buy-

ing a small hotel with a restaurant just outside of Ottawa. That's what it did for us."

Said the Green and White's Ken Charlton, "I wasn't paid when I started. The year after I was—$125 for the season. I was right halfback on offense and safety on defense. I punted and returned punts. I played 60 minutes per game all of my career. I never sat out any part of a game."

At the end of the season, Saskatchewan head coach Harry "Black Jack" Smith was fired. Characteristically blunt, Charlton explained why. "He did a lousy job, that's why. He didn't do a good job with the club we had."

His successor, Glen Dobbs, had no head coaching experience. The 1952 Roughriders finished last with a 3–13 record. Dobbs was soon out of a job, and in 1953 his playing career also came to an end.

But to have played in the national classic was very special to him. "I thought it was great. To me it was the national championship. I discussed the thing to find out how Saskatchewan people felt about it. They were just lovers—they loved their football team. It was theirs and they felt that way. I did, too.

"It was a labor of love for us up there in Saskatchewan. We had all the good things in the whole wide world. I'm sorry I got my leg hurt real bad and couldn't finish up like I wanted to. It took me a couple of years to get completely over my knee injury.

"It was just a great time in our lives. Mr. Kramer offered me a job to stay up there and work with his corporations. But I came home and went to work on my farm, raising my cattle. I still get a letter or two every month from somewhere up in Canada after all those years."

Lancaster, Jackson and the Golden Years

After winning the Grey Cup in 1951, Ottawa missed the play-offs three years in a row. Crowe was fired after the 1954 season, his successor, Chan Caldwell, the following year. Frank Clair signed on in 1956, and four years later Ottawa's golden era began.

Great teams have great quarterbacks. At the beginning of their gilded age, Ottawa had three outstanding quarterbacks. Two of them, Ron Lancaster and Russ Jackson, would end up in the Hall of Fame. The third, Frank Tripuka, starred with the Saskatchewan Roughriders from 1953–58 before being traded to Ottawa.

Another Hall of Famer was involved in the deal. Ottawa traded a defensive tackle named Jim Marshall to Saskatchewan for Tripuka. After the 1959 season, needing a quarterback, Saskatchewan sent Marshall to Cleveland for Bob Ptacek. When the Minnesota Vikings entered the NFL, they chose Marshall in the expansion draft. Jim Marshall would be inducted into the NFL Hall of Fame in Canton, Ohio.

Russ Jackson wasn't drafted as a quarterback. "When I went to Ottawa," he recalled, "I did not make it as a quarterback. I made it as a defensive back in 1958. Only injuries to Hal Ledyard and Tom Dimitroff, who were the two Americans at that time, got me into the quarterback role late in 1958.

"I never had the feeling that Frank Clair didn't think I could do the job. It took some time to earn the full confidence of everybody, but I think that's true for any quarterback. I was in the right place at the right time, sure. That's true with any sport, I think. You can be in the wrong place at the wrong time and never get the opportunity."

Jackson's first contract for $4,700, with a $500 bonus and a ticket back and forth to Toronto to go to school, was, he said, "A pretty good one in those days."

Also joining the Ottawa Riders in 1958 was running back Ron Stewart from Queen's University. At 5'7" and 180 pounds Stewart overcame his small stature to become one of greatest players in CFL history, appearing in four Grey Cups, winning three. Stewart won the Outstanding Canadian Schenley Award and was chosen the Canadian Male Athlete of the Year in 1960. An Eastern All-Star in 1960, '61 and '64, Stewart was inducted into the CFL Hall of Fame in 1977. He is one of 10 Ottawa players to have his number retired.

At Montreal on October 10, 1960, Stewart set the still-standing CFL single-game rushing record of 287 yards, doing so on only 15 carries. "Everything seemed to unfold that day," he recalled. "When a team combines to produce that kind of result, on a personal basis you have to be pretty happy with your performance. The record has held up pretty well."

Ottawa began and ended the decade of the 1960s by winning the Grey Cup. The team to beat in 1960 was Toronto, led by Tobin Rote. The Argos finished first with a mark of 10–4, their first play-off appearance in five years. Ottawa was 9–5, scoring 400 points, at that time the second-highest total in Eastern Conference history. In the semifinal they easily dispatched the Alouettes 30–14 and then shocked Toronto by winning the first game of the final 33–21 at Lansdowne Park.

The double blue came roaring back at home, erasing the 12-point deficit and surging into a total point lead of 8. But despite falling behind 20–0, Ottawa wasn't finished. Reeling off three straight touchdowns, the Riders won the game 21–20, the round 54–21, and sent the Argos back to oblivion.

The 1960 Grey Cup would be played in Vancouver. Ron Stewart couldn't wait for the game to begin. "As a young fellow I was pretty excited about going all the way out to Vancouver to play in a Grey Cup game. When you're a younger man, getting to the national final is a big deal."

For rookie Ron Lancaster it was business as usual. "In high school and college I'd had a pretty good history of always being with a championship team. It didn't really surprise me that we got there. After being there in 1960 and not again until 1966, I realized it is a lot more difficult to get to the Grey Cup than I thought it would be as a rookie. As a rookie I was just happy to be on the football team.

"I knew the Grey Cup was the championship game, but I didn't have any idea what it meant to the country. It was just another football game, and as a rookie you don't really understand its importance."

Ottawa's opponent was Edmonton, survivor of a brutal Western Final. They were in no shape to play the Rough Riders, who were sympathetic to their plight. Said Lancaster, "In those days, with the West playing a two-game total-point semifinal and a best-of-three final, and with the weather conditions and the closeness of the games, it's a wonder the West ever won a Grey Cup.

"You don't realize it until you play out West. You think it's cold down East, but usually at that time of year you were playing on mud whereas in the West they were playing on frozen fields. The bumps and bruises take a tremendous toll on your players. You ended up playing the total-point series on a Saturday and a Monday and turned around and played Saturday, Wednesday and then Saturday in your final. You were playing five games in 14 days. You were asking an awful lot from an individual to perform in the most important games of the year and then turn around a week later and play in the Grey Cup game when he hasn't recovered from his injuries. It was always amazing to me how the West did so well in the Grey Cup. The players had to be something else."

Facing Edmonton was a strong Ottawa squad. "We had Dave Thelan and Ronnie Stewart," said Bob Simpson. "Both were extremely good. We also had a very, very strong offensive line: Kaye Vaughn, Fred Robinson at guard, Bruno Bitkowski at center, Milt Graham and Tom Jones. I was on the left end and Billy Sowalski was on the right. We had a good running attack. We ran the ball and controlled the ball."

Offensive Star Ron Stewart played defense as Ottawa defeated Edmonton in the 1960 Grey Cup.

Ball control was truly the name of the game in the 1960 Grey Cup as Ottawa outrushed Edmonton 247 to 49 yards. Stewart had 99 of them. The ground game, Jackson said, "was our style. We were a running team. If you look at the people (and taking nothing away from them—Bill Sowalski was playing offensive end as well as Bobby Simpson; Davey West was a flanker) we did not have a team that was geared to throw the ball a great deal. We felt it was important to control the ball and not give the Edmonton Eskimos a chance to score a lot of points."

They didn't. The Westerners' sole touchdown came on a 63-yard pass and run from Jackie Parker to Jim Letcavits. Ottawa scored two majors, the first by Bill Sowalski. "That was a fake off a reverse we had run throughout the season," said Jackson. "It was the first time we ran it that game. It should have been a running play, but I decided we were going to fake it. Bill was all alone in the end zone. I recall him saying that the ball took so long to get there he was afraid he was going to drop it. He was all alone in the end zone.

"Our second touchdown was scored by lineman Kaye Vaughn, the only touchdown of his college and professional career. He recovered a fumble in the end zone."

Gary Schreider added a field goal and convert. Final score: Ottawa 16, Edmonton 7.

The Eskimos were certainly hurting although Jackie Parker said they lost because Ottawa was the better team. "That's very kind of him," said the Eastern Riders' Bobby Simpson. "That day they had to actually pick Johnny Bright up and carry him off the bus. I know they shot him up. When I saw him on the field he was running, but he was hurting. Parker was hurting. Getty was playing quarterback instead of Jackie. They had a couple of linemen hurt. They were beat up. There's no question about it. You could have tossed a coin on who would win if we were all in shape."

Ron Stewart agreed. "The Eskimos were pretty well beaten up. Had they been a healthier team it might have been a different ball game."

Jackson wasn't so charitable. "Well, you could look at injuries in any one game. If you make it to a Grey Cup game, you may be nicked or beat up, but you're there to do the best you can and produce an effort. Whether they were beat up or we were beat up, who knows? We had people injured, they had people injured. It happens at the end of the year."

The 1960 Grey Cup win was especially sweet for Bobby Simpson, who had won before. "In 1951 I was very young. It was all new to me. I wasn't really prepared to know what was going on then. But in 1960, after 10 years, I was prepared and I knew what it was. There are not that many who get a chance to play in a Grey Cup. I was lucky enough to win twice."

During the next five years Ottawa was always the bridesmaid, never the bride, with five straight second-place finishes. Asked to describe those years of trying to catch up with Hamilton, Russ Jackson laughed and replied, "Discouraging. You know, we had a lot of good teams, but we could just never beat Hamilton or cross that threshold to get to the Grey Cup. It was discouraging in the early '60s. Then in the late '60s we became the dominant team. We were unbeatable at home and went to the Grey Cup three times."

The breakthrough came in 1966, when the Rough Riders finished on top for the first time since 1951 with a record of 11–3. Known for their great offense, the team was also strong defensively, surrendering an average of less than two touchdowns per game.

Jackson explained what turned the also-rans into winners. "It's always personnel. The coaches were the same. We had so much talent offensively and defensively with a group of players like Margene Atkins, Vic Washington, Whit Tucker and Ronnie Stewart. We never went into a ball game in the last half of the '60s thinking that we could lose. You go with that feeling. You know you're going to find a way to win rather than find a way to lose."

The architect of the 1960s Rough Riders was former Alouette great Red O'Quinn. He explained the circumstances by which he took over in Ottawa. "I retired in 1959 and went to work for the United Aircraft Corporation, Pratt and Whitney. I had been with them for two years when Barry O'Brien, the president of the Rough Riders, called me about the job with Ottawa. So I said, 'What the heck, I'll take a shot at it and see how long it lasts.' It lasted about 10 years."

In those days teams didn't have personnel directors. Instead, said Red O'Quinn, "We all had a lot of contacts, guys who would call us with information, particularly if they heard that a top-flight player was getting into academic trouble or anything like that. We'd put him on our negotiation list. That's how we got people like Bo Scott and Vic Washington. They came to us because of their inability to pass. In those days you had to wait until your class graduated before the NFL would take you. You'd have to sit around and do nothing or come to the Canadian Football League. A lot of them did."

Meanwhile the prairie Riders were going through a dry spell. Under

George Terlip and Frank Tripuka they went 1–15 in 1959 and 2–12–2 in 1960 under their successor, former Rider running back Ken Carpenter. In 1961 New York Giant legend Steve Owen came to town. The Riders moved up a notch to fourth with a mark of 5–10–1. The following year he guided them to their first of 15 straight play-off appearances. His work complete, Owen retired, replaced by Bob Shaw, who stayed two years before heading for Hogtown. His successor was Eagle Keys.

Even in the dark days of the late 1950s, Roughrider General Manager Ken Preston was slowly but surely putting together a powerful football team. Already there were Hall of Famers Ron Atchison, Bill Clarke and Al Benecick, as well as Reggie Whitehouse. Defenders Wayne Shaw and Garner Ekstran arrived in 1961 along with perennial All-Star center Ted Urness.

The nucleus of the offense was assembled in 1963. Along with Ron Lancanster came receiver Hugh Campbell and running backs Ed Buchanan and George Reed. In 1964 tackle Clyde Brock, flanker Gord Barwell, tight-end Jim Worden and defensive back Bob Kosid came aboard. The following year saw the arrival of place-kicker and guard Jack Abendshan, linebacker Wally Dempsey, defensive back Ted Dushinski and receiver Alan Ford. The major acquisitions of 1966 were defensive lineman Ed McQuarters and tackle Tom Benyan.

Assistant Coach Jack Gotta described the 1966 Roughriders. "That team was pretty solid all the way around. You think about George Reed, Eddie Buchanan, Ronnie Lancaster, the corps of receivers we had and tight-end Jim Worden—those guys were as good as any who ever played in the league.

"And then defensively, such solid guys as Wally Dempsey and Garner Ekstran just played hard all the time. They were tough guys. Everybody picked up on it.

"Football is a great team sport. Those guys had that. Black, white, young, old, Canadian, American—everybody got along. We had some bright people on that football club. Ronnie Lancaster was a student of the game. I don't think George Reed ever blew an assignment. Everybody took such pride in what they were doing."

Added Alan Ford, "We had a pretty good crew. We were pretty close-knit. The coach can't do that, the general manager can't do that—it's got to be the guys in the locker room. You need to have guys who are leaders. There was no "I" in George Reed, there was no "I" in Ron Lancaster. Those were the guys who carried the team in terms of that "we" stuff.

"George worked harder than anybody else at practice. Ron would never miss practice. Both would play hurt. If you've got leaders, it really makes a big difference. Ron would do what he felt was necessary to get ready to play, and other people would notice that and follow along with him."

Something to Behold

As the 1966 season began, the Roughriders' challenge was to accomplish what no other Saskatchewan team had done before: win the Grey Cup. Like Ottawa, Saskatchewan had topped their division for the first time since 1951, finishing with a mark of 9–6–1. Hugh Campbell's 102 points on 17 touchdowns led the league in scoring, and he finished second to Terry Evanshen in receiving with 66 catches for 1,109 yards. Ron Lancaster and George Reed were number one in passing and rushing yardage, but Russ Jackson beat out Lancaster for the Schenley Award for Most Outstanding Player.

The Bombers beat Edmonton in the semifinal 19–8 and went to Regina for the first game of the best-of-three Western Final, losing 14–7. Back in Winnipeg for game two, with the Roughriders hoping for a sweep, the man of the hour was the Riders' Ed McQuarters. Late in the game Saskatchewan trailed Winnipeg 19–14. The Bombers were moving in for the kill and, said McQuarters, "We had a blitz on. The blitz called for me to go outside while my defensive end was supposed to loop in behind me.

"Instead of the offensive lineman dropping back for a pass (I think he blew his assignment), he fired out. When I started to loop around, he was right there. He sort of knocked me off stride, so I ended up being out of position actually, and Don Gerhardt, the defensive end, was where I was supposed to be and hit the quarterback, Kenny Ploen. Wally Dempsey also hit Ploen and the ball hit the ground. Because I was out of position, I saw it. It took one bounce, I was there and sort of scooped it up and took off.

"When the Grey Cup was over we were back in Regina at a party and I remember Eagle Keys saying to me, 'You know, Ed, if that had been the regular season, you would have got a zero on your grade because you were out of position.' I said, 'Thanks, Eagle!' But he was right—I wasn't where I was supposed to be. Anyway, the zero turned into a Western Final win for us and a Grey Cup win later on."

Ed McQuarters played so well that in just over eight years he made All-Canadian three times, won the Schenley for Most Outstanding Lineman in

1967 and was inducted into the CFL Hall of Fame in 1988. "I was told by Eagle that they had brought me to Saskatchewan late in '66 with the idea of trading me to Edmonton for defensive back John Wydraney. Once I got here and I looked pretty good, the trade never happened."

Only two Roughriders had any Grey Cup experience, the quarterback and the coach, Eagle Keys, who prepared carefully for the 1966 Grey Cup. "Unless you're prepared to dedicate yourself to the Grey Cup game," Keys said, "you don't deserve to win it. If you don't prepare and discipline yourself, you'll lose it because of mistakes. And you don't want to make mistakes and lose it because you went down there to have a good time.

"The two teams that go to the Grey Cup are glad to be there. But I always felt that there's no sense being there if you don't win it. To feel like a Grey Cup champion you have to win the Grey Cup."

Great Rider veteran Ron Atchison said, "Eagle took us way out of town when we were in B.C. We were in a quiet place. It was the best preparation we could have had for the game. I think it made quite a difference."

Hugh Campbell believed Eagle Keys' experience was an important factor in preparing the Riders for the Grey Cup. "The important thing in having been to the Grey Cup," he counseled, "is how to cope with the carnival going on around you. That's the advantage. Even a team that loses once or twice gains experience at coping with the circus.

"As a player in the Grey Cup, I remember being amazed at the number of photographers. It was beyond the sports media. It was a happening. Everyone was there. Everything was Grey Cup. That was a new thing for us. We were a bunch of wide-eyed guys. Eagle had to cope with that."

Observed Ron Lancaster, "The biggest thing in a Grey Cup is to try to keep everybody from getting caught up in the festivities that go on. Now I don't want to say that you isolate them and don't let them see anything. But somehow you have to put it in the right perspective and treat it like another football game. It's a mistake to try and put too much emphasis on it, and it's also a tremendous mistake to down play it. You have to acclimatize the players to the feelings of the festival going on at Grey Cup, yet not to the point where it overshadows the football game."

Grey Cup week 1966 was business as usual for Lancaster. "Eagle would never change the way we did things all year. He was a believer in doing certain things, and we prepared for that game the same as any other.

"Both teams are going to be ready to play. Heck, you can't hardly wait for that day. That's what you're playing for from the start of the season. Man, it's tough getting there. That's the thing you find out."

The Riders were incredibly uptight. Jack Abendschan inadvertently contributed to victory by breaking the tension. Explained Alan Ford, "Abendschan slipped and fell during the introductions. The track was muddy, so when he got up and ran out he had this big brown spot on his rear end. Of course the guys would never let him forget that."

The heavily favored Eastern Riders jumped into a 14–0 lead. Early in the first quarter Russ Jackson combined with Whit Tucker on a 61-yard pass and run for a touchdown and an 85-yard strike to Tucker for Ottawa's only other touchdown in the second. Moe Racine kicked a convert and Bill Clime added a single.

Covering on both plays was Saskatoon native Dale West, who played two years at Arizona before finishing at the University of Saskatchewan. When asked about the Tucker touchdowns, West laughed. "Thank-you for reminding me of that. I was involved in both of them. On the first one I don't know if I had not been paying attention to the films or what, but I saw Ronnie Stewart going through a three back and I came up and supported, which I never did for six or seven years of my career, so I don't know why I did it then. Tucker ran by me and got a touchdown. Larry Dumelie got blamed on TV, but I knew it was me.

"On the second one I had Tucker man to man and was okay with him down the field. Jackson came up toward the line of scrimmage, and I thought he was going to run across, so I came up. He threw it over my head. For six or seven years CTV had that picture of me chasing Tucker to the end zone in their intro for every CFL game, which really made me feel good."

Russ Jackson described the two touchdowns succinctly: "Broken plays." Reacting to the suggestion that West blew the coverage, he replied, "Nah, he didn't. We just found a little extra time, and when you do that with receivers like Tucker, they're going to find some open space out there."

George Reed agreed with Jackson. "They *were* broken plays. A lot of times when people feel bad about a play, you also have to give somebody else the credit. Obviously sometimes the offense makes a great play. Jackson flung it out there, and Whit Tucker had great speed and was able to catch up with the ball and put it in the end zone. Jackson must have had time to deliver the ball, so the offensive line must have blocked not bad, and Whit Tucker made a great catch—so, hey, there's six points."

Jack Gotta also thought Ottawa's two touchdowns came on broken plays and agreed that rather than fitting Dale West for goat horns, Tucker deserved the credit. "Whit Tucker had great instincts, especially as a deep threat," he insisted. "He would break it off and get deep. Some guys were taught differently: if the play is breaking down, break your pattern, turn and come back to the quarterback. Most guys are taught that way. In Whit's case he would change directions. If he was running a break pattern to the right, he might just straighten it out and head right up the field. With that cannon he had, Russ could get it to anybody anywhere on the field."

Down 14–0, Saskatchewan's Dale West struck back, picking off an errant Jackson pass. "The end came out and got tangled up with Ted Dushinski and went down," he recalled. "The ball came to me and I took it to the 9-yard line. Then Ronnie threw one to Jim Worden for the touchdown."

Ottawa defensive back Bob O'Billovich saw the interception differently. "It was really interference against Ted Watkins. Dale West made the pick, and the officials gave him the interception and didn't call the interference. That seemed to get the Roughriders rolling on us, and then we couldn't stop them in the second half."

Said Alan Ford, "Jim Worden was telling Ronnie all the time that he could beat Gene Gaines. Ronnie threw a pass to him when he was wide open in the end zone. Worden came back saying, 'I told you I could beat him deep.'"

"Basically they won," said Gene Gaines "because Ronnie Lancaster was a great actor. He ran the play action pass on us, and we stuck our noses in places where we shouldn't have. We were a very aggressive team, and we wanted to get up because Lancaster had the great runner in George Reed. So we thought he was going to give the ball to George most of the time. He stuck the ball in George's gut and then pulled it out, and the next thing you know the tight-end Jim Worden is down the field and bang—touchdown. We all took a bite out of it. We all took the bait."

At the end of the first quarter the teams were tied. Early in the second quarter, Ottawa's Tucker scored his other touchdown. Trailing again, the Westerners were not concerned. Ron Atchison explained, "I would say that in the Grey Cup, the game is won before you ever get on the field. We were down, but we never even thought of losing. We were beating them on the line. We were 6-point underdogs, but we had a real good feeling. After four or five minutes into the game, I could tell you whether we were going to win or lose.

"By the time they get to the Grey Cup the teams are pretty evenly matched. You've got good men everywhere. So it's a matter of who is really going to take charge. That's an inner thing."

Saskatchewan tied the score on a strange touchdown by Alan Ford. Lancaster fired the ball toward the end zone. At the last moment Bob O'Billovich got his hands up to deflect it away or make the interception. Instead, as Alan Ford recalled, "The ball went right through his hands. That took a little speed off it, made it just like a knuckle ball landing in my lap. It was probably the easiest reception I ever made, the one I'll remember the longest."

"We were in a three-deep zone," said Ottawa's O'Billovich, "and I was playing deep third to my side. Hugh Campbell ran an out on my side. The outside ran an out and the inside guy ran a corner, where he went in and then came back out to the flag on the corner. I reacted to the throw. I saw Ronnie rolling out, and I could see where he was going. I left my coverage deep outside because I went to the ball. If I had made the play and held on to the ball, I would have been a big hero because that wasn't even my responsibility.

"I don't think Ford could have caught the ball if it hadn't been deflected right into his lap because he slipped and fell down in the end zone. So it was just the luck of the draw that when I wasn't able to squeeze the ball it would fall right into his lap."

Although the teams were tied 14–14 at the half, an ominous sign for Ottawa had to be the fact they were held to a single first down in the second quarter.

In the second half Saskatchewan added two more touchdowns and a single, making the final score 29–14. Lancaster completed a 5-yard touchdown pass to Hugh Campbell, and George Reed ran it in from 31 yards out. Reed described the play. "We had run that play a time or two before, and I was very angry at myself because I probably should have gone all the way. I just tripped up.

"It was simple. It was the one where we had a cross block between the center and the guard. They got me through a hole, and I said, 'Well, we've got to try and put this game away,' and I was lucky enough to score a touchdown." Reed carried the ball 23 times in the game for 137 yards.

Although the offense scored 29 points, defense made the difference. "Our defense was the best mainly because of Ed McQuarters," concluded Atchison. "He was a one-man wrecking crew. He was the guy who led us farther than we'd ever been before. He led us to the Grey Cup. He had that power. He could disrupt a whole team because he had such great strength and speed."

"Ottawa couldn't do anything," said Dale West. "They couldn't run against us, and their passing game was marginal at best. We were getting a real good rush out of the front, and the defensive backs were doing a wonderful job. We were really swarming. We could have had three or four more interceptions."

Wayne Shaw, from Davidson, Saskatchewan, was football's angry young man. "The Grey Cup itself should be an incentive," he said. "I played way over my abilities all my career because I never accepted the fact that Americans were better than Canadians. That always pissed me off. As a linebacker, if you're really angry, you play harder.

"In 1966 our defense probably played way over its head. Russ Jackson was one hell of a athlete. He could throw, he could run. We played really hard as a team because everybody had us picked to lose. The media was so sure Ottawa was going to win that they were all set up on their side."

That just made the victory sweeter for George Reed. "They had already given the Grey Cup to Ottawa, so it was quite a thrill to go in and show them that we belonged on the same field. We won the game and then watched everybody's disbelief that we won it."

What went wrong? "We were emotionally drained because Bill Smyth, our assistant coach, had died suddenly in Ottawa during the semifinal week," Russ Jackson said. "We had won first place. We then had to go and play Hamilton in a two-game total-point semifinal in which we played terrifically.

"There was an air strike at that time and we had to go by Chicago and Seattle and bus up from Seattle to Vancouver. That's not an excuse because certainly Saskatchewan deserved full value for their win.

"At half time the score was 14–14, and our whole offense consisted of scrambling through broken plays. Whit Tucker got behind the defense, and I happened to catch him for two touchdowns. But Saskatchewan controlled the game, controlled the ball. We just were drained emotionally and didn't have a whole lot going for us. It was just one of those things that happen in life and you live with it."

Bob O'Billovich provided his analysis of the game. "I thought the key was Jim Worden, who caught some balls on us inside. Also the Riders ran the ball in the second half on us. George Reed ran it right up our butts.

"That was the year we lost Coach Smyth. He died before we went into the play-offs against Hamilton. We only had Al Bruno and Frank Clair as coaches, and Bruno was a receiver–defensive back-type coach. Coach Smyth had run the defense and coached both lines.

The Wheat Province went wild when the Roughriders defeated the Rough Riders to win their first Grey Cup in 1966.

"So in the Grey Cup game we had to make adjustments to our defensive line. They were taking wide-line splits. Our defensive line was splitting out with them instead of canceling the gap. Nobody really got the word to our players for adjustments, and that's why George ran the ball up our rear ends."

Some suggested that Ottawa lost because they got caught up in the festivities and didn't pay attention to the business at hand. "I don't think that's true," argued Ron Stewart. "Getting to the national final is what it's all about. We knew that. We just played a particularly good team that day. I think a factor though was the death of our line coach, Bill Smyth. Also we had to come from behind in Hamilton to beat them and get to the Grey Cup. We had shot our bolt. The Grey Cup was kind of anticlimactic."

The celebrations surrounding Saskatchewan's first Grey Cup were something to behold. Green beer flowed everywhere. Meanwhile veteran Reggie Whitehouse took the Grey Cup on a tour of Vancouver bars, ending up in Trader Vic's. Ron Lancaster didn't join in the festivities. "I couldn't have handled that. The Cup belonged to the guys who had played that long and finally had an opportunity to win. They had a ball."

Ed McQuarters, nursing an injury, didn't go either. "I went the whole year with St. Louis and the Riders and didn't get any more than the normal bumps and bruises," he recalled with irony. "After the Grey Cup, in the dressing room, of course, there were bottles of champagne all over, and just as I took a sip, Garner Ekstran hit me on the back, and I ended up chipping my tooth. That was the worst injury I got all year."

McQuarters had no idea at the time what the Grey Cup meant to the people of the province. "That was my first year in Saskatchewan. Not until after I got back to Regina and was there about a week did I start to realize the significance of it to Saskatchewan people. The folks just went wild. My phone never quit ringing. It was something to behold."

Hugh Campbell summed up that wonderful year. "I remember most of it vividly. I remember the excitement of the challenge of playing Ottawa and Eagle Keys telling us we may never get this opportunity again and we'd better take advantage of it and Jim Duncan telling us you only get to be champion once—sometimes you stay there, sometimes you don't. You only have that first time once. That was a thrill.

"I remember a few of the practices leading into the Grey Cup game and how the team was up awfully high, awfully quick, and then we seemed to relax after a while, and I really felt confident going into the game.

"And then in the game," Campbell continued, "I remember Garner Ekstran going off side the first couple of plays because we were so keyed up. Ottawa scored a quick 14 points and it looked like we were doomed. I remember Don Gerhardt intercepted a pass and we got some confidence and momentum going.

"I remember Ed Buchanan catching a long pass on a pick play we had worked out to take advantage of Ottawa's man defense. And, of course, George Reed just romping through them.

"I remember afterward the great satisfaction. We could hardly live with ourselves we were so proud to have beaten Ottawa because they were heavily favored and Saskatchewan had never won.

"I remember Reggie Whitehouse stealing the Cup and how we all went downtown with it to Trader Vic's. My parents were there. It was a pretty proud night."

Alan Ford felt the same way. "As a kid growing up I watched the Riders. I never thought I'd be playing in a Grey Cup, let alone playing on the Roughriders. I was in the band as a kid, marching all the time. I remember telling Atch when I joined the team in 1965 that when I used to march out to play the national anthem, I'd look over and see him standing there. That shows you how old he was."

He added an ominous note. "Since 1966 was the second year I had played and we had a fairly young team, I thought we were going to win this thing another five or six times."

It was not to be. Saskatchewan wouldn't win another while Ottawa's Jackson, Stewart and company wouldn't lose. After a devastating 1967 Western Final against Calgary, Saskatchewan faced the ever tough Tiger-Cats in the Grey Cup. Played in Ottawa as part of Canada's centennial celebrations, the score was 24–1. The Riders were lucky to get 1.

Things went wrong from the moment they arrived in Ottawa. "In 1967," Keys said, "we went to Ottawa and we had no facilities whatsoever. The weather conditions were bad, but had we stayed in Regina, where we could have had a cleared field to practice on, we would have been far better prepared. They put us on a practice field, but it was just like a skating rink. Hamilton, though, stayed home until the last moment."

Some believed that any chance the Riders had disappeared when Ed Buchanan dropped a pass in the second quarter. Dale West recalled, "It's strange. I had a good feeling about the '66 Grey Cup. In '67 I was worried because we'd had a hell of a tough series with Calgary, and I don't think between the two teams we could have fielded a healthy team. We had played on three frozen fields. We had so many guys down and knicked. It was a lousy day in Ottawa, just a terrible day. We didn't know what footwear to put on. It was really tough.

"But there was a big turning point in the game. Ronnie lays one up for Eddie Buchanan, who's wide open, and hits him right in the hands. He drops it. That was a chance maybe to get some momentum going. But we were never in the game after that. Hamilton was a tough opponent. They'd dare you to come at them. We tried but we weren't very successful."

George Reed said, "I think there was one turning point in that game. Ed Buchanan was wide open, and Lancaster laid the ball perfectly into his hands. I don't know what would have happened after that, but I think if Ed Buchanan had made that catch and took it in for a touchdown, it could have been a different ball game because it could have really deflated them. That was the big play that turned the momentum in the game."

While Ron Atchison had that good feeling before the 1966 Grey Cup, he said, "I knew within two minutes into the 1967 game we were going to lose. The first time that Hamilton had to kick the ball, the kicker ran between Ken Reed and me and we could have killed him. I made the attempt to hit him, but Ken Reed didn't, so he went between us.

"I said, 'Why the hell didn't you hit him, Ken?' He said, 'I didn't want to cause a penalty.' So I said, 'Look, if we're going to worry about causing penalties, we're in big trouble. We could have killed that son-of-a-bitch. He might not have kicked the rest of the game.' I thought that was a bad omen.

"George Reed was slipping around and he wouldn't change his cleats. The field was very bad. And, of course, Buchanan dropped that midfield pass. It didn't look good at all, and it was really just a disaster."

Ed McQuarters was frustrated that day. "No matter how hard we tried, nothing worked. Hamilton kicked us. They whipped us. I guess the game-winning touchdown was scored over me. I mean, there I am, I'm dug in. I just had the feeling they were going to come right at me, and sure enough they did. No matter how hard I fired out and stopped the offensive lineman, they still just bowled me right over and scored the touchdown right over top. I felt kind of silly, but you have those days."

Wayne Shaw mentioned the unmentionable. "In 1967 we're down 24–0. We should have had another quarterback in there for a little while. Ronnie was all shook up when he threw a touchdown pass to Eddie Buchanan and he dropped it. It's not the end of the world, but Ronnie couldn't get going. Not that anybody's a better quarterback than Ronnie, but somebody else should have gone in for once."

Lancaster said, "We hit that long pass to Buchanan early, and he dropped the ball. It was just one of those days when we didn't get anything going, whether you say our offense faltered or say Hamilton's defense didn't allow us to get going.

"But I was kind of disappointed and surprised to be shut down that way. We just didn't think anyone could beat us that easily. Hamilton did a great job on us that day."

Did Lancaster think Buchanan was the goat? "I didn't play very well," he said. "But people who did all the criticizing never got to a Grey Cup. Ed Buchanan did. He dropped that pass, which may or may not have been a key play. Someone asked me after the game what the importance of it was. I said that if he had caught that pass, we would have lost 24–8."

That was Buchanan's last year with the team. It was widely believed that Keys vowed to get rid of him. "That's not true," Eagle growled. "I didn't say that. But Ed didn't like the cold weather. On a warm day he would have caught it."

Lancaster concurred. "Eagle didn't get rid of Buchanan. He wasn't that kind of guy."

Ed Buchanan died from Lou Gehrig's Disease in 1993.

Allan Ford scored Saskatchewan's only point on a still-standing record 87-yard single. It means little to him. "It just means I had a good wind, I guess. I happened to hit it, it bounced and away it went."

Back at home Wayne Shaw noticed a difference in people's attitudes. "I was a salesman in Regina. After the 1966 Grey Cup I couldn't do many sales because I partied all winter. After the 1967 Grey Cup, I'd go make sales calls. Now, Regina's a great city for football. When I was a young, shy guy, it helped me overcome my shyness. I know guys bought from me because I played football.

"But after the '67 game, I'd go make a sales call, and guys would give me a half-hour spiel about why we lost the game. Then they'd say, 'I'm too busy. I've got to do something else.' And I wouldn't make a sale. They were mad at me. The same thing happened in '69. After '72 I couldn't stand it anymore, so I went to Winnipeg."

The following year living legend Ron Atchison called it a day. The Saskatoon junior had arrived in Regina in 1952. "I started at $1,000 and a job. The job was more important than the money made playing football. You played football for the fun of it, but the job was what you really were interested in. I finished at $15,000. There was $1,100 for the 1966 Grey Cup, but we spent it all going and coming. There never was very much money in it. It was good for me because I was a carpenter by trade. I used my football money to buy up houses. I had a little rental business. It was a real good life, the best part of my life."

When he first arrived, he became the victim of a veteran's prank. The rookie Atchison took on one of the most feared men in the game. "Martin Ruby told

Saskatchewan punter Allan Ford set the record for the longest punt in the 1967 Grey Cup.

me that if I went up and socked Blue Bomber Buddy Tinsley a couple of good ones, he'd quit. He talked me into giving Tinsley the best forearm shot I could. 'He'll just die,' Ruby said.

"So I started out to do what I was advised. I caught Tinsley a couple of times looking the other way and I gave him the forearm across the side of the head. He couldn't believe what was happening. I saw him in the line asking some of the guys. He was pointing at me. I didn't know what he was saying.

"At the end of the half, he grabbed me under the front of the shoulder pads and lifted me right off the ground and said, 'Look, Ollie, I'm going to get you in the next half.'

"I wondered where he got the Ollie idea from. I looked down at my helmet and here I was wearing a helmet with "Ollie" on it. I went into the dressing room and took off the "Ollie" and put on "Atch." In the second half he was still looking for Ollie. Tinsley was quite a ballplayer."

The rookie soon learned some tricks of the trade. "We were playing Edmonton, and Gene Kiniski kept punching me in the stomach. I taped a thigh pad on my stomach and he darn near broke his hand."

Atchison played against the great Eskimo teams of the '50s and Bud Grant's Blue Bombers of the '50s and '60s. In his estimation the Eskimos were the best. "They had Bright, Kwong and Miles. They were the scourge of the league. That goes back to before the Riders had any black ballplayers. We were just starting to get black men on our team. We were the last to do so.

"I remember trying to find out why there were no blacks on our team because we had had one black ballplayer here before my time. People said the women chased him so damn much the executive said they'd never have another one."

Atchison was first an All-Star in 1956. Then nothing happened until the next decade when he made it five years in a row, 1960–64. Despite two artificial hips and a bad knee, Atchison loved being a Roughrider. "It gave me a way of life. If you didn't have football you were just another one of the masses. Football makes you a bit of a hero. I still enjoy it. When I go places people come up and say hello and say how much they enjoyed those years. That makes you feel good." Atchison was inducted into the CFL Hall of Fame in 1978.

In 1968 the Riders romped home in first place, 5 points ahead of Calgary, but in the final the Stamps shellacked the Roughies 32–0 in Regina and then beat them 25–12 in overtime back in Calgary to gain their first berth in the Grey Cup since 1949. Their opponent would be the Ottawa Rough Riders.

Swan Song

In 1968 Ottawa finished in first place, 2 points ahead of Toronto, scoring a league-high average of 30 points per game while surrendering 20. Linebacker Ken Lehmann won the Schenley for Outstanding Lineman while Whit Tucker was runner-up for the Canadian award. The Riders were led, of course, by Russ Jackson, described by his general manager, Red O'Quinn, as "a great quarterback. He could do it all. He was smart, he could run, he could throw deep.

"When he first started playing he had trouble taking something off the ball. He practically knocked a receiver down with it if he was 10 feet away. But he overcame that. He got to be able to throw it to whatever place you wanted it. He was, in my opinion, the greatest all-around quarterback."

Jackson's supporting cast included his old running mate Ron Stewart as well as Bo Scott, Whit Tucker, Vic Washington and Margene Atkins. The Riders were strong on defense with Moe Racine, Ken Lehmann, Jerry Campbell, Marshall Shirk, Jay Roberts, Don Sutherin, Joe Poirier, Wayne Giardino, Roger Perdrix and Gene Gaines.

They faced a Calgary team that featured a superb passing attack with quarterback Peter Liske and receivers Terry Evanshen, Herm Harrison and Gerry Shaw. Evanshen and Harrison both had over 1,000 yards. Defensively they were led by the incomparable Wayne Harris as well as Frank Andruski, Larry Robinson, Don Luzzi, Joe Forzani, Jim Furlong, Fred James, Granville Liggins, Herb Schumm and Dick Suderman. Lanny Boleski and Bob Lueck were outstanding offensive linemen. Ed McQuarters singled out Lueck as the best he ever played against.

Ottawa's Gene Gaines was impressed with the Calgary squad. "Peter Liske was a good passer who understood the Canadian game. He had great ability and was very mobile. And he had the good receivers in Terry and Shaw and Herm. Herm was a tower of power. He was a very strong receiver."

What Calgary didn't have was much of a running attack. Dave Cranmer had broken his leg in the Western Final and his replacement, Rudy Linterman, didn't last through the first quarter of the Grey Cup. The Stampeders were a one-trick pony.

They were leading 14–4 at the half. Nevertheless Liske capped off a drive with a 1-yard quarterback sneak for a touchdown. Later he hit Evanshen for a 21-yard major, and the Stampeders led 14–4 at the half.

Ottawa had five scoring chances in the first half. Wayne Giardino had blocked a punt in the first quarter, but the ball rolled into the Calgary end zone, where the Stamps gave up a point. Don Suthern added a 27-yard field goal.

When the Riders went to the dressing room at half time, there were no worried men singing a worried song. Said Jackson, "We felt we had a good enough offensive team to come back. During that last eight or nine years of my career, we always felt we could score points. Being behind a few points was never a problem as it is with some teams."

Gene Gaines agreed. "We felt very secure because we had a pretty potent offense. That in turn made us a very effective defense because we could do a lot of things knowing full well our offense could always bail us out."

Ottawa got on track in the third quarter after taking advantage of another Stampeder punting problem. Unable to get the ball away, Calgary's Ron Stewart was tackled at the 55-yard line. Jackson finished a drive with a quarterback sneak. Calgary 14, Ottawa 11. Then the Riders broke it open when Vic Washington turned potential disaster into triumph.

Russ Jackson explained. "We got two big plays. The first one was where we had the wide pitchout to Vic Washington, who fumbled the ball. The Calgary defense sort of hesitated, and the ball bounced back to Vic, who took it about 60 yards for a touchdown. The other play was to Margene Atkins, a touchdown pass that we had practiced the previous week but had not put on our list for the game. It was sort of a semiroll to the right. Margene lined up on the right and went back against the grain. The Stampeders were playing a combination zone–man defense. That defense was just beginning to come into the league then, and Calgary was very proficient at it. I felt we could take advantage of it and it worked. The play went for about a 60- or 65-yard touchdown. It was probably a 45- or 50-yard pass in the air.

"So those two long touchdowns really broke their back, I think," Jackson concluded. "The one to Margene gave us a 10-point edge that made it a little easier for the defense to settle in and not be under the pressure they might have been."

Late in the game the Stamps' Dick Suderman recovered a Bo Scott fumble deep in Ottawa's end. Liske completed his second touchdown pass to Evanshen and the game ended Ottawa 24, Calgary 21.

The 1968 national classic was a rehearsal for one of the greatest performances in Grey Cup history, Russ Jackson's swan song. It was also an opportunity for the Ottawa Riders to avenge their 1966 Grey Cup loss defeat at the hands of the Saskatchewan Riders.

Vic Washington was the Most Valuable Player in the 1968 Grey Cup, when Ottawa defeated Calgary 24–21.

Russ Jackson's swan song in 1969 was one of the greatest performances in Grey Cup history.

The Rough Riders of Jackson and Stewart were destiny's darlings. You didn't have to convince Saskatchewan coach Eagle Keys. "There are some games you get the feeling you're not going to be allowed to win," he drawled. "That was one of them."

Again the Rough Riders fell behind early. Saskatchewan took a 9–0 lead on a 27-yard Lancaster to Ford touchdown pass plus a safety touch. The Westerners added two singles in the third quarter, but that was it. The Russ and Ronnie show kicked into high gear.

First of all Jackson finished a long drive by completing a 12-yard pass to Jay Roberts for a touchdown. Soon after, Jackson tossed a short one to Ronnie Stewart, who ran 80 yards for the major, putting Ottawa into a 14–9 half-time lead. Their third touchdown came when Jackson eluded a fierce pass rush on the 12-yard line and found Jim Mankins alone in the end zone.

Jackson admitted it was a broken play. "We were rolling right and McQuarters had me right in his grasp. I happened to get lucky and get away from him. I came back across the grain and Mankins was standing there just over the goal line."

Ottawa's last touchdown came in similar fashion. This time Saskatchewan's Cliff Shaw had Jackson in the grasp, but he somehow got the ball to Stewart, who ran 32 yards for the score. Jackson described what happened. "They were blitzing. We didn't throw the short pass a lot. We threw the ball downfield a lot of times. We were not into dump-and-run a lot. I believe Saskatchewan's strength and their whole game plan was to come on and make me dump the ball. Fortunately Stewie let the blitz get free, and I knew where he was going. He got there, he caught the pass and went about another 40 yards for a touchdown." The final score was Ottawa 29, Saskatchewan 11.

Ottawa was well prepared to play Saskatchewan because Russ Jackson had announced he would retire at the end of the season. "It was a very emotional time for me personally and, I'm sure, for some of my teammates who'd played with me for a lot of years because I'd announced at the start of the season it was going to be my last year. A lot of people thought it was a contract thing, but it wasn't. It was my last year. After we got to the Grey Cup and I won the Schenley Award again, I knew the pressure was on everybody to make it a fairy tale ending, which it turned out to be."

Gene Gaines pointed out that guys on the other side of the ball played pretty well, too. "We played a pretty sound defensive game. We felt if we could control the ball on offense and keep George Reed between the 30-yard lines we would have a chance. That's the way it worked out."

Alan Ford had a great day for the Roughriders in a losing cause. "I scored a touchdown on a 12- or 13-yard reception. And I had a single. I dropped a long pass in the end zone that I should have caught. After that I caught a 35-yard pass and kicked about a 45-yard single before the end of the second quarter." Ford also set a Grey Cup record with a 78-yard kickoff return, eclipsed in 1991 by Rocket Ismail.

Ford was full of praise for Ronnie Stewart. "He was amazing. You'd dump a little pass to him and he'd take off. The field was bad, but it didn't seem to bother him. Holy smokes, he really had a field day."

Some felt the slippery field hurt Saskatchewan because their key to success was getting to Russ Jackson, but Ford wasn't buying it. "I don't think it amounts to a hill of beans. Sometimes teams live on it, like Edmonton does. On their grass field, when it gets to play-off time, everybody worries about the kind of shoe and all that other crap. They think Edmonton has special shoes. If they do they've kept them well hidden. But they sure let that be known, same as we do with our field."

"That was a bad field," said George Reed. "But it was Ottawa's year to win. Ron Stewart and those guys had a great game, and we just never got anything going. Their defense played well. They shut us down completely after we went up 9–0. I think a lot of it had to do with them adapting to the condition of the field faster and better than we did. More power to them. "

Campbell agreed with Eagle Keys' comment that some games you get the feeling you're not going to be allowed to win. "In 1969 I felt like the game was a movie in which we were supposed to be the victims—like a wrestling match where it was decided ahead of time the other guy was going to win. There was a big sensational thing over the fact that Russ Jackson was retiring. It was his last game. It just seemed like everyone got on his bandwagon. That was Ottawa's game.

"I only had that feeling one other time, and that was when Ron Lancaster played his last game here in Edmonton. I felt that no matter what we did, it was meant to be that Lancaster would win his last game."

"I felt we should have won the 1969 Grey Cup," said Coach Keys. "I don't think the best team won that day. But one thing about football a lot of people don't understand is that anytime you go into a one-game situation you can have a good game or a bad game. It's just like Minnesota never having won the Super Bowl. During the season they may have been a heck of a lot better than the team they played in the Super Bowl, but on that particular day, they weren't the best team. Why? Who knows? Why are some people lucky in a card game and others aren't?"

Responsibility for staging the Grey Cup rests with the commissioner's office, and in 1969 Jake Gaudaur was presented with some special problems. "The game was in Montreal at the peak of the FLQ problem," Gaudaur said. "Leading up to that, people had been shot and killed in Montreal. There were threats that the FLQ was going to stage a march and walk toward the Grey Cup parade. In my mind's eye I could sort of see them running into the Saskatchewan band halfway down that parade going in the opposite direction. Day after day I had to sit there wondering whether I should pull the game out of Montreal. There were a lot of conflicting opinions.

"Finally the word came from Ottawa two weeks before the Grey Cup that a decision had been made. The Grey Cup was not going to be disrupted because the FLQ thought it would be counterproductive to their cause. So we took a gamble and went ahead and played the game in Montreal.

"That game was played down in the old Autostade," Gaudaur continued. "Around that stadium, built for Expo '67, there were a lot of light standards with little pods. There were both cameras and sharpshooters in those pods.

"As a final condition of staging the game in Montreal, I went to meet with Mayor Drapeau and demanded his assurance that there would be adequate protection at the stadium site. He assured me there would be. So, as we always did at that time, I would get together with the local police forces and work out security plans with them related to potential kinds of problems. For a few years on either side of 1969 we had to have those kinds of concerns, particularly with Trudeau at the game.

"I had said we needed good crowd control down on the field. With three minutes to go, I'm looking down at the field, and all of a sudden I see all these police in riot gear coming out of the entrance. There were enough of them there to ring the field shoulder to shoulder. I just about died. I guess they made a decision to overprotect.

"There were always some special situation that arose concerning the Grey Cup. I guarantee it never ran itself. The day after the Grey Cup was over, I would have a meeting with our people, and we would start planning for the next Grey Cup. Back in those days, unlike now, we had to do everything for the Grey Cup. Regardless of where the game was played, it was run by my small staff and me in the league office. It took an awful lot of planning."

After the 1969 Grey Cup, for example, the trophy was stolen. "What I did along the way," said Gaudaur, "was take the original Grey Cup and put it safely in the Hall of Fame, where nobody could touch it, and had a replica produced. I did that the year after it was stolen and recovered by the Ottawa police early in 1970. At that time I decided we shouldn't lose the symbol of what we were supposed to be all about and decided to protect it in that way.

"Traditionally what happened back then was the team that won the Grey Cup took it back to their place and used it for promotions or whatever they wanted. There was high potential for it being stolen and lost forever."

For Ottawa's Russ Jackson, 1969 was an incredible year. Along with the Grey Cup he won the Schenleys for Most Outstanding Player and Canadian. He was the Grey Cup Most Valuable Player. He was honored as Canada's Outstanding Athlete and was awarded the Order of Canada.

Jackson looked back at his Grey Cup years. "The first one was kind of neat in 1960 because we were all young Canadian kids. You dream of winning a Grey

Cup when you're a kid in Canada. That one was special. For me personally the one in 1969 was just as big, having won in '68 and having said I was going to retire."

Why were those Ottawa teams so good? "I just think we stayed together a long time. Continuity breeds success. You trust each other, you understand each other, you know the strengths and weaknesses of each other. That was part of our success.

"We had all kinds of leaders. The coaches didn't have to say a whole lot when things were going bad. The guys took over and made sure that everybody understood what the expectations were. It is important for any team to have those leaders in the clubhouse — not clubhouse lawyers but the guys who know when to say something and how to say it."

Some believe Jackson was the greatest of them all. "It's nice to be considered in the top group," Jackson replied. "I don't think anybody can pick the best. I've never been a believer in saying who is the best of this, the best of that. We all played in different eras. The games were different. If you're considered and your name comes up when you're talking about the best, you figure it must have been a pretty good time.

"I'm also a believer that if you were good in one era, you would be good in another one. You would have adjusted to whatever the requirements were."

Soon after Jackson retired, Coach Frank Clair did the same, and an era came to a close. In 1970 the Rider teams went in opposite directions. Under Jack Gotta, faced with a huge rebuilding job, Ottawa finished last with a record of 4–10. Saskatchewan was first in the West, winning 14 games, a single-season franchise record. They confidently awaited semifinal winner Calgary, who had defeated the Eskimos in Edmonton.

Footprints in the Snow

Saskatchewan's confidence was misplaced. The Stampeders rolled into Regina and over the Roughriders 26–11. Back at McMahon Stadium in Calgary for the second game of the Western Final, the Stamps were at the Rider 23, trailing 4–3 with 39 seconds left when Ken Frith caused Jerry Keeling to fumble. Ed McQuarters picked up the loose ball and ran 80 yards to the end zone.

Given a second life, the Riders returned to Taylor Field. Despite losing Lancaster with broken ribs, the Riders were confident that backup quarterback Gary Lane could lead them to their fourth Grey Cup appearance in five years.

Game three was held on a nasty day in Regina. By the time the fourth quarter rolled around, the teams were playing in blizzard conditions. With under a minute to go, the Roughriders were clinging to a 14–12 lead.

The Riders punted. The Stampeders got it down to the 25, where on the last play of the game into the teeth of a ferocious gale, Larry Robinson kicked the field goal that sent the 14–2 Riders packing and the 9–7 Cowboys to the Grey Cup.

In Saskatchewan's opinion the final score should have been 21–12. George Reed had scored one touchdown, Gary Lane another. In both cases the officials ruled that the ballcarrier hadn't made it over the goal line. Lane squeezed in by the out-of-bounds marker. Everyone but the referee could see his footprints in the snow.

"Both Gary Lane and I were in the end zone," Reed stated emphatically. "In those days I guess they didn't clean the goal line off, and the officials didn't give us the touchdown. When you're in the end zone from the waist up it is a touchdown. I don't know what the officials were looking at or thinking about, but it's just one of those things.

"Then Larry Robinson kicked the field goal and knocked us out. That was probably our best team. That was the one game that hurt the most in my whole career. It's still bitter, it still sits there in my stomach."

McQuarters felt the same way. "We had the darn thing won. When Robinson kicked that damn ball, we turned around and looked and it was way outside of the goalposts, but the wind was blowing just right and just hard enough to push it back in. There goes our 14–2 season. That was pretty disheartening."

"That was probably the worst defeat for our team," said offensive lineman Gary Brandt. "The biggest play of the game was Robinson's field goal. He knew damn well he couldn't kick it. We talked to him in the off-season about it, and he said it was a hope and a prayer. I don't think he was that good a kicker. I talked to some of their guys afterward, and they were more shocked than we were that they had won."

After the 1970 season Eagle Keys left Saskatchewan to coach the Lions. He was succeeded by former Lion coach Dave Skrein. In his first year at the helm, the Roughriders tied Calgary for first with a mark of 9–6–1. After winning the semifinal over Winnipeg, they lost two straight to the Stampeders. Meanwhile back East Jack Gotta's Rough Riders were third, losing the semifinal to Hamilton.

In 1972 Gotta's club finished in a tie for first with Hamilton, each at 11–3. After dispatching the Alouettes in the semifinal, the Riders beat the Ti-Cats 19–7 in the first game of the Conference Final. Not quite ready for prime time yet, Ottawa lost the rematch 23–8 and the round 30–27.

Meanwhile Saskatchewan had their worst season in 12 years, finishing third at 8–8. But they squeaked by the Eskimos 8–6 and moved on to Winnipeg. For the first time since 1949 the Western Final was a single game.

Winnipeg was up 21–0 at the half and scored again early in the third quarter. Ron Lancaster remembered it well. "We were down 14 points late in the third quarter. Jonas threw a pass to a fullback somewhere around our 10-yard line. If he catches the ball he walks in. But he drops it. They kicked a field goal and made it 24–7. They missed that touchdown and a chance to put it away, and for some reason we got rolling after that. Things started going our way. We came back and tied it, and we had the ball and were moving down to kick the winning field goal.

"We got it down into field-goal range. On the last play Jack missed it. Paul Williams kicked it out. I caught it and kicked it in. Williams got it and kicked it out and they got called for no yards. We got another shot, Jack kicked it through and we won."

Gary Brandt loved every minute of it. "Winnipeg was supposed to have been better than we were. Their head coach was Jim Spavital. I hated him. But they had a really good defensive line. I played against Joe Critchlow. At half time they were kicking our ass. They were yapping at us the whole game. They were really feeling pretty confident, as well they should have.

"At half time we went into the locker room and nobody said anything," Brandt continued. "We just all had a Coke and guys who smoked had a cigarette. We just thought about the game.

"The second half we got a few breaks and George started running the ball real well. All of a sudden things changed. Joe Critchlow and those other guys who were yapping in the first half stopped talking. At the end we weren't surprised we had won. The second half we just dominated them."

After a miserable first half, luck was a lady for Saskatchewan, according to Ford. "Jim Spavital probably thought Wayne Shaw interfered with Mack Herron when he was coming out of the backfield. They had Herron going up the seam, and Wayne Shaw just tackled him. They threw the ball and there was no penalty. Then, when Abendshan missed the field goal and they kicked it out, they got called for no yards."

If Only They had Listened to Wayne Shaw

It would be tempting to say that the Roughriders' luck ran out in the Grey Cup played in Hamilton against the Tiger-Cats. But that wouldn't be true. Not only did the hometown team play a good game, Saskatchewan coach Dave Skrein made coaching errors that cost the Roughriders a victory.

The game featured tough, grind-'em-out football for 58 minutes, producing a 10–10 tie. George Reed described his day. "It was a good day. I thought the game was going along quite well. I thought we should have won the game. Probably that was my second most bitter defeat because I thought we were controlling the ball, controlling the tempo of the game.

"The referees gave Hamilton a touchdown. Dave Fleming was clearly out of bounds and everybody sees that now, but he got a touchdown he shouldn't have got.

"We had a turning point in that game: we punted when we shouldn't have. We were down deep in our end on about our 35-yard line. We had a third and 1 or 2 to go for. We went for it and made it with ease. We got close to midfield and we had the same situation, a third and 1, and the coach elected to punt. We always got 1 or 2 yards when we wanted to get them. If we had gone for it they wouldn't even have had a chance to come back and win the game."

Lancaster agreed. "The thing we never understood as players was how, late in the game, we received the kickoff and got it out to the 35-yard line or thereabouts. On third and 1, we gambled and made it. On the very next series we came up third and 1, 10 yards farther out, and we didn't gamble. We kicked the ball, giving it back to them, and they moved it down and scored a field goal and won."

Some of the players were mystified at another decision Skrein made. With 1:51 left in regulation time, Hamilton had the ball on their 15-yard line. Ti-Cat quarterback Chuck Ealey had yet to complete a pass to his tight-end Tony Gabriel. He then completed three passes of 27, 12 and 15 yards to him, moving the ball to the Saskatchewan 41. After running 2 yards, Ealey hit Garney Henley for 12, moving the ball to the Rider 27. On the last play of the game Ian Sunter kicked a 34-yard field goal to win.

How did Gabriel get loose? Wayne Shaw, still angry about it 25 years later, explained. "We had a middle linebacker by name of Steve Svitak, who was a big, tough American but a rookie in 1972. He was good on the run, but completely lost on the pass.

"All day long I'm playing on Tony Gabriel. Late in the fourth quarter Gabriel had not caught one pass. I could handle him. I was hitting him off the line all day and I was with him. My job was to play on him, hit him off the line and cover him into the curl zone, 10 or 12 yards deep.

"Steve Svitak, on the other hand, would keep dropping deep. I kept telling him, 'Don't drop so deep.' I was especially worried when Garney Henley was put there. If they didn't go deep, which was not our responsibility, they were going to hit either Gabriel or Henley short for a 10- or 12-yarder. That's exactly what they did.

"Now what happened is that I hit Gabriel. I stop in the curl zone. I'm with him. I saw Ealey looking inside at Garney Henley, who had lined up outside and came into the hook zone. I was in the curl zone with Tony Gabriel. I saw Ealey looking at Henley. I looked—no sign of Svitak. I made a step inside and Ealey threw to my guy.

"I made a mistake trying to cover up. We stopped them. They didn't score. I went on the bench. The offense went out but didn't do anything. Skrein sent Bill Manchuk, who then was only in his second year, into my position. I was standing beside Skrein. I was not happy, but I didn't say anything.

"Chuck Ealey dropped back and threw the ball to Tony Gabriel. I said, 'Skrein, let me in there. I'll hit him. This is my last year, my fourth Grey Cup. I won't let him off the line. I'll take a penalty, anything.'

"Three times in a row Ealey hit Gabriel, and Skrein wouldn't say a word to me. I've never been so pissed off in my life—and I liked Skrein. After the game I went into the dressing room having a battle with myself. I wanted to go into the bloody coach's room and smack him one.

"There is no way I'd have let Gabriel catch three passes on me. I mean, they might have thrown to someone else, and 101 other things could have happened, but I was not going to let him catch those three passes on me.

"If they had played Bill Manchuk earlier in the season, then maybe he could have covered. Manchuk was faster than I was, but he couldn't cover Gabriel. Skrein quit and never coached again, as far as I know.

"I moved to Winnipeg the next year. John Payne became Saskatchewan head coach then, and Jim Spavital, who had been our defensive coordinator, was the new coach in Winnipeg. After their training camp Spavital phoned me up. He had some linebackers hurt. He wanted me to play for Winnipeg. I went out for three practices, but Payne didn't want to trade me.

"Payne was the guy who told Skrein to put Manchuk in for me. Late in the Grey Cup game Payne thought I was over the hill and shouldn't play, and he put in a young guy. Then he wanted me back. I could never figure that out. And I liked John Payne, too."

How was Gabriel able to get loose? Gary Brandt said, "Wayne Shaw was playing the right outside linebacker position the whole game. Wayne Shaw was an All-Star as far as we were all concerned. Dave Skrein knew they were going to try to pass all the way down the field. For some reason he decided to pull Wayne and put Manchuk in. Hamilton exploited that move and passed all the way down the field and kicked the winning field goal. Wayne Shaw was so mad—and rightly so—that he wouldn't even come back with us from Hamilton.

"I really felt sorry for Wayne because guys like him got us there. Wayne played the whole game. He was an exceptional ballplayer. The Ti-Cats were shrewd ballplayers. They saw somebody going in that hadn't been playing and picked up on it. Had Wayne stayed in there, things may been different. The Ti-Cats may not have tried those plays."

Alan Ford saw it the same way. "At that time in the game, our coaching staff made a change and put Bill Manchuk in for Wayne Shaw. Wayne sort of overplayed that area. He didn't play really true in the zone. He followed Gabriel all over the place whereas Bill played it a little truer and that left some seams in there."

Ti-Cat linebacker Mark Kosmos observed, "Tony Gabriel came into the league in 1971. I played against him when I was in Montreal. I found Tony very easy to keep on the line of scrimmage. I don't think he ever experienced people that would not let him off the line. Later he learned to come off the line and became one of the all-time CFL greats. If somebody gave him a break like they did in '72 and '76 and gave him room, he was going to kill you."

Saskatchewan's Allan Ford mentioned another key play. "We were marching. We ran a little check across the middle. Ron was going to throw it to me. I was about 10 yards down the field for a first down. He threw it. Angelo Mosca knocked it down because he'd got knocked back off the line of scrimmage so far that he was standing 2 yards on his side of the line. He shouldn't have been there. We punt, and, boom, they come all the way back on the last drive. We would have run the clock out or at least got some more points, so they would have had to score a touchdown."

George Reed thought Garney Henley made the difference. "Tony made some big catches, but the guy who made the biggest catch as far as I was concerned was Garney Henley. He made the catch standing on top of his head and put them into position for Ian Sunter to kick a field goal. That was a bitter defeat. It was tough to forget '72."

With Hamilton coming down the field was there a sense of panic? "Oh, yeah!" said Ford. "When you see the clock going and they're moving, the tendency is to change the defense. You try to fool them or at least get out of a defense that's been causing you problems. Usually it's not the defense. Someone's not playing the defense the way it is supposed to be played."

Ed McQuarters didn't quite agree. "The prevent defense—I don't know who invented the darn thing, but it's useless. You may as well just play your regular game because you've got a better chance if you don't just sit back."

Roughrider veterans had marveled at the thorough preparation of Eagle Keys. They found Dave Skrein was more laid back. It is hard to imagine Keys making the mistakes Skrein did. Skrein hadn't done his homework, costing his team the Grey Cup.

You Gotta Go with Jocko

Over the next three years Saskatchewan would lose the Western Final to Edmonton. The Ottawa Rough Riders were 4–10 in 1970, 6–8 in 1971 and 11–3 the following year. Gotta won his first of three Annis Stukus Trophies in 1972. He expected to pick up where he left off in 1973, but they lost their first four games. Jack Gotta was sure he would be fired early in the season. He had inherited the Riders at the end of the Jackson era and turned them from also-rans into contenders. They won 11 of their next 12, including the Eastern Final and Grey Cup.

Despite losing several key players to retirement, Jocko was optimistic about the future. "Ottawa always had a core of good Canadian talent, and geographically you could just whip down the Eastern seaboard or into Ohio or lower Michigan in nothing flat, so recruiting was relatively easy. You could get athletes there."

"The guys just kept picking up," Gotta explained. "They started eliminating mistakes. We worked so damn hard in practices. Some of the American players took awhile to adapt to the Canadian game. Then they got really good."

Dick Adams credited Gotta with the turnaround. "Probably the number one thing that turned the season around was that Jack Gotta walked in and said he believed in the players and it was really up to us to start playing the way we were capable of playing. We won 9 out of the next 10 games. We had a pretty good group of veteran guys who had been there a couple of years, so it was time to line up and play to our capabilities, I guess."

The only offensive category the Riders led in 1973 was scoring, helped by Gerry Organ's 123 points. Although Hugh Oldham, Rhome Nixon, Jim Evenson, Jim Foley, Art Green and Jerry Keeling were solid performers, clearly Ottawa's strength lay on the defensive side of the ball. This was reflected in the All-Canadian team. No Riders made it on offense, but four made it on defense: tackle Rudy Sims, linebacker Jerry Campbell and defensive backs Dick Adams and Al Marcelin. Gerry Organ won the Most Outstanding Canadian Award.

After winning the Grey Cup in his rookie year with Montreal, finishing runner-up to Wayne Harris in the Schenleys, Mark Kosmos got caught in the middle of the Bob Ward–Sam Etcheverry controversy. Team loyalties were divided between Assistant Coach Ward and Etcheverry, who thought that Ward was undermining him with the tacit blessing of team owner Sam Berger. Kosmos was traded to Hamilton, where he won his second Grey Cup. His sojourn in the Steel City was short.

"When I went into Hamilton they made me a middle linebacker although I was an outside linebacker. Jerry Williams was the head coach. He was one of those bright guys. I think by profession he was a lawyer. I always thought that his defenses were as difficult as could be.

"I used to joke that the reason we won the Grey Cup in 1972 was because we didn't understand the defenses, so we went out there and just played on ability. We had some good guys on defense and we won. In '73 we started to understand Williams' defenses and we began to lose."

The following year Kosmos was on the bubble. The end came, ironically, after a game against Ottawa. "Ottawa had lost their first four games. They were playing in Hamilton. I could feel the heat from the coaches.

"Rick Cassata and I still joke about the play. It was a situation where, as a middle linebacker, you had to make a decision based on something happening in the backfield: either you're going to be rushing or picking up a guy out of the backfield. I assessed the situation and rushed. I was hitting Rick about the time he was letting it go to my man. They scored a touchdown and the next day I was released. Ottawa picked me up."

Kosmos was getting discouraged. "I had been to two Grey Cups in three years and had been to the Schenleys the other year, yet I found myself getting traded all the time. When I got to Ottawa I thought I'd play that year and retire. Then we had a phenomenal year in 1973 and I fit right in. I went back to the outside position. I had good linebackers and Wayne Smith and Rudy Sims were playing in front of me. We had the Capital Punishment team. When I got to Ottawa we were just getting ready to play Edmonton. We won that game and then whipped off a series of wins."

Kosmos loved playing for Jack Gotta. "I appreciated the freedom the coaches would give you. We were playing Montreal, and I was getting cracked back because of the position the coaches put us in. I was having a guy outside of me. I'd tie up with Peter Della Riva, and then Larry Smith would crack back on me. They'd go around the end because I was the outside contain. I got to the sideline and said to Coach Gotta, 'We can't be in that position, we're going to get ourselves killed.' He said, 'What do you want to do?'

"I'd never heard a coach say that before. So I said, 'When they go into that position we should shift. I will go out on Larry Smith, which will give me the position to be the outside contain again. Everybody will move over one.'

"Gotta just said, 'Who's going to call it?' And I said, 'Soupy'll call it. He'll be able to see it when they're coming out.' We went to that system and shut them out, the only shutout game I can remember being in. Jack Gotta would let you play your game—especially with the characters we had in Ottawa."

One of those characters was quarterback Rick Cassata. During Grey Cup week he pulled off a practical joke that fellow Italian Jack Gotta swallowed hook, line and sinker. Kosmos told the tale. "Rick was my roommate for that Grey Cup. He came into our room the day before the game and his eye was black. I said, 'What's wrong?' He said, 'I got into a fight in the sauna with Tom Laputka, and that's it, I'm not playing.' Jerry Keeling was injured, so Rick was our only quarterback. And I said, 'What are you talking about?' He said, 'I'm not going to play.' Then I looked at him and he said, 'I rubbed a newspaper on my eye.'

"Jack Gotta was out at the television station, but Rick had told one of the coaches he was leaving. They found Jack at the studio and he came rushing back to our room, almost pleading with Rick. Rick says, 'I don't give a shit. Listen, if Laputka plays, I'm gone.' And this was one of our big, strong defensive linemen. Cassata said, 'That's it. I'm packing my bag.' I'm sitting off to the side, not saying a word. Gotta was almost in tears.

"Here's his opportunity to coach a Grey Cup team, and here's his only quarterback saying, 'Screw this. I'm leaving. This guy punched me in the face.' This went on for at least 10 minutes the day before the Grey Cup when you think you've got to be concentrating on the game. That's what kind of team it was."

Gotta remembered things differently. "Rick never threatened not to play. I could always relate to Rick. I'd always kid him. I'd say, 'Come over here, you hot-headed Italian. You're southern Italian, I'm northern. We always have to think for you guys down south on the bottom of the boot.'

"I said to him, 'What the heck's wrong with you? We're not looking for arguments out of you. We're looking for you to be the leader. Rick was such a competitive guy, such a good-hearted guy. He was really emotional and would do things to get himself into a jackpot. A lot of times he'd start to get a little carried away. He had some great skills, but he could be his own worst enemy."

Not on Grey Cup day. Cassata played one of the finest games of his career, leading the Rough Riders to a 22–18 win over Edmonton, bringing Ottawa its eighth Grey Cup.

The team with the healthy quarterback won the day. Ottawa's Jerry Keeling had a knee injury, so Cassata had to go all the way. Because Bruce Lemmerman banged up his elbow in the play-offs, Edmonton was relying on Tom Wilkinson to go the distance as well. He didn't.

Edmonton began on the ground. Early in the first quarter Calvin Harrell picked up 13 yards and Roy Bell 38 for 6 points. Cassata countered with a 38-yard touchdown pass to Rhome Nixon, evening the score. Dave Cutler put Edmonton back in the lead with a field goal, making the score at the end of the opening quarter 10–7 for the Westerners.

Giving the quarterback a rough ride was characteristic of the Capital Punishment gang. On Edmonton's first possession of the game, defensive end Wayne Smith was penalized for roughing the passer. Ten minutes later Smith nailed Wilkinson again. Wilkie was just about out of bounds when Jerry Campbell hit him in the face with a forearm. Seconds after Wilkie hit the ground, Wayne Smith smashed him in the ribs. Ottawa was penalized 15 yards for roughing, a small price to pay for getting Wilkinson out of the game. The injured Bruce Lemmerman entered the fray.

"We were a tough football team, very similar to Hamilton but better athletes," said Kosmos. "Wayne Smith—when he wanted to play, no one could stop him. Rudy Sims—in that Grey Cup Wilkinson was lining up, and he had that cadence that would make you jump off side. Rudy wasn't worried about the 5-yard penalty, but I know Wilkinson started to worry about Rudy when he jumped off side. Rudy didn't hit the center, he hit Wilkinson. Rudy was about 260 pounds, and he pounded Wilkinson a couple of times on that cadence. I don't know many people who would stand there and let this guy bounce off you."

According to Dick Adams, there was no intent to injure. "That was just part of the game. Everybody was playing hard, playing all out, leaving everything on the field, not taking anything back in the locker room. I just know the quarterbacks for Edmonton kind of took a beating that game. Let's put it that way."

Gotta had planned to get really physical with both Wilkinson and Lemmerman. "Let's get to them and really pound them. That was the point we really tried to get through to the players," he commented.

The only scoring in the second quarter came when Eskimo punter Gerry Lefebvre fumbled the ball in the end zone and conceded a safety, and on the last play when Gerry Organ kicked a 46-yard field goal. Ottawa led by 2 at the half.

In the third quarter Ottawa's Jim Evenson rumbled 18 yards for a major and Organ added a field goal. In the last minute Tom Wilkinson threw to Lefebvre for a touchdown. Earlier, Lefevbre had kicked an 85-yard single, the second longest punt in Grey Cup history. The final score was Ottawa 22, Edmonton 18.

Kosmos had that feeling. "I never felt as sure about a game as I did about that one. I just thought we were a better team. I thought we could win because we were physically stronger than the other team. We won it on the defensive line."

Kosmos couldn't remember a game that had the same level of intensity. "In one situation their quarterback had fumbled, and I came running up and dove on the ball. I got it in one hand and pulled it in and had this big recovery around our 20-yard line.

"I was so emotionally into the game that I got to the sideline all excited about the play, and Jake Dunlap came up behind me and whispered, 'What did you think it was? A wallet?' I couldn't enjoy the joke because I was so wrapped up in the game."

Jack Gotta looked back. "I can remember vividly when we won the Grey Cup in '73 after a horrendous start of 0–4. I got hung in effigy in both official languages in Ottawa. We went through all that and then we won 11 out of 12, including the championship."

But team owner David Loeb didn't care. "That's right," said Gotta. "And I know the money David Loeb made when I was the head coach there. He was way over a half million dollars. I didn't share in any of those profits and neither did our players.

"I went to him and told him that I had one more year to go on my contract. I was getting $28,000 and I asked him for an extension and a little bonus as part of the extension. I asked for five and five—that is, $10,000 more for the next year. I would have gone from $28,000 to $33,000 on an extended contract with $5,000 to sign the thing. This was when bonuses were just starting to come in and I wanted to get in on it.

"He said, 'No, you've got one more year to go on your contract and that's it.'

"I had made some statements about how we'd had a horrendous start but came out of it to win the championship," Gotta continued. "I said I know the money that's been made here. I said I didn't think I was asking too much because other coaches in the league were getting substantially more, but I said I wasn't using that as a bargaining chip. I said I had two youngsters and I'd like to continue my career here. I didn't want to move.

"Just prior to when I went in to see Loeb (this was about a week after the Grey Cup) I had got calls from the World Football League. The first one was from Ben Haskins from Winnipeg, who had a franchise in Hawaii. It's a great place out there, but I knew it would be a hard place to sell football. So I said, 'No, I think I'm going to continue to stay here.'

"A few days later I got a call from Bill Putnam. He asked me about coming to Birmingham. Well, I was fully aware of Alabama football with Bear Bryant, who was a great coach, a legend. I investigated Bill Putnam. I always liked to watch hockey. He started the Philadelphia Flyers and the Flames in Atlanta. He was a businessman in Philadelphia and the youngest vice president in the history of Chase Manhattan Bank in New York. He was a Texan by birth and education, a super guy. When I talked to different people I knew in hockey such as Sammy Pollock, they said, 'Hey, this is an ace guy. Talk to him.' So I talked to him. He asked me if I would be interested in coaching in the World Football League. I said I thought I would because I was kind of miffed over my meeting with Loeb. But I said before I could do anything more I said I would like to talk with Mr. Loeb again. So I went to see him again.

"I asked, 'Is it all right if I pursue other avenues if you're not going to extend my contract?' He said, 'You can do whatever you want.'

"So I shook his hand, walked out of there and got on the phone right away to Bill Putnam. We met in New York, where he gave me the contract.

"I saw David Loeb again and I said, 'I think I'll be leaving.' He said, 'Do what you want to do.' So I did."

Gotta's successor, George Brancato stayed with the club for 11 seasons, compiling a record of 82–90–4. He made the play-offs 10 straight years and had two Grey Cup appearances. The first time he missed postseason play, he was fired.

The Great George Reed

In 1976 Saskatchewan and Ottawa both finished on top. The Western and Eastern Riders would meet in the Grey Cup for the fourth and last time. Saskatchewan was without George Reed. Although he had signed a two-year contract in January 1976, he had announced his retirement before training camp opened. Still a remarkable physical specimen at 36, the bruises were taking longer to heal, the injuries seemed more painful. His personal pride and his good sense told him it was time to quit. Bud Grant referred to him as the second-best fullback ever next to Jim Brown.

George Reed made All-Canadian nine times, an achievement unequaled by any other offensive performer. He won the Schenley in 1965. Reed scored 137 touchdowns. His 134 rushing majors are 56 more than second-place Normie Kwong. He had 11 seasons of rushing for more than 1,000 yards. He had the most consecutive 1,000-yard seasons (6) and then another (5). He is the all-time leader in regular season yardage from scrimmage with 18,888. George Reed had the most 100-yard rushing games at 66. He and Johnny Bright hold the record for most play-off touchdowns at 19. Reed holds the record for most play-off rushing yards (2,584) and most in a play-off year (529) as well as most rushing play-off touchdowns (18). His 346 Grey Cup yards are second only to Leo Lewis.

Given his eleven 1,000-yard seasons, the only athlete he can be compared to in terms of outstanding performance over a long period of time is Gordie Howe. George Reed was remarkable. He is also a very proud man, especially of his race. Reed wouldn't accept racism to get along by going along. He fought back, sometimes alienating people who believed racial prejudice didn't exist in Saskatchewan. Roughriders white and black knew that wasn't true.

Although Reed realized early on that the black prophet wasn't as honored in his own land as the white one, he had no complaints about his teammates.

When asked why those Roughrider teams were so good, he replied, "We had a very close-knit group of guys who just didn't want to be defeated. We worked very closely together and believed in each other. When you have that you can accomplish a lot of things. We were good because we believed nobody could beat us. We always had the philosophy that if we got beat, that if the time ran out and we couldn't do any more, the game didn't really beat us."

George Reed's best year came in 1965. "It was my best year stats-wise and from the standpoint of the team because we had to win a couple of games at the end of the season to get into the play-offs, which meant a lot to the team. The game against B.C. I had 200 and some yards (the total was 268) and then I followed it up with about 150 against Edmonton.

"In those great years of 1965 and '66 I was a marked man, and still no one could stop us. The one year that Paul Dudley got hurt all we had in there was guys blocking, and I knew Eagle was going to feed me the ball. I think the last year before I retired was probably as good a year as any I had. I wound up with almost 1,500 yards, and I thought I played very well."

In 1970 Reed cracked a bone in his leg. "I played until we clinched first place. Then they found the crack in my leg and I took three games off. I probably could have kept on playing. I had played eight games on it. If that hadn't happened, I probably would have had 12 straight years of 1,000 yards."

Reed survived his career relatively unscathed. "I have a little twinge in my knee once in a while, but outside of that I feel good and healthy. I try to keep my weight down. I'm fairly injury free."

The loss of George Reed would be felt in the Grey Cup of 1976. When the Roughriders needed a first down on the ground, they couldn't get it.

Gabriel, Blow Your Horn

Grey Cup day in Toronto was windy and cold. In many ways it was a strange Grey Cup. Like 1972 it was the old veteran Ron Lancaster against a downy-cheeked youngster, this time second-year man Tom Clements out of Notre Dame. Lancaster had won the Schenley Award as the CFL's Most Outstanding Player. Most pundits made the Western Riders 5- to 7-point favorites. Like 1972 the man of the hour would be Tony Gabriel, the 1976 winner of the Schenley for Outstanding Canadian, and like 1972 Saskatchewan coaches would make key mistakes.

Saskatchewan let Ottawa have the wind and the ball in the first quarter. Art

Green started off with 15 yards on three carries, the last one nullified by holding. After an incompletion Ottawa punted and Saskatchewan started out on their 40.

After picking up a first down, Steve Molnar ran to the Ottawa 50, where he fumbled. Wonderful Monds picked up the ball and ran 60 yards for a touchdown, but the ball was ruled dead. On the very next play Molly McGee fumbled, and Ottawa recovered, giving them first down at their 45. Both Western Rider fumbles were caused by linebacker Larry Cameron, who, with Mark Kosmos and Al Brenner, played a very strong game that day.

After a drive was again stopped by a penalty, Gerry Organ was wide on a 57-yard field-goal try, leaving Saskatchewan to scrimmage at the 7. Kosmos stopped McGee at the line. On second down Lancaster went back into the end zone to pass, scrambled to elude Kosmos and slipped and fell at the 1. Footing on the slick field would be a problem all day for Saskatchewan. (This was the third Grey Cup in which they couldn't find the right footwear. Their opponents didn't seem to have that problem.)

Bob Macoritti kicked from 14 yards deep in his end zone. Ottawa couldn't move the ball and had to settle for a 31-yard Organ field goal at 9:27. Ottawa 3, Saskatchewan 0.

The Roughriders scrimmaged at the 35. After two incomplete passes Macoritti got away a 40-yard punt into the wind. The stiff breeze held the ball up for a second or two. Canadian Rookie Bill Hatanaka fielded the ball on the run. Ted Provost lunged desperately at him. The rookie easily brushed him aside and outraced Lou Clare and Macoritti 79 yards to the end zone for what was then the longest punt return in Grey Cup history. In 68 seconds, Ottawa had scored twice to jump into a 10–0 lead.

The second quarter belonged to Saskatchewan. Starting at their 48, Lancaster alternated hits and misses: to McGee for 23, to Leif Petterson for 14 and 12. First down at the 13. An incomplete followed by 9 yards to Petterson. Third and a foot at the 4.

For 13 years, whenever the Riders needed a yard, George Reed always came through. It was second nature to Lancaster to call the fullback's number in this situation rather than his own, although twice during the Western Final he kept crucial drives alive with quarterback sneaks. Not this time. Fullback Steve Molnar piled into the line. Ottawa held.

Ottawa punted two plays later and the Riders took advantage of good field position to put 3 points on the board. But a golden opportunity had been lost. The Riders had to rely on Ron Lancaster's arm, and he had a magnificent day, as did his primary receivers Petterson and Bob Richardson. However, their inability to pick up short yardage on the ground was their undoing.

Saskatchewan's next possession was set up by Steve Mazurak's 24-yard punt return. From the Ottawa 45, Molnar picked up 8 yards, McGee 1. Faced with another crucial third and 1, Lancaster picked up the first down even though Ottawa was off side. Saskatchewan scrimmaged from the 31. A 16-yard strike to Mazurak brought them to the Ottawa 15. Lancaster then threw left to Mazurak, who ran across the middle and got a great block from receiver Rhett Dawson to make it to the end zone. Tie ball game.

Three plays later Ted Provost, who played a great game for Saskatchewan, intercepted Clements at the 51, returning it 26 yards. Lancaster promptly hit Bob Richardson at the 10. The big tight-end shook off Ron Woodward and thundered into the end zone. At 12: 43 the score was Saskatchewan 17, Ottawa 10. At half time, Lancaster was 15 of 21 for 170 yards and two touchdowns. Ottawa's Tom Clements had picked up a miserable 25 yards passing. The football universe was unfolding as it should.

To start the second half, Ottawa gave Saskatchewan both the ball and the wind. Mark Kosmos made the call. "Being the captain, I went out at half time to call which end of the field. When I said we'll defend that end, it was as if Ron Lancaster was going to do cartwheels. He just couldn't believe it. In my mind I can almost see him saying to the officials, 'You heard him. He said he wants to defend that end of the field and he doesn't want the ball.' Ronnie was just excited."

For Ottawa coach George Brancato, the decision was simple. "Everybody wants the wind in the fourth quarter."

Kosmos said the Easterners made some key adjustments at half time. "That week we were watching what the Roughriders were doing with their tight-end Bob Richardson, who was about 260 pounds. We always blitzed. I loved to blitz, and I was calling the defensive plays. We blitzed with the outside linebackers, leaving the middle linebacker to roam.

"Before the game I said, 'Listen, we're going to keep getting killed if we let these tight-ends go downfield when we're blitzing because we're not slowing anybody down at the line. If we let these guys run free, they're going to kill our secondary guys. One of the coaches didn't agree.

"So we got into that game and his approach wasn't working. They carried our secondary guys. On one play Richardson carried a couple of guys into the end zone, and at half time George Brancato said, 'What do you think?'

"I said, 'Why don't we let the outside linebackers play on the tight-ends? It's better for me at 235 pounds to be playing on Richardson than it is for a 180-pound defensive back to be trying to cover him.' That's what we did."

The strategy worked to some extent, holding Lancaster to 7 completions in 14 attempts for 93 yards and no touchdowns.

Saskatchewan opened the third quarter by picking up where they left off. Lancaster drove from his 36 to the Ottawa 43. Bob Macoritti kicked a 51-yard field goal to widen the lead to 10. Ottawa replied immediately with a 40-yard 3-pointer of their own into the wind. On Saskatchewan's next possession, Macoritti missed a 43-yarder with the wind. That was all the scoring in the third quarter although Gerry Organ gave his team an opportunity to narrow the gap when, with about a minute left in the third, Ottawa was third and 10 at their 37. To everybody's surprise, particularly the opposition, Organ ran for 52 yards. He did it entirely on his own according to Brancato.

One of the players back to block on the punt was Kosmos. "We're in the huddle. As we're breaking the huddle, Gerry says, 'Get ready.' I don't know what he means by that. The next thing the ball goes by me because I'm an upback, and he says, 'We're running.' He goes for 52 yards."

To no avail. With a first down at the Saskatchewan 21, Clements promptly threw an interception to Cleveland Vann. A play later the quarter ended with Saskatchewan holding a 7-point lead.

Although Saskatchewan had had the wind in the third quarter, Ottawa had picked up six first downs to their four, and the teams had traded field goals. The Easterners had the upper hand going into the final frame.

Things started to go wrong for Saskatchewan on their first series of the final quarter. On a punt from the Ottawa 52, Gary Brandt snapped the ball high. Macoritti jumped up and pulled it down but was almost tackled by Kosmos. He dribbled the punt away. Ottawa took over on their 54.

The teams exchanged two bucks and a kick, but Saskatchewan was being punted into poor field position because of the wind. Ottawa started at the Roughrider 50. Clements evaded a fierce rush, rolled to the sideline and hit Jim Foley for 14 yards. Three plays later Organ kicked a 32-yarder. Halfway through the fourth, the score was 20–16.

From Saskatchewan's 35, Lancaster threw to Leif Petterson for 11 yards.

Scrimmaging from the 46, he hit Petterson again for 9 more. On second and 1, Lancaster again eschewed the quarterback sneak and gave it to Steve Molnar. He slipped and fell a good yard short. Macoritti punted. Ottawa took over at their 26.

Tom Clements only had two good drives in the entire game, but they came at the right time. Behind excellent protection, he threw to Jeff Avery for 13 yards. After an incompletion he threw to Art Green for 16. Green ran for 4 to the Saskatchewan 51. Then Tony Gabriel got off the line, cut across the middle, cradled Clement's picture-perfect pass and ran 41 yards to the Roughrider 10.

On first down Green picked up 2. On second down Clements carried down to the 2-yard line, where he fumbled. The ball was ruled dead. With third and goal at the 1-yard line, the magnificent seven of Frank Landy, Tim Roth, George Wells, Jesse O'Neal, Cleveland Vann, Bill Manchuk and Roger Goree held. Saskatchewan took over on their 1-yard line with 1 minute and 32 seconds left to play.

On first down Tom Campana sliced off tackle for 5 yards. Lancaster called the same play again. This time only 1 yard. Macoritti punted. Ottawa took over at the Saskatchewan 35.

Art Green ran for 1 yard. With 40 seconds left Gabriel got off the line, cut across the middle and caught one for 10. With 20 seconds left and a first down, Gabriel faked inside, ran to the end zone and caught the touchdown pass that gave Ottawa their ninth and final Grey Cup. Ottawa 23, Saskatchewan 20. Tom Clements had 151 passing yards in the second half, 104 of them on their last two possessions.

Throughout his career Ron Lancaster was the best comeback quarterback in CFL history. Trailing late in a game he would reach into his bag of tricks and snatch victory from the jaws of defeat. But he always did it passing, and in 1976 he was picking Ottawa's secondary apart. For Lancaster, however, protecting a lead late in the game was another matter. Then he became conservative and went into a shell. He did that against Ottawa, and it cost him a Grey Cup.

Kosmos wasn't just surprised at Saskatchewan's conservative strategy at that point in the game. "I was shocked. I'm calling all the defensive plays. I remember us getting in the huddle and I said GAP defense. That's almost like a goal-line defense. If Ronnie would have thrown the ball the guy would still be running. None of our guys were playing the pass. They had to know that we were going to play the run."

George Brancato said, "What I thought would happen was that they'd give up 2 points, kick off and get us out of field position because there was less than a minute left in the game. They surprised me when they kicked the ball and we took over in good field position at their 35."

Alan Ford explained the ill-fated strategy. "We knew we needed one first down to run out the clock. We had lost our tailback—he'd been hurt—so Campana was in for Molly McGee. The first play we ran we picked up 5 yards. It was second and 5. If you pick up 4, you'll probably go for it. If you don't pick it up, you know you're still going to force them to use a time-out. You're going to run some of the clock off anyhow. I think the percentages were that you should keep the ball on the ground and try to pick up the first down. If you throw you stop the clock and you punt the ball away. What was the best way to pick up the first down? We'd done a pretty good job of blocking on the run."

That was the first mistake. Not giving up a safety was the second mistake. In the process of conceding a safety, Macoritti could have run all over the end zone before stepping out, taking at least another 20 seconds off the clock. Ottawa would likely have got the ball on the ensuing kickoff at about their own 40- or 45-yard line with 50 seconds left.

John Payne's third mistake was his strategy against Tony Gabriel. Everyone in the ball park knew Clements would go to Gabriel, but they couldn't stop it from happening. But remember 1972, when Wayne Shaw kept Gabriel in check by hitting him at the line? It was the same John Payne who was then the Saskatchewan defensive coach who made the decision to pull Shaw and get somebody with more speed on the big tight-end. The decision didn't work earlier and it didn't work later.

Said Ottawa's Mark Kosmos, "If the situation had been reversed and I had been playing against that team, Tony Gabriel would never have left the line of scrimmage. Tony was never touched that entire play. In those days you could hit people coming off the line, and receivers were fair game. They were just targets out there.

"Everybody knew the ball was going to Tony. Tony was running free as a bird, and Tommy laid it right into him. I don't remember a big rush on Tommy either."

Tony Gabriel described the dramatic moment. "I'd been hit hard on the previous play by Cleveland Vann, and I was dazed and seeing stars. I got back into the huddle, and Tom Dimitroff had sent in Gary Kuzyk, the wide receiver

Tony Gabriel and friends celebrate his winning catch in Ottawa's 1976 Grey Cup victory over Saskatchewan.

with a play from the bench. Time was counting down and Tom Clements shouted, 'No!' and called the play that won the Grey Cup.

"It was a Fake 324, fullback through the four hole and a tight-end slash. Ironically, in the set Saskatchewan was in defensively, Roger Goree was off the line of scrimmage, and they had a defensive end line up over me. That allowed me to escape the line. Ray Odums followed our wide receiver and left my area empty.'

"When the ball was coming my heart was pounding and my eyes were open wide. If I had dropped that pass I may as well have retired right then."

Because Gabriel was seen running away from Ted Provost, Provost has been wearing the goat horns ever since, a knock against him that he doesn't deserve. According to George Brancato, "It was the corner, the outside guy [Odums]. He jumped on the underneath guy. It was a four-deep defense and the corner didn't get back. Tony broke for the corner. Provost was actually in a good position, taking the middle away. But he had no help on the outside. You usually blame the guy closest to the ball. The fan does and probably most of the press do, too. In this case it just so happened that the guy closest to the ball was not really responsible. He was just chasing."

Bob O'Billovich, unfairly labeled the goat in 1966, might award one horn to Provost. Asked if Provost was the culprit, Obie replied, "He was and he wasn't. Tony Gabriel had been running that deep crossing route. He had about six catches in that game on that route over the middle. And because they were in four deep, Provost was in that inside quarter on that side of the field. Ray Odums was the corner on that side.

"What happened was the route that Tommy called was one where Gabriel cut in front from deep outside. Odums jumped the out. In that defense that's the play you'd give up, but, of course, when you're in your own end zone, you've got to play tighter so you don't give them a touchdown.

"Provost saw Tony start to make his move over the middle, and he thought he was going to run that crossing route again. He kind of jumped at that initial move and then Tony broke it back to the corner. Because Odums jumped the out, and Provost had already taken the bait, there was nobody there.

"Tony ran a great route, but if Provost had stayed back in his quarter, he would have had a better chance at making the play. Odums should have made it tougher. Four deep, you shouldn't get beat deep."

Ron Lancaster felt the game should never have come down to the last minute. "We had a chance to score when we had a first and goal at the 4 and didn't get it. If we had taken advantage of our opportunities, the last minute wouldn't have mattered. But we didn't get it done. We had chances to put that game away and we didn't do it."

Why didn't Saskatchewan throw a pass or concede a safety touch on their last series? "I really don't know that," conceded Lancaster. "The coach made the decision. I thought we were out far enough that all we had to do was punt the football down the field, cover it, and they weren't going to have enough time to score the touchdown. If we gave them the safety and kicked the ball, they would be in field-goal range with a first down or two. I thought we did everything properly. Ottawa just made the plays when they had to make them."

While Gary Brandt agreed Coach Payne would have called the critical play, he said, "In terms of throwing or running, Ronnie called all his own plays. If the coach sent in a play Ronnie still had the authority to call it off. Ronnie

called 95 percent of all the plays we ran. I would have thought those were decisions of Ronnie, and I would never to this day question if they were good decisions or not. You have to remember that I was an offensive lineman. We weren't
paid to think."

"In his later years I kind of knew how we were going to do on a day depending upon Ronnie's moods. He was so critical to our whole team. In his early
years he was jacked up all the time, but in the later years sometimes something
would piss him off—say, for example, he would throw an interception early in
the game—and he'd get really mad because maybe the receiver ran the wrong
route.

"I would kind of have a sense of how much harder it was going to be for us
to win a game, depending on his attitude. When he was fired up in the huddle,
things were kind of magical. He could get things done for us. In that Grey Cup
I would never have questioned anything he said in the huddle. It was just a joy
playing with him and, of course, George, too. I was pretty lucky."

But not in Grey Cups. Gary Brandt had four appearances, four losses. The
1976 loss was the hardest one to take. "In 1972 during that last series," he said,
"you could see it going by you. In 1976 we thought we were good enough to beat
anybody. We weren't overconfident, but we did have confidence, whereas in '67
and '69 you could see at the start of the game we were going to get dominated.

"The '76 Grey Cup meant more to me than any of them because I was in
the twilight of my career, and I thought it was about high time we won a Grey
Cup game. That year was the beginning of the end of an era. A lot of us had
played a long time together, and the team was starting to disband. If we were
going to win, it that had to be the year."

Brandt retired the following year. Alan Ford retired right after the Grey
Cup. "When I came back to Regina from the College of Pacific in 1965, I started the second game playing in Edmonton and hurt my knee. I missed the rest
of the season except for the last game and then came back for the one play-off
game we had. From then on I was a starter until my last year in '76. I played in
179 straight games.

"In 1976 I injured my neck in training camp, and I just couldn't function
by the last game of the season, so that was my retirement bell. I didn't play in
the Grey Cup. I watched it from the press box.

"The Grey Cup games in '72 and '76 were the real disappointing ones. I
thought we were the better team in both cases, and we lost both of them on

essentially the last play of the game. But that's what's so great about our game. It's never over till it's over, but it's heartbreaking."

The triumphant Ottawa Roughriders were also closing out an era. They would meet Montreal in the play-offs for the next five years, 1977–81, and the Als would win four of them. Mark Kosmos hung them up the year before.

The passion Kosmos had for the game shines through in part of a poem he wrote. "I wrote two sports poems. I woke up in the middle of the night and wrote them down. Some of the lines were

> *A game in which you gave your all,*
> *and strived for one great goal,*
> *that when you walk on that field of green,*
> *all knew you gave your soul.*

"That's what the game meant. You weren't making any money, so it wasn't that. The respect you earned on the field was almost like a paycheck. The last lines of the poem are

> *Now I sit and wonder,*
> *surely it's a dream I'm in,*
> *for no feeling like the one I've shared*
> *was ever meant to end."*

David Versus Goliath

In 1981 Ottawa was 5–11, 13 points behind Hamilton in second place. After beating the Als in the semifinal, they upset Hamilton late in the fourth quarter when quarterback J.C. Watts hooked up with Pat Stoqua for an 102-yard pass and run touchdown.

The Rough Riders prepared to meet the 14–1–1 Eskimos, the greatest CFL team of all time, in Montreal. Edmonton was trying to become the only team to win four straight Grey Cups. What should have been a hopeless situation turned out to be one of the most glorious days in the 114-year history of the Ottawa franchise.

How does a head coach instill confidence in a team facing a hopeless situation? "We actually had played pretty well against Edmonton during the season," said George Brancato. "Toward the end of the season we started to get hot. J.C. Watts started to finally shake his injuries and play well.

"We were really loose the week before. Nobody expected us to win. I don't think the game was even on the boards for betting because everybody was sure Edmonton was going to win. Edmonton might have been pressing, or they might have thought they had an easy shot at it and didn't come to life until the second half."

Said Bob O'Billovich, "It's easy to get players motivated for those kind of games. When you're the hopeless underdog, I think it's easier than when you're heavily favored because nobody expects you to win. Psychologically I think that works to your advantage. The other guys start reading about how much better they are, and sometimes they aren't ready to play the way they should be. By play-off time we were a lot better than our record indicated. We knocked off Hamilton in Hamilton when they had the second-best record in the league."

One of Ottawa's stars was defensive end Greg Marshall, an Eastern All-Star four times, an All-Canadian twice. He won the Schenley for Outstanding Defensive Player in 1983. He described the team's frame of mind during Grey Cup week. "We actually were pretty confident about our chances. We knew we could play with them. We didn't have anything to lose. Nobody expected us to win, so we were just going to go out and play hard and see what happened. We knew that it would be hard not to be a little bit overconfident if you were in Edmonton's situation. If we could get something going early we thought we'd have a chance."

That's exactly what happened. In the first quarter Gerry Organ made field goals of 34 and 37 yards to give Ottawa a 6–0 lead. A minute and a half later, capitalizing on a turnover, Jim Reid finished off a drive with a 1-yard touchdown. In the second quarter Sam Platt ran 14 yards for a major, giving the Eastern upstarts a 20–0 lead. All the mighty Eskimos could produce was a single on a missed field goal.

Edmonton got back in the game in the third quarter with touchdowns by Jim Germany and Warren Moon. In the final frame Organ notched a 28-yard field goal. Ottawa 23, Edmonton 15. With four minutes left Moon engineered a long drive for the 6 points and then threw to Marco Cyncar for the 2-point conversion. Soon after, Cutler kicked the winner from 27 yards out. Final score: Edmonton 26, Ottawa 23.

Marshall explained their first-half success. "We played a good field-position game, making Edmonton start their drives deep in their own territory. Our defense controlled the ball. We didn't have any turnovers. We really got after them. We pressured Warren Moon quite a bit and didn't allow them to run the ball very much either. We just played a very solid team game in the first half.

"At half time we were all kind of disappointed that we had to come in because we had things going so well and knew that the Eskimos were the type of team that was going to regroup and come out that much better in the second half. We talked about some of the things we might see from them and tried to prepare for them."

In the dressing room Brancato told his players to keep doing what they were doing. "I think more or less they did. We came out and got a pass interception right away and took the ball into field-goal range and got a field goal right at the start of the third quarter. And then that was it. Edmonton woke up."

Marshall thought mistakes turned the game in favor of Edmonton. "To me the key to the game was a turnover deep in our territory when they got the ball. They kicked a field goal to make it 20–4. Shortly after that we fumbled the ball on about our own 10-yard line. They recovered and were able to take it in on a third down play for a touchdown. That got 7 points real quick and got back in striking distance."

Did Marshall feel the game slipping away? "Obviously we were concerned, but if you had told us before the game that it was going to come down to the last three minutes of a tied game, would you take your chances? You'd say sure you would because everybody was expecting us to lose by 30 points.

"I still felt good about the things that we were doing," Marshall continued. "We just needed to make one play. Unfortunately we weren't able to make that play. Edmonton did and won the game."

A key mistake made by an official had an effect on the final outcome. Ottawa pivot J.C. Watts had completed a pass to Tony Gabriel at the 55, but it was called double interference. The ball went back into Ottawa's end, where Watts was sacked. Ottawa punted, Edmonton got the ball in good field position and moved in for the kill.

Gabriel recalled what happened. "I was coming back to the ball, and Gary Hayes was draped all over me. I made the catch, but the official called double interference. That official never worked another play-off game. I came out after that play. I had been wearing a brace, and I was hurt and sore. It was a disappointing way to end my career, not only because of the penalty but because we had a 20–1 lead and let it slip away."

Marshall was incensed at the call. "Probably the worst call in the history of the CFL," he said. "That call was utterly ridiculous. In retrospect it really did cost us an opportunity to win the ball game. To this day, every time I see it, I can't believe it was called that way."

Observed O'Billovich, "We were at about our own 25, and it was second down. Gabriel was going downfield, and Edmonton had a little defensive back named Gary Hayes covering him. J.C. laid it up. Hayes was crawling all over Tony. Gary was about 5'10", Tony was 6'4". Tony was warding him off with his one hand and caught the ball with the other hand for a big gain.

"The official called double interference. I'd never heard of that call and have never seen it made since. It was just a terrible call because we know a tie goes to the receiver. It was just a travesty, the worst call I've ever seen in a championship game."

Brancato agreed. "It was definitely defensive interference. We would have had a first down just over midfield, and anything could happen there. The score was tied. We would have had a shot at winning it."

In spite of the officiating, Greg Marshall praised the opposition. "Warren Moon played an excellent second half and made some great plays. I remember in particular when they went for the 2 points to tie it up. I thought he made a great play.

"I was playing defensive end and gambled," Marshall continued. "I took an inside rush on the two backs that were trying to get the corner for him. I thought I had a pretty good angle to Moon, but he made a move and got outside and was able to throw the pass to get the 2 points. That was just one of several big plays he made in the second half. Wilkie came in near the end of the first half and maybe calmed things down a bit. But he only put 1 point on the board. Warren Moon was definitely the catalyst in the second half.

Marshall also praised his teammates. "A lot of guys had been traded or cut by other teams and ended up in Ottawa. They were very grateful for the chance to continue playing. When they got that chance they made sure they gave their best effort, and it showed in the outcome of the game."

Coming so close to pulling off the biggest upset in Canadian sports history was something the Ottawa Rough Riders could feel very good about. "I suppose," said George Brancato, "but a loss is a loss. It's hard to take, especially a Grey Cup loss. It hurts to lose a game like that."

Greg Marshall agreed. "At the time we walked off the field the loss was a bitter disappointment because we had come so close and had let it slip through our grasp. The thing I remember is thinking that I was going to get back here again and get another chance. Well, I never did. Hopefully, as a coach, I'll get another chance someday." Greg Marshall did in 1997 as Saskatchewan's defensive coordinator.

The 1981 Grey Cup game was the last hurrah for the Ottawa Rough Riders. They never had another winning season although they did finish at .500 in 1982 and '92 and made the play-offs seven times. They won only once in post-season play.

After Brancato was fired in 1984, the Riders went through 10 head coaches and several general managers and directors. On July 24, 1991, the entire board of directors resigned, dumping the franchise into the league's lap. On October 19 of that year, Bernie and Lonie Glieberman from Detroit brought the team from the CFL. In February 1994 local entrepreneur Bruce Firestone purchased the team from the Gliebermans but sold it to Chicago businessman Horn Chen 13 months later. After losing a bundle in 1995, Horn Chen stopped the cash flow, leaving the Ottawa orphans once again on the doorstep of the CFL. The absentee owner began to be called the Mysterious Horn Chen because only John Tory, Larry Smith and Jeff Giles ever saw him.

The CEO of the Rough Riders, Garth Roberts, asked Leo Cahill to come in and save the franchise. Cahill had always been able to put people in the seats. On July 7, 1996, he talked about the beginning of the end of the Ottawa Rough Riders. "I came over here not knowing what I was getting into, really."

For example, said Cahill, reports about fan support were deceiving. "What happened, especially with the last two or three owners, was that they gave a lot of tickets away in order to encourage fan support. Last year at some games they had 20,000 people, but 9,000 were freebies. If this city was really stepping up to buy season tickets, I don't think the franchise would have had those problems all those years. It just isn't our problem — it's been a problem for 10 years. I don't know what the answer is.

"If you were lucky enough to win your first five games and get a legitimate 20,000–25,000 people to come to the ball games, you'd be in pretty good shape. But when you lose your exhibitions and first two regular season games, you have to do something to improve the situation."

It didn't improve. Despite frantic postseason efforts to save the franchise, the Ottawa Rough Riders were no more.

A Curse Settles Upon the Land

Fortunes for the Western Riders over the next decade mirrored those of their Eastern namesakes. Not only were the Riders unable to get back to the Grey Cup for 13 years, they didn't even make the play-offs for a record 11 straight years. Even the Great Depression had only lasted 10 years.

The 1988 Schenley Most Outstanding Offensive Lineman was Saskatchewan veteran Roger Aldag. "My first year was 1976, the year we went to the Grey Cup," he recalled. "I played a couple of games, I hurt my ankle and I went on the injury list. I was on the sidelines at the Grey Cup and I thought, 'Gosh, this is great. I should be here next year, too.' But it never happened."

It was an amazing stretch. One would have thought during that period that a rival team might come down with injuries and allow the Roughriders to slip into third place. One would think that a team would manage at least one lucky break or two in 10 years. Adding to the despair of the people of the Wheat Province, Saskatchewan in the 1980s suffered the worst economic downturn and the poorest crops since the Dirty Thirties.

John Payne resigned after the 1976 season, replaced by Jim Eddy, who went 8–8 and finished fourth in 1977 but was fired after a 0–6 start in 1978. Walt Posadowski completed the season with a mark of 4–5–1.

Ron Lancaster explained the demise of the Roughriders. "The 1976 season was kind of our last hurrah. A whole lot of guys were getting up there. The team probably needed to make some changes each year leading up to '76, starting to replace players, but we didn't do it because we had a pretty good nucleus of players. We reached the plateau in 1976 and started down the other side. Management decided that 1976 was going to be our last shot at this thing. We were going to try to win it all, and if we did, there were going to be a whole lot of guys going out as champions. We didn't win it. It was time to change the personnel."

When the team started losing in 1977, Lancaster bore the brunt of criticism. "People around here aren't used to losing," he said. "They haven't seen a team struggle as much as we have recently. They can't quite understand it. A lot of people are under the impression you can dress 32 dummies up in green and white and expect them to win. That isn't true at the best of times, and it surely isn't true this year. To execute you have to have the horses. We have had the horses, but we've changed them so often that it's just about impossible to get things going the way we want to."

In 1978 Lancaster played the last of 20 distinguished seasons. He had set practically every passing record, most of which still stand, played in six Grey Cups, won two Schenleys and was All-Canadian four times. His opponents accorded him rare and unique respect. They thought he was the smartest quarterback they had ever faced.

However, the prophet is often without honor in his own land. He was often booed and jeered in Regina, despite having led his team into the play-offs a record straight 15 times. When he made his farewell tour of enemy ball parks, the fans in those cities accorded him the greatest reception possible. But the greatest winner in Roughrider history was booed during his final appearance as a player at Taylor Field.

Lancaster took over as head coach, winning four games in two years. Offered a contract for 1981, he at first accepted but then changed his mind and went on to become the best TV football color man the networks ever had.

He was replaced by Eskimo assistant Joe Faragalli. Sharing quarterbacking duties were veterans John Hufnagel and Joe Barnes. In an exciting 1981 campaign, the two became known as J.J. Barnagle. The team almost made the play-offs, losing on the last game of the season 13–5 at rain-swept Empire Stadium. Still they finished with a 9–7 record. Faragalli was named Coach of the Year, defensive end Vince Goldsmith won the Schenley for Outstanding Rookie and Joey Walters caught 91 passes for 1,715 yards to make All-Canadian.

The 1981 Riders were assembled by General Manager Jim Spavital, formerly an assistant coach with Saskatchewan and Calgary and a head coach in Winnipeg. He had arrived in Regina the year before. Given the talent on the field, Spavital thought the team should have done better. Believing the team lacked discipline, Spavital privately decided to fire Faragalli, but before he got around to it, the media made Faragalli Coach of the Year. Certainly there would have been a huge outcry if the popular Papa Joe had been sent packing after the season.

But Spavital's fears were confirmed. The team fell into the basement the next year with a record of 6–9–1. During the off-season Faragalli traded Joe Barnes to Toronto because Barnes wanted to start all the time. When John Hufnagel stumbled out of the gate, the coach started rookie Joey "747" Adams, a quarterback with an arm like a cannon. Unfortunately he was about as smart as a cannon and would soon prove to be the coach's undoing.

Still the 1982 Roughriders were second only to Edmonton in total offense, first downs and passing yardage. Joey Walters led the league with 101 receptions for 1,670 yards. Five Riders made All-Canadian.

But reflecting their lack of discipline, they were first in fumbles, interceptions, penalties and losing the ball on downs, and defensively they were the Easy Riders with the fewest sacks in the league. They also gave up the most yards and were able to thwart a third-down gamble only once.

The case of Joey Adams was instructive. Faragalli said he repeatedly urged Adams, a college track star, to run more, but he refused because he had such great confidence in his arm. He was a passer.

After ending a four-game losing streak by beating Calgary 53–8, Faragalli said, "If they play 60 minutes of football, they can beat anybody. When this team plays up to their capabilities, I don't worry about a thing. This is the first time this year we've played a whole game of football. Look at the results."

Papa Joe was too nice a guy to put an end to the country club atmosphere and cut the cancer from the club. It cost him his job. Blindness had forced Jim Spavital to relinquish his position of general manager, and his replacement, John Herrera, late of the L.A. Raiders, fired Faragalli in August 1983, replacing him with Assistant Coach Reuben Berry. The first thing Berry did was cut Adams.

Berry was 10–15–1 over a season and a half and didn't make the play-offs. At the end of the 1984 season, the Rider executive cleaned house, firing Herrera and Berry, replacing them with Bill Quinter and Jack Gotta. It wasn't a marriage made in heaven, and the two disagreed on just about everything. Quinter had never been a general manager before, and Gotta was used to running his own show. The team went 11–22–1 under them and the play-off drought continued.

Once again the executive cleaned house, this time bringing in former Rider great and IPSCO executive Bill Baker as general manager. He would stay only two years before becoming the fifth commissioner of the CFL.

The Promised Land

Baker faced a gargantuan task. The team had sold only 12,756 season tickets for 1987 and was virtually bankrupt. Tired of losing, the faithful stayed away in droves. The first thing Baker did was convince the players to accept $700,000 in salary cuts. Then he hired Winnipeg offensive line coach John Gregory to succeed Gotta. Gregory had never been a head coach at the professional level.

"Coach Gregory is a man of character," Bill Baker explained. "He is an unusual guy with a lot of personality and enthusiasm. We get along very well, and yet we also argue pretty hard sometimes and have some good debates. But in the end we have the same approach to getting things done and the same enthusiasm for the game."

The 1987 Riders won five games. They scored the fewest points with all their quarterbacks combining for only 12 touchdowns. The defensive stats were almost as bad, but they were on the field most of the time.

In 1988 the Riders got off to a 3–0 start. They had an outstanding defense with Gary Lewis, Bobby Jurasin, Rick Klassen and Vince Goldsmith on the line with James Curry going in and out. The linebackers were Dave Albright, Eddie Lowe and Stephen Crane. Albright explained their initial success. "Winning is contagious. Things are beginning to turn around here. We've brought in some veteran players from winning programs. We now have a winning attitude instead of a losing one."

And win they did, finishing tied for first place with Edmonton, each with marks of 11–7. The play-off drought was over, but the Riders lost the semifinal 42–18 to the Lions in Regina. Their hunger deepened.

Not since the days of Ron Lancaster had the Riders been as strong at quarterback. Sharing the duties were Kent Austin and Tom Burgess. A quarterback controversy is a given in Regina, and 1989 was no exception. Although Burgess had been getting more playing time, many people thought Austin should be the starter. "I don't agree," Coach Gregory stated emphatically. "Each has special things he does. I like Austin, I like Tommy. Tom Burgess threw 19 touchdown passes, Austin 9. Austin completed 58 percent of his passes, Burgess 47 percent. Burgess throws the hot routes fantastically. Anytime you blitz Tom, you've got a chance to get beat badly. But he doesn't throw very well against zone coverages. Austin throws very well against zone coverages but has trouble with the blitz. Both have a big area to improve on. Whichever one makes the biggest improvement will be the quarterback."

Austin started the season against Calgary, played miserably and was replaced by Burgess, who brought the team from a 14-point deficit with less than two minutes remaining to win 32–29.

Through the first third of the season, Burgess threw 19 touchdown passes. The Riders started off 4–1 but then lost four straight. On September 16, trailing Toronto 24–9 at the end of the third quarter, Gregory pulled Burgess and gave Austin another chance. Saskatchewan won 29–24. The following Sunday Austin got his first start since opening day, leading the team to a 48–35 win over Edmonton. He started the rest of his career in Saskatchewan.

Austin ended up second only to Lancaster in completions, yards and touchdown passes. He set team records for most attempts and completions in a season and a game, and the most yards in a game — 558.

Two weeks after their impressive performance against the Eskimos, the Roughriders reached the low point of their season when they experienced a crushing defeat at the paws of the Lions, losing after time had expired. "There were 7 seconds left and we were up by 5 points," said Coach Gregory. "All we had to do was let them catch the ball and tackle them and the game was over. They were going into a very strong wind. Dunigan threw a Hail Mary up there and one of our players was called for extremely obvious pass interference. By then the clock was out. The next play they threw the ball into the end zone, and we were called for pass interference again, which gave them the ball on the 1-yard line. They ran a quarterback sneak. Dunigan fumbled, but someone else fell on it and that's how we lost the game.

"A lot of the fans thought that game was the end of the season for us," Gregory continued. "But we hadn't lost heart because we felt we had a good football team. We pulled up our bootstraps and went on from there.

"I have to look at 1989 as one of the most interesting seasons I've ever coached. If I was ever proud of myself as a coach in accomplishing something, I was proud of the fact that we were able to hold everybody together. That loss could have been disastrous, but we were able to keep together and keep working."

The culprit in the B.C. game was the Riders' All-Star safety Glen Suitor. "People were on his butt because they didn't think he was a hitter," said Gregory. "All of a sudden he was going to try and prove he was. He tried to make a big play, and it actually ended up being a bad play. Glen is a good guy and was a really good player. He was just trying to do something as a result of the pressure on him."

Saskatchewan closed out the regular season by losing to Edmonton 49–17. A quick exit from the play-offs seemed guaranteed.

But no. Beginning the most magical period in Saskatchewan Roughrider history, they went into Calgary and knocked off the Stampeders 33–26. The key play came on a second and long at the Stampeder 46. Austin ran a draw with little-used Canadian fullback Brian Walling, who ran it in for the winning touchdown.

Surely that would be it, for next the Riders would face Edmonton, who'd had a record-setting season of 16–2 and had defeated the Riders twice during the regular season. The Eskimos were well-rested and ready. But the underdog Roughriders upset the mighty Eskimos 32–21.

Kent Austin wasn't surprised at the outcome. "We had really played well against Edmonton in the regular season. A lot of people didn't realize that we beat them in the preseason and once during the regular season at home. So we felt that even though they had a better record than ours, one of their two losses that year was against us.

According to Gregory the Riders were lying in the weeds. "The last game of the year we went up and played Edmonton with a completely skeleton crew because we had lots and lots of injuries and we knew we were in the play-offs. They beat us pretty good, but we were stronger than we looked.

"Then, when we went over to play Calgary, we were still really banged up. We had to play Brian Walling in the backfield. Our third-string quarterback Jeff Bentrim had to play slotback because Ray Elgaard was still out. So we still had a lot of struggles when we went to Calgary. But I knew if we could get by Calgary we'd have all our horses back for the Edmonton game. I really felt we could beat Calgary, but about Edmonton I wasn't so sure."

The CFL's all-time leading receiver Don Narcisse looked back at the 1989 play-offs. "Nobody expected us to win," he said. "The game that really brought everyone together was when we beat Calgary. We had Jeff Bentrim playing slotback. He was our third-string quarterback. We had a guy like Brian Walling coming in and making a 55-yard run. That put the determination in us. We said, 'We can do it, we're only one game away, we go there and play Edmonton and you never know what will happen.' We weren't that good a team, but we were together as a team. Things just worked out fine."

The underdog Roughriders headed for Toronto to meet Hamilton at the Grey Cup christening of SkyDome to meet Hamilton, the only team they couldn't beat during the season. A dozen members of the 1986 Grey Cup champions were still in Hamilton in 1989. Al Bruno said his Ti-Cats preferred to play Edmonton. Given the outcome maybe Bruno knew something nobody else did.

Hamilton had defeated Saskatchewan 34–17 on a stormy July night in Regina. On August 18 in Hamilton they won 46–40 with a blocked kick playing an important role. The losing quarterback in both cases was Tom Burgess.

Saskatchewan had led the league in passing yardage and touchdown passes. The Ti-Cats had been second in passing yardage and completions. Neither team had a good pass defense. Everything pointed to a shoot-out of epic proportions.

Saskatchewan had a superb offensive line with Mike Anderson, the center (his father, Paul, played for the Riders in the 1950s), Bob Poley and Roger Aldag the guards, Vic Stevenson and Ken Moore the tackles. They would face Grover Covington, Mike Walker, Ronnie Glanton and Tim Lorenz. The Ti-Cat linebackers were Frank Robinson, Darrell Corbin and Pete Giftopoulos, who had been drafted by Saskatchewan in 1988 but refused to report.

The Rider wide-receivers were Don Narcisse and Mark Guy, the slotbacks Jeff Fairholm (son of former Alouette Larry Fairholm) and Ray Elgaard. Tim McCray and Milson Jones were the backs and Kent Austin was the quarterback. John Gregory explained why. "Although there was a fan conflict about which quarterback we were going to play, I knew we were going to play Tommy Burgess against a blitzing team and Kent Austin against a zone team. Hamilton was a zone team. They were in all kinds of different zones and coverages.

"A lot of people questioned me. In fact they even had a pick-the-quarterback contest in the newspaper, and everybody called in, which I was very upset about. My thought was with the guys on the field. The Ti-Cats were a zone team, and I really felt Kent would give us the best chance to win. He played a great football game."

Austin would be attacking a Hamilton secondary comprised of Will Lewis, Stephen Jordan, Jim Rockford, Sonny Gordon and Lance Shields. They had a long afternoon.

Saskatchewan's defensive front four were Bobby Jurasin and Chuck Klingbeil, Gary Lewis and Vince Goldsmith. They faced center Dale Sanderson, guards Jason Riley and Darrell Harle, and tackles Miles Gorrell and Mike Dirks. The Rider linebackers were Eddie Lowe, Dave Albright and Dan Rashovich. The secondary of Steve Wiggins, Larry Hogue, Glen Suitor, Richie Hall and Harry Skipper would defend against wide-outs Wally Zatylny and Tony Champion, slotbacks Rocky DiPietro and Richard Estell, running backs Derrick McAdoo and Jed Tommy, and quarterback Mike Kerrigan, the hero of Hamilton's Grey Cup win in 1986.

Terry Baker and Dave Ridgway would do Saskatchewan's kicking, Paul Osbaldiston for Hamilton.

Said John Gregory, "I felt good about the game before it ever started. I was positive we were going to win. I think our players did, too. At the press conference the day before, I said the game will probably come down to a last-second kick, and there isn't anybody I'd rather have kicking the ball than Dave Ridgway."

Despite the Roughriders' confidence, the early going wasn't promising. On Hamilton's second possession they moved from their 54 to the Rider 35 and kicked a 42-yard field goal. Four plays later, a Kent Austin pass was deflected into the arms of Frank Robinson. The Cats kicked their second 3-pointer to lead 6–0. Saskatchewan replied with a single.

Hamilton scrimmaged at the 35. Off-side Saskatchewan moved it to the 40. McAdoo picked up the first down. Kerrigan hit Winfield for 15 and 19. At the Rider 28, Kerrigan threw to Estell for 15. Then it was into the end zone for Tony Champion. Hamilton led 13–1 at the end of the quarter.

Kent Austin wasn't worried. "I felt we had a good offense. We certainly had enough weapons to put points on the board. Offensive football in the Canadian league is very much a matter of tempo. The sporadic start didn't allow us to get into a groove. Once we put a couple of first downs together, we ended up having an unbelievable second quarter."

The fun began on Saskatchewan's second possession of the second quarter. Starting at their 48, Austin hit Jeff Fairholm for 22 yards. Testing the secondary, Austin missed on a long bomb to the end zone but then connected with Ray Elgaard for 16. After an incompletion at the 24, it was a strike to Don Narcisse to the 5. Ray Elgaard then caught one for a touchdown. Hamilton 13, Saskatchewan 8.

"We ran a corner route and he made a great catch, but he was quite open on the play," recalled Gregory. "Of all the players I've had, I consider Ray Elgaard one of the top professional football players. He was a tough guy. He prepared well. The tougher the game the better he played."

Said Austin, "He made a great catch on the 16-yarder. The ball was a little high. Hamilton broke the coverage and Ray got behind them on a corner, but without that great catch over the middle we probably would have been kicking a field goal. Ray made many of those before."

Elgaard was also more impressed with the 16-yarder he caught at the Hamilton 24. "I scored a touchdown, but that wasn't a particularly memorable catch. But I did catch another pass that was a pretty big play for us. We were down at the time, and we weren't really rolling. Kent threw me a ball that I had to extend forward on, and I snagged it. It seemed that after we scored on that drive, we were just playing pitch and catch."

So was Hamilton. After taking the Rider kickoff to their 53, Kerrigan picked up a first down to Estell. He completed a pass to DiPietro at the 30 and then to McAdoo for the touchdown. Hamilton 20, Saskatchewan 8.

The Riders were not to be outdone. With first down at their 35, Austin dropped back to pass and found Jeff Fairholm streaking down the left side. At the moment he caught the ball, a flag came down, but the second-year slotback broke through the interference and ran 75 yards for the touchdown. Hamilton 20, Saskatchewan 15. That was the signature play of the 1989 Grey Cup.

Fairholm was a study in concentration. "On the catch I made for the touchdown, I didn't even know I had been interfered with. I didn't even know the guy was on my back. I just caught the ball, ran for a touchdown, looked back and saw the flag and thought, 'Oh, my God, somebody held.' I had no idea that the guy was all over my back until I saw the film the next day."

The catch was the biggest moment of his professional career. "It will always be in my memory, there is no doubt about that. Every day I look at that football I caught."

"We caught Hamilton in a man-to-man situation," explained Austin. "The safety was really cheating with my eyes. We picked that up in the first quarter. We sent Jeff on a streak route, and I looked the safety back to the field, and Jeff got behind his man. Really the only chance he had was to kind of pull Jeff down. He got an interference call on it, but Jeff still pulled away from him and caught the ball. The ball came over his outside shoulder and he kind of looked back. It was a tough catch."

Don Narcisse felt the Fairholm touchdown gave the team a big lift. "A lot of us were never in that situation, never had a chance to play in a Grey Cup, and here we were trailing. I remember one time watching the instant replay and saying to a guy, 'Hey, get yourself into the game. We don't need none of that.' When Jeff Fairholm made that long touchdown, everybody got excited. I think everybody was sitting back, waiting for a big play, and once that big play came, it was just like 'Hey, it's not that bad after all.' Everybody contributed to it and it was just wonderful."

Hamilton was not impressed. With two strikes of 9 and 15 yards to Tony Champion, five runs for 37 yards by McAdoo and an 11-yard completion to DiPietro, Kerrigan marched his team 71 yards for a touchdown. Hamilton 27, Saskatchewan 15.

So what? said Saskatchewan. Three passes to James Ellingson plus strikes to

Narcisse and Elgaard brought the Riders to the 5, where Austin found Narcisse alone in the end zone. At half time the scoreboard read Hamilton 27, Saskatchewan 22.

Saskatchewan had launched an all-out aerial attack. Austin was 11 for 16 and three touchdowns in the second quarter. He went exclusively to the air, he said, "because we got down and Hamilton kept scoring. We didn't run the ball one time in the second quarter. We couldn't afford to. We had to keep scoring to keep pace with those guys and stay in the game. We got on a roll with the passing game in the second quarter, and we didn't get away from it."

Early in the second quarter Hamilton's left corner, Lance Shields, went down and didn't return. He was replaced in the secondary by receiver Earl Winfield. According to Austin they didn't try to exploit the situation. "We had a pretty decent game plan going in. Our line blocked really well in the second quarter, and our receivers were beating their guys. Jeff got behind the defense on a deep ball. Narcisse was running some great routes. Ray got behind the coverage on his touchdowns. It just was a combination of everyone working together, protecting the quarterback, and the receivers reading the coverage properly and getting open.

"We had the good game plan—what we called Full Fill—throwing where the defense would dictate a certain progression on the field for us. We played together two or three years before that Grey Cup so we had a pretty good idea of what we were going to do."

Saskatchewan coach John Gregory admired Lance Shield's replacement. "Hamilton had to put one of their receivers, Earl Winfield, in as a defensive back. Once I got over there and coached him I realized that was no problem because he was an outstanding player. Earl moved over on defense, but he was such a marvelous athlete I don't think that hurt them at all."

Not so, said Don Narcisse, describing his second-quarter touchdown. "Winfield was a receiver, and I had it in my mind that no receiver was going to go out there and cover me. I'll always come out on top when a receiver is covering me. I beat him on a little hitch route, a little 5-yard hook. I came back for the ball, and the ball was there."

Still he didn't buy the argument that injuries to Hamilton's secondary made his job easier. "We got in a groove, we started making the plays, we started doing what we had to do, and it didn't matter who was out there," he insisted. "We took advantage of whoever they had out there anyhow."

It all evens out, said Rider secondary coach Dick Adams. "We lost a player also, so we had a young guy [rookie John Hoffman] playing out on the corner for us."

Surely the kind of shoot-out that was taking place would make a secondary coach nervous. "To be honest I did get a little bit upset," said Adams, "but they had real good receivers and quarterbacks, and we knew the game was going to be a shoot-out from the word go. From the opening whistle we knew the ball was going to be in the air.

"I felt confident our guys were going to win the thing. I had played the game in my mind the night before and saw that we were going to win. But there were going to be some great plays during the course of the game. In the end it was going to come down to a Dave Ridgway field goal to win it anyway."

Half time, according to Coach Gregory, was not a time for great speeches. "I quit doing that when I was down in college," he said. "Once in a while you have to try to upset the team or change their attitude, so you go in and holler and scream at them, but most of the time preparation wins for you rather than Knute Rockne speeches."

In the third quarter the teams traded field goals on their first possessions. At the 10-minute mark Terry Baker pinned Hamilton at their 3-yard line with a thunderous punt. Three plays later Osbaldiston conceded a safety touch.

After the ensuing kickoff, Saskatchewan scrimmaged at their 33. After a 2-yard gain by Tim McCray, Austin hooked up with Narcisse on a 47-yarder to the Hamilton 28. The Cats took an interference call on the next play and McCray crashed over from the 1.

Narcisse talked about the big play. "It was a hook route. The defensive back I was playing against, Shields, had his ankle broken or whatever because they had Winfield playing cornerback at one period of time and then they put Shields back in. I knew his ankle was bad and I skimmed him up. I gave him a good move, caught the ball and ran with it. It's something you practice, something you dream about, and it happened."

Was Austin still convinced that the injury to Shields wasn't critical? "They had their corner hurt," Austin said, "but I don't know if that was necessarily the turning point. I just think we really got on a roll offensively. Not to take anything away from Hamilton, but they were going to have a hard time stopping us the rest of the game. It really wouldn't have mattered who was there.

"The idea of trying to take advantage of a rookie or a replacement is very overrated," insisted Austin. "Most times if you try to key on one side of the field, it ends up backfiring. We spread the ball around pretty well that day. I think most good offenses do that. When you get distracted because of one injury and then you focus on nothing but that, you end up sacrificing the rest of your offense."

At the end of the third frame the Roughriders had their first lead of the game, 34–30. A minute and 12 seconds later, Ridgway kicked a 25-yard field goal.

Starting at the 35, Hamilton's Kerrigan fired a pass upfield but was picked off by Glen Suitor at the Ti-Cat 51. Surprisingly the Grey Cup interception wasn't the highlight of his career. "The highlight for me from a personal standpoint was the game before that, the Western Final," he recalled. "I had take some criticism for that play against B.C., where I hit David Williams late on the last play of the game that gave the Lions a first down. Matt Dunigan scored and they won. That was with about five games left in the season. I took a lot of heat from the media and fans. Being named defensive player of the game in the Western Final was a real highlight for me. It was good for my family, too. We went through the phone calls from irate fans and a lot of things like that. It was nice that my wife got a little pressure off her."

Austin drove the Riders toward the Hamilton goal line, where an interception was thrown—by Ray Elgaard. "We ran a reverse pass," said Gregory. "It was a run–pass option. He should have run. It was kind of a trick play that didn't work. He threw it down to the 2- or 3-yard line. The primary receiver was absolutely wide open. Ray threw it to the secondary receiver for some reason. The thing that was too bad is we probably could have gotten a field goal out of it."

Added Austin, "That was right after we got an interception by Suitor. We were up by 7 and in scoring range, so that was a big turnaround for Hamilton because had we gone in to score we may have pulled away from them."

The teams twice exchanged punts. At the 8:39 mark, Osbaldiston kicked a 47-yard field goal to close the gap to 4. Ten plays later, Ridgway replied with a 20-yarder of his own, making the score Saskatchewan 40, Hamilton 33 with 1:58 left in regulation time.

Austin thought that drive was critical. "It helped us maintain the atmosphere and the tempo. It helped show Hamilton that they were going to have to keep scoring to stay with us."

Can do, said Hamilton pivot Kerrigan. Starting at the 35, he threw to Lee

Knight for 18 and to DiPietro for 9. McAdoo ran for 6. After an incompletion Saskatchewan was called for interference at their 11. McAdoo went for 2 followed by an incomplete pass. With third down and 8, Kerrigan threw into the right side of the end zone. Tony Champion made a dazzling over-the-shoulder catch while falling backward to the turf. The convert was good. With 44 seconds left the score stood Hamilton 40, Saskatchewan 40.

"The guy who probably didn't play very well that game would have been Harry Skipper," said Dick Adams. "He made some plays, but he also was the guy who got picked on the most, too. Tony Champion made one of the greatest catches I've ever seen for the touchdown, and Harry's right there beside him. I can get mad at Harry, but, on the other hand, you have to admire the catch Tony made with the bad ribs and everything."

Saskatchewan ran the kickoff back to their 36. There was no thought of playing conservatively, hoping for a win in overtime. For once in the last minute of a Grey Cup, the Riders attacked.

"When Kent went out there," recalled Gregory, "we told him to use the clock wisely, which he always did. They were probably going to play zone, so we told him to read the coverage and hit the spots. That's exactly what he did.

"The Tiger-Cats were trying to overload on Elgaard. Kent hit Elgaard on a wheel route for about 20 yards. When Hamilton called the zone to Elgaard's side, Kent threw backside and hit two big plays to Mark Guy."

"On the first play of that drive," said Austin, "I went to Narcisse on a stop and go and overthrew everybody, but that was really more to send a signal to Hamilton that they weren't going to squat on a route. There were three more passes. Elgaard caught one, Guy, two.

"I didn't feel like they could stop us. There was plenty of time to get into scoring range for the best kicker I ever played with. I knew if we got close, Dave Ridgway would make it. We actually drove it down there into pretty decent range for him. It was a pretty easy kick for him although in that type of pressure situation, no kick is easy.

"Before that Ray Elgaard made a big second-down catch on the sidelines that kept the drive alive, and then Mark Guy came through with a big catch. On the first one over the middle, he took a good hit from the safety but held on to the ball."

With the ball on the Hamilton 26, Austin went down on one knee to stop the clock. The teams exchanged time-outs. Then at 14:58 of the fourth quarter, before 54,088 anxious fans, the greatest moment in the history of Saskatchewan sports took place: The Kick.

The snap was back. Suitor put the ball down as Ridgway moved toward it. For a split second the great domed stadium was silent. Then, as the ball flew toward the goalposts, the crowd roared. When the ball split the uprights, all Saskatchewan fans followed the ball to cloud nine.

But 2 seconds remained on the clock. Ridgway kicked off. Steve Jackson punted it back down the field to Glen Suitor, who ran it out of bounds. The greatest Grey Cup of them all was over. The final score: Saskatchewan 43, Hamilton 40.

Dave Ridgway talked about the kick. "There's no doubt there was a tremendous amount of pressure. If there's one thing that really helped me it's that there's a thing that athletes get into called the Zone. It is a psychological outlook at the situation in which you get tunnel vision and you become so focused on what you are doing. Fortunately, throughout most of my career, I've found myself in the Zone, and 1989 was no different.

"I was totally oblivious to the meaning of what that kick was until after the fact. Then I sat down and said, 'Holy Cow! That was a big kick!' It was an afterthought.

"When we got out on the field, there were two time-outs, and I asked my holder, Glen Suitor, to talk to me about something other than football. He got me laughing and before I knew it, it was time to attempt the kick. I get a strange kick out of doing it. I like walking on the field in that situation, and I expect to make it.

"Still I would rather that game hadn't come down to a field goal because that's an awful lot of pressure on one person's shoulders. I just don't see living in this province if I had missed in that situation."

Kent Austin was sensational, completing 26 of 41 passes for 474 yards and three touchdowns, winning him the Grey Cup Most Valuable Player Award. His 474-yard performance is the third best in Grey Cup history, his three touchdowns one short of Russ Jackson's 1969 record. Austin's performance was one of the best in Grey Cup history.

Mike Kerrigan wasn't exactly a shabby Tabby, completing 23 of 35 passes for 303 yards and three touchdowns.

Al Bruno analyzed his team's defeat. "We got demoralized by the fact we got our best defensive back hurt, and Saskatchewan picked on us. We had to put Winfield in there after that, which really hurt us. The play where Fairholm

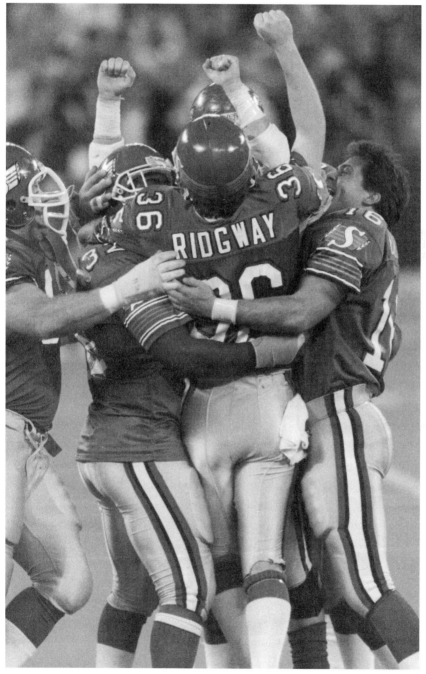

Dave Ridgway and friends celebrate after the 1989 field goal that brought Saskatchewan its second Grey Cup.

caught that long touchdown pass killed us. We blew the coverage. Our guy [Rockford] tried to grab him, but Fairholm went right by him. That really turned the game around. It's one of those embarrassing things. You have the guy, but all of a sudden he dekes you. You try to grab him, you miss him and he scores. Suitor's interception hurt us, too. Take that last pass when Saskatchewan went down there and hit that final field goal: we knocked the hell out of that new receiver and he still caught the ball. We should have won that Grey Cup. If we had gone into overtime, we would have won. I know we would have."

Austin paid tribute to another facet of his team's success. "Mark Guy gave us great field position and so did Tim McCray on a couple of kickoffs. We had real good special teams that year. We also had good defensive special teams, especially in covering the ball. They played very well."

Dick Adams had had that feeling the night before the Grey Cup. "It was a premonition, a dream. I had really played the game the night before and saw what the outcome was going to be—that it was going to be a close game and we were going to win it with a field goal at the end."

Saskatchewan always livens up a Grey Cup. The record SkyDome crowd rocked and rolled for an hour before game time and until well after the last Roughrider left the field. At one hotel, The Torch, the caped crusader with the gun-powder on his helmet, strode through the lobby with his minions in tow. At another inn a wandering band of musicians spotted Ron Lancaster and George Reed and played a rousing chorus of "On Roughriders."

At the ball park the Rider fans delighted everyone with their fresh-faced enthusiasm, their small-town friendliness, their good-natured ribbing of the opposition. There were banners from Lancer, Lanigan, Roger Aldag's home town of Gull Lake, Weyburn and even Regina and Saskatoon.

They were matched in their all-consuming delight in the festivities by the die-hard fans from Hamilton, who also knew how to party hearty. Trying as best they could to ignore the revelry in their midst, even a few staid Torontonians joined in the fun.

Don Narcisse was dazzled by it all. "It was a lot of fun. I was young and I didn't really understand. Because I had never really been on a winning team, had never won a championship, I really didn't get a chance to understand. Now, after playing the game for 11 years, I understand, and I want it back so much. And getting the type of Grey Cup ring they gave us—nobody else has come close to getting one like ours."

Dick Adams saluted the Riders' fans. "You talk about feelings and the people from the province. Saskatchewan fans are everywhere. There are Saskatchewan fans in the Maritimes, in Ottawa.

"We went to the play-off game in Calgary and a bunch of the Green Riders showed up over there. It was an awesome sight. We came from behind and won. Then we went into Edmonton for the Western Final, and there was just an eerie feeling in the stadium. I don't know that I've ever had that feeling—the feeling almost like that of a player, where the butterflies are churning and you're ready to go to war right there.

"Then all the people came in singing 'Green is the Color' and we walked out of there a winner. It was unbelievable. We thought that was probably the best we could hope to see until all of a sudden we walked into the SkyDome and the place was green. Having had the good fortune to coach in Saskatchewan for five years, I can say that there isn't any place like Saskatchewan to go as a player or a coach because fans get into it, the province is behind you. When you get into the play-offs there are going to be fans showing up in the other city to support you. It's a fun place."

Jeff Fairholm said, "I loved playing in Regina. The fans there are great. I liked the smallness of the city. I was able to get to know a lot of people. Hey, I was having fun doing what I loved to do. It couldn't get much better than that."

As a player or general manager, Alan Ford has been part of every Saskatchewan Grey Cup in the modern era except 1951. He compared the two winning teams, 1966 and 1989. "It's never the same as being a player. I think there are probably four levels of enjoyment: player, coach, manager and fan. Obviously the closest to it is the player, the next closest is the coach and then comes management. I think I enjoyed 1989 more because it was for our fans.

"You can't get any lower than after the B.C. game when we lost with no time left on the clock," Ford continued. "It looked like we weren't going to make the play-offs. And then to just keep battling back. Everybody in Saskatchewan identified with the team—that's the way this province is.

"If we're fortunate enough to get to another Grey Cup and win it, it will be its own game, but nothing will match the way things went in '89."

Said John Gregory, "The thing I always appreciated about the players in Saskatchewan was that they played hard. A lot of times I think they played over their heads. And the fans—although they liked to pick the quarterback for you—were great. I was really proud for the Saskatchewan people who supported that team so strongly. It was interesting how it affected everybody from the farmers to the meat cutters to the presidents of banks."

Indeed. After 10 years of low wheat prices, rural depopulation, crop failures and losing football teams, winning the Grey Cup was just what a beleaguered people needed to enter the last decade of the century with confidence. The 23-year Grey Cup drought was over.

The Roller Coaster Riders

The new decade dawned full of promise for the Saskatchewan Roughriders, but in 1990 they finished third again with a 9–9 record. This time the Eskimos were ready for them, winning 43–27 in the semifinal.

The following year the Riders returned to their familiar spot in the basement with a record of 6–12. John Gregory was fired in August, when the team was 1–6. He was replaced by Don Matthews, who had returned from the Orlando Thunder of the World League of American Football. He was 5–6 the rest of the way.

In 1992 the Riders returned to .500 and were on the verge of eliminating the Eskimos in the semifinal in Edmonton when fate intervened—the kind Saskatchewan fans have learned over the years to dread. Lining up for a game-winning field goal, Dave Ridgway slipped and fell on his duff. No solace was found in the Eskimos' loss to Calgary in the Western Final.

Saskatchewan went 11–7 in 1993 but still only finished third behind Calgary and Edmonton. They lost the semifinal to the Eskimos 51–13. Austin had his second-best year in Rider livery, completing 405 of 715 passes for 5,754 yards and 31 touchdowns. Despite his performance he was booed throughout the season. His wife suffered abuse at the hands of some fans, and Austin wanted out. Saskatchewan traded him to Ottawa for Tom Burgess, defensive back Anthony Drawhorn and linebacker Ron Goetz. Ottawa then moved Austin to B.C. for Danny Barrett, where he went on to win his second and last Grey Cup.

Proving that hell hath no fury like a province scorned, Austin received a rude reception when he returned to Taylor Field for the first time in a Lion uniform. He was unmercifully booed. The month before *Regina Leader-Post* readers overwhelmingly picked him as the province's most disliked sports personality. A radio announcer urged fans who sat behind the visitors' bench to take eggs to the game to throw at him.

All of this for a man who helped the team win only its second Grey Cup in

84 years, a quarterback who dueled with Doug Flutie for the league lead in every passing category, who led the Green and White to the play-offs in six of the seven years he was there, and who was the second greatest quarterback in Roughrider history.

Don Matthews exercised the escape clause in his contract and left to become the head coach and director of football operations of the expansion Baltimore Colts. He was replaced by Ray Jauch. The Riders were 11–7 in 1994, finishing fourth in the expanded Western division. They lost the semifinal 36–3 to Calgary. A key to their successful regular season play was leading the league in the giveaway–takeaway category at +27.

Jauch opened the 1995 campaign with a veteran team and high hopes although he had lost all-purpose running back Mike Saunders and quarterback Warren Jones, defensive back Anthony Drawhorn and linebacker Ray Bernard to free agency and Gary Lewis and Glen Suitor to retirement. Jones later returned.

Saskatchewan hopes rested on the shoulders of Tom Burgess, who played miserably. After six games the Riders were 1–5, and Burgess had a passing efficiency rating of 39.6. The year before his rating was 90.2 after six games. When asked what was wrong with the Roughriders, Coach Jauch replied, "Let's put it this way: you've got to spread the fertilizer around before you get good crops." The team ended up with a record of 6–12.

The signs were ominous in 1995. Early in the season Ray Jauch was bowled over at the bench by a player and tore his knee ligaments. In the second game the Riders had the Eskimos on the run at Taylor Field when a thunderstorm struck, knocking the power at 9:17 of the third quarter. In a torrential downpour both teams fled to their darkened dressing rooms with the home team leading 16–3. The hot Roughriders cooled off, the Eskimos used the ensuing 36 minutes to regroup and went on to a 26–19 victory in overtime. Nothing went right for the rest of the year.

Except Don Narcisse. The unassuming native of Port Arthur, Texas, and graduate of Texas Southern University came to the Roughriders in 1986 from St. Louis of the NFL. At 5'9", 170 pounds, he is small, not particularly fast but remarkably durable. Narcisse holds the record for most consecutive 1,000-plus–yard receiving seasons at 7 and most consecutive games catching a pass. He ranks first in receptions.

In 1997 Narcisse explained how, against all odds, he has had such a great professional career. "Determination. Growing up, everybody was always saying I was too small or too slow. Nobody ever gave me anything. I always worked hard at it. It has always been instilled in me that I've got to be better. I'm never satisfied with myself.

"I concentrate on the football. You get a guy who runs fast and his thinking is 'I'm going to catch it and run.' My thinking is 'I'm going to catch it first, and I'm going to run next.' My concentration is such that I know if you throw the ball to me it's going to be my ball. Being a receiver you've got to have an attitude that you can beat anybody. One on one, it's time for me to do my job. Just throw it my way and I'll catch it."

What records does he cherish the most? "The record for consecutive 1,000-yard seasons and catching a pass in every game. Catching a pass in every game—that's me. I like to contribute every time I go on the field. I'm looking forward to being the all-time leader in receptions. Until I'm number one I can't feel that my dream has come true. If I get the 1,000-yard and consecutive-game records, they will be a plus for me."

He made an interesting point. "When you look at the all-time list for receptions, seven of the first eight are slotbacks. I'm the only exception. It is harder for a wide-receiver to get the ball than it is for slotbacks because they are right by the quarterback. It is easy for him to dump the ball off to them. I'm a wide-out who has been playing in Regina, where the wind blows about 60 miles an hour, so I've often only had two quarters of football to catch passes. Also, I've had at least 20 quarterbacks throughout my career.

"When you have a rapport with the quarterback, you can just run your routes. When I was playing with Kent Austin, it was like, 'Hey, I'm going to run this route, and if it's not open I'm just running into another area. Because we were on the same page, he'd throw it. He knew me so well and what I could do. Working with Kent Austin for seven years was a real plus."

In 1995 Dave Ridgway was struggling through his worst year since 1986. For the last two games of the season, Jauch decided to give Paul McCallum a chance. He was good on 11 of 15 field-goal attempts. But typical of the Queen City, the kicking change created an ugly situation in Regina. Again the media got involved in a name-that-kicker contest. Naturally the author of the 1989 Grey Cup victory came out on top. Familiar with the ways of the Wheat Province, the media attention didn't particularly perturb Ray Jauch.

What did bother him was Ridgway's public reaction to his benching and his request that General Manager Alan Ford intervene with Jauch on his behalf. Ford did so. Determined not to allow the inmates to run the asylum and believing that both the general manager and kicker should know better, Jauch refused to budge. At the end of the season he quit in disgust.

Jauch was vindicated when Ridgway retired. His career was over. But the club's handling of the situation cost them a Hall of Fame coach.

Jauch was succeeded by Jim Daley, a native of Ottawa with five years experience as a CFL assistant. Going into the season with three untried young quarterbacks, all of whom were injured at one time or another, the team finished with a record of 5–13. During the off-season the club almost went under, saved only by a desperate season ticket drive and an infusion of NFL cash. During the off-season Daley acquired veteran Reggie Slack from the Blue Bombers. He would live and die with Slack and second-year man Kevin Mason.

The coaching staff wanted and started Slack, the fans and media wanted Mason. The controversy raged throughout the 1997 season. Daley explained why he signed Slack instead of staying with the original plan of bringing his young quarterbacks along. "We wanted to get a quarterback with some experience and he has that. He understands our game. He's very mobile, which I think you need in our league. He has a strong throwing arm and tremendous leadership skills. Everywhere he's been, the players have really liked playing with him."

In training camp Daley thought the offensive line would be a strong point, but that wasn't the case. After a 22–13 loss in Calgary, where it appeared Slack had performed poorly, Daley said he didn't pull Slack earlier because the line played so badly it would have been a disgrace to pull any quarterback. In Edmonton a couple of weeks later, Slack got hurt and Daley again criticized his offensive line. Although the target of relentless criticism, Daley refused to allow public opinion to choose his quarterback. He was determined to do what was best for the football team no matter how uncomfortable it got for him personally.

An important addition to the team was All-Canadian linebacker K.D. Williams, who the Bombers' new coach Jeff Reinebold had cut and run out of town with a torrent of disparaging remarks. "There were things said there that were pretty uncommon for a coach to say about a player," Daley said. "We aren't worried about those comments. We will make our own evaluation on K.D., and we will make our own decisions about him. We think K.D. is a good player, a good person and we think he's going to be a great addition."

Arriving in Regina in the Ottawa dispersal draft was another linebacker, Lamar McGriggs. Both Williams and McGriggs were holy terrors on the field and in the dressing room. When they made charges about racism among the coaching staff, Jim Daley had had enough. Although desperately needing both players, he traded them to Hamilton, where Williams was cut soon after.

Daley discussed what happened. "Their comments in the *Globe and Mail* article gave a totally inaccurate picture of our team. It is unfortunate that they were printed in a national newspaper. Those comments—even if only partly attributed to them—put them in a situation where they had to be traded. It took no time to decide that. During the course of a year there are a lot of things that can be said in a locker room, but there's a line you cross. Certainly those comments, painting the picture they did, made it impossible for them to function with our players."

As for desperately needing them at that point in the season, he replied, "You don't make a decision based on needs because then you are compromising your values. You make the decision based on what is right and wrong, and then you adjust to it."

Daley's action so galvanized the team that they made the play-offs and, reminiscent of 1989, headed for Calgary. No one gave them a chance against the powerful Stampeders despite the fact Calgary had been very inconsistent and Saskatchewan had beaten them earlier in the year. In the earlier 21–19 win in Regina, the key to victory had been the running of Reggie Slack.

In the semifinal Stamp quarterback Jeff Garcia went down with a knee injury in the first quarter. Although his replacement, Dave Dickenson, played well, the Stamps again fell victim to Slack's running, and the underdogs went on to win 33–30, their first play-off win since 1989.

Shades of 1989 again, the Riders went on to meet the even more powerful Edmonton Eskimos, a team they had played well against during the regular season, a team also plagued by inconsistency.

Slack opened the scoring with a 5-yard touchdown run. Curtis Mayfield scored on a 37-yard touchdown pass from Slack and then returned a punt 95 yards for his second touchdown. Edmonton replied with majors by Darren Flutie and Eddie Brown. The Riders led 24–15 at half time.

Four times Edmonton drove deep into enemy territory but could only manage two field goals and a single. With less than two minutes to go, Slack ran 14 yards for the clinching touchdown. The Eskimos struck back 21 seconds later with one of their own by Henry Williams and a 2-point conversion by Flutie. The final score was Saskatchewan 31, Edmonton 30.

Everybody was flabbergasted at this incredible turn of events. Everybody, that is, except Jim Daley and his Roughriders. "We knew early in the season that all four Western teams were going to have a chance at going to the Grey Cup," Daley insisted. "When we played Calgary and Edmonton in the regular season or play-offs, it was never a matter of being worried about being underdogs. We had beaten Calgary and Edmonton and lost to them as well. We felt that in the play-offs we had to play great football but that it was realistic for us to be going in with every confidence that we could win those games. And we did."

The slogan for the eighty-fifth Grey Cup was "Party in Your Parka." Saskatchewan fans from all over the country converged on Edmonton to have the time of their lives. Come Grey Cup day, Commonwealth Stadium was a sea of green. Although the Riders had rained on Edmonton's parade by knocking the host team out of the big event, the good people of Alberta's capitol became instant Saskatchewan fans. (Deep down most of them are anyway.)

Saskatchewan's Grey Cup opponent would be the powerful Toronto Argonauts. Even though many thought the eighty-fifth Grey Cup should be labeled the mismatch of the century, the Riders were not afraid. "The odds being all in favor of Toronto was not a real concern because, one," said Coach Daley, "any team going into the Grey Cup with Doug Flutie as their opponent would be the underdog, and, two, we had played Toronto earlier in the year and beaten them. Our guys were very much looking forward to playing them. We were on a bit of a roll ourselves, and we were optimistic that we could compete with them. The odds didn't have any bearing on our confidence."

The festivities got under way with an ominous sign for Saskatchewan. The public address announcer began the introduction of the Roughrider offense by calling out the name of center Carl Coulter. Nothing happened. No one appeared. Sensing what lay ahead, had the Roughriders decided to stay in their dressing room? *Au contraire.* After what seemed like an eternity, Coulter emerged from the tunnel prepared to meet his doom.

And doom it was. The final score: Toronto 47, Saskatchewan 23.

Saskatchewan coach Jim Daley's Grey Cup strategy was simple. "We wanted to be able to run the option in specific situations, and we also wanted to be able to get Reggie outside the pocket. That was our main focus. Unfortunately the opening kickoff in the third quarter went for a Toronto touchdown. That changed the game. The last possession of the second quarter the Argos got a long kickoff return after we had scored, and they were able to get three points off it. So in two kickoff returns we gave up 10 points in the course of 35 seconds. We did score 23 points, but Toronto getting up early in the third quarter really limited our ability to have Reggie run. We had to go to the air more.

"We just gave up too much field position on special teams, and, of course, Doug Flutie had an outstanding game," Daley conceded. "For us to play within our game plan, we needed a close game.

"There were a lot of positives, but Toronto played a great game. Their special teams put their already great offense in great field position. Special teams changed the momentum. Whatever could go wrong did go wrong."

Injuries to the secondary didn't help matters. "Vince Donelson had a knee injury to the patella tendon," said Daley. "Todd McMillan separated a shoulder and Terell Ulmer separated his shoulder. Terell came back in and finished, but he was way off his game with his shoulder hanging. We didn't get McMillan and Donelson back."

Cal Murphy summed it up. "The whole thing boils down to number two. When you have Flutie, that has to help. He's the guy who oils the engine, who gets it going. There were so many times there when you think you've got him and he comes out of it, just like when he had Pinball Clemens in the end zone. You think you've got him, and all of the sudden he flips the ball out to the side. It's just too much."

From the verge of extinction to the Grey Cup. For the Saskatchewan Roughriders, 1997 was a wonderful year. And, oh yes, they made money, too.

The more typical Saskatchewan nightmare occurred the following year. After opening the season with wins over Toronto and Edmonton and a loss to Montreal, they won only three more games the rest of the way, finishing 5–13, 8 points out of a play-off spot. Things started going wrong immediately. Jim Daley cut sure Hall of Famer Bobby Jurasin in favor of rookie R-Kal Truluck, who had a sensational game in the home opener against Toronto. Unfortunately he sustained a concussion and was out for the year.

The only bright spot for the Roughriders in 1998 was Don Narcisse, who became the leading receiver in CFL history. At the end of the season, Jim Daley was fired and replaced by offensive coordinator Cal Murphy.

Six games into the 1999 season, the Roughriders were 1–5 and the cries of anguish in the Wheat Province could be heard across the country. Quarterback

Reggie Slack had been suspended for missing the team flight to Hamilton. It was revealed a few days later that Slack had a medical addiction that had caused him to miss the plane. He had received treatment earlier in the year with the full knowledge of Allan Ford and Cal Murphy. Slack's replacement, Steve Sarkisian, struggled as a starter. Fans stayed away in droves to express their displeasure, placing the fragile franchise in danger of folding. Saskatchewan with the Roughriders? Unthinkable. But Cal Murphy had pointed out before the 1999 campaign that it had been 25 years since the Riders had finished first. If the team doesn't start winning, the unthinkable may become thinkable.

Meanwhile, in Ottawa a group interested in bringing the CFL back to the nation's capitol was confident of success.

CHAPTER 6

Calgary

Go Stamps Go!

AT EVERY GREY CUP SINCE 1948, CHUCK WAGONS, country bands, white Stetsons and pancake breakfasts have been a familiar site. Hosts of the annual Greatest Outdoor Show on Earth, the Stampede, Calgarians invented the Grey Cup Festival in 1948, when the West first challenged for national bragging rights. They know how to party.

With cowboys and Indians hootin' and hollerin', the wild westerners came east that year to show support for their beloved Stampeders. Whistle-stopping through Medicine Hat, Morse, Moose Jaw, Moosomin, Brandon, Bagot and Beausejour, through Burwash, Britt, Barnesdale, Barrie and on to Toronto, the Grey Cup Special picked up steam and turned the Canadian Rugby Union championship game into the nation's premier sporting event.

Although 49 Grey Cups have been played since then, the Stampeders have made it to the party they created only nine times, winning on four occasions.

In the 53-year history of the Calgary Stampeders, success has come in three distinct waves, the first soon after their creation, when they represented the West in Toronto in 1948–49. The second wave came between 1960 and 1971, when they made it to the national classic three times. The third has been the 90s. The Stampeders have owned the '90s with seven first-place finishes in nine years and four trips to the title game.

Senior football began in Calgary in 1909 when the Tigers joined the Alberta Rugby Union. The Calgary Canucks played during World War I, followed by the Fiftieth Battalion team formed in 1923. The Tigers were back from 1928–31, succeeded by the Altomahs and then the Bronks. The Calgary Stampeders were born September 29, 1945.

There was no league play that year, but Calgary beat Regina 3–1 and 12–0 in the semifinals before bowing 9–6 to Winnipeg and losing the right to represent the West in the Grey Cup.

Former Roughrider Dean Griffing was Calgary's first head coach. Under his direction the Stamps finished first in 1946 and second in 1948, both times losing the final to Winnipeg. He was succeeded by Les Lear, a rough and tough customer who had been in four Grey Cups with Winnipeg. Lear was the first Canadian to star in the National Football League, first with the Lions and then the Rams. He signed with Calgary for $8,000 a year.

Rather than fill his import quota with downy-cheeked collegians, Lear chose gnarly old pros: quarterback Keith Spaith, center Chuck Anderson, receiver Woody Strode and tackle John Aguirre. Lear picked up home-brew Winnipeg veterans Bert Iannone, Norm Hill, Harry Hood and Fritzie Hansen. Former Blue Bomber Dave Berry had signed with the team right after the war.

Berry explained how he became a Stampeder. "I played for Winnipeg, but when I came back after the war there was no place for my mother and father to live. My mother was in Lethbridge, where my dad was stationed during the war, and my dad was up in Calgary because he was working for the government. They couldn't get a house anywhere.

"I bumped into Pappy Rowe and Dean Griffing, and I told them the circumstances. They said if I decided to play with them they'd get me a house. I said, 'You get me the house and I'll play for you.' So they got me a veteran's home, which I was entitled to get.

"I played for the Stampeders under the regular system they had, which was that the money they made, they split up. For the whole season Pappy Rowe, Hal Harrison and I were the most expensive players on the team. We each made $47.50 for the whole season."

Barry enjoyed playing for his first Calgary coach, Dean Griffing. "He was a gentleman. He was hard as a rock, but he was a good man and a fair man. When you did things wrong, he let you know. When you did things right, he let you know. That's what I liked about him."

He didn't feel the same way about Griffings' replacement, Les Lear. "Let me put it this way: if I passed Les Lear on the street, I wouldn't say hello to him. If I found out he was putting on a coaching clinic a hundred miles away, I'd be the first guy there."

So he was a great coach but not a very good person? "That's a nice way to put it," Barry said. "He was tough and rough, but he was unfortunately a little dirty. He expected us to be the same way. I couldn't see it. Why the hell would you put a guy out of the game or put him out of football for life or some stupid thing? You clip him and you could put him out for life.

"Mind you, let us not say in the years I played that if someone did do something to me that I couldn't break even by the end of the season. I'd get him sometime—but to hurt him, not to maim."

Lear transformed the way the game was played, using, for example, a four-man line on defense. "When we pulled it against Ottawa," Berry recalled, "one of their linemen said, 'Where the hell are the rest of your guys?' I said, 'Come on through and you'll find them.'"

With quarterbacks like Frankie Albert, Eddie LeBaron, Eagle Day, Peter Liske, Jerry Keeling, Doug Flutie, Jeff Garcia and Dave Dickenson, the Stampeders have always been known as a passing team throughout their history. Lear began that tradition with Keith Spaith and Woody Strode. While other teams ran twice as much, as Berry explained, "Calgary, in essence, brought in the passing attack. The ratio between passing and running with us was 60–40. The other teams really hadn't seen a passing game like Spaith and Strode put on. The typical strategy was usually two bucks and a kick, or a run, a pass and a kick. We used the pass the way they do today."

Soon after, quarterbacks like Lindy Berry, Jack Jacobs and Glen Dobbs arrived on the CFL scene to counteract Calgary's considerable success.

In 1948 the Stampeders went undefeated, a record no other CFL team has equaled. (The only other professional football team to enjoy an undefeated season has been the 1972 Miami Dolphins.)

In going 12–0, the Stampeders outscored Saskatchewan and Winnipeg 218–61. Their only close calls came in three games against Saskatchewan, all won by a single point. In the first game of the Western Final, the Stamps and Riders played to a 4–4 tie. Calgary earned their first trip to the Grey Cup by winning the second game 17–6.

Dave Berry evaluated the 1948 team. "Half of them were veterans and half were rookies. I was 27. I was ancient. Woody Strode was 36, Spaith was getting along, Pappy Rowe, David Adams, Chick Chickowski, Bert Iannone—all those guys were in their late 20s or early 30s."

Another member of the 1948 team was the legendary halfback Fritzie Hansen, who Berry said, "was the greatest ballplayer this country has ever seen," even at the ripe old age of 35. "As a matter of fact, if he hadn't caught Saskatchewan's Gabe Patterson we wouldn't have gone to the Grey Cup. Patterson, who was only 22 years old, picked up a fumble and took off, and Fritzie took after him after giving him a 10-yard head start. He caught him on the 40-yard line. He could run, old Twinkle Toes. I loved him like a brother. It broke my heart when he died.

"Fritzie was the greatest football player we ever had!" Berry insisted. "Can you imagine what he'd have done in his youth if he had had unlimited blocking in front of him? He would have made records that would never have been broken."

Berry was Canadian football's first defensive specialist. "In '46 and '47 I played receiver, but in '48, when the new rule came in about unlimited substitution, because my eyes were going (I had to wear glasses and at that time you didn't wear glasses and play football) Les Lear said, 'How would you like to play defense—strictly defense?' I said, 'You've got it,' making me the first player in Canada to play only on defense. All the other guys played both ways.

"We had this rule whereby you could go in and out. So we got to the Grey Cup and we got into problems because the East didn't have that rule. The East and West then were absolutely separate leagues, and the East didn't have unlimited substitution.

"In the Grey Cup I had to report in one play before I went on. It could be second down with 20 yards to go, and I'd have to report in because I went in on the kick. If we made a first down I had to stay on. That's why in the Grey Cup I actually caught a pass when I was strictly a defensive end."

One of the rookies on the 1948 team was halfback Pete Thodos. A star with the junior Vancouver Merelomas, his lifelong friend recommended him to the Stampeders. Still, as he explained, it took a twist of fate to give Thodas a 10-year career in professional football.

"Rod Pantages went back to Calgary, and he was asked by Les Lear if he could recommend anybody, so he recommended me. It so happened I was on my way to a logging camp, but I went out with the boys the night before, so I missed the boat. Then this fellow called me and said they wanted me to come to Calgary to try out. I said, 'Fine.' If I hadn't missed the boat, I would have missed football. Strange, isn't it?"

Unlike Berry, Thodas spoke of Les Lear in glowing terms. "He was hard-nosed, rough, tough. What he said he meant. He'd always stick by his ballplayers. I thought he was terrific. A lot of people didn't like him, but I sure did.

"He was very innovative, coming up here with the forward pass system he had played under in the States. From then on, Canadian football became more of a passing game instead of two bucks and a kick."

In addition to his halfback duties, Thodas played defensive back and returned kickoffs and punts. He set a record for kickoff returns of 816 yards in 1952, including 219 yards against Winnipeg in a 41–20 losing cause October 5.

Thodas would handle the ball 12–15 times a game. "I wasn't a big star, just a little star," he said with a chuckle. As for playing both ways, he said, "Once you were on the field, you never left it. That's the way it was in those days. For the Grey Cup that year we were allowed to dress 19 people. There wasn't a lot of substitution."

He assessed the strengths of that 1948 Grey Cup team. "The strength was in the quarterback, Keith Spaith. He had a great arm. We had some veterans in Harry Hood, Paul Rowe, Rube Ludwick, Johnny Aguirre, Bert Iannone, Chuck Anderson and Woody Strode. They had some experience. Woody, Chuck, Johnny and Keith had played down in the States for different professional teams. Rube, Harry and Bert all played for Winnipeg prior to coming to Calgary. That was the nucleus, and then the team added the spice, if you will, in Pantages, Normie Kwong, Ced Gyles, Jimmy Mitchener, Normie Hill and me."

The train ride to Toronto and the Grey Cup game was an adventure in itself. "Every time we stopped," said Berry, "we got off the train and did calisthenics. I remember we stopped at one town and there must have been four feet of snow—it was snowing like hell—and we'd run from the end of the train to the engine and back and then do exercises until the old guys said, 'All aboard.' And then we got aboard.

"Wives went along (mine didn't because we had a bunch of kids at home), but the guys couldn't even talk to them until coming home. Once the game was over, the rules were out the door, so coming back was a little different. That was wild and woolly. But before that, no fooling around. You bunked with the team and you ate with the team and you stayed with the team. You didn't go running around looking for your wife or anybody else.

"We were billeted in a place called the Pig 'n' Whistle Inn out in Oakville," Thodas recalled. "We practiced at Appleby College. I think they had something like six or seven regulation football fields. They had quite a facility."

Thodas got a kick out of his coach's paranoia. "God, it was funny. Les Lear wouldn't allow planes to fly over our practice. He took us down to the basement in this school and he closed all the doors. The team was all down there, and he brought out film of an Ottawa game and we watched it. In those days you either didn't have film or weren't allowed to have film. I don't know which. Anyhow, we watched the film, and in particular we watched how Ottawa liked to pull that sleeper play. Of course, we pulled it on them."

The cuisine left much to be desired. "And then eating cheese sandwiches everyday. I can recall the guys all getting teed off with their cheese sandwiches. Chuck Anderson just said to hell with it, took off and left camp. They sent Bert Iannone after him to bring him back. We would have been without a center."

The Stampeders certainly weren't down east on a holiday. "We were on the field at 8:30 in the morning," said Thodas, "and we worked out until about 11:00. Then we went for lunch. Back on the field at 1:30 and off by 4:00. Friday afternoon we bussed in and stayed at the Royal York. We had horses and chuck wagons down there. We made pancakes on the street or the fans did. It sure woke that old town up. There was nothing in the lobby because they cleared all the furniture out after they were riding their horses in there."

Before the game began, said Berry, "We were told to play our game, play our position and don't get too many stupid penalties. That's all. Do it right and you'll win. Do it wrong and you'll lose."

The Stampeders did it right, winning the Grey Cup 12–7 on their first try over the favored Ottawa Rough Riders.

To score their first touchdown, the Stampeders gave the Riders a dose of their own medicine with the sleeper play that Ottawa had made famous. With a minute left in the first half, Spaith and Strode combined on a pass play to the Ottawa 14-yard line. Stampeder Norm Hill lay on the ground by the sideline when the team went into the huddle. When the ball was snapped Hill headed for the end zone. The ball hit Hill's hands and bounced in the air. A Rider defensive back knocked him flat on his back. The ball fell in his lap for the touchdown.

Said Thodas, "I was left halfback and Normie Hill was left end, so he'd be right beside me in the huddle. Johnny Aguirre, who was playing left tackle, was opposite me. We got back into the huddle and I said, 'Where the hell's Norm Hill?' And Johnny Aguirre grabbed me and said, 'Get your ass in the end position.' He pulled me where Norm would normally be standing. I said, 'What's going on?' and he said, 'He's out there sleeping it.' And I said, 'You've got to be joking.'

"Keith threw the ball and there he was. Johnny Aguirre knew it and nobody else. I think there was mud on the ball. It squirted and he popped it up. It finally fell into his arms and he sat down in the end zone."

Tony Golab kicked a single for Ottawa, making the score 6–1 for the West.

In the third quarter, Rider quarterback Bob Paffrath plunged over to give his team a 7–6 lead. Shortly after, the Stampeders capitalized on a lapse in judgment to set up the winning score. Paffrath threw an overhand lateral pass to Pete Karpuk, but it was wide. Karpuk thought it was an incompletion. Woody Strode picked it up and headed for the goal line.

Dave Barry recalled, "Woody set it up, but he didn't know it was a lateral pass. There were four of us there—the coach, me, Archie McGillis and another player—and we were screaming, 'Woody, pick it up, pick it up!' And he picked it up and took off. They were going to tackle him at about the 25 when he lateraled to Michener, who ran down to the 10-yard line. The next play the Rough Riders were so damn confused that Thodas just went bang, touchdown, right up the middle. He was a halfback, a good player and a nice guy."

Thodas looked back on his big Grey Cup moment. "Bob Paffrath threw the ball to Pete Karpuk. He thought it was a forward pass, which it wasn't. It was a lateral pass even though he threw it overhand. So the ball was still alive. Woody picked it up, started running and lateraled to Michener. I'm right beside Michener and I'm telling him to lateral it to me, but he swallowed it at the 10-yard line.

"Then they called an off-tackle play and I went across. I met Pete Karpuk on the goal line with the best straight-arm I ever made. Sportswriter Jim Coleman had me down as the best back of the day. I averaged 7.5 yards a carry and caught five for five. I had a good day."

In the 1948 Grey Cup, Normie Kwong was a wide-eyed rookie. Forty years later he would play a pivotal role in saving the Stampeders and the CFL. The Calgary native had played junior football with the North Hill Blizzard.

"I knew I wasn't going to start," he recalled, "but it still was an exciting time to be there. You hoped against all odds that you would play a lot. Of course, there were other veterans ahead of you at the time. I went in for about four plays. That was just because Les Lear made sure everybody got into the game so they could say they played in a Grey Cup. The following year, though, I started the game and played most of it."

Kwong admired his first pro coach. "Les Lear didn't have the assistant help that later people had. He operated largely on heart and was the most inspiring coach I had in my career."

Kwong remembered the origins of the Grey Cup festival. "I was part of the original start-up of Grey Cup week. We went down to Toronto ahead of the fans, of course, but we came back with them on the train.

"It was a really spontaneous time. Everything happened just because someone thought of it at the time. Nothing was planned. On the way back people met us at every little whistle stop along the way, and the coach made sure that one or two players were always there to greet the people no matter what time of night. There were people there right across Canada."

The Stampeders picked up where they left off the following year, winning 10 straight before finally losing 9–6 to Regina in Calgary. Along the way the Stamps set the still-standing record of 24 straight wins. Including postseason play, they had gone 27 games without a loss. They would win the rest of their 1949 regular season games, finishing the two years with a remarkable record of 23–1.

Berry down-played the streak. "There was the normal pressure to win. The coach didn't lay it on the line and say you've got to win this one because this is the twenty-seventh game. He said go out and win. We won 26 games before we lost, and we didn't lose again until the Grey Cup. We lost two games in two years."

"Going into the 1949 season, the papers started to play up the winning streak," recalled Thodas. "Just as soon as we lost one game we got panned to hell. I thought, 'What's this all about? You lose one game in 24 and get panned?' But that's the way they were. What are you going to do? You've got a team that is the Grey Cup champion and has gone on a winning streak, and I guess when you lose the big one they start panning you."

Calgary won the first game of the 1949 Western Final against Saskatchewan 18–12. They lost the return match 9–4 but took the series 22–21. Barely. With seconds left on the clock, Saskatchewan lined up for a chip-shot field goal that would win the right to go to the Grey Cup. Buck Rogers missed it. But wait. Les

Lear had gone off side, so the Riders had a second chance. This time former Stampeder Del Wardien would do the honors. He also missed. The Stampeders headed to Toronto to face the Montreal Alouettes.

The Varsity Stadium playing field, according to Dave Berry, was a mess. "It was muddy. It was really bad—slippin' and slidin' and goodness knows what."

Pete Thodas said, "There was only one patch where you could really get some traction and that's where the snow was. Whenever we had a chance we'd run down to the snow. The rest of it was really bad. It was melting and they didn't have a tarp on the field. It affected the play terribly in certain positions on the field because you couldn't get your footing. And the ball was sitting in a puddle and then Keith had to turn around and throw it. It had to be difficult."

Berry explained how field conditions helped determine the outcome. "We were on the Alouettes 10-yard line, and Harry Hood ran it right down to the 2. Riley Matheson had gone down and blocked a guy about 8 yards down the field. Conditions were so bad they slid another 5 yards and the referee called him for blocking over 10 yards. Even in the pictures it shows that he was only about 8 yards down the field when he hit the guy. The referee called it and that was the end of that."

Soon to be a living legend in Calgary, Ezzret "Sugarfoot" Anderson was in his first year as a Stampeder. Forty-eight years later he would still be a regular fixture in their dressing room. The Kentucky State graduate from Hot Springs, Arkansas, told how he came to Canada. "Woody Strode and Les Lear came down to Los Angeles and got me. They were looking for another end. I had retired after playing 10 years. I was in the Pacific Coast League and had gone over to the Rams to try out, but the guy over there told me I wouldn't make it. They had Hall of Famer Jim Denton, they had Crazy Legs Hirsch coming in from Chicago and Tom Fears was just getting out of school. So I went with Woody and Les Lear."

He, too, held his coach in the highest regard. "He was one of those top-notch coaches. I call him Canada's Vince Lombardi, a no-nonsense guy. Lear was the first Canadian to play in the NFL, a noseguard with the Rams. Lear was a playing coach in 1949. He played middle guard."

Naturally Sugarfoot went both ways. "I played end on both sides of the ball. I'm the first guy who crossed that line, who made All-Pro both ways. When we started the game, Les Lear would kiss us good-bye and say, 'I'll see you at the end of the game if they don't take you out on crutches.'"

Anderson, too, was unimpressed with the conditions at Varsity Stadium on Grey Cup game day. "The field was nothing but ice, and that affected us. You could only block 10 yards in those days. Harry Hood took the ball across the goal line, but Herb Trawick, a big tackle for Montreal, pulled John Aguirre into that zone. I told the referees what was happening but nothing was done.

"When you cross the goal and it's called back and you try again, nine out of 10 times you don't make it. Something happens. You miss the field goal or a guy drops a pass. That's what beat us in that game. We played on ice."

Montreal's great running back Virgil Wagner scored two touchdowns and Herb Trawick and Bob Cunningham one each to lead the Alouettes to a 28–15 win. Ches McCance added three converts and a field goal, Fred Kijek a single. Harry Hood and Sugarfoot Anderson scored Calgary's touchdowns. Vern Graham converted both. Keith Spaith kicked a single and Aguirre tackled Cunningham in the end zone for a safety touch.

Sugarfoot recalled his particular moment of Grey Cup glory. "There was a fumble on a pitchout coming my way. I knew this guy wanted to take me inside, so I just backed out and let him go inside and stepped around him. I read the quarterback's eyes, what he was looking at. He pitched out and the guy fumbled it. I just picked it up and ran 40 some yards for the touchdown."

That Grey Cup also was memorable for Normie Kwong but for another reason. "In 1949, when I went in, I was probably too nervous to be effective. That taught me to never choke up in big games. I was very fortunate to have Les Lear as a coach because he told me that he thought I had froze in that game. From that moment on I made up my mind that I would never choke in a big game, and I don't think I ever did."

Years later, Dave Berry was still steaming about the officials. "At the start of the second half, Montreal kicked to us. It was a short kick and Normie Hill went for the ball. One of their players tripped him and another one fell on the ball. That's interference. You can't do that. But the referee let it go. We argued like hell, so we got a 15-yard unsportsmanlike conduct penalty tacked on, so that they ended up on our 10-yard line. That was the winning touchdown, by the way. If you look it up you'll find that the same guy made both calls, and he never umpired again.

"I'm not saying for one second that we should have won the game," Berry continued. "I'm just saying the referee shouldn't have won it. You can't take anything away from the Alouettes as a team. Virgil Wagner was a great player. So was Herb Trawick."

What about Alouette quarterback Frank Filchock? "He had a hell of a game," said Thodas. "But he was not only great offensively, he was fantastic on defense. On one play I'd come out from left half, gone down the field and broke out to the left, and he covered me like a blanket. If he hadn't I would probably have made a first down because I was only a yard or two short, but he just enveloped me. I couldn't make it. That was second down. If I had made it, we would have had the ball on their 15-yard line and who knows what would have happened? Filchock was the difference in the 1949 Grey Cup, no question about it."

Sugarfoot Anderson described the trip to Toronto and back. "We went down to Toronto and back with the fans on the train. We had a bar car and a dance car. They took horses and cows to Toronto for the parade and they rode their horses into the Royal York Hotel. On our way back we stopped in Medicine Hat and some fans let all the horses and cows out. We were delayed there three or four hours while they rounded them all up and got them back on the train.

"We had a great time. I'll never forget it. There were thousands of people at the station when we got back to Calgary. You'd think we had won the game. It really shook me up. They closed the schools and the town down."

What kind of bonus did he get for playing in the Grey Cup? "I'll tell you what kind of bonus we got. Do you remember those old Hudson Bay coats? His and hers? The ones with the red, black and yellow stripes? That's what we got. And we got a little bitty old ring from People's Credit Jewellers. Wasn't nothing to write home and tell nobody about. I think it had a 15-point diamond on it."

Woody Strode and Sugarfoot Anderson were the first blacks to play in Calgary. Anderson had few encounters with racism though he recognized that his status as a football player affected peoples' attitudes. "For example, our country club here didn't allow Jewish or black people," he said, "but they said Woody and I could come. That kind of struck me as a little odd and I never did go. If I hadn't been a Stampeder, they wouldn't have let me in, so I just didn't go. Coming from Arkansas, nothing that happened to me in Calgary was anything to write home about."

"In Canadian football," said Berry, "the players didn't give a damn if you were red, white, yellow, pink or black as long as you pulled your weight. Winnipeg was kind of strange, though. One year they wouldn't let one of the Negro players in the hotel. Coach Les Lear said, 'He doesn't stay here, nobody stays here.' That ended the argument."

Ten Lost Years

The 1950s were the decade of the damned for the Stampeders when the team missed the play-offs every year but 1952 and 1957, and when they managed a winning percentage of only .346. Lowlights of that lost decade included trading Normie Kwong to Edmonton in 1951 for Reg Clarkson, who didn't last a season in Calgary, as well as coming to the conclusion that Johnny Bright was injury prone and shipping him to Edmonton in 1954. The China Clipper played 10 seasons in Eskimo livery, Bright 11. Together they gained 18,735 yards, scored 146 touchdowns and won three Grey Cups for the Green and Gold.

One of the best all-round athletes in history, Johnny Bright arrived in Calgary in 1952. The native of Fort Wayne, Indiana, was All-State in high school football, track and basketball. At Drake University he set 20 football, basketball and track records. He was the leading rusher in U.S. college football and was the first draft choice of the 1951 Philadelphia Eagles. He played pro basketball with the Harlem Globetrotters. He pitched a no-hitter in the World Professional Fastball Tournament.

Johnny Bright led the Western Conference in rushing four times, including his rookie year, 1952. He won the Schenley in 1959. He was an All-Star six times. Only Saskatchewan's George Reed ran farther, but Bright played in an era when players went both ways.

At Drake University, Bright was the victim of one of the ugliest racial incidents in the history of American collegiate sports, when he was the first black to play in a football game against Oklahoma. The Sooners expressed their resentment by deliberately smashing his jaw. Because there were no Oklahoma hospitals that would admit a black man, he had to endure an all-night train ride back to Des Moines, Iowa, before he could receive treatment. A photographer won a Pulitzer Prize for his picture of the incident.

After missing the play-offs two years in a row, the Stampeders opened the vault to sign him. When the Eagles wouldn't even come close to Calgary's offer, Bright came to Canada. Although happy and fulfilled north of the 49th, he regretted not playing in the NFL. "If I harbor one doubt in my mind as an athlete, it is not having played in the NFL," he said. "And, you know, whenever you do something, you want to do the big apple, the biggest, whether you are accepted or not.

"I played with Hugh McEleney, Frank Gifford and Ollie Matson in the East–West Game," Bright continued, "and I received as many votes as any of those guys did for the outstanding player award. They went on and became All-Pros in the NFL. There is no doubt in my mind that I could have performed as well in the NFL as they did.

"But certain situations develop in your life. Certain uncontrollable, unforeseen things happen, and you are channeled in a direction that you have no control over. Then sometimes, when you try to change that direction, you're at the point where it is too late. Things have gone against you."

The ultimate, tragic example of Johnny Bright's recognition of the role of the unforeseen came in 1983 when he entered an Edmonton hospital to have an irritating bone chip removed from his knee, injured during his playing days as an Eskimo. On December 14, at age 53, he died of a sudden, massive coronary while being administered an aesthetic prior to surgery. The medical examiner's office said he died of cardiac arrhythmia, an irregular heart beat caused by blocked arteries. An autopsy had revealed Bright's heart was double the normal size.

Two months before his unexpected demise, Bright had been operated on by orthopedic surgeon Dr. John Huckell, who terminated the procedure because arthritis caused by an old football injury made the joint too tight to treat. Bright had agreed to a second operation because the injury was interfering with his normal life.

The circumstance of Johnny Bright's death was typical of the life led by this extraordinary athlete and individual. Never content to do anything at less than full speed, he had to have the knee fixed so his body could keep up with his mind. Battling the odds all his life, full of determination and optimism, it was no surprise to those who knew him that he had a heart twice the normal size. Given what he had to overcome, Johnny Bright had to have twice the heart of ordinary men just to survive. It was also typical of his life that, in the end, he was done in by an incredible stroke of bad luck, the kind of luck that dogged him throughout his illustrious career.

Though Bright was, after all, an All-American, a Harlem Globetrotter, a no-hit pitcher in a world championship, an All-Star football player, a Schenley Award winner, a successful coach, and a respected educator and a beloved citizen of his community, he was in many ways a tragic figure. He was a giving, loving man whose marriage ended in failure. He was acknowledged as one of the greatest football players who ever lived on either side of the border, but he felt his achievements as an athlete weren't really appreciated. No matter what he accomplished, it was always in some way flawed. His life was one of triumph and tragedy.

His upbringing in an Indiana ghetto shaped his life. With an ironic chuckle, he described his formative years. "I would probably say the one advantage that I find in my life is the things I had to learn growing up in a slum area, where you had to fight to get to school if you wanted to go because you were an uppity kind of guy if you were looking for an education. In the slum you didn't do that. You hung around the street corner, and you went out and mugged somebody or you stole at night. That was your group identity, and anybody who didn't do that was ousted or became a different kind of guy.

"And somehow that wasn't my cup of tea. I knew that even at the age of 10 or 11. As far as the gang I ran with, I put certain limitations on what I would get involved in. It became a very disheartening thing because I was actually ostracized by a lot of guys as I grew up. But consequently it paid a dividend for me. I had been used because I liked people, because I was easy going. I felt that all people were good and decent. That lulled me to sleep.

"I learned the lesson of being able to be down, kicked and come back, and try again and keep a little self-pride and self-dignity and go on and win."

Although victimized by racism in Canada on many occasions, Bright rejected the notion that the overt racism of the Deep South was somehow preferable to the sneaky, covert kind in Canada because at least you knew where you stood. "I never felt in the northern states or in Canada that my life was in danger, but that wasn't the case down south. There they'd kill you and throw your body in a swamp for being a different color."

Bright was content in Calgary, but bad luck led to his trade to Edmonton. "When I first went there in 1952," he recalled, "I was Calgary's golden boy, and I could do no wrong. But I went through a series of unfortunate and uncontrollable situations such as receiving a ruptured appendix during a game for which I had to have an emergency operation.

"During the off-season I used to dive quite a bit competitively, and I hit the water at the edge of the pool wrong and I dislocated the caps of my shoulder. In May I had to play with a chain on my shoulder, and consequently I damaged that shoulder quite severely during those 16 games of the CFL season. I had to have an operation on it.

"Sportswriters claimed those were football injuries. Suddenly I—who had played sandlot, junior high, high school and college and had never been injured except for that Oklahoma situation—became, in their words, injury prone.

"So all of a sudden, the Messiah (if that's the correct expression) who would lead Calgary out of the wilderness was not functional as far as the football public was concerned. Prior to that my time in Calgary was deluxe. I still have a very, very warm spot for Calgary. I never lost it."

Soon after the end of the 1952 campaign, the football world was saddened to learn of the death of halfback Harry Hood. "Hood was 25 when he died," said Dave Berry. "He and I were very good friends. Whenever we went on the road, he and I would sit down with Mickey Hajash and Mel Wilson and play bridge. We'd play bridge for hours.

"I played against him in high school. When I was with the RCAF Blue Bombers, he was with the United Service team, and I played against him again. He played during '46 and '47 with Winnipeg, and in 1948 he came with us. I was never so happy in my life. I got tired chasing that guy all over the field. He was an excellent ballplayer. If he had lived, he would have made the Hall of Fame, no doubt about it."

"He had cancer," recalled Thodas. "Very strange. Harry Hood was a nice guy, but he palled around with Keith. They had their own little group. Other than practice and games, Rod Pantages and I never saw him socially. Anyhow, he came out to Vancouver and was staying at the Georgia Hotel. He phoned both of us up and asked us to come on down. We said fine and went down.

"We wondered why we weren't going out for dinner or a drink. We just sat in his room. He started talking about the past, the Grey Cups in '48 and '49. Then he started talking about his father, who passed away from stomach cancer. I said, 'Oh, gee, that's too bad.'

"That's all the conversation there was. The next thing I know, he's back in Calgary and he's in the hospital and he's got cancer of the stomach. I phoned Rod and said, 'Isn't that amazing? I guess he came out here knowing he's going to pass away, knowing he can't beat it, and he's going around saying good-bye to everybody.

"Ten years later Rod and I are out of town and Les Lear phones. He's in town and phones Mamie Pantages and my wife, Marjorie, asking for us. He says, 'Well, tell them I came to say hello. I'll be back in a couple of weeks and I'll get in touch with them.' He never did call back, and he died, too, about two months later."

Hood's is one of five Stampeder retired numbers. The others belong to Willie Burden, Tom Forzani, Wayne Harris and Stu Laird. Les Lear was inducted posthumously into the CFL Hall of Fame May 6, 1974.

Lear was fired after the 1952 campaign, replaced in turn by Bob Snyder, Harry Seimering, Jack Hennemier and Otis Douglas, who was given the pink slip in 1960 on the team's way to the play-offs.

Pete Thodas remembered Bob Snyder well. "We were playing Edmonton, and they were using the Split-T. He tried every type of defense he could, but nothing worked. Apparently he was on a first-name basis with Frank Leahy of Notre Dame. He kept phoning Frank, who would tell him to do this or do that. Finally he phoned Frank and said, 'Nothing's worked. What should I do?' He said, 'The only thing I can tell you is use the Split-T against them and see how they defense it.'"

Calgarians were full of optimism going into 1953 because of the signings of San Francisco 49er great Frankie Albert at quarterback and promising rookie running back John Henry Johnson. Johnson won the Jeff Nicklin Memorial Trophy as the player in the Western Conference deemed most valuable to his team. He left at the end of the season for a Hall of Fame career in the NFL with the Pittsburgh Steelers. Albert also left, in his case after an abysmal year. Eddie LeBaron, another NFL veteran, replaced him with equally unimpressive results.

In 1954 Stampeder fullback Howard Waugh ran for 1,043 yards, becoming the first player in CFL history to rush for over 1,000 yards.

Four games into the 1956 season, Hennemeir was fired, replaced by Otis Douglas, who kept the job until two games into the 1960 season when New York Giant legend Steve Owen took over. Douglas never had a winning season with the Stampeders although he did make the play-offs in 1957. That year General Manager Bob Masterson punched player Harvey Wylie on the train to Winnipeg. Club president Red Dutton went to Winnipeg, fired Masterson and installed Jim Finks in his place.

Finks would stay until 1965, when he left for the National Footbal League, where he turned the Minnesota Vikings into perennial champions before rebuilding the Chicago Bears and guiding the New Orleans Saints into the only successful period the team enjoyed. While at the helm of the Stampeders, he assembled the team that would appear in three Grey Cups in four years, proving once again that the key to football success is the man occupying the front office.

A Glimmer of Hope

The decade of the 1960s began on a high note when the Stampeders moved into McMahon Stadium. Under the direction of Frank and George McMahon, financing was raised, and in 103 days the stadium went from the sod-turning to completion. The team playing at the new facility was a contender with Joe Kapp at quarterback and Lovell Coleman, Earl Lunsford and Gene Filipski in the backfield. Lunsford won the Western Interprovincial Football Union rushing title with 1,323 yards. Tony Pajaczkowski and Don Luzzi were All-Star linemen, and Harvey Wylie made the dream team at safety. The Stamps finished third, losing the semifinal round to Edmonton 70–28.

Kapp's life and career had almost come to an end the year before. A ritual of all training camps is rookie night, when the newcomers have to sing a song or entertain in some way to the hoots of derision of the veterans. At the 1959 rookie night, Kapp and Doug Brown got into an argument and Brown cut the rookie's face open with a broken beer bottle. Brown came within an inch of his jugular and it took the team doctor hours to remove the glass and sew him up.

Despite making the play-offs, Coach Steve Owen was fired, replaced by Glen Dobbs' brother, Bobby. It was a year of controversy with several players walking out of training camp, upset with the severity of Dobbs' approach. Later on, All-Star Clare Exelby demanded to be traded, and Joe Kapp, Ron Morris and Ernie Warlick refused to sign new contracts. Exelby and Morris ended up in Toronto, Warlick played out the season and went to Buffalo of the American Football League and Kapp was traded to B.C. for Bruce Claridge and Ed O'Bradovich. Kapp's successor was Jerry Keeling, who would quarterback the team to victory in the 1971 Grey Cup. Before that he would be displaced by two other pivots, Eagle Day and Peter Liske. During that time Keeling made the All-Star team as a defensive back five times.

Joining the Stampeders in 1961 along with Keeling were Larry Robinson, who won the Rookie of the Year Award, and Wayne Harris, who became the greatest linebacker in CFL history. Harris made the All-Star team that year for the first of 11 consecutive seasons.

Earl Lunsford set a new CFL rushing record of 1,794 yards that same year but didn't win the Schenley. In fact he wasn't even the West's nominee, that honor going to Jackie Parker. Tony Pajaczkowski won for Most Outstanding Lineman.

The 1961 Stampeders finished third, advancing to the final by beating

Edmonton 27–26 on the round. But they were no match for the Blue Bombers, losing two straight by a combined score of 57–15.

On to 1962. At 9–6–1, the Stampeders had their best record since 1949, finishing three points behind the Bombers. After demolishing Saskatchewan in the two-game semifinal 43–7, they beat Winnipeg 20–14 in the opening game of the final, losing game two in Winnipeg 20–11, setting up game three and the most heartbreaking moment in Calgary Stampeder history.

The author of that moment was Calgary native Harvey Wylie, who had joined the Stamps in 1956. He made the Western All-Star team as a defensive back five straight years, 1959–63, and was All-Canadian in '62 and '63. He won the Schenley for Outstanding Canadian in 1962. Wylie ranks eighth all-time in kickoff return yardage and returns. He still holds the record for most touchdowns on kickoffs with five. He was elected to the CFL Hall of Fame May 24, 1980. Harvey Wylie was a great football player. Unfortunately he is best remembered for the last game of the 1962 Western Final.

With less than a minute to go and Calgary leading 7–6, Jim Furlong punted for the Stampeders. He was knocked flying, but no penalty was called. If the flag had come down, the Stamps would have had a first down and had a chance to run out the clock. Instead the Bombers marched to the Calgary 10-yard line. On the last play of the game, Winnipeg's Gerry James tried a 17-yard field goal.

Furlong managed to deflect it wide into the end zone. Instead of falling on the ball and conceding the point or picking it up to punt it out, Wylie kicked the ball right into Farrell Funston, who fell on it for the game-winning touchdown. The final score was Winnipeg 12, Calgary 7.

Postseason misfortune continued the following year when the second-place 10–4–2 Stampeders demolished Saskatchewan 35–9 in the first game of the two-game semifinal series in Calgary. Even Saskatchewan fans thought the situation hopeless, leaving Taylor Field half empty for the opening kickoff. By half time, cars were streaming toward the ball park from all over the city, and the Riders were playing in front of a full house by the time the fourth quarter began. Pulling off one of the greatest comebacks in football history, the Roughriders rallied to beat Calgary 39–12, winning the series 48–47 and handing the Stampeders another crushing disappointment. Along Calgary's Eighth Avenue the word *choke* began to creep into coffee shop discussions.

Earl Lunsford retired before the 1964 season. During his distinguished six-year career, he became Calgary's leading rusher and the tenth-leading rusher in

CFL history with 6,994 yards. His average of 1,165 yards per season is third behind Mike Pringle's 1,275 and George Reed's 1,240. On Labour Day 1962 the "Earthquake" scored five touchdowns against the Eskimos. Lunsford won the rushing title twice and was an All-Star three times. He ranks twelfth in rushing touchdowns with 55 and fifth in 100-yard games with 28. His 1,283 yards in 1956 represent the third-best rushing performance by a rookie. Lunsford would go on to be the general manager of the Blue Bombers and Stampeders. He was elected to the CFL Hall of Fame on May 13, 1983.

The Stampeders had a tremendous 1964 season, going 12–4, but still finished second to the powerful B.C. Lions. After getting revenge by routing the Roughriders 76–40 on the semifinal round, they lost to the Leos in three games.

On September 10, 1964, GM Jim Finks resigned to become the general manager of the Minnesota Vikings. Director Pat Mahoney took over as acting general manager. Bobby Dobbs coveted the position. At the end-of-the-season team party, President George McMahon announced that Rogers Lehew, Finks' assistant, would be the new general manager. Dobbs got up almost immediately, made his way to the microphone and quit. He was succeeded by the cerebral Jerry Williams.

Calgary repeated their 12–4 performance in 1965, this time finishing first for the first time in 16 years. Winnipeg beat Saskatchewan in the semifinal and headed for Calgary, where they lost 27–9. The Bombers won the next two games 15–11 and 19–12 to advance to the Grey Cup for the sixth time in nine years. Another great season had ended in frustration for the Calgary Stampeders.

Bomber coach Bud Grant conceded that for most of the 1965 season the Stampeders were the better team, but come play-off time the Bombers were the best. Stampeder receiver Herm Harrison agreed. "Calgary did that a lot. They'd come out of the chute and play hard all year, but for some reason, when the play-offs came, they would tighten up. I just couldn't believe it. Even in my first year I was hearing all the stories. All I heard was Harvey Wylie, Harvey Wylie. And I'm thinking, 'God, this guy's an All-Star who makes one bad play and everybody talks about it.' They still talk about that play today."

Harrison told how he joined the Stampeders in 1964. "I was actually too small to play in the NFL. When I graduated from college, I was about 170 pounds. And they said, 'Herm, we'd like to use you as a tight-end, but you're just too small.'

"So Rogers Lehew, who had been down in my senior year and put me on Calgary's negotiating list, said, 'Herm, you can play in Canada.'

"I came up as a wide receiver and almost didn't make the team. The coach said, 'Herm, we've got to let you go. We've got Pete Manning and Bobby Taylor. We just can't use you. I asked, 'What position are you looking to replace?' He said, 'We need linebackers.' I said, 'Look, I've got one week left. Will you try me at linebacker?' He said, 'All right, come see me this afternoon.' I went out and Dobbs taught me some things. We had a scrimmage that afternoon. He was really impressed with me in the scrimmage. He said, 'Herm, I want you to really concentrate on learning this.' And that's how I ended up making the team.

"The next year Bruce Claridge, who was the tight-end, popped his collarbone and Eagle Day said to the coach, Jerry Williams, 'You've got to put Herm in.' Eagle Day and I always practiced together when everybody would leave the field. 'But he's playing linebacker.' Eagle said, 'He can do both.'

"I went the last seven games both ways. Then Jerry Williams said to me, 'Herm, when you come back next year, I'm not sure where I'm going to play you. I'll have you play the first half on offense and the second half on defense.

"Opening up the second half in a game against Regina, Ronnie Lancaster did a half-roll away and threw back across the field. I picked it off, went down the sideline and scored. I remember the coach saying to me when I walked over to him, 'You're really making this difficult, aren't you?' He said, 'Know your linebacking duties. Don't forget them, but I've got to play you at tight-end. With those hands you're just too valuable to us.' So they kept me at tight-end."

"Ham Hands" Harrison went on to become All-Western six times and an All-Canadian three. He was inducted into the CFL Hall of Fame in 1993. In nine seasons the Arizona State graduate caught 443 passes for 6,693 yards and 43 touchdowns.

In 1965 linebacker Wayne Harris won his first Schenley for Outstanding Lineman. He had been runner-up to John Barrow in 1962. He would win again in 1966, '70 and '71. He recalled how he came to the Stampeders. "I was drafted by the Boston Patriots and put on Calgary's negotiation list for the CFL," he said. "I had a friend who played up here, Donny Stone, and I also knew a trainer at the University of Arkansas who at the time worked up here in training camp with Otis Douglas. That was long before me, but he sort of recommended Calgary. I talked to Donny somewhat about it. He said it was a great league to play in. I didn't really want to go East, I liked the West better, so we packed our things up and came to Calgary."

Harris had been nicknamed Thumper in high school in El Dorado,

Arkansas. Asked about his strengths as a player, he replied, "I don't know. I felt I had real good fundamentals coaching when I started playing football in high school. A lot of things you do on the field become reaction things. I think that was from the coaching and the techniques I picked up, trying to read the triangle, as it was referred to back in those days, amongst the running backs. I didn't read the offensive line that much. I played the football. I was always looking into the backfield. I had great leg strength.

"I was a fairly quiet type of guy and still am, I guess. I was never a big rah, rah fan. I encouraged guys to play the best they could. I didn't overstress it like some people do."

Harris led by example and became defensive quarterback. "Under Jeff Thompson and Bobby Dobbs I called all the plays. Then, when Jerry Williams took over, well, basically, we got some calls in from Dick Monroe."

"In all my years I never played with or against a linebacker who, pound for pound, was as good as Wayne Harris," said Herm Harrison. "He was unbelievable. He wrote down everything on every player. He started me doing that. When I was playing defense my first year, he had me watching every running back, what hand he put down, how much his weight was shifted forward or sideways, and I recorded it all. I watched them. That's why sometimes you could yell, 'It's coming here,' or 'It's going up the middle' because they tipped it off out of habit. Wayne had everything written down. That's what made him so good. He did his homework."

What Wayne Harris probably had was a photographic memory. While it was true he knew all his opponents' tendencies, he insisted that he never wrote anything down.

From the time Wayne Harris arrived until the present day, the Stampeders have always been strong defensively. Number 55 described their defense of the '60s and early '70s. "We had a unique defense, I think. We played a lot of what we called a 5–3 or 4–3. The 4–3, which came the '50s, was really a great defense for the running game. We did a lot of stunts off the 4–3. Then we shifted to the 5–3 and 5–2. You had a great mixture of running game—not just strictly passing. Quite a bit of it was a running game."

Not so much in Calgary. Although Lovell Coleman averaged nearly 1,500 yards rushing between 1963–65, the leading Cowboy rushers to the end of the decade averaged only 534 yards per season. The Stampeders lived and died with the pass. The numbers are instructive. In 1966 Peter Liske threw for 2,177 yards, the next year for 4,479 and the year following for 4,333. With superb receivers like Terry Evanshen, Gerry Shaw and Herm Harrison, the Stamps put on a dazzling aerial circus every time they played. Their ground attack was practically nonexistent.

Harrison evaluated the three quarterbacks he played with. "The quarterback that made me was Eagle Day. Eagle was the one who talked them into putting me at tight-end because no one had really seen me in action catching but him.

"But Pete Liske was the kind of quarterback who would say, 'Okay, Herm, what would you like to do today?' And I used to always say, 'Just throw deep to me once.' Everybody thought I was too slow to really go deep. He said, 'Herm, I just can't do it right now. We don't have that much time for you to get deep.'

"But in 1968, on my birthday, we were playing Saskatchewan. He said, 'Herm, today you can do anything you want.' He threw deep to me and I caught it. I said, 'I told you I could get deep.' And he said, 'I was afraid of that. Now you're going to want to go deep all the time.'

"Liske was the kind of guy who would say, 'I'm going to try something.' He didn't follow form. He'd just say, 'Okay, what can you do?' I'd tell him and he threw it.

"Each of those quarterbacks threw a different ball. Jerry Keeling threw a heavy ball. When that ball came in there, you'd better be waiting for it because it was a heavy ball. Pete threw a floater that would hit your hands very softly. Eagle Day could thread a needle. Anything up to 15 yards he could thread a needle. He was that accurate. He said, 'Herm, all you need is one step and I'll have the ball there.' So each had his little individual techniques and I enjoyed them all. I really did enjoy them all."

The top five passers in Stampeder history are Doug Flutie, Jeff Garcia, Peter Liske, Jerry Keeling and Eagle Day.

The 1966 Stampeders slipped back to fourth place and out of the play-offs. Running backs Ted Woods and Coleman were lost for the season with Achilles tendon problems. Jim Furlong, Harrison and Shaw missed several games as well. Day had such a poor season that he was released in favor of Liske.

The club bounced back in 1967, finishing on top with a record of 12–4. After winning the first game of the finals against Saskatchewan 15–11 in Calgary, the teams returned to Regina for one of the coldest play-off games on record, one in which disaster struck for Calgary, when Terry Evanshen broke his leg. The event proved to be a turning point.

"Terry could go deep," said Harrison. "He was so elusive. Without him we didn't have that deep threat. When he got hurt it seemed like the morale of the team just went down. Up until that point we were right in the game, putting pressure on them, everything. But when the injury occurred, you could see heads dropping.

"And that's one thing the coach said. 'Look, I know we're missing Terry, but you've got to be able to carry this thing on without him. But it was just tough for a lot of guys to get up."

Said Wayne Harris, "That was one of the coldest games I can recall playing. There was a lot of snow on the field. It had been warm during the day before, and it melted and started freezing at night. It was kind of like a skating rink out there but with a lot of moisture so you got completely wet. With the wind factor the temperature was like 40 below." The Stamps lost 11–9.

Back in Calgary for game three, George Reed carried 35 times for 201 yards to lead the Roughriders to victory. Denied again, the Stampeders prepared for 1968.

The only bright spot of the 1967 campaign was winning two Schenleys, Evanshen for Outstanding Canadian and Liske for Most Outstanding. Jerry Williams was Coach of the Year.

The 1967 campaign marked the first of five straight Calgary–Saskatchewan Western Finals. Wayne Harris loved those years. "I really enjoyed those games. Saskatchewan probably had the best team in the CFL during that period of time. We always gave them a battle. I never did go back to see how many games we won. (Including play-offs, Calgary was 12–13–1) It seemed like they may win the close ones, but then we'd come back and kick the heck out of them the next game. They had a great offensive line and, of course, George Reed, Ron Lancaster and Hugh Campbell. They were a very balanced football team, very strong.

"If you selected an All-Star offensive line, you wouldn't have a better line than what they had in those days," Harris observed. "We had a good team, too, and we always had a lot of good tussles with them. They offered that challenge to us. A lot of times we were successful and other times we weren't. But we had some good battles."

Calgary's Jim Furlong agreed. "They had a tremendous football team. They were always hard-hitting. We used to go out there and try to beat each other's heads in. But strangely enough, they were always clean games. No cheap shots."

"I used to say," said Harrison, "if they ever wanted to sell the CFL to the U.S. they should have taken some of those games and put them on video and sent them to all the major networks. It would have been an unbelievable showing for Canada."

Going into 1968 the Stampeders had not won the Grey Cup in 20 years and had gone 19 years since playing in one. Losing three of their last four games to finish with a record of 10–6, the Stampeders hardly looked like the team that would end the drought, especially since they led the league in team losses while having the fewest yards rushing and on kickoff returns. But they peaked at the right time.

In the sudden-death semifinal, they dispatched the Eskimos 29–13. Then they went into Regina and walloped the 12–3–1 Roughriders 32–0. Back home at McMahon Stadium, they took the Riders into overtime, winning 25–12.

Return to Glory

Facing Ottawa in the 1968 Grey Cup, the Stampeders outpassed the Riders 258 yards to 185 and enjoyed a big edge in first downs, 24–13. But Ottawa had the only edge that counted: on the scoreboard.

Peter Liske propelled Calgary into a 14–4 lead during the first half by capping off a drive with a 1-yard plunge for a touchdown and completing a 21-yard pass to Evanshen for the other one. In the first quarter Wayne Giardino broke through to block a Calgary punt. A Stampeder fell on the ball in the end zone, conceding a single point. Ottawa's Don Sutherin added a 27-yard field goal a few minutes later.

Early in the third quarter, the Riders smothered Calgary punter Ron Stewart at midfield, taking over on downs. Russ Jackson engineered a drive down to the 1-yard line, where he scored Ottawa's first touchdown of the game. They missed the convert. Soon after, Jackson pitched out to Vic Washington, who dropped the ball. It bounced right back into his hands, and he scampered 80 yards for a touchdown. Jackson closed out the Ottawa scoring by combining with Margene Atkins on a 70-yard pass and run for a major. In the fourth quarter, Calgary's Dick Suderman recovered a Bo Scott fumble, setting up a Liske to Evanshen touchdown. The final score was Ottawa 24, Calgary 21.

The key play for Ottawa was the run for a touchdown by Vic Washington. Jackson thought that when the ball came loose, the Stampeders hesitated for a second, allowing Washington to run by them. Wayne Harris somewhat disagreed. "They were running a sweep play. The ball was dropped and came back up into his hands almost immediately. Washington had a lot of speed. Evidently our defensive backs reacted to the fumble and probably came up. The ball came up and, well, he deked them and was gone."

After leading by 10 points at the half, Calgary had let Ottawa off the hook. "Washington's touchdown sort of got them coming back," explained Harris. "And they had a super football team. Russ Jackson was a great quarterback, a very good ball handler. He could hide a football better than any quarterback I'd seen or played against. It was very hard to follow the ball the way he handled it. He was very smart, and he was a good running quarterback."

Calgary was in no shape to play Ottawa or anyone else. Their running back Dave Cranmer had been injured in the play-offs. His replacement, Rudy Linterman, went out with torn knee ligaments in the first quarter, and Herm Harrison also was playing with an injury. If all that wasn't bad enough, a third of the team came down with the flu. If it hadn't been for bad luck, Calgary wouldn't have had any luck at all.

"None at all," moaned Harrison, "none at all. There were a lot of guys not feeling good. It was unbelievable. I broke five ribs in the first five minutes of the game. I still tried to play, but it just wasn't there. I was surprised that we held our own as well as we did."

Harrison was the leading receiver in the league that year catching 67 for 1,306 yards. His inability to perform was a severe blow.

At the end of the season, Liske and Coach Jerry Williams signed with the Philadelphia Eagles. Harrison was sorry to see Williams go. He had relied on the leadership of his ballplayers and allowed for their input. "That's exactly the way he was," Harrison said. "Jerry Williams, bless his heart, was just one of those kinds of guys. Even the racial things that existed—Jerry would separate that. He'd have a meeting and say, 'I've got to find out what's happening. How do you guys feel?' He talked about it. We thought he was just coming to the black guys, but he was talking to the white guys, too. Then he'd get us all together and say, 'I've had this meeting with both of you. Everything seems to be okay.' If there was a problem, he'd say, 'Let's address it now,' which I thought was just perfect.

"Williams was innovative," Harrison continued. "He was the one who started splitting the tight-end out, making him an integral part of the receiving corps. Most of the tight-ends in the league at that time were always in tight.

"I remember going into Montreal and playing against John Baker. In the first quarter he had my nose all bleeding. Coach Williams said, 'Move out a little bit more and see just how far he's going to come with you.' So I moved out 10 yards and he came out about 8. Williams said, 'A-ha!' and started to change the plays. We began to run on Montreal and killed them because the guy was trying to get out to me.

"Then Williams said in the second half, 'Herm, go way out—18–20 yards.' That was something Montreal hadn't seen before. The next game he had incorporated me into that entire system. That's the way he was. He was very, very bright.

"You know what else he did that was really unique? He would put four basic defenses on the board, call all the receivers in (anybody who had anything to do with the ball) and say, 'I want you to design any play you can that would beat these defenses. I'll use it in a game.' We had plays like the Harrison Special, the Shaw Special, the Evanshen Special.

"Evanshen Special on two—everybody knew it because we ran it in practice. Williams said, 'If you can beat the defense in practice, you can beat the other team on the field.' That was Williams' attitude. I respected the man so much for that.

"He'd come to me and say, 'Herm, what can you do?' I'd tell him and he'd go right to the quarterback and tell him to throw it to me. Bingo.

"He was so smart. He used to say things and Granny Liggins used to say, 'Coach, can you break that down a little bit more?' Williams was using all these big lawyer terms and Granny would say, 'Coach, what does that mean?' Williams would explain and Granny would say, 'Coach, how come you don't say it like that in the first place?' He was always teasing Jerry about that."

Williams was succeeded by Jim Duncan, an assistant from the staff of Eagle Keys. As hard-nosed and down to earth as Williams was cerebral, Duncan nonetheless achieved impressive results, making two trips to the Grey Cup in three years.

His first year at the helm, 1969, wasn't one of them. His old team, the Roughriders, were the class of the CFL at 13–3. Calgary was second, 8 points behind. After beating the 5–11 Lions in the semifinal 35–21, the Stampeders bowed to superior firepower, losing two straight to Saskatchewan 17–11 and 36–13.

The 1970 Roughriders were even better, finishing first with a mark of 14–2. The Stampeders finished at 9–7, good for third place. In the semifinal Jerry

Keeling teamed up with Gerry Shaw for a last-minute touchdown to eliminate the Eskimos 16–9. The Western Final would be David against Goliath.

Most accounts of the 1970 Western Final focus on Larry Robinson's last-second 32-yard field goal into a 40 mile-per-hour wind in a Regina blizzard, giving the upstart Stamps an upset victory over the heavily favored Roughriders, who swear to this day that both George Reed and quarterback Gary Lane had touchdowns taken away by officials suffering from snow blindness. They thought Robinson was incredibly lucky.

But the game wasn't a single, sudden-death final. It was the third of a best of three. The Stampeders could argue that the Roughriders were lucky to get another chance to win in the third game, since Calgary defeated the Riders 28–11 in the first game in Regina. At McMahon Stadium, Calgary trailed 4–3 with 39 seconds left in regulation time. The Stamps had moved into field-goal range at the 23, when Jerry Keeling fumbled after being hit by Ken Frith. Shades of 1966, Ed McQuarters scooped it up and ran 80 yards for a touchdown, saving Saskatchewan from the embarrassment of being eliminated by a third-place team in two games straight.

"In the second game back in Calgary," recalled Harrison, "we didn't have a man to cover George Reed coming out of the backfield. They had never run George Reed deep. But Eagle Keys ran George out of the backfield and down the alley. Then they ran a wide receiver through the center. Once he passed the linebacker, there was an opening. George caught two or three passes and was killing us.

"In the third game we put the strong-side linebacker on George and shut it down. The coach said, 'If you've got to tackle him at the line of scrimmage, tackle him.' Saskatchewan should have gone to another game plan because we had that strategy cased and dominated them."

As for Saskatchewan's disallowed touchdowns, Wayne Harris said, "They had the ball on our 3 or 4. George thought he got in, but we didn't think so and the referee didn't think so."

Opposing Calgary for the 1979 Grey Cup were the Montreal Allouettes, who had gone 7–6–1 and had defeated Toronto and Hamilton in the play-offs. For the first time, both Grey Cup contestants were third-place teams.

Calgary got on the scoreboard first after recovering a fumbled punt at the Montreal 15-yard line early in the first quarter. Keeling completed a 10-yard pass to Hugh McKinnis, who took it in from the 5.

The Alouettes responded with a touchdown of their own on what appeared to be a broken play. Gambling on third and 1 deep in the Calgary end, Terry Wilson broke through and grabbed halfback Moses Denson around the legs. Denson saw Ted Alfen in the end zone and threw him the ball. Wayne Harris explained what happened. "It was a sweep. Terry Wilson was closing in on him pretty fast, but he got the ball away. That was a popular play back in those days. It wasn't really a broken play. It was one of those plays you hope everybody goes asleep on that works. You might use it at a time when you really need to make something happen."

The Als went to the dressing room at half time with a 9–7 lead, thanks to a 21-yard field goal by George Springate. Larry Robinson closed out Calgary scoring with a third quarter field goal. Montreal added touchdowns by Tom Pullen and Garry Lefebvre to win 23–10.

The field in 1970 was a terrible mess. Harrison said, "Gerry Shaw picked up a handful of sod and walked back to the huddle and said, 'Look at this—this is what we're playing on.' I couldn't believe it. We should have won that game. But you know something? I'll tell you what losing did for us: I knew that in '71 we were going to win it. I knew we'd be there. I didn't know if we'd win the Grey Cup, but I knew we'd be there because that team was virtually the same as in '70 and it was just the conditions that beat us."

Wayne Harris concurred. "They had that bad turf on there. They had just resodded the field, and, of course, at that time of the year you'd never get it tied down. There was no traction to speak of."

Harrison led the league in receiving again in 1970 and again sustained broken ribs in the Grey Cup, this time courtesy of a hit by Mark Kosmos, which forced him to the sideline in the second quarter.

Wayne Harris won his third Schenley as Outstanding Lineman. He would win another in 1971. The Stampeder defense that year surrendered a league low 218 points, an average of less than two touchdowns per game. Eight Stampeders made the All-Star team on defense.

Calgary and Saskatchewan tied for first in 1971 with records of 9–6–1. Winnipeg was 4 points behind. The Stamps regular season record against the Riders was 1–1–1, but it was hard to tell which Calgary team would show up for post-season play, the one that started the season at 8–1 or the one that finished at 1–6. It was the first one. In the Western Final, the Stampeders eliminated the Roughridrs in two straight, 30–21 and 23–21.

For the first time Calgary would play a Grey Cup in the West, in Vancouver, against the favored Toronto Argonauts. Again the weather was bad, raining cats and dogs. Along with Wayne Harris, who was nearing the end of a distinguished career, was a group of grizzled old veterans who knew this would likely be their last chance to win the Cup. The Stampeders had brought home the trophy on their first try in 1948. Every other team had won the Grey Cup at least once since then.

Defense dominated the 1971 Grey Cup. While Calgary's Wayne Harris rightfully became the first defensive performer to win the Most Valuable Player of the Game Award, Toronto's defense played just as well. After all, the final score was only 14–11, and the double blue defense came up with three interceptions. It was truly a game that could have gone either way.

The offensive star of the game for Calgary was running back Rudy Linterman, who set up both Stampeder touchdowns with his running and receiving. In the first quarter, after a long Linterman run, Keeling hit Herm Harrison in the end zone for a 13-yard touchdown.

Harrison described the play. "It was something we had set up. The wide receiver and the slot ran deep. They would create an alley. I would come right down between them in that alley, and then I would cut across the middle because they were clearing out all those guys. We had worked on the play in practice, we had worked on it in pregame. Jerry Keeling said, 'Herm, it's there, it's there,' because Dick Thornton was cheating on the speed side. So he said, 'Herm, I've got to turn and hit you before you get to Dick.' And that is exactly what he did. As a matter of fact, as soon as I caught it, Dick bumped me.

"Years later Dick brought that up. He phones and says, 'We've got to have a golf game, Herm, because I've got to beat you. You scored a touchdown on me in the Grey Cup and I'll never forget that.'

"So he reminded me. He said, 'I was supposed to come up on you, but I figured with your speed I could still get there. But Jerry pulled up and threw it too fast.' And that's exactly what happened." Calgary 7, Toronto 0.

Linterman set up Calgary's final major, scored by Jesse Mims on a 6-yard run in the second quarter. Ivan McMillan nailed an 11-yard field goal, making the score at half time Calgary 14, Toronto 3.

Special teams accounted for the Argo touchdown, coming in the third quarter when Jim Silye fumbled Zenon Andrusyshyn's punt. Joe Vijuk picked it up and lateraled to offensive lineman Roger Scales, who ran 36 yards for the only major of his career. Near the end of the third quarter, the Argos' McMillan tried a 31-yard field goal but was wide. Calgary conceded the single, making the score after three quarters the Stampeders 14, the Argos 11.

Near the end of the final stanza, Dick Thornton intercepted a Keeling pass and ran it back to the Calgary 14, where he was tackled by former All-Star defensive back Jerry Keeling. Bill Symons swept to the right and lost 3 yards. Then Leon McQuay ran his fateful sweep to the left, fumbling the ball to preserve Calgary's win. The final score was Calgary 14, Toronto 11.

Wayne Harris remembered the McQuay play well. "They had run a sweep play before, and we nailed them for a loss. They decided to run a sweep to our right on the next play. We had them hemmed up pretty good, and all of a sudden the ball popped loose and we recovered. McQuay definitely wasn't going to get back to the line of scrimmage. Everybody still refers to that game as the one Leon McQuay gave to us, but it wasn't him.

"The Argos had only crossed the 55-yard line twice, maybe three times, the whole day," Harris continued. "We had a super defensive unit that year. The Argos may have kicked a field goal to tie it, but they definitely weren't going to score a touchdown on that run."

Harris didn't agree with Leo Cahill's explanation that while Calgary made a lot of mistakes, Toronto made more. "I don't know if they made mistakes. We just had a tough defense at that time. We had John Helton and Fred James at tackle, and Craig Koinzan and Dick Suderman on the ends. They were a good front four. We had good linebackers in Joe Forzani and Jim Furlong. I think it was our defense shutting them down more than anything else that caused them to make mistakes. We dropped a punt that led to the one touchdown they got. Beyond that, they only kicked a field goal and a single against us. We held them in check all day."

They had to. Calgary only picked up one first down in the entire second half.

The 1971 Grey Cup was the first played on artificial turf, a good thing considering all the rainfall. While the receivers complained about the hydroplaning effect of the soaked field, all that water didn't bother Harris. "I wore the longest cleats I could get. I always did, all through my career. I didn't find the traction that bad. It didn't affect our defense."

"Toronto and Calgary were both good teams," said Harrison. "I was looking for a real good game because Toronto was hot. But I felt we had the team, too, to be there. Everybody says, 'If it wasn't for the McQuay play. . . .' I say, okay, I hear what everybody's saying, but I say, 'Do you realize before Leon McQuay fumbled we were winning anyway? A lot of people don't think like that. They think the fumble is what caused the Argos to lose, but we were winning. The best they could have done if they hadn't scored or got the first down was kick a field goal to tie the game. But a lot of people don't realize that. They think because he fumbled we went ahead. We were always ahead."

Calgary won, according to Harrison, because of defense. "I couldn't believe the way our defense played. They weren't to be denied. They were all over Theismann. They even broke his nose in that game. They were just running him down. As fleet of foot as he was, he hardly ever had the opportunity to show it because the defense was all over him."

Harrison contended that a change in Calgary Head Coach Jim Duncan's attitude was crucial to success. "You know what the whole difference in that game was? I said to Jim Duncan, 'You can't put the pressure on these guys like you did the year before. You've got to turn these guys loose and let them do what they would do in a regular game.' The coaches had made the Grey Cup game seem like it wasn't a football game. That put so much pressure on the guys that everyone got uptight. So we went to Duncan and said, 'There's too much pressure. You've got to loosen up and let us be ourselves.' And he did.

"I know that was hard for Jim to do because he was such a disciplinarian, but he came to the guys and said, 'We've come this far. There's nothing I can tell you now. You've got to go and do what you do best. The curfew's off this week. Do what you've got to do. Do what you feel comfortable with.' That's the way he treated us. And I thought that was the big difference. I really did.

"Boy, I'll tell you when we hit that field, I'd never seen more pumped-up guys. I think what happens with a lot of coaches is that they put too much stress on curfews and all that stuff. They don't do it during the regular season, so why should they do it in the Grey Cup?"

Was Grey Cup experience a factor in Calgary's win? "A whole bunch of us were getting very long in the tooth," said Harris. "Certainly there weren't going to be many more opportunities to play in very many more Grey Cups, if any. We started on the slide after that year. The players got older, a little bit slower, and it was time to rebuild, I suppose.

"In my case, 1971 was my twelfth year. Keeling and Robinson, the same. Some of our defensive backs had been around 10 years or so. We were really an old, veteran football team."

"Our best team was 1971," insisted Harrison. "I thought the '71 team could have beaten an NFL team. The defense was just awesome. Everybody was playing as a unit and was dedicated to the game. It was all attitude. Nobody put himself forward as a stand-out. The team effort was so strong. It always seems we won as a team rather than one individual making an exceptional play."

Wayne Harris retired at the end of the 1972 campaign, one spent mostly on the sideline due to an injury sustained when a teammate fell on him in Regina. But he retired pretty much unscathed. "I never did have my knees cut or anything," he said. "My neck hasn't bothered me since I retired. No operations. I took a few bumps and got a few crooked fingers, but I was very lucky."

The opponent he admired most was Ron Lancaster. The feeling was mutual. "You could never fool him twice," said Number 23. "You'd get him early in the game and try to come back and do it later, and it didn't work. He just had that sixth sense that enabled him to play the game better.

"One time we ran a play where Harris had to take a fake from George Reed, and I'd pitch to the back going around the end. I could see the doubt in Harris's eyes. He knew something wasn't right, but he swallowed it. In the fourth quarter we ran the same play to the other side and he nailed it. He knew the first time something wasn't right. The second time he didn't bite at all. That's something you can't teach, and he had it. He wasn't the biggest, strongest or fastest — he was just maybe the best."

Herm Harrison called it quits at the same time as Wayne Harris. Harris settled in Calgary, where he became an active member of the team's board of directors.

Chicken Feathers

The 1972 Stampeders tumbled into fourth place. Coach Jim Duncan faced the 1973 season without Wayne Harris, Herm Harrison, Hugh McKinnis, Terry Wilson and Dick Suderman, who was traded to Edmonton. When quarterback Peter Liske returned from the NFL, agreeing with W.C. Fields that any place was better than Philadelphia, Jerry Keeling was released and picked up by Ottawa, where he won his second Grey Cup ring.

While hoping for a stellar career in the NFL, Liske took his release from the Eagles in stride and came back to the CFL. "It doesn't matter where you play as long as you get a chance to play," he concluded. "You learn to put that sort of thing in prosper perspective. When you play you want to win football games wherever you are. I've been in the NFL, I've won football games there I've proved to myself that I can do it. After that I don't care where I play and win football games."

Liske found the sledding tough in 1973. The fans expected him to step right in and turn the team around, but, he explained, "You have to know your personnel. You have to know the capabilities of your backs, their speeds, their reactions, the way they cut. You have to know what patterns your receivers run best and get the timing down on those pass plays."

The Penn State graduate rated football intelligence as the number one attribute of a good quarterback. "You really have to study the game. Football is tremendously complicated. The people in the stands have no idea how much is involved. So naturally you have to be intelligent—at least as far as football is concerned."

Liske disputed the theory that all professional quarterbacks are relatively equal in skill level. "That's not true at all. There are differences in size, speed and agility that dictate the way you play." Still he agreed that "the quarterback's quality and success are really inseparable from that of the team."

The 1973 edition of the Stampeders was terrible, going 5–8. After Jim Duncan explained a loss by saying, "You can't make chicken salad out of chicken feathers," General Manager Rogers Lehew gave him his walking papers, replacing him with Offensive Coordinator Jim Wood.

When management makes a coaching change, it is usually hoped that a new spirit of determination will take hold in the players. Even with only five wins, the Stampeders still had a chance to make the play-offs. However, the team played no favorites. They were as capable of losing for one Jim as another. Saskatchewan initiated Wood into the head coaching ranks by licking the Stamps 34–7.

Lehew hadn't expected a sudden reversal of form. The Cowboys switched horses in the middle of the stream to pacify the fans, who were staying away in droves. Duncan had worn out his welcome and was going to go the way of all coaches, so by firing him with three games left, Lehew hoped to fill those 8,000 empty seats. Attendance was somewhat improved for the last home game, a 14–10 win over Edmonton. Calgary finished the season by losing to the Lions 15–7 and missing the play-offs.

In 1974 GM Lehew left to become the assistant general manager of the Detroit Lions. He was replaced by Earl Lunsford's Winnipeg assistant, Gary

Hobson. Looking to the future, Hobson said, "Compared to some other clubs in the league, our problems aren't really that great."

The feisty little Hobson was determined to clean house. "Some of our veterans are going to have to go. That's pretty tough on Jim Wood, but I'm behind him all the way. We're going to rebuild from the ground up."

One of the veterans who left before the 1974 season was Jim Furlong, ending a 12-year career with the Stampeders. An All-Star linebacker in 1965, Furlong contributed to the club in many ways, including punting. Furlong was a Lethbridge boy, one of the many quality athletes turned out by Jim Whitelaw at Lethbridge Collegiate Institute. After graduating from LCI, he went to Tulsa University, where he came under the tutelage of Glen and Bobby Dobbs.

Over his 12 years in Calgary, the Stampeders made the play-offs nine times with three trips to the Grey Cup. "Winning the Grey Cup in 1971 had to be my biggest thrill," Furlong said, "although getting there in 1968 was just about as big. That year we beat Saskatchewan in overtime in the third game. That was a tremendous night."

The low point in Furlong's career came in his rookie year. "My first year in the league was in 1962, and we were playing Winnipeg in the third game of the finals. That's the time when Harvey Wylie dropped the ball in the end zone and Winnipeg won. I was really disappointed after that one because I was sure we were going to win.

"Losing in the Grey Cup hurts, and overall it was disappointing to me that we didn't win more. We had good teams after 1962 that should have won more, but so many times, just like in the 1965 finals against Winnipeg, we blew it. We just blew it."

Furlong rated Saskatchewan's Lancaster as his toughest opponent and teammate Harris as Lancaster's toughest opponent. "Ron was the smartest quarterback in the league. If I lined up at linebacker one foot over from where I had been throughout the season, he'd spot it and do something to me. But Wayne Harris was the greatest ballplayer I ever saw. He wasn't the rah, rah type—he led by example. But was he ever quick! It was really something to behold the cat-and-mouse game Harris and Lancaster played with each other."

Canadians like Furlong, Larry Robinson, Gerry Shaw, the Forzanis, Tony Pajaczkowski, Terry Evanshen, Basil Bark, Fred James and Harvey Wylie, to name but a few, were the backbone of the Stampeders. It is a given that you can't be successful in the CFL without good Canadians. Coaches and general managers made that point over and over, but when it came to contract time, they sang another song. Furlong often felt like a second-class citizen. "The general managers always gave you the same old story: you're a Canadian," Furlong said. "You know we can't pay you as much as an American. We're operating this club on a shoestring. We have to save our money for imports.

"It's hard to generalize, but I'd say that Canadians got paid 25 to 30 percent less than an import of equal ability. Some of us were in Regina over one winter for a broom-ball game with the Roughriders. We got to talking money. It was ridiculous what they were paying Bill Baker. He wasn't getting anywhere near what most imports were getting. But you know, we were our own worst enemies. When we signed a contract, the general manager told us not to tell anyone what we were making. So you never really knew about the other guys. That really worked to the advantage of the clubs.

Furlong didn't think a Canadian general manager would make any difference. "They're brainwashed to the system of getting Canadians on the cheap. This really bothered guys like Robinson and me, when we were playing just as well or better than Americans, but the general manager wouldn't give us their kind of money."

Still, as he looked back, he said, "I made a lot of friends. I experienced something that few other Canadians have experienced. If I had to do it all over again I certainly would. It was a good life."

The Stampeders started the 1974 season with the veteran Liske and rookie Joe Pisarcik at quarterback. The Stamps were still a one-trick pony, living and dying with the pass. Mostly dying.

After training camp Jim Wood said, "We have failed to establish a running game. We know we cannot win without one, and we failed to get one. One guy quit camp, Jesse Mims was suspended, others didn't work out." As to relying on the aerial attack, he said, "Potentially we have possibilities in the passing department."

The Stamps went 1–7 over the first half of the season. The seventh loss came at the hands of the Tiger-Cats, 27–0. It was then that Wood decided that Calgary's future did not lie with Liske. The veteran pivot had no faith in the running game, wouldn't throw the deep out pattern and wasn't very enthusiastic about his head coach. The end really came when he waved the short-yardage team off the field in Hamilton and then threw three incompletions from the Ti-Cat 5. In October Liske was traded to the Lions for quarterback Karl Douglas and back Henry Sovio.

The most important new face arrived halfway through the season, a wonderful running back named Willie Burden. In half a season Burden picked up 541 yards. He would become the third leading rusher in Stampeder history behind Earl Lunsford and Lovell Coleman.

During the 1975 preseason Burden looked magnificent, prompting a Medicine Hat writer to predict he would win the Schenley Award that year. According to Wondrous Willie, he almost didn't play football at all. "I started playing when I was a sophomore in high school. I didn't play when I was in junior high although I did go out for the team. A funny thing happened — I went out on the field for a couple of days and the coach was giving out uniforms. I didn't get one because I hadn't played the year before. I thought that my football career was ending right there."

At North Carolina State, the 5'11", 200-pound Burden ran for 2,529 yards in three years, being acclaimed the Atlantic Coast Conference Player of the Year for 1973. Detroit drafted him in the sixth round, but things didn't go well in Motown. "I was drafted by the Lions," Burden recalled, "and I stayed during the entire preseason camp. About five days before the first league game, I was cut. I had injured my knee in my last year of college in 1973. I didn't get it operated on until the following spring. It was kind of late, considering that training camp opened in July. Although I made a lot of progress, my knee had not come along as well as I thought it should have. Even so, I thought I could have made the team in the shape I was in."

Although disappointed at not sticking with the Detroit Lions, he said early in 1975, "I just want to play football. Any American coming out of college wants to prove he can play in the NFL. But I enjoy the game, whether in the NFL or CFL. Since I've been exposed to the type of game up here, I really like it. Who is to say where the best place to play is? It's what I want to get out of the game as an individual. I have a chance to play here. I'm appreciative just because I enjoy playing the game so much."

Burden felt the dimensions of the Canadian field helped him. "I think probably more than anything else the wider field helps me. You can run a sweep. In the NFL you can run only so far before you get to the sidelines. Here you've got farther to go. You can outrun the pursuit and turn the corner and pick up 5 or 6 yards whereas in the NFL you'd only get 1 or 2. Overall the Canadian game is much more exciting than the NFL. The three downs make it more exciting, too, because you have to open up and go for longer gains."

Willie Burden certainly met Calgary's need for a ground attack. An exciting, elusive runner. He possessed unnatural balance and an uncanny ability to find his opening. He didn't overpower people. Instead he slipped along, picking up yards where a lesser back would not. Burden had a great sense of timing. On top of all that, Jim Wood described him as an "honest ballplayer" who always gave his best, a total team man.

Jack Gotta said, "Burden was so great. He made my job so much easier. We're going to Regina to play a preseason game. A rookie comes up to me. 'Coach, how are we supposed to dress? Do you have a dress code?' I talked to the whole team and said if you've got a problem with anything, check with Willie, just check with Willie.

"So our guys are coming on the airplane and they're dressed well. They're not sneaking mickeys on in their bag. There's practice the next day at a bad hour. You want to get things done. The first thing you do after the guys are stretched out is give the ball to Willie. First running play—*whop!*—away he goes. The night before he had carried 22 times and they pounded the crap out of him. All of a sudden your practice is set for the day. The others follow his example. Here's the best guy last night going like hell the next day. Give me a team of Willie Burdens."

What made Willie run? "The more I carry the football the better I do," he said. "If I only carry the ball 5 or 10 times I feel I really haven't got myself into the game. The more involved I get, the more excited I get. I really get motivated. When I get hot out there, I like to keep going."

Like any talented professional, Willie liked to talk about his craft. "I'm not as crisp in my blocking as I should be or I know I'm capable of being. You have to be good at running, blocking, catching and carrying out the fake. To be a real good running back, you have to work on all those phases of the game.

"You've got to get to the hole first of all. You should not miss any holes because this can ruin the confidence your teammates have in you. You've got to get there when you're supposed to. You've got to time the thing out. You've got to work on this with the people up front. Timing just doesn't happen. It's not instinctive.

"No one can do it alone. You work together as a unit. If one part of the team breaks down, the whole play breaks down. You've got to have confidence in each other. If the guys up front feel you're going to run through the holes they make, they're going to make more holes. If you know a hole is waiting for you,

you're going to run with more authority. I have a lot of confidence in our offensive line."

The native of Raleigh, North Carolina, ran for over 900 yards in his first seven games of the 1975 season, stringing together five consecutive 100-yard plus games. Only Johnny Bright, Willard Reaves and Mike Pringle had more consecutive 100-yard games. Before the 1975 season ended, Burden would have ten 100-yard–plus games, a record equaled in 1984 by Reaves, Robert Mimbs in 1991 and equaled and surpassed by Mike Pringle in 1997–98. Burden set a single-season rushing record of 1,896 yards, a mark that stood until Pringle ran for 1,972 yards in 1994, and he was fourth in scoring with 15 touchdowns.

Burden's achievements in 1975 were even more remarkable considering that the Stampeders won only 6 games and missed the play-offs for the fourth year in a row.

In 1975 Calgary hosted the Grey Cup for the first time, and the highlight for hometown fans was the Schenley Awards when their man Willie beat out the Ordinary Superstar Johnny Rodgers for the Most Outstanding Player Award.

In addition to his contribution on the field, Burden was a delightful teammate, always upbeat and smiling and giving credit to others. He was outstanding at community relations. Burden was a superstar in life as well as on the field.

Burden missed several games to injury in 1976 but still picked up 962 yards. In 1977 he bounced back with 1,032 yards, third in the league behind the Jims, Edwards of Hamilton and Washington of Winnipeg. Burden also picked up 611 yards on 63 pass receptions.

In 1978 Burden again came down with the injury bug, picking up 627 yards rushing and 307 receiving. His figures in '79 and '80 were about the same. Hobbled by injuries in 1981, the great Stampeder retired. He is now his alma mater's athletic director.

Although several Stampeders have posted more impressive numbers over their careers, his is only one of five uniforms the team has seen fit to retire. He is also on the Stampeders' Wall of Honour.

Following the disastrous 1975 campaign, Jim Wood was fired in favor of his assistant, Bob Baker. On September 12, after losing to the Lions 30–15, Calgary's record stood at 0–7–1. On September 13, at the age of 49, General Manager Gary Hobson died of a heart attack. No one had worked harder to produce a winner and sell tickets. In the end the stress of losing proved fatal.

Hobson's enthusiasm for the CFL was that of a super fan. A native of Winnipeg, Hobson graduated from Kelvin High School and played junior football for the Westons and Rods. He also coached football, leading the Fort Garry Lions to six provincial and three national championships.

For 26 years he worked for the Manitoba Telephone System. He served several terms as an alderman and member of the police commission in Winnipeg. He got into the professional game when Earl Lunsford hired him to coordinate Blue Bomber player development. In 1970 he became the assistant general manager, coming to Calgary in 1974.

While in Vancouver for the last game of his life, he told Bob Ackles that he had been to the doctor earlier in the week and had been given a completely clean bill of health. Ackles said that Hobson was in good spirits and looked just fine. He was sorely missed by the Canadian football fraternity.

When the Stampeder record hit 0–10–1, assistant GM Joe Tiller took over as head coach with President Roy Jennings assuming front office responsibilities. With a new quarterback in town, former Penn State All-American and Denver Bronco John Hufnagel, the Stamps ended the longest losing streak in team history by beating Winnipeg 22–10. They then tied the Lions at 31 and knocked off the Eskimos 36–28. The final game of the season they were at home to the Roughriders. Ron Lancaster engineered a brilliant last-minute comeback to win 33–31 and clinch first place. With a record of 2–12–2, the worst year in Calgary Stampeder history ended.

Jocko

Better days were just ahead. Jack was back. Jack Gotta had been raised in the iron country of northern Michigan. He had spent his high school years in Ironwood, which is across Lake Superior from Thunder Bay. He didn't play high school football because he was too small. After graduation he took a sales and management course at General Motors Institute. When he got up to 180 pounds he played for a semipro team in the area. His uncle recommended him to Michigan State, but locals Bump and Pete Elliot, All-Americas at the University of Michigan, had begun their major college coaching careers at Oregon State. A professor from his hometown and a friend of his father's also urged Gotta to go west young man. So he did.

At Oregon State he got a science degree and a military commission because, he said, "I was really keen at that time on flying. I wanted to fly jets. I wanted to shoot down every Commie north of the Yalu—that was my main commitment in life. But when I went to preflight training and I had gone up in some jets several times, I discovered I had an ear problem. It was just the rapid change of altitude.

"I saw the flight surgeon after the second time, and he said I might have had a problem as a youngster. I remembered I had earaches as a kid, but I figured everyone did. So I went up for the third and fourth time and the same thing persisted, so they recommended that I switch into multi-engine school and fly the bigger aircraft. But that wasn't for me. I just wanted to complete my couple of years of active duty, which I did as a lieutenant, and get out of the service. I played two years of service football. I made the All-Services team. We had a really good service football team. Many guys went on to play in the NFL, and some guys came to Canada."

After leaving the service Gotta tried out for the NFL-champion Cleveland Browns. Near the end of training camp Gene Filipski was cut and headed for Calgary. Coach Otis Douglas asked Filipski who else was on thin ice down there, and he mentioned his roommate, Jack Gotta. When the Browns released him a week later, Jack got a call from Calgary.

"It was kind of funny," he recalled. "I'm being paged in Toronto's airport, and I don't know anybody in Canada. It was a call from Green Bay, and this guy wanted me to put everything on hold. He said, 'We'd like to pick you up, so come on down here.' Does that mean you're going to pick up the contract I had at Cleveland? It was for $7,000, an excellent contract way back in those days. That was as much as guys who were all-pro in the NFL were making.

"Anyway, he said, 'No, we just want to bring you in and see how things work out.' I said I had a guaranteed deal to go to Calgary and I was going to take that, which I did. There were seven games remaining in that '56 season, and I played those games in Calgary. I said that at the end of the year I would come back down and that I wouldn't ink a contract other than for the '56 season. At the completion of the year, I compared contracts. There was no comparison in the contract I was offered to come to Calgary in 1957 and the one Green Bay offered me."

Gotta began his pro career at the late age of 26. In his first full season, 1957, he made the All-Star team on both sides of the ball. He made the dream team again in 1958 as a defensive back. After the 1959 season he was traded to Saskatchewan.

"What happened is that I got hurt," Gotta said. "I dislocated my shoulder, and they didn't want to pay me even though I had been a good performer. I came back at the tail-end of the year after getting the proper treatment for it and staying out of the games.

"The night I came back, I played both ways, and I played pretty well. In fact I was given one of those Hudson Bay coats for being named player of the game. The next day Calgary had to name the 11 imports they were going to play in the last three games of the season, and I wasn't named as one of those players. I couldn't believe it. I guess they thought the shoulder could be knocked out again.

"So I went in there and said some things I shouldn't have said and I was on my way to Saskatchewan. If I had gone to Green Bay I'd have never ended up in Calgary. If I hadn't got hurt I'd have never ended up in Saskatchewan and met the girl I married and had the family we have. What would have happened I don't know."

Gotta stayed in Regina until halfway through the 1964 season. He played the last seven games with Montreal and then retired, joining the staff of Eagle Keys a year later. After a failed business enterprise in Kelowna, Gotta ended up with Frank Clair in Ottawa in 1968 and succeeded him as head coach when the professor retired a year later. When General Manager David Loeb wouldn't renegotiate his contract after winning the Grey Cup in 1973, Gotta went to Birmingham of the World Football League.

Although there were several paths not taken in his career, he clearly regretted one of the choices he didn't make. "The one thing I wonder about," he said ruefully, "is when I was down in the World Football League and I had been offered the head coaching job of the Chicago Bears by Jimmy Finks. This was just before we won the World Bowl Championship game down there. We won that game, and I talked to Jimmy again and said, 'Give me a little time to think about it,' and I thought, 'Well, the group in Birmingham was lobbying and trying to get into the NFL. Memphis, with John Bassett's money, was trying to get in.'

"And the league folded, but I thought we could resurrect it. It looked like Memphis was going to take certain players from some of the teams in the World League that folded. Birmingham had the other half of those players. It looked like we had a real good chance to get into the NFL. If that was the case I would have been in a great position going into the NFL with the Birmingham entry as the coach at the same time Seattle and Tampa Bay did. But we didn't go in because they did.

"I turned a job down to coach the Chicago Bears," Gotta said wistfully. "I look back at that and wonder if I should have gone to Chicago. The next year I had a chance to go to Atlanta as interim head coach. You turn those down, and, of course, the door never opens again. Maybe it shouldn't.

"The only time I regretted a decision was turning down Jim Finks. I had the highest regard for him. That was a decision I wrestled with more than any other."

He explained at the time why he went to Calgary in 1977. "I could have gone to a couple of other places. But I thought Calgary had a number of quality football players. The other thing that appealed to me was the city and the province itself. I like living out here. My four children and my wife like outdoor living, and this environment affords that. I want my family's formative years to be spent here.

"I'm paid well, I've got a good contract, and I'm dealing with good people here. I think we can do the job here. We can turn this team around. Our players and coaches really give me a positive feeling."

Gotta was also the Stampeders' general manager. "I think having both jobs will avoid the conflicts that happened here in the past. When I came in here as a visiting coach in the past, I'd hear the coaches on one radio show and the general manager on another show, and they would be contradicting each other and taking credit or assessing blame. I'd never been around a situation like that before."

Gotta looked forward to his first campaign in Calgary in 1977. "I just hope we can catch a play-off spot. For us to improve 100 percent means we win four games. I want us to do better than that."

Gotta didn't, finishing 4–12 and in last place. Suffering a rash of injuries to offensive personnel like Tom Forzani, Willie Armstead, Bob Viccars and Willie Burden, the Stampeders had to field a makeshift lineup most of the season. Although they moved the ball well, the limitless substitution cost them dearly when they got into the red zone. Said quarterback John Hufnagel, "We were moving the football, but when we needed that extra yard to get into the end zone, we always, for some reason, faltered."

Looking toward the 1978 year, Hufnagel said, "Maybe we weren't a very mature team last year. Maybe this year we'll be a lot better. If we have a relatively injury-free season, maybe we'll get together and be more productive."

They were. The 1978 Stampeders finished second with a mark of 9–4–3.

They were second in points scored, first downs and total offense. In 1977 they had averaged 15 points per game, in 1978, 24 points per game. Defensively they gave up the fewest yards in the Western Conference.

Rookie running back James Sykes rushed for 1,020 yards. Sykes also led Stampeder receivers with 50 catches for 614 yards. Sykes, guard Harold Holton, and defensive linemen John Helton and Reggie Lewis made All-Canadian. For Helton it was his seventh selection in eight years. Jack Gotta won his third Coach of the Year Award. Only Don Matthews has won more.

After trouncing the Bombers 38–4 in the semifinal, the Stampeders headed for Edmonton. It was the first time the two teams had met in the Western Final. Kickers Cyril McFall and Dave Cutler traded first quarter field goals. In the second stanza, Stampeder corner Ray Odums intercepted Tom Wilkinson and returned it 53 yards for a touchdown. The Esks evened up the score with a major by Jim Germany.

Although the Stampeders had the wind in the third quarter, they could only manage a field goal. In the final 15 minutes, the wheels fell off the chuck wagon. Three penalties for 30 yards kept a 66-yard Eskimo drive going, resulting in Germany's second touchdown. Dave Cutler converted three turnovers into 9 points. The final score was 26–13 for Edmonton.

Calgary continued to improve in 1979, finishing second with a mark of 12–4. Edmonton was 12–2–2. Calgary quarterback Ken Johnson ranked third in passing behind Dieter Brock and Warren Moon with 176 completions for 2,344 yards and 19 touchdowns, the second-highest total in the league. He completed 56.4 percent of his passes. His favorite targets were Tom Forzani and Willie Armstead.

After beating the Lions 37–2 in the semifinal, it was off again to Edmonton. In a span of 1 minute and 33 seconds Warren Moon threw touchdown passes to John Konihowski and Brian Kelly. Otherwise the name of the game for the Green and Gold was defense. Calgary's J.T. Hay kicked two field goals and a single for all of the Stampeders' scoring. The final score was 19–7.

The Stamps were victimized by questionable officiating. In the second quarter Calgary pivot Johnson hit Armstead with a long pass down to the Eskimo 6-yard line. After making the catch Armstead fumbled. While one Eskimo held him, another fell on the ball. The Eskimos should have been called for defensive holding or interference. A touchdown at that point would have changed the tempo of the game. Also, in the second quarter, an Edmonton drive that ended in a touchdown was kept alive at midfield when John Helton was called for roughing the passer after he laid Warren Moon down as gentle as a feather.

Jack Gotta said the only way to win the West was to finish first and host the Western Final, vowing to do exactly that in 1980. Instead he appointed his friend Ardell Wiegandt as head coach while retaining the position of general manager. Wiegandt was a hard-nosed former U.S. Marine Corps drill instructor who soon lost the respect of his team. The Stamps slipped back to third and lost the semifinal to Winnipeg 32–14.

The following year Jerry Williams was brought in as offensive coordinator, implementing a system the players openly criticized as too difficult to master. Shades of Mark Kosmos' comments about Williams in Hamilton, the Stampeders were most successful when quarterback Ken Johnson ignored the system and went with their bread-and-butter flair passes to James Sykes.

After a loss to Montreal dropped their record to 5–7, Gotta fired Wiegandt. He fired the wrong man. Jerry Williams' offense was last in the conference in points and yardage. The defense was the stingiest in the CFL in yardage surrendered and third in points given up. The team went 1–4 the rest of the way, including a 44–6 shellacking in Winnipeg the last game of the season.

At the insistence of the board of directors, Gotta returned to the sidelines in 1982, leading his club back to the play-offs with a mark of 9–6–1 and third place. They were wiped out by Winnipeg 24–3 in the semifinal. In 1983 the club finished 8–8 on the final game of the season, losing 27–23 to the last-place Roughriders. The defeat cost Calgary a play-off spot.

In a scenario of you can't fire me, I quit, Jocko launched a preemptive strike by demanding a new contract and a substantial raise. He got neither, bringing the Jack Gotta era in Calgary to a close. During his seven years with the team, he won 44, lost 37, tied 4 and made the play-offs three of the five years he coached. He left the team with a big bank account. Media, fans and most players were sorry to see him go. Living just outside Calgary in Cochrane, he remains a popular figure in the foothills city to this day.

When Gotta had returned to the bench in 1981, the directors had hired a banker, Walter Prisco, to run the business side of the team. The critical personnel area had been run by Gotta's Assistant General Manager Joe Tiller in a most effective fashion. But after Prisco was appointed, Tiller resolved to leave and did so when a coaching job opened up at Purdue University. Previously

Tiller had been offered the GM's position in Regina when Jim Spavital took the job.

After Gotta cleaned out his office, he was replaced with Steve Buratto, a man with no head coaching experience. Calgary also made him general manager. Buratto made horrendous personnel judgments. Although short of receivers he forced Tom Forzani into retirement. He then traded All-Canadian middle linebacker Danny Bass to Edmonton for Tom Scott, who was over the hill. At a free agent camp, Lionel James, who went on to star with San Diego, was deemed not good enough to play in the CFL.

The team went 6–10 and wound up in the basement. An example of the comedy of errors that gripped the franchise was the debacle over Tom Forzani's sweater. Calgary's last game was at home October 20 against the Lions. Herm Harrison and other members of the executive had arranged to retire Forzani's Number 22. At half time Tommy Scott, who wore Number 22, would switch to 26. Forzani would be brought out and the number would be retired. That's what happened, even though the top management of the team knew absolutely nothing about it because they had been opposed to honoring Forzani in that fashion.

On the Brink of Disaster

Attendance fell by an average of 8,198 seats between 1982 and 1984. The club lost over $1 million, placing the future of the franchise in a very precarious position. Before the 1985 campaign Earl Lunsford was hired as general manager. The first thing he did was sign 34-year-old quarterback Joe Barnes.

"Some people believe that when you rebuild, you start with the defense," he explained. "I've always believed the quarterback is most important. Without him you won't win games or put people in the seats. We have to prove to the people here that we are committed to winning. Joe Barnes is an important part of that." To get Barnes the vault was opened to the tune of $1 million, the most Calgary had ever paid for a football player.

Before the start of the 1985 season, Buratto had said, "I don't think it's unrealistic for us to dream about getting into the play-offs." After losing five of their first six games, Lunsford fired Buratto, replacing him with former Blue Bomber head coach Bud Riley. Under his crusty direction, the team was 2–8, finishing last at 3–13. Attendance fell again, and by September the Stamps were $400,000 in the red.

"We budgeted back in January to average 24,000 people per game over the season," said Lunsford. "We thought we'd lose 2,000 season ticket holders because of the negative attitude here, but instead we lost 7,000."

Attendance averaged 14,878 per game, the worst mark in over 25 years by a substantial margin. The game in October when Wayne Harris, John Helton and Paul Rowe were inducted onto the Wall of Fame, the Stampeders had the poorest crowd in modern team history.

The team was bankrupt. Former great Gerry Shaw joined Doug Hunter, Bill Tanner and Brian Ekstrom to save the Stampeders. They had $2 million and approached the province and city council for a matching grant. Premier Don Getty agreed, but Calgary city council turned the proposal down.

Former personnel director Ed Alsman was fronting for a wealthy individual who wanted to buy the team. But Alsman made it clear he would be general manager if his patron bought the club and Earl Lunsford would be out. Some members of the executive were opposed to the Alsman bid because they wanted to protect Lunsford.

A meeting between the Alsman group and the executive was called off because the football directors didn't show up. A second meeting was canceled. The Alsman group finally met with the executive, but because of short notice and an unreasonable deadline, it did not have time to do business properly. The Alsman group withdrew, but speculation was that the result might have been different if Alsman hadn't stated that he would be the manager and Lunsford would be out.

A "Save Our Stamps" campaign began in earnest. With a telethon, contests, appearances by present and past Stampeder greats, 22,400 season tickets were sold. There was money in the bank for a couple of years. Lunsford remained as general manager with entrepreneur Vern Siemens installed as a volunteer, unpaid president to oversee the business operation of the team.

In 1986 the league also revised the play-off structure so that if the fourth-place team in either Conference had a better record than the third-place team in the other Conference, then they would make the play-offs instead of the third-place team. In 7 of the previous 10 play-off years, if that rule had been in place, the number four team in the West would have made postseason play.

To lead the Stampeders into 1986, Lunsford chose as head coach Bob Vespaziani, formerly an assistant with Ray Jauch, Cal Murphy and Don Matthews. He quickly assembled a talented team. With Rick Johnson at quarterback and 11 newcomers in the lineup, the Stamps were 11–7, tied with the Bombers for third place. They drew the short straw and ended up, under the new format, playing the first-place Eskimos. In the second quarter Johnson was injured and couldn't continue. Despite losing their quarterback, the Stampeders played hard before bowing 27–18 to the inevitable.

Calgary had gone from 3–11 and bankruptcy to 11–7 and a full treasury in 12 months. The future looked bright. Instead they got off to a terrible start in 1987, losing six of their first eight games. Part of the problem was at quarterback. Rick Johnson wasn't sharp in the early going due to lack of conditioning after off-season surgery and losing weight for, of all things, a Hollywood screen test. When Rick Worman became the starter, Johnson complained publicly at every opportunity. Teammates chose sides in the dispute.

As losses piled up, finger-pointing and dissension grew. Some players complained that the defensive system of Dan Daniels was too complicated. Others extremely loyal to offensive coordinator Lary Kuharich felt he should play a bigger role. Vespaziani, in only his second year as a pro head coach, lost control of his squabbling colleagues. Team unity and chemistry were gone.

With falling attendance and a player revolt imminent, the board of directors demanded wholesale changes. They were partly moved to action after the team's second win at Ottawa. Trailing by 26 points to the Riders, Kuharich came to the sideline from the press box to engineer the comeback. The players presented him with the game ball, pointedly ignoring their head coach. At an annual Stampeder–media steak barbecue, Kuharich openly courted executive members and the press. For Vespaziani the handwriting was on the wall.

President Vern Siemens believed the very existence of the franchise was at stake if radical surgery wasn't performed at once. In what came to be known as the McMahon Stadium Massacre, Vespaziani, Lunsford and Personnel Director Bud Riley were fired. Many questioned the timing of the move. The Stampeders cleaned house just two days before playing B.C. After the Lions, the Stampeders would have a 17-day break before meeting the Eskimos on Labour Day. Why not wait until after the B.C. game? Why wasn't the deed done right after the Ottawa encounter? The problem was Earl Lunsford. When the executive told him to swing the ax, he refused. Days went by while the directors tried to convince their general manager that the execution was necessary. Lunsford refused and loyalty to his friend Vespaziani cost him his job.

How could the head coach go from hero to bum in only half a season? People change. A Stampeder veteran, known as a loyalist to his coach and not a clubhouse lawyer, said Coach Vee had to go. "He couldn't make a decision. He was a changed man, hostile to his players, the media and the public. Many of us tried everything to help him, but he wouldn't accept our help." Vespaziani also had personal problems. The father of five had recently separated from his wife of many years.

Vespaziani was replaced by Lary Kuharich. The Stamps won five of their next six games and finished the season in second place at 10–8. Inspired by their coach, who talked about putting a "sword in their hands" they headed for Edmonton full of optimism, only to lose the semifinal 30–16.

Again the team had every reason to look forward to next year, but typically it was one step forward and two steps back as they fell to the basement with a mark of 6–12. Coach Q, as he was called, turned out to be Dr. Jekyll and Mr. Hyde. He could be charming and rational one minute and in a total rage the next, and the victim of his aggression would have no idea why. Two of his victims were popular veterans J.T. Hay, the special teams captain, and Bob Poley, captain of the offense. Kuharich cut both, blaming the decision on the CFL salary cap. But he did it after September 1, meaning, as six-year veterans, they had to be paid their full salaries to the end of the season. He also cut quarterback Rick Worman without ensuring an adequate replacement.

The players' Dr. Jekyll had turned solidly into Mr. Hyde. But Kuharich was in the first year of a three-year contract as director of football operations. Making matters worse was the fact that his six assistants had two-year deals, unheard of in the CFL. What could Calgary do? Hope Kuharich was a misunderstood genius and send him to charm school? The team couldn't afford to clean house. Although Kuharich treated his new general manager, Normie Kwong, shamefully at times, the China Clipper swallowed his pride and kept Kuharich on.

That appeared to be a wise decision as Calgary rebounded to 10–8 and a second-place finish in 1989. During the season Kuharich continued to exhibit bizarre behavior that made him impossible to work with in the clubhouse and a public relations disaster in the community. That year the Stampeders fumbled 41 times. "The situation may be part and parcel of the players being too uptight, too tense," offered defensive coordinator Wally Buono.

The last straw came during the semifinal against Saskatchewan. Whenever the Roughriders visit Calgary, the stadium looks like a Rider home game with so many people wearing green and white. When other teams are in town, they revert to their red and white jerseys and cheer the Stampeders on. All Calgary coaches have learned to live with the large number of Roughrider fans who live in Calgary, knowing they are essential to the financial well-being of the team.

At one stage of the game, when the Riders had made a good play and loud cheers came from the stands behind the Stampeder bench, Kuharich turned around and gave them the middle finger salute. They responded with a cascade of snowballs. The Riders went on to upset the Stamps 33–26. It was no comfort to Coach Q that they also upset Edmonton and won the Grey Cup.

A few days later, amidst rumors of his Calgary coaching demise, Kuharich cleaned out his office in the middle of the night and fled to Vancouver, where he was quickly introduced as the new coach of the B.C. Lions.

Galloping to Greatness

With Kuharich gone, the golden age of the Calgary Stampeders was about to begin, but first the team had to solve its problems at the gate. Attendance in 1986 after the "Save Our Stamps" campaign had averaged 27,286 per game. In 1989 the average was 22,003. Once again the team was in dire financial straits. Normie Kwong, a CFL legend and part owner of the NHL Flames, was so highly regarded in the community that he was able to single-handedly keep the team alive. If the Stampeders had folded it is unlikely the CFL could have survived. It is not an exaggeration to credit Kwong with saving both his team and the league.

Under tremendous pressure to sell season tickets, Kwong could have opted for the big name coach who might provide a quick fix. Instead he chose a man with no head coaching experience. He chose to promote Wally Buono.

Born in Italy in 1950, Buono's family had moved to Montreal in 1953. Because his mother couldn't afford to look after Wally and his brother, the boys were put in an orphanage for a time until she could reclaim them. After playing minor and high school football in Montreal, Buono went to Idaho State. He played linebacker for his hometown Alouettes from 1972–81, appearing in five Grey Cups and winning two. After four years as an assistant in Montreal, he joined Bob Vespaziani's staff in Calgary in 1987.

Going into the 1999 campaign, Buono's record is 115–46–1, a winning percentage of .713, third best in CFL history behind Hugh Campbell and Pop Ivy. His average of 12.78 wins per season is unmatched. His teams have finished first every year except 1991 and 1997, including five straight from 1992–96. He's taken Calgary to the Grey Cup four times, winning twice. His record would be remarkable in any era but especially in one of free agency.

Buono has managed to accomplish all this during the most turbulent, upsetting period in the team's history. First of all came the near bankruptcy of the club in 1991 and its purchase by the flamboyant, erratic Larry Ryckman. Next came Ryckman's collapse and the new ownership of Sig Gutsche. Each year Buono has had to replace a half a dozen starters, including All-Canadians like Harold Hasselbach, Junior Thurman, Darryl Hall, Kent Warnock, Karl Anthony, Doug Flutie, Dave Sapunjis, Bruce Covernton and Jeff Garcia. Wally Buono is one of the greatest coaches in Canadian football history.

In addition to Buono, General Manager Kwong hired the brilliant bird dog Roy Shivers to find American players. His acquisitions included Allen Pitts, Kelvin Anderson, Marvin Coleman, Alondra Johnson, Marvin Pope and Darryl Hall. Kwong also lured out of retirement the greatest personnel man of them all, Frankie Morris, to help with Canadian scouting and recruiting.

In 1995 Stan Schwartz became the team's vice president and general manager of administration, keeping the franchise alive during the fall of Ryckman's financial empire. His rock-solid reputation for honesty and his good common sense allowed the Stampeders to move smoothly into new ownership. The Medicine Hat native was appointed president of the club February 12, 1996. Thanks to Schwartz and Buono, the Calgary Stampeders could rival the Eskimos as the flagship franchise in the CFL.

When Buono took over in 1990, he talked about what had to be done to bring a championship to Calgary. "One, you've got to work on attitude so everyone is at least thinking in the same direction. Two, you have to get the kind of people who respond to you. Three, you have to get good people, good football players, good athletes.

"People ask why we can't beat Edmonton. My direct answer is that the Edmonton organization has been at it for 30 or 40 years. You look at Hugh Campbell. He's the product of Norm Kimball, who was there for 25 years. That's why they are very successful. Their approach and their organizational skills are far better than those of anyone else.

"Get good people that you have confidence in and allow them to build the organization. That's one thing I really stressed when I talked to Norm Kwong and the board before I got the job.

"It's not so important who you hire," Buono insisted. "But be stable from the top down or be filtering people up so that if you do make a change at the top you do so without changing the philosophy or disrupting the organization."

Buono's 1990 Stampeder team had nine rookies in the starting lineup, including an entire corps of receivers consisting of Derrick Crawford, Allen Pitts, Dave Sapunjis, Pee Wee Smith and Shawn Beals. Crawford and Smith were also outstanding return men. Defensively Buono went with rookie linebackers Joe Clausi and Henry Smith as well as end Harold Hasselbach and defensive back Darryl Hall. Second-year men included defensive end Will Johnson and cornerback Junior Thurman. Johnson made All-Canadian five years in a row. Veterans Walter Ballard, Mitchell Price, Kent Warnock, Matt Finlay, Greg Peterson, Dave McCrary and Ron Hopkins rounded out the defense.

The Stampeders' O-line was anchored by 16-year veteran Lloyd Fairbanks in his tenth season in red and white. Leo Blanchard, who had spent nine seasons with Edmonton, and six-year veteran Mike Palumbo were the guards, and 12-year man Kevin Powell was the other tackle. Tom Spoletini was in his sixth year at center. Calgary protected quarterback Danny Barrett, who first came to the team in 1983 out of Cincinnati as a receiver. He was backed up by Terrence Jones, a gifted athlete who never came close to fulfilling his promise, and the steady but slow Rick Worman. The running backs were Anthony Cherry and Andy McVey.

Calgary opened at B.C. with a 38-point overtime tie. They then won five out of six, lost two in a row and then won six of their remaining nine games to finish atop the Western Conference standings for the first time since 1971. They met the Eskimos in the final.

In what would become a familiar pattern, Calgary and Edmonton would have trouble winning Western Finals at home. In their first meeting of the decade, Edmonton waltzed into McMahon and beat up on the Stampeders 43–23.

The Stampeders still had to learn how to win the big game. "They've played in big games and won, and they've lost a big play-off game," said Buono. "They understand there is a difference between winning and losing and that there's really not that much. The winners learn to win, the losers learn to lose."

When asked how to coach a winning attitude, most coaches say that if they knew, they would bottle it and make $1 million. Not Buono. "Let me put it this way," he said. "Supposedly we were a losing franchise, and now we are perceived as winners, so obviously somebody's doing something right. You don't coach it, but you have to stress it. You have to plant the seed in people's minds.

You have to keep watering and fertilizing it so it grows. Winning doesn't happen by chance. A lot of things cause winning and one of them is talking to the players about winning and letting them know it is there.

"We have some winners here now. Frankie Morris is a winner. Don Sutherin is a winner. All of a sudden your organization has winners and guess what? They don't think about losing, they think about winning. Part of the process is to surround yourself with winners because they think positively. They know that sometimes things don't go their way, but it's no big deal. They get around that and get the job done."

As for the 1991 Stampeders, Buono said, "We should be a good enough football team that we should be thinking nothing but Grey Cup because we have enough skill, enough depth, enough talent. The players have won enough here now to understand that winning is there and that they just have to go out and get it."

Buono looked back on his first year as a head coach. "I learned that the things I valued the most, truth and honesty, paid dividends — being able to look a man in the eye and know you haven't wronged him for any reason. I think that goes a long way.

"The emotional drain was a surprise to me. It is difficult always being in a position of authority, where you're always making decisions. That gets very wearing."

In the West the road to the Grey Cup has usually gone through Edmonton. Facing the 1991 campaign, Buono felt that finally Calgary was the team to beat to get there. "I feel that way. Maybe I'm the only one but that's okay," he said.

Buono made six changes on defense in 1991, adding Karl Anthony and Errol Tucker to the secondary, Dan Wicklum and Alondra Johnson at linebacker and Stu Laird and Tim Cofield on the line. Tucker and Cofield were rookies.

Derrick Crawford broke his leg and was replaced by rookie Carl Bland, who caught 56 passes for 903 yards. Anthony Cherry was released in favor of B.C. veteran Keyvan Jenkins, who responded with 801 yards, Calgary's best total in four years. Buono made three changes to the offensive line, putting Doug Davies at center, Bill Henry at guard and Ken Moore at tackle. Danny Barrett returned at quarterback. The receivers were Pitts, Beals, Marshall Toner and Sapunjis.

The 1991 Stampeders went 11–7, finishing two points behind the Eskimos. They ranked fifth in points, seventh in total offense, last in rushing but second in passing. Defensively they ranked fifth. They went 11–7 because they made few mistakes while taking advantage of the miscues of their opponents. Calgary led the league in the giveaway–takeaway category with +20, 12 ahead of Saskatchewan.

The Stampeders were led by Allen Pitts, perhaps the greatest receiver in CFL history. In 1990 Pitts had caught 65 passes for 1,172 yards. He was the league's first newcomer since Terry Evanshen in 1966 to rack up over 1,000 yards (although B.C.'s Matt Clark and Argo Rocket Ismail would do it the following year). In 1991 Pitts picked up 1,764 yards while setting a CFL record with 118 receptions. Seven times he would go over 1,000 yards.

Pitts has been an impact player since his arrival in the CFL. What is really remarkable is that he was out of football four years before arriving in Calgary. Graduating in 1986 from Cal State Fullerton, he attended two L.A. Ram camps but failed to make the grade. Then he got the call from Calgary. "I attended an open camp in May 1990 in Irvine, California," he recalled. "Roy Shivers was in charge of American personnel, and he knew me from college days. Things went well, I was invited up to Calgary, and they signed me to a contract."

Despite being away from the game, Pitts was convinced he could play professional football. "I made up my mind in May of 1989 to give it one more chance. I looked at it realistically and decided that I wasn't going to be ready in 1989 because I wasn't in the proper condition mentally or physically to give it my best shot. I prepared myself for the 1990 season. It was a slow process, but with a lot of determination, faith and prayer, things worked out for me."

He described what it takes to be an outstanding receiver. "Never being satisfied, always looking for ways to improve," he concluded. "What also helps is that I've been very fortunate to be able to pretty much pick up on reading defenses well, which helps me after the ball is snapped. I'm already on the run and reading whether they are in man coverage or zone. I have really good eyesight, which helps.

"To be a great receiver, you have to believe that in tough circumstances you know you can get the job done. It's that type of attitude along with God-given ability that carries some people to a higher level than others."

Having a good quarterback also helps. Setting a record made Pitts partial to Danny Barrett, but he learned to adjust to Doug Flutie, Jeff Garcia and Dave Dickenson. Despite his impressive credentials, Pitts has never been the Western nominee for Most Outstanding Player.

Danny Barrett, like Allen Pitts, also knows what it's like to get little or no respect. At the University of Cincinnati, they tried to make him a defensive back, in Calgary a wide receiver. After languishing on the bench in Toronto, he asked to be traded. The only team that would take him was Calgary. Their quarterbacks were hurt and they needed someone to back up and guide their rookie, Terrence Jones. Like the old song said, "You'll have to do until the real thing comes along."

Never regarded as number one, always seen as a stop-gap measure, Danny Barrett established himself as Wally Buono's starting quarterback for a couple of seasons. Barrett explained how he landed in the CFL. "Jerry Keeling had an opportunity to see me play for the University of Cincinnati on cable TV against Miami, and he thought I had the skills to play in Canada. We ran a pro-type offense, but we also moved the pocket quite a bit. Calgary gave me a free agent tryout in Las Vegas. Again I wasn't one of the top guys they brought in, but I looked on it as an opportunity to join a pro football squad. As it turned out I landed a contract, and I've been trying to better myself ever since then. When I came out of university I thought I had the skills to play in the NFL. Obviously I didn't because no one gave me even a phone call about it."

The personable Barrett had a simple explanation for why, in 1991, in Calgary he became a nine-year overnight success. "Every time I've been given a chance to play longer than a few minutes I've come through and really performed because that gave me confidence. If you instill confidence in a person, he's going to do what's necessary to win football games. I appreciate what the Calgary coaches have done for me as opposed to the past, where if you weren't spectacular in the first quarter, they yanked you out.

"I was never a flashy quarterback. Toronto was always looking for spectacular players to bring in more fans. When we go into cities to play and they have the big-name quarterback, that makes me want to have a great game to show that not only can I compete with those guys, I can beat them, too.

"As far as getting a lot of publicity," Barrett continued, "I want the Stampeders as a team to get all the attention, to show that we are a complete team. I'm just one part of it. There is so much talent with you on the field. I just get the ball to my teammates and they make things happen. I've been playing the game long enough to know that great stats and publicity don't mean very much. I'm past that now. I want to win a Grey Cup ring."

To be a successful quarterback, he said, "You must be patient and not turn the ball over. That's what I pride myself on. Don't hurt your team. There are good enough offenses playing against us who can hurt us, so I try not to give them any advantage at all.

"If possible, try to eliminate the sacks. Football is a game of field position, and you don't want to be backed up in your own end. If you eliminate sacks and don't turn the ball over, you can dictate field position and scoring."

He again referred to patience. "First and foremost in the Canadian game, you must be patient and take what the defense gives you. Because it's basically two-down football, you take what they give you and don't force things. That was not something I learned earlier in my career. I was trying to make things happen that weren't there.

"I try to learn all facets of the game. I'm a good student of the game. I have an excellent coach in John Hufnagel. I've really learned a lot from him such as the little things about reading defenses that I may have overlooked in the past. He's really helped me try to be a smarter quarterback.

"I just want to be the total package, that's all, just a total package," Barrett concluded. "Whatever is necessary to get the job done, I want to be able to do it. I pride myself on studying the game and myself as well. Reading defenses is very important, especially with 12 men on the field, because they can give you so many different looks. If you're aware before you start the play what the coverage will be, it helps you get rid of the ball a whole lot faster. I've gotten away from tunnel vision, where I would hone in on one receiver. Now I'm able to go to secondary receivers a whole lot better.

"You've got to have a lot of confidence in yourself but you also have to have poise. You can't get rattled easily."

Barrett usually didn't. Throughout his 14-year career, Barrett threw 3,029 passes and had 91 picked off, an average of 1 interception per 33 passes, the best ratio in CFL history. In 1990–91 Barrett had the fewest interceptions in the league. In '91 he didn't have one picked off until the fifth game and ended the season with six.

When Doug Flutie became available after 1991, Barrett was traded to B.C. When B.C. acquired Kent Austin in 1994, Barrett headed for Ottawa. He rejoined the Stamps in 1996 and became their quarterback coach the following year. In 1998 he returned to B.C. as a player coach.

Ranked fifteenth all-time in passing, his greatest day as a pro came August 12, 1993, at B.C. Place, when he passed for a record 601 yards against Toronto. Matt Dunigan shattered the record with 713 yards a year later.

Barrett led the Stampeders north for the 1991 Western Final. Calgary had only managed one play-off win in Edmonton in their history, that coming in the

1970 semifinal. In an entertaining shoot-out, the Esks were up 36–31 with less than a minute to play when Barrett went back to pass and hit Pee Wee Smith on the fly for a 68-yard pass and run for a touchdown. For the first time in 20 years the Calgary Stampeders were Grey Cup bound. For the first time ever, the game would be played in Winnipeg.

The temperature was –19°C at kickoff, and the mood of Calgary fans by game's end was as low as the temperature. Although the Stampeders had had the fewest turnovers during the season, Barrett was intercepted three times by the Toronto Argonauts. The usually stingy special teams came up short all day.

On Calgary's first possession Ed Berry intercepted and ran 50 yards for a touchdown. Lance Chomyc added the convert and a single before Barrett marched his team down the field for their first major score. The teams traded field goals in the second quarter, making the score at half time Toronto 11, Calgary 10.

Mark McLoughlin kicked the Stampeders into a 14–11 lead in the third quarter, but Matt Dunigan responded with a 48-yard touchdown pass to Darrell K. Smith. With Chomyc's earlier single, Toronto led 19–14 after 45 minutes.

Early in the final frame Chomyc added a 19-yard field goal. Barrett brought the Stampeders back, completing a drive with a 13-yard touchdown pass to Pitts. Toronto 22, Calgary 21.

McLoughlin kicked off, and, in the play of the game, Rocket Ismail returned it 87 yards for the score. Toronto 29, Calgary 21.

On the ensuing kickoff the ball bounced off Keyvan Jenkin's foot and Toronto recovered. Two plays later Dunigan hit Paul Masotti in the end zone for Toronto's final touchdown. In 58 seconds the hopes and dreams of two decades of Calgary football were dashed.

Barrett didn't give up, marching from his 31 to the Argo 2, 77 yards in 9 plays. A couple of running plays would bring them the major, and Calgary would be 8 points down with lots of time to even the score. Instead they decided to pass.

"On the touchdown before," Barrett explained, "I had isolated Pitts on Brazely, and I thought I could do it again." The pass went incomplete. Surely this time Andy McVey or Jenkins or Barrett would carry the ball. No. Barrett dropped back to pass and was brought down on the 11-yard line.

"I looked the wrong way, and by the time I saw my receiver it was too late," Barrett lamented. That series hurt us more than anything else. When I got sacked that probably cost us the ball game."

Offensive Coach John Hufnagel made the decision to throw. "We had a short passing play that we were pretty sure would work," he said. The rest is history. Toronto 36, Calgary 21.

Canadian player of the game Dave Sapunjis (4 catches for 45 yards) wasn't critical of the calls. "We were very confident in our receivers against their DBs. That was when using five or six receivers was coming into the league. We started it. Their defense wasn't used to that. So, when we got to the 2-yard line, we thought we would spread them apart and throw a quick pass. That was our game plan. It didn't work."

All-Canadian defensive end Will Johnson wasn't so forgiving. "We're not coaches. We're just players, and we have to accept what the coaches do. With 2 yards to go, I'd have run a sweep or a quarterback sneak or a quick-hitting dive play."

Led by Johnson, the Stampeder defense played well that day. "We played well, very well," he insisted. "The Argos double-teamed me on both sides with a back and a tackle. Mainly they'd spin it away from me. But I hit Dunigan a couple of times. One time that I hit him he coughed up the ball into the air, and Tim Cofield caught it and got a few yards before an offensive lineman grabbed him. They didn't really do anything to us. We defensively took control of the game. We just should have scored on defense. Special teams killed us."

Calgary kicker Mark McLoughlin discussed the impact of cold weather on the kicking game. "When you have weather like that, what happens is the ball hardens. It's almost like kicking a brick. You can't control it, you can't direct it, so what you do is just line up and try to kick it straight as possible and hope it maintains its line."

He appreciated Argo coach Adam Rita's strategy of sky-kicking the ball. "That worked. When you're kicking hard footballs in that type of weather, you're not going to get a whole lot of distance on the ball, so if you try to kick it normally for depth it is not going to happen. So that was a very good strategy, kicking the ball in the air and hoping the receivers would have a hard time handling it."

Not being on the field much means a place-kicker really has trouble keeping warm. "I grew up in Winnipeg, but Grey Cup day was probably the coldest I can remember. On game day you did what you had to do to keep warm. I kept on the move all the time, jogging up and down the sidelines."

Being the kicker can be a lonely job, he conceded. "We never get wrapped up with the offense or defense, regardless of whether we're behind or winning.

We have our area down by the kicking net, and that's usually where we stay. There is no need for us to be getting in the way or being part of the X's and O's because that's not something we need to concern ourselves with. We just need to focus on our job, try to keep our minds clear and try to keep loose."

He agreed with Dan Ferrone that if you're winning you don't feel the cold. "If you're winning it's not as cold, if you're losing it's colder. I think Toronto had the game in hand pretty much when Ismail ran the kickoff back. Basically they had it wrapped up.

Dave Sapunjis felt the same way. "I don't think the weather affected us. I think that we'd gotten used to it over the week. It was extremely cold, it was bitter. But our defense was designed for any weather just like their offense was."

Sapunjis wasn't surprised Dunigan played. "You never know what's going on in the opposition dressing room. We didn't know how healthy he was. Things were pretty quiet. Rita's always kept things pretty quiet when he's coaching his club. We didn't know how serious Dunigan was, and when he stepped on the field, well, it really didn't surprise us. I was surprised to hear after the game that he had a broken bone or a separation and he played with it."

To Sapunjis, special teams were the difference. "Ever since that Grey Cup I've always said when we've gone to the Grey Cup or play-offs that special teams should be ready because sometimes it comes down to them. My first Grey Cup in '91, I believe, was lost because of special teams.

"Rocket's touchdown sort of put us away. We still had a chance to come back and make it interesting at the end, but when you get beaten so badly on special teams it starts to drain you on the offensive and defensive sides of the ball. That really hurt us. Our emotions just dropped and we lost our energy."

McLoughlin analyzed their defeat. "Special teams played a huge factor, but I think there was a lot of veteran leadership on the Argos. They had a lot of guys who had been to the Grey Cup before. As a fairly young team in 1991, we had just come off a very big emotional high in the Western Final up in Commonwealth Stadium. I think when we got to the Grey Cup, we said, 'Boy, we're here, let's enjoy this.' Maybe we approached the game the wrong way. Maybe we thought we could carry on and let the emotion ride from the week before, but we weren't able to do that.

"I think the very first play was an interception for a touchdown, and then there was a fumble. Those turnovers were very uncharacteristic of us. It's a mental thing when things like that happen. But we were down right off the bat. It was tough for us to come back. Plus Toronto was a very good team that year as well. They deserved to be in it and win it."

In Buono's first year as head coach, Calgary lost to Edmonton in the final. In his second year they beat the Eskimos but lost the Grey Cup to Toronto. Looking ahead to 1992, Buono wanted his team to turn it up a notch and take that final step. "The whole thing about the other notch," he explained, "is that the players have been there and understand what the other notch is. Now they know that although the road is tough the goal is attainable. It takes a lot of skill, but they have that. They know what must be done. The Grey Cup is now their focus whereas in the past I don't think they truly believed they could do it."

Since the end of Buono's first year, 14 of the 24 starters had been replaced. Buono made eight changes to a lineup that had won the West. Tim Cofield was replaced by Harold Hasselbach, Dan Wicklum by Marvin Pope and Errol Tucker by Kenton Leonard. Lloyd Fairbanks, Leo Blanchard and Bill Henry were replaced on the offensive line by Rocco Romanao, Lou Cafazzo and rookie Bruce Covernton. Shawn Beals was released, Derrick Crawford was back after breaking a leg and Dave Sapunjis became a starter at slotback. The biggest change was at quarterback with Doug Flutie replacing Danny Barrett.

On his way to winning his first Most Outstanding Player Award with B.C. in 1991, Flutie set new season records for pass completions and yardage, 466 for 6,619 yards. He threw for 38 touchdowns. His 63.8 percent completion rate was the best in the league.

The Stampeders started the 1992 season with four wins in a row. Flutie, hailed as the conquering hero, was typically modest. "I've been on a roll," he allowed, "and the media and fans think it is all the quarterback, and it's not. You're dependent on the people in front of you. If you don't have time to throw the ball, you can't get the job done. If you don't have guys working to get open and catching the ball, you still don't get it done. There is too much emphasis on the quarterback."

Flutie stressed the fact that he was playing relaxed. "The key to reading defenses is that if you are relaxed you just see things. If you're tense you're taking specific reads and reacting to that whereas a veteran quarterback or a guy who is relaxed out there drops back and notices the position of the free safety or the deep drop of a linebacker. It's second nature to him. He can see other things."

Flutie compared the CFL and NFL. "It's a different game, that's for sure.

Doug Flutie—three Grey Cup wins in four tries, six Outstanding Player Awards.

When you have a seven-man front and a five-man secondary, the majority of the time there's a free safety in the middle of the field. That kind of simplifies the reads. However, the open areas on the field are different than in American football. The width of the field opens up bigger seams, but it also makes you throw that long ball to the wide side a lot, which is harder on your arm.

"The 20-second clock hasn't been bad. I got a good feeling for that relatively quickly. Having three downs was the biggest adjustment. With only three downs, I became very paranoid about calling running plays.

"In the NFL you're definitely a robot. Everything is signaled in from the sidelines. Everything is predetermined. Up here you have a lot more responsibility. You are in total control. Because it is a passing game, the ball is in your hands a lot more."

Echoing Danny Barrett, Flutie concluded, "Patience is the toughest thing for a quarterback. To be able to just dump the ball off to a back when people drop deep or to take the 5-yard gain when it's there or throw the ball away when it isn't there—that's the toughest thing to teach."

His greatest strength? "Just making the right reads and getting the ball to the person who's open, I guess. Doing the right thing at the right time."

In 1998 Flutie quarterbacked the Buffalo Bills into the AFC play-offs and won a spot in the Pro-Bowl.

After their fast start in 1992, Calgary split the next eight before finishing the season with seven straight wins and a final mark of 13–5, good for first place. After scraping by Saskatchewan 22–20 in the semifinal, the Eskimos hooked up with Calgary for their third consecutive Western Final.

As usual it was a thriller. With a minute and a half left, the Eskimos were leading 22–16. Then Flutie went to work, marching to within the shadow of the enemy goalpost via strikes to Sapunjis and Pitts. With time running out Flutie audibled to tackle Ken Moore and slipped, minus a shoe, into the end zone behind him. Shoeless Doug Flutie had found a way to win. The final score was 23–22. After the game the former All-American and Heisman Trophy winner said the comeback was his greatest moment in football, even greater than the play that made him famous, the "Hail Mary" touchdown pass that beat Miami 47–45.

Flutie completed 396 passes for 5,945 yards and 32 touchdowns during the season, all totals second to Kent Austin, but his 57.6 percent completion rate was the second worst of his CFL career. Flutie also ran for 669 yards and scored 11 rushing touchdowns. He won the Most Outstanding Player Award and made All-Canadian along with Allen Pitts, Rocco Romano, Will Johnson, Junior Thurman and Darryl Hall.

On to Victory!

In the Grey Cup against Winnipeg in Toronto, Flutie was flawless. Winnipeg's strength lay on the ground with rookie running back Michael Richardson, who led the league in rushing with 1,153 yards. If Calgary could jump into an early 10-point lead they would force Winnipeg out of the running game and render the Bomber defense less effective by making it play cautiously.

That is exactly what happened. Calgary scored on four of their first five possessions, making the Bombers' Matt Dunigan put the ball in the air. Richardson picked up only 21 yards in the first half and 27 overall. Although the ground game was their forte, Winnipeg only ran the ball once in the second half.

The Stampeders took an early lead when Mark McLoughlin kicked a 37-yard field goal. Four minutes and 29 seconds later he missed on a field-goal attempt and picked up a single. Four minutes later, Flutie finished a drive with a 35-yard pass to Dave Sapunjis.

"It was a simple corner pattern," the Western Ontario grad recalled. "They were playing a man-to-man defense, which meant that their defensive player was one on one with me. I beat him inside. I know Flutie didn't see the ball after he released it. He just let it go to the area I normally am in. It was a perfect pass. It was a romp, really."

McLoughlin kicked two 17-yard field goals in the second quarter to give Calgary a 17–0 lead at the half.

The third quarter was scoreless. At 2:36 of the fourth, Flutie completed a 15-yard pass to Pitts for a touchdown. "It was called a 144X-Smash," said Pitts. "I'm the X receiver and that's a corner route by me. The Bombers were in man coverage that play. I just beat the guy, and Doug did a real good job of putting the ball in a very good spot."

With 6:37 left in the game, Winnipeg finally got on the scoreboard, when Troy Westwood kicked a 46-yard field goal. Four minutes later, Gerald Alphin scored their only touchdown. The final score: Calgary 24, Winnipeg 10. The Stampeders had won their second Grey Cup.

Flutie was the Player of the Game. He completed 15 of his first 20 passes and 17 of 25 by the half. He finished the game with 33 out of 49 for 480 yards and two touchdowns, the second-best performance in Grey Cup history. Dave Sapunjis was again the Canadian Player of the Game with seven receptions for 85 yards and a touchdown. Honorable mention should have gone to Derrick Crawford. After a banner 1990 season, Crawford had shattered his ankle in the first game of 1991. He was never quite the same until that Sunday at SkyDome, where he played brilliantly, catching six passes for 162 yards. It was his finest day in a Stampeder uniform.

The 24–10 score flattered Winnipeg. "We moved the ball a whole lot, yes," agreed Pitts, "but we didn't finish off drives like we should have."

Said Calgary's Sapunjis, "We absolutely dominated that game. We probably should have put up 42 points. We marched the ball down every time we had to. We just didn't put it into the end zone every time. Defensively we stopped them."

Blue Bomber Stan Mikawas agreed with Sapunjis. "Flutie did a number on us. He's very elusive and very fast with his release and his speed. We just couldn't stop him, and our offense couldn't get anything on the board. It was exactly opposite to what we did in Edmonton in 1990."

Mikawas assessed the tactics to stop Flutie. "We tried a number of things," Mikawas said. "The best way to do it is to react. The faster you can get to him — in other words the better the pressure — the better chance you'll have. We tried it. We had guys all over him, and he still completed passes."

Mark McLoughlin scored half of Calgary's points, demonstrating that no matter how dominant the offense, the place-kicker always has to be ready to perform. "In 1992 it seemed like we just controlled the game from the very outset," he said. "And to me, personally, the outcome was never in doubt. I knew we were going to win that game just by the way we were controlling the football. But the score was a lot closer than the play indicated."

McLoughlin described how the team prepared for the 1992 Grey Cup. "We took a very low-key approach during that week. We went into the game with a tremendous amount of confidence. We weren't really concerned about what Winnipeg was going to do, we were just concerned about what we were going to do. Once Doug got hold of the ball, that was it."

While Flutie was spectacular, Matt Dunigan was not. "Dunigan didn't have a good day," said Sapunjis. "You know what? They did not have good coaching that game. We were surprised at how they played us. They were playing linebackers on guys like me, and we beat them every time."

Dunigan insisted he was just missing by inches. Calgary's Will Johnson disagreed. "I don't think so, not in a Grey Cup game when you lose 24–10. Our guys were playing well. They didn't score a point until the fourth quarter, and to be honest I think they were given that touchdown."

The key to victory in 1992? "I don't believe there was a key," said Johnson. "I don't think Winnipeg was that good. They were the team in the East. There was no competition in the East."

McLoughlin described what it was like to win. "It was a great feeling. It was also a bit of a relief, too, because it's a long year. These guys go through a lot physically and mentally. It is a lot easier for me to go through a season than it is for the other players. But still, the bottom line is the team goal, and that is winning the championship. When you have an opportunity to do that and experience it, it's a great relief, and it really doesn't sink in for a while.

"When we got back to Calgary with the Cup and had the parade, that's when it started to sink in. When you have the off-season to enjoy that — to take the Grey Cup around to different functions, different schools, let other people share in the win — that's when it really hits that you've accomplished a tremendous goal."

For Wally Buono and his Stampeders it was two Grey Cup appearances in three years. Everybody was talking dynasty. But while they dominated the 1992 Grey Cup, they got out of the West by the skin of their teeth. Buono was not concerned. "Some of the greatest games I ever had as a player were in the Eastern division final. When you play the final, the game is usually very close or it's a complete blowout. Did Edmonton's defense fail because they couldn't stop Doug Flutie in the last 38 seconds? I don't think so. You've got to give the players credit. Great players rise to the occasion and do great things. That is what Doug did."

Still the coach didn't think Doug Flutie was the difference in terms of the Stampeders being Grey Cup finalists in 1991 and winning it all in 1992. "It had nothing to do with Flutie, really. Not to say that he wasn't very important. The intention of our players from January 1 to November 29 was to be the Grey Cup champion. So the focus from the beginning of each workout until the end was to be the champion.

"Everybody in June has aspirations to go to the Grey Cup that may be short-lived. You start struggling and you realize it won't happen. That's not the way it was with us. Our theme was—and will be again—playing in and winning that big game in November. When you get that focus, your mind, your body, your actions reflect that. You could be lucky and accidentally win the Grey Cup. But I think the teams that are prepared to win it and expect to win it have the advantage.

"What are the biggest things this team has? I think two things: one, they've got the skills. If you've got the skills, all you have to do is go out and do what is natural for you. Two, you have to have the determination to want to do it again. The reason our veterans accepted pay cuts in the off-season wasn't the desire to be nice to me—it was to return and win again as a team. The players would take a pay cut because they expected to make it to the Grey Cup."

In preparation for the 1993 season Lou Cafazzo moved over to defense, replaced by Todd Storme. Carl Bland, an outstanding possession receiver, gave way to Brian Wiggins and Will Moore. Pee Wee Smith was relegated to second string. On defense Kent Warnock retired, overcome by chronic injuries. His place was taken by import Eric Johnson. Greg Peterson also retired, replaced by Guelph Griffin Greg Knox. Darryl Hall went to the NFL. Greg Eaglin and Gerald Vaughn were added to the secondary.

Buono was particularly high on Knox. "Tom Higgins and I went to the Vanier Cup and liked him. The knock against him was that he had some injuries. We had a priority list for the draft, and we felt if he was available in the fifth or sixth round, we would take him. He was and we did.

"Greg started 10–12 games as a rookie last year, and he played very well. His confidence level will be much higher this year, and he'll really feel like part of the team. Greg is competitive. He's a pretty tough kid. When there is an opportunity, that's when you'll see what kind of player you have. If he seizes the opportunity like I think he will, his career will take off."

And so it did. Knox made All-Canadian in 1994.

From Ecstasy to Agony

The Stampeders came out of the starting gate like Secretariat in 1993, winning 10 in a row. They hadn't lost since September 27, 1992, their winning streak of 17 games the fifth longest in league history. The streak ended at Commonwealth Stadium on September 10, when they lost 29–16 before 54,324 fans. Calgary was hit by the injury bug, losing Pitts, Jenkins and Thurman for the rest of season.

The Cowboys responded to adversity by winning their next four and five of their remaining seven to finish first with a mark of 15–3. The top four Western teams made the play-offs, so it was Calgary versus B.C. and Edmonton against Saskatchewan. Calgary won 17–9, the Eskimos 51–13. The Alberta entries prepared to meet in the Western Final for the fourth year in a row.

Calgary's record was deceptive. Besides losing Pitts, Thurman and Jenkins, Will Johnson was on the limp and Matt Finlay was in constant pain. Edmonton had played extremely well since beating Calgary on September 10 and had won the last regular season game against the Stamps 39–21. While Calgary had lost at home only once in two years, the Eskimos were a better team on a bad field.

As it turned out, field conditions weren't bad—they were worse. The few days leading up to the Western Final were bitterly cold with snow. Long-time observers couldn't remember more daunting weather for a football game than that of the Western Final. The artificial turf would be sorely tested.

The Stamps started in dramatic fashion with Pee Wee Smith returning a punt 64 yards for a touchdown three minutes into the opening quarter. Mark McLoughlin added a field goal to give Calgary a 10–0 lead after one quarter of play. In the second frame Edmonton scored a touchdown on a 73-yard pass and run from Damon Allen to Jim Sandusky. Edmonton added a single before Calgary replied with a field goal. Calgary led 13–8 at the half.

Half time was extended to allow the stadium crew to clear the snow off the field. That seemed to be all Edmonton needed. Damon Allen completed touchdown passes to Sandusky, Eddie Brown and Jay Christensen while the Esks' defense held Calgary to 2 measly points. The final score was Edmonton 29, Calgary 15. Flutie left the game in the fourth quarter complaining about cold hands. It was an even harder loss for the Stampeders because the Grey Cup in 1993 was to be played in Calgary. To lose the right to defend their title in their stadium to their arch enemy was a bitter pill to swallow.

The 1994 Stampeders were even more impressive throughout the regular season, winning 12 of their first 14 games and 3 of the last 4, finishing on top for the fourth time in five years. Again Wally Buono had to replace key people, losing Harold Hasselbach to the NFL, Karl Anthony and Ken Watson to Baltimore and Andy McVey and Keyvan Jenkins to retirement. When asked what he wanted to improve for 1994, Buono replied, "I'd like to improve how we handle –40-degree weather, but I don't think we can find a way to practice that."

A worry had to be Allen Pitts, who had broken his leg the year before. "I went to L.A. on April 10 and worked Allen out," said Buono. "We were very pleased with his progress. He reassured me that he would be ready to go and be as effective as he once was. Tremendous speed has never been Allen's forte. It's his size, his demeanor, his ability to get open. None of that has changed. He might even be a step faster because of all the hard work and rehab he's done."

Sure enough Pitts had his greatest year as a pro in 1994, catching a record 126 passes for 2,036 yards and 21 touchdowns. He led the league in receptions, yards, yards from scrimmage and touchdowns. Needless to say he was All-Canadian.

Flutie won the Outstanding Player Award for the fourth time. He completed 403 passes for 5,726 yards and 48 touchdowns. He led the league in passing attempts, completions, yards and passing touchdowns. He set the CFL record for attempts, completions and yards in one season. In just five years Flutie had become the eighth-leading passer of all time in the CFL.

On July 27 Calgary's opponent was Winnipeg. As a backdrop to former greats Earl Lunsford and Tom Forzani being inducted onto the Wall of Fame, Flutie led the Stamps to a 58–19 win, the most points in club history. Calgary scored 50 of those points in the first half, when Flutie threw six touchdown passes and ran for two others. "It was one of those nights when everything works for you," said a delighted Flutie.

The following week the Stampeders took on the undefeated B.C. Lions.

This time the score was 62–21. On August 19 they beat Saskatchewan 54–15, a week later Toronto 52–3. On Labour Day they pounded the Eskimos 48–15. Through the first half of the season, the Stamps averaged 43.5 points per game while surrendering 16.5. It was the greatest run of offense in CFL history.

The Cowboys coasted home in first place with a mark of 15–3. With another four-team play-off, Calgary faced Saskatchewan in the semifinal, winning 36–3. The Stamps were jubilant to learn that B.C. had upset the dreaded Eskimos 24–23, ignoring the fact they had beaten the Lions by only a single point the last game of the regular season.

To make matters worse for the Leos, both their quarterbacks, Danny McManus and Kent Austin, were hurt. They came into Calgary on a hope, a wing and a prayer. Lions' coach Dave Ritchie ended up being convinced of divine intervention. On the last play of the game, on a snowy McMahon Stadium field, Lions' pivot McManus hit Darren Flutie in the end zone. David 37, Goliath 36.

For Mark McLoughlin the loss was the most devastating of his career. "We had a lot of opportunities, and personally I had a lot of opportunities to contribute to a victory in that game. A couple of those drives—if we could have ended them with field goals—probably would have given us the margin of victory we needed. It didn't happen, so it ended up being a B.C. Grey Cup. I guess for the sake of the league it turned out to be very positive."

Approaching the 1995 season, Wally Buono was a frustrated man. He had the third-best winning percentage in CFL history. Doug Flutie and Allen Pitts were rewriting the record book. His Stampeders had finished first every year but one in the 1990s. They should have been regarded as one of the best teams of all time, but they weren't because they only had one Grey Cup to show for all their brilliance.

Buono looked ahead to 1995. "We'd like to improve our pressure on the opposing quarterback. I'd like to establish a running game sooner in the year. The biggest thing is that I'd like to win the games that are most important.

"In the last four years we played in four Western Finals. We won two, we lost two. We should have won all four. The tragedy of our sport is the fact that you play one game to get on to the next step and sometimes that isn't the game in which you are at peak performance.

"Last year defensively we played as consistently as anybody in the league for as long as I can remember, yet when it came to the Western Final we didn't play anywhere close to the level we played at during the season or in the semifinal, where our defense dominated a good Saskatchewan team. I don't know what happened. I wish I did. We talked to the players at half time and mentioned that it was important to get back to being more dominant. Sometimes what you say doesn't happen.

"How can we improve? By winning the Western Final and Grey Cup," Buono concluded. "Can we win more than 15 games? We talked about that last year at this time. We won 15. I guess the issue for this year is whether we can win three play-off games."

Like everyone else, the Calgary club lost key players to free agency and retirement. Gone were corners Junior Thurman and Douglas Craft, receivers Will Moore and Brian Wiggins, offensive linemen Doug Davies and Ken Moore, as well as backup quarterback Steve Taylor.

The O-Line was revamped with Bruce Beaton, Denny Chronopoulous, Jamie Crysdale, Bobby Pandelidis and Rocco Romano. Bruce Covernton missed most of the season with an injury and never fully recovered. Terry Vaughn and Tyrone Williams replaced Wiggins and Moore, who went to the NFL, and Marvin Coleman and Al Jordan started on the corners. Marvin Pope replaced Ken Walker at defensive end with Anthony McLanahan replacing Pope at linebacker.

No matter the changes, Calgary still had Flutie. Again the Stampeders got off to a fast start, winning their first seven games. In the next game, at home to the Birmingham Barracudas, disaster struck. After breaking the 30,000-yard career passing mark, Flutie injured his elbow and was unable to answer the bell for the third quarter. The Barracudas went on to win 31–26, ending Calgary's 27 home-game winning streak. Flutie had surgery the following week. His doctor said he was out for the season. Surely the Stampeders were doomed.

When Jeff Garcia replaced Flutie in the third quarter, sportswriters scrambled to find out something about this red-headed kid from California. No one worried about Calgary's second-string quarterback because Flutie had never missed a game in his CFL career. (After returning from his injury, he wouldn't miss another.)

Showing the self-assurance of an old veteran, Garcia proceeded to win six games in a row, including the Labour Day Classic against Edmonton, where he threw six touchdown passes, equaling the record held by Pete Liske and Doug Flutie. Calgary's newest hero took it all in stride. "Today was just a dream come true," he said. "I know it's a big game for the province, but I've been through many big games in college, games where we were highly overmatched. But in this situation we were not overmatched.

"The main thing I try to do is play within myself. I have tremendous athletes around me, especially great receivers. The thing is to get the ball to them and let them do what they do best. With that kind of supporting cast, I don't need to go out and make everything happen. I feel confident in them, and that helps me calm down and get comfortable."

Knowing how good he was, it must have been frustrating sitting on the bench before Flutie got hurt. "I think that was something I was dealing with early on," Garcia conceded. "I knew I was going to get opportunities to play late in games because of the manner in which we were able to put teams away. Was I content with that? Not really. But I was in a situation where I was backing up the best quarterback in the league. I was learning and growing within the system. I pretty much felt that I was just going to wait out my remaining years on my contract. I never really saw what was coming, but I was prepared for it."

Calgary finished at 15–3 atop the Northern Division. In three years Calgary's regular season record was 45–9, the best winning streak in CFL history.

But it was play-off time. This time the Stamps left nothing to chance. In the new play-off format to accommodate American expansion, all the Canadian teams were in one division. Calgary faced Hamilton in the semifinal. Against all odds Doug Flutie was back but turned the ball over five times before being booed off the field at half time. Garcia returned, winning a surprisingly close game, 18–15. Was the Cowboy collar getting tight?

Edmonton had been thoroughly whipped by the Stampeders the first week of September, losing 51–24 on Labour Day, and four days later back at Commonwealth Stadium by a score of 33–17. Nevertheless the Eskimos hadn't lost since then, including their 26–15 play-off win over B.C. For the fifth time in six years, Edmonton and Calgary would meet in the division final. This time the Stamps got King Kong off their back, walking all over the Eskimos 37–4.

Despite his early return from elbow surgery, Flutie played the game of his life in the Northern Final. He threw short over the middle to Vince Danielson, Sapunjis and Pitts. He went long to Terry Vaughn and Tyrone Williams. Occasionally he took off with the ball, putting moves on defenders that would male a bullfighter green with envy. He was magnificent.

The competitive fires burn deeply in this man who was stung by the booing he took in the semifinal. He was hurt by suggestions in 1993 that Calgary had lost the final because he couldn't handle the cold. He looked forward to vindication in Regina against Don Matthews' Baltimore Stallions.

Showdown in Saskatchewan

The Stallions, also finishing at 15–3, would be a formidable opponent in the 1995 Grey Cup. Baltimore was fifth in points, seventh in total offense. They led the league in rushing but were dead last in passing. They had a better giveaway–takeaway ratio than Calgary and had fewer penalties.

Baltimore was led by running back Mike Pringle, who had set the CFL rushing record in 1994 with 1,972 yards and was runner-up to Doug Flutie for the Most Outstanding Player Award. He found a home in Baltimore after being cut by Edmonton and traded by Sacramento.

In 1995 Pringle again led the league in rushing with 1,791 yards. He also picked up 2,359 all-purpose yards and beat out Dave Sapunjis for the Outstanding Player award. Sponge caught 111 passes for 1,655 yards and 12 touchdowns, winning the Canadian Player Award. Baltimore also had Chris Wright, who picked up 2,450 all-purpose yards.

To win the Grey Cup, Calgary's Will Johnson, Stu Laird, Marvin Pope and Gonzalo Floyd would have to win the war in the trenches against Baltimore's mammoth offensive line of Shar Pourdanesh, John James, Mike Withycombe, John Earle and Neal Fort, who weighed an average of 305 pounds. The Stampeder defensive line averaged 250 pounds.

Calgary had led the league against the run and had held Pringle to 50 yards when they beat Baltimore 25–15. Calgary also was first in total offense, points and passing. Baltimore's pass defense ranked ninth in yards and twelfth in completions.

Baltimore's strength was rushing. Calgary had trouble running the ball. Baltimore's weakness was pass defense. The Stampeders were tops in that department. If it came down to field goals, Stallion Carlos Huerta made good on 79 percent of his kicks, Stampeder Mark McLoughlin on 83 percent. Baltimore's punter, Josh Miller, was clearly superior to the Stampeders' Tony Martino.

Calgary's ace in the hole would be Flutie. Not one Baltimore defender believed in his heart that Flutie could be stopped.

The Stampeder defensive strategy would be to box in Tracy Ham and force him to throw. But overlooked in all the statistical analysis was one interesting fact: although poorly regarded as a passer, Stallion quarterback Tracy Ham had the third highest career percentage completion rate in CFL history.

The Stampeders' Matt Finlay was playing his last game. His spirit was willing, but his flesh just couldn't take it anymore. Finlay looked back to the beginning of his distinguished career. "I was drafted by Montreal in '86," he recalled. "Montreal folded, of course. I was there for one week. Willie Pless was injured, and Bob O'Billovich told me at that time I would be there and be part of their system. A week later Willie came off his injury and Toronto traded me to Calgary. I think they planned all along to only use me for the week.

"It was a disappointment, I guess, Toronto being my hometown and my family being there, but it would have been really difficult to play in my hometown. I've seen that here in Calgary. For me getting out of Toronto was a good move.

"When I was in Grade Nine in Mississauga, I told my mother that I was going to get a scholarship in the States. She said that was fine. I don't know whether she believed me or not, but I did end up getting a scholarship to Eastern Michigan. Two years later I told my Dad I was going to play pro. He said that's great, but make sure you get your education, which I did. It all worked out."

Finlay paid a high price for his career. "I tore a bicep," he said. "It's going to be that way forever. That's not going to change. My knee is slowly getting better, but it'll take some time. I'm wearing a brace now and will until I retire. My Achilles tendon is pretty bad right now. It's hard to run, so I don't do much of that during the week, only in games.

"Pain is part of the game. I've always played with pain. In college I had knee surgery and two shoulder surgeries."

One of his greatest admirers was another outside linebacker, Wally Buono. "I've seen the progression of Matt Finlay from a rookie to a very seasoned football player who right now is one of the premier linebackers in the league.

"Watching Matt Finlay mature, not only as a football player but also as a leader, has been very rewarding to me," Buono continued. "Matt is a consummate pro. He's always well prepared. He leads by example, keeping the other players motivated. He helps them to be sharp on the field. He's worked extremely hard to get where he's at. He's had a good career."

Finlay talked about getting ready for Grey Cup 1995. "Experience is certainly going to help us cope with the jitters. Guys who have been there before don't get as nervous. They'll be able to settle down quicker. But this is the second year in a row for Baltimore, so we can't use that as an advantage. About half our team has been to two Grey Cups. This is my third.

"The largest crowd in Canadian sports for the year is watching the game. If you think about it, it could get to you. A great number of people are watching you, and one wrong move could mean a loss for your team. The reality is there is a lot more pressure. Someday you are going to look back and think that if I'd made this play we might have won the Grey Cup. But the game of football is pressure."

Hugh Campbell said that blaming a loss on one play is too simplistic. "That's very true," said Finlay, "but personally you don't want to be the one who makes the mistake. What do people remember about Toronto and Calgary in 1971? Leon McQuay fumbling the ball. Whoever said one play didn't win a game is probably right, but one person is remembered for losing the game if he made a mistake in a close game."

Finlay agreed that shutting down Baltimore's running attack and having good coverage on special teams was essential to victory. "That's been basically our game plan all year. By concentrating on the run we try to make teams one dimensional and throw the ball, especially with teams that have great running backs like Pringle. If you can shut him down that really limits what they are able to do. Even Ham running is not all that bad because he's not going to beat you alone. He needs a tailback to do the running.

"What we're really concentrating on is special teams. Baltimore is excellent in all aspects of special teams play. They have who I consider to be the premier returner in the league in Chris Wright. If you're not careful, he'll blow right by you for a touchdown. Baltimore has the premier punter in the league. He gets the ball down the field in a big way every time. So we are going to need big returns on our side and we're going to have to limit their returns. At best we're looking at a draw for our team. We can't let them win the battle of the special teams because that could make the difference in the game."

The Grey Cup game unfolded exactly as Finlay predicted.

After leading his team into the play-offs, Jeff Garcia was the odd man out. "Hopefully I'll get an opportunity to play in Sunday's game," he offered. "I'm preparing like it's any other game, not trying to overemphasize it even though in the back of my mind I know it's for all the marbles.

"The coaches told us they want us to enjoy the week, to have a good time because we are deserving of it and worked very hard to get here. Have some fun early on, but definitely don't lose sight of why we're here. Stay focused and go about preparing for the game just like any other." Garcia didn't play a down.

His offensive coordinator, John Hufnagel, knew Garcia would be disappointed. In the 1984 Grey Cup, when Tom Clements had lost a contact lens and had to come out, it was Hufnagel who went in and got the Bombers untracked. When Clements got another lens, Hufnagel returned to the sideline. He made sure Garcia understood that his value to the team wasn't diminished because Flutie was starting.

Hufnagel thought the Satmpeders' Grey Cup experience was an advantage. "At home or in a normal week, you have them in the meetings, you have them going home. Things just run their normal course. Here it is tough to stay focused. That's what the players have to fight through—staying focused enough to prepare themselves for the big game. I think that the more experience you have at it, the smarter you are and the better you're able to handle the distractions.

"Both teams are going to be challenged by their coaches: 'Hey, this is it. This is what we've worked for. This is the Grey Cup, a chance to prove how good we are. We don't want to disappoint the fans.'"

No team has ever said they came out flat when they lost a Grey Cup, not surprising to Hufnagel. "I think it would be very difficult to say you came out flat for the biggest game of the season, sometimes the biggest game of your career. I mean, you may come out and not play well, but I can't see being flat.

"The worst thing is being too concerned about making a mistake. If you're going to be that concerned about it, you're not going to be flying around. This is what mental preparation is all about. If you make a mistake, just don't make it again, but at least you're flying around and creating havoc, hitting people and knocking people down.

"Grey Cup is a special couple of days. You're trying to remain as calm as possible and focus yourself. Come game time, it's an exciting moment, an exciting day."

In Regina it was a windy day. The theme for Grey Cup '95 was "Huddle Up in Saskatchewan," but the really cold weather never materialized. Grey Cup week had been unseasonably balmy, but early Sunday morning a ferocious wind blew in.

Said Commissioner Larry Smith, "The only problem I had as commissioner was in Regina in 1995 when the wind got up to about 85 kph. Our insurance on the temporary stands covered us to 90 kph, and we had a backup plan to take

20,000 people into a hockey rink and watch it on the screens. That was a little scary. But the winds abated and stuck about 75, so we were okay."

Calgary received the opening kickoff, returning it to the 40. With the wind at his back Flutie threw 13 yards to Sapunjis. Tony Stewart lost a yard, Flutie threw incomplete and Calgary took a roughing penalty. Martino punted 43 yards to Chris Wright at the Baltimore 28. Wright returned it 82 yards for a touchdown. With 2:12 gone, the score was Baltimore 7, Calgary 0.

Tony Stewart fumbled the ensuing kickoff, recovered by Stallion Tracey Gravely. Baltimore moved from the Calgary 47 to the 36, where they lined up for a field-goal try. Dan Crowley bobbled the snap and was sacked for an 8-yard loss. Taking over at their 44, Flutie completed a 16-yarder to Vaughn and 8 and 11 to Stewart, bringing the ball to the Stallion 28. After two incompletions McLoughlin kicked a 35-yard field goal.

Two possessions later, Flutie moved the Stamps from their 51 to the Baltimore 25, where McLoughlin added a 32-yarder. At the end of the first quarter the score stood at Baltimore 7, Calgary 6.

Starting at their 35, Baltimore moved to the Calgary 47, where Tracy Ham threw a screen pass behind Gerald Alphin. Will Johnson picked it off and ran to the enemy 3. Flutie surprised everyone in the ball park by throwing to Marvin Pope for the touchdown. Seconds into the second quarter, Calgary led 13–7.

Baltimore struck back. Starting at the Stallions' 47, Ham completed an 18-yarder to Robert Drummond. He then hit Robert Clark at the 23. First down incomplete. Second down, Pringle was wide open and dropped it. Huerta kicked a 30-yard field goal.

Five minutes later Calgary was set to punt. Players were looking at each other and throwing up their hands, indicating confusion on the Calgary line. Sure enough, O.J. Brigance blocked the punt, Alvin Watson picked it up and ran to the end zone. Baltimore 17, Calgary 13 — both Stallion touchdowns coming on special team breakdowns. Baltimore added two more field goals to take a half-time lead of 23–13.

Baltimore had the wind in the third quarter. On their third play Miller kicked an 80-yard single. Doug Flutie then went to work. Flutie for 9, Stewart for 10 and then for 2. Flutie to Pitts for 10. Stewart 5, Flutie to Sponge for 7, to Vaughn for 22. Flutie took it the rest of the way on three plays. The 65-yard drive ate up six and a half minutes into the wind. The score was Baltimore 24, Calgary 20.

After a penalty Baltimore started out at their 18. Ham completed five passes to the Calgary 14. Pringle picked up 1 and then Ham ran 13 yards for the major, making the score at the end of the third quarter 31–20 for Baltimore. A key play was a third and 1 at the Calgary 49. Ham was awarded the first down over the strenuous objections of the Stampeders. Given Calgary's momentum at that point, the placement of that ball likely cost them the Grey Cup.

Even though they had the wind at their backs, Calgary was shut out in the final quarter while Carlos Huerta added two field goals. The final score was Baltimore 37, Calgary 20. Canada's Grey Cup had fallen into American hands.

Tracy Ham completed 17 of 29 for 213 yards, ran for 24 and a touchdown and was named Player of the Game. Dave Sapunjis, 8 for 113 yards, was the Canadian Player of the game for the third time.

One play in particular stood out in Sapunjis's mind. "We had what we called a hitch pass, which is basically a 15-yard pass along the line of scrimmage, where I take one step and then come back. I look at Flutie, he throws me the ball and I have to run with it.

"And so I caught it. It was only a 1-yard gain at the time. I broke a couple of tackles and turned it into a 35-yard gain. That was maybe our biggest offensive play of the game. I was out there working hard and making things happen."

Calgary had trouble getting by Baltimore's 25-yard line. "They stopped us down there quite well," Sapunjis agreed. "They played a defense where they just dropped guys back and let us try to pick it apart—and we didn't. We struggled from the 25-yard line in. It wasn't any one player. As a unit we didn't move the ball when we had to."

Sapunjis analyzed the game. "I think, first of all, we were always chasing Baltimore. Chris Wright returned a punt all the way for a touchdown. The game started off as a special team problem like it did in '91.

"Defensively we had a scheme where we were going to let Tracy Ham sit in the pocket and throw. Well, we did that, and he tucked the ball underneath and ran with it.

"It was just like that play in 1991 when Rocket returned it all the way. The guys on the sideline were trying to get going, and all of a sudden they broke a big play and our emotional level dropped. It hurt us, for sure. Both '91 and '95 were similar in the fact that the other team's special team dominated."

Coach Buono agreed with that assessment. "It is tough to recover when you play a good football team. Maybe we weren't on top of our game either. Defensively I thought our guys hung in there very well. Offensively we had some drives, but we were not as consistent throughout the night as we would liked to have been. It is tough to spot any team 14 points on special teams and think you're going to win."

Buono analyzed the special team breakdown. "The first one, Wright hit a crease. That happens with a good returner. He found a crease and got into the open field. On the blocked punt I think there was miscommunication. They were moving around, one of our guys let somebody through and he blocked the punt."

Dave Sapunjis described the mood at half time. "I think we were happy to be only down 10 points. We came into the locker room and said we can win this thing if we go out there and start playing better. We knew we could only play better. We couldn't play any worse.

"And then we went out there and, hey, we had a great drive at one point in the third quarter. We marched the ball down and scored. We made it pretty close, and all of a sudden you could feel the energy on the sidelines being lifted. We were ready to go out there and win. But then they marched the ball down and scored."

Sapunjis agreed with Flutie starting the game. "I think you had to go with Doug. We talked about that all week, and I said you have to go with his experience. Go with the leadership, go with the guy who has played in the Grey Cup and won. If he really struggles, then maybe bring in Jeff. Doug played well enough to win. I think the guys around him didn't play well enough to win."

Winning the Canadian Player of the Game three times and the Outstanding Canadian Award twice were the highlights of Sapunjis's career. "I take great pride in playing well in the big games. I've been named the league's Outstanding Canadian twice, and that's not a feat many have accomplished. It's something I take a lot of pride in, and when I finish this game I hope I'll be known as one of the best Canadian receivers ever."

Will Johnson disagreed with the Stampeders' strategy to contain Tracy Ham. "The plan was to box him in and let him throw out of the pocket. We didn't want to let him run. But any quarterback, no matter how lousy, is going to pick you apart if he stays in the pocket for a long time."

"Because Tracy is so successful running the ball," said Greg Battle, who spent many years chasing him, "a lot of people don't realize he is also a good passer. As he gets older he'll run and scramble to find receivers who are open because it is hard for a defensive back to cover a guy for 6 or 7 seconds. That usually results in a very big play."

Johnson thought Calgary's defense should have been going after him, trying for the sack. Why didn't he? "I did later on, but the other guys are more coach-conscious whereas I'm more win-oriented. I've been in the league a long time so I do what I think it takes to win.

"If you're pushing a guy back into the quarterback on almost every play and bumping him, then you've got him. If you're not getting any push up the middle, it's useless. So I've got to pass rush. I've got to get off what the coach is saying and do what it is going to take to win this thing.

"I've had my battles with Tracy Ham. When I first came into the league we had our battles, and I ended up winning because he ended up leaving Edmonton and we ended up beating them often."

Stallion coach Don Matthews agreed with Johnson. "It is a surprise that anyone uses that strategy. Tracy Ham or any scrambling quarterback hurts you when you get conservative on your pass rush. When we played against Tracy we sent our front four with reckless abandon after him. We also played a lot of zone, so if he scrambled we were going to treat him like a flare back and just keep him under 5 yards.

"We felt the worst thing we could do was play man coverage with a lot of our defensive backs with their backs to Tracy. Every time you do that you have to slow down your pass rush, which affords him more time, and that's when he's dangerous. Tracy's very bright. He's a remarkable talent and a quality guy. If you try to keep Tracy in the pocket and make him throw, he'll kill you. You've got to go get him."

Matthews followed his own advice against Calgary's Flutie. "We played a lot of three-man rush and kept everybody looking at him because we didn't want him to scramble. On man-to-man coverage you have everybody running off, so when the quarterback scrambles, eight of your players never see him go because they are in coverage. In zone those eight players are looking at him, and they go get him when he takes off." Flutie ran the ball 10 times for only 45 yards.

When the observation was made that Ham had lots of time to throw, Calgary coach Wally Buono replied, "I think that was part of our plan for keeping Tracy boxed in. The defensive line was doing pretty much what we asked them to do, pushing the pocket, trying to stay in front. Overall, the majority of time we did keep him in the pocket. There were times he did have time to throw the football, but I don't think his throwing really hurt us. I think it was more the fact that we gave them some big plays.

"We wanted our D-line's pass rush to be a little bit more under control so that we didn't have Ham running all over the place as he did on his touchdown. At times we did give him a little more time, but that wasn't the key factor. The key factor was the two special teams plays and our inability to catch the football and keep drives alive.

"We let them score in the third quarter," Buono continued. "We were trying to get momentum, and it was critical for our defense not to give up any points in the third quarter. We did, which neutralized the touchdown we got. We sawed off with them. That's not what we wanted to do. We wanted to win the third quarter to put our offense in a position to get points in the fourth quarter. But Baltimore put that ball in the end zone, which was a big demoralizer.

As far as Mark McLoughlin was concerned, the reason Calgary lost was simple. "We were outplayed," he concluded. "Bottom line, we were outplayed. When Baltimore needed to make the big plays they got them, and when we needed to make the big plays we didn't."

Still Grey Cup '95 was memorable for the Calgary kicker. "I really enjoyed the week in Regina. The fans were fantastic. It's unfortunate we didn't get to play the day before because the weather was beautiful and then, of course, game day they had that tremendous wind.

Coach Buono summed up his feelings about the loss. "I'd be more disappointed if we had played our best and lost. We made a lot of mistakes, and in a game of this nature, playing a team as good as the Stallions, if you make mistakes you end up losing. But this team has had a tremendous run. We had a lot of adversity this year. We fought through it and put ourselves in the position to be Grey Cup champions. Today we fell short."

Given all the changes the Stampeders have had to make every year, Dave Sapunjis thought the team had done remarkably well. "I think it is a real tribute to the organization, the coaching staff, the players. Wally's always said—and we talk about it—that he maintains a core group of people here: Stu Laird, Allen Pitts, Will Johnson, Alondra Johnson, me. This is sort of a core group of guys that are out there working hard every day. The new guys come in here, and when they see the veterans working hard, they start feeding off that.

"Plus we have great fans, great community support. You go to other cities like Toronto and the CFL isn't big time for them. Out here it is. So we feed off that. This is a great organization to play for and a lot of great players have come in and out of here."

With six months to think about it, Buono looked back at Grey Cup '95. "Maybe if the wind had waited three or four hours, it might have been a different game. We could have controlled our punting game better if that had been the case. You've got to be at the right place at the right time. The circumstances have to be right for you.

"When we played the first part of the game, I knew we were not at our best. But I felt as the game progressed that we started to come out of it. I thought in the third quarter that we started to take control of the game. Then Tracy Ham broke away.

"But there was a play way before that. It was third down. Baltimore went for it and made it by an inch. They could very easily not have made it by an inch. If they didn't make it, we not only had the momentum because we had just scored, but because we had just taken the ball away from them.

"I think Tracy Ham was intent on making his mark. He's a great athlete who has been criticized for not been able to win the big game. Obviously his motivation was extremely high."

During the off-season, free agent Doug Flutie left Calgary to sign with Toronto. Sig Gutsche bought the club. Matt Finlay's battered body finally gave out and he retired. Marvin Pope tried the NFL, failed and came back. Tony Stewart was traded to Hamilton.

The 1996 Stampeders would have Jeff Garcia as starter with a young phenom from the University of Montana, Dave Dickenson, in reserve. Once again Calgary finished first and once again they lost a heart-breaking Western Final at home to the Eskimos 15–12, Garcia going down with a leg injury in the second quarter.

Before the 1997 season began, Allen Pitts smashed his hand in a bar fight but returned to the team in September. Dave Sapunjis, Stu Laird and Rodney Harding retired. Hobbled by a chronic back problem, Will Johnson was released and signed by Saskatchewan. When the Riders came to town in August, Johnson blew out his knee and retired. Pee Wee Smith was cut.

Like all the teams in the Western Conference, the 1997 Stampeders were inconsistent. They finished in second place but looked confidently ahead to knocking off Edmonton and heading north for the Grey Cup. Instead they were defeated by the Cinderella Roughriders and their most disappointing season of the decade was over.

Redemption

Still, when the 1998 campaign got under way, the Stampeders were the most talented team in the country. Wally Buono had signed a contract extension. Jeff Garcia and Dave Dickenson were both outstanding quarterbacks, Allen Pitts, Vince Danielson, Terry Vaughn and Travis Moore were the best receiving corps in the league, Kelvin Anderson was coming off two straight 1,000 plus yard rushing seasons, the offensive line of Jamie Crysdale, Rocco Romano, Fred Childress, Jay McNeil and Rohn Meyer was first-rate.

The Stamps fielded a veteran defense with a front seven of Jermaine Miles, Ray Jacobs, Bronzell Miller, Steve Anderson, Darryl Hall, Anthony McLanahan and Alondra Johnson and a secondary of corners Marvin Coleman and Willie Hampton, defensive backs Eddie Davis and Jack Kellogg, and safety Greg Knox. Tony Martino and Mark McLoughlin led formidable special teams.

But in the past—particularly in 1993–94 and 1996–97—having the best players in the league wasn't enough. There was something missing. In 1997 in particular, little things seemed to go wrong all the time. The team was out of kilter. Some players, particularly on defense, seemed to believe they only had to throw their helmets out on the field to win. The 1998 Stampeders underwent an attitude transformation that led them to their fourth Grey Cup championship.

When asked the difference between '97 and '98, Mark McLoughlin replied, "One word that comes to mind is *focused*. From the first day of training camp, the veterans were determined to get back to the Grey Cup and win it. The veterans stepped forward and provided the leadership."

Said Wally Buono, a week after returning in triumph from Winnipeg, "I don't know how many guys believed they could win the Cup in 1997. This year everybody believed they should win it. Maybe that was a good way to put it in perspective.

"I think the veterans this year really felt they played good football pretty much the whole year, and when it was all said and done, we should be the team that would be hoisting the Cup because we were good enough.

"In 1997 there was a lot of turmoil, which was unsettling all around, all the time. I spent a lot of time putting out fires, trying to mend fences, trying to create what really wasn't there. In 1998 the big thing we always talked about was keeping focused on the goal ahead, which was to be Grey Cup champions."

Did the chemistry on defense improve because of certain individuals? "Maybe the individuals that weren't here more so than the individuals that were here," Buono explained. "The guys I thought were key were Darryl Hall, Steve Anderson and Alondra Johnson. Obviously A.J.'s new attitude, his rededication to himself and his teammates, was a big part of it. I think that by changing one or two guys last year, we took one or two thorns out of the sides of everybody, which helped everything to be just that more congenial."

Gone was Alondra Johnson's side-kick Marvin Pope. Choosing his words carefully, Buono said, "Marvin Pope was not a positive force, especially last year. I don't know how many people he brought with him. I think it was a good separation because of that. That was one of the main reasons I had no consideration for bringing him back."

Although the Stampeders racked up their seventh first-place finish of the decade, it wasn't clear sailing to the Grey Cup. Safety Greg Knox was unable to overcome injuries sustained the year before and had to retire at the end of the season. His replacements, Dave Van Belleghem and Greg Frers, missed several games due to injury. At one time Vince Danielson, Travis Moore and Greg Vaughn were on the injury list together. Pitts was hurt at the beginning of the season, Marvin Coleman, Jermaine Miles and Bronzell Miller later.

In training camp the Stamps had looked invincible at linebacker, but Anthony McClanahan sustained a spinal cord injury that ended his career. Canadian linebacker Raymond Biggs also went down for the count. Buono brought in former Roughrider Henry Newby and Blue Bomber Shonte Peoples, and they soldiered on.

Seven Stampeders made All-Canadian, including Jeff Garcia, Kelvin Anderson, Terry Vaughn, Allen Pitts, Fred Childress, Alondra Johnson and Tony Martino. Four were finalists for the five league awards. Vince Danieleson lost the Top Canadian Award to Hamilton's Mike Morreale, Kelvin Anderson was bested by Mike Pringle for Most Outstanding Player, Ti-Cat Joe Montford beat Alondra Johnson for the Defensive Player Award, but Fred Childress was named Outstanding Offensive Lineman. (Danieleson would be named the Outstanding Canadian on Grey Cup day.)

The most talented Stampeder, Allen Pitts, has never represented the West in the awards. In fact only twice has he even been his team's nominee. And yet in 1998 Pitts moved into second-place all-time in yards receiving with 12,297 and receptions with 792. He set a new record for touchdowns with 101.

After easily disposing of Edmonton in the Conference Final, the Calgary Stampeders headed for Winnipeg. They carried their new attitude into Grey

Cup week. In 1995, in Regina, Coach Buono had imposed no curfew. On the Thursday morning about 7:00 A.M. when team officials were coming down for a meeting, several players were just getting in after an evening of revelry. By their own admission they partied too much and weren't all that focused on the game. In 1998 things were different. A curfew was imposed.

"That was my idea," said Buono. "I talked to the captains about it. Whether that was a big issue or not, I really don't know. Just the fact they even were willing to listen showed that their intentions were better. Maybe the disappointment we shared in the middle '90s had a lot to do with their mental framework than a curfew.

"They came wanting to win, and if that meant they had to be in a couple of nights, it wasn't going to be a big deal. A couple of them probably went out anyway after we checked. But enough of them cared. If you get enough to care, the players will discipline themselves."

Although Jeff Garcia publicly complained about teammates entertaining women into the wee hours of the night, as a whole this was a more disciplined, committed club than the one that lost to Baltimore 1995. And given coaching errors, special teams breakdowns and the talent of the Stallions, in all likelihood the Stamps would still have lost even if they had been sequestered at St. Michael's retreat house in Lumsden.

Grey Cup '98 was an intriguing match-up, another Battle of Alberta, pitting the Calgary Stampeders against Edmonton East, aka the Hamilton Tiger-Cats. The Stamps would face the dynamic duo that broke their hearts in 1994 and 1996, Danny McManus and Darren Flutie. Add in old nemesis Ron Lancaster as coach and the cast was complete. Hamilton's defensive coordinator, Don Sutherin, formerly of Calgary, knew how to stop the Stampeders.

The Westerners were loaded with veterans. Fifteen had played in the '95 Cup, seven in '92 and six in '91. Only four Ti-Cats had been in the big game, including kicker Paul Osbaldiston. The Stamps knew what it took to win a Cup and how long the off-season is when you lose.

The teams were a good match. Calgary was first in points and total offense, Hamilton second. Calgary yielded the second fewest yards, Hamilton was third. Hamilton surrendered the fewest points, Calgary was second.

Hamilton's offensive line of Seth Dittman, Val St. Germain, Carl Coulter, Chris Burns and Dave Hack gave up 15 sacks, the second lowest total in CFL history. Calgary's Garcia and Dickenson went down 40 times. Tony Martino,

Marvin Coleman and Terry Vaughn gave Calgary the edge on special teams. Paul Osbaldiston and Mark McLoughlin were great veterans. Osbaldiston was fourth all-time in scoring with 2,130 points, McLoughlin fifth with 2,126. Call the place-kickers even.

If there was a dark cloud on the horizon for Hamilton it was their fifth-place standing against the run. Also the Stampeders would wear their black uniforms in which they had never tasted defeat.

Come kickoff time, it was a balmy 10°C with a west wind of 28–37 kph. Wally Buono addressed the troops. "I told them, 'We have worked awfully hard to get here, and let's make the most of the opportunities. Let's not come back in here with any regrets.'"

In the Eastern dressing room Ron Lancaster said, "We've probably got further than a lot of people thought. The opportunity to win a Grey Cup isn't there every year. You've worked your tail off to get here, let's finish it off right."

Lancaster knew what it was like to get close but not drink from the Cup. "I can remember my rookie year when I got there," he recalled. "And it took me six years to get there again. It is hard to get to the Grey Cup game, and when you get there, you've got to take the opportunity to win it. Even if you've got a lot of young guys and you think you've got a good team, it is not easy to get back there. It's hard."

Calgary won the coin toss, keeping the wind in the second and fourth quarters.

Calgary opened the scoring at 3:02, when Orlando Steinhauer conceded a single after Mark McLaughlin missed on a 48-yard field-goal try. Four minutes later, Osbaldiston kicked the Cats into the lead with a 24-yard field goal. Soon after, McLoughlin was good from 34 yards out. After 15 minutes Calgary led 4–3, but the Stampeders were on the Hamilton 3-yard line.

In the second quarter, whatever could go wrong for the Stampeders did go wrong. Kelvin Anderson capped the 86-yard, 8-play drive with a 3-yard plunge into the end zone. But the snap went awry, and the convert was no good. Calgary 10, Hamilton 3. Danny McManus replied by marching from his 24 to the enemy 13, where Osbaldiston's 20-yard field goal reduced Calgary's lead to 4 points.

Six plays later, Bobby Olive clearly fumbled Tony Martino's punt, but the referee blew the call. On second and 11 at the Hamilton 20, Greg Frers intercepted McManus, but was called for interference. Wally Buono disagreed. "The referee called us for jamming. I couldn't see it. I thought it was a great play. We did a nice job of disguising what we were doing, but the referee made the call."

With passes to Darren Flutie, Andrew Grigg and Mike Morreale, the Cats drove to the Stamps' 39. McManus then read the blitz brilliantly and hooked up with Ron Williams for a 35-yard touchdown. Hamilton 13, Calgary 10.

Calgary came back, moving the ball to the Hamilton 42, where they lined up for a field-goal attempt. But it was a fake! Dave Dickenson hit Kelvin Anderson right in the bread-basket, but he dropped it. When Calgary got nowhere on their next possession, Martino went back to punt on his 24. The snap was high, and Martino rushed to get it off. It dribbled 23 yards, where the Stampeders were called for no yards. On the final play of the half, Osbaldiston kicked a 40-yard field goal, making the score Hamilton 16, Calgary 10.

Buono was not concerned. "The issue we addressed was the fact that when you look at it, everything really went against us—not in a negative sense but in the what-else-can-go-bad sense—but we were only behind by 6 points. In my mind, 6 points was just one play. I felt very confident, and I challenged the guys individually to go out and do what they knew they could do. I thought they responded very well to it.

"There are highs and lows, there is excitement and relief. At half time some of the guys were getting a little bit edgy, but we calmed them all down until they just relaxed. 'It's no big deal, it's just 6 points and there are still 30 minutes to be played. Let's not come back in here regretting the next 30 minutes.' I thought the players recaptured their focus very well.

"I didn't feel there was any need to panic," Buono explained. "There was no need to point fingers at anybody. The big need was for us to understand what had occurred and to go out and do something about it."

Like Buono, Hamilton coach Ron Lancaster was not concerned. "The game's going to go 60 minutes, and Calgary didn't get to the Grey Cup by laying down," he said. "I didn't feel at half time that either team had control of the game because they were down 6, so there was no reason for us to be concerned because we were up 6. There were still 30 minutes of football to be played, and in this league that's an eternity.

"You never make any drastic changes at half time," Lancaster observed. "You take the game plan you went in with and cut it down to the things that you are executing well and that you think will be good for you the second half. You go in trying to cover all situations, and each quarter you cut it down a bit. If you

Stampeder quarterback Jeff Garcia drinks from the Cup after beating Hamilton 26–24 in the 1998 Grey Cup.

execute your game plan better than them you'll win. If not, you're going to get beat."

Hamilton continued to have the upper hand through the first half of the third quarter but only came away with 2 points. On their opening drive with a third and 5 at Calgary's 52, Lancaster ordered a direct snap to Jarrett Smith, who ran for 20 yards. Three plays later, Osbaldiston missed a 32-yarder.

It was two and out for Calgary. Starting at their 35, McManus moved his team to the Stamp 46, from where Ozzie hoofed a 66-yard single, making the score 18–10 Ti-Cats.

Then Calgary's Garcia and Anderson went to work, marching 75 yards in 14 plays for a touchdown. Anderson picked up 25 yards on the ground and 15 through the air. Garcia took it in from the 1 on the final play of the third quarter. With the convert, Hamilton's lead was cut to 1 point.

Why did those plays with Anderson work then and not earlier? "Sometimes it's the defense that's called," he said. "It's how they've adjusted, it's the fatigue factor. That drive took about seven minutes. The longer the defense is on the field, the more at a disadvantage it is. That's why you want first downs. One builds to two, two to four, four to eight, and pretty soon you're in the end zone.

"We did show them a couple of different formations, which worked to our benefit," Anderson continued. "We put in a tight-end formation with a tackle over, which they hadn't seen. We took Duane Forde out of the formation and put him in at receiver, which made them adjust their front. Those were just the subtle things that went a long way to help us hurt them."

Calgary took the lead at 4:28 of the final frame, when McLoughlin kicked a 22-yard field goal, set up by Aldi Henry's 26-yard interception return. McLoughlin added another 3 points on Calgary's next possession, this one from 32 yards out. With 5:45 remaining, the Stampeders led by 5.

Starting at his 35, Hamilton's McManus threw incomplete. He then hit Grigg for 15. Incomplete again. McManus ran for 9. Third down on the Calgary 51, a 2-yard quarterback sneak. Danny Mac then threw a short pass to Archie Amerson, who took it 47 yards to the 2-yard line. On third and goal, Ron Williams scored. The 2-point conversion attempt failed when Steve Anderson batted the ball down at the line of scrimmage. Hamilton 24, Calgary 23. Two minutes and 2 seconds remained.

"I knew as soon as we scored that there was too much time left on the clock," concluded Ron Lancaster.

The Stamps started out at their 30-yard line with 1:57 remaining in the game. Garcia hit rookie Aubrey Cummings for 12 and Travis Moore for 9. After a quarterback sneak for 2 yards and a first down, Garcia completed the last pass of the game to Moore for 13 yards. First down at the Hamilton 44 with 57 seconds to go. Garcia ran for 8 and 3. At the 32, Anderson carried for 2. Garcia ran 3 yards into the middle of the field. Mark McLaughlin and Dave Dickenson took to the field.

Like all great kickers, McLoughlin lives for the moment the big game is on the line. He went down his mental checklist and prepared to kick. "I was calm," he insisted. "I'd known for about the last three minutes that I'd have to make that kick."

Unlike Glen Suiter and Dave Ridgway in 1989, all was silent that moment in Winnipeg. Asked what he and Dickenson talked about before the kick, McLoughlin replied, "Nothing."

The ball was snapped and put in place. McLoughlin swung through it and drove it to the end zone. Calgary 26, Hamilton 24.

For Winnipeg native McLoughlin, this was the sweetest Grey Cup of all. Referring to his father, who died suddenly of a heart attack the year before, he said, "If only Dad would have been here to see me. But he was here. Without a doubt my dad was right by my side when I kicked it. I wish he could have been here physically to share this moment with me, but I know he was here in spirit."

Mark McLoughlin celebrates his game-winning field goal with teammate Greg Knox.

The king of the quarterbacks praised the Stampeders' Jeff Garcia, who was named the Grey Cup MVP. "He took care of the ball very well on that last drive," said Lancaster. "He hit open receivers. He didn't throw into any trouble, and when it wasn't there he ran with it. When Calgary got across midfield and he was getting close to field-goal range, he did an especially great job of protecting the ball.

"We just stayed with our basic game plan, but they did a real good job of executing on that last drive. That's a sign of a good team. They didn't make any mistakes when things were on the table. We did not make the play when we needed to make it on the last drive.

"It was just one of those games where things that we did during the year we didn't get done in that particular game," Lancaster concluded. "When we had guys open we usually would hit them downfield. A couple of times Dan threw it a little too far in the end zone and under threw Archie Amerson in the end zone. We didn't sack their quarterback, we didn't knock any passes down — things that we did most of the games all year.

"Now, you can say Calgary did an outstanding job and that's probably what happened. They didn't allow us to do the things we did so well. And yet it still came down to a last drive to win the game."

As for the winning field goal, Coach Buono said, "It is something we practice every week: the holder goes back, kneels down, Mark kicks the field goal and life goes on. We said one time this year that we were going to have to do that to win a big game. I can mention another big field goal in 1991 up in Commonwealth Stadium that Mark kicked. That was a tremendous win because that gave this organization a lot of confidence, which carried us into the '90s."

Buono praised the Tiger-Cats. "They were a lot like us. I don't know that they were as explosive on offense as we were, but defensively they were every bit as good if not better than us. They played hard on teams. On offense they had the combo of McManus and Flutie that has always hurt us."

If Calgary had lost the 1998 Grey Cup, the Stampeders of the '90s would forever be labeled the greatest team that never was. In the weeks following their victory, the team shared the Cup with the people of Calgary. Because of the enormous pressure to win, Grey Cup 1998 was especially meaningful for Wally Buono. "For me, it was a very satisfying win for a lot of reasons. I was happy for the players, I was happy for the organization, but I was also happy for myself in a very nonselfish way.

"To see the city really enjoy the victory was tremendous. It is a pleasure to see people get so much joy out of touching the Cup. Sometimes we participants don't realize what a great joy and pleasure it is to the average fan."

As the century draws to a close, the Calgary Stampeders remain the team to beat in the Western Division. During the fifth game of the 1999 season, the Stampeders lost their third starting quarterback, yet remained in first place, indicative of the tremendous strength of their organization. The Stampeders are averaging over 30,000 tickets at the gate and are on pace to set a new season attendance record and turn a profit.

This happy situation has resulted from the shrewd management of Head Coach Wally Buono, who continues to put a winning team on the field, as well as the marketing genius of Ron Rooke and President Stan Schwartz, who are winning young people back to the park with ticket packages and deals they can afford. They are guaranteeing a fan base for years to come while NHL attendance in the city continues to decline.

Calgary has always been a great football city. Team success in the '90s obscures the fact that the team missed the play-offs eight times in the '50s and six times in the '70s. Even during those bleak periods, support for the team was strong. Ticket sales have averaged 27,000 per game over the last 20 years, a figure exceeded only by the Edmonton Eskimos.

With their pancake breakfasts, staged shoot-outs, country and western music, square dancers, and colorful cowboys and horses in the parade, nobody livens up the Grey Cup festival more than Calgarians. Hosts of the first Grey Cup in the new millennium, the Stampeders promise to get the twenty-first century off to a rip-roaring start. Yahoo!

INTO THE MILLENNIUM

The Canadian Football League is moving into the new millennium with a renewed sense of confidence. Certainly there are concerns with attendance in Toronto, Vancouver and, to some degree, in Hamilton. Ownership is doubt in our largest city.

History tells us that fans will only take so much, that a point can reached where they will withdraw their support. That happened in B.C. in the '70s, Calgary in the '80s and Ottawa in the '90s. That is a real possibility in Saskatchewan.

But football is king in Calgary and Edmonton, alive and well in Winnipeg and on the brink of prosperity in Montreal. The venerable old league may soon return to the nation's capitol. Interest in our oldest professional sports league remains high. Celebrations of recent years demonstrate how strongly the Grey Cup is embedded in the national psyche.

While the National Hockey League and major league baseball live in a fool's paradise of spending and salaries, the CFL long ago weathered that storm, imposed the salary cap and got its house in order. During its darkest hours, the game has been sustained by Canada's greatest sporting event: the Grey Cup. The league's selling of the rights to the Grey Cup game and festival has not only nourished fan interest in the CFL from coast to coast, but has helped franchises to regain their financial footings.

Our love affair with Canadian football and the Grey Cup will continue to grow. Not only is football flourishing at the minor, high school and university levels, but the CFL remains a success on television and at the gate for the majority of teams. As we hear more and more about the globalization of sports, as our Canadian hockey teams tragically move south of the border, as baseball dies in Montreal and as more Canadiana disappears into the American maw, our unique brand of football and its national championship—the Grey Cup—will be considered more than ever a cherished part of our culture, something near and dear to the Canadian heart.

My hope is that we are returning to the atmosphere of our centennial year, which was a glorious explosion of everything Canadian. In 1967, before NHL and baseball expansion, the CFL was our only truly national league and the Grey Cup our only truly national sporting event. Though under-funded, under-appreciated by some and belittled by those who crave for the NFL, the CFL will be the league that survives in Canada. It has always been the little engine that could. I look forward to the centennial celebration of the Canadian Football League in 2009 and to the one hundredth playing of the Grey Cup in 2012. The centennial should be quite a party!

NAME INDEX